Second Edition

Basic Methods of Policy Analysis and Planning

Carl V. Patton
Georgia State University

David S. Sawicki
Georgia Institute of Technology

PRENTICE HALL
Upper Saddle River, NJ 07458

Library of Congress Cataloging-in-Publication Data

PATTON, CARL V.
    Basic methods of policy analysis and planning / Carl V. Patton,
David S.Sawicki.—2nd ed.
        p.   cm.
    Includes bibliographical references and index.
    ISBN 0-13-060948-X
    1. Policy sciences.   I. Sawicki, David S.   II. Title.
    H97.P38   1993
    361.6′1—dc20   92-38957
                                                            CIP

Acquisitions Editor: Julie Berrisford
Editorial/production supervision and
    interior design: Marianne Peters
Cover design: Maureen Eide
Manufacturing Buyer: Mary Ann Gloriande
Prepress Buyer: Kelly Behr
Supplements Editor: Sharon Chambliss
Editorial Assistant: Nicole Signoretti

 ©1993, 1986 by Prentice-Hall, Inc.
Upper Saddle River, NJ 07458

Printed in the United States of America

20   19   18   17   16   15

ISBN   0-13-060948-X

Prentice-Hall International (UK) Limited, *London*
Prentice-Hall of Australia Pty. Limited, *Sydney*
Prentice-Hall Canada Inc., *Toronto*
Prentice-Hall Hispanoamericana, S.A., *Mexico*
Prentice-Hall of India Private Limited, *New Delhi*
Prentice-Hall of Japan, Inc., *Tokyo*
Prentice Hall Asia Pte. Ltd., *Singapore*
Editora Prentice-Hall do Brasil, Ltda., *Rio de Janeiro*

Contents

Preface   xi

PART ONE: **METHODS**

1   **The Need for Simple Methods of Policy Analysis and Planning**   1

Quick, Basic Policy Analysis   2
Learning the Methods of Policy Analysis and Planning   6
Practical Principles for Beginning Policy Analysts   8
Summary   18
Organization of the Book   19
Glossary   19
Exercises   20

2 The Policy Analysis Process   21

Types of Policy Analysis   23
The Role of the Analyst   26
Ethical Considerations   30

*Values in Analysis, 32   Ethical Analysis, 33
Ethical Principles and Rules, 39   Guidelines for
Professional Conduct, 42*

The Analytic Process   46
Basic Policy Analysis in Six Steps   52

*Step One: Verify, Define, and Detail the Problem, 54
Step Two: Establish Evaluation Criteria, 57
Step Three: Identify Alternative Policies, 58
Step Four: Evaluate Alternative Policies, 60
Step Five: Display and Distinguish among
Alternative Policies, 61
Step Six: Monitor and Evaluate the Implemented
Policy, 63*

Summary   64
Glossary   66
Exercises   66
Source Material   67
Exhibits   68

3 Crosscutting Methods   74

Identifying and Gathering Data   77

*Sources of Data, 78   Literature Review, 81
Library Search Methods, 82   Getting Started, 84
Federal Government Information, 87
Legal Searches, 91   Management Records, 95
Observation, 96*

Interviewing for Policy Information   97

*The Investigative Approach, 98   Structure and
Closure, 99   Choosing the Interviewees, 100*

*Making Contact, 101   Conducting the
Interview, 102   Using Your Time Efficiently, 104*

Quick Surveys   105

*Types of Surveys, 107   Survey Methods, 107
Questionnaire Construction, 108   Sample
Selection, 109*

Evaluating Data and Information   109

*Estimating Data Quality, 110   Document Analysis,
111   Determining Truth from Interviews, 113*

Basic Data Analysis   113

*Descriptive Data Analysis, 114   Graphic
Techniques, 115   Tables, 124   Maps, 127
Descriptive Statistics, 129   Association or
Correlation, 130   Measures of Significance, 133*

Communicating the Analysis   134

*Getting It on Paper, 136   Using Graphics to
Communicate, 137   Organizing the Report, 138
In-Person Communication, 140*

Summary   141
Glossary   141
Exercises   143

4   Verifying, Defining, and Detailing the Problem   147

Identifying and Defining Problems   148
Developing the Problem Statement   151
Back-of-the-Envelope Calculations   154
Quick Decision Analysis   158
Creation of Valid Operational Definitions   163
Political Analysis   168
The Issue Paper versus First-Cut Analysis   176
Summary   178

Glossary   178
Exercises   179

---

5   Establishing Evaluation Criteria   186

The Process of Establishing Evaluation Criteria   188
Several Important Economic Concepts   191

*The Free Market Model, 192   Costs, 194
Benefits, 195   Standing, 196   Externalities, 199
Elasticity, 200   Marginal Analysis, 201
Equity, 204*

Commonly Employed Evaluation Criteria   207

*Technical Feasibility, 208   Economic
and Financial Possibility, 210   Political
Viability, 214   Administrative Operability, 218*

Summary   219
Glossary   220
Exercises   222

---

6   Identifying Alternatives   227

Sources of Alternatives   231
Searching for Alternatives   233

*Researched Analysis and Experimentation, 234
No-Action (Status Quo) Analysis, 235
Quick Surveys, 237   Literature Review, 238
Comparison of Real-World Experiences, 238
Passive Collection and Classification, 238
Development of Typologies, 239
Analogy, Metaphor, and Synectics, 239
Brainstorming, 241   Comparison with an
Ideal, 244*

Creating Alternatives   245

*Feasible Manipulations, 246   Modifying Existing
Solutions, 248*

Pitfalls to Avoid   251
Summary   253
Glossary   255
Exercises   255

7   Evaluating Alternative Policies

257

Forecasting Methods   258

*Extrapolative Techniques, 260   Theoretical
Forecasting Techniques: Modeling, 268
Intuitive Forecasting Techniques, 273*

Evaluation Methods   275

*Discounting, 276   Three Measures of Efficiency, 280
Sensitivity Analysis, 284   Allocation Formulas, 289
Quick Decision Analysis Revisited, 295*

Political Analysis   301

*Political Feasibility Analysis, 302   Implementation
Analysis, 307   Scenario Writing, 313*

Uncertainty   315
Summary   317
Glossary   318
Exercises   319

8   Displaying Alternatives and Distinguishing among Them

332

Problems in Selecting the Best Policy   333
Conflict between Individual and Collective Rationality   335
The Problem of Multiple Criteria   337
Several Methods of Dealing with Multiple Criteria   339
Basic Comparison Methods   339

*Paired Comparisons, 341   Satisficing, 341
Lexicographic Ordering, 341   Nondominated-
Alternatives Method, 341   Equivalent-Alternatives
Method, 343   Standard-Alternative Method, 347*

Matrix (Scorecard) Display Systems   349

*Goeller Scorecard, 350   Alternative-Consequence
Matrix, 351*

Other Matrix Methods   353

*Goals-Achievement Matrix, 353   Variations on
GAM, 354   Planning Balance Sheet, 354
Which Matrix Method Should Be Used? 355*

Weights, Rating Systems, and Index Numbers   355
Summary   357
Glossary   359
Exercises   360

9   Monitoring and Evaluating Implemented Policies   362

Types of Policy Failures   365
The Policy Evaluation Continuum   368
Types of Ex-Post Evaluation   369

*Before-and-After Comparisons, 376   With-and-
Without Comparisons, 376   Actual-versus-Planned
Performance Comparisons, 377   Experimental
Models, 378   Quasi-Experimental Models, 379
Generalizing from Quasi-Experimental Designs,
384   Cost-Oriented Evaluation Approaches, 385*

Which Method Should Be Used?   386
Principles of Quick Evaluation   388
Summary   393
Glossary   394
Exercises   395

PART TWO: CASES

10   Downtown Development   398

Introduction   398
The Assignment   399
Background Information   399

11   Defending against Accusations of Prejudice   401

Introduction   401
The Assignment   401
Background Information   402
The Data and Data Problems   403
Learning Objectives   403
Exhibits   403

12   Solid-Waste Collection Methods   411

Introduction   411
The Assignment   412
Exhibits   412

13   Campus Parking Policies   421

Introduction   421
The Assignment 422
Background Information   422
Guidelines for Analysis   426
Final Report   427
Source Material   427
Exhibits   428

14   Emergency Aid for Home Fuel: Developing
     an Allocation Formula   435

Introduction   435
The Assignment   436

The Specific Tasks   437
Source Material   438
Exhibits   438

15   A Tax on Paper Diapers   446

Introduction   446
The Assignment   447
Underlying Themes   447
Learning Objectives   448
Source Material   448
Exhibit   449

16   Public-Private Development: Underground Atlanta   450

Introduction   450
The Assignment   451
Issues and Actors   451
Exhibits   452

Bibliography   463

Index   475

Preface

Basic Methods of Policy Analysis and Planning presents quickly applied basic methods for analyzing and resolving planning and policy issues at state and local levels. Quantitative and qualitative methods are combined in a systematic approach to addressing such policy dilemmas. Besides methods, the book presents the rationale and process of policy analysis as well as policy application cases.

This second edition contains three new policy cases, and three of the previous case examples have been revised substantially. The other cases, as well as the examples used throughout the book, have been updated. Dozens of new end-of-chapter exercises have been added. Moreover, the policy analysis and planning literature has been brought up to date through the inclusion of references and examples from more than 150 new books and articles. In an effort to reflect current literature and practice, new sections have been added on ethical considerations, the types of policy actions that can be taken, and who has standing in policy analysis.

The book is divided into two parts. Part One presents quick, basic methods in nine chapters—organized around the steps in the policy analysis process. It also includes a review of the policy analysis and planning process and serves as a guide to recent literature on policy analysis and planning methods. Part Two presents seven policy cases, which range from brief mini-cases that can be solved in a day or two to longer, more complex cases that may take up to 25 hours of analytic time. The cases, like the methods chapters, are intended to lead the reader to integrate quantitative and qualitative approaches. Methods chapters include glossaries and exercises. All exercises and cases are taken from real experiences, and they have been used successfully in instructional settings at three universities.

An *Instructor's Manual* is available to authorized persons free-of-charge. Faculty members may request the *Instructor's Manual* from the publisher by letter. Request the *Manual* on your university letterhead. Contact Prentice Hall, College Operations, Englewood Cliffs, New Jersey 07632.

Most of the methods presented here have long been used by planners and analysts. We did not invent them, and in many cases it is impossible to identify who did. Rather, we have each spent more than twenty years applying these methods, learning which work the best, discovering how others should be modified, and developing realistic exercises and cases that support the learning of these quickly applied methods.

This book, then, is for students and analysts who seek to learn quick, basic methods that can be applied to a range of policy problems. It should be especially useful for the beginning analyst or the person starting the study of policy analysis and planning. The book assumes no prior knowledge of advanced mathematics or economics on the part of the reader. We deliberately avoided methods that require such knowledge, but the reader who has these skills can certainly apply them to the exercises and cases. We also avoided methods that involve extensive research. Our point is that many of today's most important policy problems are resolved quickly, and time is seldom available for researched analysis. Planners and analysts must use quick, basic methods in order to generate, test, and even advocate alternatives in the time available and with the resources at hand—if they are to have an impact on public policy. The methods in *Basic Methods of Policy Analysis and Planning* respond to this need.

Preparing a book such as this requires the assistance of many people. The most important and critical were the students who experienced drafts of the text, exercises, and cases. They provided many ideas about how to improve their usefulness. For that we are grateful. We also appreciate the suggestions from our colleagues, Prentice Hall reviewers David Forkenbrock and Allan Feldt, and Stanley Wakefield and Tom Aloisi of Prentice Hall. We owe a debt to a number of policy analysts and scholars who have guided our thinking over the years as teachers or colleagues—Eugene Bardach, Robert Behn, Aaron Wildavsky, and Arnold Meltsner, to name a few. Their ideas are reflected in this text, attributed, we hope, in all cases, perhaps inadvertently used without attribution in some.

In the preparation of the first edition, extraordinary help was provided by Amy Helling who edited a number of drafts of chapters, prepared most of the glossaries, contributed many chapter exercises, and acted as a critical, perceptive colleague during the writing of the book. Jane Patton undertook a number of tedious and necessary tasks including proofreading drafts, requesting permissions, and checking references. Janet Tibbets converted early drafts from several wordprocessing systems to a common format and produced the final draft of the manuscript.

In the development of the second edition, we were assisted by Karen Horton and Dolores Mars of Prentice Hall, as well as by Prentice Hall reviewers Barbara Lukermann, William Russell Mangun, and Barbara Ray who provided helpful advice on restructuring the book. Comments on and contributions to new sections of the text were provided by James Bacik, Richard Bolan, Sharon Bostick, Stanley Carpenter, Jerome Kaufman, Richard Leacy, David Lindsley, Gretchen Patton, Richard Perry, Catherine Ross, and Leslie Sheridan. Amy Yard assisted with the preparation of the manuscript, and Pearl McHaney and Leigh Kirkland proofread the final copy.

Carl V. Patton, Georgia State University
David S. Sawicki, Georgia Institute of Technology

PART ONE: METHODS

Chapter One

The Need for Simple Methods
of Policy Analysis and Planning

Our increasingly complex society confronts us with more and more difficult policy problems that are not easily solved.[1] Although these problems may be "attacked" or "addressed," often they have no clearly correct answers. Some authors characterize the problems of modern society as "squishy," "fuzzy," "subjective," and "wicked" and as often having the following attributes:

1. They are not well defined.
2. They are seldom purely technical or purely political.
3. Their solutions cannot usually be proven to be correct before application.
4. No problem solution is ever guaranteed to achieve the intended result.
5. Problem solutions are seldom both best and cheapest.
6. The adequacy of the solution is often difficult to measure against notions of the public good.
7. The fairness of solutions is impossible to measure objectively.

There are many examples of complex problems. What is the best location in a state for a maximum-security prison? Should a ban on phosphorus that

[1] For an overview of these problems, see David G. Gil, *Unravelling Social Policy: Theory, Analysis, and Political Action towards Social Equity*, 4th ed. (Rochester, VT: Schenkman Books, 1990).

1

has proven ineffective in improving water quality be lifted? A city council is considering offering tax breaks for developers willing to build offices in certain sections of downtown. Should the mayor veto the plan? The county executive has proposed a $70 million expansion of the metropolitan airport. Should the county board of supervisors support this plan? These problems will be answered: That is, decisions will be made. Even if the decision is to do nothing, it will still have consequences for citizens.

How will decision makers make their decisions? On the basis of what information will they act? To whom will they listen: lobbyists, constituents, policy advisers? The number of trained professionals employed in government and in the private sector to offer advice on these matters is growing. They usually call themselves planners, policy analysts, or public managers. This book is for people who want to work in this area or who are working in this area and wish to improve their analytical skills. It is called *Basic Methods of Policy Analysis and Planning* because it is intended as the first book a beginning analyst will use in building a portfolio of methods to approach knotty public policy problems.

QUICK, BASIC POLICY ANALYSIS

We believe there is a set of systematic procedures or policy analysis methods that can be used to attack contemporary policy problems. We also believe there is a subset of these methods that are basic methods, yielding quick results and serving as theoretically sound aids to making good policy decisions. Some people might argue that the variety of public policy problems is so great that no one set of systematic procedures could be developed for dealing with all of them. Critics might also say that the geographic and political context for these problems is so far-ranging that they don't have much in common, thus defying any standard approach. Yet a process for approaching these problems has evolved and has been applied. Called the *rational model*, one simple version takes the form of Figure 1-1, in which problem definition leads to the identification and evaluation of alternatives followed by policy implementation. There is evidence that when time and resources are available, the analytical process does take this or an acceptably similar form. Most often, however, this rational problem-solving process is not followed because of the pressures of time, limited knowledge, and constrained resources.

This book is different from others in that we present only quickly applied methods, those that can be useful when there is no time for researched analysis. Policy analysts are often required to give advice to policymakers in incredibly short periods of time, in contrast to university researchers and think-tank consultants who are hired specifically to conduct intensive research on public policy issues. Some have called this latter type of work *policy studies* or *policy research.* Analysts doing this work are typically given comparatively large budgets and long periods of time to produce results, and they work with large sets of data.

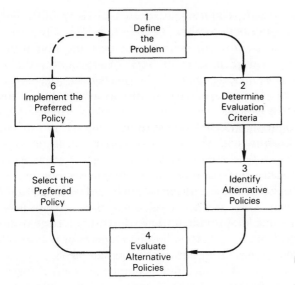

Figure 1-1   The Classical Rational Problem-Solving Process

Consequently the methods they use are different from those used by staff who work for decision makers on a day-to-day basis. The terms *researched analysis* and *quick analysis* were coined to describe this difference.[2] Since we have included in this book only methods that we feel are both quick and theoretically defensible, we consider them to be highly useful for completing a short-term assignment or for taking the first cut at a longer-term project. Thus, we call them basic methods, and the product of their application basic analysis.

[2] The origin of these terms is unclear. Robert D. Behn and James W. Vaupel introduce the terms formally in *Quick Analysis for Busy Decision Makers* (New York: Basic Books, 1982), pp. 3–7, but the phrase "quick and dirty analysis" has been used for years and has long been incorporated into the curricula of schools of public policy and planning. Our interest in basic, quick analysis grew in large measure respectively from a classroom assignment and involvement in a local transportation issue. Patton had learned a number of quick, basic methods while in Graduate Planning School at the University of Illinois in the late 1960s, and these skills were further developed at the University of California, Berkeley's Graduate School of Public Policy, where quick analysis was an integral part of the core curriculum. Students were regularly assigned one-, two-, or three-day and week-long problems where the goal was to learn to do the best job possible in a completely unfamiliar area within the time available and with the resources at hand. Patton described his approach to quick analysis in Carl V. Patton, "A Seven-Day Project: Early Faculty Retirement Alternatives," *Policy Analysis* 1, no. 4 (Fall 1975), 731–53, and has taught quick, basic methods to undergraduate and graduate planning students since 1976. Sawicki became involved in quick analysis after conducting research and policy analysis on a transportation issue. Although the research was published as "Express Transit Systems Analyzed," in the *Journal of Transport Economics and Policy* 8, no. 3 (September 1974), 274–93, it was having no impact. So he boiled down sixty pounds of computer output and a 200-page report to a 25-page report. Still no one listened. Then he pared it to ten pages, and several key legislators read it. Then he reduced it to two pages and gave testimony in front of a legislative committee. It had some impact. Then he was interviewed in a one-minute spot on the evening news: His hard work finally had an impact on the decision that was made. Having learned many valuable lessons from that experience, Sawicki has been learning and teaching quick, basic methods since then.

The goals of persons who produce researched analysis are different from those of persons who produce basic analysis. Certain to be critically reviewed by their peers, researchers seek the truth behind problems and nonintuitive, or even counterintuitive, solutions. Fellow researchers are impressed with the complexity, elegance, and precision of the analysis. For quick, basic analysis the goals are much more practical. The goal may be simply to inform public decision makers well enough so they don't get caught in major errors. An example might be to assist the mayor of a large city who must decide whether to side with the director of public works in defending the cost of garbage collection when an opponent claims the cost to be double that of other cities of comparable size. Somewhat more idealistically, the goal might be to inform decision makers well enough so that a more enlightened discussion of public policy occurs and better policy is adopted as a result. On a practical level, quick, basic analysis may be all that is justified for a one-time local problem where the cost of a large-scale study would exceed the benefit from the precise solution or where for political reasons the best technical alternative has little chance of being adopted.

The process of basic analysis is much more complex, in some respects, than that of researched analysis. Researched analysis is rather well codified; there are routine steps of exploration and accepted standards of scientific behavior. On the other hand, the most compelling feature of basic analysis is whether the consumer understands it, is able to follow its logic, and as a result is able to formulate better policy. This means that there is an interplay between the basic analytical routines themselves, the process for interacting with clients, and the communications tools used to convey the results of analysis. This is why some authors describe basic analysis as craft rather than science. Success is measured by the quality of public debate and the efficacy of the policy adopted. Therefore, basic analysis must be responsive to the policy problem. Methods must be selected for their ability to attack the client's problem in the time available without obfuscation.

Much has been written about the differences between policy analysis and planning. To avoid a tortuous review we will highlight what is important for users of this book. Some might say that the differences are well described by the phrases *researched analysis* and *basic analysis,* with planning being the former and policy analysis the latter. This, like other simple dichotomies sometimes proposed, is inadequate. First, were the pertinent literature in both fields to be reviewed, one would find that policy analysis has concentrated primarily on problems of the federal level of government, while planning has focused on those of state and local governments. Although this is an accurate statement about the literature, this dichotomy, too, has relatively little meaning for our purposes. State and local governments adopt policies, and the federal government often develops plans. Some critics would say that policies are more broad and abstract, require more information and analysis, and have wider ramifications than plans, but others would argue the opposite. The answer depends on the level of government: One's tactics may be another's policies and yet another's plans. This semantic difference is not very important. Most practicing planners and policy analysts use both basic methods and researched methods in their work, whether that is in public or private practice.

More telling perhaps is the historical development of each field and the resulting differences in the paradigms of their processes.[3] Classic comprehensive planning includes the following elements:

1. An extensive inventory phase, usually for gathering data on the natural geography and environment, on the physical infrastructure, and about the demographic and economic characteristics of the resident population
2. A search for alternative solutions, which may be described as exhaustive, but in fact is severely constrained, with significant alternatives eliminated before presentation to the client (the public)
3. The preparation of a plan
4. An unspecified client: "the public interest"
5. A subject-oriented, as opposed to a problem-oriented, scope (e.g., the transportation system versus congestion of the downtown loop)
6. A rather long time horizon (at least ten years)
7. An apolitical approach to the process of implementation

Policy analysis, on the other hand, includes this parallel set of characteristics:

1. An inventory or search phase, limited in scope and directed at a particular issue
2. A constrained search for alternatives, which are then all usually evaluated and displayed to the client
3. The preparation of memoranda, issue papers, policy papers, or draft legislation
4. A particular client, be it a chief executive, an elected official, a public interest group, a neighborhood, or a bank, likely to have a particular perspective on the problem
5. An issue or problem orientation, described alternatively as a reactive posture
6. A time horizon often compromised by terms of elected officials and uncertainty
7. A political approach to getting things accomplished

The comprehensive planning process has more in common with researched methods, and the policy analysis process has more in common with basic methods. However, several additional points should be made. First, policy analysis is,

---

[3] For related discussions see Rachelle Alterman and Duncan MacRae, Jr., "Planning and Policy Analysis: Converging or Diverging Trends?" *Journal of the American Planning Association* 49, no. 2 (Spring 1983), 200–215; Robert A. Heineman, William T. Bluhm, Steven A. Peterson, and Edward N. Kearny, *The World of the Policy Analyst: Rationality, Values, and Politics* (Chatham, NJ: Chatham House, 1990); David S. Sawicki, "Teaching Policy Analysis in a Graduate Planning Program," *Journal of Planning Education and Research* 1, no. 2 (Winter 1982), 78–85; and David L. Weimer and Aidan R. Vining, *Policy Analysis: Concepts and Practice* (Englewood Cliffs, NJ: Prentice Hall, 1989).

in a sense, only part of a larger policy planning process. Analysis itself is the breaking up of a policy problem into its component parts, understanding them, and developing ideas about what to do. Many activities beyond analysis are involved in the policy development process, and the term *policy analysis* may often be used when *policy planning* would be more appropriate.

Second, the two descriptions suggest that policy analysis is much more reactive than planning, always happening after someone has spotted a problem or proposed a solution. This is a reality of policy analysis at present; it may be a result of a shortage of resources for analysis in government. Someone must take the first step in creating or designing the plan, policy, or program, and this role of the professional planner in government has been severely neglected.

Third, planning is conducted because of the concern for the appropriate use of resources in the long run and the concern for the larger public interest. As noted above, the policy analysis paradigm specifies work for a single client. That client might be an embodiment of the public interest, like a mayor taking a particularly heroic stand on an issue seen as vital to city residents. Or the client might hold a very personal agenda, like reelection, that could well work in opposition to the public interest.

Finally, our reason for including *policy analysis and planning* in our title was not to imply that we would cover researched methods as well as basic methods. To the degree that the two can be separated, we will cover only basic methods. Rather, we chose our title because the activities of policy analysts and planners in state and local governments are the subject of this book. How the professional label reads is moot.

LEARNING THE METHODS OF POLICY ANALYSIS AND PLANNING

Methods courses are usually taught by supplying students a toolbox of analytical techniques (e.g., forecasting methods and regression analysis) that can ostensibly be applied to policy problems. There are many drawbacks to this approach. It creates the sense that all that needs to be done is to discover the proper match between problem type and specific method and then crank out a solution. This is seldom the case. It also fails to acknowledge that the complex problems facing governments are usually multifaceted and require multiple, not single, analytical approaches. Problems examined this way usually lose their context and become mathematics problems rather than policy problems.

In reaction to this approach to learning methods, some have said that since each problem is unique, what is needed is a "proper frame of mind" to do analysis. In other words, there is no standard method that can be used to approach these problems; each time an approach must be created new. Our position lies between these two. We believe that a standard procedure exists for addressing these problems. We also believe that a number of fundamental or basic methods can be used within this procedure to analyze complex problems.

We have brought these basic methods together in this book for the beginning policy analyst.

We believe these basic methods cannot be effectively learned without a context. Thus, in this book we describe the process of policy analysis and planning and explain a number of basic methods appropriate to each step in that process. Each method is illustrated with examples. The end of each process chapter contains practice problems. The second part of the book contains policy cases, which will take from 15 to 25 hours each to resolve. For each policy case, unlike the more directed exercises provided with the process chapters, readers are on their own in delineating the problem, choosing an approach, and adopting methods of analysis. This combination of traditional learning and learning by doing was selected with several goals in mind. We hope each user of this book will:

1. Learn to recognize situations in which specific basic methods can be applied quickly and appropriately
2. Become competent at using methods of analysis and designing approaches to policy problems
3. Learn how to communicate the results of analysis to appropriate decision makers

We hope that in the process of attaining these goals our readers will also:

- Learn the language of policy planning
- Learn to write with organization, clarity, and precision
- Learn to use supporting documentation (maps, charts, graphs) effectively
- Learn to speak publicly, delivering critical information concisely
- Learn to develop simple models that are supported theoretically and empirically
- Learn to evaluate the distributional aspects of policies and programs
- Learn to incorporate political factors into analysis
- Learn to advocate uncomfortable positions
- Learn to work under time constraints and to allocate analytic resources
- Develop management skills and the ability to work in, and/or direct, a team
- Learn how to obtain policy-relevant data through efficient search techniques and persistence
- Practice the sifting and synthesizing of mountains of seemingly irrelevant reports and memoranda
- Practice using secondary data sources
- Develop quantitative analytic skills
- Develop skills for qualitative analysis
- Learn to design effective program implementation guidelines
- Learn to cope with uncertainty in a policy context by being flexible and tolerating false starts and dead ends
- Learn to read and understand legislative language
- Learn how to develop a program of researched analysis for staff
- Learn to be skeptical of their own solutions as well as those of other analysts

Some people might argue that these skills are best learned on the job. We contend that because a standardized process has emerged and because practitioners of policy analysis and planning have developed a number of basic methods, it is more efficient to learn and practice these methods before facing them in real life.

What role do other courses play in learning to do policy analysis? For those who expect to work on state and local government problems, two other streams of learning, besides methods, are important. The first is the process of policymaking and planning. How do governments work, laws get passed, and administrative rules get initiated? How do professionals within organizations function in providing analysis and advice to decision makers, be they elected or appointed officials? How can the process of analysis involve various constituencies and public and private groups? Courses in planning, government, administration, and management as well as some interdisciplinary programs are directed toward these concerns. The second essential element is a knowledge of the economic, geographic, and social structures of urban and regional systems. How do cities and regions grow and decline? Which of their problems might be addressed by governments? Courses in urban and regional economics, human ecology, sociology, geography, and interdisciplinary offerings address these questions. The analytical methods portion of a planning or policy analysis curriculum usually involves courses in descriptive and inferential statistics, use of the computer on larger data sets, and courses containing a potpourri of researched analysis techniques such as survey research methods, linear programming, cost-benefit and cost-effectiveness analysis, input-output techniques, modeling, and simulation. Some curricula offer courses containing more generic methods for policy analysis and planning, such as forecasting and prediction, alternatives generation, and techniques of program monitoring and evaluation.

This text should be used early in the analyst's career. After learning basic methods of policy analysis and planning, the analyst will be ready to move on to coursework in more advanced analytical techniques and techniques of researched analysis that require more time, resources, and usually larger information bases and data sets.

PRACTICAL PRINCIPLES FOR BEGINNING POLICY ANALYSTS

Learning how to approach policy problems and how to choose appropriate basic methods during the policy process takes time. There is no substitute for practice. Our first bit of advice, then, is to begin thinking like analysts and planners. As you read the daily news, reflect on the problems confronted by governments and ask how you would approach those problems, what information you would need, and what basic methods might be appropriate. Over time, as you develop the habit of looking at policy problems analytically, you will gain confidence in your ability to understand such problems. The following suggestions should help as you begin to undertake policy analysis.[4]

1. Learn to Focus Quickly on the Central Decision Criterion (or Criteria) of the Problem. What factor of the problem is most important to your client? On what criterion is the decision likely to be made? Will it be minimizing the cost of some service? Or might it be to spend more effectively the funds now allocated to the activity? Perhaps it will be to broaden the base of those being served by the program. On what basis can we judge the merits of alternative policies or programs? Identifying the central "nugget" of the problem is essential. In the case of Underground Atlanta (Chapter 16), for example, you will be forced to confront the many possible objectives, implicit and explicit, that are part of that major public/private festival marketplace development.

In some cases the criterion can be inferred from legislative intent; in others you might have to exhume it from a mountain of seemingly patternless reading material. When working on exercises or case studies, you will have no real client from whom to extract "the nugget." On the other hand, the client often has no idea what the central decision criterion is. The difficulty is that public policies often have multiple and competing objectives, and the objectives are often extraordinarily ill-defined. Beginning analysts must learn to focus quickly, or valuable analytical time will be wasted.

If beginning analysts are to survive, it is essential that the sea of ambiguities—extensive reading material but none with priority, reams of undifferentiated data, the blank writing pad, the motionless pencil, and the microcomputer in the "off" position—be recognized and overcome. Getting started is difficult, but focusing on the central decision criterion will help to identify needed information. It is better to make a bad start than to make no start. You can and should recycle: After several hours of work, does your central decision criterion still ring true?

There are, of course, dangers in choosing the nugget prematurely. There is a tendency to choose the one that can be defined and measured most easily (e.g., least cost) while possibly ignoring more important but less quantifiable goals and impacts and forgetting about who pays and who benefits from the policy. There is also a distinct possibility that several competing and equally valid decision criteria exist, and that early focusing will dismiss the alternatives forever.

2. Think about the Types of Policy Actions That Can Be Taken. There are various direct and indirect actions that governments can take to address public policy issues when the private market or government does not allocate goods efficiently or there are equity or distributional problems. Some actions involve monetary policies; others involve nonmonetary policies.

---

[4]For both pitfalls to watch for and an analytical checklist, see Hugh J. Miser and Edward S. Quade, eds., *Handbook of Systems Analysis: Craft Issues and Procedural Choices* (Chichester, Eng.: Wiley, 1988), pp. 619–56.

Table 1-1 Types of Policy Actions

	TYPES OF POLICY ACTIONS	
	Direct	Indirect
Monetary	Provide	Tax
	Purchase	Subsidize
Nonmonetary	Prohibit	Inform
	Require	Implore

Source: Adapted from Michael O'Hare, "A Typology of
Governmental Action," Copyright © Journal of Policy
Analysis and Management 8, no. 4 (Fall 1989), 670;
reprinted by permission of John Wiley & Sons, Inc.

As a planner or analyst you should understand the range of potential policies, even though policy instruments are typically selected because of familiarity, traditions, or professional biases.[5] Several schemes have been proposed for categorizing these types of policy actions.[6] A recent conceptualization by O'Hare appears to be the most useful in helping to categorize the types of actions that might be taken.[7] We have adapted that conceptualization as Table 1-1. We suggest that when faced with a policy issue, you use this direct-indirect/monetary-nonmonetary framework to help you identify possible policy actions.[8]

Within the category of direct monetary policies, a government can directly provide a good or service itself through bureaus, departments, corporations, or special districts, such as fire and police protection, education, and recreation. It can also purchase such a good or service from the private sector, other governments, or the nonprofit sector, or it can license an organization to provide the service. Governments can allocate, stockpile, ration, or auction these goods or services as well.

In the area of indirect monetary policies, governments can enact commodity and excise taxes, tariffs, fines, quotas, or fees, or they can establish pricing mechanisms. They can also provide compensation, subsidies, welfare payments, vouchers, grants, loans, tax credits, exemptions, insurance, or similar mechanisms.

Direct nonmonetary policies include the prohibition or restricting of actions by rules, regulations, standards, quotas, licensing, deregulation, or legalization,

---

[5] Stephen H. Linder and B. Guy Peters, "The Design of Instruments for Public Policy," in *Policy Theory and Policy Evaluation: Concepts, Knowledge, Causes and Norms*, Stuart S. Nagel, ed. (New York: Greenwood Press, 1990), p. 104.

[6] Edith Stokey and Richard Zeckhauser, *A Primer for Policy Analysis* (New York: Norton, 1978), pp. 322–23; and Weimer and Vining, *Policy Analysis*, pp. 125, 173.

[7] Michael O'Hare, "A Typology of Governmental Action," *Journal of Policy Analysis and Management* 8, no. 4 (Fall 1989), 670–72.

[8] But for an overview of problems with such classifications, see Linder and Peters, "Design of Instruments," pp. 109–16.

such as environmental laws and safety regulations. Governments can also require certain actions, although there are very few policies that can truly require action; rather, they are prohibitions that look like obligations. O'Hare states that the only real obligations in U.S. society are compulsory education, jury duty, and revealing ourselves to the census.[9]

Indirect nonmonetary policies include educational, informational, and promotional efforts to modify behavior. They also include stronger measures to cajole or implore.

In Chapter 15 an environmental group has proposed a 10% tax on paper diapers, probably jumping to the policy conclusion before doing any analysis. First you must confirm the goals of intervening in the market. What was the intent of the environmental group? Then review the range of policies and combinations of policies and how they might attain the stated objectives.

Rarely do alternatives fall cleanly into only one category. More often they fall into two or more categories, and generic policies must be customized to fit particular situations. In addition, each policy may have limitations and drawbacks in the intended application that must be addressed. It is, nonetheless, useful to have this classification scheme in mind when thinking about potential policies.

Moreover, as O'Hare pointed out, there is decreasing certainty in the effectiveness of the policy actions as we move from the upper left to the lower right of Table 1-1. When the government provides or purchases a good, the outcome is relatively certain. When we adopt policies based on education or cajoling, the outcome is less certain.[10]

3. Avoid the Toolbox Approach to Analyzing Policy. Some disciplines specify analytical routines in detail for many circumstances. This may encourage some people to begin work on a policy problem because it lends itself to their favorite method. Ideally the problem should dictate the methods, not vice versa. This book is intended to help avoid the toolbox approach. Because problems are complex, beginning analysts can be very apprehensive about which method to use. We advise using the simplest appropriate method, and using common sense to design a method if one doesn't already exist. Combine methods if you must. Use more than one whenever possible. Apprehension often forces us back to the methods with which we feel most comfortable, but try to avoid this tendency.

The principal tools of the policy planner are logic, common sense, and experience with particular substantive areas. It helps to be practiced in data analysis, rational problem solving, and other specific skills. But more often than not we design our own approach or methodology to policy problems. This kind of creativity becomes easier the more policy analysis we do and the more we learn what the clients, be they real or simulated (in exercises and cases), find understandable and useful to their deliberations. If the methods applied are not

---

[9] O'Hare, "Typology," p. 671.
[10] Ibid., p. 672.

transparent, the client is forced to either accept or reject the results without understanding.

In Chapter 11 you will be asked to analyze whether an owner of a number of large apartment complexes has discriminated in his rental practices. Invariably, a few students are familiar with the social science literature on discrimination as well as formal measures of racial segregation. Some will attempt to force their use on this problem, usually with poor results. In fact, this case presents a great opportunity to invent your own method, based on a sound concept of discrimination, and to use it in analyzing the situation and explaining it to the client.

Doing the exercises and completing the cases in this book, seeing others' approaches to the same problems, and understanding the deficiencies of one's own methods are efficient ways to obtain experience in policy analysis.

4. Learn to Deal with Uncertainty. Neophyte analysts are tempted to isolate each parameter of a policy problem and then establish their most likely future values. Having tacked down the key parameters of the problem (because the task is never-ending, many spend most of their allocated time on this phase), they believe the problem can be solved. This approach is often a waste of time. Therefore, we describe basic methods of decision analysis and sensitivity testing that can aid in analyzing important parts of a policy problem even if you cannot find values for certain variables. This will be illustrated with a popular policy question: Should a city waive property taxes for a number of years on certain downtown properties in order to encourage their redevelopment? Our experience shows that most beginning analysts spend all their time trying to find out (for sure) whether the tax abatement will cause the development. Almost no time gets spent trying to analyze what the costs and benefits of such a program would likely be if it were instituted and did or did not cause development. Learning to live with and work with uncertainty is a must for policy analysts. Uncertainty is present in nearly every public policy problem.

In Chapter 10 you will be asked to give advice on whether to put a parcel of downtown land up for bid, or to build a city-owned parking garage on the site. Even in this very simple urban policy problem, uncertainty permeates. Handling that uncertainty, and giving good policy advice despite it, will be a significant challenge for you.

5. Say It with Numbers. Much of this book deals with using numbers to understand and resolve problems. Most policy problems have an associated data base, and it is important to use these data in gaining insights about the problem. The most basic mathematical operations—addition, subtraction, multiplication, and division—can yield powerful insights. Division, for example, can tell you how much a service costs per capita. When analyzing the case on solid-waste collection (Chapter 12), you will undoubtedly want first to perform a number of simple mathematical operations. How much garbage is collected in how much time? By crews of what sizes? Using how many of what kinds of trucks? In streets or in alleys? Using what type of trash container? Compared to other cities, how do these numbers look? High, low, equivalent? What critical data are obviously missing but essential to this first-cut analysis?

Of course, not all critical factors can be measured empirically. Some are intangible, but this does not necessarily make them unimportant. Even if, in the last analysis, intangibles are found to be central, the quantitative analysis will supply a good base upon which other analyses can be done. Carol Weiss made the point this way:

> Any participant who has no data or evidence to support his/her group's position is at risk of being brushed aside; any group whose case rests on faulty data or flawed analysis can be more easily overwhelmed. Of course, the existence of powerful patrons and supporters can rescue even an analytically weak case, but where many groups vie, where power is roughly equally distributed, or where important actors have not yet taken a stand, analytic evidence is often of significant value.[11]

6. *Make the Analysis Simple and Transparent.* Does the analysis inform your clients? Do they understand it and as a consequence make better decisions? These central questions should be asked about any policy analysis. To achieve these goals, the analysis must be *simple.* This doesn't mean simple-minded, but rather, not complex, convoluted, or impossible for a bright, well-informed client to follow. *Transparency* is another attribute of effective analysis. This means that if any models or calculating routines are used, the client should be able to see how they work, step by step, not simply be given the results of the internal machinations of a "black box." Simplicity and transparency go hand in hand.

Using a gravity model to predict retail sales provides a good example of this principle. In judging the impact of a proposed suburban shopping mall on the downtown of a medium-sized city, planners employed a typical gravity model to assess changes in shopping patterns (Table 1-2). Those familiar with such models will know that the results shown in Table 1-2 are the product of running data through a mathematical formula, a formula whose various parameters should be clear and transparent and open for discussion, criticism, and possible testing with data by others. The mall is both generating more total business and drawing business away from elsewhere, including downtown. Unfortunately, Table 1-2 shows only the results of analysis. To be consistent with our principle, the factors in the formula need to be defined, the data used to generate the results should be listed, and a rationale for using this model in the given context should be provided. In some reports the analyst may want to confine such detail to an appendix, but it should always be made available so that consumers of the analysis can follow the logic and check the factors being used and their

---

[11] Reprinted by permission of Greenwood Publishing Group, Inc., Westport, CT, from Carol H. Weiss, "The Uneasy Partnership Endures: Social Science and Government," in *Social Scientists, Policy, and the State,* ed. Stephen Brooks and Alain-G. Gagnon © Greenwood Press (New York: Greenwood Press, Praeger Publishers, 1990), p. 100.

Table 1-2 Reilly's Law of Retail Gravitation
Applied to the Upland Mall

SIZE OF PROPOSED MALL	RESULTING DISTRIBUTION OF ANNUAL RETAIL TRADE		
	Downtown	Mall	Other
Don't build	$56 M	$ 0	$17 M
Build 10,000 square feet	$49 M	$14 M	$14 M
Build 20,000 square feet	$35 M	$42 M	$11 M
Build 40,000 square feet	$21 M	$63 M	$ 8 M

M = Millions of dollars.

measurement. If it is too complicated to explain, it should not be used in analyzing policy.

In Chapter 14 you will be asked to develop a mathematical formula to allocate a state project budget to the many counties of that state. The funds are to be used to assist the elderly and poor with their energy bills. There are endless numbers of indicators of the counties' needs for these monies, and countless possibilities for expressing these needs in a formula. However, you will want to develop a formula that is, at the same time, intellectually defensible, politically acceptable, efficient, effective, and yet understandable to the appointed and elected officials who are the clients for your analysis.

7. Check the Facts. It is important to develop a healthy skepticism for widely held beliefs and established facts in matters of public policy. Such beliefs and facts have a way of becoming baseline information for anyone who begins to study a policy problem. Yet they are not always reliable. It takes time to feel confident enough to challenge existing authorities, but uncovering erroneous or uncorroborated facts can prevent your analysis from compounding the error. A few tips for checking the facts include the following:

1. Analyze the sources of the facts. Is the position of the author served by the facts?
2. Never rely on a single source. Use people, reports, and the analysis of others to corroborate the facts. Use independent sources.
3. Understand how the facts were generated. If the method wasn't clear, discount the facts greatly.
4. Since you can't check everything, check the facts most closely associated with the central decision criterion.
5. Since facts often depend on definitions, check the critical ones. If the claim is that a majority of all city families are in poverty, how are *majority, city, families,* and *poverty* being defined and measured? Can you generate the same facts by using these definitions and assumptions?

Many planning and policy analysis issues revolve around population projections. Too often the projections of prestigious agencies are taken as facts and become bases upon which other analyses are performed. A smaller city within a metropolitan region had done this by relying on the projections of a respected regional planning agency. The regional totals were projected objectively, with the agency using the latest birth, death, and migration rates. These totals, however, were allocated to communities on the basis of the regional agency's plan. The plan itself was at odds with what had been happening for the previous decade. The plan was designed to encourage centrality and dense development, but the region was becoming more spread out and more decentralized. The plan was a normative statement about the agency's desired growth pattern, but the agency had no power to implement its plan. The resulting population projection for the small city was, then, much higher than could be expected. Until a sharp analyst reviewed the fact base (including the population projection), analyses were being done under the assumption that the agency's city-level projections were a forecast of trends.

In Chapter 15 you will be asked directly to check the facts surrounding an assertion by an environmental lobbying group that using paper diapers costs the American public over $7 billion a year, a billion of which is a public subsidy of diaper producers and consumers. The tips given above plus many others in this book should help you develop your own fact base for this case.

8. Learn to Advocate the Positions of Others. There are three principal reasons that taking a position different from your own can be beneficial. This is not to suggest that analysts should be amoral. Rather, your willingness to advocate other sides of the issue can have several positive results: (1) It can raise the level of debate, bringing out the merits of both sides and displaying the problem and alternative solutions in all their complexity. This can help lead to compromises, where if left as simple arguments or arguments based on clashing values alone, the problems may remain irresolvable. (2) This approach can improve your analytical skills and your facility with unfamiliar subject material, in the process perhaps causing you to reexamine what you have considered to be established truths. (3) This approach can also strengthen the tradition of an advocacy process where a strong challenge to an established policy—even a good policy—can result in a better policy. Competitive or advocacy processes are built into some of our most important institutions: the courts, Congress, and free enterprise. These systems rely on conflict in order to function, and their achievements would be far fewer if they had to wait for consensus or had vested a single entity with the responsibility to take a comprehensive view.

Analysts should take the opportunity to learn from lawyers whose professional training teaches them to assume either side and to play within the rules of the legal and political process. Majone believes that a "policy analyst is a producer of policy arguments, more similar to a lawyer . . . than to an engineer or scientist."[12] He further argues that there is nothing intrinsically wrong with

---

[12] Giandomenico Majone, *Evidence, Argument, and Persuasion in the Policy Process* (New Haven: Yale University Press, 1989), p. 21.

putting together a convincing argument, and if analysts are unable or unwilling to provide such arguments, decision makers will look to others for assistance.[13]

Learn to make up for a lack of substantive knowledge—in housing, health, environment, transportation, land use—by substituting an efficient learning process. Like lawyers, students of policy analysis need to be able to develop a case from any perspective and with limited prior substantive knowledge of the problem area. Policy analysts need to know how to learn efficiently about substantive problem areas because most analysts will encounter problems that shift during their lifetime, if not daily.

In Chapter 11 you will be working for the owner of many apartment complexes. He has been accused of discriminating against nonwhites in his rental practices. Many policy students' first reaction to this case is to assume the worst about the landlord. After all, housing segregation is a reality in most cities in the United States. Thus, the students would rather work against this businessman than for him. But the assignment is to work for him and to represent his interests the best you can. You will learn firsthand how a statistical argument is constructed, and you will be forced to analyze your own ethical standards in the process.

9. *Give the Client Analysis, Not Decisions.* Policy analysts and planners usually give advice to their clients; they do not make decisions for them. This has important implications for the types of analyses that are done and, even more importantly, for the methods of communicating the results of analysis. The client will make the final choice and should be able to reanalyze the policy data. This means that critical assumptions, values, and uncertainties must be reported. When the analysis is done well, the decision maker will be able to weigh the consequences of changes in assumptions, values, and uncertainties and come to an independent conclusion. In some cases the client will be seeking a recommendation, but this is typically the case only with skilled analysts who have developed a long-term relationship with their client.

In Chapter 13 you will be asked to develop policies for parking on a college campus. Because most college students have been directly affected by campus parking policies, those working on this case usually cannot resist offering their preferred solutions to the problem. However, the case should serve to remind you that no matter how personally you might be involved in a case, you should offer your client (in this case the president of Georgia Tech) analysis, and maybe recommendations, but never decisions. In many cases, students offer only one solution to the problem, leaving no options for the president.

This point about providing analysis rather than decisions can be sharpened with an illustration. It was proposed to build a bridge to replace an existing ferry service over a river that separated the downtown of a major metropolitan area from its hinterland. The analysis showed that the critical variables in deciding

---

[13] Ibid., p. 19.

between the new bridge and maintaining the existing ferry were the amount of time saved by commuters and how it was valued, the uncertainty of the cost of the bridge, and the assumption that traffic would remain at levels that could be adequately served by the existing ferry fleet. Good analysis would detail these factors for decision makers and assess the consequences of varying assumptions about each. Poor analysis would simply recommend action. The key is learning to present detailed information in a format that decision makers find understandable and persuasive.

10. Push the Boundaries of Analysis beyond the "Policy Envelope." Often problems come in very circumscribed forms. Someone has already decided what the problem is and what the alternative solutions are. The analyst may be able to expand both the problem definition and alternative solutions. For example, if traffic congestion is the specified problem and three alternative freeway locations are the possible solutions under consideration, a good analyst might raise questions concerning overall traffic efficiency and equity and advocate adding several mass-transit options to the freeway alternatives. For new and junior analysts this may not be possible, but at least the bounds should be explored. If the results are good, consider introducing them into the formal analysis. A major portion of our potential contribution is taken from us if we are handed the problem definition. Almost nothing remains if we are also given the allowable set of alternative solutions.

In Chapter 15 an environmental lobbying group has proposed a 10% tax on paper diapers. As a policy analyst you should examine the intended purpose of that tax. What result was it expected to achieve? Then you should push the boundaries of the analysis, not simply recommending yes or no on the proposed tax, but analyzing other policy tools and alternative definitions of the problem.

11. Be Aware That There Is No Such Thing as an Absolutely Correct, Rational, and Complete Analysis. Quality of analysis can be judged only in the context of time and resources available. Students working on practice problems or cases often complain that they are never given enough time to complete the analysis satisfactorily and that teachers have unrealistic goals for what can be accomplished in the time allotted. Students fail to believe that so little time would be devoted to analyzing "such an important policy" in the field. Many of the problems in this book are, however, drawn from field experiences where practicing analysts had little time and limited resources. Only in practice can the twin constraints of time and resources be appreciated. Even if resources and time were unlimited, the analysis would seldom be absolutely correct and complete. There would still be the issues of uncertainty and competing value systems.

The analyst must ask clients the level of analysis they desire: one person-hour or ten; one person-day or seven; a month or a year of how many people's effort? Analysts must be prepared to examine a problem at any of these levels, making recommendations where appropriate about the optimal amount of effort for each level of inquiry. Time and resources should be spent in amounts that garner the maximum marginal gain in information per dollar spent. Usually two or three levels of analysis can be identified for a policy problem, and an appropriate budget and work program can then be designed for each.

The case of the proposed parking garage (Chapter 10) can illustrate this point. Should the city clear a vacant downtown parcel and build a large municipally owned parking structure? At the first level we may have less than ten hours in which to analyze the idea. The work program would probably concentrate on verifying the total cost to the city of building and operating the structure and estimating the revenues it might generate by using fee structures and utilization rates from several adjacent lots. Given more time, say 40 hours, the analysis might be broadened to include an examination of the opportunity costs of building the garage; that is, the benefits lost by not selling the land to a private developer who would build a 20-story tax-generating office building. A sensitivity analysis might also be performed on the garage's proposed pricing schedule and expected utilization rate to see if the decision to build holds under pessimistic scenarios. With a work program that might stretch to six months and include several staff members, it would be possible to inventory the city's private and public parking facilities for pricing practices and utilization rates by location and relate this information to an overall plan for downtown development. Major secondary effects such as the impact on mass-transit ridership and retail shopping could also be explored. If still more time were available, it might also be possible to enter into more detailed negotiations with potential buyers of the downtown site and get written commitments to various types of development. The overall impacts of those proposed developments could then be compared to the parking-garage alternatives.

This last level looks very much like what we have described as researched analysis. However, drawing the line between basic and researched analysis is very difficult. Most policy problems can be approached on various levels, given different time and resource constraints, and useful advice can be given to decision makers at all levels of analysis. The analysis can get more comprehensive and detailed as resources and time increase, but even when detailed analysis is done, questions remain. In the parking-garage example, these might include the uncertainty over utilization rates and the effect on mass transit and retail activity, as well as uncertainty about possible alternatives to the garage and their impacts on employment and property taxes.

SUMMARY

This chapter provided an overview of the rationale for using simple methods for analyzing policies and plans. The point was made that decision makers often need answers quickly and will make decisions with available data. Policy analysts and planners can help to improve the quality of decisions by providing quick, accurate, and timely analyses. We described the primary differences among the classic rational problem-solving approach, researched analysis, comprehensive planning, and the policy analysis approach. We also provided a number of practical principles for beginning analysts.

We hope that beginning analysts will grow comfortable with the idea that they can provide clients a product that aids decision making, no matter how limited are time and resources. It is a matter of designing the work program to maximize information and analysis within given constraints. Getting good at this takes time and comes with experience. Practicing on sample problems and case examples is an ideal way to begin.

ORGANIZATION OF THE BOOK

We believe that, since policy analysis and planning is a craft, an important part of learning is practice. We also believe it is important to experience a continuum of learning from the most abstract and basic to the real and complex. This book is intended to be the first one that a student of policy analysis will use in connection with learning about methods of policy analysis. Previous coursework in statistics and economics is appropriate but not essential. Courses in modeling, survey research methods, linear programming, input-output analysis, econometric methods, and other researched methods will most appropriately follow use of this text. The book itself contains a continuum of learning experiences. Chapter 2 describes the process of policy analysis in some detail and introduces a minicase exercise that will be referred to throughout the book. Chapter 3 begins a series of seven chapters that describe steps in the policy process and explain associated basic methods that have proven useful in the field. Each of the chapters in this first part of the book ends with exercises.

The second part of the book contains case problems. Unlike the exercises in the previous chapters, little direction is given about which methods should be applied. However, a substantial problem description and clear directives on the needs of the client are provided.

People who read the entire book, practice the exercises, and solve the cases should gain confidence in their ability to approach policy problems, be ready and receptive for advanced courses in researched methods, and be well on their way to a career in a most exciting field.

GLOSSARY

Basic Analysis or Basic Methods   a subset of policy analysis methods, comprising quickly applied but theoretically sound ways to aid in making good policy decisions.

Comprehensive Planning   classically, a process in which an extensive inventory phase is followed by alternatives development and the preparation of a plan. The client is usually the general public, and often the preparer's perspective is supposed to be comprehensive, considering all pertinent factors and viewpoints. Most plans have rather long time horizons and attempt to maintain political neutrality.

Policy Analysis   a process that usually begins with problem definition rather than the broader inventory phase of the planning process. It also yields alternatives, but the final document is likely to be a memorandum, issue paper, or draft legislation. It has a specific client and a single point of view, a shorter time horizon, and an openly political approach. The final product of such a process is called a *policy analysis*.

Policy Analysis Methods   systematic procedures for attacking specific problems with specific purposes. They include *researched methods* and *basic methods*.

Policy Envelope   the constraints within which the analysis is to be performed. These may include a problem definition, values for certain parameters, and even a set of alternatives. These constraints can sometimes be altered during analysis if warranted.

Rational Model   (or rational problem-solving process) a process for approaching policy problems in which problem definition leads to identification and evaluation of alternatives, which is followed by implementation.

Researched Analysis or Researched Methods   a subset of policy analysis methods, requiring substantial budget, time, and data to achieve results. Many researched methods are well codified and are taught in advanced methods courses in planning, policy analysis, sociology, or economics curricula. Examples include survey research, model building, and input-output studies.

EXERCISES

1.   In order to begin to practice quick analysis, make a list of 15 problems that you believe could be resolved using basic methods of policy analysis and planning. Compile this list in 30 minutes or less.

2.   You work as the special assistant to the mayor. Clip from one week's worth of newspapers as many articles as possible that address public policy issues. Identify the central decision criterion of each issue.

3.   Categorize the problems you identified in Exercise 2 according to those that you believe can be solved through quick analysis and those that require researched analysis. Explain briefly why you categorized each problem as you did.

4.   Rank the problems you identified in Exercise 2 according to their political importance to the mayor. Rank them also according to their importance to society. Explain to the mayor why the differences exist and which issues ought to be attacked first.

5.   As policy analyst to a U.S. senator, identify 10 problems that need to be addressed by federal policy. As sources you might use back issues of national weekly news magazines.

6.   Categorize the problems that you identified in Exercise 5 according to those you believe can be solved through quick analysis and those that require researched analysis. Explain briefly why you categorized each problem as you did.

7.   Rank the problems you identified in Exercise 5 according to their political importance to the senator. Rank them also according to their importance to society. Explain to the senator why the differences exist and which issues ought to be attacked first.

8.   Using the list you developed in either Exercise 2 or 5, think about the types of policy actions that might be taken. Use the typology presented in Table 1-1 to identify the various direct, indirect, monetary, and nonmonetary policies that might be considered for three of the issues.

Chapter Two

The Policy Analysis Process

Chapter 1 introduced the concept of policy analysis as the *process* through which we identify and evaluate alternative policies or programs that are intended to lessen or resolve social, economic, or physical problems. However, the term *policy analysis* is also commonly used to refer to the *product* or outcome of the analytical process. This could be a bound, illustrated report, but more often it is a memo, position paper, or draft legislation. The analytic process and conclusions drawn from the process might also be presented orally and visually. Together, the process and product is oral and written persuasion through which the analyst seeks to inform others about the insights gained during examination of the policy problem.[1] The primary emphasis of this book is on the policy analysis *process*— how the analysis is formulated and conducted, and the methods used in the analysis. However, the product and its presentation are discussed at several points because their quality can be as important as the analysis they describe. A good presentation improves a good product.

We do not intend to belabor the definition of policy analysis, since the term, like the field, continues to evolve. The term *policy analysis* was probably first used

---

[1]Giandomenico Majone, *Evidence, Argument, and Persuasion in the Policy Process* (New Haven: Yale University Press, 1989), p. vii.

in 1958 by Lindblom,[2] although the concept of the policy approach was also discussed by Lasswell in 1951,[3] and the practice of policy analysis can be traced back to budget issues in the time of Jesus Christ[4] and even to public laws in Mesopotamia in the 21st century B.C.[5] Lindblom was referring to a type of quantitative analysis involving incremental comparisons in which nonquantitative methods are included in recognition of the interaction of values and policy.[6]

Over the years policy analysis has also been defined as:

- A means of synthesizing information including research results to produce a format for policy decisions (the laying out of alternative choices) and of determining future needs for policy-relevant information[7]
- A complex process of analyzing, intervening in, and managing the political conflict that is inextricably related to urban change[8]
- The systematic investigation of alternative policy options and the assembly and integration of the evidence for and against each option. It involves a problem-solving approach, the collection and interpretation of information, and some attempt to predict the consequences of alternative courses of action[9]
- The choice of the best policy among a set of alternatives with the aid of reason and evidence[10]
- Client-oriented advice relevant to public decisions[11]
- Determining which of various alternative public or government policies will most achieve a given set of goals in light of the relations between the policies and the goals[12]

[2] Charles E. Lindblom, "Policy Analysis," *American Economic Review* 48, no. 3 (June 1958), 298–312.

[3] Harold D. Lasswell, "The Policy Orientation," in *The Policy Sciences: Recent Developments in Scope and Methods*, ed. Daniel Lerner and Harold D. Lasswell (Stanford, CA: Stanford University Press, 1951), pp. 3–15.

[4] Lawrence E. Lynn, Jr., "Policy Analysis in the Bureaucracy: How New? How Effective?" *Journal of Policy Analysis and Management* 8, no. 3 (Summer 1989), 373–77.

[5] William N. Dunn, *Public Policy Analysis: An Introduction* (Englewood Cliffs, NJ: Prentice Hall 1981), pp. 8–9.

[6] Lindblom, "Policy Analysis," pp. 298–312. For additional historical perspectives see Peter deLeon, *Advice and Consent: The Development of the Policy Sciences* (New York: Russell Sage Foundation, 1988), pp.14–51; and Theodore J. Lowi, "Four Systems of Policy, Politics and Choice," *Public Administration Review* 32, no. 4 (July/August 1972), 298–310.

[7] Walter Williams, *Social Policy Research and Analysis: The Experience in the Federal Social Agencies* (New York: American Elsevier, 1971), p. xi.

[8] Dennis A. Rondinelli, "Urban Planning as Policy Analysis: Management of Urban Change," *Journal of the American Institute of Planners* 39, no. 1 (January 1973), 13.

[9] Jacob B. Ukeles, "Policy Analysis: Myth or Reality?" *Public Administration Review* 37, no. 3 (May/June 1977), 223.

[10] Duncan MacRae, Jr., "Concepts and Methods of Policy Analysis," *Society* 16, no. 6 (September/October 1979), 17.

[11] David L. Weimer and Aidan R. Vining, *Policy Analysis: Concepts and Practice* (Englewood Cliffs, NJ: Prentice Hall, 1989), p. 1.

[12] Stuart S. Nagel, "Introduction: Bridging Theory and Practice in Policy/Program Evaluation," in *Policy Theory and Policy Evaluation: Concepts, Knowledge, Causes and Norms*, ed. Stuart S. Nagel (New York: Greenwood Press, 1990), p. ix.

- An applied discipline which uses multiple methods of inquiry and argument to produce and transform policy-relevant information that may be utilized in political settings to resolve public problems[13]
- A form of applied research carried out to acquire a deeper understanding of sociotechnical issues and to bring about better solutions. Attempting to bring modern science and technology to bear on society's problems, policy analysis searches for feasible courses of action, generating information and marshaling evidence of the benefits and other consequences that would follow their adoption and implementation, in order to help the policymaker choose the most advantageous action[14]

TYPES OF POLICY ANALYSIS

Policy analysis can be done before or after the policy has been implemented. An analysis can be conducted to anticipate the results of alternative policies in order to choose among them, or it can be conducted to describe the consequences of a policy. Descriptive policy analysis refers to either the historical analysis of past policies or the evaluation of a new policy as it is implemented. Descriptive policy analysis has also been termed *ex-post,*[15] *post hoc,*[16] or *retrospective*[17] policy analysis. This after-the-fact analysis can be further broken down into two types: retrospective and evaluative, with retrospective analysis referring to the description and interpretation of past policies (What happened?) and evaluative policy analysis referring to program evaluation (Were the purposes of the policy met?). For example, a study of past student loan default rates among students of different majors would be a retrospective study. A study of default rates among students with particular characteristics to see if they matched those that had been anticipated when the program was set up would be an evaluative policy analysis.

Policy analysis that focuses upon the possible outcomes of proposed policies has been called *ex ante,*[18] *pre hoc,*[19] *anticipatory,*[20] or *prospective*[21] policy analysis. This analysis prior to the implementation of policies can be subdivided into predictive and prescriptive policy analysis. Predictive policy analysis refers to the projection of future states resulting from adopting particular alternatives, while

---

[13] Dunn, *Public Policy Analysis*, p. 60.

[14] Edward S. Quade, *Analysis for Public Decisions*, 2nd ed. (New York: Elsevier Scientific, 1982), p. 5.

[15] Michael Carley, *Rational Techniques in Policy Analysis* (London: Heinemann, 1980), p. 37; and Robert L. Lineberry, *American Public Policy: What Government Does and What Difference It Makes* (New York: Harper & Row, 1977), p. 86.

[16] Lineberry, *American Public Policy*, p 5.

[17] Dunn, *Public Policy Analysis*, p. 51; and Michael B. Teitz, "Policy Evaluation: The Uncertain Guide," Working Paper no. 298 (Berkeley: University of California, Institute for Urban and Regional Development, September 1978), p. 5.

[18] Carley, *Rational Techniques in Policy Analysis*, p. 37; and Lineberry, *American Public Policy*, p. 86.

[19] Lineberry, *American Public Policy*, p. 86.

[20] Teitz, "Policy Evaluation," p. 5.

[21] Dunn, *Public Policy Analysis*, p. 51.

prescriptive policy analysis refers to analysis that recommends actions because they will bring about a particular result.

Majone takes the distinction even further, limiting prescription to instances where the problem has a definite solution and there exists a well-defined procedure for achieving the solution. When the policymaker is unclear about the nature of the problem or when there is no standard way to choose among alternatives, then the analyst gives *advice*. When the analyst uses the language of advice to redirect the policymaker's attitudes, preferences or cognitive beliefs, this is *persuasive* advice.[22]

Thus, prescriptive policy analysis involves displaying the results of analysis *and* making a recommendation. The assumption here is that the analyst understands the client's values, goals, and objectives[23] and that the client expects or will at least tolerate a recommendation rather than a list of options.

A study forecasting the impact of changing the student loan interest rate on the savings behavior of borrowers and their parents would be a predictive policy analysis. A study to recommend what interest rate should be charged on student loans to cause potential borrowers to use family resources before borrowing would be a prescriptive analysis.

Descriptive analysis is often incorporated into prospective policy analysis. In order to design and evaluate new policies, the rationale for and the impact of past policies must be understood. Implemented policies must be monitored and evaluated in order to decide whether to continue or modify them and to generate information that will be useful when similar policies are proposed in the future. In the student loan example, descriptive analysis about past borrower behavior would be an important ingredient of an analysis of possible revisions to loan policies. However, the process and methods described in this book are intended primarily for use in predictive and prescriptive policy analysis, to help analysts examine the probable consequences of implementing new policies.

The principal tasks in prospective policy analysis include the identification and verification of complex problems, the quantitative and qualitative comparison of alternative ways to redress problems, and the assemblage of this information into a format that policymakers can use when making decisions. *Policy analysis* is thus a systematic evaluation of the technical and economic feasibility and political viability of alternative policies (or plans or programs),[24] strategies for implementation, and the consequences of policy adoption. A good policy analysis

---

[22] Majone, *Evidence, Argument, and Persuasion,* p. 38. For the relationship between the senior analyst and the client see Arnold J. Meltsner, *Rules for Rulers: The Politics of Advice* (Philadelphia: Temple University Press, 1990).

[23] Goals are typically considered to be broader and more general than objectives. Objectives are usually stated in quantifiable terms.

[24] Distinctions can be made among the words *plan, program,* and *policy,* but there is little agreement in the literature. The following distinctions may be helpful to readers not familiar with the literature. A *plan* is a general scheme of action or a procedure to obtain a desired end. A *policy* is a settled course of action to be followed by a government body or institution. A *program* is the specific set of steps that must be taken to achieve or implement a policy. A plan can include policies and programs. A policy may include programs. We will not belabor the differences in this text. The words will be considered as synonyms.

integrates quantitative and qualitative information, approaches the problem from various perspectives, and uses appropriate methods to test the feasibility of proposed options.

Methods and technical tools such as decision analysis, discounting, and modeling play an important role in policy analysis. However, policy analysis is more than the technical tools used to help inform decision makers. It is also the process that guides the selection and use of methods and tools, that recognizes the goals and values of the client, affected individuals, citizen groups, politicians, and units of government, and that provides a clear explanation of the issue being debated. It also involves explicitly stating the criteria that will be used to evaluate possible policies, the means for generating and evaluating alternative policies, specific ways to implement these policies, and how to assess the results of the analysis.

Clearly policy analysis is more than a technical, quantitative process. In fact, it has been argued that *politics* dominates policy analysis.[25] Whatever the balance, policy analysis involves both quantitative and qualitative analysis:

> ... if the purpose of policy analysis is not simply to find out what is good or satisfactory policy but to ensure that the policy will actually be chosen and implemented, the traditional skills are not sufficient. The analyst must also learn rhetorical and dialectic skills—the ability to define a problem according to various points of view, to draw an argument from many different sources, to adapt the argument to the audience, and to educate public opinion.[26]

As we look to the future of policy analysis, we do not see a lessening of the use of quantitative analysis. Rather, we see a greater involvement in the process of analysis of the groups and individuals to be affected by the policy, a much more open and visible or transparent process, more emphasis on negotiation, and a greater explicit recognition of the role that values play in the entire policy process, from the selection of the issues to address, to the types of alternatives selected, to the policy indicators selected, and to the respective weights given to economic, technical, and political criteria.[27] Moreover, the issue of the ethics of policy analysis will be addressed increasingly, although whether progress in this area will translate into better public policies is yet to be seen.

What, then, constitutes a good, complete policy analysis? The definitions presented above suggest that a good policy analysis addresses an important problem in a logical, valid, replicable manner, and provides information that can be used by decision makers in adopting economically viable, technically feasible, ethical, and politically acceptable policies that will resolve public issues.[28]

---

[25] deLeon, *Advice and Consent*, p. 106.

[26] Majone, *Evidence, Argument, and Persuasion*, p. xii.

[27] See also deLeon, *Advice and Consent*, pp. 104–22; Duncan MacRae, Jr., *Policy Indicators: Links between Social Science and Public Debate* (Chapel Hill: University of North Carolina Press, 1985), pp. 293–325; and Miriam K. Mills, *Conflict Resolution and Public Policy* (New York: Greenwood Press, 1990), pp. vii–xv.

[28] See also Hugh J. Miser and Edward S. Quade, "Toward Quality Control," in *Handbook of Systems Analysis: Craft Issues and Procedural Choices*, ed. Hugh J. Miser and Edward S. Quade (Chichester, Eng.: Wiley, 1988), p. 649; and Nagel, "Introduction," pp. x–xiii.

THE ROLE OF THE ANALYST

Policy analysts can be found at all levels of government, in private consulting, and within academe. DeLeon believes that hundreds of millions, and more likely billions, of dollars are spent annually on policy analyses.[29] Policy analysts work for state planning and budget bureaus, governors' offices, and legislative committees. They work for city managers, planning and development agencies, boards of education, finance departments, and federal departments and agencies.[30] Most often these analysts are staff assistants, and their assignments usually vary from day to day or week to week. They typically work on remedies to specific problems for immediate application. Their jobs involve a large measure of producing evidence and arguments to be used in the debate over alternative governmental actions.[31]

Analysts may be housed within an agency or they may be part of an external organization,[32] such as a private consulting group, a commission, a think tank, or a university unit. When they are part of an ongoing agency they may become so closely identified with the programs of the agency that their analyses may not suggest much change from the status quo, may have a bias toward defending that agency's positions, and may not be able to evaluate policies objectively. Consequently, it is often argued that independent contractors, outside agencies, or other third parties can produce policy analyses that are more objective.[33]

People become policy analysts because they want to work on interesting problems, to apply their technical knowledge, to be useful, to make an impact, to make a decent income doing something they find enjoyable, and to be near power or possibly to have power.[34] MacRae and Wilde believe that informed citizens can be their own policy analysts.[35]

Meltsner has classified policy analysts as three types: the technician, the politician, and the entrepreneur.[36] The technician is a researcher with excellent

---

[29] deLeon, *Advice and Consent*, p. 106.

[30] Policy analysis is also being institutionalized in other countries. See Richard Hofferbert, *The Reach and Grasp of Policy Analysis: Comparative Views of the Craft* (Tuscaloosa: University of Alabama Press, 1990).

[31] Majone, *Evidence, Argument, and Persuasion*, p. 7.

[32] For more on this "third community," see Evert A. Lindquist, "The Third Community, Policy Inquiry, and Social Scientists," in *Social Scientists, Policy, and the State*, ed. Stephen Brooks and Alain-G. Gagnon (New York: Praeger, 1990), pp. 21–51.

[33] Robert A. Heineman, William T. Bluhm, Steven A. Peterson, and Edward N. Kearny, *The World of the Policy Analyst: Rationality, Values, and Politics* (Chatham, NJ: Chatham House, 1990), pp. 41–42.

[34] Arnold J. Meltsner, "Bureaucratic Policy Analysts," *Policy Analysis* 1, no. 1 (Winter 1975), 115–31; and Meltsner, *Rules for Rulers*, pp. 30–41.

[35] Duncan MacRae, Jr., and James A. Wilde, *Policy Analysis for Public Decisions* (North Scituate, MA: Duxbury Press, 1979), pp. 4–5. See also William D. Coplin and Michael K. O'Leary, *Public Policy Skills* (Croton-on-Hudson, NY: Policy Studies Associates, 1988).

[36] Arnold J. Meltsner, *Policy Analysts in the Bureaucracy* (Berkeley and Los Angeles: University of California Press, 1976), p. 4.

analytical skills but few political skills who would "rather be right than on time." The politician is the analyst-turned-bureaucrat striving for personal advancement who is more attuned to politics than analysis. The entrepreneur, highly skilled both analytically and politically:

> ... knows how to work with numbers and people ... does not let his immediate client constrain him ... sees the public interest as his client ... has strong normative views of the scope of government activity ... is concerned about distribution as well as efficiency ... is much more aware than other analysts that his preferences guide the selection and solution of analytical problems.[37]

Most analysts we know, and the students we teach, view themselves as, or would like to become, entrepreneurs.[38] They seek to exercise both technical and political skills.

Becoming an entrepreneur rather than a bureaucrat is not easy. Meltsner has found that analysts in bureaucracies are susceptible to bureaucratic influences because "(1) they are members of an emerging profession without enforceable standards and sanctions; (2) they lack an adequate base of knowledge and associated theoretical paradigms; (3) they have tenuous communication networks; and (4) they are low resource, low status political actors."[39] With a lack of social and political support from outside the bureaucracy, they succumb to bureaucratic forces, folkways, and incentives. Because it is important to combine technical and political skills early in a career, both types of methods are included in this book to help the beginning analyst become the type of analyst who can work with numbers *and* people.

The beginning analyst faces a number of challenges. Not only must textbook knowledge be put into practice, but the analyst must learn about the operation of the agency and the political system. In the process of interviewing hundreds of administrators, Bellavita found that most of them learned what they knew about organizations through books, courses, role models, and experience, with experience being the most significant source of knowledge.[40] In addition to reading and coursework, and short of gaining actual experience, the analyst can observe analysts and managers at work and learn about their experiences. In this vein, Bellavita asked a number of seasoned administrators what they now know about organizations that they would like to have known earlier in their careers. Among the points are the following:[41]

---

[37] Ibid. pp. 36–37.

[38] For a counter view in which the technician may be effective see Heineman, *World of the Policy Analyst*, pp. 27–28.

[39] Meltsner, *Policy Analysts*, pp. 11–12.

[40] Christopher Bellavita, "Preface," in *How Public Organizations Work: Learning from Experience*, ed. Christopher Bellavita (New York: Praeger, an imprint of Greenwood Publishing Group, Inc., 1990), p. xiv. Reprinted with permission; all rights reserved.

[41] Adapted from Christopher Bellavita, "Learning from Experience," in *How Public Organizations Work* (New York: Praeger, an imprint of Greenwood Publishing Group, Inc., 1990), pp. 209–10. Reprinted with permission; all rights reserved.

- Organizations are driven by the self-interest of their members and thus conflict is endemic to them.
- As a manager there are limits to your ability to influence other people's behavior.
- Organizations have multiple realities (i.e., political, social, economic, legal).
- Organizations have multiple levels of discourse; many levels of conversation are taking place simultaneously.
- Learn by listening and by thinking about the theoretical implications of a significant event after it has happened.
- Understand yourself, and your motivations, values, and beliefs; to help others you first need to know where you stand.

Although policy analysts may sometimes become advocates for a particular policy, they more often remain analysts, striving to provide their employer or client an evaluation of alternatives that can be used as one of perhaps several inputs to formulating a decision. Policy analysts may be asked for advice, and sometimes they can set an agenda, but most often the decision is reserved for the agency director, the legislative committee, the governor, or the mayor.[42] In addition to these people at the top, policy is made by the so-called street-level bureaucrats such as school teachers, police officers, social workers, judges, prosecutors, zoning administrators, and other government workers in the process of carrying out their day-to-day responsibilities.[43]

Not only may the analyst have trouble gaining the ear of decision makers, it has even been said that "most policy actors run in totally opposite directions from what many policy analysts advocate,"[44] and analysis is undervalued and underutilized.[45] Moreover, Wildavsky argues that the life of a public servant is likely to become more difficult as he or she acts as the go-between for politicians who disagree over what constitutes the public interest. Wildavsky expects that in the future public servants will be even more vulnerable than they are today to attack as a result of conflicts over visions of what ought to be done.[46] In a similar vein, Bellavita used the word *hero* to describe administrators whose accomplishments exceeded the normal range of experience and who should serve as models for future administrators in the public sector.[47]

---

[42] For guidance for those analysts who advise leaders, see Meltsner, *Rules for Rulers.*

[43] Dennis J. Palumbo, *Public Policy in America: Government in Action* (San Diego: Harcourt Brace Jovanovich, 1988), pp. 19–21, 93–95.

[44] Hok Lin Leung, *Towards a Subjective Approach to Policy Planning & Evaluation: Common-Sense Structured* (Winnipeg, Canada: Ronald P. Frye, 1985), p. 19.

[45] Robert H. Socolow, "Failures of Discourse: Obstacles to the Integration of Environmental Values into Natural Resource Policy," in *When Values Conflict: Essays on Environmental Analysis, Discourse, and Decision,* ed. Laurence H. Tribe, Corinne S. Schelling, and John Voss (Cambridge, MA: Ballinger, 1976), pp. 1–33.

[46] Aaron Wildavsky, "Ubiquitous Anomie: Public Service in an Era of Ideological Dissensus," *Public Administration Review* 48, no. 4 (July/August 1988), 753–55.

[47] Christopher Bellavita, "The Hero's Journey in Public Administration," in *How Public Organizations Work* (New York: Praeger, an imprint of Greenwood Publishing Group, Inc., 1990), pp. 43–66. Reprinted with permission; all rights reserved.

The analyst who does not understand the relationship with the client, especially the analyst responsible to an elected official, is likely to be frustrated and disappointed. Often political factors will prevent a technically superior alternative from being selected. Lineberry provides the caution: "It does not stretch a point too much to say that politicians usually listen more carefully to voters than to analysis, whereas the opposite is true of experts. In essence, the question is whether a policy should be adopted because a majority prefer it or because it is the rational thing to do."[48] Occasionally the two positions are synonymous, but the analyst must also expect instances when they are not.

That the decision usually falls to others does not necessarily negate the influence of the analyst who will be involved in the interpretation of problems, the establishment of a fact base, and the identification and evaluation of alternatives. The way the analysis is packaged or presented can influence decisions. Moreover, basic assumptions may introduce biases into the analysis. Thus, to maintain credibility the analyst must identify underlying assumptions, keep accurate records, use multiple sources of information, and employ replicable methods and models.

In real life most policy analysis topics are identified by top officials, politicians, and agency officials who seek to understand the costs and benefits of policy decisions they must make. These problems may be assigned to staff for analysis, or staff may provide data for the decision maker's analysis. In either case, but especially when assigned the task of conducting the study, the analyst has a right to expect some guidance from the executive or client including the following, which we derive from our experience and suggestions from the Urban Institute.[49] The client or manager should:

1. Assist in the identification of problems and issues
2. Delegate responsibility and authority for the study to a specific individual or group
3. Provide adequate staff and fiscal resources
4. Indicate a time frame for completing the analysis
5. Review the objectives, evaluation criteria, alternatives and constituencies included for political ramifications
6. Periodically check on progress
7. Review results and use the relevant findings

Not all managers will meet all of their obligations. On occasion you may find that these responsibilities have been neglected so badly that they jeopardize the validity and usefulness of your work. What to do depends on your relationship to the client who requested you to do the analysis. If you are an influential senior adviser, you may be able to alter the context within which you are working by appealing to the client directly or to your superior. If you are a junior-level

[48] Lineberry, *American Public Policy*, p. 33.
[49] Harry Hatry, Louis Blair, Donald Fisk, and Wayne Kimmel, *Program Analysis for State and Local Governments* (Washington, DC: Urban Institute, 1976), pp. 10–11.

staff member, you may well have to live with the problem and profit from the experience.

ETHICAL CONSIDERATIONS

In the preceding sections we suggested that policy analysts and planners deal with ethical considerations, and, as you will see, virtually all of the case studies in this book involve ethical issues as well.[50] Planners, analysts, experts, and advisers are confronted with ethical issues on a daily basis. Many of these issues are addressed and resolved without controversy, such as those related to administrative decisions, bureaucratic procedures, and rules of behavior regarding clients and supervisors. The more complex issues are those related to the moral implications of our methods, the ethical content of the criteria built into decision models, and those ethical issues inherent in the evaluation of major policy alternatives.[51]

A typical ethical dilemma is presented in Figure 2-1.[52] In this case, the mayor is not satisfied with the results of a planning analysis because of the impact the findings might have on the community. The consultants who prepared the report refuse to change it to suit the mayor. The mayor then tells a staff analyst to rewrite the report. The staff analyst is thus presented with an ethical dilemma and is faced with conflicting responsibilities to multiple moral constituencies, including the mayor, the community, the profession, and self. Although the consultants refused to rewrite their report, they may face another ethical dilemma if the staff member rewrites the report and the mayor releases it.

Such ethical dilemmas or moral problems arise because of clashes among ethical or moral principles: for example, among client loyalty, the public interest, fairness, equity, efficiency, justice, the law, and professional autonomy.[53] One

[50] The case-study method has been proposed for teaching ethics for the same reason we use cases; that is, "to make abstract principles come alive . . . to test and apply principles rather than simply collect them to support a general proposition." John A. Rohr, "Ethics in Public Administration: A State-of-the-Discipline Report," in *Public Administration: The State of the Discipline*, ed. Naomi B. Lynn and Aaron Wildavsky (Chatham, NJ: Chatham House, 1990, pp. 114–15). For case examples, see Joan C. Callahan, ed., *Ethical Issues in Professional Life* (New York: Oxford University Press, 1988); William N. Dunn, ed., *Values, Ethics, and the Practice of Policy Analysis* (Lexington, MA: Lexington Books, 1983); Frank Fischer and John Forester, eds., *Confronting Values in Policy Analysis: The Politics of Criteria* (Beverly Hills: Sage, 1987); Norman Krumholz and John Forester, *Making Equity Planning Work: Leadership in the Public Sector* (Philadelphia: Temple University Press, 1990); and Martin Wachs, ed., *Ethics in Planning* (New Brunswick, NJ: Center for Urban Policy Research, 1985).

[51] Martin Wachs, "Introduction," in *Ethics in Planning*, ed. Martin Wachs (New Brunswick, NJ: Center for Urban Policy Research, 1985), pp. xiii–xiv.

[52] For other examples of ethical dilemmas, see Callahan, *Ethical Issues in Professional Life*, and Nagel, "Introduction," p. xix.

[53] Richard S. Bolan, "The Structure of Ethical Choice in Planning Practice," *Journal of Planning Education and Research* 3, no. 1 (Summer 1983), 23–34; Elizabeth Howe and Jerome Kaufman, "Ethics and Professional Practice," in *Values, Ethics, and the Practice of Policy Analysis*, ed. William N. Dunn (Lexington, MA: Lexington Books, 1983), p. 9; and Peter Marcuse, "Professional Ethics and Beyond: Values in Planning," *Journal of the American Institute of Planners* 42, no. 3 (July 1976), 264–74, reprinted in Wachs, *Ethics in Planning*, pp. 3–24.

Oldport: The Hazards of Population Projections

In Oldport the mayor retained a planning firm as consultant to develop a comprehensive twenty-year plan for urban renewal, housing, schools, and social service facilities. The planners' preliminary report projected moderate population growth but a dramatic and continuing shift in racial composition, with minority groups reaching a majority in twelve years. A black majority was predicted within five years in the public schools.

The mayor reacted strongly to the preliminary report. If these findings were released, they would become a self-fulfilling prophecy. All hope of preserving an integrated school system and maintaining stable mixed neighborhoods or developing an ethnically heterogeneous city with a strong residential base would disappear.

The planners were asked to review their figures. They agreed to use the lower range of their projections—minority dominance in the public schools after eight years and a majority in the city in sixteen. The mayor was not satisfied. He told the planners either to change the figures or to cut them out of the report. They refused, feeling they had bent their interpretation of fact as far as they could. Without a discussion of these facts, the balance of the report could not be professionally justified.

The mayor lashed out at them privately for professional arrogance, asked a professional on his own staff to rewrite the report without the projections, and ordered the consultants not to release or disclose their findings on race under any circumstances.

Source: Excerpted from Peter Marcuse, "Professional Ethics and Beyond: Values in Planning," Reprinted by permission of the *Journal of the American Institute of Planners* 42, no. 3 (July 1976), 265.

Figure 2-1   A Typical Ethical Dilemma

moral principle pulls one way, and another pulls the other, creating a "conflict of duties."[54]

In order to deal with ethical issues, planners and analysts adopt a normative moral theory or perspective.[55] In deciding about the policy action to take in the Oldport example, the staff analyst might adopt the criterion of the greatest good for the greatest number, the greatest benefit to the least advantaged, that lying with statistics is always wrong, that lying is acceptable to achieve a good end, that economic costs and benefits should be weighed, or that we know what is right by intuition.[56]

The issue, however, is not that policy analysts and planners are confronted with ethical dilemmas. The real point is how to practice analysis in an ethical manner, which includes addressing such matters as what is the right thing to do, what is good, whose values are to be pursued, whose goals are to be sought, and to what extent a client is served instead of the public or common good.[57] Planners and policy analysts need to understand ethics because they will be making choices about conceptual analytic frameworks, alternative actions and policies, and their own behavior.[58]

---

[54] William K. Frankena, *Ethics* (Englewood Cliffs, NJ: Prentice Hall, 1963), p. 2.

[55] For good introductions to the language and definitions of ethics see Callahan, *Ethical Issues in Professional Life*, pp. 3–25; and Frankena, *Ethics*.

[56] Elizabeth Howe, "Normative Ethics in Planning," *Journal of Planning Literature* 5, no. 2 (November 1990), 123–24.

[57] We are not talking about obviously morally indefensible actions such as stealing, malfeasance, misfeasance, and nonfeasance in office.

[58] Peter G. Brown, "Ethics and Education for the Public Service in a Liberal State," *Journal of Policy Analysis and Management* 6, no. 1 (Fall 1986), 59.

Ethical issues also include questions of intergenerational and international justice, not only those questions involving contemporaries.[59] The ethical choices we have to make are often very subtle, involving what we analyze, how we approach it, what information we present, how we work with clients, and generally how we act as professionals.[60]

Values in Analysis

Very few planners and analysts today would argue that their work is value free. In fact, in most fields, practitioners increasingly recognize both that their work is highly value laden and that there are limits to technical knowledge.[61]

Most contemporary writers on policy analysis also recognize that analysis has a substantial normative component, since through its use we seek information about the consequences of actions and their impact on people. As Dunn has stated: "The aims of policy analysis include but go beyond the production of facts; policy analysts also seek to produce information about values and their attainment through reflective action."[62] We believe that few, if any, policy analysts and planners still cling to a strict objective, value-neutral view of policy development. In fact, Majone has pointed out that in the decisionist view, rational policy analysis can begin only after the relevant values have been identified, and that these values change over time as a result of the policymaking process.[63]

Not only is it generally recognized that values play a role in analysis, but Heineman and colleagues argue that values and beliefs are used as heuristic shortcuts in decision making, especially in the development of foreign policy,[64] and Leung notes that "a policy is a concrete expression of values, which involves the distribution of resources and powers."[65]

Even in his early chapter on "The Policy Orientation," Lasswell wrote that the analyst must clarify values:

> The policy-science approach not only puts the emphasis upon basic problems and complex models, but also calls forth a very considerable clarification of the value goals involved in policy. After all, in what sense is a problem "basic"? Evaluations

[59] Timothy Beatley, "Environmental Ethics and Planning Theory," *Journal of Planning Literature* 4, no. 1 (Winter 1989), 18–22; and Brown, "Ethics and Education," p. 58.

[60] Howe and Kaufman, "Ethics and Professional Practice," p. 9.

[61] Rosemarie Tong, *Ethics in Policy Analysis* (Englewood Cliffs, NJ: Prentice Hall, 1986), pp. 12–38.

[62] William N. Dunn, "Introduction," in *Values, Ethics, and the Practice of Policy Analysis*, ed. William N. Dunn (Lexington, MA: Lexington Books, 1983), p. 1.

[63] Majone, *Evidence, Argument, and Persuasion*, p. 24; see also Leung, *Towards a Subjective Approach*, pp. 35–38.

[64] Robert A. Heineman, William T. Bluhm, Steven A. Peterson, and Edward N. Kearny, *The World of the Policy Analyst: Rationality, Values, and Politics* (Chatham, NJ: Chatham House, 1990), pp. 60–61.

[65] Leung, *Towards a Subjective Approach*, p. 39.

depend upon postulates about the human relations to be called desirable. For purposes of analysis the term "value" is taken to mean "a category of preferred events," such as peace rather than war, high levels of productive employment rather than mass unemployment, democracy rather than despotism, and congenial and productive personalities rather than destructive ones.[66]

Although the value-laden nature of planning and policy analysis is understood, practice has not seen much systematic consideration of the impact of ethical values on decisions. This task has proven difficult because policy analysis has grown out of empirically based disciplines built on scientific objectivity and assumed value neutrality. But some analysts have attempted to include normative concerns in their work. This mixed nature of policy analysis was described by Fischer and Forester:

> On one hand it is empirical but not rigorously scientific in the classical sense of the term. On the other hand it is fundamentally concerned with the realization of norms and values, but it is not ethics per se. Policy analysis lies squarely (if uncomfortably) between science and ethics.[67]

Ethical Analysis

Ethics did not become a popular topic until quite recently.[68] The scientific management approach of the late 19th and early 20th centuries and the professionalism of politics and public administration pushed out the ethical considerations that had been brought about by the Pendleton Act of 1883.[69] The rapid growth of policy analysis after World War II was driven primarily by operations research, systems analysis, and applied economics, which Dunn calls "disciplines particularly resistant to ethical reasoning and valuative discourse."[70] It was not until the decline in confidence in social institutions and the Watergate issue in the 1970s that ethics reemerged as a topic of concern, which continues today as a result of the lack of confidence in government.[71] The 1970s also saw discontent with the way in which normative issues were being considered in policy analysis,

[66] Harold D. Lasswell, "The Policy Orientation," in *The Policy Sciences: Recent Developments in Scope and Methods*, ed. Daniel Lerner and Harold D. Lasswell (Stanford, CA: Stanford University Press, 1951), pp. 9–10.

[67] Frank Fischer and John Forester, "Volume Editors' Introduction," in *Confronting Values in Policy Analysis: The Politics of Criteria*, ed. Frank Fischer and John Forester (Newbury Park, CA: Sage, 1987), pp. 10–13.

[68] Douglas Amy, "Can Policy Analysis be Ethical?" in *Confronting Values in Policy Analysis: The Politics of Criteria*, ed. Frank Fischer and John Forester (Newbury Park, CA: Sage, 1987), p. 53; and Dunn, "Introduction," p. 1.

[69] Terry L. Cooper, *An Ethic of Citizenship for Public Administration* (Englewood Cliffs, NJ: Prentice Hall, 1991), p. 115; and Michael L. Vasu, Debra W. Stewart, and G. David Garson, *Organizational Behavior and Public Management*, 2nd ed. (New York: Marcel Dekker, 1990), p. 364.

[70] Dunn,, "Introduction," p. 1.

[71] Vasu, Stewart, and Garson, *Organizational Behavior and Public Management*, pp. 366–67.

in particular, that techniques such as policy analysis assumed general agreement on societal priorities and values that did not exist.[72]

The literature on ethics has expanded greatly in recent years, but the coverage has been called "chaotic," and ethics has been said to overlap with many other topics—"personnel, budgeting, administrative law, and so on."[73] Not only have the journals in virtually all fields published articles or even special issues on ethics, but numerous journals are devoted primarily to ethics.[74] Even with all of this publication activity, there is no commonly accepted definition of ethics or moral thinking in the field of policy analysis.

Within the broader literature of ethics there are three kinds of moral thinking: *descriptive*, which attempts to develop a theory of human nature that bears on ethical questions; *normative*, which addresses what is good or right in a particular case or as a general principle and leads to a normative judgment; and *critical* or *meta-ethical*, which addresses logical, epistemological, or semantical questions dealing with the establishment and justification of ethical and value judgments.[75]

The issues raised by the Oldport example fall into the area called "normative ethics," which has been defined as "a systematic inquiry into the *justifications* for individual conduct and institutional practices and modes of thought."[76] Normative ethics thus addresses the justifications for behavior and provides guidelines for selecting a policy that is good or right, rather than seeking a causal explanation of behavior. Although facts are integral to moral decision making, normative ethics focuses on value judgments as opposed to facts.[77] "Normative ethics provides guidelines for deciding what makes right acts right."[78]

How do we decide whether a policy is morally right? It is widely accepted that rules cannot define ethical or morally correct action. We cannot be guided simply by traditional or customary practices. Rather, we must reflect on the principles that will govern our actions. Although law, prudence, economics, religion, authority, and opinion/bias/taste can be relevant to ethical decision making, they alone are not sufficient.[79] We have to engage in moral *reasoning*. But what kind of principles can we draw upon to support this reasoning? Theories of

---

[72] Amy, "Can Policy Analysis be Ethical?" pp. 46–47.

[73] Rohr, "Ethics in Public Administration," p. 97.

[74] Rohr reviews the ethics literature and cites a half dozen ethics journals plus a number of texts and case books in "Ethics in Public Administration," pp. 99, 115, but many others are available as well. For an overview of issues at the federal level, see Anne Marie Donahue, ed., *Ethics in Politics and Government* (New York: H. W. Wilson, 1989).

[75] Frankena, *Ethics*, p. 4.

[76] Brown, "Ethics and Education," p. 57; see also Eugene J. Meehan, *Ethics for Policymaking: A Methodological Analysis* (New York: Greenwood Press, 1990).

[77] Callahan, *Ethical Issues in Professional Life*, pp. 6–7.

[78] Howe, "Normative Ethics in Planning," p. 123.

[79] Callahan, *Ethical Issues in Professional Life*, pp. 10–14.

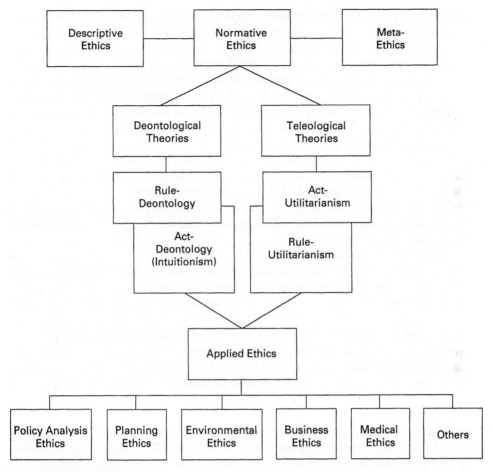

Figure 2-2   Ethical Theories

normative moral obligation are generally classified as teleological and deontological (Figure 2-2).[80]

   Teleological theories are concerned with the goodness of outcomes. They hold that the moral value of an action is a function of the *consequences* of that action, that is the nonmoral good rather than the act itself.[81] Teleological theories

---

[80] Jerome Kaufman suggested an earlier version of this figure. Theories that will not be addressed include Marxism, critical theory, and communitarian theory.

[81] Callahan, *Ethical Issues in Professional Life*, p. 19. The moral theory "consequentialism," sometimes seen as a subset of teleological ethics, holds that actions are right or wrong according to the consequences they produce. See James F. Childress and John Macquarrie, eds., *The Westminster Dictionary of Christian Ethics* (Philadelphia: Westminster Press, 1986), p. 122.

may be concerned with consequences to self (egoistic), to others (altruistic), or to everyone (universalistic). In order to decide whether something is right, good, or ought to be done, we must first have some view of what is good in the nonmoral sense and then decide whether the act in question can bring about the good.[82]

Deontological theories are concerned with process. They hold that an act or behavior is judged right or wrong according to the nature of the act, regardless of the consequences.[83] Deontologists believe that an act can be morally right even if it does not produce the greatest balance of good over evil.

Deontological and teleological theories may be rule based or act based. In rule-based theories, the ethical principles are used to generate rules that guide the behavior of individuals. In act-based theories, individuals use the general ethical principles to make decisions in particular situations.[84] Act-based theories are flexible enough to deal with conflicts and exceptions but pose the problem of too many exceptions. The rule approach avoids the problem of too many exceptions, but is rigid.

One universalistic teleological theory, *act-utilitarianism*, holds that an act is right if, and only if, it brings about the greatest happiness for the greatest number of people, without regard for the distribution of the good or bad. We decide what alternative to select based upon the net happiness produced. This theory is the basis for benefit-cost analysis. As attractive and often used as this approach is, it has been criticized because of the difficulty of defining happiness, the rationale for pursuing it for the greatest number of people, the possible unjust distribution of pleasure and pain, the difficulty of comparing the relative happiness of people, and allowing for too many exceptions to agreed upon principles.[85]

Rule-deontology theory focuses on rules, rights, and actions that are right in themselves, rather than on outcomes. That is, it focuses on right and wrong, rather than benefit and harm. Among the rule-deontologists is Kant, who proposed a rational rule non-self-interest theory. There is also Rawls, who proposed a theory of justice based on individual rights to basic liberties and the distribution of greater benefit to the least advantaged available through equal and fair access to offices and positions.[86] The rule-deontology approach is criticized because moral rules that must bind under *all* circumstances are violated on a regular basis in contemporary society, and this approach has little to say about policy outcomes.[87] While the influence of deontology theory on the practice of planning

---

[82] Frankena, *Ethics*, p. 13.

[83] Ibid., p. 14.

[84] Howe, "Normative Ethics in Planning," p. 127.

[85] Tong, *Ethics in Policy Analysis*, p. 82; see also Heineman, Bluhm, Peterson, and Kearny, *World of the Policy Analyst*, p. 71; and Howe, "Normative Ethics in Planning," p. 129.

[86] For a planning application of Rawls's theory see Timothy Beatley, "Applying Moral Principles to Growth Management," *Journal of the American Planning Association* 50, no. 4 (Autumn 1984), 459–69.

[87] Tong, *Ethics in Policy Analysis*, pp. 84–86; see also Howe, "Normative Ethics in Planning," p. 141.

and policy analysis has been limited, it appeals to many people in a culture dominated by Judeo-Christian religious traditions in which all people are held to the same rules.[88]

Callahan believes that most of us would categorize ourselves as deontologists, but that in practice we often function teleologically; for example, whenever we weigh pros and cons we "attempt to produce good results without considering seriously enough what moral values might be sacrificed in the process."[89]

In practice, neither of these two approaches is completely satisfactory, so alternative middle-ground approaches have been developed, among them *rule-utilitarianism* and *act-deontology* (intuitionism), upon which codes of ethics have been based.

In rule-utilitarianism, the principle of utility is applied to rules instead of to individual acts. It allows moral rules to coexist with, and be justified by, the principle of utility. It allows for individual exceptions to moral rules because of good consequences, and where several institutionalized rules conflict, the principle of utility can be used to decide between them. Unfortunately, the issue of collective goods is not at the center of this ethical theory.[90]

Act-deontology approaches are less rigid versions of rule-deontology because choices between competing ethical principles can be made in certain situations. Intuitionism, one form of act-deontology, recognizes that there are many ethical principles that should be obeyed, but that sometimes these may conflict with one another, and each individual must choose in each instance what is intuitively right. Many planners and policy analysts think of ethics in these terms, but the theory provides no guidance on how to choose, and ethical intuition could easily be overwhelmed by "personal preference, self-interest, political pressure or . . . 'pragmatic eclecticism.' "[91]

Planners and analysts have emphasized different theories, depending upon their backgrounds and the moral communities of which they are a part. Economists tend to emphasize efficiency, lawyers emphasize rights, planners emphasize deontological values such as equity or environmentalism, and policy analysts emphasize the utilitarian cost-benefit approach.[92]

Kaufman classified planners into four categories of ethical involvement: the ethically unaware, the ethically hyperactive, the ethical relativists, and the ethical hybrids.[93] The first group could identify only the grossest ethical issues. The second group was highly sensitive and tended, like deontologists, to see their behavior as right or wrong. The relativists were more like teleologicalists

---

[88] Howe,"Normative Ethics in Planning," p. 127.

[89] Callahan, *Ethical Issues in Professional Life*, p. 21.

[90] Howe, "Normative Ethics in Planning," p. 142.

[91] Ibid., pp. 144–45.

[92] Bolan, "The Structure of Ethical Choice in Planning Practice," pp. 23–34; Howe, "Normative Ethics in Planning," p. 146.

[93] Jerome L. Kaufman, "Hamelethics in Planning: To Do or Not to Do," *Business and Professional Ethics Journal* 6, no. 2 (1989), 68–69.

and focused on the consequences of their actions. The hybrids sometimes adopted a deontological stance and other times a teleological one. Howe believes that we think in terms of act-deontology when faced with problems of "professional ethics" but in terms of act-utilitarianism when faced with a policy to analyze.[94]

It seems clear that one common ethical theory for the policy fields is unlikely to emerge, much less a set of ethical rules. Many planners and policy analysts seem to act on the basis of multiple theories. They both try to do good and act truthfully, loyally, and efficiently. Applying different moral theories has been criticized, however, as creating dissonance. Tong argues that rather than a set of moral or ethical rules, policy analysts need to develop a moral point of view that helps them live up to a set of self-imposed moral ideals. She notes that the same ethics should govern both our private and professional lives, that analysts should be guided by an ethic of virtue based on personal integrity, and that analysts must cultivate virtues specific to their professions. These moral virtues are derived either from justice or benevolence. Tong identifies both obligations to the client and to third parties as important to professional life.[95]

If there is not a common definition of ethics in policy analysis, is there, nonetheless, a consensus on the primary ethical concern for professionals and practitioners? In a review of definitions of ethics from contemporary literature, Vasu, Stewart, and Garson identify the notion of *obligation* as the common theme, with obligation seen as related to who bears the obligation, whether it is a positive or negative obligation, and whether the effort to shape ethical decision making is internal or external to the individual or organization.[96]

The concept of *responsibility* was identified by Cooper as the central concern in administrative ethics.[97] When we are confronted with a problem about what ought to be done, he says we are experiencing the need to define our responsibility in the administrative role, with there being two kinds of responsibility, objective and subjective responsibility. Objective responsibility derives from legal, organizational, and societal demands on our role as an administrator, whereas subjective responsibility is based on an inner drive composed of beliefs, values, and predispositions about how we should act. It is in confronting conflicting, competing, and inconsistent responsibilities that ethical dilemmas are typically presented to us.

A related view is given by Rohr, who has argued that there is an emerging consensus on the nature of the ethical problem that faces the political servant—the responsible use of administrative *discretion*. He believes that "through admin-

---

[94] Howe, "Normative Ethics in Planning," p. 146.

[95] Tong, *Ethics in Policy Analysis*, pp. 94–136.

[96] Vasu, Stewart, and Garson, *Organizational Behavior and Public Management*, pp. 368–81.

[97] Terry L. Cooper, *The Responsible Administrator: An Approach to Ethics for the Administrative Role*, 3rd ed. (San Francisco: Jossey-Bass, 1990), pp. 58–83.

istrative discretion a career civil servant participates in governing a democratic society without being directly accountable to the electorate."[98]

Ethical Principles and Rules

How do we use these various concepts to guide ethical decision making? It would seem helpful to have a set of rules or guidelines to follow, but the answer is not that easy. Ethics cannot be determined simply by reference to a set of rules; it is an ongoing process. Over time, individual decisions about ethical issues lead to the development of an operational ethic.[99] Tong has argued that ethics is as much about virtues as it is about rules, and about character as it is about conduct. She states: "If a person is not interested in developing his moral character, probably he will not care about articulating and following justified moral rules. Similarly, if a person does not care about moral rules, most likely he will not be interested in moral character."[100]

Nonetheless, a number of fields have developed codes of ethics or statements of principles or guidelines, including the American Society for Public Administration,[101] the International City Management Association,[102] the American Institute of Certified Planners,[103] the Operations Research Society of America,[104] the National Association of Social Workers,[105] the National Society of Professional Engineers,[106] and the National Association of Environmental Professionals.[107] Being relatively young, the Association for Public Policy Analysis and Management has yet to develop a code of ethics. Such codes, of course, are interpreted variously by practitioners, and there is a wide gap between the codes and practice[108] and between the beliefs of practitioners and students.[109]

A traditional and basic ethical principle in public service is that of doing no harm, which, although easily stated, may require considerable ethical analysis to determine what constitutes an injury to the various parties involved in an ethical

[98] Rohr, "Ethics in Public Administration," p. 119. See also Bolan, "Structure of Ethical Choice in Planning Practice," pp. 24–29.

[99] Cooper, *Responsible Administrator*, pp. 5–6.

[100] Tong, *Ethics in Policy Analysis*, p. 9.

[101] Rohr, "Ethics in Public Administration," p. 98; Wachs, *Ethics in Planning*, pp. 353–54.

[102] Rohr, "Ethics in Public Administration," p. 98.

[103] Wachs, *Ethics in Planning*, pp. 335–45.

[104] Howe and Kaufman, "Ethics and Professional Practice," p. 25.

[105] Callahan, *Ethical Issues in Professional Life*, pp. 459–60.

[106] Ibid., pp. 460–64.

[107] National Association of Environmental Professionals, "Code of Ethics and Standards of Practice for Environmental Professionals" (Alexandria, VA: National Association of Environmental Professionals, February 1978).

[108] Howe and Kaufman, "Ethics and Professional Practice," pp. 22–23.

[109] Sue Hendler, "Ethics in Planning: The Views of Students and Practitioners," *Journal of Planning Education and Research* 10, no. 2 (Winter 1991), pp. 99–105.

dilemma. In contrast, there is the obligation to do good, which may not be accepted by all administrators. There are also midrange positions where an administrator might be able to correct harm caused by others,[110] or the utilitarian view that harm should be outweighed by good, such as in benefit-cost analysis.

After reviewing a number of models of professional-client relationships, Tong concludes that the *fiduciary* model is the most appropriate.[111] This is the model of doctor–patient and lawyer–client relationships. It recognizes the superior knowledge that experts hold and in turn imposes special obligations on them, but acknowledges that the clients and policymakers have the final decision-making power. A key element of the relationship between expert and client is trustworthiness, which flows from the virtue of justice and includes honesty, candor, competency, diligence, loyalty, and discretion or confidentiality.

In addition to the obligation to one's client, the analyst has an obligation to third parties. Since the analogy between doctors or lawyers and policy analysts is not perfect (because the policymaker is merely the immediate recipient of the policy expert's services and the public is the ultimate recipient of these services), that obligation is difficult to specify. In this view, the policy analyst has a number of basic obligations to third parties, including duty over self-interest, not manipulating or deceiving participants, and not harming them.[112] Cooper emphasizes the role of the public administrator as the citizen-administrator who acts on the behalf of other citizens in performing certain public functions, subordinating technical expertise to the obligations of fiduciary citizenship.[113]

Within the field of public administration, *citizenship* has been seen as the source for ethical norms with a distinction made between legal citizenship and ethical citizenship. Ethical citizenship expands on the legal citizenship of qualifications, rights, and obligations by constitutions and statutes by adding the social, economic, and political aspects of life. Under this definition, the qualifications, rights, and obligations of citizens are defined and prescribed by the values, norms, traditions, and cultures of a community.[114]

Tong concludes that the ultimate client is the people and that the analyst has a threefold obligation: "to bring to public attention government policies that they believe may threaten the public health and welfare, to speak out when they believe that public debate is being needlessly hampered by the misrepresentation or suppression of information, and to share the information with as many citizens as they practically can when public debate is not as well informed as it could be."[115] But citizens also have an obligation to listen, to learn, to participate, and

[110] Vasu, Stewart, and Garson, *Organizational Behavior and Public Management*, pp. 372–77.

[111] Tong, *Ethics in Policy Analysis*, pp. 89–92; see also Cooper, *Ethic of Citizenship for Public Administration*, pp. 163–69.

[112] Tong, *Ethics in Policy Analysis*, pp. 115–28.

[113] Cooper, *Responsible Administrator*, p. 278; and Cooper, *Ethic of Citizenship for Public Administration*, pp. 4–5.

[114] Cooper, *Ethic of Citizenship for Public Administration*, p. 6.

[115] Tong, *Ethics in Policy Analysis*, pp. 133–34.

to play a role in the policy process. Unfortunately few citizens participate actively in governance, which Cooper identifies as both an ethical as well as political act.[116]

There is also an increasing recognition that policy analysis involves advocacy.[117] In addition, analysts and experts are playing even stronger roles in influencing decisions. Fischer, among others, has argued that experts and professionals are playing larger roles in actually making policy and the practice of policy analysis is becoming increasingly adversarial.[118] There may be a positive role for advocacy and adversarial actions. Rather than the impartial pursuit of the public interest, Lindblom argues for the principle of thoughtful partisanship, in which the analyst:

> . . . acknowledges that his work is guided by a selection of some among other possible interests and values; who, so far as feasible, reveals his selection; who makes no claim that his values or interests are good for everyone, who, in other words acknowledges that they are to a degree injurious to some people; and who believes that it is impossible for him to do otherwise without deceiving himself and those who use his work. I do not mean someone who lies, conceals evidence, or violates conventional standards of scientific integrity except as just stated.[119]

He is simply pointing out the fact that everyone is a partisan and places the interests and preferences of some people over those of others, and that we should recognize it explicitly, rather than hide behind a "myth of nonpartisanship." If there is a shared interest, that will be disclosed through the "competition of ideas" among the partisans. The best a society can do, Lindblom says, is "acknowledge conflicting versions and work out—politically, not analytically—a resolution."[120] Moreover, ethical analysis helps us identify assumptions we hold in common with others, discard other assumptions, locate areas of consensus, and identify where factual research will not add to the decision because the dispute is over values.[121] Heineman and colleagues are concerned, however, that advocacy, while a perfectly legitimate activity for analysts, may tempt them to manipulate data or findings, especially when high stakes are involved.[122]

To this point we have seen that values play an important role in informing policy analysis, that there are competing theories of ethical behavior, that objec-

---

[116] Cooper, *Ethic of Citizenship for Public Administration*, pp. 2–3, 92.

[117] Bruce Jennings, "Interpretation and the Practice of Policy Analysis," in *Confronting Values in Policy Analysis: The Politics of Criteria*, ed. Frank Fischer and John Forester (Newbury Park, CA: Sage, 1987), p. 131.

[118] Frank Fischer, "Policy Expertise and the 'New Class': A Critique of the Neoconservative Thesis," in *Confronting Values in Policy Analysis: The Politics of Criteria*, ed. Frank Fischer and John Forester (Newbury Park, CA: Sage, 1987), p. 122.

[119] Charles E. Lindblom, "Who Needs What Social Research for Policymaking?" *Knowledge: Creation, Diffusion, Utilization* 7, no. 4 (June 1986), 350.

[120] Ibid., p. 354; see also Tong, *Ethics in Policy Analysis*, pp. 105–12.

[121] Brown, "Ethics and Education for the Public Service," pp. 61–62.

[122] Heineman, Bluhm, Peterson, and Kearny, *World of the Policy Analyst*, p. 30.

tivity and neutrality are not likely, and that partisanship and advocacy are realistic modes for identifying competing values as well as common interests. But the questions remain: How should analysts conduct their professional lives? What values should guide us?

Guidelines for Professional Conduct

Weimer and Vining suggest that analysts consider three values in the conduct of their professional lives: "analytical integrity, responsibility to client, and adherence to one's personal conception of the good society."[123] They note that the centrality of these values will vary depending on the role of the analyst, whether that person is an objective technician, a client's advocate, or an issue advocate.[124] The objective technician focuses on prediction, keeps a distance from clients, and identifies relevant values, but leaves the trade-offs to clients. The client's advocate vigorously promotes the client's interest, takes advantage of analytic ambiguities to advance the client's position, and selects clients with similar views of the world. Issue advocates look at analysis as a means to move toward their conceptions of the good society. They select clients opportunistically, emphasize ambiguity, and exclude values when the analysis does not support their position.

Rather than adopting one of these roles, Weimer and Vining suggest that the analyst should try to keep all three under consideration. The ethical issue, they believe, is deciding how much of each value can be sacrificed when conflicts arise; that is, determining the minimal duties required under each of the values. They argue for the development of an ethos for the profession of policy analysis:

> As teachers and practitioners of policy analysis, we should explicitly recognize our obligations to protect the basic rights of others, to support our democratic processes as expressed in our constitutions, and to promote analytical and personal integrity. These values should generally dominate our responsibility to the client in our ethical evaluations. Nevertheless, we should show considerable tolerance for the ways our clients choose to resolve different value conflicts, and we should maintain a realistic modesty about the predictive power of our analyses.[125]

We believe, however, that there is something to be said for the process of developing a code of professional ethics. The exercise itself can help to clarify the ethical dilemmas in the profession, elucidate the various approaches to normative ethics, and encourage more consideration of ethics in analysis.[126] Moreover, an ethos, as the differential characteristic of a people, is the result of their adherence to an ethical code, either explicit or implicit.

---

[123] Weimer and Vining, *Policy Analysis*, pp. 16–18.
[124] Kaufman, "Hamelethics in Planning," pp. 66–77.
[125] Weimer and Vining, *Policy Analysis*, pp. 27–28.
[126] See Sue Hendler, "Professional Codes as Bridges between Planning and Ethics: A Case Study," *Plan Canada* 30, no. 2 (1990), 22–29.

Tong sees analysts learning to balance between the external goods of the institution that employs them and the internal goods of the practice that absorbs them; that is, between power, prestige, and money and the satisfaction of doing the best job possible.[127] She proposes that policy analysts ask themselves the following questions:

> Am I giving my client this advice because it reflects reality or because it is what he or she wants to hear? Am I using a certain methodology because it is accepted by those who wield the power in my professional association or because it provides the most accurate results? Do I keep my clients' confidence simply because doing so can promote my career? Does getting ahead mean more to me than doing my job as well as possible?[128]

Similarly, Lindblom suggests the following four principles that should guide analysts:

1. Instead of the pursuit of the public interest, partisanship.
2. Instead of a preoccupation with feasible solutions, a variety of studies.
3. Instead of serving the needs of officials alone, help for the ordinary citizen.
4. Instead of recommendations, a tailoring of research to meet varying specific critical needs.[129]

Our position is that analysts and advisers influence policy in many ways, including how they define the problem, specify alternatives, present data, select examples, and frame recommendations. This presents a major moral role for analysts. From time to time, however, it has been suggested that analysts or advisers are not responsible for the consequences of the advice they give, since a decision maker has decided whether to act on the advice. This argument follows the legal view that one who merely advises others is generally not liable for any harm others commit. But a person who *induces* others to act is generally held liable.[130]

Thompson has analyzed this position and developed three criteria, that taken together, he believes, could form a set of necessary and sufficient conditions for ascribing responsibility to advisers. An adviser is responsible (1) only if the advisee would not have acted in a particular way but for the advice or omission of advice; (2) the adviser could reasonably be expected to foresee that the consequences would follow from the advice; and (3) the harm the advice

---

[127] Rosemarie Tong, "Ethics and the Policy Analyst: The Problem of Responsibility," in *Confronting Values in Policy Analysis: The Politics of Criteria*, ed. Frank Fischer and John Forester (Newbury Park, CA: Sage, 1987), p. 194. Note that Meltsner distinguishes between integrity to one's field and loyalty to a superior/client. Meltsner, *Rules for Rulers*, p. 156.

[128] Tong, "Ethics and the Policy Analyst," p. 209.

[129] Lindblom, "Who Needs What Social Research?" p. 363.

[130] Dennis Thompson, "Ascribing Responsibility to Advisers in Government," in *Ethical Issues in Professional Life*, ed. Joan C. Callahan (New York: Oxford University Press, 1988), p. 283.

causes is greater than the harm that would result from the adviser not performing as required by the position held.[131]

In getting to the point of how policy analysts and planners can incorporate ethical analysis into their work, we come to the conclusion that planners, analysts, and advisers are responsible for the consequences of their advice and that a set of rules and regulations will not be sufficient. Rather, planners and analysts need to develop a framework for thinking about ethical issues in various aspects of their professional lives.

The preceding overview suggests to us that there are four perspectives from which ethics should be considered: (1) that of the individual analyst, (2) in relation to employers and clients, (3) in relation to colleagues and the profession, and (4) in relation to third parties and the general public.[132]

Figure 2-3 summarizes the ethical questions related to each of these areas that we believe analysts and planners should ask when evaluating possible actions. Rather than being hard and fast rules, these questions should serve as a framework for decisions.

How does one make an ethical decision with the information presented above? How would the Oldport staff analyst decide whether to revise the report? Much would depend on the analyst's moral makeup; that is, the extent to which the analyst is ethically aware, and the degree to which the analyst is a deontologist or teleologist or a combination of both.

A deontologist might conclude that the figures must not be altered. A teleologist might decide that doctoring the figures is permissible because of the outcome that will be avoided.

In this situation rule-utilitarians would ask whether the application of a rule would result in a good consequence. They would ask: Of the rules, which would generate the best results? Act-deontologists would make a decision between competing ethical principles. They would choose the principle that is intuitively right.

The decision would also depend on the balance the analyst puts on obligation to client and community and the extent of advocacy, whether client- or issue-oriented.

Faced with competing loyalties and clashes among principles, the Oldport analyst could work through the list in Figure 2-3 and balance the clashes among the ethical principles and among the conflict of duties. Although there is no one correct answer, using the list will allow the analyst to see more clearly the decision to be made.

After going through this analysis, it may be that the analyst would decide to disagree with the mayor. What can planners or analysts do when the wishes of their clients conflict with their own views of what is right and wrong? In this regard, Weimer and Vining present a conceptualization involving three domains

---

[131] Ibid., p. 288.

[132] These are also the four general areas addressed in the code of ethics of the American Institute of Certified Planners.

1. In Relation to One's Self
   - Am I recognizing values explicitly?
   - Am I using the most responsive methods?
   - Do I use multiple methods to reveal alternative approaches?
   - Will my action result in increased knowledge?
   - Will I lose my job and harm my family?
2. In Relation to Employees and Clients
   - Am I exercising independent judgment?
   - Am I working within my competencies?
   - Will I be respecting confidences?
   - Is there a conflict of interest?
   - Will this action respond to my client's needs?
3. In Relation to Colleagues and the Profession
   - Am I treating colleagues fairly?
   - Must I share this information with the analytic community?
   - Is this simply a stock solution?
   - Will this action reflect negatively on the profession?
4. In Relation to the General Public
   - Will this action cause unjustified harm?
   - Will this violate anyone's rights?
   - Have I hidden any partisan views?
   - Have I properly involved citizens?
   - Does this action seek the long-run positive benefit?
   - Am I providing full, clear, and accurate information?

Figure 2-3   A Framework for Ethical Analysis

with areas of intersection (Figure 2-4). The analyst may work to change the organization from within (Voice), may attempt to undermine the organization (Disloyalty) or may leave the organization for another (Exit). Actions that involve more than one domain include leaking information, resigning and disclosing information, issuing an ultimatum, and speaking out until silenced. In their text, Weimer and Vining discuss the ethical implications of the various actions. Without repeating their discussion fully, actions of disloyalty or sabotage are in most instances judged unethical; decisions to exit, although ethical, may not be effective; and speaking out or protesting, while ethical in some instances, may also not be effective.[133]

It seems to us that only in the most severe circumstances would quitting an organization bring about desired change.[134] Outside the organization, only the most senior person with an independent power base can be effective. Most of us, as limited as our power and influence might be, probably have the greatest chance of affecting the ethical decisions of our organizations by working for change from within, by raising ethical issues in our own analyses, and by encour-

[133]Weimer and Vining, *Policy Analysis*, pp. 20–24. See also Tong, *Ethics in Policy Analysis*, pp. 128–33; and Bok on whistleblowing and lying: Sissela Bok, "Whistleblowing and Professional Responsibilities," in *Ethics Teaching in Higher Education*, ed. Daniel Callahan and Sissela Bok (New York: Plenum Press, 1980), pp. 277–95; Sissela Bok, *Lying: Moral Choice in Public and Private Life* (New York: Pantheon Books, 1978).

[134]See Meltsner, *Rules for Rulers*, pp. 133–60.

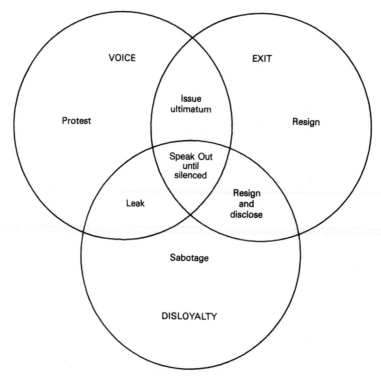

Figure 2-4 Alternative Responses to Value Conflicts
Source: David L. Weimer and Aidan R. Vining, *Policy Analysis: Concepts and Practice,*
2nd ed., © 1992, p. 22. Reprinted by permission of Prentice Hall, Englewood Cliffs, NJ.

aging our colleagues to do likewise. Furthermore, we believe that organizations take on the personality of their members. Our best hope is for analysts and planners who develop strong personal decision-making ethics and who can influence positively the organizations of which they are a part. Certainly policy analysts and planners have an obligation to do more than simply follow orders:[135]

> Policy analysts need not be passive victims of their bureaucratic environment. They can, if they so choose, respin the bureaucratic web within which they are entangled.[136]

THE ANALYTIC PROCESS

How is a policy analysis conducted? There is no single, agreed-upon way. A number of practitioners, researchers, and teachers have described policy analysis models. Some of these processes have been criticized because they follow the

[135] Sue Hendler, "Ethics in Planning," p. 104.
[136] Tong, "Ethics and the Policy Analyst," p. 205.

ideal, rational-model approach—a method, some argue, that cannot be followed.[137] We will return to this argument, but first what have these experts said about the process of policy analysis?

Policy analysis has been characterized as art, craft, compromise, argument, and persuasion, activities that depend to a large extent on the skill, judgment, and intuition of the analyst.[138] Beginning analysts have to develop these skills by doing analysis, and a framework can help. Keep the following summaries of the policy analysis process in mind when we describe the steps in that process in later chapters.

Quade identifies the five most important elements in the policy analysis process as problem formulation, searching for alternatives, forecasting the future environment, modeling the impacts of alternatives, and evaluating (comparing and ranking) the alternatives. He points out that policy analysis is an iterative process in which the problem is reformulated as objectives are clarified, alternatives are designed and evaluated, and better models are developed. He suggests that the process continues until time is up or money runs out.[139]

In writing for the citizen as a potential analyst, MacRae and Wilde argue that each analysis of a policy choice involves a set of common elements: definition of the problem, determining the criteria for making a choice among alternatives, generating a range of alternative policies, choosing a course of action that will cause the policy option to be implemented, and evaluating the policy after it is in effect.[140]

In their primer on quantitative methods for policy analysis, Stokey and Zeckhauser suggest a five-step process as a starting point: Determine the underlying problem and objectives to be pursued, lay out possible alternative courses of action, predict the consequences of each alternative, determine the criteria for measuring the achievement of alternatives, and indicate the preferred choice of action.[141] The authors recognize that the analyst may not

[137] For a critique of the rational model see Robert Formaini, *The Myth of Scientific Public Policy* (New Brunswick, NJ: Transaction Books, 1990); Leung, *Towards a Subjective Approach to Policy Planning & Evaluation: Common-Sense Structured*, pp. 5–19; and Timothy W. Luke, "Policy Science and Rational Choice Theory: A Methodological Critique," in *Confronting Values in Policy Analysis: The Politics of Criteria*, ed. Frank Fischer and John Forester (Newbury Park, CA: Sage, 1987), pp. 174–90.

[138] Peter W. House, *The Art of Public Policy Analysis: The Arena of Regulations and Resources* (Beverly Hills: Sage, 1982); Laurence E. Lynn, Jr., *Designing Public Policy: A Casebook on the Role of Policy Analysis* (Santa Monica: Goodyear, 1980); Majone, *Evidence, Argument, and Persuasion*; Meltsner, *Policy Analysts*; Quade, *Analysis for Public Decisions*; and Aaron Wildavsky, *Speaking Truth to Power: The Art and Craft of Policy Analysis* (Boston: Little, Brown, 1979).

[139] Quade, *Analysis for Public Decisions*, pp. 47–62; see also Hugh J. Miser and Edward S. Quade, eds., *Handbook of Systems Analysis: Overview of Uses, Procedures, Applications, and Practice* (New York: North-Holland, 1985); and Hugh J. Miser and Edward S. Quade, "Craftsmanship in Analysis," in *Handbook of Systems Analysis: Craft Issues and Procedural Choices*, ed. Hugh J. Miser and Edward S. Quade (Chichester, Eng.: Wiley, 1988), p. 23.

[140] MacRae and Wilde, *Policy Analysis*, pp. 7–12.

[141] Edith Stokey and Richard Zeckhauser, *A Primer for Policy Analysis* (New York: Norton, 1978), pp. 5–7.

move in an orderly manner from one step to another and may have to work back and forth among the steps, but they hold that all five areas must be present in an analysis.

A similar process is described by the Urban Institute for state and local program analysis: Define the problem, identify relevant objectives, select evaluation criteria, specify the client group, identify alternatives, estimate the costs of each alternative, determine the effectiveness of each alternative, and present findings.[142] This process breaks apart some of the steps identified by other authors. In other formulations, problem definition includes the identification of objectives and client groups, and the evaluation of alternatives includes cost, effectiveness, and other measures.

Weimer and Vining divide the policy analysis process into two major components: problem analysis and solution analysis, to suggest that both parts of the process must be given ample attention. Within the problem analysis portion they include understanding the problem, choosing and explaining relevant goals and constraints, and choosing a solution method. Within the solution analysis portion they include choosing evaluation criteria, specifying policy alternatives, evaluating alternatives in terms of criteria, and recommending actions. They also indicate the necessity for both information gathering to support the analysis and communicating useful advice to clients.[143]

These and other policy analysis approaches resemble the ideal, rational decision-making process found in many fields. For example, the process defined in a multidisciplinary textbook on decision making includes the following steps: Define the problem, identify the alternatives, quantify the alternatives, apply decision aids, choose an alternative, and implement the decision.[144] Like other formulations of the decision process, this one includes the iteration of steps when a given step cannot be completed because of a lack of information. Moving back and forth among steps can lead to more precise problem statements and the identification of additional alternatives.

The rational model is also prescribed for solving strategic problems in business. It, too, includes the familiar steps: Diagnose the problem, define objectives, generate alternatives, assess consequences, select the "best" alternative, preimplement the "best" solution (identify side effects or unintended consequences), and implement the "best" solution.[145] Similar rational problem-solving

[142] Hatry, Blair, Fisk, and Kimmel, *Program Analysis*, pp. 1–7; see also Palumbo, *Public Policy in America.*

[143] Weimer and Vining, *Policy Analysis*, p. 183.

[144] Percy H. Hill, ed., *Making Decisions: A Multidisciplinary Introduction* (Reading, MA: Addison-Wesley, 1978), p. 22.

[145] Harvey J. Brightman, *Problem Solving: A Logical and Creative Approach* (Atlanta: Georgia State University Business Press, 1980), pp. 219–21.

approaches have been prescribed for many fields over the decades, including economic development,[146] design,[147] urban and regional planning,[148] systems analysis,[149] and public administration.[150]

Can anyone, especially a fledgling analyst, follow these processes? They require a clear statement of goals and objectives (This is often difficult to obtain from an individual, much less from an organization or public body), an identification of the full range of alternatives that could be used to achieve the goals (How do we know when all options have been considered?), and the computation of the costs and benefits of these options (How can we ever determine such values for hundreds of possible options?). The ideal process is not only mentally demanding, but time-consuming and costly as well.[151] By the time the analyst cycles through the process, the problem may have been resolved by other means, may have disappeared, or may have become too big to deal with.[152] Furthermore, organizations cannot usually afford to conduct complete analyses.[153] In the day-to-day world of policymaking, the need for quick, roughly right decisions requires that compromises be made within the rational model. Simon argues that good or acceptable options, not necessarily the best, are selected because the cost of the search will outweigh the benefits.[154] Lindblom holds that decision makers cannot make the simultaneous comparisons required by the rational model so they adopt an incremental approach, making successive limited comparisons, selecting options that are at least a little better than other possibilities.[155] Etzioni proposed the mixed scanning approach as a compromise between the rational and incremental approaches, in order to look comprehensively at issues but also to focus in on those areas that appear to be the most promising for detailed

[146] Jan Tinbergen, *Economic Policy: Principles and Design* (Amsterdam: North Holland, 1956).

[147] Don Koberg and Jim Bagnall, *The Universal Traveler* (Los Altos, CA: William Kaufman, 1974), p. 17.

[148] William I. Goodman and Eric C. Freund, *Principles and Practice of Urban Planning* (Washington, DC: International City Managers' Association, 1968).

[149] Wladyslaw Findeisen and Edward S. Quade, "The Methodology of Systems Analysis: An Introduction and Overview," in *Handbook of Systems Analysis: Overview of Uses, Procedures, Applications, and Practice*, ed. Hugh J. Miser and Edward S. Quade (New York: North Holland, 1985), pp. 117–49.

[150] Marshall E. Dimock, *A Philosophy of Administration: Toward Creative Growth* (New York: Harper & Row, 1958), p. 140.

[151] Charles E. Lindblom, "The Science of 'Muddling Through,'" *Public Administration Review* 19, no. 2 (Spring 1959), 79–88.

[152] Lineberry, *American Public Policy*, pp. 29–30.

[153] Martin Meyerson and Edward C. Banfield, *Politics, Planning, and the Public Interest* (New York: Free Press, 1955).

[154] Herbert A. Simon, "A Behavioral Model of Rational Choice," *Quarterly Journal of Economics* 69 (February 1955), 99–118.

[155] Lindblom, "Muddling Through."

analysis.[156] And Paris and Reynolds, arguing that policy analysis is not a science, propose that policy arguments be evaluated through a rational ideology that links normative experiences and perceptual data to allow us to determine favored policies.[157] Since policies often involve funding, the rational decision process is also compromised by the incremental nature of the budget process,[158] through which existing programs are likely to be continued and major changes are slow to occur.

The rational model and policy analysis itself have been criticized severely because of their unrealistic demands and overstated claims. Robert Formaini has written:

> ... scientifically-based (i.e., *justified*) public policy, a dream that has grown ever larger since the Enlightenment and that, perhaps, has reached its apogee towards the close of our own century, is a myth, a theoretical illusion. It exists in our minds, our analyses, and our methods only because we seek to find it and, typically, we tend to find that which we seek.[159]

Moreover, after spending a great deal of funds on policies and programs, there still is the question of whether much has resulted from these efforts.[160] Hofferbert notes that many major governmental policy efforts have not had noticeable results; for example, teen-age job training programs and efforts to reduce drug and alcohol consumption.[161] And Formaini points to the failure of government policy analysis to formulate an optimum response to the 1976 swine flu episode.[162]

But in contrast, Schwarz has argued that government programs have had a beneficial impact on American life, for example, in reducing poverty and improving health. Beyond this, he argues, most Americans depend on help from government policies, that voluntary action is not sufficient, and that government policies have had a more positive effect than commonly recognized.[163] Quigley and Scotchmer also argue that policy analysis makes an impact, citing a number

---

[156] Amitai Etzioni, "Mixed-Scanning: A 'Third' Approach to Decision-Making," *Public Administration Review* 27, no. 5 (December 1967), 385–92.

[157] David C. Paris and James F. Reynolds, *The Logic of Policy Inquiry* (New York: Longman, 1983).

[158] Aaron Wildavsky, *The Politics of the Budgetary Process*, 2nd ed. (Boston: Little, Brown, 1974); and Aaron Wildavsky, *Budgeting: A Comparative Theory of Budgetary Processes* (Boston: Little, Brown, 1975).

[159] Formaini, *Myth of Scientific Public Policy*, p. 1.

[160] Heineman, Bluhm, Peterson, and Kearny, *World of the Policy Analyst*, pp. 43–44.

[161] Richard Hofferbert, *The Reach and Grasp of Policy Analysis: Comparative Views of the Craft* (Tuscaloosa: University of Alabama Press, 1990), pp. 14–17.

[162] Formaini, *Myth of Scientific Public Policy*.

[163] John E. Schwarz, *America's Hidden Success: A Reassessment of Public Policy from Kennedy to Reagan*, rev. ed. (New York: Norton, 1988).

of recent instances in which analysis mattered.[164] And in a large-scale quantitative analysis of 58 cases, Bryson and colleagues demonstrated that planning and planners have made a substantial positive impact on the creation of desirable outcomes in major projects.[165] Moreover, there may be indirect impacts of policy analysis on decisions through the process of enlightenment.[166]

Alternatives to and modifications of the rational model have been proposed by various authors, but no competing paradigm has emerged as dominant. Alexander, however, suggests that a contingency approach which synthesizes research findings with normative prescriptions has the best prospect of supplanting the rational model.[167] Most of today's writers on policy analysis as well as practitioners advocate the use of a variant of the rational model, one that integrates the scientific-technical approach with the normative-political approach.[168]

A strict rational model cannot be followed, because many apparently rational decisions have to be compromised because they are not politically feasible. A rational, logical, and technically desirable policy may not be adopted, because the political system will not accept it. The figures don't always speak for themselves; there is often a lack of consensus on basic values, and good ideas do not always win out. Analysts and decision makers are constantly faced with the conflict between technically superior and politically feasible alternatives, and they often have to include argument, persuasion, and political efforts in their analytic processes.[169]

Nagel has summarized the evaluations of policy studies, many of which also apply to policy analysis, noting that it is criticized for having both too many and too few of the same characteristics.

---

[164] John M. Quigley and Suzanne Scotchmer, "What Counts? Analysis Counts," *Journal of Policy Analysis and Management* 8, no. 3 (Summer 1989), 483–89.

[165] John M. Bryson, Philip Bromiley, and Yoon Soo Jung, "Influences of Context and Process on Project Planning Success," *Journal of Planning Education and Research* 9, no. 3 (Summer 1990), 183–95; see also Peter A. Hall, "Policy Paradigms, Experts, and the State: The Case of Macroeconomic Policy-Making in Britain," in *Social Scientists, Policy, and the State*, ed. Stephen Brooks and Alain-G. Gagnon. (New York: Praeger, 1990), pp. 53–78; Evert A. Lindquist, "The Third Community, Policy Inquiry, and Social Scientists," in *Social Scientists, Policy, and the State*, ed. Stephen Brooks and Alain-G. Gagnon (New York: Praeger, 1990), pp. 21–51; and Laurence E. Lynn, Jr., "Policy Analysis in the Bureaucracy: How New? How Effective?" *Journal of Policy Analysis and Management* 8, no. 3 (Summer 1989), 373–77.

[166] Heineman, Bluhm, Peterson, and Kearny, *World of the Policy Analyst*, p. 44.

[167] Ernest R. Alexander, "After Rationality, What? A Review of Responses to Paradigm Breakdown," *Journal of the American Planning Association* 50, no. 1 (Winter 1984), 62–69.

[168] John M. Bryson, *Strategic Planning for Public and Nonprofit Organizations: A Guide to Strengthening and Sustaining Organizational Achievement* (San Francisco: Jossey-Bass, 1988); Heineman, Bluhm, Peterson, and Kearny, *World of the Policy Analyst*; Majone, *Evidence, Argument, and Persuasion*; Hugh J. Miser and Edward S. Quade, eds., *Handbook of Systems Analysis: Craft Issues and Procedural Choices* (Chichester, Eng.: Wiley, 1988); and Weimer and Vining, *Policy Analysis*.

[169] Palumbo, *Public Policy in America*, pp. 79–80.

Those conflicting characteristics include being (1) a temporary fad or stale material, (2) too practical or too theoretical, (3) too multidisciplinary or too narrowly focused on political science, (4) too quantitative or too subjective, (5) underutilized or overutilized, and (6) too liberal or too conservative.[170]

He answers these charges by arguing that policy studies (analysis) combines diverse ideas so that the field is better able to deal with the systematic evaluation of alternatives. Moreover, he says, policy studies scores well on a number of dimensions.

It has a long-term philosophical foundation, originality, a theoretical side, a practical side, an important political science component that involves all fields of political science, a multidisciplinary component that involves all fields of knowledge, especially the social sciences, a qualitative value-oriented side, a quantitative, reasonably objective way of dealing with analytic problems, an ability to get utilized when deserved in the light of democratic processes, nonutilization when deserved in the light of those same democratic processes, value to conservative policy makers, and value to liberal policy makers.[171]

Since this is a book about methods of policy analysis, we obviously believe there is merit in systematic analysis. However, we, like other policy analysts, admit that real people don't act as the models say they should. When we explain how analyses are conducted, we are reporting how they should be conducted. We do not suggest that the policy analyst should rigidly follow the steps in the rational model. Often it cannot be done. We do think that beginning analysts can use a process outline as a guide or framework for analysis and that they ought to work through each step in the process. Others have made similar arguments for the rational model (or a compromise of it) and have suggested furthermore that it allows others to evaluate the analysis,[172] cuts problems down to manageable size and reduces subjectivity,[173] and informs citizens.[174]

BASIC POLICY ANALYSIS IN SIX STEPS

We have incorporated ideas from a number of overlapping descriptions of policy analysis with our own experiences to create the six-step process shown in Figure 2-5: problem definition, determination of evaluation criteria, identification of alternatives, evaluation of alternatives, comparison of alternatives, and assess-

---

[170]Stuart S. Nagel, "Conflicting Evaluations of Policy Studies," in *Public Administration: The State of the Discipline*, ed. Naomi B. Lynn and Aaron Wildavsky (Chatham, NJ: Chatham House, 1990), p. 421.

[171]Ibid., pp. 458–59.

[172]Stokey and Zeckhauser, *Primer for Policy Analysis*, p. 6.

[173]Quade, *Analysis for Public Decisions*, pp. 11–12.

[174]MacRae and Wilde, *Policy Analysis*, pp. 4–5.

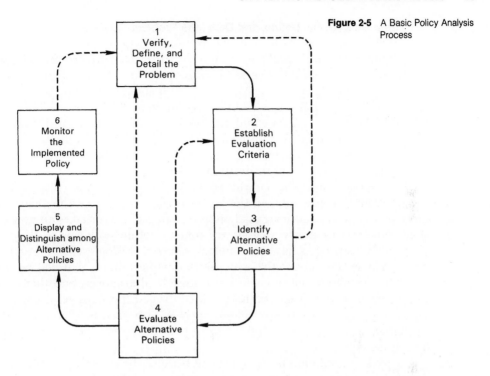

Figure 2-5 A Basic Policy Analysis Process

ment of outcomes. These are the major steps in the process, but each step could be broken into smaller components. The basic methods that can be used at each step are presented in Chapters 3 through 9.

Analysts may take various routes through the policy analysis process because of differences in training, the time available for analysis, the complexity of the problem, resource availability, and organizational affiliation. Most analysts first approach a problem by using the methods and outlook of their discipline. Economists often first see the problem in terms of economic costs and benefits, persons trained in sociology may first look at the differential impact on groups of citizens, and attorneys may first look at the legal aspects of the problem. The less time available, the more likely that steps in the process will be collapsed or skipped. Complex problems may seem to require the delegation of tasks and the use of specialists, but if resources are short, the work will be done in-house. Analysts in large organizations will likely have access to consultants, technical support staff, and specialized equipment and may often deal with only part of the problem; those in small organizations are less likely to have such support and are more likely to conduct most of the analysis themselves.

Compromises of the model often have to be made, and we expect people who read this book to devise their personal versions of the policy analysis process after gaining some experience. However, as a point of departure, we suggest six basic steps.

Step One: Verify, Define, and Detail the Problem

When faced with problems in our personal lives, we are often frustrated by the many angles that have to be considered and the conflicting nature of possible solutions. The more people we consult about a problem, the greater the number of factors that are brought to our attention. The more we delve into the problem, the more aspects we find that need evaluation. The same dilemma arises in policy analysis. Don't accept the initial problem statement without question. It may be only the tip of the iceberg, a part of a larger problem, or one that cannot be influenced by the client or decision maker.

Since conditions change, the policy analyst must continually ask whether the problem that precipitated the analysis still exists. Often the analyst has to redefine the problem during analysis as it changes form or takes on new dimensions. Students of policy analysis are told to define problems so they can be resolved. This process has been dubbed *backward problem solving.*[175] Analyze the best available data about the issue, settle on the criteria that will be used to evaluate alternative policies, think up possible alternatives, and then redefine the problem so that it can be reduced, controlled, perhaps resolved, with the information and resources on hand. Such an approach is often demanded by the immediacy of problems and the short period during which the analysis must be conducted.

Problem definition is often difficult because the objectives of the client are not clear, or stated objectives appear to be in conflict. Sometimes client and analyst may not understand each other because of differences in terminology or jargon. But often organizations cannot or will not make clear statements of objectives. This is a special problem for public organizations, which may have multiple missions, serve many clienteles, and attempt to respond to changing or conflicting public sentiments. Furthermore, power, including the power to determine organizational objectives, is diffused in large organizations and sought after by competing factions. An apparently simple contemporary problem illustrates some of the difficulties inherent in problem definition.

In some states, a driver's license can be obtained at age 18, but if a person has successfully completed a driver education course a license may be obtained at age 16. Teen-agers have the highest accident rate of any group of drivers. A political candidate has called for "reducing the carnage on our highways." (See Figure 2-6.) What is the problem? Note that the answer depends on who's asking. You and your client may want to consider the perspectives of some constituencies and not others, but it pays to think about all possible viewpoints as you start out. Then narrow them down quickly, using a defensible rationale.

Is the problem one of an excessive accident rate among teen-age drivers? Or is it more specifically the deaths and injuries that occur as a result of some

[175] G. Polya, *How to Solve It* (New York: Doubleday, 1957), pp. 225–32; and Wildavsky, *Speaking Truth to Power,* pp. 2–3.

West Says Keep Driver Ed, Don't Up Driving Age

CAPITOL CITY—Raising the driving age in the state to 17 and abolishing mandatory drivers' education is the wrong way to solve the problem of accidents among inexperienced young motorists, says Secretary of State Chris West.

Drivers' education programs should continue in the schools, West said Monday. And instead of raising the driving age, she said teen-agers under 18 should be given provisional licenses that can be yanked if they violate traffic laws.

West, in news conferences at the Statehouse and elsewhere, responded to comments made last week by the Democratic candidate for governor, Pat Karl.

Karl said the driving age should be raised to 17 from 16 as a way of "reducing the carnage on our highways."

Teen-agers have the highest accident rate of any group of drivers and West said there are about 287,000 16- and 17-year-olds with drivers' licenses in the state.

Karl also said the state should do away with mandatory driver education programs, but West also disagreed with that.

"Raising the driving age to 17 or 18 discriminates against responsible, mature young drivers who need to drive to school or work," West said.

West's opponent in November, Democratic state Treasurer Val Lawrence, essentially agrees with West's position and disagrees with that of Karl, an aide to Lawrence said.

Of licensed 16- and 17-year-olds in 1991, West said about 31,500 had one moving violation against them, and another 10,400 had collected two tickets. Under West's provisional license idea, a youngster's driving privilege would be suspended for three months after a first ticket. A second ticket within a year for someone under 18 would mean the loss of a driver's license for a year.

West has been studying the provisional license plan since last spring with the State Motor Vehicle Laws Commission. Neither she nor the Commission has yet introduced any concrete proposal in the form of specific legislation.

Driver education is a valuable tool in teaching young people how to drive, West said.

Many school districts across the state complain that the state falls short of reimbursing them for the actual costs of driver education. The state will finance the programs this fiscal year with $16 million, West said. The money comes from a combination of portions of the fee for drivers' licenses, instructional permits for 15- and 16-year-olds enrolled in drivers' education, and a surcharge on fines for conviction of traffic offenses.

West said insufficient state financing would be an inadequate excuse to abolish mandatory driver education courses. Young people who do not complete classroom and behind-the-wheel drivers' education must be 18 to obtain a driver's license in this state.

Source: Adapted from an article in a midwestern newspaper.

Figure 2-6 A Typical Policy Problem

of these accidents? A variety of factors may contribute to the problem: driver education programs that do not adequately prepare teen-agers for unsupervised driving, a license examination that does not distinguish prepared from unprepared teen-agers, unsafe second- and third-hand vehicles driven by teen-agers, and teen-agers driving while intoxicated. School districts might define the problem as the high cost of driver education. Parents of teen-age motorists might define the problem as the high cost of insuring their safe teen-age motorist because insurance rates have been pushed up by unsafe teen-age drivers. Facing such a range of possibilities, the analyst must verify, define, and detail the problem, making sure that it can be addressed by policies over which the relevant decision maker (often the client) has control.

Assuming that a problem exists, the analyst will try to determine its magnitude and extent. For example, how many teen-age auto fatalities per mile driven are there each year? How does this compare with other age groups? How long has the difference, if any, existed? How does this compare with other locales? Quick, rough calculations, sometimes referred to as back-of-the-envelope calculations, can set boundaries on the problem. Search for similar analyses by others. Use both documents and people. Contact the people who prepared the reports and seek additional material from them. The analyst can also use basic decision analysis (described in Chapter 4) to estimate possible economic and political impacts of changing existing policies.

Part of the problem definition is understanding the positions and influence of various individuals and groups. So the analyst asks: Who is concerned about the problem? Why? What are their stakes in the issue? What power do they have to affect a policy decision? These groups are often surprisingly many and diverse.

In the teen-age accidents case, the affected and interested parties or stakeholders could include the politician who initiated the discussion of the problem and who saw it as a possible campaign issue; driver education instructors, who might lose their jobs if driver education courses were dropped; school districts that must bear the cost of driver education; the police, who enforce traffic laws and investigate accidents; parents, who are concerned about the safety of their children; and of course, the teen-agers themselves, who are concerned about their driving privileges.

The list of attentive or stakeholder groups might also include motor clubs concerned about driver and passenger safety; school parent–teacher organizations, concerned about the health and lives of teen-age drivers and the cost of driver education; auto body shops, which repair teen-ager-inflicted damage; insurance companies, which are concerned about risk taking; the farm lobby, which values farm teen labor mobility; and, of course, society which has made an investment in the education of teen-agers.

Finally, the analyst needs to know whether enough information is available to conduct an analysis and whether there would be benefit in collecting more data. Approximately how much effort would be required to answer the basic questions, and what would a more in-depth study require?

The challenge at this stage of policy analysis is to state the problem meaningfully, to eliminate irrelevant material, to say it with numbers, to focus on the central, critical factors, and to define the problem in a way that eliminates ambiguity. After this effort (which must be done quickly to make the best use of money, talent, and time), the analyst should know whether a problem exists that can possibly be resolved by the client, should be able to provide the first detailed statement of the problem, and should be able to estimate the time and resources the analysis would require. Later, as alternatives are generated and analyzed, other aspects of the problem may be identified that will call for a redefinition of the problem.

Step Two: Establish Evaluation Criteria

How will the analyst know when the problem is solved or when an appropriate or acceptable policy is identified? How will possible policies be compared? Any proposed policy will have a variety of impacts and may affect various groups differently. Not only will policies that are acceptable to one group possibly be unacceptable or harmful to another group, but a policy that appears acceptable when judged on the basis of cost, for example, may become unacceptable when its environmental impacts are considered.

In order to compare, measure, and select among alternatives, relevant evaluation criteria must be established. Some commonly used measures include cost, net benefit, effectiveness, efficiency, equity, administrative ease, legality, and political acceptability. For example, one alternative may cost less than the others or may fall within a budget constraint. One alternative may yield a greater net economic benefit than another. One may provide the greatest benefit from the available funds. One may be the least expensive way to obtain a particular objective. One may benefit or harm certain individuals, groups, or organizations more or less than other options. Some of the alternatives will be more difficult to implement than others. One may require more administrative skill or time than is available. Some may require changes in the law. Some may be unacceptable to all involved. The political dimensions of the problem that will affect a solution must be identified, as the alternatives will vary in political acceptability.

Where does the analyst obtain the decision criteria? Sometimes the client provides them, either directly as measures or indirectly through a statement of goals or objectives. In the former case it is the analyst's job to make the criteria specific enough so their attainment can be measured. In the latter case we have to deduce criteria and confirm them with our client. On occasion (perhaps more often than not) the decision maker will not or cannot identify goals, objectives, or criteria. Consequently the analyst will have to infer what they are. The analyst will also have to specify criteria relevant to the public interest, to groups that may become involved in the problem in the future, and to opposing interests.

Seldom are all criteria equal, so the analyst must indicate those that are most relevant to the parties involved. When the alternatives are evaluated later, it will be important to note the extent to which the criteria salient to the various individuals and groups involved are satisfied by the alternative policies. The relative importance of the decision criteria then becomes central to the analysis.

What would be possible evaluation criteria in the minimum-age-for-drivers problem? To enumerate possible criteria, it may be helpful to think about this problem from the perspective of the possible groups involved.

From the viewpoint of society at large (the public interest) the teen-age accident rate (annual number of accidents per thousand teen-agers or number of accidents per thousand miles driven) may be an appropriate criterion, as well as such criteria as the teen-age auto fatality rate and the driving-while-intoxicated arrest rate. Parents may favor criteria such as insurance costs (the additional cost for insuring a teen-age driver) in addition to accident, death, and driving-while-intoxicated rates. Other criteria may attempt to measure parental convenience (not having to chauffeur their teen-agers). Criteria important to school districts could include driver education costs (cost per pupil per year) and parental attitudes (change in level of satisfaction with school district management). Teenagers would likely favor such criteria as personal safety (teen-age accident rate) and mobility (miles traveled per week). Politicians and state officials would be concerned about the above criteria but would probably add administrative, legal, and political criteria (staff increases needed to implement the option, number of laws to be changed, and popularity with voters).

The analyst will have to identify those criteria that are central to the problem under analysis and most relevant to the key participants in the decision process. The analyst seeks criteria that meet these specifications, but sometimes criteria are determined by the data that are available. Nonetheless, specifying evaluation criteria and deciding the dimensions along which the alternatives will be measured cause the analyst to clarify the values, goals, and objectives of the interested and affected parties and to make explicit both the desirable and undesirable outcomes. By stating the criteria in advance, we are setting up rules that have to be followed when comparing alternatives. Stating evaluation criteria early also helps avoid the temptation to rationalize preferred options later. New criteria may be unearthed during later stages of the analysis, but the analyst must explicitly recognize the addition of those criteria.

Step Three: Identify Alternative Policies

By this stage in the process, the analyst should have an understanding of the values, goals, and objectives not only of the client but also of other involved parties. Knowing what is sought, and having identified the criteria to be used in judging alternatives, helps the analyst generate alternative policies. The analyst will most likely already have a list of possible alternatives. If the client had a favorite policy in mind when assigning the problem, the analyst may have deduced this. The no-action alternative (continuation of the status quo and minor modifications to the status quo) is a policy that deserves consideration. During the problem-identification stage similar problems elsewhere may have been located, and the solutions tried in those locales can be considered. The analysts who were involved in those problems may be able to suggest other possible policies.

The list of possible alternatives for even a relatively well-defined problem can be long, especially when variations and combinations of alternatives are considered. A first set of alternatives for the teen-age auto accident problem might include the following:

1. Raising the minimum age at which a driver's license can be obtained
2. Issuing to teen-agers restricted licenses that permit driving only during daylight hours to school or to work
3. Issuing to teen-agers provisional licenses that would be revoked if traffic laws were violated
4. Enforcing current traffic laws more strictly
5. Eliminating driver education courses
6. Revising driver education offerings
7. Making the driver's license examination more stringent for teen-agers
8. Enforcing more strictly the laws regarding the drinking of alcoholic beverages
9. Requiring that vehicles be equipped with sensors that would prohibit their operation by intoxicated individuals
10. Maintaining the status quo

Variations and combinations of these alternatives are also possible, and the details of each option would have to be specified. For example, driver education might be continued and only provisional licenses be issued to teen-agers. Or the minimum age for obtaining a driver's permit might be raised, driver education might be dropped, and the driver's license examination might be made more stringent. Another combination might be retaining driver education and issuing restricted licenses to teen-agers who successfully complete a driver education course. Details to specify would include whether to raise the minimum age to 16½, 17, 17½, or higher, whether to restrict driving by time (daylight hours only), purpose (work or school), or both time and purpose, the type and number of laws violated that would result in the suspension of a provisional license, the length of suspension, and so on.

Generating and combining alternatives may reveal aspects of the problem not identified earlier. Examining alternatives used by others in analogous situations may provide additional insights into the problem. It may be necessary to redefine the problem because of this new information, and the reformulated problem statement may lead to a revision or addition of evaluation criteria. The challenge at this step in the analytic process is to avoid settling prematurely on a limited number of options.

Thinking hard may be the most profitable way to identify alternatives, especially when time is short. Alternatives can also be identified through researched analysis and experiments, through brainstorming techniques, and by writing scenarios. Typologies describing the various groups that might be affected may reveal alternatives specific to particular groups. Seemingly unconventional alternatives should not be overlooked. What may have been unacceptable in the past may be more acceptable today. Testing these extremes may also provide data about the acceptability of less dramatic measures and about how basic policies might be modified. Since values and assumptions of participants change over time, yesterday's unacceptable options cannot simply be discarded today without analysis.

Step Four: Evaluate Alternative Policies

The linchpin in the policy analysis process is the evaluation of alternative policies and the packaging of policies into strategies and programs. What are the expected impacts of each policy? To what extent does each policy satisfy the evaluation criteria?

The nature of the problem and the types of evaluation criteria will suggest the methods that can be used to evaluate the policies. Avoid the toolbox approach of attacking every evaluation with your favorite method, whether that is decision analysis, linear programming, or cost-benefit analysis. It has been said that when the only tool an analyst has is a hammer, then all problems will look like nails. Some problems will call for quantitative analysis. Others will require qualitative analysis. Most problems will require both. In the teen-age traffic accident problem, a cost-effectiveness study could be conducted to estimate the least expensive way to cut in half the teen-age auto accident rate, or a cost-benefit analysis could be used to determine whether there would be a net economic benefit from raising the minimum licensing age to, say, 18 years, by comparing possible savings on such items as auto operation, maintenance, repair, insurance, and traffic enforcement with such costs as income lost to teen-agers who can no longer drive to work, the value of time that will be spent by parent chauffeurs, and the value of teen-age mobility and status. But for such a problem, the alternatives may also have to be evaluated for equity. Will farm and small-town teen-agers and families bear a greater burden because of less access to mass transportation? Options will also have to be examined from a political perspective. Would citizens, through their political representatives, support an increase in the minimum driving age? Given sufficient time, researched methods such as a citizen survey might be used to gauge support for various options. When time is not available for such undertakings, we must use simple prediction and forecasting techniques and elementary models to illustrate the effects of the options, sensitivity analysis to estimate the impact of changes in basic assumptions and parameters, and quick decision analysis to provide probability estimates of the outcomes of various sequences of decisions.

This evaluation step may reveal alternatives that satisfy most or all of the major criteria, and it may reveal others that can be discarded with little additional analysis. Some alternatives will call for further examination. Additional data may have to be collected. During this stage it is important for the analyst to recognize the difference between economically or technically feasible and politically acceptable alternatives. Policy formulation, the designing and evaluation of alternatives or policy options, is aimed at defining the problem appropriately and ferreting out feasible and effective solutions. Whether any of these solutions can be implemented is essentially a political question. In the teen-age driver example, if the alternative, eliminating driver education and increasing the minimum age for obtaining a license, was found to be the most cost-effective life-saving policy, would the change be supported by the parents of teen-age drivers, school administrators, teacher unions, farm groups, and so on? Such information must be brought into the policy evaluation stage, since policies should not be compared without reference to prospects for implementation.

The policy evaluation step is also a point in the analysis where we may discover that the problem no longer exists as we defined it or as it was defined for us. Information discovered during the identification and evaluation of policies may reveal new aspects of the problem, which may in turn call for additional or different evaluation criteria. Although it may be disheartening to discover new angles to the problem at this stage, it is essential to recycle through the analysis. The prospect of finding, during the evaluation step, that the problem has been incompletely or inaccurately defined reaffirms the suggestion that a first-cut analysis be conducted quickly during the problem-definition phase. Several fast iterations through the policy analysis process may well be more efficient and effective than a single, more detailed one.

Step Five: Display and Distinguish among Alternative Policies

Depending upon the analyst–client relationship, the results of the evaluation might be presented as a list of alternatives, an enumeration of criteria, and a report of the degree to which the criteria are met by each alternative. This is not to suggest that the numerical results can or should speak for themselves. Even in this somewhat neutral presentation format, the order of criteria, the sequence of alternatives, and the space given to various options can influence decisions.

The results of the evaluation might be displayed in a number of other ways. We will show later how matrices can be used as a format for comparison, to provide a quick visual means of highlighting pros and cons. When criteria can be expressed in quantitative terms, value-comparison schemes might be used to summarize the advantages and drawbacks of the alternatives. Evaluation results can also be presented as scenarios, in order that quantitative methods, qualitative analyses, and complex political considerations can be melded. Such scenarios describe the alternatives, report the costs of the options, identify who wins and who loses under each alternative, and play out the economic, political, legal, and administrative ramifications of each option.

For a problem that involves quantitative and qualitative information such as the teen-age accident problem, it is unlikely that the results of the analysis can be presented as a numerical summary. Furthermore, there may be no agreement on the relative importance of criteria. In such a case, a comparative matrix could be used to summarize the analysis. Along one axis would be listed the alternatives, along the other axis, the criteria. The cells would contain net benefits in dollars where appropriate, number of lives saved, change in the teen-age auto accident rate, and so on. Such a format permits the decision maker or client to assess the options and to use the analysis to make a policy choice. In those cases where the client or decision maker has clearly stated objectives (or when the analyst has obtained agreement on objectives), ranking or weighting schemes may be appropriate, but the analyst has to be aware that personal biases can easily enter such summation schemes.

Some clients prefer that the analyst present a strong argument for the superior option, and in some instances the analyst may feel that a particular option has such overwhelming merit that a special case must be made for it. In these cases, scenario writing may be the preferred tool, since it allows the analysis to be placed in a larger context, can give life to a dull analysis, can excite, can anger, can move a person to action. As the analyst develops experience and gains the confidence of superiors and clients (moves toward becoming an entrepreneur), this phase of analysis may involve more advocacy and contain an explicit ranking of alternatives.

Keep in mind the difference between a technically superior alternative and a politically viable one. Sometimes the preferred alternative, in a technical sense, is known, and the task is to deal with political opposition. Use political feasibility analysis to display the pros and cons of alternatives and to answer such questions as: Do the relevant decision makers have the interest and influence to implement the policy? Would a less comprehensive (suboptimal) policy that addressed part of the problem and could be carried out by fewer participants have a better chance of success? What will the client have to give up or promise in order to have the policies implemented? Will new administrative mechanisms be required? Since policy is not made or implemented in a vacuum, others may have to be persuaded to make related decisions. Several units of government may need to cooperate.

Rarely will there be only one acceptable or appropriate alternative. Not only will different options appeal to various interested parties, but two or more alternatives may bring roughly similar results. None of the alternatives is likely to be perfect, as problems are rarely solved. More often their severity is reduced, the burden is more evenly distributed, or they are replaced by less severe problems.

Policy analysts work under time constraints. As a result, they take shortcuts. They estimate. They overlook alternatives and variables. Most policy analyses are incomplete. Because analysts make recommendations under conditions of uncertainty, these uncertainties must be reported and possible side effects must be identified. Will the proposed policy cause problems worse than those it addresses? It has been said that "every solution breeds new problems."[176] If so, is the client willing to accept them? Are there ways to mitigate such unintended consequences? If raising the age for a driver's permit causes more teens to ride buses and the subway, will this increase fear among older transit riders? Will the transit systems and local governments be able to alleviate these fears? If the preferred alternative is cracking down on teens who violate traffic laws, will

---

[176] Brightman, *Problem Solving*, p. 50.

the court system be able to process the cases? A worst-case scenario or worst-case worksheet can be prepared to lay out what could go wrong with the implementation of each option.

Having learned a great deal about the issues and alternatives by this point in the process, the analyst must again ask whether the correct problem was identified, whether important components of the problem have been ignored, and whether real alternatives have been evaluated. Have conditions changed that might call for revising the assessment of alternatives? Are new options available? Have better data become available? Should portions of the analysis be redone using these data? Accuracy checks should be conducted.

Supporting technical studies may be needed that did not seem necessary earlier. It is unlikely that an analysis will reach this point without peer review, but if it has, and if the project is not top secret, others (nonprofessionals as well as experts) ought to be asked to criticize the analysis for logical inconsistencies, math errors, general blunders, and political feasibility.

Finally, what remains to be done to implement the preferred policy? Tasks and responsibilities must be assigned. Plans for monitoring and evaluating the implemented policy should be made.

Step Six: Monitor and Evaluate the Implemented Policy

In most instances, the policy analyst, planner, or expert is not involved directly in the implementation of the preferred alternative. Typically, agency operating staff actually put the policy into operation, although to varying degrees the analyst will be involved in developing implementation guidelines and procedures. Analysts design the bus rather than drive it, so to speak. On the other hand, the policy analyst should be involved in the maintenance, monitoring, and evaluation of the implemented policy.

Even after a policy has been implemented, there may be some doubt whether the problem was resolved appropriately and even whether the selected policy is being implemented properly. These concerns require that policies and programs be maintained and monitored during implementation to assure that they do not change form unintentionally, to measure the impact they are having, to determine whether they are having the impact intended, and to decide whether they should be continued, modified, or terminated.

Although we have chosen to focus primarily on preprogram aspects of policy analysis, postprogram evaluation is also important. The quality of preprogram analyses can be improved if we understand how to conduct postprogram evaluations, and if we have an idea of how and why policies and programs fail. With this knowledge, policy maintenance, monitoring, and evaluation procedures can be designed to forestall some of these failures.

It is important for the analyst to realize that policies can fail either because the program could not be implemented as designed or because the program was run as designed but did not produce the desired results because the underlying theory was incorrect. Policy or program evaluation has tended to look primarily at theory failure, but we must not dismiss the possibility that a program could not be implemented as designed. In the teen-age driver problem, evaluation activities would have to consider whether the new policy was implemented as designed. If the option selected was to restrict teens to daytime driving, is it being enforced? If it was to enforce the drinking age, is this law being adhered to? If the decision was to issue provisional licenses, are they being revoked after violations? If we find that the policies are being implemented properly, then we can conduct an evaluation to determine whether the policy is having an impact on the teen-age driver accident or death rate. Possible evaluation designs would include comparison of relevant rates before and after implementation of the policy and comparing rates in a test state with a control state. Because establishing a control or comparison group may be impossible, the evaluation might instead take the form of a time-series analysis from a year before the change in policy through at least a year of the policy.

Although postprogram evaluation is typically characterized as "researched analysis," policy analysts are often called on to conduct such evaluations quickly and to reconstruct the evaluation data after the programs have been operating for some time. Such assignments require that the analyst call upon many of the basic, quick methods of preprogram policy analysis.

SUMMARY

This chapter was meant to provide a framework for thinking about policy analysis and a process for conducting policy analyses. The quality of the analysis depends greatly upon the identification of an important, precisely stated problem formulated so that relevant data can be collected. The policy analysis process consists of six basic steps: (1) defining the problem, (2) establishing evaluation criteria, (3) identifying alternative policies, (4) evaluating alternative policies, (5) displaying and distinguishing among policies, and (6) monitoring policy outcomes. Rather than a rigid lock-step approach, the process involves feedback and iteration among the six activities.

Subsequent chapters present basic methods for analyzing policies. We describe crosscutting methods appropriate at various steps in the policy analysis process as well as methods most often used in specific steps in Chapters 3 through 9 (Table 2-1). We organize the methods according to the steps in the process because we believe that policy analysis is more than methods and techniques. It is a way of thinking about problems, of organizing data, and of presenting findings. Policy analysis involves craft and creativity, and policy analysts develop their own styles and their own personalized ways of orchestrating information. However, we believe beginning analysts can develop a set of basic skills and a general approach that will provide a foundation for analytical development. We encourage you to solve the practice problems and to use the case studies to apply the methods discussed in the chapters that follow.

Table 2-1 Basic Methods by Steps in the Policy Analysis Process

Steps in the Process	Method
All steps	Identifying and gathering data
	Library search methods
	Interviewing for policy data
	Quick surveys
	Basic data analysis
	Communicating the analysis
1. Verifying, defining, and detailing the problem	Back-of-the-envelope calculations
	Quick decision analysis
	Creation of valid operational definitions
	Political analysis
	Issue paper/first-cut analysis
2. Establishing evaluation criteria	Technical feasibility
	Economic and financial possibility
	Political viability
	Administrative operability
3. Identifying alternatives	Researched analysis
	No-action analysis
	Quick surveys
	Literature review
	Comparison of real-world experiences
	Passive collection and classification
	Development of typologies
	Analogy, metaphor, and synectics
	Brainstorming
	Comparison with an ideal
	Feasible manipulations
	Modifying existing solutions
4. Evaluating alternative policies	Extrapolation
	Theoretical forecasting
	Intuitive forecasting
	Discounting
	Sensitivity analysis
	Allocation formulas
	Quick decision analysis
	Political feasibility analysis
	Implementation analysis
	Scenario writing
5. Displaying alternatives and distinguishing among them	Paired comparisons
	Satisficing
	Lexicographic ordering
	Nondominated-alternatives method
	Equivalent-alternatives method
	Standard-alternative method
	Matrix display systems
	Scenario writing
6. Monitoring implemented policies	Before-and-after comparisons
	With-and-without comparisons
	Actual-versus-planned performance
	Experimental models
	Quasi-experimental models
	Cost-oriented approaches

GLOSSARY

Act-Deontology a theory of ethics in which choices can be made between competing ethical principles in certain situations.

Act-Utilitarianism an ethical theory that holds that an act is right if, and only if, it brings about the greatest happiness for the greatest number of people.

Anticipatory Policy Analysis see *Prospective Policy Analysis*.

Deontological Theories ethical theories that are concerned with the process of making moral decisions.

Descriptive Policy Analysis analysis after the fact. Also called "ex post" and "post hoc."

Ethics a branch of philosophy that deals with questions of morality, moral problems, and moral judgments, involving three kinds of thinking: descriptive, normative, and critical or meta-ethical.

Evaluative Policy Analysis a subcategory of descriptive policy analysis, that answers the question: "Were the purposes of the policy met?"

Ex Ante see *Prospective Policy Analysis*.

Ex Post see *Descriptive Policy Analysis*.

Intuitionism a form of act-deontology ethical theory in which each individual chooses in each instance what is intuitively right.

Normative Ethics addresses the justifications for behavior and provides guidelines for selecting a policy that is good or right.

Plan a general scheme of action or a procedure to obtain a desired end. Often used as a synonym for *Policy* and *Program*.

Policy a settled course of action to be followed by a government body or institution. Often used as a synonym for *Plan* and *Program*.

Policy Analysis a systematic evaluation of the technical and economic feasibility and political viability of alternative policies, strategies for implementation, and the consequences of policy adoption.

Post Hoc see *Descriptive Policy Analysis*.

Pre Hoc see *Prospective Policy Analysis*.

Predictive Policy Analysis a subcategory of prospective policy analysis that limits itself to projecting future states likely to result from adopting various alternatives.

Prescriptive Policy Analysis a subcategory of prospective policy analysis that recommends actions because they will bring about a particular result.

Program the specific steps that must be taken to achieve or implement a policy. Often used as a synonym for *Policy* and *Plan*.

Prospective Policy Analysis analysis before the policy has been implemented. Also called "ex ante" and "pre hoc."

Retrospective Policy Analysis a subcategory of descriptive policy analysis that answers the question: "What happened?"

Rule Deontology a theory of ethics that focuses on rules, rights, and actions that are right in themselves, rather than on outcomes.

Rule Utilitarianism a theory of ethics in which the principle of utility is applied to rules instead of to individual acts.

Teleological Theories ethical theories that are concerned with the goodness of outcomes.

EXERCISES

Teen-Age Driver Auto Accident Rates

Teen-agers have the highest accident rate of any group of drivers. This results in expensive auto repairs. The more serious dimension of the problem, however, is deaths and injuries. At the national level this problem is so serious that it has been termed "the major health problem for teen-agers in the United States." Almost half of all deaths in the 16- to 19-year-old age group are the result of motor vehicle crashes. A person under 21 years of age is nearly twice as likely to die in an alcohol-related crash than is an older person. Teen-age drivers involved in accidents injure not only themselves but their own passengers, as well as other drivers and those drivers' passengers.

Approximately one-half of the states provide direct financial support to high schools that teach driver education, and almost as many states allow teen-agers to obtain driver's licenses at a younger age if they have successfully completed driver education. Typically 16- and 17-year-olds may obtain a driver's license if they successfully complete the course. In a few states 15-year-olds who complete the course can obtain a license. Without such a course one usually has to be 18 years old to obtain a driver's license.

Politicians and officials in various states are concerned about the high accident rate among teen-age drivers. In this chapter you were introduced to the debate on the topic between Secretary of State Chris West and challenger Val Lawrence (see Figure 2-6).

The exhibits that follow give a brief overview of the problem. Although they do not present the entire picture, they provide information about some of the problem's key dimensions. Your assignment is to conduct a full-cycle policy analysis, from verifying and redefining the problem, through specifying evaluation criteria and alternatives, to conducting the evaluation of alternatives. The selected source materials that are cited will provide a data base for your analysis, but you may need to locate data and information specific to the problem as you define it. Assume that your client is either Secretary of State Chris West or challenger Val Lawrence.

You are to solve the problem within one week, using the six-step policy analysis process. Address each of the following items in a paper not to exceed 12 pages, double spaced. Each individual item should not exceed three pages, double spaced. In addition, prepare a cover memo and executive summary. Separate findings from recommendations. Use subheadings, avoid jargon, be succinct, and present statistics clearly. Do the best job you can within the time available.

1. Verify, define, and detail the problem for your client. Has the problem been identified correctly?

2. Establish the evaluation criteria against which you would test possible alternative solutions.

3. Identify as many relevant alternative policies as possible.

4. Evaluate these alternative policies, giving the pros and cons and expected as well as unexpected consequences of each.

5. Devise a method to display the alternatives and select the preferred alternative from the perspective of your client.

6. Explain how you would monitor the results of the policy after it is implemented.

SOURCE MATERIAL

BARNES, GRACE M., and JOHN W. WELTE. "Predictors of Driving While Intoxicated among Teenagers." *Journal of Drug Issues* 18, no. 3 (Summer 1988), 367–84.

HACKER, GEORGE A. "Taxing Booze for Health and Wealth." *Journal of Policy Analysis and Management* 6, no. 4 (Summer 1987), 701–8.

KARPF, RONALD S., and ALLAN F. WILLIAMS. "Teenage Drivers and Motor Vehicle Deaths." *Accident Analysis and Prevention* 15, no. 1 (January 1983), 55–63.

LEIGH, PAUL, and JAMES T. WILKINSON. "The Effects of Gasoline Taxes on Highway Fatalities." *Journal of Policy Analysis and Management* 10, no. 3 (Summer 1991), 474–81.

LUND, ADRIAN K., ALLAN F. WILLIAMS, and PAUL ZADOR. "High School Driver Education: Further Evaluation of the DeKalb County Study."*Accident Analysis and Prevention* 18, no. 4 (1986), 349–57.

PATTON, CARL V. "A Seven-Day Project: Early Faculty Retirement Alternatives." *Policy Analysis* 1, no. 4 (Fall 1975), 731–53.

PHELPS, CHARLES E. "Risk and Perceived Risk of Drunk Driving among Young Drivers." *Journal of Policy Analysis and Management* 6, no. 4 (Summer 1987), 708–14.

WELLS, JoANN K., ALLAN F. WILLIAMS, NANCY J. TEED, and ADRIAN K. LUND. "Belt Use among High School Students." Arlington, VA: Insurance Institute for Highway Safety, January 1989.

WILLIAMS, ALLAN F. "Nighttime Driving and Fatal Crash Involvement of Teenagers." *Accident Analysis and Prevention* 17, no. 1 (January 1985), 1–5.

WILLIAMS, ALLAN F., and RONALD S. KARPF. "Teenage Drivers and Fatal Crash Responsibility." *Law and Policy* 6, no. 1 (January 1984), 101–13.

WILLIAMS, ALLAN F., RONALD S. KARPF, and PAUL L. ZADOR. "Variations in Minimum Licensing Age and Fatal Motor-Vehicle Crashes." *American Journal of Public Health* 73, no. 12 (December 1983), 1401–03.

WILLIAMS, ALLAN F., DAVID F. PREUSSER, ADRIAN K. LUND, and SHARON J. RASMUSSEN. "Cars Owned and Driven by Teenagers." *Transportation Quarterly* 41, no. 2 (April 1987), 177–88.

EXHIBITS

West Proposes Limit on Teen-Age Drivers

Secretary of State Chris West has proposed a provisional driver's license for teen-age drivers that would require some to do additional safety course work if they receive traffic violations.

West explained the proposal Friday at the 30th Annual State Traffic Safety Seminar essay contest luncheon.

The legal driving age should not be raised from 16 to 18, West said, because this would penalize the good drivers in this age group for the irresponsible actions of the bad drivers. She said provisional licenses should be considered as a possible alternative to a higher driving age.

Under the proposal now being studied by a state commission, they would receive restricted driver's licenses which would require notification of parents when a youth receives a traffic ticket, West said. Further coursework would also be required in some cases.

West said the proposal is an attempt to "isolate the bad driver while not punishing the good driver." She said she hoped the General Assembly would consider the measure next year.

Commenting on other legislation, West said that the new tougher drunk driver law, which went into effect January 1, has resulted in increased arrests. She said a 25 percent drop in the traffic fatality rate for the first three months of this year, compared to last year, can be attributed in large part to the new law.

West called traffic safety "the most serious problem we have in our society," and said education of young people is the best way to promote safety. "We can pass laws, police can enforce them, judges can convict, but it won't solve the problem," West said. "The real solution is a change in society's attitude."

West, who was appointed secretary of state in January to replace Lynn Schultz, is running for reelection against Val Lawrence.

Source: Adapted from an article in a midwestern newspaper.

Lawrence, West Differ on Few Election Topics

For all the noise they've been making, you'd expect Secretary of State Chris West and her election opponent, Val Lawrence, to disagree a little more than they did Friday.

But, in speaking at a forum sponsored by the State Press Association, the two agreed that their records as state officials will be important in the campaign, that the state needs even tougher drunk driving laws, that there should be no increase in the minimum driving age, that schools should continue to teach driver's education, that there should be some kind of mandatory auto insurance, and that they would work for increased efficiency in the secretary of state's office.

The two concurred so frequently, in fact, that Lawrence once said, "I wish my husband would agree with me as much as you do, Chris."

West said that in her 20 months as secretary of state she's improved traffic safety and the integrity and efficiency of the office.

Lawrence meanwhile said she made the

state treasurer's office "a very vital part of state government" by introducing special loan programs for farmers, home mortgages and home improvements.

West said she didn't agree with raising the driving age from 16 to 17, but did favor granting a "provisional" driver's license [to 16- and 17-year-olds]. Under that proposal, she explained, young drivers would lose their license for three months with their first offense. Lawrence said she proposed the same idea in December.

Lawrence said drunk drivers should lose their license for two years, upon conviction. West said she will be coming out with new, strict drunk driving proposals next week.

West said eliminating driver's education from high schools would be "a drastic mistake." Lawrence said, "We have to have a strong driver's ed program."

The biggest disagreement came when the candidates were asked about suggested increases in motor fuel taxes and license fees in order to pay for road improvements.

"We don't need higher taxes in this state, we need more taxes," Lawrence said. "The real culprit is unemployment. If we get our people back to work, we won't have to raise any taxes."

West, meanwhile, said the tax increase issue was not for her to decide, but was a legislative issue.

Source: Adapted from an article in a midwestern newspaper.

Teenagers

As both drivers and passengers, teenagers are disproportionately involved in motor vehicle crashes, compared with people of other ages. Even though they drive less than older people (except those 70 and older), teenagers have very high numbers of motor vehicle crashes and crash deaths. This edition of Fatality Facts addresses the problem.

- 5,749 teenagers (13-19 year olds) died from motor vehicle crash injuries in 1991. This represents a 10 percent decline since 1990, with male teenagers accounting for more of the decline than females.

- Forty-two percent of the motor vehicle crash deaths in 1991 (2,398) were drivers of passenger vehicles (cars, pickups, cargo and large passenger vans, and utility vehicles). The death rate for male teenage drivers (14 per 100,000 people) exceeded the rate for females (6).

- Passenger vehicle occupants comprise most (81 percent) teenage motor vehicle deaths. An additional 8 percent are pedestrians, 6 percent are motorcyclists, 2 percent are bicyclists, and 2 percent are occupants of other vehicles.

- Teenagers comprised 10 percent of the U.S. population in 1991 and 14 percent of all motor vehicle deaths.

- Teenage motor vehicle deaths involve mostly people of driving age (16-19), but 18 percent involve 13-15 year olds.

- More than 40 percent of the deaths of 16-19 year olds from all causes in 1989 occurred from motor vehicle crash injuries. These injuries comprised almost half (48 percent) of the deaths of females 16-19 years old.

- More than twice as many male teenagers as female teenagers are killed in motor vehicle crashes.

- From age 13-15 to 16-19, the increase in motor vehicle deaths per 100,000 people is dramatic for both males and females (more than a twofold increase).

Teenage Motor Vehicle Deaths

	Male	Female	Total*
1981	6,014	2,301	8,315
1982	5,354	1,969	7,323
1983	4,850	1,955	6,805
1984	4,947	2,005	6,952
1985	4,715	2,022	6,737
1986	5,280	2,182	7,466
1987	5,107	2,186	7,293
1988	5,036	2,204	7,242
1989	4,528	2,158	6,688
1990	4,420	1,944	6,364
1991	3,882	1,865	5,749

*Total includes sex unknowns.

Teenage Motor Vehicle Deaths, 1991

Age	Deaths
13	200
14	324
15	486
16	919
17	1,061
18	1,367
19	1,392
Total	5,749

Fatality Facts 1992
Published by the Insurance Institute for Highway Safety

More than twice as many male
teenagers as female teenagers are
killed in motor vehicle crashes.

Teenage Motor Vehicle Deaths by Type, 1991

Age	Passenger Vehicles*	Motor-cyclists	Pedes-trians	Bicyclists	Other/Unk*
13	111	5	37	29	18
14	208	19	57	25	15
15	353	24	67	20	22
16	802	36	55	14	12
17	919	52	60	16	14
18	1,163	91	75	9	29
19	1,125	144	85	16	22
Total	4,681	371	436	129	132

*Columns include sex and seating positions unknown.

Passenger Vehicle Deaths by Age, Sex, and Seating Position, 1991

	Drivers			Passengers		
Age	Male	Female	Total*	Male	Female	Total*
13	7	1	8	57	41	98
14	22	4	26	97	73	170
15	37	27	64	142	134	276
16	264	149	413	207	163	370
17	335	156	491	249	163	412
18	504	189	693	286	159	445
19	513	190	703	257	146	404
Total	1,682	716	2,398	1,295	879	2,175

*Totals include sex unknowns.

Distribution of Teenage Motor Vehicle Deaths by Time of Day, 1991

	Percent
Midnight - 3 am	20
3 am - 6 am	8
6 am - 9 am	8
9 am - Noon	5
Noon - 3 pm	9
3 pm - 6 pm	14
6 pm - 9 pm	15
9 pm - Midnight	20

Distribution of Teenage Motor Vehicle Deaths by Day of Week, 1991

	Percent
Sunday	18
Monday	10
Tuesday	10
Wednesday	10
Thursday	11
Friday	17
Saturday	23

Percent of Fatally Injured Drivers with BACs ≥ 0.10 Percent, 1991

Age	Male	Female
13-15	10	9
16-17	17	12
18-19	36	18
20-24	52	32
25-34	57	39
35-54	48	22
55+	16	5

Percent of Fatally Injured Passenger Vehicle Drivers with BACs ≥ 0.10 Percent

	Driver Age		
	16-20	21-30	>30
1981	50	63	44
1982	49	63	42
1983	46	61	39
1984	41	56	38
1985	35	54	36
1986	37	56	35
1987	29	55	36
1988	31	56	34
1989	33	53	34
1990	33	56	35
1991	33	55	34

About half of all teenage
motor vehicle deaths occur
between 9 pm and 6 am.

Driver Deaths per 100,000 People, 1991		
Age	Male	Female
0-12	0	0
13	<1	<1
14	1	<1
15	2	2
16	15	9
17	19	10
18	29	11
19	26	10
20-24	25	8
25-29	19	6
30-64	12	5
65-74	14	5
75+	24	6

Passenger Deaths per 100,000 People, 1991		
Age	Male	Female
0-12	3	3
13	3	3
14	6	5
15	9	9
16	12	10
17	15	10
18	17	10
19	14	8
20-24	11	5
25-29	6	3
30-64	2	2
65-74	2	5
75+	5	7

- Male 18-year-old drivers of passenger vehicles have higher death rates than any other group — 29 per 100,000 people, or more than twice the rate for males 30-64 years old.

- In 1991, 2,175 teenagers died as passengers in cars, pickups, cargo and large passenger vans, and utility vehicles. The death rate for male teenage passengers (11 per 100,000 people) exceeded the rate for females (8).

- The passenger death rate for females peaks at age 16-18 (10 per 100,000). For males, the death rate peaks at age 18 (17 per 100,000). After the teenage years, passenger deaths begin decreasing dramatically.

- Twenty percent of all passengers who die in motor vehicle crashes do so when a teenager is driving. Most teenage passenger deaths (63 percent) occur in crashes in which another teenager is driving.

- More than half (58 percent) of all teenage motor vehicle deaths occur on weekends (Friday, Saturday, and Sunday).

- About half of all teenage motor vehicle deaths occur between 9 pm and 6 am.

- Male drivers 16-19 years old were involved in 43 nighttime fatal crashes per 100 million miles traveled in 1983 — about 4 times the rate for men 30-54 years old.[1]

- Female drivers 16-19 years old were involved in 26 nighttime fatal crashes per 100 million miles traveled in 1983 — more than 3 times the rate for female drivers 30-54 years old.[1]

- Teenage drivers with blood alcohol concentrations of 0.05-0.10 percent are far more likely than sober teenage drivers to be killed in single-vehicle crashes — 18 times more likely for males, 54 times more likely for females. Drivers who are at least 25 years old and have similar blood alcohol concentrations are 9 (males) to 25 (females) times more likely to be killed in single-vehicle crashes, compared with sober drivers.[2]

- Teenage bicyclists comprised 15 percent of all the bicyclist deaths that occurred in 1991.

- Motorcyclist deaths begin rising during the teenage years. Teenagers comprise 14 percent of all motorcyclist deaths.

Motorcyclist deaths begin rising during the teenage years.

Motor Vehicle Deaths as a Percent of All Deaths, 1989		
Age	Male	Female
0-4	2	2
5-9	26	24
10-12	25	23
13-15	24	29
16-17	36	49
18-19	40	46
20-24	32	30
25-34	17	15
35-54	5	4
55+	1	<1

Distribution of Teenage Motor Vehicle Deaths by Month, 1991	
	Percent
January	6
February	6
March	8
April	7
May	9
June	10
July	10
August	11
September	8
October	9
November	8
December	6

Percent of Teenage Deaths Occurring at Night (9pm - 6am), 1991		
Age	Male	Female
13-15	35	36
16-17	47	39
18-19	58	48

THE INFORMATION IN THIS FACT SHEET IS BASED LARGELY ON ANALYSIS OF DATA FROM THE U.S. DEPARTMENT OF TRANSPORTATION'S FATAL ACCIDENT REPORTING SYSTEM. FOR FURTHER INFORMATION, SEE THE FOLLOWING REPORTS:

[1]Williams, A.F. 1985. Nighttime driving and fatal crash involvement of teenagers. Accident Analysis and Prevention 17:1-5. (Note: Some of the information in this report has been updated for inclusion in Fatality Facts.)

[2]Zador, P. 1991. Alcohol-related relative risk of fatal driver injuries in relation to driver age and sex. Journal of Studies on Alcohol 52:302-10.

INSURANCE INSTITUTE FOR HIGHWAY SAFETY

July 1992, Editor Anne Fleming

Insurance Institute for Highway Safety
1005 North Glebe Road, Arlington, VA 22201
(703) 247-1500

The Insurance Institute for Highway Safety is an independent, nonprofit public service organization that develops and evaluates ways to reduce motor vehicle losses. The Institute's work is wholly supported by the nation's property and casualty insurers, individually and through their trade associations.

Chapter Three

Crosscutting Methods

This chapter presents crosscutting methods, those that can be useful at all steps in the policy analysis process. They can be used to start quickly on basic policy analysis and planning. Thus, you will want to refer back to these methods later. Some of them are basic to all research and analysis and may already be familiar to you. They are extremely important nonetheless and may be as critical to the accuracy and success of your quick analysis as are the more complicated concepts presented in later chapters. Included are procedures for identifying and gathering data, conducting specialized interviews, preparing basic statistical analyses, and communicating results. We focus here on methods that are useful when time is too short for researched analysis. Selecting the appropriate method is always difficult. When we are faced with problems that are both technical and political, or that must be answered quickly, selecting the best method can be especially hard. The analyst must be right the first time. We cannot usually collect much original data or revise erroneous data. Time for cleaning, coding, and analyzing large, complex data sets is usually not available.

In selecting methods, analysts are guided by what clients want to know, by the time available for analysis, by professional knowledge of the factors affecting the policy decision, by the complexity of the issue, and by the data available. Although we strongly believe that the analyst should strive to "say it with numbers," we also recognize that sometimes a strategy, rather than numbers, is needed.

For persons entering policy analysis from scientific fields, this constant need to do things quickly with the best information available may be unsettling. Persons entering policy analysis from the humanities may be especially disappointed if they expected policy analysis to be scientific. Nevertheless, on many occasions, the only analysis that can be done is a quick one, using available data. An analyst for Cleveland's Department of Community Development made the point this way:

> When I first came to work at the Cleveland City Planning Commission almost seven years ago, posted on the wall was a quote from Tom Johnson, Mayor of Cleveland during a happier time in Cleveland's past. The quote said "A good executive always acts quickly and is sometimes right." At the time, this bothered me very much. I had just graduated from planning school and had come to my first job in a big-city planning agency armed with the usual arsenal of analytical techniques. . . . Merely to act quickly and be sometimes right did not seem like a very lofty aspiration to me. . . . I felt that it was possible to be right considerably more often than sometimes. Furthermore, this shooting-from-the-hip sort of approach seemed to be the very antithesis of what planning was all about. After a few months of real world experience I learned that in government decision making, as in other parts of life, the race usually goes to the swift, and he who hesitates is lost.[1]

Planners and analysts have to work fast because politicians, for whom they work, are under pressure to take positions on issues about which they know little. Again Linner's observations are poignant:

> [Politicians] can't afford to deliberate for very long lest they be accused of being indecisive or wishy-washy. Therefore, when a mayor asks . . . for advice, he's not interested in T-tests or levels of confidence. He wants a quick answer from someone whom he suspects knows a little bit more about the issue than he does. If he's told that he'll have to wait six months for a study, he'll probably ask someone else the next time.[2]

Analysts can respond quickly by using the methods presented in this book: back-of-the-envelope calculations, quick decision trees, and discounting of future costs and benefits. However, politicians may not be as interested in quantitative analysis as in a position they can justify, and there may not even be time for quick computations. But even if this is so, the analyst need not stand by helplessly. The following example from Cleveland illustrates how the analyst can help

[1] John Linner, "Planning and the Political Process: A View from the Trenches" (Paper presented at the 1979 American Planning Association National Conference, Miami, FL, 1979), p. 1.
[2] Ibid., p. 2; see also Carol H. Weiss, "The Uneasy Partnership Endures: Social Science and Government," in *Social Scientists, Policy, and the State*, ed. Stephen Brooks and Alain-G. Gagnon (New York: Praeger, 1990), p. 102.

politicians serve the interests of their constituents even without quantitative analysis:

> [The] business community began pushing for the construction of a new airport. This was not to be an ordinary airport, but a "jetport" on an island which would itself be constructed in Lake Erie. The jetport would serve as the primary landing point for supersonic aircraft traveling between Europe and the eastern part of the United States. This was viewed as the kind of massive public works project that would revitalize the local economy and lend prestige to the entire Cleveland area—sort of a Grand Coulee dam for an urban area. Politically, it was irresistible. There would be tens of thousands of construction jobs for several years. Local companies would have an opportunity to supply some of the hundreds of millions of dollars of material required to build it. Local banks would buy the bonds needed to finance the project, and local law firms would earn handsome fees as bond counsel. In short, this would be the kind of project that would promise so much for so many people that few politicians would dare oppose it, even if it made no sense whatsoever. The local media supported the idea and began pushing the mayor for his position. Obviously, there were a number of complicated questions surrounding the issue. What effect would it have on Lake Erie? What would the noise levels be like in nearby city neighborhoods? Would access roads cut through existing residential areas and require massive relocation of families? What would happen to Cleveland's existing airport, which was almost ready to begin a $90 million capital improvement program? Is it possible to build a large island several miles out into Lake Erie? Getting the information to answer these questions would take years of study. So rather than advising the mayor to say nothing or to pledge his unqualified support, we advised him to stipulate a list of conditions that would have to be met if the project were to go forward. The most important of these were (1) that the jetport would be part of the city of Cleveland so that workers would pay income taxes to the city and (2) that a specified percentage of the jobs would be filled by city residents. The mayor adopted our recommendations as his official position on the project.[3]

Although analysts take pride in their ability to think on their feet and respond quickly, some of this haste might be avoided if planners and analysts involved themselves earlier. By the time analysts are invited to work on a problem, others may have spent a great deal of time on a proposed solution. This investment tends to make those involved less willing to consider a new alternative. Analysts also need to anticipate issues and to do preliminary work before issues become crises. This permits the analyst or planner to contribute constructively as a problem emerges as important. The astute analyst will have information that others need and want and thus will become centrally involved in the analysis. On the other hand, an analyst or planner cannot become deeply involved in every problem that arises or examine all aspects of every issue. Developing quick answers to important problems demands that the analyst adopt a consistent point of view rather than trying to examine every aspect of the problem from every affected party's perspective. The problem must be cut down to a size that can be

[3] Linner, "Planning and the Political Process," pp. 2–3.

handled during the time available and for which data are available or can be collected quickly.

In those situations when data need to be collected or analyzed, sophisticated, time-consuming approaches may have to be ruled out. Simple counts and basic tabulations may answer the question. Before undertaking researched analysis we should certainly exhaust the existing data. The methods we use will depend on the data available, the time available, and the type of problem. The ideal process described in Chapter 2 must often be compromised. Analysts may examine a limited number of alternatives, consider only the roles of major actors, leave some political consequences unaddressed, or fail to resolve implementation issues before policy adoption. You must judge whether such omissions will critically flaw the particular analysis. Existing data must be gathered quickly but be analyzed appropriately. This chapter presents procedures for identifying, gathering, and analyzing existing data, for conducting specialized interviews and quick surveys, for producing basic analyses, and for communicating the results.

IDENTIFYING AND GATHERING DATA

Quick analysis usually begins with a search for existing information in such places as the U.S. Census, federal and state agency reports, policy journals and periodicals, and the work of other analysts. Quick analysis largely consists of putting the pieces together. Locating the pieces and finding the way they match is a primary job of the analyst. During problem definition, the analyst will begin to identify the types of data needed and should make a list of possible data sources. In general, use existing data, and if other data are needed, gather first those that are most easily obtained from the fewest sources. That is, seek data from archives, records of public hearings, legislative history, observation, and similar sources before undertaking time-consuming interviews or before launching a survey that could be both expensive and time-consuming. It is better to analyze roughly appropriate existing data exhaustively than to conduct a superficial analysis of hastily collected new data. Collecting original data and undertaking survey research have important places in policy research, but techniques such as the specialized interview are much more useful in quick, basic analysis. Do not overlook colleagues,[4] other informed individuals, advocacy coalitions,[5] and issue networks[6] as sources of data and information. Since one seldom has

[4] William A. Niskanen, "Economists and Politicians," *Journal of Policy Analysis and Management* 5, no. 2 (Winter 1986), 234–44.

[5] Evert A. Lindquist, "The Third Community, Policy Inquiry, and Social Scientists," in *Social Scientists, Policy, and the State*, ed. Stephen Brooks and Alain-G. Gagnon (New York: Praeger, 1990), p. 36.

[6] Weiss, "Uneasy Partnership Endures," p. 105; but note that these are not neutral sources, see Arnold J. Meltsner and Christopher Bellavita, *The Policy Organization* (Beverly Hills, CA: Sage, 1983), p. 19.

time to become an expert during a quick analysis, it is essential to draw upon the knowledge of those who are. Establish communication networks so that when important issues arise, you know where important data are kept, what data are collected by whom, and who is a good source for particular types of information.

When faced with a new policy problem, the tendency is often to collect as much information as possible. However, there is not sufficient time to collect everything; restrict yourself to data related to aspects of the problem over which the decision maker or your client has control. Quickly search several obvious sources to uncover basic data. These data will lead you to other sources of basic information. With these data as background, a conversation with the client can help narrow the search and make it more fruitful.

What strategy should be used to identify and gather data? At first data seem scarce for most assignments. However, the opposite is often true after the analyst has had time to search. Begin the search by thinking about the problem, about who is likely to become involved, and about similar problems from the past. Outline the current situation, the characteristics of the problem, and list key individuals and organizations. The blanks in such an outline become the first draft of questions to be answered and also produce a better understanding of the problem and data needs. These data needs can be filled through a review of the literature, through analyses of statistical reports and agency documents, and through observation and interviewing.

Sources of Data[7]

Providing a list of all possible sources of data would be impractical, and such a list would be outdated quickly. Instead, this section suggests ways to think systematically about data sources. Figure 3-1 is a checklist that gives an overview of the range of data sources. The major headings suggest the broad categories of data available to planners and policy analysts. Although the agency or office in which you work may maintain its own library, information will usually be kept only on a limited range of issues. When new or unusual problems arise, you will need to search for specific facts that address these problems. Success depends on creativity in thinking about a problem and ferreting out the most appropriate and reliable data.

Existing data fall into several major categories: the vast amount of existing data stored in libraries, reports published regularly by governmental agencies, occasional data and reports published by public and private organizations, and the balance of information collected and stored by units of government, private organizations, and special interest groups.

---

[7] Portions of this section appeared originally in Carl V. Patton, "Information for Planning," in *The Practice of Local Government Planning*, 2nd ed., ed. Frank S. So and Judith Getzels (Washington, DC: International City Management Association, 1988), pp. 473–77.

- *Libraries*
  - Federal depository libraries
  - Local libraries
  - University libraries
  - State libraries
  - Agency libraries
  - Other major libraries through interlibrary loans
- *Federal Agencies*
  - Department of Agriculture Statistical Reporting Service
  - Department of Commerce Bureau of the Census and its Regional Offices and State Data User Centers
  - Department of Commerce Bureau of Economic Analysis
  - Department of Health and Human Services
  - Department of Housing and Urban Development
  - Department of Labor Bureau of Labor Statistics
  - Internal Revenue Service Statistics of Income Division
  - National Center for Education Statistics
  - National Center for Health Statistics
  - Social Security Administration
- *State Agencies*
  - State planning agency
  - State departments of transportation, health, education, etc.
  - State budget bureau
  - State archive
  - State library
  - State license bureau (automobile and other)
- *Local Agencies*
  - Local and regional planning agencies
  - Departments of public works, building inspection, zoning, etc.
  - Community development departments
  - City and county assessors' offices
  - County extension agencies

- Law enforcement agencies
- Public health offices
- Social service agencies
- School districts
- Housing authorities
- *Other Public and Quasi-Public Bodies*
  - Water and sanitary districts
  - Gas and electric companies
  - Telephone companies
  - Transit districts
  - Park and recreation districts
  - Public health districts
  - Economic development districts
  - University research and policy institutes
- *Survey Research Organizations*
  - University-affiliated organizations
  - Private survey research firms
  - Radio and television stations
  - Newspapers
- *Private Organizations*
  - Chambers of Commerce
  - Boards of realtors
  - Voters' leagues
  - News media organizations
  - F.W. Dodge Division of McGraw-Hill Information Systems Company
  - Rand McNally Map Services Company
  - Sanborn Map Company
  - R.L. Polk Company
  - Donnelly Marketing Information Services
  - Real Estate Data, Inc.
  - Dun and Bradstreet Software
  - Woods & Poole Economics, Inc.
  - Alexander Research and Communications, Inc.
  - Conference Board
  - Consulting firms
  - Think tanks
  - Interest groups
  - Trade and professional associations
  - Labor unions

Source: Updated version of Figure 3-2 from the first edition of *Basic Methods of Policy Analysis and Planning*, and Carl V. Patton, "Information for Planning," in *The Practice of Local Government Planning*, 2nd ed., ed. Frank S. So and Judith Getzels (Washington, DC: International City Management Association, 1988), p. 474.

Figure 3-1   Data Source Checklist

   Libraries.   The primary source for data is the municipal, county, or university library. Libraries are also maintained by most states and major governmental agencies. Federal reports and statistics can be examined at federal depository libraries located in major cities and at major universities. Local, university, and state libraries are sources for U.S. Census data; indexes, abstracts, and guides; government publications; and laws and statutes. Agency libraries are sources for internal reports and often maintain general libraries on the agency's primary area of concern. For example, the state department of education may have a library of education statistics, and the state department of health may have a library of vital statistics. If the most accessible library does not have a certain report or data set, the item can often be obtained through an interlibrary loan.

Federal Agencies.   Although reports and statistics from federal agencies can often be obtained from a library, if time is available the federal agency should be consulted directly because most libraries hold only a fraction of what a federal agency produces. Most planners and analysts are already familiar with data from federal agencies such as the Department of Commerce Bureau of the Census, the Department of Commerce Bureau of Economic Analysis, the Department of Housing and Urban Development, the Department of Health and Human Services, the Department of Education National Center for Education Statistics, the Department of Agriculture Statistical Reporting Service, and the Department of Labor and its Bureau of Labor Statistics, but numerous other agencies can provide policy data, including the Statistics of Income Division of the Internal Revenue Service, the National Center for Health Statistics, and the Social Security Administration.

State and Local Agencies.   Most states publish a directory of agencies, but even then users learn only through experience which ones have appropriate data and how to get it. Agencies of potential help include the state planning agency, the bureau of the budget or its equivalent, the state archives, the state library, and the state departments of transportation, health, and education. Analysts in these agencies can often provide reports on similar problems elsewhere in the state and in other states as well.

Local agencies are also sources of data, including planning, zoning, public works, and code enforcement departments, as well as school districts, housing authorities, assessors' offices, and similar groups.

Other Public and Quasi-Public Bodies.   Most agencies, public and private, regularly collect data on their own activities. For example, the transit agency can provide data on transit usage; the park district can provide data on park use and sometimes even on user attitudes and characteristics; and water, sanitary, and other utilities can provide data on household characteristics. School districts also collect policy-relevant data on population changes, financial trends, and household characteristics. Even if these agencies do not have precisely what you want, they can often indicate other sources that do.

Survey Research Organizations.   Many research organizations collect data continuously on particular topics. Universities often have survey research centers, either as independent units or affiliated with departments of urban affairs or political science. In addition to surveys undertaken for specific clients that may be released for public use, these units sometimes conduct annual or biennial omnibus surveys. These data may be available on disk or tape as well as in printed form. The survey research unit is often able to reformat the data or produce custom reports from the data on file at reasonable rates.

Similar data and services are also available from private firms, with the difference that the data more often are proprietary. Nonetheless, private survey research firms often have high-quality data sets on a variety of public topics.

Radio and television stations and newspapers and magazines often conduct their own surveys. These surveys tend to cover popular topics, including citizen opinions on current issues, housing and office vacancy rates, and economic trends. Often these surveys are nonrandom and nonscientific, and must be interpreted with caution.

Private Organizations. Special interest organizations regularly collect and make available relevant data. Local and state chambers of commerce assemble data on business activities and trends; boards of realtors collect housing data; voters' leagues produce community guides; the F. W. Dodge Division of McGraw-Hill collects data on the construction industry; Rand McNally produces city maps and population data; the Sanborn Map Company provides detailed city block maps for insurance and other purposes; the R. L. Polk Company and Donnelly Marketing Information Services prepare and sell population, economic, and housing data for selected metropolitan areas; the Conference Board collects data on emerging business trends and issues; and numerous consulting firms regularly provide information on population and economic trends, parking and transportation issues, retail sales volume, office and hotel occupancy rates, and similar topics. Some other organizations give away data related to their particular interest. Names, addresses, and telephone numbers for national nonprofit organizations are listed in the *Encyclopedia of Associations* by Gale Research. Gale Research also publishes a *Research Centers Directory* and an update called *New Research Centers*. The telephone directory can also yield the names of organizations that deal with aspects of the problem under study. A list of private companies that have repackaged Census data to meet special user needs is available from the Census Bureau's National Clearinghouse for Census Data Services.

Literature Review

The adage "There is nothing new under the sun" applies in policy analysis. Most problems have been addressed by someone else in another setting. Your problem is finding out about it. Since the policy field has developed its own journals, you might begin by checking these sources for work on your topic. You will probably want to subscribe to one or more of the key journals as well, including the *Journal of Policy Analysis and Management, The Public Interest,* the *Policy Studies Review,* the *Policy Studies Journal,* the *Journal of Public Policy,* and *Canadian Public Policy.*

If you are located near a library, the reference librarian may be able to locate relevant studies for you. Computer-based reference systems are being developed at many libraries, and this will make locating useful material much easier in the future. You may also be able to purchase a computer-generated review of literature titles and subjects, but this can be expensive and may not be produced quickly enough. Perhaps the most efficient approach is to conduct the literature search yourself, in order to identify only relevant sources quickly. Unlike a bibliographic search for a research paper or thesis, an exhaustive search is not needed. If one is not careful, the literature review can use time that could be more profitably spent on other phases of the analysis. The key is to identify whether data, documents, and reports exist, whether they can be obtained, and whether additional library searching would be profitable. Even if relevant documents exist, you may not be able to obtain them in time to use them. Often the best sources have to be photocopied and obtained through the mail. Occasionally they may be proprietary documents that cannot be released. With this possibility in mind, the analyst should seek needed information from multiple sources.

Even when the literature search is fruitful, and the documents are obtained in time, be warned that the data they contain may be outdated, may not be transferable to your problem, and may contain misleading solutions. Do not be influenced by the solutions of other analysts merely because their work is in print. Rather, use their work to suggest possible alternatives, related issues, and sources of other data. Never simply accept the work of others as the right solution.

A good reference librarian can make short work of a literature search. If you don't have access to one, you can begin your literature review by searching the library card catalog, abstracts, indexes, guides to periodical literature, and reference guides. Scan journals in the relevant field. Footnotes to current articles will cite key documents, book reviews will guide you to current work in the field, and authors of articles and members of journal editorial boards will guide you to persons and organizations engaged in research on the topic. Be selective about the sources searched and the topics on which to collect data, and think carefully about the time invested in each area. The search process is iterative. As Bardach has noted, documents lead to people and people lead to documents; documents lead to other documents, and people lead to other people.[8]

Library Search Methods[9]

During the past decade, major libraries have made important changes in the way that searches are conducted. For example, instead of searching in a card

[8] Eugene Bardach, "Gathering Data for Policy Research," *Urban Analysis* 2, no. 1 (April 1974), 121–24.

[9] Mary Ravenhall provided useful comments on this portion of the chapter for the first edition. Richard Leacy updated the references for the second edition, and Leslie Sheridan and Sharon Bostick provided useful comments on the second edition.

catalog, library patrons use computer terminals to search data bases by author, subject, or key words for books and periodicals. Years of publication may also be specified. In some online systems, the AND/OR/NOT commands permit a search to be more specific. If you are searching for information about water pollution, you could ask for all documents with "pollution" in their titles. This might produce an enormous list of relevant titles. You could display the first 20 titles found and then decide to limit the search further. You could, for example, limit your search by asking only for those citations with "pollution" AND "water" in their titles.

You may use the NOT command to eliminate publications about subjects that you do not wish to cover. If you were not interested in ocean pollution, you could search for "pollution" AND "water" NOT "ocean." You could focus on lake and river pollution by asking for "pollution" AND "water" AND ("lake OR river") NOT "ocean." You should be aware that the NOT command will remove all publications having the designated term even if those publications also include other material relevant to your work. In some systems, it is possible to use the NOT command to eliminate publications in a language you do not read.

Most planners and analysts have access to such computer-based systems. Increasingly, large segments of library holdings are included in these systems. In order to make effective use of them, analysts must define the problem, identify relevant terms, and discover the jargon of the field being examined. Although the local public library may not yet have such a system, the academic libraries in your vicinity should have them. In addition to these electronic library catalogs are more than 500 computerized numeric and bibliographic data bases that are commercially available. Most can be accessed through your library's user service center computer or your microcomputer if it has a modem. Arranging for personal access to a commercial data base will take several weeks and will require a contractual arrangement with the vendor. Having obtained access, you will then need to acquire code books and training manuals. To become a proficient user, attendance at a vendor-sponsored training session is necessary. Many libraries offer a fee-based service to search the data bases for you. Among the more widely known bibliographic data-base searching services are Knight-Ridder's DIALOG, and Maxwell Online BRS Information Technologies' BRS and Orbit.

Augmenting the vendors of computerized bibliographic reference data bases are the numeric source data-base service organizations. They include Data Resources Incorporated, the WEFA Group (which came about through the merger of Wharton Econometrics Forecasting Associates and Chase Econometrics), and Citibase. Subscribing to any of these services permits access to their data bases as well as customized data services including economic analyses and projections. The larger service organizations have hundreds of data bases available on their systems. Many of the guides, indexes, and information sources that will be cited later are available on-line. These include, for example, *American Statistics Index, PAIS International in Print,* and *NewsBank Library.*

Although we believe that today's planners and analysts must be computer literate, we also know that the traditional library search is often the only way to obtain needed information. Such a search may be necessary because the analyst is still defining the problem or the needed information may not be available on-line.

Getting Started

When beginning to work in any new area, the term-paper approach learned in junior high school can be very useful. Look up the topic in a dictionary and an encyclopedia. Begin with a standard English-language dictionary such as *Webster's, Random House,* or *American Heritage* and the *Encylopedia Americana* or *Encyclopedia Britannica.* This simple step will assure that you spell the key words and terms correctly, will give you information about the nuances of the key words and phrases used in the field, and will generally help you get started thinking about the problem. Usually these sources will contain enough information to allow you to lay out several pages of facts and figures about the problem. Don't hesitate to write a rough draft based on these sources. You will be writing only for personal consumption and will soon have additional information that will supersede these basic facts. With modern microcomputer and word-processing technology, you can easily update this information at any time.

Having learned something about the topic from these sources, you might next want to consult a specialized dictionary or encyclopedia. Specialized dictionaries and encyclopedias are published for U.S. government, U.S. politics, U.S. and foreign legal terms, international relations, sociology, urban planning, urban development, other social sciences, and applied technology. There are also dictionaries of acronyms and initialisms. You can find a list of these sources in *Guide to Reference Books* by the American Library Association.

Specialized dictionaries and encyclopedias provide more detail on the topic and include bibliographies of titles on the subjects covered. Many of the encyclopedia articles are signed, and you may want to look for other works by their authors or possibly contact them on the telephone.

At this point you should develop a list of subject terms to guide your search. Check the terms against the *Library of Congress Subject Headings*, the *Readers' Guide to Periodical Literature*, the *New York Times Index*, and other indexing services.

Most readers will be familiar with the process used to locate books in a library card catalog. Most card catalogs have author, title, and subject sections. In some libraries, subjects and authors are filed together in a common catalog; in other libraries, they are in separate catalogs. It is usually more efficient to begin a search in the subject catalog. Searching under subject headings may yield other terms related to your topic. You may then want to look up these terms to see if useful titles are cataloged under them. Titles filed under subject headings may reveal new authors working in your area. It may be helpful to see what other materials they have published. The author card, and in some libraries the subject and title cards as well, lists all the subject headings under which a book is listed. These subject headings could be used to identify useful related material. This cascading process allows the researcher to investigate any topic thoroughly. Similar information is available in automated card catalogs.

Journals.   Most policy problems will involve current or recent events. Encyclopedias and books tend to provide a historic foundation about the issue, but the time lag in publication means that the most recently printed information will be available in journals or newspapers. The major journals in a field can be identified by asking a librarian, serials director, or an expert in the field and by consulting *Ulrich's International Periodical's Directory.* To get your bearings, you might want to skim the contents of the past year or two of the key journals in the field to see if the problem has been the subject of either an article or a book review.[10] Skimming will also provide more key words, author names, and other clues about how topics in the field are described.

Since it would be impractical to skim more than a few journals per field, you will want to make use of the abstracts and indexes that cover journal contents. Use the list of key words, topics, and subject headings developed thus far in your search.

The *Readers' Guide to Periodical Literature* covers major nontechnical periodicals. The *Readers' Guide,* which is available on compact disk read-only memory (CD-ROM), is a good place to start almost any journal search. You're practically guaranteed to find articles on your topic. Most libraries will have the major periodicals indexed in the *Readers' Guide.* Other sources, also on CD-ROM, are the *Academic Index* and *Academic Abstracts.*

Indexes, Abstracts, and Guides.   Indexes, abstracts, and guides to the scholarly literature are prepared for virtually all technical fields. Indexes provide common word access to the contents of journal articles, while abstracts provide summaries of books or articles. Guides are annotated bibliographies to journal and monographic literature; they often contain an introduction to the subject, an explanation of the classification system used, and instructions about locating information sources. The major indexes of use in policy analysis include the *PAIS International in Print,* the *Index to Current Urban Documents,* the *Social Sciences Index,* the *Social Sciences Citation Index,* the *ABC Political Science and Government Index,* and the *New York Times Index.* These titles provide an avenue into the contents of articles in the primary journals covering social, economic, political, and governmental issues. Other more specialized indexes are prepared for journal literature in such disciplines as architecture, business, criminology, transportation, urban affairs, and urban and regional planning.

Abstracts can be especially helpful because they summarize the journal articles. Depending on the size of your library, you will be able to find abstracts

[10] For a list of policy and related journals see David L. Weimer and Aidan R. Vining, *Policy Analysis: Concepts and Practice* (Englewood Cliffs, NJ: Prentice Hall, 1989), pp. 221–22, 225.

for policy sciences, urban affairs, public affairs, economics, energy, education, political science, social sciences, sociology, psychology, public administration, business, and management. Some of these abstracts are available on-line and on CD-ROM.

Dissertation Abstracts International, Comprehensive Dissertation Index, and *Masters Abstracts* are useful sources to identify research that is either current or unavailable in the print literature. Information about recently completed dissertations may also be found in journals for various fields, including journals in economics, political science, transportation, business, and finance. Information about dissertations in process can be found in journals and newsletters of some professional societies. If you find reference to a dissertation that covers your problem area, you most likely will be able to obtain it from University Microfilms International in Ann Arbor, Michigan. While your local libraries, both public and academic, probably do not have the dissertation, they may be able to borrow it for you on interlibrary loan. It will take a while to obtain a copy. You may be able to track down the author by contacting the school attended and obtain a copy directly from that source.

Guides to the literature can be found for virtually all fields. The library catalog will identify the guides to most policy fields, including public policy, urban policy, energy, land use, water, housing and urban development, environment, economics, criminology, political science, urban planning, philosophy, psychology, and other social sciences. Current issues are usually kept on the shelves in the reference room of the library. Guides in the area of public policy include *Urban Policy: A Guide to Information Sources,* Volume 6 in the Urban Studies Information Guide Series; *Public Policy: A Guide to Information Sources,* Volume 13 in the American Government and History Information Guide Series; *Guide to Library Research in Public Administration* by Simpson; *Recent Publications on Government Problems* by the Merriam Center Library in Chicago; and the *Council of Planning Librarians Bibliographies.*

Another useful source for contemporary information is the annual review. Such reviews (collections of important recent articles) are published in the areas of policy studies, politics, political science, criminal justice, education, evaluation, sociology, psychology, law, national priorities, and benefit-cost analysis.

Research in process is often reported at conferences. Guides to conference proceedings might be consulted to see who is working in a particular area of interest. Several guides to consult would include the *Conference Publications Guide, Proceedings in Print, Directory of Published Proceedings* (United States), *Index to Conference Proceedings Received* (Great Britain), and *Yearbook of International Congress Proceedings.* Conference presentations are often listed in periodical indexes as well.

Newspapers. Newspapers are major sources of information for anyone working with current policy issues. Libraries subscribe to major newspapers, but many planners and analysts believe it is money well spent to subscribe to a major newspaper such as the *Wall Street Journal, New York Times, Washington Post, Chicago Tribune, Los Angeles Times,* or *New Orleans Times-Picayune.* A good combination is the *Wall Street Journal* or the *New York Times* and a reputable regional newspaper. Your library will probably have one or more newspaper indexes, which, like the periodical indexes, will let you locate articles about recent events. The *Newspaper Index* covers major newspapers including the *Boston Globe, Washington Post, Chicago Tribune, Denver Post, San Francisco Chronicle, Los Angeles Times, Houston Post,* and *New Orleans Times-Picayune.* Indexes are also published for the *Wall Street Journal* and the *New York Times.* The *New York Times* index contains substantial abstracts. The *NewsBank Urban Affairs Library* indexes selected articles in 120 local newspapers.

It may also be useful to identify local media, both broadcast and print, which will have details about community activities. Back issues of a town newspaper will contain the history of local activities and provide insight into both key players and positions taken on issues of importance to the area. *Gale Directory of Publications and Broadcast Media: An Annual Guide to Publications and Broadcasting Stations, Including Newspapers, Magazines, Journals, Radio Stations, Television Stations and Cable Systems* is an alphabetical listing by state and city or town of all media.

Federal Government Information

Finding information in U.S. government publications and related nongovernmental publications is a chore, simply because so much material is produced each month. Your task will be much easier if your library has a documents division and a documents librarian who is willing to help locate newly published items. Assuming that you have to conduct the search yourself, begin by looking in the *Monthly Catalogue of United States Government Publications,* which is also available on-line and on CD-ROM. This catalog lists publications by author, agency, subject, and title. Your library may hold the document you locate in the *Monthly Catalogue.* If not, you can order it from the Superintendent of Documents using the code number given in the *Monthly Catalogue. New Books,* a bimonthly service of the U.S. Government Printing Office, lists new government publications available from the Superintendent of Documents. Items on most policy topics can be found in a typical issue. Even if you do not know about a specific publication or author, examine the list of government authors in the *Monthly Catalogue.* There is a good chance that one of the many Senate or House committees, if not a government agency or commission, will be working on your topic. If you are unsure of the agency that would be assigned to work in the area of your problem, consult the *United States Government Manual,* which lists agency and department missions. Do not be restricted by this listing, however, since federal agencies often take on tasks and assignments that overlap and would seem to be more fitting to another federal unit. Names, addresses, and telephone numbers of government agencies and personnel can be found in the *Official Congressional Directory,* the *Congressional Staff Directory,* and the *Federal Statistical Directory.*

Other sources for government documents include *Government Reports Announcements and Index* by the National Technical Information Service and the *CIS Index to Publications of the United States Congress* by the Congressional Information Service. Recent congressional events can be located through the *Congressional Index*, the *Congressional Information Service Index and Abstract*, and the *Congressional Quarterly Weekly Report* (and the annual review titled *Congressional Quarterly Almanac*).

Technical reports and data sources for state and local governments can be found in some of the sources already mentioned, such as *PAIS International in Print, Government Reports Announcements*, and the *Index to Current Urban Documents*, but other sources include *The Municipal Yearbook, The County Yearbook, National Civic Review, Legislative Research Checklist*, and the *Monthly Checklist of State Publications*. Do not overlook the U.S. Census Bureau reports on city and state governments, such as the *State and Metropolitan Area Data Book*, the *County and City Data Book*, the *Congressional Data Book*, the *State and Metropolitan Data Book, City-Government Finances*, and *State Government Finances*. Names, addresses and telephone numbers for state agencies and officials can be found in *The National Directory of State Agencies* and *State Administrative Officials Classified by Function* (one of several supplements to *The Book of the States*). Similar information on think tanks and interest groups can be found in *The Capital Source* published by the *National Journal*.

A number of published guides make locating official statistics less tedious. Be aware that sources change, but Hoaglin and colleagues suggest good starting places would include the *Guide to Federal Statistics: A Selected List*, the *American Statistics Index*, the *Statistical Abstract of the United States*, the *Guide to U.S. Government Statistics* and the *Statistical Reference Index: A Selective Guide to American Statistical Publications from Private Organizations and State Government Sources*.[11] International data can be located through the *Index to International Statistics*.

The information functions of the U.S. government have been grouped together by responsible agency and broad topic in Figure 3-2. Many nongovernmental sources may also be useful in locating government information. Several of the primary ones are listed in Figure 3-3.

Data of particular use to local and regional planners and analysts are included in the U.S. Census. Readers may be familiar with the general types of information collected through the decennial Census: population and housing statistics, by census blocks and tracts, for minor civil divisions, summarized at metropolitan, county, and state levels. (See Figure 3-4.)[12] The 1980 Census made available more detailed and accurate data than ever before for small geographic areas under a new series of reports called *Summary Characteristics for Governmental*

---

[11] David C. Hoaglin, Richard J. Light, Bucknam McPeek, and Michael A. Soto, *Data for Decisions: Information Strategies for Policymakers* (Cambridge, MA: Abt Books, 1982), pp. 167–68. For a list of additional sources see Weimer and Vining, *Policy Analysis*, pp. 228–34.

[12] For data sources on the economy, urban development, housing, and environmental issues, see Patton, "Information for Planning," pp. 479–82.

- U.S. Government Printing Office (GPO). *The Monthly Catalog of United States Government Publications.* Covers the publications of the Congress, the executive agencies, and the federal judiciary. Printed, cataloged, and distributed by GPO. The publications are available in those libraries that are part of GPO's Depository Library Program. There are depository libraries in every congressional district.
- National Technical Information Services (NTIS). *Government Reports Announcements and Index.* Covers technical reports sponsored by the military and civilian executive agencies as well as some technical literature produced by foreign governments if that literature is of interest to the U.S. government. Materials included are available from NTIS in Springfield, Virginia, or from a source listed in the bibliographic citation of a title.
- U.S. Department of Energy (DOE). *Energy Research Abstracts.* Comprehensive catalog of materials covering all areas of energy, regardless of language or country of origin. Includes nongovernmental literature.
- National Aeronautics and Space Administration (NASA). *Scientific and Technical Aerospace Reports (STAR).* Covers governmentally sponsored literature in all disciplines of space technology regardless of language or country of origin. Citations are available from NTIS or a source listed in the bibliographic citation.
- American Institute of Aeronautics and Astronautics (AIAA). *International Aerospace Abstracts (IAA).* Covers nongovernmentally sponsored literature in all disciplines of space technology regardless of language or country of origin. Sponsored by NASA and produced on alternate weeks to *STAR.*
- National Library of Medicine. *Index Medicus.* Covers "3,000 of the world's biomedical journals" in all related fields, regardless of language, country of origin, or sponsoring source. Information on availability of material is given in a section titled "Access to Articles Cited."
- U.S. Patent and Trademark Office. *Official Gazette . . . : Patents*; and *Official Gazette . . . : Trademarks.* Cover patents and trademarks awarded only by the U.S. government.
- National Archives and Records Administration. *The United States Government Manual.* Includes primary office holders, addresses, telephone numbers, and references to enabling legislation for the legislative, judicial, and executive branches of government. Also includes the *Declaration of Independence* and the *Constitution of the United States.*
- Congress. Joint Committee on Printing. *Official Congressional Directory.* Gives information on the organization and membership of both the Senate and the House of Representatives. Includes descriptions of congressional districts, biographical sketches of members, personal office and committee staffs with addresses and telephone numbers. Gives other information of use to the members of Congress such as a breakout of the executive departments and independent agencies, diplomatic delegations, the federal judiciary with a biographical sketch of federal judges, international organizations, and the press corps assigned to Washington, DC.
- U.S. Census Bureau. *Statistical Abstract of the United States.* Provides a statistical, demographic, and economic compendium with detailed subject index on all demographic and economic aspects of the United States. Includes some foreign data.
- U.S. Census Bureau. *County and City Data Book.* Covers all "states, counties, cities of 25,000 or more, places of 2,500 or more." Summarizes data from economic and demographic censuses supplemented by vital statistics and some public service data.
- U.S. Census Bureau.*State and Metropolitan Area Data Book.* Covers "metropolitan areas, central cities, states." Drawn from both economic and demographic censuses as well as public service data sources from other agencies.

Note: Each of these titles is separately indexed by personal or corporate author, subject, and report/contract number where appropriate. Explanatory material in each title will provide information about its structure, bibliographic data, and coverage.

Figure 3-2 Key Federal Government Information Sources

- Congressional Information Service. *CIS Index to Publications of the United States Congress.* Covers the hearings, reports, and documents of the Congress. Information about local communities is frequently included in the hearings. Source of material is indicated in each citation.
- Congressional Information Service. *American Statistics Index.* Covers statistical data from the federal agencies mostly located in the Washington, DC, area. Source of material is indicated in each citation.
- Congressional Information Service. *Statistics Reference Index.* Covers statistics excluding those from the federal government. Includes materials from/about major cities and other topics of concern to planners and analysts.
- Congressional Quarterly. *Congressional Quarterly Weekly Report.* While focus is on the legislative activities of Congress, coverage includes both the executive and judicial branches as well as other public issues of major concern to the federal government.
- Congressional Quarterly. *Congressional Monitor.* Covers news digests and schedules of congressional meetings including abstracts of the *Congressional Record.*
- Greenwood Publishing Group. *Index to Current Urban Documents.* Covers the official publications of local governments. These publications are available both from Greenwood Publishing or the governmental agency issuing the publication.
- International City Management Association. *Municipal Year Book.* Covers statistics and some articles about local government organization.
- National Municipal League. *National Civic Review.* Examines actual problems with the solutions developed by local governments.
- National Association of Counties, and International City Management Association. *The County Year Book.* Covers articles and data pertinent to current issues facing county governments.
- Public Affairs Information Service. *PAIS International in Print.* "A selective list of the latest books, periodical articles, government documents, pamphlets, microfiche, and reports of public and private agencies relating to business, economic and social conditions, public policy and administration, and international relations published in English, French, German, Italian, Portuguese, and Spanish throughout the world." Supersedes *PAIS Bulletin.*

Figure 3-3 Primary Nongovernmental Information Sources

Figure 3-4 Selected Census Data Available to Analysts

- *Population and Housing Census:* Advance reports. U.S. summary and all fifty states: final population and housing unit counts for the United States; regions, states, counties, congressional districts, and incorporated places. Includes breakdown by race.
- *Population Census:* "Number of Inhabitants." All 50 states; gives land area for states and counties. Population counts for states, counties, metropolitan statistical areas (MSAs), townships, and places. Breaks population down into urban and rural inhabitants.
- *Population Census:* "Characteristics of the Population." Data on age, marital status, race, and household characteristics of inhabitants of states, MSAs, counties, and incorporated places.
- *Housing Census:* "General Housing Characteristics." Data on occupancy, tenancy, plumbing, and rent for housing units by state, urban/rural, counties, MSAs, and incorporated places. Some characteristics broken down by race of residents.
- *Population and Housing Census:* Block statistics. For MSAs and other selected areas in the 50 states and Puerto Rico: Population and housing characteristics by block.
- *Summary Tape File 1A:* For states, counties, places, townships, census tracts, and block groups. Data on age, race, sex, and household relationships and housing characteristics.

Units. Furthermore, detailed unpublished data for neighborhoods were made available to participating localities through the *Neighborhood Statistics Program.*

The Neighborhood Statistics Program was discontinued with the 1990 Census. It has been replaced by the *User Defined Areas Program* (UDAP). UDAP allows data users to identify block or tract groups and subject categories for which data are required. Geographic areas must be delineated so that confidentiality will be maintained. The Census Bureau then prepares a report for the customer on a fee-for-service basis. These reports are never placed in the public domain, requiring each report to be purchased even if a similar or identical one has previously been prepared.

In the 1990 Census the entire country was blocked and tracted. The expansion of the contents and number of *Block Statistics Reports* allows data to be regrouped for geographic areas whose boundaries do not correspond to those of Census tracts. New questions were added to recent Censuses to yield a self-identified Hispanic population, data on the physically and mentally disabled, and information on journey-to-work. These improved data for smaller geographic areas may be especially useful for local planners and policy analysts. Intercensal data for selected subpopulations and locales are also collected and are reported in *Current Population Reports.* Printed data may be obtained at state data centers, which also provide access to data available only on computer tapes. Data are now available on floppy disks and compact disks for use with microcomputers.

Legal Searches[13]

Many policy problems contain a legal aspect that will require the use of the law library. Universities with law schools have law libraries that can be used by the general public, sometimes with special permission and at restricted times. The same approach applies to the law library as to the general library. Get your bearings by clarifying legal words and phrases in a legal dictionary, looking for recent similar problems in legal periodicals, consulting a specialized treatise, and finding relevant cases and statutes.

A legal search is important because federal, state, and local laws may restrict the plans and policies that may be developed and specify the procedures through which they can be implemented. The search can reveal regulations that can be changed, and it will allow the planner and analyst to communicate with lawyers.[14]

The U.S. Constitution limits all laws; it specifies the powers of the federal government as well as the powers of state governments. No law at any level may violate the provisions of the Constitution. Federal and state governments enact statutes; local governments enact ordinances. Statutes and ordinances grant au-

---

[13] Clyde Forrest provided useful comments on this portion of the chapter for the first edition. Richard Leacy updated the references for the second edition.

[14] Annette Kolis Eagleton, *Fundamentals of Legal Research for Planners* (St. Louis: Washington University Press, 1978); and Dwight Merriam, "Demystifying the Law: A Planner's Guide to Legal Research," *Practicing Planner* (June 1979), 4–7.

thority to agencies to issue regulations to carry out the provisions of laws. Statutes, ordinances, and regulations are all subject to judicial review through individual cases. The result of this process, which is called adjudication, is case law. Case law is developed through the federal and state court systems. Case law establishes, or reinforces, precedent that may be used by a litigant in a subsequent case to support a legal argument. *Shepard's Citations* provides references to previous decisions that may affect current cases. Another helpful source is *The American Digest System*, which groups decisions by subject and by legal principles. The higher the court, the more definitive the decision. Federal laws may grant authority to state and local governments. State law regulates the authority of state agencies and delegates authority to local governments.[15]

In the area of law, the beginning analyst will have to rely on dictionaries, encyclopedias, and well-known, well-documented cases. Law treatises and casebooks provide court cases, interpretations, and references. Such sources are available on land use, the environment, housing, and similar topics with which policy analysts and planners deal.

Consult a legal dictionary to determine what specific terms mean and how topics are defined. Legal works and phrases are defined in *Black's Law Dictionary: Definitions of the Terms and Phrases of American and English Jurisprudence, Words and Phrases;* and *Ballantine's Law Dictionary with Pronunciations.* A law encyclopedia can provide a quick overview of the legal aspects of a policy issue. Unlike general encyclopedias that cover a little about everything, a law encyclopedia covers most relevant topics in some detail, with substantial technical material and extensive case citations.

Examination of a law dictionary, a law encyclopedia, and a treatise should provide sufficient background for the preparation of a detailed problem statement. We recommend that you put your ideas in writing at this stage, even if you do not feel comfortable with legal jargon and you are overwhelmed by the many citations and technical discussions. Sort through this material to discover the central concepts, critical problems, and key words and phrases.

After you have an idea of the legal issues that may affect the policy issue, you will want to search for useful information in legal periodicals. Legal periodicals are both general and subject specific. They contain articles by attorneys and professors, notes and comments on topics and cases by law students, and book reviews. The articles are well documented. As with the nonlegal periodicals, the articles identify experts working on the topic and other relevant literature. Several hundred legal periodicals are published; their contents are referenced by subject and author in the *Index to Legal Periodicals*, and on *Legal Trac*, available on CD-ROM.

You may also wish to consult legal "reporters" that are prepared on a weekly basis by commercial firms. They provide information on recent decisions,

---

[15] Eagleton, *Fundamentals of Legal Research.*

statutes, and regulations. Case reporters and annotations provide similar information on appellate decisions.

The preceding sources provide background on the law, interpretations, citations, and so on. To find the law itself, you need to determine whether you are seeking a statute (federal or state) or ordinance (local), an administrative or agency rule or regulation (federal, state, or local), or a judicial decision.

Federal statutes can most easily be located by using the *Statutes at Large*, the *U.S. Code Annotated*, or the *Federal Code Annotated*. The last two are commercial publications, have useful indexes, and are updated regularly. The official governmental source of federal law in subject, or codified arrangement, is the *U.S. Code*, but the time lag of publication makes it less useful. Similarly, judicial decisions appear in a variety of publications. *U.S. Law Week*, a commercial publication, provides references to U.S. Supreme Court opinions and the major federal laws adopted each week. The *Digest of Public General Bills and Resolutions* by the Congressional Research Service of the Library of Congress reports on current and pending legislation. Copies of bills before Congress and laws that have been enacted are available from depository libraries and from law libraries. They may also be obtained from congressional offices.

Federal regulations are published first as proposed language for public comment and then as a final rule in the *Federal Register*, a daily publication. Annually all current regulations are prepared in subject, or codified, arrangement in the *Code of Federal Regulations*. These federal regulations cover agency administrative rules and operating procedures. States and local governments also publish the regulations of their agencies and departments.

State laws are published on an annual basis, and each state's official code lists all laws of the state in effect at the time of publication. The official codes are supplemented annually. Commercial firms also publish unofficial, annotated codes for most states. Laws passed during legislative sessions are made available through law services as enacted. Local ordinances are enacted or changed less frequently and are available from the municipality.

West Publishing Company and Mead Data Central are the two primary commercial sources for federal and state legal materials. These materials include statutes, regulations, and judicial decisions. A law library most likely will have access to both of these services; however, a large academic library may also have access to them.

Supreme Court decisions are available from four primary sources: *United States Reports, United States Supreme Court Reports Lawyers' Edition, Westlaw,* and *Lexis*. Each of the sources has its own structure, common word indexing, and codified access tools. (See Figure 3-5.)

Federal and state court decisions, as well as statutes and regulations, are all part of both the *Westlaw* and *Lexis* on-line data bases. There are paper copy publications for the decisions of all courts, state codes and sessional laws, and regulations. Large libraries are likely to have only isolated series. Any one of the

- Supreme Court of the United States. *United States Reports.* Includes bound volumes of cumulated decisions for each term of the Court, and individual paper copy decisions for those too recent to be in a bound volume. For very current decisions, the Supreme Court has an on-line system called Hermes, which is accessed by depository libraries. All decisions include separate opinions from the justices when issued.
- Lawyers Cooperative Publishing. *United States Supreme Court Reports Lawyers' Edition.* Includes bound volumes of cumulated decisions for each term of the Court, with paper copy issues for more current decisions. All publications include separate opinions from the justices when issued as well as briefs of litigants.
- West Publishing Company. *Westlaw.* Includes decisions of the Court and separate opinions of the justices when issued. Does not include briefs of litigants.
- Mead Data Central. *Lexis.* Includes decisions of the Court and separate opinions of the justices when issued. Starting in 1979 includes briefs of litigants for those cases orally argued before the Court.

Figure 3-5 Supreme Court Data Sources

on-line systems will give the user comprehensive access to federal and state legal materials.

Federal district court decisions are available in print from West Publishing Company's *Federal Supplement*, while federal appeals court decisions are available in West's *Federal Reporter.* The state court decisions are published officially by the states or are available in print in regional reporters published by the West Publishing Company as the *National Reporter System.* Individual reporters are available for New York and California. Late-breaking decisions and current legislation cannot be located in printed materials because of publication lags; however, they can be located quickly through the on-line services noted above.

Legal material in casebooks, law journals, law encyclopedias, and reporters will be summarized and interpreted to some extent. When you locate a relevant case, however, you may have to analyze the case for your own needs. Learning to understand an edited opinion and to analyze a case takes several weeks of instruction. Thus you may want to seek help with this analysis. If you decide to analyze a case, Eagleton suggests you examine it by six components that are usually part of any case.

1. *Facts.* The court will set forth who has a claim against whom; for what reason the suit is brought; and what set of circumstances gave rise to the claim.
2. *History of the Case.* The court will briefly outline which agencies or courts have considered the case, if any, and its disposition.
3. *Issue(s).* The court will set out the question(s) before the court. . . . Each question should be answered in the case.
4. *Applicable Law.* The court will describe previous cases, administrative decisions, and statutes and regulations which bear on the issues in the case.
5. *Law Applied to Case at Hand.* The court may then compare, contrast, and reconcile the facts of the case with the applicable law. The court may also reject applicable law and make new law for reasons such as "changing social and economic conditions."
6. *Conclusion and Holding.* The court's answer to the questions or issues raised in the case is called the court's holding and is the most important part of the case.[16]

---

[16] Ibid., pp. 21–22.

Summarizing the data from a case will assist you in determining the possible effects of the law on proposed policies. You should be able to determine whether the proposed policy has a history of legal difficulties and what the outcome has been when similar policies were enacted elsewhere. If this search reveals legal problems, however, your research dollars may be well spent in obtaining legal counsel and advice.

Other important legal material may be found in books on the subject, so you will want to conduct a search through the law library catalog. Bibliographies are also available on most legal topics; law libraries will have a substantial collection of them. The law librarian is the best source for guidance because these types of materials are often kept in vertical files or may be cataloged in mysterious ways. The law librarian can also help you acquire materials not available in the library. You may request material from another library, or you may order it from the publisher. Either way you are likely to experience some delay in obtaining it; therefore, you may find it helpful to seek similar information from other sources.

Management Records

Agency files can contain a wealth of policy-relevant information. The key is to locate the files and gain access to them. Organizations such as school districts, hospitals, housing agencies, and most public organizations regularly keep program information, but, as would be expected, the quality of this information varies greatly, and recording may lag behind collection. Beware of categories or definitions not consistent with your needs, missing categories of data, tabulations by unequal time periods, and changes in record-keeping practices over time. It is also important to ask how the data were recorded. Has someone been in charge of data recording, and what efforts have been made to standardize collection and reporting? Be aware that the existence of a computer-based data system does not assure quality data. If the data are collected and entered by staff who are also judged by the data they report (e.g., caseload volume, throughput data, or other process measures), the reporters may consciously or unconsciously bias the data.

Many public agencies are required to collect and submit data to public scrutiny, and these requirements have several important effects. While the requirements increase the availability of data, the data requirements themselves empower certain viewpoints over others. Innes argues that even more importantly, these requirements change the terms of debates by shaping agendas, framing the norms of discourse, and influencing which values form the basis for choice.[17]

Despite the possible shortcomings of agency or program records, do not dismiss them. They may be the only source of historical or trend data, and the time and effort required to restructure and check the data may be well spent.

[17] Judith Innes, "The Power of Data Requirements," *Journal of the American Planning Association* 54, no. 3 (Summer 1988), 275–78.

We advise a quick check of the quality and consistency of the data, such as using them to produce a simple analysis or replicate a known fact. This exercise will give you a clue as to whether a further investment in this data source would be worthwhile.

When using data collected by others, the analyst is at the mercy of persons who may or may not have collected the data objectively, selected the proper measures in the first place, supervised the recording of observed data (e.g., housing conditions) in a consistent manner, trained the interviewers to ask survey questions properly, or checked the questions for possible ambiguity. Even deeper problems exist. Are the measures true indicators of the concepts we want to examine, and are they valid and reliable over time?[18] These questions are discussed in Chapter 4.

When using management files, we are faced with the question of how to select those cases we want to study. Depending on the size of the file, we may use all the data or select a sample of cases. When selecting a sample, many of the typical problems of selecting a random sample apply, but special problems also exist. A sample of court files from all cases active on a given day will overrepresent long drawn-out cases because they are active for more days. Systematic sampling may be biased by the method used to number cases. For example, the recorder may record particular types of cases with a certain range of numbers. Selecting cases by physical means (e.g., using a ruler to select files located every six inches in randomly ordered files) will result in the overrepresentation of thicker files.[19] Sampling decisions will require prior consultation with the staff who maintain the files. Be aware also that pieces of files may have to be combined to make a full record.[20]

Observation

The use of observation in research has been well documented in *Unobtrusive Measures* by Webb and colleagues.[21] Observation is an important source of policy data, both postprogram data for use in documenting program impact and preprogram information. Instead of asking people how they feel about a given issue, their behavior can be monitored. Do usage patterns indicate a preference for particular types of recreation facilities? Are people observing the new speed limit? A thoughtfully designed observation may produce useful data in a brief period, but observation becomes a researched method when we observe an activity over time, develop standardized recording procedures, devise predetermined categories for recording data, and take other steps to assure that the data collected are representative. This is not to suggest that such steps are not

---

[18] For additional cautions see Hoaglin et al., *Data for Decisions*, pp. 159–65.

[19] Ibid., pp. 155–56.

[20] Ibid., pp. 156–57.

[21] Eugene J. Webb, Donald F. Campbell, Richard Schwartz, and Lee Sechrest, *Unobtrusive Measures: Nonreactive Research in the Social Sciences* (Chicago: Rand McNally, 1966).

necessary, but that the analyst must weigh the cost of researched observation against the combination of quick observation and other methods.

Observational studies are more often used in monitoring policies than in the design of policies, but limited observational data may be collected for policy analysis. Observation can provide quick insights into the operation of a program or into problems experienced by a group or organization, but observation can also have a Hawthorne effect, causing those persons being observed to change their behavior because they are being studied. Observation can be time-consuming; its accuracy depends on the competence of the observer; the observer has little control over extraneous variables; observations are difficult to quantify, and they are usually based on small samples.[22] The data collected may provide only anecdotal, but potentially useful, information. Observation can help us gain insights into problems and can help us check the quality of data from other sources.

Data collected by observation can include that from windshield or sidewalk surveys, mechanical counting (e.g., traffic volume counting), demonstration of preference in selection of goods or items, physical forces such as the wearing away or erosion of surfaces, and even satellite images.[23]

INTERVIEWING FOR POLICY INFORMATION[24]

We have already indicated that interviewing knowledgeable people is an important way to identify and gather data. Survey research methods, standardized questionnaires, and large-scale interviewing efforts have long been used to collect planning and policy data.[25] These researched methods are usually employed to collect data from a random sample of persons in a large population. In contrast to such mass interviewing efforts is *elite* or *specialized* interviewing, in which nonstandardized information is collected by the analyst from selected, key individuals who have specialized knowledge of an event or process.[26] This nonstandardized interviewing has also been termed *intensive* interviewing.[27] A related, semistandardized approach has been called *focused* interviewing.[28]

---

[22] Kenneth D. Bailey, *Methods of Social Research* (New York: Free Press, 1978), pp. 215–48.

[23] Ibid., pp. 219–48; and Webb et al., *Unobtrusive Measures*.

[24] The first draft of this section was written with James D. Marver under the title "Interviewing for Policy Analysis."

[25] For an excellent text on traditional interviewing techniques see Herbert H. Hyman, *Interviewing in Social Research* (Chicago: University of Chicago Press, 1975).

[26] For a discussion of the type of interviewing where one does not use a predetermined questionnaire, see Lewis Anthony Dexter, *Elite and Specialized Interviewing* (Evanston, IL: Northwestern University Press, 1970), and Jerome T. Murphy, *Getting the Facts: A Fieldwork Guide for Evaluators and Policy Analysts* (Santa Monica: Goodyear, 1980). Eugene Bardach discusses many of these issues in his article "Gathering Data for Policy Research." His article focuses upon the broader question of how to go about collecting data. Also see Olaf Helmer, "Using Expert Judgment," in *Handbook of Systems Analysis: Craft Issues and Procedural Choices*, ed. Hugh J. Miser and Edward S. Quade (Chichester, Eng.: Wiley, 1988), pp. 87–119.

[27] Murphy, *Getting the Facts*.

[28] Robert K. Merton, Marjorie Fiske, and Patricia L. Kendall, *The Focused Interview: A Manual of Problems and Procedures* (New York: Free Press, 1956).

Policy analysts often use elite interviewing as a quick, basic data collection method. They rely upon this approach under a variety of circumstances—in particular for short-term projects, for new topics, in instances where there is little or no literature, where respondents would be reluctant to put certain answers in writing, where quantitative information is difficult to obtain, and where hired interviewers may be insensitive to the complexities of an emerging policy problem. In these situations, policy analysts need to obtain the insights of experts, including agency personnel, program participants, and people who have access to unpublished materials.

There are a number of useful sources about how to conduct personal interviews. We will not review this literature but will outline how such interviewing techniques can be used in quick analysis. Be cautioned, however, that elite or intensive interviewing would be inappropriate for collecting a sample of citizen opinion, for gathering data for statistical analysis, or for obtaining other types of sample data. Do not grasp onto this as the only way to collect the data needed. Keep an eye open to other methods. If interviewing is the appropriate method, we suggest you adopt an investigative approach.

The Investigative Approach

Policy analysts try to answer applied rather than theoretical questions while working under time constraints foreign to most traditional researchers. These facts result in the policy analyst's need for an investigative approach to data collection. Often the analyst must quickly obtain data that have never been organized or tabulated. Experts in the area may be the best source of such information; they will often know where to locate unpublished material or who else to contact. They can help the analyst define the problem by reacting to initial ideas. The expert can provide information to help the analyst construct a survey instrument, if one will be needed, and to compile the list of persons to interview. More often, however, analysts are dealing with problems that defy the use of structured interview schedules. There may be too many unknowns and too much politically sensitive material. The analyst must be able to probe, to delve into apparent inconsistencies, and to get a feel for the way in which major actors think about the issues confronting them.

In our own work, interviews have been essential sources of information. In analyzing policies regarding the educational assessment and placement of handicapped children, planning and budgeting for infrastructure replacement, and the early retirement options of academics, we relied on interviews as both primary and supplementary methods. In each of these cases, only a limited number of individuals was knowledgeable about the policies in question. The lack of published material made it initially difficult to define the problems, and, most important, time was scarce. In these and in other studies we typically began our investigations with interviews. This strategy permitted us to test our conclusions on individuals who could easily see through faulty logic or misinterpreted facts.

If beginning analysts follow several principles, they will collect more accu-rate, consistent information. While there are no absolutes, analysts who are aware of these principles have a better chance of obtaining useful information in new or changing areas. When one first undertakes this type of investigation, questions about whom to interview, how to make initial contacts, and how to obtain sensitive information are certain to arise.

One's data collection strategy should be shaped by an adequate understand-ing of what information is required to undertake the analysis. Under most cir-cumstances, one or more of the following types of information will be necessary: (1) historical data, (2) basic facts, (3) political information, (4) forecasts and projections, and (5) additional contacts and materials.

Historical Background and Context.   Follow the issue's evolution through primary turning points to determine the policy components that have remained most salient. Concentrating on those aspects of the issue's history that have most influenced the present will help one gain a more accurate understanding of the current context.

Basic Facts.   Facts are needed for problem documentation and for the evaluation of alternatives. The more precisely stated the problem, the more credible the analysis. For example, determining the best way to provide access to environmentally sensitive areas of a nature preserve may depend on the number of persons frequenting the preserve.

Political Attitudes and Resources of Major Actors.   To undertake the politi-cal components of the analysis, gather information concerning the feasibility of alternatives, the influence and power of various actors, and the policy preferences of these persons.

Ideas about the Future.   You will not wish to produce work that will be quickly outdated, so forecasts and predictions of trends will increase the use-fulness of the analysis.

Additional Contacts and Materials.   Every interviewee should be consid-ered as a source for further contacts and recommendations about additional materials and documents. However, in highly politicized issue areas, interviewees cannot always be expected to cooperate, for there is a natural reluctance to recommend persons with countervailing views and perceptions.

Structure and Closure

Only after information needs are determined can we decide upon the most appropriate strategy for meeting them. An important decision to make is the extent to which the interview format will be structured or unstructured and whether the questions will be closed- or open-ended. In a structured interview, the interviewer has a predetermined set of questions that is asked, while an unstructured format allows questions to be asked in response to earlier answers. The latter format gives the analyst more opportunity to probe and to pursue apparent inconsistencies. The questions themselves can be open-ended, allowing for a range of responses, or closed-ended, forcing the interviewee to choose from among a limited set of responses. Each type of question and format has its advantages and disadvantages; generally the analyst's choice will depend upon both the question being addressed and how much is already known about the subject. Especially in the early stages of analysis, the interviewer will want to give the subject freedom to raise new issues.

The style and status of the interviewee must also be taken into account. Some experts may not wish to answer a predetermined set of questions or to be locked into a set of answers. If the subject matter is complex or delicate, the interviewee may not accept structure. Experts interviewed on a complex issue will often prefer to tell anecdotes or stories, thus permitting themselves a chance to describe the subtleties and nuances of the policy issue.

Also consider the type of information needed. Where attitudinal data are required from a large sample of persons, both structure and closed-ended questions are necessary for tabulation and analysis. On the other hand, when the analyst is trying to comprehend the political environment of an issue, much more flexibility must be allowed. Information of this type need not be in a fixed format for analysis, so the analyst can sacrifice symmetry to gain added depth and understanding.

Choosing the Interviewees

Many types of people may have to be interviewed. Some may have the basic facts that are required for the analysis of alternative policies; others may have experience in related areas and may be able to extrapolate to new policy areas. Your review of key documents will have provided a list of potential contacts, but it is not always possible to determine which experts are best for which purposes. Contacts inside the agency and advice from other analysts can be especially helpful here. Interviewees may be chosen not only for *what* they know but for *whom* they know. Even if they do not have the sought-after information themselves, they may be able to direct the analyst to someone who does.

In most cases it is more efficient to seek information (say, for technical analysis) from staff persons not too highly placed. Executives and higher-level managers are less likely to have the time to obtain this for the interviewer; they may not even know if it exists or where it might be located. On the other hand, these persons may need to give their approval before the required data can be released. The more senior individuals may have a more sophisticated understanding of the political arena, but they may also be more reluctant to speak openly. Aides at or near the operational level of a bureaucracy may know less, but they may speak more freely, both because they feel less threatened and because they are more interested in the interview than their superiors would be. If you have an appointment scheduled with an expert who then substitutes a subordinate, try to meet the expert, even if only briefly, so you can follow up later. Try to avoid group interviews. If subordinates are brought in for technical knowledge, try to elicit the supervisor's general ideas first, then those of the subordinate.

Making Contact

Sometimes to obtain an interview one need only appear at an agency and ask questions. More often one will need to phone ahead to schedule interviews. Occasionally you will need to make a formal request on letterhead. Of course, the more formal one is forced to be, the longer quick analysis will take. Fortunately interviews are usually not that difficult to obtain. Perhaps the only general rule is that you may have to wait longer for appointments with busier people, but even this rule has exceptions. Very seldom have we been unable to obtain needed interviews. At times we have been surprised at the speed with which we have been able to schedule appointments with high-ranking corporate officials. More often it has been middle-level staff that prove difficult to see. Interview teams may have to abide by more formal procedures,[29] but individual analysts should contact prospective interviewees directly, recognizing certain limitations. Agency directors and their deputies are busy, have full calendars, schedule far in advance, and sometimes must break appointments. The analyst may be put off indefinitely as a result of the official's overcrowded calendar. So that the expert recognizes the analyst's name when contacted for an interview, it is useful to precede phone calls with a letter that briefly introduces you, spells out the reason for your interview request, and indicates that a phone call will follow. It helps if you have been referred by someone of consequence or a mutual friend. You might begin the request for an interview by saying: "I'm calling at the suggestion of Senator West."

Secretaries effectively screen visitors for their bosses. If you are consistently thwarted by a secretary, try reaching the potential informant when the secretary is absent: before eight or after five o'clock, times when the boss is likely to answer the phone. It is sometimes also useful to arrive unexpectedly during those hours. If it is clear that the analyst has gone out of the way to stop by the office, the official may make an effort to cooperate. One of the authors was on the way to a prearranged interview and noticed a familiar name on a door when the elevator stopped at a lower floor. It was a person who had been too busy to agree to an interview. After completing the scheduled interview the analyst stopped by the person's office and was sympathetically admitted to what turned out to be an extended and very valuable interview.

There are nonetheless times when the analyst must be somewhat more

[29] Murphy, *Getting the Facts*, pp. 47–53.

assertive. It can be useful to make clear that a reluctant interviewee's perspective is as yet unrepresented in the analysis, which already includes the views of adversaries. One of the authors' reluctant interviewees did not cooperate until being told that similar information had been obtained elsewhere and that the analysis would soon become public. Upon hearing this, he quickly made time available to meet and to verify the accuracy of the information already collected.

If you happen to make contact with the expert by telephone when arranging the interview, use this as an opportunity to open the conversation, for what is learned then need not be pursued again in the scarce personal interview time. Moreover, the more you learn before the interview, the more penetrating will be your interview questions. Knowledge about the expert's background will also help you interpret the interview. Be prepared for the person who prefers to talk by telephone. In some cases, you can present the topic to the expert in a way that makes it so interesting that you will be invited in for a personal visit. In any case, try to keep these telephone conversations as informal as possible, thus increasing the possibility of further discussions. As an entree to additional interviews with the same person, ask permission to call again in the event that more questions arise.

Conducting the Interview

Regard the interview as an exchange. The more the interviewee can learn from the analyst, the more the interviewee will try to help. What you learn from one expert can be used to elicit further information from others. How is a successful interview conducted? How is the interview started? In what order should questions be asked? What should be done when the expert refuses to answer or avoids questions? There are few hard and fast rules, but the following guidelines have enabled the authors to obtain successful interviews.

Time is usually scarce, so you will want to get to your questions quickly. However, most interviews will begin with a pleasant exchange meant to ease tensions. Accept the coffee that is offered, mention the weather, and do whatever else would put you both at ease. Thank the person for giving you the appointment, explain briefly and generally why you are there (the expert is not likely to recall what you wrote in a letter or said over the phone), and get down to business.

It is probably best to begin with simple, factual questions and move toward more complex ones. The simple questions can get the ball rolling, get the expert thinking about the topic, and get you into the note-taking mood. Save the more difficult, controversial questions for near the end of the interview, but try to end on a pleasant note by returning to more neutral questions or by summarizing some of the more positive aspects of the interview. The questions themselves should be devised in advance; guidance provided for survey research questions applies here. Keep the questions simple, short, and as clear as possible. Make sure they are not loaded or accusatory. Use terms that are familiar to the person being interviewed. You may want to use an interview guide to jog your memory, but the value of elite or specialized interviewing is the ability to go with the flow of the conversation, to follow up on new issues as they are raised, and to probe for additional information. An interview guide can contain topic headings and concepts to cover, but it probably should not contain a list of questions to which you have to refer. The questions should be memorized but should be introduced into the conversation in a manner that does not interrupt the flow of the conversation.

After having conducted a few interviews, it should be easy for you to keep the conversational ball rolling. You can encourage the expert to continue, to explain, to go into detail by paying attention, by taking notes, by smiles, nods of the head, poised pencil or pen, silence, by paraphrasing the response, and through similar cues. It is important, however, to maintain control of the interview. If the expert gets sidetracked, do not hesitate to interrupt and say in a gentle but firm way that because of time constraints you need to get back to the main topic. However, before doing this, make certain the expert is really off the track, not shifting to an important, related issue.

Generally a friendly, supportive, knowledgeable, attentive, and perhaps skeptical interviewer is most effective. Skepticism should be expressed by probing and asking for more details rather than by adopting an adversarial role. However, do not allow inadequate answers to stand. Ask for evidence and for examples.

What should be done if the expert refuses to answer or evades a question? First, reword the question. Follow with silence. An awkward period of silence may cause the interviewee to reply. After it is clear that the question has been understood, but the expert chooses not to reply, ask what part of the question is offensive. This may yield a response, but the answer may not fit the question. This can occur not only during such probing, but at other times as well. Interviewees tend to interpret questions and supply answers they have used before. Be sure the interviewee knows the focus of the inquiry and understands the intent of the question.

If the information being sought is critical, and the expert is the only source for it, you might try offering a plausible response that puts the expert in an unfavorable light. You might disagree with the answers to related questions. You might continue to press the point. These actions should be taken only with the realization that they may anger the expert, will likely eliminate this person as a source of information, and may earn you an unflattering label that could affect your future interviewing.

Ending an interview can be as important as the information gained during the encounter. The proper ending can assure continued contact with this expert and can reveal other people to contact and documents to obtain. As the interview is concluding, summarize the main points, ask the expert to agree or disagree, repeat what the expert has promised to forward to you, and ask for the names of other people and documents that may be helpful. The interviewee should be thanked on the spot, but a thank-you note should also be sent. The note can be used to ask for additional information, to remind the informant about promised materials, or to keep the lines of communication open and your name in mind.

Using Your Time Efficiently

Policy analysts must often interview very busy or important persons who, in most cases, will try to keep the interview time as short as possible. Accordingly, try to make the most of available time. By learning as much as possible outside the interview, such as by telephone, more time is left for probing. Sometimes the length of the interview can be extended if the informant is enjoying the interview. To some extent this forces the analyst to give the subject a certain amount of flexibility, but care must be taken to avoid a rambling stream of consciousness, especially if a tape recording is to be transcribed.

Where time is very short, a recorder is quite practical, for the analyst need not slow down the interview by taking notes. The more complex a policy issue, and the greater the quantity of data provided, the more useful a recording becomes to ensure accuracy. It also permits the analyst to listen carefully and to follow up any unexpected comments or inconsistencies. On the other hand, transcribing tapes is time-consuming and costly, and sometimes information will be lost due to malfunctions. In addition, some interviewers believe that a recorder inhibits frankness, especially when dealing with sensitive material. If you suspect this would be the case, or if you feel uncomfortable with the equipment, it would be best to avoid the recorder. Instead of recording on the spot, you could take brief notes and immediately after the interview use them to reconstruct the interview on tape or paper. After practicing with a recorder you will be able to decide for yourself whether it is worth the effort and possible cost. We suggest you rely on written notes, even if a tape is made. Listening to the tape takes as much time as the interview, but it can be used to check quotations, facts, and figures. Notes cannot be taken verbatim. Use shorthand notations instead, concentrating on impressions and major points. Leave ample space in the notes to be filled in later. Gaps in the notes should be filled in immediately after the interview. This is also a good time to write or record additional ideas or questions generated by the interview, to summarize the main points covered by the expert, to analyze the relationship of this new information to previously collected data, and to list unresolved points and items that should be checked through a follow-up phone call to the expert.

The interview can also be used as an opportunity to collect other data. The agency you are visiting may be a source of useful reports and documents, and the interview can also provide the opportunity for observation.[30] During the course of the interview you might request annual reports, rules, regulations, and other typical documents. If you find out about these documents before the interview, you can request them by name. During the interview you may learn

---

[30] Murphy, *Getting the Facts*, pp. 111–21.

about internal reports, memos, or agency files that may be useful. Furthermore, you may discover documents by other agencies during the interview. Record the names of these documents so that they can be more easily obtained from the issuing agency. If you can call the document by name, it's harder for an agency official to claim it doesn't exist. It is also helpful to ask experts for suggestions to the key literature on the topic. Scan their library shelves for useful books and reports. Stop at the agency publication office to pick up official reports. Collect everything that is offered. This will save time later.

Observation can also generate information during interviews. Murphy has labeled as "transient observation" quick, undisguised observation such as that which takes place at meetings or during interviews. Props such as books, photographs, plaques, bulletins, and posters can give insight into the background and interests of the person being interviewed and provide clues to a relaxing opening to the conversation.[31] The behavior of the interviewee may also provide useful nonverbal clues. The expert may become nervous, bored, or agitated by a certain line of questioning, which may suggest you should probe deeper, postpone further discussion of that aspect of the conversation, or follow up on the topic with other persons who may have opposing views.

Interviewing knowledgable people is only one way to obtain policy-relevant data, although we believe that it is an appropriate method for use in investigating new topics, for politically sensitive areas, and for situations in which data are needed quickly. Remember, however, that you will not be dealing with a random sample of respondents, so generalizations must be made with caution. Do your best to get input from a variety of informants. Throughout the process be careful not to ask leading questions and otherwise generate data that merely support your preconceived ideas. Although elite interviewing can yield valuable insights, the need remains for triangulation through multiple sources of data and information.

QUICK SURVEYS[32]

When conducting basic, quick analyses, planners and analysts typically do not have time to employ full-blown survey research methods. On occasion, however, they do conduct quick surveys. When collecting data quickly, shortcuts are often taken, many of which affect the validity of the data collected. When time is available, scientifically valid surveys should be conducted. By this we mean a systematic survey of a population (the topic under study, not necessarily a human population) to collect policy-relevant data not available elsewhere. Usually these data are collected from a sample of the population rather than from the entire

---

[31] Ibid., pp. 115–18.
[32] Portions of this section appeared originally in Patton, "Information for Planning," pp. 483–85.

population. Unfortunately, over the years, a great amount of nonscientific data collection has been called survey research. Data collected from a biased or limited sample will not yield information that can be generalized to the entire population. It will yield data about only the group that has been sampled; for example, people walking past the corner of Fifth and Vine Streets, members of Basic Methods 101, or the subscribers to *Analysts' Digest.*

Even with the difficulties involved in conducting a survey quickly, often without adequate resources, planners and analysts are nonetheless called upon to carry out such activities. The information in this section is provided as an overview of survey research methods. The practicing planner or analyst might conduct quick surveys for several purposes. Other policy analysts might be surveyed to collect standardized data about how they handled a particular policy problem. Political actors might be surveyed to collect information on their attitudes toward alternative policy actions. Citizens might be surveyed to obtain information about consumer preferences. Often clients and superiors come to a policy problem with set ideas, and one way to obtain baseline information is through a survey. Even if a survey must be conducted quickly, the following principles should be kept in mind.[33]

To provide useful information, a sample survey must be designed to collect data from a *representative* sample of the population. That is, all the subjects in the relevant population (e.g., households, autos, mayors, etc.) must have a known probability of being selected. If the sample is a random one drawn from a complete list of identifiers for the full target population, the results will be reasonably reliable and can be used to draw conclusions about the entire target population. Some compromise inevitably occurs; the list may not be complete, or the sample may not be entirely random. Good survey research practices, however, ensure that the results are approximately correct and allow the degree of error to be estimated.

If survey data are required, for example, to obtain citizen opinions on a policy option or update population and household data for a rapidly changing neighborhood, an agency could contract for survey research services or undertake its own research. Deciding whether to conduct outside or inside survey research depends on funds and skills available and often on timing. There is no fixed rule. Sometimes a commercial unit can conduct a survey more quickly, less expensively, and more accurately than an operating agency, especially if the agency does not regularly conduct surveys. Although some agencies do normally conduct their own surveys, an in-house survey is not necessarily the least expensive approach. For example, even if several interns are available, training and

---

[33] For further elaboration see Earl R. Babbie, *Survey Research Methods*, 2nd ed. (Belmont, CA: Wadsworth, 1990); Don A. Dillman, *Mail and Telephone Surveys: The Total Design Method* (New York: Wiley, 1978); Floyd J. Fowler, Jr., *Survey Research Methods* (Newbury Park, CA: Sage, 1988); and Nancy I. Nishikawa, "Survey Methods for Planners," in *The Planner's Use of Information: Techniques for Collection, Organization, and Communication,* ed. Hemalata C. Dandekar (Stroudsburg, PA: Hutchinson Ross, 1982), pp. 32–55.

supervisory costs, as well as start-up costs for what may prove to be a one-time event, must be taken into account. On the other hand, an agency that plans to conduct regular surveys may want to establish an in-house mechanism for doing so. For a first survey, it might be wise to hire a consultant to help design both the survey approach and the analysis of the results.

Types of Surveys

Before conducting a survey it is necessary to decide how the results will be used. Will they be used to describe a single point in time or a situation over a period of time? The first type of survey is cross-sectional; the second is longitudinal. A cross-sectional survey collects data on a single population or on several target populations at one point in time. The characteristics of these populations can then be examined on a number of dimensions—for example, income, education, homeownership, or age—and comparisons can be made among the populations and their subgroups. When data are being collected to compare subgroups, it is a good idea to take a disproportionately large sample from those subgroups that may make up only a small fraction of the population, such as certain racial or age groups. This can help to ensure enough responses to permit statistically meaningful analysis. These oversampled groups must then be adjusted mathematically back to their proper proportion of the population when the results are reported as comparisons among subgroups.[34] This is called *stratified sampling*.

Longitudinal surveys collect data on one or several subgroups over time, to permit comparison, for example, between responses before and after the introduction of a policy. Trend analyses can be made using data for several time periods. Planners and analysts are often asked to produce such analysis only after a policy has been initiated; it is then necessary to construct ex-ante data from existing records.

After the type of survey is chosen, the next step is to determine the survey method.

Survey Methods

Each of the three basic survey methods—mail, telephone, and in-person— has advantages and disadvantages. Mail surveys are the most common of all approaches, and their familiarity is also their drawback. Recipients tend to ignore them, and without a great deal of follow-up effort, a 15% response rate is average. Often, a nonrepresentative sample will result. For a hotly debated local issue, however, the response rate may be higher. A variety of techniques can be used to encourage recipients to respond. First, mail surveys that are brief are

---

[34] Gary T. Henry, *Practical Sampling* (Newbury Park, CA: Sage, 1990), pp. 129–33; and G. William Page and Carl V. Patton, *Quick Answers to Quantitative Problems: A Pocket Primer* (Boston: Academic Press, 1991), pp. 115–31.

more likely to be completed. Second, methods can be used to attract and retain the attention of recipients. For example, the survey might have a cover letter from a prominent person; respondents might be given token gifts (such as magazine subscription or theater tickets); or those who do not respond might be called on the telephone and encouraged to participate. An advantage of mail surveys is that they require less staff time to administer than do other data collection techniques.

Telephone surveys are becoming more popular as the costs of other survey approaches increase. Respondents to this approach are obviously limited to persons with telephones. If the telephone book is used as the source of names, individuals with unlisted numbers will not be surveyed. A technique called random-digit dialing permits calls to be made within specific geographic areas without the need for a list of telephone numbers. Although telephone surveys require a staff of several persons if the calls are to be completed within a reasonable period of time, new computer systems allow interviewers to code respondents' answers as they are given, thus reducing staff time for data entry and coding. Much survey research by commercial firms is now conducted by telephone. Properly conducted telephone surveys can yield relatively high response rates, but the list of questions must be kept reasonably short and uncomplicated.

In-person interviews are a third method of obtaining policy data. Structured personal interviews are preferable when data are being collected about complicated issues or issues with a visual or historical component. Interviews need to be used in situations in which respondents tend not to have telephones, are not well educated, or do not usually answer mail surveys. They are also used when the survey data are to be related to physical data about the housing unit of the respondent (e.g., the condition of the structure).

As would be expected, in-person interviews are the most expensive form of survey research. Higher response rates and more detailed data have their costs. Nonetheless, there are times when this is the most reasonable approach. In-person interviews do, however, require larger and more highly trained field and supervisory staffs than other methods, if the data are to be collected quickly enough for timely decisions.

Questionnaire Construction

An agency that wishes to conduct its own survey may want to obtain help with questionnaire design and construction. A number of texts are available on the topic,[35] but a consultant might also be considered. The survey should be pretested before being used in the full study. Be sure that respondents can understand and answer the questions, that the survey does not take too much time, and also that the data can be analyzed.

---

[35] Dillman, *Mail and Telephone Surveys*; Fowler, *Survey Research Methods*; and Paul J. Lavrakas, *Telephone Survey Methods: Sampling, Selection, and Supervision* (Newbury Park, CA: Sage, 1987).

Sample Selection

How large the sample should be is the question most often asked by beginning analysts. The principle is to take a sample only large enough to yield data at the level of accuracy and confidence needed. That is, if you want to know the median income in an area plus or minus $500 and are willing to risk being wrong in 5 out of 100 samples, you will need a smaller sample than if you want to know the median income plus or minus $100 at the same risk level. Technically, sample size is related to the confidence interval (plus or minus $500) and the confidence level (5 out of 100) that are acceptable to those undertaking the survey. For most local studies, a sample that results in 400 usable returned questionnaires yields data that give a good approximation of the value for the full population. Of course, the sample has to be truly random. Simple random sampling uses a random number table or takes every nth element from a list. Several other sampling methods are available also. Stratified sampling can be used to select random samples from subpopulations of the target population. In large areas, cluster sampling is used to reduce expenses, by first randomly selecting small geographic units and then sampling households from those units.[36]

Although a quick survey may be useful from time to time, the time and cost for survey research may reduce its value in quick analysis. If a quick survey is to be conducted, the basic principles of survey research methods must be followed, if the survey results are to be reliable.

EVALUATING DATA AND INFORMATION

Policy analysts and planners collect both raw data and data that have been transformed into information and evidence. Early in the data and information collection process, it is difficult to distinguish between data and information. Often we wind up with more data than can be used in the time available. Therefore, it is important to evaluate their quality. Some data may be wrong, even falsified, but even good data will vary in quality. The best data should be analyzed first to conserve time and money. How does the analyst evaluate the quality of data on an unfamiliar topic? This is a common dilemma for a new analyst. First, make an effort to locate multiple sources of the same information. Are the data consistent? Be sure to determine that the data were collected independently and are not merely separate reports of the same data sources. After the information has been collected—say, from a review of the literature, specialized interviews, a culling of archives, and perhaps a quick survey—the data should be cataloged, collated, or somehow placed in an order that will permit comparison.

---

[36] Henry, *Practical Sampling*, pp. 33–59; and Page and Patton, *Quick Answers to Quantitative Problems*, pp. 33–59.

Estimating Data Quality

Analysts must be creative in order to locate and obtain data. Since many possible sources exist, it is important to identify the most appropriate sources quickly and to evaluate the quality of the data. The checklist in Figure 3-6 is intended to guide your thinking about the quality of the data you discover.

For each set of data, assign a score of either +, 0, − in response to each of the questions below. Discount those sources that rate extremely poorly, unless you have nothing else to use. In the latter case, use these data with their limitations in mind and bring these limitations to the attention of your client. At a minimum the following questions should be asked about the data.

What Data Were Collected?   Attempt to obtain original data that respond directly to the problem at hand. Often the data that are available have been reformatted, summarized, or edited. Have the definitions remained the same over time? If the original data are not accessible, use the reorganized data as one of several indicators.

Where Were the Data Collected?   Try to obtain data for the same or a comparable area. If the data are for the same locale, have the geographic boundaries remained constant over time? If the data are for another area, is that location sufficiently comparable to permit the data to suggest useful alternatives and potential solutions? Since no two locales, agencies, or organizations are identical, such analogous data must be used cautiously.

How Were the Data Collected?   Try to use data that were collected in a systematic manner by impartial persons who would not be directly affected by the findings.

Figure 3-6 Data Quality Checklist

- What data were collected?
  - Original/secondary data
  - Same/different definition
  - Multiple/single indicator
- Where were the data collected?
  - Same or comparable/dissimilar locale
  - Same/different geographic boundaries
  - Similar/noncomparable program
- How were the data collected?
  - Systematically/haphazardly
  - Random sample/nonrandom sample
  - Impartial third party/program personnel
- Why were the data collected?
  - Ongoing monitoring/response to a crisis
  - Response to an internal need/fulfillment of an external requirement
- When were the data collected?
  - After planning/during a crisis
  - Recently/in the past
- Who collected the data?
  - Trained/untrained personnel
  - Experienced/inexperienced personnel
  - High-level/low-level staff
  - Highly/not highly regarded staff
  - Organized/unorganized director
  - Skilled/unskilled communicator

Why Were the Data Collected?   Seek data that are collected regularly for a legitimate, recognized purpose. Hastily collected data gathered to address a need during a crisis should be scrutinized before being used.

When Were the Data Collected?   Current data are to be preferred, but this preference must be balanced against the preference for data collected as part of a well-planned, fully conceptualized process. Not only may crisis data contain errors because of the haste with which they were collected, but they may also reflect an aberration in the long-run trend.

Who Collected the Data?   Was the person or organization trained in data collection and well versed in the topic being studied? Did he or she have prior experience in the area? Did the person have the ability to command resources that would assure a quality study? Are the data presented clearly? The lack of clear labels, footnotes, and so on should cast doubt on their accuracy. Is the source highly regarded for other work in the area?

Document Analysis

Taken together, library materials, documents obtained from informants, and other sources will yield a great deal of information. Do not be surprised to find that the documents contain conflicting information.

Bailey has provided some guidance for analyzing documents, suggesting that there are two main types of analysis: the relatively unstructured and non-quantitative case-study approach, and the structured content-analysis approach that yields quantitative data. He suggests that unstructured methods are more likely to be used on personal documents and structured methods on nonpersonal documents or, in our case, public documents. As policy analysis involves primarily nonpersonal, public documents, the content-analysis approach may prove more useful. The goal of content analysis is "to take a verbal, nonquantitative document and transform it into quantitative data."[37] The results are usually presented in tables in the same manner as survey data. In social science research, content analysis might involve counting how often certain words or phrases appear. In policy analysis, content analysis might involve identifying communication networks, preferences, patterns of voting, and so on. Thus, the analyst would devise a set of mutually exclusive and exhaustive categories and record the frequency with which each category occurs in the documents. Selecting categories and recording units (e.g., single word, theme, sentence, etc.) and a system of enumeration (whether the item appears or not, the amount of space given to it, the strength of the statement) have been detailed before.[38] For quick analysis,

---

[37] Bailey, *Methods of Social Research*, p. 276.
[38] Ibid., pp. 279–88.

however, basic categorization and counting may be the more appropriate approach.

In preparing to do a quick analysis, the analyst often sifts through a pile of reports and extracts relevant data. This task can be made manageable. If you have not already developed your own method for analyzing a pile of documents, you soon will. We offer the following suggestions from our experience.

Record Ideas.   As ideas and concepts come to mind during reading, jot them down. Some analysts use large file cards. Others write out the ideas on sheets of paper that are placed in categorized file folders. We use our microcomputers with appropriate software.

Record References.   List references to check and other documents to obtain. Write down all of this; don't rely on your memory. Eventually you may have more references than it will be possible to check.

Record Names.   List authors, actors, and organizations that you will want to contact.

Have a Purpose.   Know what you're looking for. Have a list of questions you will want answered.

Place the Documents in Priority Order.   Select the ones that appear most useful (most general, most introductory, easiest to read) to examine first. Quickly skim each document. Examine the table of contents. Quickly look at the charts and graphs.

Develop Categories.   Prepare a matrix or other system in which to record data, and sources of data, by key categories.

Record Facts.   List what you find. Put it in numbers when possible, but do not copy large sets of numbers. Record their essence and make note of where they are located.

Set Deadlines.   Don't let this task drag on into time needed for analysis. Make a schedule for the completion of the first-cut review.

By all means avoid becoming so totally engrossed in this task that you try to read all documents in detail. You must quickly decide whether the documents will contribute to the analysis. Documents are important sources of policy information, but be aware that they have many of the same limitations as management records and interview data. Material is selectively placed in the documents by fallible human beings who make errors, who forget, who confuse sequences of events, and who may even choose not to include some information. Even the reports of hearings, committees, and study groups are sometimes edited, and the printed account may not accurately reflect the tone or context of the hearings, Documents must be compared, tested against data from other sources, and used with caution.

Determining Truth from Interviews

An interview provides the informant's view of things. How do we judge the truth? For one thing, we may be seeking the interviewee's view of an event or interpretation of a rule or regulation. In this case, and in many others, there may be no absolute truth. Furthermore, the elite or intensive interview should not be the only source of information, and the findings from the interview can be checked against other facts. The general rules for evaluating information discussed in the introduction to the chapter apply here. The credibility and reliability of the source must be judged. Dexter[39] and Murphy[40] suggest a number of tests that we incorporate below with our own ideas about judging the value of interview data.

1. Is the account plausible, reasonable, and coherent?
2. Is the story consistent, or does it contain contradictions?
3. Is the account specific, precise, and detailed?
4. Does the story fit together; does it correspond to known facts?
5. Is the account based primarily on direct experience, or is it a second- or third-hand account?
6. Does the expert have an ulterior motive in presenting a particular view of the situation?
7. Did the informant have reason to give an account that would please you?
8. Would anything have prevented the expert from responding candidly?
9. Is the expert knowledgeable, informed, and clear-headed?
10. Is the informant self-critical?

Answers to these questions will help you evaluate the veracity of information obtained through interviews. As with all types of information, the need remains for the use of multiple sources of data, peer review, and careful interpretation. Only if we obtain good data can we place confidence in the analyses we perform with it.

BASIC DATA ANALYSIS

Much of the intelligence collected about a public policy issue will be empirical data that must be translated into information and evidence before it can be used. This is what Altman had in mind when he referred to public bodies as being

---

[39] Dexter, *Elite and Specialized Interviewing,* pp. 119–38.
[40] Murphy, *Getting the Facts,* pp. 67–72, 171–80.

"data rich and information poor."[41] Clients and analysts may be inundated with numerical data but have virtually no information until the facts are analyzed, interpreted, and effectively communicated. Below we present several methods of basic data analysis—quick techniques that can be used to discover the meaning in a set of data and, just as important, techniques that help convey the meaning of data to clients.

Statistics enable us to describe a set of data and also to make statements about a population from sample data. *Descriptive statistics* provide ways to assemble, tabulate, and summarize data so their meaning can be more easily understood. Techniques for grouping the data, describing their characteristics, identifying relationships among variables, and presenting and displaying the data using graphs, tables, and maps will be covered. *Inferential statistics* are used to make generalizations about a population from sample data. They indicate how likely it is that relationships or associations found in the sample data describe characteristics in the population from which the sample was taken—or, in statistical terms, whether the findings are significant.

It is not our intention to provide a short course in statistics. We have concentrated on other basic methods of policy analysis. Many fine books explain descriptive and inferential statistics. A number of other sources offer less traditional approaches to the use of statistics to explore policy.[42] There is no substitute for a firm grounding in statistics for policy analysts. You will need it eventually, so it is best to get it early and use it often. However, we do not feel that a course in statistics teaches all the quantitative skills a beginning analyst needs, especially if the emphasis is on inferential statistics to the exclusion of basic methods of data analysis and communication.

Descriptive Data Analysis

Basic data analysis, as defined by its principal developers,[43] refers to a process for sifting through a body of data and searching for patterns and relationships in order to gain insights about the phenomena the data describe. Basic data analysis is included as part of this chapter on crosscutting methods because it is a body of techniques used in almost every step of the policy analysis and

---

[41] Stanley M. Altman, "The Dilemma of Data Rich, Information Poor Service Organizations: Analyzing Operational Data," *Journal of Urban Analysis 3*, no. 1 (April 1976), 61–75; see also Giandomenico Majone, *Evidence, Argument, and Persuasion in the Policy Process* (New Haven: Yale University Press, 1989), pp. 47–48.

[42] Edward R. Tufte, *Data Analysis for Politics and Policy* (Englewood Cliffs, NJ: Prentice Hall, 1974); Edward R. Tufte, ed., *The Quantitative Analysis of Social Problems* (Reading, MA: Addison-Wesley, 1970); Judith M. Tanur et al., *Statistics: A Guide to the Unknown* (San Francisco: Holden-Day, 1978); William B. Fairley and Frederick Mosteller, *Statistics and Public Policy* (Reading, MA: Addison-Wesley, 1977); and Lawrence P. Witzling and Robert C. Greenstreet, *Presenting Statistics: A Manager's Guide to the Persuasive Use of Statistics* (New York: Wiley, 1989).

[43] John W. Tukey, *Exploratory Data Analysis* (Reading, MA: Addison-Wesley, 1977); Tufte, *Data Analysis for Politics and Policy*; Tufte, *Quantitative Analysis of Social Problems*.

planning process. It is especially important when defining problems and evaluating alternative solutions.

A knowledge of statistics is essential for doing basic data analysis, but the analyst's attitude is equally important. One needs to be inquisitive about what the data might show, creative about developing routines that reveal patterns in the data, and open to conclusions that might be drawn. Simple, thoughtfully reported percentages, ratios, and charts and graphs can often lead to powerful insights.[44]

An important point should be emphasized here. The major goal of standard statistical texts is teaching inferential statistics, not data analysis. That is, the student is properly taught how to infer characteristics of the population from which the sample was drawn—for example, assuring that the mean family income of sampled households is the same as the mean family income of the population of households from which it was drawn. The second goal of standard textbooks is to test hypotheses—for example, whether the elderly pay a higher percentage of income for housing. This second goal joins the first when the data used to test the hypothesis are sample data. The question is then whether the results achieved are a product of a real relationship between the two variables, here housing cost and age of resident, or whether the results are a product of a nonrepresentative sample. These types of questions are often of concern to policy analysts as well, but they spend as much or more time on the basic questions of whether the data show anything. In other words, hypotheses don't already exist; policy analysts look at raw data to discover patterns or meaningful relationships that might exist.

We have previously discussed the process of identifying, finding, and collecting relevant data. These activities are also part of basic data analysis. Data identification, analysis, and display are, of course, inextricably interwoven.

Graphic Techniques

Graphic methods are an essential part of data analysis, and today's microcomputer software allows the analyst to produce camera-ready artwork quickly. Visual displays of numerical information can often provide more insights than tabular summaries of numerical data, for analysts as well as for clients. Quantities of data can often be rapidly summarized graphically. Altman developed a typology of common comparisons and associated graphic displays.[45] His summary is reproduced as Table 3-1. Altman suggests that there are basically five types of comparisons that we might want to illustrate: (1) components or proportions of the topic being examined, (2) number of items or differences, (3) frequency

[44] W. Edwards Deming, "Making Things Right," in *Statistics: A Guide to the Unknown*, 2nd ed., ed. Judith M. Tanur (San Francisco: Holden-Day, 1978), pp. 279–88.

[45] Stanley M. Altman, "Teaching Data Analysis to Individuals Entering the Public Service," *Journal of Urban Analysis* 3, no. 2 (October 1976), 211–37.

Table 3-1 Altman's Typology of Graphic Displays

Comparison Type	Key Words	Graphical Form	Typical Comparisons
1. Component	• Contribution • Share • Proportion • Percentage of total	Pie chart	Proportion of tax revenue by major sources Share of municipal budget by operating department Percentage of population in urban, suburban, rural areas
2. Item	• (Item) A more (less) than B • Differences • Rank A is greater (less) than B	Bar chart	Number of employees by department Tax revenue from major sources Operating costs for different field offices of public service organizations
3. Frequency distribution	• Variation • Distribution • Concentration • Relative frequency	Histogram Dot diagram	Number of families in different income classes Distribution of county governments by property tax rate Variation in the population of counties in a given state
4. Corelationships	• A is related to B • A increases (decreases) as B • A does not increase (decrease) with B	Scatter diagram	Hospital respiratory admissions related to air pollution index Number of state employees related to size of state population Consumer expenditures increase with disposable income
5. Time series	• Trends • Since • From (date) to (date) • Verbs, such as Fluctuate, Change • Nouns, such as Rise, Decline, Growth	Time series—plotting a curve which shows how the quantity of an item varies with time	Changes in annual municipal budget Trends in amount of refuse collected Seasonal variations in unemployment

Source: Stanley M. Altman, "Teaching Data Analysis to Individuals Entering the Public Service," *Journal of Urban Analysis* 3, no. 2 (October 1976), 217.

distributions of characteristics, (4) corelationships between variables, and (5) time-series or trend data for an item. He proposes that six graphic forms can be effectively used to describe these comparisons, with pie charts most useful for illustrating proportions, bar charts for items, histograms and dot diagrams for frequency distributions, scatter diagrams for corelationships, and time-series curves for trend data. We have applied these six graphic forms to data that describe the neighborhoods in a hypothetical city and will discuss their use below.

For maximum effectiveness, the preparation of graphics should be part of both the analytical and communication processes. Preparing useful graphics involves four basic steps: formulating hypotheses or theories about what the data might show, choosing measures, developing the layout, and plotting or entering the data and completing the graphic with title, scale, key, date, source, and explanatory notes. Like all other aspects of planning and policy analysis, this process is iterative. You will often have to return to the theory-formulation step, which may in turn require different measures when a graphic you've begun to sketch doesn't support your hypothesis. If you don't spend excessive amounts of time on any one step, you won't be tempted to skip the important ones.

Formulating a Hypothesis. A common problem in many locales is the high cost of housing and the question of the affordability of shelter, especially for renters. Assume that a municipality, Sun City, is faced with proposals to increase the availability of rental housing or to subsidize the cost of rental housing, and that you are asked to present an analysis of the problem to city council. You have a feeling that the problem may affect only certain income groups and only certain neighborhoods, and you have access to data on gross annual household income and annual housing costs (rent) for households in Sun City and its neighborhoods. Basically you want to examine the affordability of rental housing in Sun City. You theorize that most households spend one-quarter of their income on housing, but guess that this may be different for high- and low-income groups. This is your hypothesis. Without one, you have no stated purpose for your graphic or analysis, and you risk spending valuable time constructing tables, charts, and graphs peripheral to your analysis.

Selecting Measures. It would be possible to begin immediately plotting housing expenditures against income for each household, using a scatter diagram. This would be time-consuming, especially if you are working with raw, ungrouped data. Instead, you may wish to check your hypothesis by using secondary data that have already been grouped and summarized. Assuming that your initial testing of the data indicates that a pattern exists, you may decide to produce a graphic that shows the relationship between rent and income by plotting dollars of rent (the dependent variable, by convention plotted on the y axis) against dollars of income (the independent variable, by convention plotted on the x axis). (When one axis will represent time, it will typically be the x axis, as time is almost always the independent variable.) Alternatively, you could express rent as a percentage of income, with the *y* axis describing this percentage. In this case, this would produce a curve with a more dramatic shape, actually turning down for higher-income families.

Identifying measures comes before preparing a layout because it often involves additional data manipulation. To express rent as a percentage of income, for example, you would have to calculate percentages for each data point. This could be a lot of work. Sketching proposed layouts, and returning to manipulate measures to fit the one that works best, may save time.

Selecting measures related only to the principal variables under consideration may not be sufficient, especially when part of the purpose of the analysis is to convey the information to lay decision makers who may have partial or unsubstantiated information about the issue. You may, in fact, find it valuable to prepare a set of graphics that leads up to the central issue—for example, graphics that show the racial and household composition of Sun City neighborhoods, household size, and so on. These graphics could provide the basis for a better understanding of the key graphic about housing affordability.

Developing the Layout. Layout involves choosing a graphic form, deciding on appropriate intervals, and labeling and plotting the data. There are many graphic forms to choose from, and experienced analysts use combinations of basic forms to fit their needs. Altman's six forms provide a useful foundation for graphic displays. The six forms could be applied to data about Sun City and its neighborhoods in the following ways:

Pie chart   Pie charts illustrate percentages of the whole. Figure 3-7 shows
                   neighborhood populations as a proportion of the total popula-

Figure 3-7 Pie Chart: Sun City Neighborhood Populations, 1990

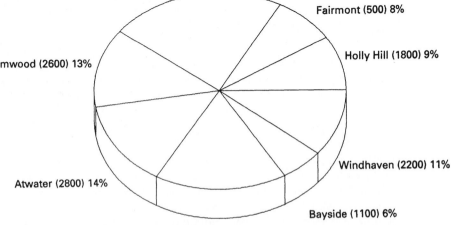

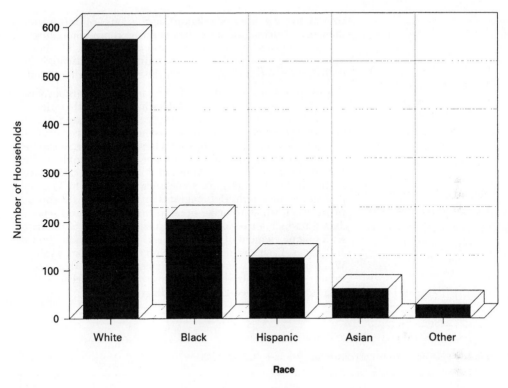

Figure 3-8 Bar Chart: Number of Households by Race, Holly Hill, 1990

tion of the municipality, where the frequencies for the categories are shown as proportions of the 360-degree circle. Pie charts are familiar to many people and present differences dramatically. However, most people have difficulty estimating the sizes of the wedge-shaped areas, and Tufte has argued that pie charts don't ordinarily add much insight and are not particularly useful.[46]

Bar chart   Focusing in on the Holly Hill neighborhood, it may be useful to know the racial composition of households, for there may be some reason to suspect red-lining or some other activity that reduces the availability of housing to a particular group of people. Figure 3-8 shows how a bar chart can be used to compare the magnitude of and differences among mutually exclusive categories of noncontinuous nominal or ordinal data. The bar chart provides both information about actual quantities and relative proportions.

Histogram   Similar to the bar chart, the histogram shows both magnitudes and differences among categories. While bar charts are drawn with spaces between the bars, because the categories are not

[46] Edward R. Tufte, *The Visual Display of Quantitative Information* (Cheshire, CT: Graphics Press, 1983); but also see Edward R. Tufte, *Envisioning Information* (Cheshire, CT: Graphics Press, 1990).

continuous (e.g., race or religion), histograms are drawn with their bars touching because they describe continuous categories (e.g., income) of interval or ratio data. Figure 3-9 shows how a histogram can illustrate the number of households in each of seven income categories for the Bayside neighborhood.

Dot diagram

Dot diagrams are used in much the same way as histograms, but they are used when the variables have many categories—for example, when income data are plotted by thousand-dollar increments rather than as ten-thousand-dollar increments as was done above. Figure 3-10 shows how a dot diagram can be used to portray graphically the number of households in the Bayside neighborhood by thousand-dollar income categories. Points in dot diagrams are sometimes connected by lines to produce a line graph. Dot diagrams or line graphs are appropriate when the data make up a function or ordered sets of data for which a rule associates with each element of the first set a unique element of the second set. These are plotted on x and y axes. Each x value must have no more than one y value. When individual x values are associated with more than one y value, and the data have not been grouped or summarized, the data can be displayed as a scatter diagram.

Figure 3-9   Histogram: Number of Households by Income, Bayside, 1990

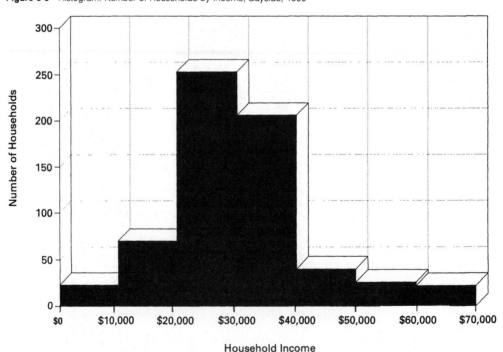

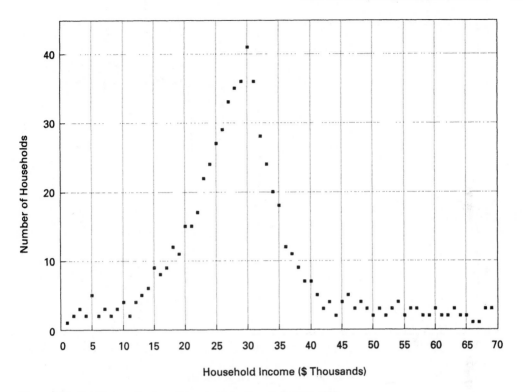

Figure 3-10   Dot Diagram: Number of Households by Income, Bayside, 1990

Scatter
diagram

Figure 3-11 is a scatter diagram for another neighborhood, Fairmont, showing the relationship between annual household income and annual rent payments. Unlike the dot diagram, this graphic is a plot of ungrouped data (which could be grouped to produce a dot diagram). Figure 3-11 might, in fact, be the type of graphic most relevant to our investigation of the affordability of housing in Sun City neighborhoods, but the other graphics can provide insights into how we might interpret this scatter diagram. For example, we might be led to investigate the relationship shown in the scatter diagram separately for each race, and we might want to compare the findings with other neighborhoods in Sun City. We also might be led to wonder whether these relationships have changed over time.

Time series

Time-series diagrams are intended to show change over time in the quantity of a variable—for example, population growth or decline, unemployment levels, or tax rates. Such data might be plotted for each year, or data for only selected years might be plotted. More than one time series can be shown on an individual time-series diagram. For example, the number of households in each neighborhood in Sun City for each of the past ten decades might be plotted. In Figure 3-12 the number

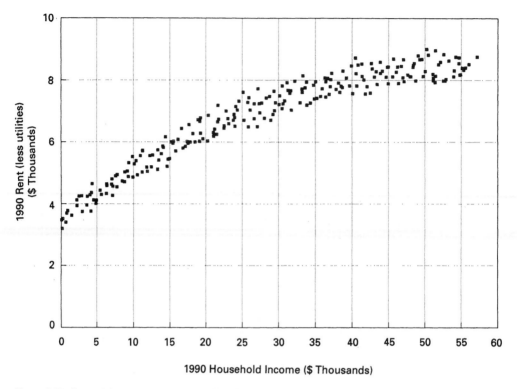

Figure 3-11 Scatter Diagram: Rent versus Household Income, Fairmont, 1990

of households for one neighborhood, Bayside, are plotted from 1900 to 1990.

These six graphic types by no means exhaust the visual display possibilities open to the analyst.[47] In addition to illustrations that display data, the analyst might find organization and flow charts useful. An organization chart can show formal and informal relationships at a chosen time. It can help the analyst or client understand the relationships of individuals or entities affecting the policy issue under discussion. A flow chart can be used to portray an entire process, or alternative processes, identifying important steps in those processes. Depending on the analyst's purpose, it may be important to highlight decision points, use time as an axis so that the relative speed of alternatives is readily evident, identify who has responsibility for each step, or attach probabilities to some or all alternative outcomes.

[47] Among other references on preparing charts, graphs, and other displays of numerical data are Mary Eleanor Spear, *Charting Statistics* (New York: McGraw-Hill, 1952); Calvin F. Schmid and Stanton E. Schmid, *Handbook of Graphic Presentation,* 2nd ed. (New York: Wiley, 1979); Darrel Huff, *How to Lie with Statistics* (New York: Norton, 1954); and Witzling and Greenstreet, *Presenting Statistics.*

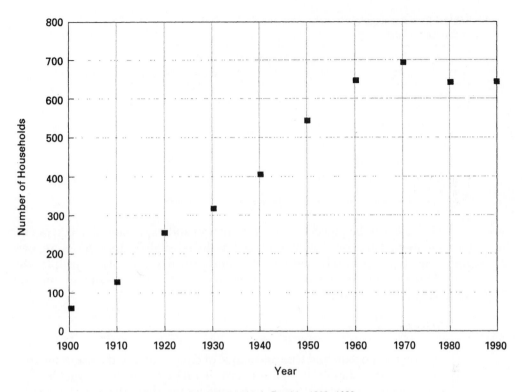

Figure 3-12 Time-Series Diagram: Number of Households in Bayside, 1900–1990

Completing the Graphic.   All graphics, even those reserved for the analyst's own use, should be properly documented. This prevents misinterpretation by others who use your work and allows you to respond to questions or challenges, whether they occur immediately or many months later. This means every graphic should be self-contained and self-explanatory. The title should provide a clear and complete explanation of what the graphic shows. If the title must be short to be memorable or catch attention, add a subtitle to complete the thought. Labels, source and explanatory notes, keys, and the date of preparation should make it possible for uninformed users to answer many questions for themselves.

When selecting the scales for your measures remember that your choice can influence conclusions. Don't be overly impressed by steep slopes or sharp peaks that you created. Use graphics as one of several aids to understanding. Once you have plotted your data, don't look only for confirmation of your hypothesis. Be alert to other interpretations. Observe trends, patterns, cycles. Note historical events that may explain aberrations. Look for the highest and lowest points, and satisfy yourself that you have a plausible explanation of why they occurred. Look also for points of intersection or greatest diversion when there are two or more dependent variables.

Table 3-2   Percentage of Household Income Paid as Rent
in Sun City in 1990

Gross Annual Income	Number of Households	Percentages of 1990 Gross Income Paid as Rent
$70,000 and over	150	19
$60,000–69,999	190	25
$50,000–59,999	890	30
$40,000–49,999	1,370	33
$30,000–39,999	2,400	34
$20,000–29,999	2,200	35
$10,000–19,999	900	25
$0–9,999	61	21

Graphics can be powerful tools for analysis and explanation. The types we have mentioned are conventional forms, but the possibilities for developing new and better types of graphics are great. Tufte provides a history of people who have done this and suggests a set of principles for those motivated to improve upon current standards.[48]

Tables

Another important and basic technique of data analysis is the use of tables.[49] Although it sounds rather straightforward, it isn't easy to develop tables that both provide insights for the analyst and convince the client that the conclusions drawn from the data are correct. Different versions of tables drawn from the same empirical information may be needed for these two purposes. The same four steps may be used to develop tables as to develop diagrams. Table 3-2 shows how a table can be used to convey a similar message as was shown in Figure 3-11, but this time for Sun City as a whole: Moderate-income households in Sun City pay a larger percentage of gross annual income than all other classes, including the poor.

Be consistent about laying out tables. Since we often work with ordinal or interval data, and they are often positive in sign, we suggest you visualize tables as the upper right quadrant of the coordinate system: the x positive, y positive quadrant. This implies that data should be ordered from low to high values along the x axis beginning at the zero point (intersection) and from low to high along the y axis. This produces the graphic shown in Figure 3-13.

This layout has the advantage that a positive correlation will yield data that tend to fall on the diagonal from lower left to upper right, and a negative

[48] Tufte, *Visual Display of Quantitative Information.*

[49] Tukey's *Exploratory Data Analysis* covers the use of tables for gaining insights. Standard statistics textbooks also cover table development. See Hubert M. Blalock, Jr., *Social Statistics*, 2nd ed., rev. (New York: McGraw-Hill, 1979); see also Page and Patton, *Quick Answers to Quantitative Problems*, pp. 13–24.

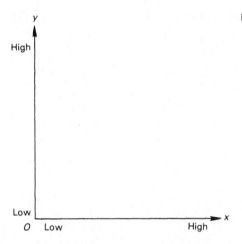

Figure 3-13 The *x* and *y* Axes

correlation will run from the upper left hand corner to the lower right, a well-established and widely used convention.

Readers are also aided if percentages are computed for all cells in complex tables but the number of cases is given only for column or row totals. Percentages in the body make the tables easier to understand and compare. Row or column totals permit individual cell values to be recomputed if necessary (Table 3-3). It is also important to indicate the missing observations (MO) that could not be included in the table and the data that are not applicable (NA). Missing observations occur, for example, when the respondent fails to answer a question. Data are reported as not applicable when the respondent skips over data that were not relevant—for example, questions about reasons for moving to a town that are skipped by persons who have always lived in the town.

In order to make visual sense out of most data, they will need to be collapsed into acceptable categories such as five-year age groupings or $5,000 income categories. The percentage of cases falling into the respective categories should be reported, with the percentages computed on the number of respondents rather than on the total number of questionnaires sent out.

When categorizing data, be sure that the categories are mutually exclusive (not overlapping) and exhaustive. Table 3-4 compares categories that are and are not mutually exclusive.

Categories that are not mutually exclusive present the problem of where to place borderline data. Is a person who earns $20,000 per year placed in the $10,000–$20,000 category or the $20,000–$30,000 category?

Table 3-5 presents income categories that are both mutually exclusive (when the data are rounded to the nearest dollar) and exhaustive.

Tables can contain text or symbols as well as numbers. This type of table is particularly useful for displaying comparisons in a condensed format. We will show in Chapter 8 how a policy analyst might use such a table to lay out the

Table 3-3 Typical Table Layout: Newcomers Wanted the Convenience of a Nearby City

	INFLUENCE OF PROXIMITY TO OUR TOWN			
Town/Period Moved	None	Some	Strong	Total
Lakeside				
1981–1990	8%	50%	42%	100% (361)
Pre-1981	38%	42%	21%	101% (272)
Total	21%	47%	33%	101% (633)
Seaside				
1981–1990	13%	41%	47%	101% (215)
Pre-1981	24%	38%	38%	100% (178)
Total	18%	40%	42%	100% (393)
Hillside				
1981–1990	38%	36%	26%	100% (202)
Pre-1981	49%	29%	22%	100% (250)
Total	44%	32%	24%	100% (452)

Lakeside:		Seaside:		Hillside:	
MO*	= 54	MO	= 103	MO	= 11
NA**	= 172	NA	= 105	NA	= 194
Gamma	= 0.54	Gamma	= 0.21	Gamma	= 0.16

*MO = Missing observations

**NA = Not applicable (have always lived in town)

Source: Adapted from Carl V. Patton and Kenneth E. Stabler, "The Small Town in the Urban Fringe: Conflicts in Attitudes and Values," *Journal of the Community Development Society* 10, no. 1 (Spring 1979), 87.

Table 3-4 Mutually Exclusive Categories

MUTUALLY EXCLUSIVE CATEGORIES	NOT MUTUALLY EXCLUSIVE CATEGORIES
Annual Income	Annual Income
$30,000–39,999	$30,000–40,000
20,000–29,999	20,000–30,000
10,000–19,999	10,000–20,000

Table 3-5 Mutually Exclusive and Exhaustive Categories

Annual per Capita Income in Dollars

$60,000 and above
$50,000–59,999
$40,000–49,999
$30,000–39,999
$20,000–29,999
$10,000–19,999
Less than $10,000

advantages and disadvantages of several alternatives, using a standard set of criteria as row headings and devoting one column to each alternative.

Maps

Maps also have great analytic potential when the policy issue has spatial dimensions. Like other forms of graphics, however, unless the analyst follows the four steps, beginning with forming a hypothesis, large amounts of time can be wasted creating colorful and irrelevant maps.

Maps can often be borrowed. Avoid these common pitfalls: poor reproduction potential, prohibition of reproduction, too much or too little detail, an inappropriate scale, extraneous information or decoration, and lack of a complete title, legend or source, and explanatory notes. Figures 3-14 and 3-15 show an example of the use of maps. Figure 3-14 shows infant mortality in the Atlanta metropolitan area for 1984–88. Figure 3-15 shows the same item plotted for the state of Georgia for the same time period.

Using maps to portray aggregated characteristics of individuals or units smaller than the areal units shown risks encountering the ecological fallacy that will be discussed in Chapter 4. Areal units shown on maps represent data groupings in the same way as income or age groupings for summarizing tabular data. It should be clear that important information can be concealed by groupings that are inappropriate (e.g., too broad).

Analysis often depends upon comparison, which can be difficult with maps. Transparent overlays are one technique that can be used with a base map that depicts basic physical features. The overlays, showing areas affected by alternatives, key resources, densities, and so on, can be used alone with the base map or in combination. This technique is especially useful when evaluating policies involving physical changes, construction disruption, flood potential, and so on.

In summary, preparing any graphic is an iterative process that typically involves trial and error. The number of trials required is usually greater if you intend to use the graphic as a tool for communicating with others as well as for your own analysis.

We suggest the following guidelines for preparing useful tables and graphics.[50]

- Give all graphics titles that are descriptive and easy to remember.
- Specify the dependent and independent variables.
- Divide the data into mutually exclusive and exhaustive categories.
- Use evenly divided categories where possible.
- Round off final data to whole numbers and percentages when this would not be misleading.

---

[50] Expanded from the first edition of *Basic Methods of Policy Analysis and Planning* with material from Page and Patton, *Quick Answers to Quantitative Problems*, pp. 14–15, 26.

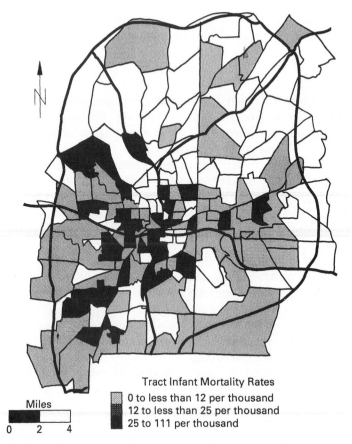

Tract Infant Mortality Rates

0 to less than 12 per thousand
12 to less than 25 per thousand
25 to 111 per thousand

Miles

0 2 4

Figure 3-14 Atlanta Region Infant Mortality Rate, 1984–1988 Average
Source: Georgia Division of Public Health.

- Report missing values and responses not analyzed because they were not applicable.
- Calculate percentages across the rows to equal 100 %, and read down the columns when interpreting the data.
- Report only row totals or column totals, as individual cell values can be recomputed if necessary.
- Time should run from left to right and from bottom to top.
- Magnitudes should run from left to right and from bottom to top.
- Label trend lines directly to reduce the amount of information that must go into a legend.
- Maps should include legends that identify the variables being presented. Orient maps with North at the top. Include a north arrow and a scale.
- Shading or tones should be selected that will photocopy and telecopy well.
- Avoid using three-dimensional graphics that distort relationships.
- Cite your sources.

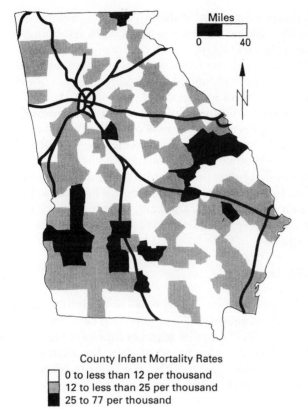

County Infant Mortality Rates

☐ 0 to less than 12 per thousand
▨ 12 to less than 25 per thousand
■ 25 to 77 per thousand

Figure 3-15   Georgia Infant Mortality Rate, 1984–1988 Average
Source: Georgia Division of Public Health.

Descriptive Statistics

Descriptive statistics, or measures that summarize attributes of a data set, are important tools of basic data analysis. The most common descriptive statistics are the mean, median, and mode as indicators of central tendency, and the range, variance, and standard deviation as measures of variation. These statistics can be computed from original data and from data that have been previously grouped into categories. Standard statistics texts cover this topic.[51]

The key, however, is not the mechanics of calculating statistics correctly, although this is important, but rather identifying those variables and their mea-

[51] Blalock, *Social Statistics*; Wilfred J. Dixon and Frank J. Massey, Jr., *Introduction to Statistical Analysis*, 4th ed. (New York: McGraw-Hill, 1983); see also Page and Patton, *Quick Answers to Quantitative Problems*, pp. 3–12.

sures that will yield insights for policy analysis. Table 3-6 presents grouped data that further explore the possible existence in Sun City of red-lining—systematic discrimination by denying loans or insurance coverage on properties in specific geographic areas. The table appears to show that when households are grouped by neighborhood of applicant, two neighborhoods, the poorer ones in terms of average household income, show low approval rates.

When statistics of individual applicants are computed, however, we see that the average income of approved borrowers is only slightly higher than that of those not approved, and that the range is extremely wide (Table 3-7). These summary statistics raise additional questions about whether the location of properties is a factor used to determine loan approval or denial, since income of the applicant is only slightly related to approval rates. The analyst should obtain additional data on approval rates by location and income of applicant for several time periods. These two simple tabulations have suggested possible avenues that the analyst might explore.

Association or Correlation

Beyond reporting percentages, which may convey important messages, it is also helpful to have an indication of the relationship between two variables or among three or more. Initially the analyst might examine frequencies to discover how often particular values occur in the set of data. For example, do persons who have had a driver education course within the past five years have different frequency-of-accident records than those who didn't have a course? Next, the analyst might cross-tabulate two variables (one independent and one dependent variable). We would like to know whether there is a pattern in the data. Do the variables vary (change) in a consistent manner? As the value of one variable gets larger, does the value of another get larger or smaller? For example, do persons with higher education levels also have higher incomes? Or do persons with higher education levels have fewer traffic accidents?

Table 3-6 Average Household Income, Loan Applications, and Approval Rates for Neighborhoods in Sun City in 1990

Neighborhood of Applicant	Mean 1990 Neighborhood Household Income	Number of Loan Applications	Approval Rate
Windhaven	$13,300	40	35%
Bayside	$24,900	40	80%
Emory	$ 9,000	30	10%
Atwater	$34,500	80	75%
Elmwood	$36,100	90	85%
Mabry	$22,100	60	75%
Fairmont	$22,700	50	70%
Holly Hill	$24,500	60	80%

Table 3-7 Average Household Income of Applicant,
Location of Property, and Approval Rates for Neighborhoods
in Sun City in 1990

Neighborhood of Property	Mean 1990 Household Income of Applicant	Approval Rate
Windhaven	$23,100	25%
Bayside	$25,800	79%
Emory	$22,800	5%
Atwater	$27,300	90%
Elmwood	$28,800	92%
Mabry	$25,000	74%
Fairmont	$24,500	75%
Holly Hill	$25,500	81%
Mean income of loan applicant	$23,100 per year	
Mean income of approved loan applicant	$24,400 per year	
Range of income of approved loan applicants	$20,700–87,200 per year	

After basic relationships are understood, the effect of a third (control or test) variable can be examined. This third variable might alter the apparent relationship between two variables. Taking a different example, we might discover a relationship between race and quality of housing: For example, black householders live in lower-quality housing. However, when the data are controlled for a third variable such as income, the apparent relationship between race and housing quality may no longer hold. Householders with similar incomes may occupy similar-quality housing no matter what their race. Analysts are usually hoping to find policy-sensitive variables, but they cannot afford to be misled, since a flawed understanding of why a problem exists may lead to a wrong solution.

A variety of statistical tests can be used to answer the question of whether two or more variables are associated or are independent. Which one to use depends on the level of the data with which we are working: *nominal*, for which some characteristic is classified into exhaustive, mutually exclusive but not ordered categories (ethnicity, e.g., with categories defined so they don't overlap); *ordinal*, for which some characteristic is classified into exhaustive, mutually exclusive and ordered categories (e.g., popularity ranking or level of education completed); or *interval*, for which some characteristic is classified on a scale which permits it to be measured exactly (e.g., age), using established units of measurement that can be added or subtracted (e.g., years). A still higher level of measurement, called a *ratio* scale, has all the characteristics of an interval scale plus a nonarbitrary zero point, so that numbers on the scale may logically be compared as ratios. By putting the data in tabular form, we can readily see associations, and basic statistics can be used to summarize the data in the contingency tables. Table 3-8 shows the final exam results for male and female students in a policy analysis class.

Table 3-8 Student Test Performance in a Policy Analysis Class

	FINAL EXAM PERFORMANCE		
Gender of Student	Fail	Pass	Total
Female	34%	66%	100% (205)
Male	54%	46%	100% (130)

Gamma = 0.39

These data suggest that females were more likely to pass the final exam than were males. A correlation coefficient could be computed to measure the strength of this **association** or correlation. Gamma or Yule's Q is a handy measure for this purpose when we are working with ordinal data.[52] Since this is not meant to be a statistics book, we won't explain how to compute gamma, which for the final exam example equals 0.39.[53]

A gamma of 0.39 indicates a moderate positive association between gender of the test taker and passing the final exam. That is, females (arbitrarily classified as "high," according to the convention shown in Figure 3-13) are more likely to have passed the final exam than males. The value of gamma ranges from -1.0 to $+1.0$, with 0.0 indicating no relationship, $+1.0$ indicating a perfect positive relationship (all persons with high scores on one variable have high scores on the other variable and all persons with low scores on one variable have low scores on the other), and -1.0 indicating a perfect negative relationship (all persons high on one variable are low on the other and vice versa).

For the above set of data, a finding that females are more likely to pass the final exam would probably merit further investigation. One explanation for the different pass rates might have to do with attendance at a review session. Thus, the data can be *controlled* for whether the test taker attended the review session prior to the exam. The data are controlled by splitting them into the group of both males and females who attended the review session and the group of both males and females that did not attend. Table 3-9 gives the pass and fail statistics when the data are recomputed in this way.

This step in the analysis indicates that the same percentage of males and females passed the exam within the group of persons attending the review session (75% passed) and within the group that did not attend the review session (33% passed). The results of controlling or testing for a third variable are not always this clear, so the partial correlation coefficient is computed to help interpret the effect of the test variable. Readers who have not had a statistics course should consult a basic statistics text to learn how to compute a partial correlation coefficient.[54] Our purpose is to indicate that insights can be gained from contingency-

[52] James A. Davis, *Elementary Survey Analysis* (Englewood Cliffs, NJ: Prentice Hall, 1971).
[53] Page and Patton, *Quick Answers to Quantitative Problems*, pp. 49–56.
[54] For example, see Davis, *Elementary Survey Analysis*, pp. 81–106.

Table 3-9   Controlling for Whether the Test Taker Attended the Review Session

DID ATTEND REVIEW SESSION				*DID NOT ATTEND REVIEW SESSION*		
	Exam Performance				Exam Performance	
	Fail	Pass			Fail	Pass
Female	40	120		Female	30	15
Male	10	30		Male	60	30
Gamma = 0.0				Gamma = 0.0		

table analysis. Based on the results of controlling the above data for a test variable, the table would be recast to show the importance of attending a review session, rather than the apparent importance of the gender of the test taker. Our new table is shown in Table 3-10.

By displaying the data this way we can see that there was a much higher proportion of successful exam takers among those attending the review session than among those who did not. This appears to be a clear and important finding. Here we have assumed that 335 persons took the exam. But suppose this 335 was but a 10% random sample of the 3,350 who actually took the exam. Other questions now surround our results. Was the sample representative? Or was this for some reason an odd sample? Do these sample results validly represent the larger population?

Measures of Significance

Inferential statistics allow analysts to make probabilistic statements about a population, even though they only have data for a small sample from that population. In the last example above, we assumed that a sample of 335 was drawn from a population of 3,350 students. We would have taken care to use unbiased procedures and to have drawn a representative sample. But despite our efforts, we might have drawn a nonrepresentative sample. This would never be clear unless we followed up by questioning all 3,350 students. The idea behind sampling, of course, is avoiding this costly alternative. Inferential statistics allow us to say how sure we are that the results obtained from our sample resemble those

Table 3-10   Final Exam Performance and Review Session Attendance

	FINAL EXAM PERFORMANCE		
Attendance at Review Session	Fail	Pass	Total
Yes	25%	75%	100% (200)
No	67%	33%	100% (135)
Gamma = 0.72			

we would have gotten had we questioned the whole population. In our example we might be able to say that we were at least 95% sure that the 42 percentage points difference in number of students who passed the exam (33% for nonreviewers and 75% for reviewers) found in the sample did not occur as a result of drawing a nonrepresentative sample, but reflects test-score differences in the population of 3,350 test takers. Such findings would be called statistically significant at the 0.05 level (95% sure).[55] However, the idea that this finding did not occur by chance is different from the idea that the finding is strong or important. Here the judgment of the analyst enters. Was the 42 percentage points difference obtained a noteworthy and significant finding? Note here the two different ways the word *significant* is used.

One last question remains. Did attending the review session cause the students to do better on the exam? In this case the answer appears to be yes. The attending students either were given answers or were given a better understanding of the material. Of course, those in attendance may have been a self-selected group of superior students to begin with; if so, what actually went on at the review may not have caused the better test results. In policy analysis both kinds of findings, mere association as well as causality, can be of interest. Sometimes it is enough to know a relationship exists without knowing what causes it. For example, one of the authors once demonstrated that neighborhoods with certain characteristics were more likely to experience certain types of criminal behavior. This kind of finding—of an association between variables—could be helpful to analysts trying to deploy police officers or determine the location of police facilities. On the other hand, the deeper question of what it was that caused crime to happen in neighborhoods with certain characteristics proved difficult to answer. To develop causal explanations usually requires a solid data base, a solid theory that comports with the findings of statistical association, and successful attempts to rule out rival hypotheses (such as self-selected superior students attending the review session). There are, then, four separate ideas that must be recognized by the analyst: statistical significance, strength of relationship or association, research significance or importance, and causality.

COMMUNICATING THE ANALYSIS

Writing is how most planners and analysts communicate with their clients. The best analysis is irrelevant if it is late, and useless if it is not understandable. What makes a good report? Simplicity. The analysis must be conveyed clearly, concisely, and without jargon. It must also be accurate, well documented, and fair.

---

[55] We could compute significance for gamma, but this requires more knowledge about sampling theory, confidence intervals, and confidence levels than we assume for basic analysis. For instructions on computing the significance of gamma, see Linton D. Freeman, *Elementary Applied Statistics: For Students in Behavioral Science* (New York: Wiley, 1965); and Davis, *Elementary Survey Analysis.* For basic information on calculating statistical significance, see Page and Patton, *Quick Answers to Quantitative Problems,* pp. 51–71.

Simplicity. Don't allow yourself to believe that your analysis is the one exception to the rule of simplicity. Presume there are no exceptions. Most analysts are *not* writing for other analysts but for readers much farther removed from the subject than they are. If you want to convince them to see things the way you do, avoid jargon. Give the information to your client in clear, concise sentences, using no more words than necessary. You may be forced to adopt a bureaucratic style requiring you to write in the passive voice and as if your report were the work of a group of people (the County Board, the Planning Commission, your agency), or in the third person, using expressions such as "this analyst" and "the author." Unless you are forbidden, write in the active voice and use "I" and "you." The active voice ("The mayor rejected our proposal.") is almost always better than the passive voice ("Our proposal was not approved."). Active constructions are usually simpler. They also avoid ambiguity. The statement "Our proposal was not approved" may leave the reader wondering where the proposal failed, unless you are careful to add "by the mayor." The passive voice is occasionally necessary but usually undesirable.

Some phrases combine the vague wordiness of the passive voice with additional vagueness, such as "it has long been known," "it is believed that," and "it might be argued that." Be specific. Avoid using vague modifiers like "very" or "somewhat." Be precise. Much of this book is about how to perform accurate, fair analysis. If, at the end of your research, you cannot be specific and precise, don't cover it up with your writing style. Present the information you have, and identify the questions to which you found no adequate answer.

Accuracy. Verify your facts. Check your calculations. Use several sources of data. Report inconsistencies. Don't go beyond the data. If you engage in speculation, be sure to indicate this. Separate fact from opinion. Accuracy also means being complete. You can't include every detail, but in selecting those to report, do not ignore facts that conflict with your personal position.

Documentation. Be sure your analysis can be replicated. Provide sufficient documentation so that your facts can be checked and the analysis can be redone by a third party to reach the same conclusion. Be critical of your work's shortcomings but not apologetic. Report the assumptions you had to make and the shortcuts you took. Apologies lead clients to believe you don't have faith in your conclusions, thereby destroying theirs.

Fairness. Report all major alternative views and explanations. Present facts that support alternative viewpoints. Don't include information solely to embarrass someone. Always cite the work of others that you used in the analysis. Do not use insulting or deprecating language. It could embarrass you in the future.

Finally, pay attention to mechanics such as spelling, punctuation, usage, capitalization, and the use of numbers. Get a reference book on style and a good dictionary. Keep both on your desk, and use them often. Create your own style sheet if your employer doesn't use one, and list in it the rules you forget most often. Many issues of style can be decided in several ways. The key is to make a choice and stick with it. Word-processing software ordinarily comes with a spell-checking facility that allows the user to catch most errors, and grammar-checking software is also available. But the user must stay alert in order to avoid the substitution of the wrong, but accurately spelled, word.

Getting It on Paper

Even good analysts may put off writing the analysis. You will never have enough data. You will have to draw your conclusions from partial proof. How does one begin?[56] We prefer to work directly on a microcomputer that allows even a poor typist to produce a higher-quality product quickly. But whether one uses a microcomputer or paper and pencil, the same basic rules apply. Work from an outline. Write about your findings as you go along. Fit these pieces into the outline to form a first draft. Fill in holes and gaps later. Some analysts develop a general idea of their writing plan, write up thoughts and findings as they occur, and file these in topic folders (either electronic or paper), to organize later as a draft report. Under either approach, you will find it helpful to work on several sections simultaneously. Keep a positive mindset while writing and avoid negative thinking.[57] Write backward. Rough out the conclusion that you expect to draw; then back up and develop the argument to reach that conclusion. If you are having trouble with one section, jump to another. The final report must be logically ordered, but it can be written in bits and pieces. You will undoubtedly find it necessary to cut and paste your rough draft. Set goals and deadlines for yourself (and rewards if necessary). Never leave your desk or microcomputer after finishing a section. Always begin the next section. This will help you avoid facing a blank sheet of paper or monitor the next time you begin to write. Finish a rough first draft without worrying too much about your writing style or things you've omitted. Revision is easier on a clean, complete draft.

Get help and advice from others. Ask people you trust to review your work. Specify whether you want them to comment on the basic logic and accuracy of what you have written, on the mechanics of your writing, or both. Not everyone is capable of editing your writing to improve its consistency and style, but most people will be able to point out portions of your written analysis that are ambiguous or difficult to understand. They may also alert you to jargon or acronyms that you included inadvertently.

Revise your writing to improve clarity and incorporate new data. Communicating your analysis, as we stressed earlier, is the only way to prevent your work

[56] For additional suggestions see Martin H. Krieger, "The Inner Game of Writing," *Journal of Policy Analysis and Management* 7, no. 2 (Winter 1988), 408–16.

[57] For tips on positive thinking see Edward Lumsdaine and Monika Lumsdaine, *Creative Problem Solving* (New York: McGraw-Hill, 1990), p. 55.

from being wasted. Set aside enough time to write your conclusions and revise them—more than once if possible. Asking for review comments before you revise will give you a fresh perspective and may improve your revision, but revise you must. Reorganize. Refine. Rethink. Never release a product without scrutinizing it. Reexamine your notes, records, and data. Incorporate facts that have become relevant since the last draft.

Write your analysis so your clients can use it *as is* for their own purposes. A paper that has to be rewritten to be distributed probably won't be rewritten. Instead, someone will summarize it, perhaps misinterpreting your conclusions. Will your client want to distribute something to the press? Include a one-page summary that could serve this purpose. Make sure it is written appropriately for public distribution. Good graphics are often borrowed and used again, and whole reports may be reused if they are concise, neat, and understandable.

Using Graphics to Communicate

A picture is worth one thousand words. You know it's true, but does your communication reflect this? There are a wide range of graphic approaches, each appropriate to different uses. Table 3-11 lists some of these.

Sometimes you should plan to use both text and graphics to convey an idea.

Table 3-11   Types of Graphics and Their Uses

GRAPHIC	USE
• Charts and Graphs	
Pie and bar charts, histograms, dot diagrams, scatter diagrams, time-series curves	Illustrating patterns in data, trends, cycles, comparisons, distribution, proportions
Organization chart	Illustrating relationships among individuals and entities
Flow chart/decision tree	Illustrating processes, options, probabilities of different outcomes
• Tables	
Numerical	Ordering and summarizing numerical data to support an argument or hypothesis or serve as a reference
Text (or mixed text, numbers and symbols)	Ordering information to permit easy assimilation or comparison
• Maps	
	Illustrating spatial location and/or distribution of items or characteristics
• Pictures	
Photos	Illustrating or documenting actual conditions, adding interest
Drawings	Illustrating how something works, what a proposal would look like

When you do this, don't confuse the purpose of each. Use prose to explain what the conclusion is and why. Don't write a description of the line you've plotted, how it rises from 1980 to 1990, takes a sharp dip and then rises again more gradually after 1991. The graph conveys this information far better.

Don't overwork a single graphic. Most charts are best when they are simple, usually containing a single idea, such as, "The number of households is increasing more rapidly than the number of people." You may develop a complex idea with a series of graphics or through the use of overlays. The idea of simplicity extends to color, pattern, and layout. Don't use many colors or patterns. Maintain generous margins and other white space around the graphic. When you use a color or pattern, use it consistently. Don't let households be the solid red line in one figure and the dashed blue line in another. Although there are color copiers, avoid making color essential to understanding in a written paper or report graphic, since not everyone has access to this technology. Patterns (a solid line contrasted with a dashed line) photocopy without losing their meaning.

All graphics should be self-contained. Readers should be able to understand them and answer their own questions about the data without having to refer elsewhere—not even to text on an adjacent page. Every graphic should have a complete title, explaining what it shows, labels (including units of measure), keys and explanatory notes as necessary to understand it, and a source note and date. Use no abbreviations unless they are defined on the same page.

Avoid tricks. *How to Lie with Statistics*[58] will tell you how to recognize some of the more common tricks, like not starting the scale of a graph at zero and changing the scale to emphasize the point you wish to make. You are striving to be accurate and don't need to rely on tricks.

You will be able to produce much of the graphic material you need on your own microcomputer. Sometimes you will need to use the graphic skills of others. Many departments and agencies have graphic artists who can turn your sketched layout (with all data, labels, and notes carefully provided) into an appealing and professional graphic, often in less time than it would take you to produce something poorer. If you do have this opportunity, take advantage of it. Remember, however, that the responsibility for the final product is yours. No graphic artist can invent data you haven't provided, and few could come up with a better general approach, since they wouldn't know the objective or the audience as well as you.

Organizing the Report

Give your readers a road map. Let them know what will be in the report. Break it into understandable pieces. Summarize. Include transitions. Make it clear to the reader why you are going from one subject to the next. Use headings, underlining, and section dividers. Don't bury recommendations. Number them

---

[58] Huff, *How to Lie with Statistics*.

and get them on the front page. Highlight the key points and the policy implications.

There is no single way to structure an analytic report. One way is to reflect the process used to produce the analysis. A report organized according to this method would contain the following sections:

1. Summary
2. Problem Definition
3. Evaluation Criteria
4. Alternatives
5. Analysis and Comparison
6. Conclusion
7. Next Steps

Each step may not get equal treatment in the final report, but preparing a draft report that contains these sections can aid your thought process, will help to identify gaps and inconsistencies, and will contribute to a more understandable final report. Be careful to write most about what is most important, not about the steps that took the most time. Just because your report is organized according to the process you followed is no reason to write about false starts or fruitless investigations you undertook.

1. *Summary.* A one-page summary statement should begin the report and should devote one short paragraph to each section of the report. Next, report on each area in more detail.
2. *Problem Definition.* Describe and explain the problem, using statistics, graphics, anecdotes, or other devices. Argue how the audience or client ought to perceive the problem.
3. *Evaluation Criteria.* Clarify "what is good." List and explain the criteria you used. Be sensitive to political constraints.
4. *Alternatives.* Describe the alternatives. Group similar alternatives and discuss the general types and variations.
5. *Analysis and Comparison.* Explain how you evaluated the alternatives using the criteria you have already described. Use basic statistics, decision analysis, mathematical formulas, scenarios, and other techniques you can defend. Test the sensitivity of alternatives to changes in parameters. Summarize and compare the alternatives. Exclude inadequate alternatives, after briefly and defensibly explaining why, and detail other alternatives.
6. *Conclusion.* Present your conclusions and recommendations. Report uncertainties and the effects of accepting your conclusions and following your recommendations.
7. *Next Steps.* Is more research and analysis needed? What specific steps should your client take next if your recommendations are accepted? Include plans for monitoring and evaluation. Offer alternative steps as well, to avoid forcing the client to choose all or nothing.

Another common approach is to put the conclusions first, providing a summary of the rationale that led to them and the results expected. Such an approach is good for a briefing document or short memo. Most clients are interested primarily in conclusions, not how you got them. Documentation of the process is important in case someone challenges your conclusions or in instances when legal requirements (e.g., for public involvement) or the presence of special interest groups will mean the process is subject to special attention. This is more likely with full-scale planning efforts, processes for awarding funds or contracts, and formulation of binding rules, regulations, and ordinances than with most applications of quick analysis.

In-Person Communication

You will often be able to communicate the results of your analysis best in person. Analysts sometimes devote their attention entirely to putting conclusions in writing, neglecting the importance of face-to-face contact in getting the message across. Don't miss an opportunity to present your conclusions in person, with the written report as backup.

Base your oral presentation on the principles for preparing effective written reports and graphics. Be clear and brief. Avoid jargon and language that might offend listeners or insult those holding other views of the issue. Use graphics to enliven your presentation and improve understanding. If you are addressing a group, your graphics will have to be large, so everyone can see them. If you are making a presentation to one person, or a very small, informal group, you may distribute copies of a handout instead.

Don't be threatening to your listeners. Recommend in a friendly way that clearly leaves the decision to them. Trying to frighten or bully people into seeing things the way you do often backfires. Similarly, though a personal appeal is more difficult to put aside than a memo, don't press too hard for an immediate decision. Explain the consequences of delay, if any, and make a clear recommendation of what decisions and actions are needed first. To avoid losing momentum you may want to include in your recommendation some actions you believe will be easy for your client to take.

No technique is more effective than a real desire to communicate, both to be understood and to understand. When you present your results in person, you can expect questions, comments, and criticisms. Make a strong effort to be receptive to these and to respond tolerantly and openly. This may be difficult if the person or group reviewing your work is inattentive, focused on details, or biased against you or your findings. Under these circumstances your responsiveness is even more important. Make your presentation interesting to the listener(s). Address their concerns early, present a summary rather than a full written report, and try to defuse controversy by preparing listeners for your ideas. Answer questions completely if you know the answer. If you don't, commit yourself as to when you will provide it. If your listeners are not as familiar with the issue as you are, their questions may be confused or confusing. If you restate the question politely, in a way that makes sense to you, you may encourage them to clarify what they want to know. If you don't take the trouble to do this, you may antagonize them, making them less inclined to accept your conclusions.

Finally, leave behind copies of your written analysis, or if the group is a large one, a written or graphic summary of the major findings. This has the advantage of allowing the audience to inspect your work at their leisure, and it allows them to use your written and graphic products in implementing your recommendations.

SUMMARY

This chapter presented a number of methods that can be used at various points in the policy analysis process. We discussed ways to identify and gather data, including library search methods and specialized interviewing techniques. Mastery of these methods permits the analyst to obtain relevant data quickly and in a format useful to future analysis. We also presented methods of basic data analysis, placing them in the context of a systematic approach to formulating hypotheses, selecting measures, developing graphic layouts and tables, and presenting information in ways that the client will find useful. We discussed the relationship between statistical analysis and basic methods, illustrated the importance of association and correlation in policy analysis, and distinguished between correlation and statistical significance.

Not only must planners and analysts have a good understanding of these methods, but they must be able to communicate their findings to clients, decision makers, and the public. Thus, we concluded the chapter with a discussion of how to communicate the analysis through graphics, report organization, and in-person communication.

The purpose in presenting these approaches is not to specify methods that must always be followed, but to present basic methods that can be adapted to a variety of means. You should develop a facility with these methods so that you will be able to select among them as needed. Having used them a few times, you will find those that are most useful to your own approach, will discover ways to modify others that make them more useful, and will devise other methods and approaches that fit your needs and your style of policy analysis and planning.

GLOSSARY

Bar Charts figures that compare the differences among mutually exclusive categories of grouped data using bar segments of differing heights. The bars describing the data categories do not touch each other.

Cluster Sampling used when it would be difficult to compile a list of elements in the population. Elements are clustered or grouped together, and then selected clusters are sampled.

Confidence Interval in making an estimate, answers the question of how far from the true value are we willing to be at a stated level of probability. Are we willing to accept a value plus or minus $1,000 of the true mean with 95% confidence, or will we accept only a value plus or minus $5 of the true mean?

Confidence Level often referred to as the significance level, answers the question how likely we are to be wrong in our estimates: 1 out of 100 times, 5 out of 100 times, 10 out of 100?

Correlation Coefficient a numerical value that summarizes the strength of relationship between or among variables.

Cross-Sectional Surveys used to collect data on groups within a single population or on several target populations. The characteristics of these populations can be examined and comparisons can be made among and within them.

Dependent and Independent Variables the independent variable is the one we suspect affects the behavior of the other, or dependent, variable.

Descriptive Statistics techniques to assemble, summarize, and tabulate data so their meaning may be more easily understood.

Disproportionate Sampling used when we wish to ensure that a subpopulation contains enough cases for analysis. In order to assure a minimum number of respondents from a particular stratum, we may take a larger percentage sample from that stratum.

Dot Diagrams figures used when the variables have many categories and the data are grouped more finely than can be effectively illustrated with histograms.

Elite Interviewing (also called *specialized* or *intensive* interviewing) a process through which the analyst collects nonstandardized information from selected, key individuals who have specialized knowledge of an event or process. A related, semistandardized approach has been called *focused* interviewing.

Focused Interviewing see *Elite Interviewing*.

Function an ordered pair of sets for which a rule associates with each element of the first set a unique element of the second set.

Gamma (or Yule's Q) a useful correlation measure when data can be structured in ordinal form. Ranges from − 1.0 to + 1.0, with 0.0 indicating no relationship between the variables, + 1.0 indicating a perfect positive relationship, and − 1.0 indicating a perfect negative relationship.

Grouped Data data that have been converted from directly measured values into categories.

Hawthorne Effect a research phenomenon in which persons being observed change their behavior because they are being studied.

Histograms figures that describe differences among categories of continuous grouped data. The bar segments describing the data categories abut one another.

Independent and Dependent Variables the independent variable is the one we suspect affects the behavior of the other, or dependent, variable.

Inferential Statistics techniques used to make generalizations about a population from sample data.

Intensive Interviewing see *Elite Interviewing*.

Interval Scale Data data classified on a scale that permits them to be measured exactly, using generally accepted units of measurement that can be infinitely divided.

Inverse (Negative) Relationship as values of one variable increase, values of the other variable decrease.

Levels of Significance guidelines that have been adopted for use in statistical analysis to aid decision making. In social science research, the traditional significance level is 0.05. That is, statistically significant results are those that would occur by chance in no more than 5 out of 100 samples.

Longitudinal Surveys used to collect data on one or several subgroups over time, to permit comparisons over time; for example, before and after a policy is implemented.

Measures of Association (such as gamma) tell us whether two or more variables are correlated and the strength of that correlation.

Measures of Significance (such as Chi Square) tell us the probability that an association experienced in a sample occurred by chance.

Nominal Scale Data data classified into exhaustive, mutually exclusive, but not ordered categories.

Ordinal Scale Data data classified into exhaustive, mutually exclusive, and ordered or ranked categories.

Pie Charts circular figures that illustrate proportions or shares of the whole.

Population a word used in statistics to describe a collection of things (e.g., households, cars, people, dogs) that are to be sampled.

Positive Relationship as values of one variable increase, the values of the other variable increase.

Random Sample a scientific, unbiased sampling procedure that assures that all units or elements in the population under study have an equal chance of being selected.

Randomness and Representativeness all members of the group being surveyed must have a known chance of being selected in the sample.

Ratio Scale Data data classified on a scale that permits them to be measured exactly using generally accepted units of measurement, and that includes a nonarbitrary zero point.

Representativeness see *Randomness*.

Scales of Measurement there are four scales of measurement for quantitative data: nominal, ordinal, interval, and ratio.

Scatter Diagrams or Scatterplots graphic representation of two variables: One is measured on the *y* (vertical) axis and the second variable is measured on the *x* (horizontal) axis. Scatterplots, an extension of the concept of dot diagrams, are also called scattergrams or scatter diagrams.

Simple Random Sampling involves selecting elements, members, or units from a group or population at random. Usually a random number table is used to select a given number or percentage of elements from a previously numbered list.

Specialized Interviewing see *Elite Interviewing*.

Statistical Sampling the process by which a portion of the whole (population or universe) is selected for examination with the intent to generalize or infer from that sample to the entire population.

Statistical Significance a measure of how likely it is that relationships or associations found in sample data describe characteristics in the population from which the sample was taken.

Stratified Sampling a sampling technique that helps assure we obtain an adequate sample size for important subpopulations by breaking the population into homogeneous subpopulations that are then sampled.

Systematic Sampling a method for selecting elements from a list to produce a random sample.

Time-Series Diagrams diagrams that show change over time for a variable.

Weighting a procedure for applying a factor or weight to the results of a sample to adjust for a disproportionate sample, to correct for a misestimate of the size of a cluster or strata, to adjust for different response rates, or to make population estimates.

EXERCISES

1. Within a four-hour period, compile a reference list (bibliography and contact persons) of key data sources for your metropolitan area. Include sources for data about at least the following:

   (*a*) Population statistics

   (*b*) Housing vacancies

   (*c*) School enrollment by level

   (*d*) Income levels

   (*e*) Unemployment rates

   (*f*) Juvenile delinquency rates

   (*g*) Transportation services

   (*h*) Bus ridership

   (*i*) Journey-to-work patterns

   (*j*) Teen-age auto accident rates

   (*k*) Driving-while-intoxicated rates

   (*l*) Tax rates

2.   All 50 states and the District of Columbia have now adopted 21 as the legal age at which one may drink alcoholic beverages. States that had a drinking age below 21 increased the legal age to 21 in order to continue to receive federal highway financial assistance. Find out when your state raised its legal drinking age to 21. Did increasing the legal age have an impact on decreasing road deaths?

3.   Obtain the figure for average household income for the city in which you live from at least four sources (such as the U.S. Census, the United Way, the Mayor's Office). Do they differ? If so, why? Address such issues as how they were collected, when, by whom, and for what purpose.

4.   Many cities face the problem of deteriorating conditions in neighborhoods surrounding the central business district (CBD). Much discussion about these problems is based on hearsay, partial data, and outdated or incomplete information. The data about such neighborhoods are often available, but not always in one place. Within one week, compile a set of data that describes the physical, social, and economic conditions and change in at least two central-city neighborhoods and relate this to the city as a whole. Work from original and secondary data sources including Census data. Include both a library search and data searches of local government agencies and bureaus. Limit the number of items or variables about which you collect data, but collect the data you do from as many sources as possible. Evaluate the quality of the data you collect. Report the range of values for each variable measured.

5.   Graphically illustrate the data you obtained for Exercise 4. Use at least the six graphic techniques (pie chart, bar chart, histogram, etc.) described in this chapter. Be sure to properly label the graphics, to cite your sources, and to give each graphic a title. Briefly summarize the conclusions you draw from these graphics.

6.   Construct a table or tables that describe the primary finding from your analysis of the data in Exercise 4. As with the construction of your graphics, label the table(s), cite your sources, and title the table(s).

7.   Contrast *mass* and *elite* interviewing methods. When would one method be preferred to the other? Give examples of possible uses for both.

8.   You have been assigned the task of investigating drug abuse for your town. You know little about the topic and decide to begin with a set of interviews of knowledgeable people. Who would be in your first round of interviews? Who would be in the second round? Whom would you leave until last? Why?

9.   Visit the dorm room of a friend, the office of a faculty member, or the living room of an acquaintance. Observe the room. Write an analysis of the person based on the objects in the room.

10.   Interview an expert to verify, correct, or modify the conclusions you drew from your graphic analysis for Exercise 4. Prepare a four-page double-spaced memo that reports your findings.

11.   Identify a legal issue arising from your analyses of the data describing the case neighborhoods in Exercises 4 and 6. This might be an issue such as zoning, parking regulations, litter abatement, noise control, or taxation. Discuss the nature of the issue with your instructor to assure that it is a legal issue; then conduct a legal search to clarify the issue and to identify applicable laws. Write a brief analysis of how the current law addresses or fails to address the problem you have identified and how the law might be modified.

12.   Distinguish between descriptive and inferential statistics. What is the importance of this difference for the practicing policy analyst?

13.   Distinguish between association and statistical significance. Under what circumstances would you use one as opposed to the other?

14. The mayor for whom you work is ready to recommend a special tax referendum to support lakefront development. The decision is based on a set of tabular data that appeared in a consultant's report showing widespread citizen support for lakefront development. The data indicated a correlation of 0.65 between support for lakefront development and a willingness to publicly fund the development. You reanalyzed the data, controlling for whether respondents reported voting in the last referendum, and found that the correlation among voters was 0.081. What advice would you give the mayor?

15. The issue of attracting industry to Seaside is heating up again. As in the past, the issue seems to pit young against old. The local press has published reports from older residents who want to keep their village a quiet, peaceful place, as it has always been. These reports have been juxtaposed with statements from younger residents who support attracting industry in the hope that property-tax increases can be forestalled. A commentator in the regional newspaper has implied that the issue is not between young and old but a result of attitudes held by newcomers to Seaside. A survey of resident attitudes is provided below. What insights do these data provide on the issue of support for attracting industry to Seaside?

All Adult Residents of Seaside

	FAVOR ATTRACTING INDUSTRY	
Age	No	Yes
50 +	30	130
< 50	110	40
Total	140	170

Adults Who Moved to Seaside Since 1985

	FAVOR ATTRACTING INDUSTRY	
Age	No	Yes
50 +	10	80
< 50	60	20
Total	70	100

Adults Who Moved to Seaside During or Before 1985 or Who Were Born There

	FAVOR ATTRACTING INDUSTRY	
Age	No	Yes
50 +	20	50
< 50	50	20
Total	70	70

16.   The following data present the test results for seven American Institute of Certified Planner (AICP) examinations. The major variables are length of professional experience, graduation from accredited versus nonaccredited planning programs, and level (master's or bachelor's) of postsecondary education. On the surface, the data suggest that a graduate degree is an advantage to the test taker. But some observers argue that graduating from an accredited planning program and years of experience are more important. Use the data to develop tables that display the test results and use them to help you discuss the relationship between passing the test and the key variables. Begin by examining the relationship between test success and level of education. Next control the data for school accreditation to see whether the relationship between test success and level of education is affected. Next control for length of experience. Finally control for both level of education and length of experience. How would you respond to people who argue that graduation from an accredited planning program and length of experience help one pass the AICP exam?

AICP Exam Results

Degree/School	Years of Experience	Number of Candidates	Percentage Passing
Graduate (planning)			
Accredited	0–5	957	66
	6+	220	70
		1,177	67
Not accredited	0–5	76	63
	6+	60	53
		136	59
Bachelor's (planning)			
Accredited	0–5	57	49
	6+	31	65
		88	55
Not accredited	0–5	29	41
	6+	6	67
		35	46

Chapter Four

Verifying, Defining, and Detailing the Problem

In Chapter 2 we explained that problem definition, including verification that a problem does indeed exist and redefinition of vaguely stated problems, is a key step in the policy analysis process. We also pointed out that as we discover new information or as assumptions change, we may have to redefine the problem. In this chapter we present basic methods the analyst can use to help define the problem: back-of-the-envelope calculations to estimate the size of the problem; quick decision analysis to identify key components or attributes of the problem; creative operational definitions to help reduce conceptual ambiguity; political analysis so that we do not ignore nonquantitative factors; and the issue-paper concept to help us decide whether further study is justified. Although these methods may be used at other stages in the policy analysis process, they are most appropriate to the quick basic analyses that must be done when we first face a problem.

During the problem-definition stage, the analyst attempts to frame the problem in concrete terms and to develop a statement that gives the client a firm understanding of the problem's technical and political dimensions. Since problems are related to values held by individuals and groups, problem definition will include normative statements of what is considered good or acceptable to various groups. We usually attempt to describe the problem with numbers, but we may also use anecdotes or scenarios to convey the message.

IDENTIFYING AND DEFINING PROBLEMS

Beginning analysts have most of their problems assigned to them. The client, supervisor, or policymaker usually imposes at least the preliminary definition of the problem. As the analyst matures, the client–analyst role becomes more symmetrical, and analysts participate more fully in identifying problems by scanning the environment and collecting information on emerging strategic issues.[1]

> ... client and analyst are a bureaucratic pair, linked to each other in responding to external demands. Both are presented with similar cues for an analytical response. It is not so much that the client tells the analyst which problem to select, or that the analyst usurps the client's prerogative, but rather that they both face similar constraints.[2]

We can approach problem definition in a number of ways. We can accept the problem as given by our client, we can take a pragmatic approach and identify those aspects of the problem that can be affected, or we can attempt to define problems by their effects on individuals and society.

The *pragmatic approach* is consistent with the perspective that a policy analysis can be conducted only when there is disagreement about how an issue or problem is being handled, and when there are alternative ways to deal with the problem. If you cannot do something about a problem, if things cannot be changed, then a person adopting this approach would maintain there is no need to do a policy analysis.[3] Using this approach, those alternative actions that can be implemented immediately are analyzed to determine the least costly way to reduce the disagreement in fiscal and in political terms.

In the *social-criterion approach* to problem definition, the analyst seeks out expressions of discontent and tries to define societal problems that should be solved. Identifying problems in this way may be more difficult because of the conflict between individual problems and societal problems, between widespread problems and serious problems, and between absolute and relative problems.[4]

Serious individual problems may not be societal problems. An individual or group may perceive an issue to be a problem; for example, lack of knowledge about a rare disease. Although the problem may be real to them, when those affected are a small proportion of the population, their problem may not be

---

[1]Ann M. Pflaum and Timothy J. Delmont, "External Scanning—A Tool for Planners," in *Strategic Planning: Threats and Opportunities for Planners,* ed. John M. Bryson and Robert C. Einsweiler (Chicago: Planners Press, 1988), pp. 145–59; and Peter Smith Ring, "Strategic Issues: What Are They and from Where Do They Come?" in *Strategic Planning: Threats and Opportunities for Planners,* ed. John M. Bryson and Robert C. Einsweiler (Chicago: Planners Press, 1988), pp. 69–83.

[2]Arnold J. Meltsner, *Policy Analysts in the Bureaucracy* (Berkeley and Los Angeles: University of California Press, 1976), p. 83.

[3]Irving Kristol, "Where Have All the Answers Gone?" in *Policy Studies Review Annual,* Vol. 4, ed. Bertram H. Raven (Beverly Hills: Sage, 1980), p. 126.

[4]Edward C. Banfield, *The Unheavenly City Revisited* (Boston: Little, Brown, 1974), pp. 1–24.

widespread enough to be considered a societal problem. In its early history, for example, AIDS was seen by most people as a serious individual problem. Only as it affected more and more people in society, including infants, children, celebrities, and sports figures, did it become perceived by most people as a societal problem.

Widespread problems may not be serious problems. Although a majority of the population may be affected by a problem—a typical example being ostensibly excessive commuting time to work—the problem may not be that serious. The solution—cutting commuting time in half—may be more costly than the problem.

Escalating standards can create relative problems that are interpreted as absolute problems. For example, when the poverty level is defined as one-half of the median income, roughly one-quarter of the population will always be in poverty. However, in absolute terms (meaning, say, the ability to obtain clothing, food, and shelter), only a portion of this quarter of the population may be in poverty. Banfield has pointed out the ironic situation in which performance is actually increasing, but standards are increasing even more rapidly, with the result that improvement looks like decline.[5]

The conflicts between individual and societal problems, between widespread and serious problems, and between absolute and relative problems make clear the importance of values in problem definition. Values are general beliefs about the relative worth of items or behaviors. It is difficult to measure values, but identifying a problem implies that certain values are not being satisfied. Problems can be verified, defined, and detailed only in relation to the values of the groups and individuals involved. The analyst must understand the values that underlie the problem definition and where they came from. Later, when the analyst devises criteria for evaluating possible options, these will also be based on the original values, usually of the affected and attentive parties.

It is easier (but still difficult) to describe general goals and measurable objectives than to list and describe values. But efforts to clarify goals and to identify objectives are often stymied because of the collective-goods dilemma described below and because ambiguous goals can benefit some parties. Consider the collective-goods dilemma from economics. Individuals and groups may be willing to take large immediate gains in exchange for losses later when they may or may not be around to pay. If they are not around, the public absorbs the future losses. This makes determining the public interest difficult, since the sum of individual preferences does not necessarily reveal what would be best, in the long run, for society.

In the classic example of the dilemma of the collective good, farmers let their cattle overgraze on the commons to gain immediate benefit, with society bearing the future cost.[6] This may be seen in other forms today; for example,

---

[5] Ibid., pp. 21–22.

[6] Garrett Hardin, "The Tragedy of the Commons," *Science* 162 (December 13, 1968), 1243–48.

the drawing down of aquifers to support development in semiarid areas, or the use of farming practices that lead to erosion. Thus, apparent solutions may be disastrous if the full dimension of the problem is not considered in the definition. Yet some clients and policymakers may prefer the narrow definition, ignoring constituencies such as future generations.

What can the policy analyst do? One can argue that all the important effects of the policy should be known in order to make a good decision. Advise your client that defining a problem so that it can be resolved is counterproductive if the unintended consequences are worse than the original condition. The press and consumer groups uncover irresponsible public and private decisions every day: the marketing of unsafe products, pollution, unfair hiring practices, and so on. These discoveries cost the perpetrators dearly in suits, damaged reputations, fines, and loss of goodwill. Policy analysis should reveal the consequences of the proposed action—intended and unintended—for everyone's benefit.

Consider also the potential value of vague goals. Inconsistent or ambiguous goals allow policymakers to support conflicting policies; for example, subsidies to tobacco farmers and funding for antismoking campaigns. Although budgets may provide implicit rankings by showing the different levels of funding for the two programs, it is important to realize that most policymakers have more than one constituency to satisfy. "Sometimes even very basic goals are not ranked because policy makers want everything and do not want to choose between policies."[7] Understanding this does not mean you can prevent it, but you can be better prepared to cope with the problem.

We have made the point that problems must be verified, defined, and reformulated. In doing so we may have implied that a problem exists, if only we can find it, and that we can do better, if we try harder. This tendency to search for a solution in the form of a new policy is to be expected. Analysts look for solutions. That's what we're paid to do. However, while defining problems, we must also recognize that "doing nothing" is also a possible policy. The do-nothing option comes in a variety of styles. We can alter perceptions by changing the standards we use to define the problem—for example, by changing the definition of poverty to include only households in the lowest 10% income category. We can wait until the public agenda changes or wait until a new problem emerges. We can decide to take no action or continue the status quo through maintenance. For example, we might decide to maintain the roads at their current quality level. We can also address the symptoms of a problem rather than the problem itself— for example, providing only temporary shelter to those unable to find work because of structural changes in the labor force. One or more of these options may not appeal to us, because they are not consistent with our values, but the status-quo, no-action, minor-treatment option may in some cases be a valid solution. It might be the best that can be done with the resources available, it might

---

[7]George C. Edwards and Ira Sharkansky, *The Policy Predicament: Making and Implementing Public Policy* (San Francisco: W. H. Freeman, 1978), p. 112.

be the most efficient (it may be the only solution whose cost does not exceed expected benefits), or it might be the only politically acceptable solution. Thinking about the consequences of taking no action may help you determine whether a problem exists, and to define it if one does.

Practitioners and academics frequently cite problem definition as the most difficult or crucial step in policy analysis.[8] Although Bardach has argued that finding the solution is more difficult,[9] others point out that we often come up with solutions to misspecified or nonproblems, generate the right answers to the wrong problem, or solve the right problem too late.[10] Clearly, choosing the right problem definition is a critical step in the policy analysis process, and one that has crucial implications for the political efficacy of the analyst and the client as well as for the policy.[11]

Problem statements set the analytic agenda, but they may also be adopted by the media, by politicians, by community groups, by task forces, and by other constituent groups. A convincing problem statement can focus resources of many groups on an important problem.

DEVELOPING THE PROBLEM STATEMENT

General steps in the problem-definition process were described in Chapter 2. We advised that the analyst verify the initial problem statement, use the best available data to cut the problem down to size, define the problem from the perspectives of interested parties, identify potential winners and losers, and conduct a first approximation of the analysis. The task of the analyst is to move from a general problem concept to specific measures of that problem, so that alternatives can be devised and evaluated.

This stage of the policy analysis process involves a number of steps. As in the overall process, these steps are not always taken in the same order, and the process is iterative. Part way through one may discover information that will call for a modification of an earlier step in the process. We will illustrate the general problem-definition process here with an example, and then later in the chapter will use a second example to describe how concepts are expressed in measurable terms.

---

[8] William N. Dunn, *Public Policy Analysis: An Introduction* (Englewood Cliffs, NJ: Prentice Hall, 1981), pp. 97–139; and Meltsner, *Policy Analysts in the Bureaucracy*, pp. 81–154.

[9] Eugene Bardach, "Problems of Problem Definition in Policy Analysis," in *Research in Public Policy Analysis and Management*, Vol. 1, ed. John P. Crecine (Greenwich, CT: JAI Press, 1981), pp. 161–71.

[10] See, for example, Carl V. Patton, "Jobs and Commercial Office Development: Do New Offices Generate New Jobs?" *Economic Development Quarterly* 2, no. 4 (November 1988), 316–25; Howard Raiffa, *Decision Analysis: Introductory Lectures on Choices under Uncertainty* (Reading, MA: Addison-Wesley, 1968), pp. 264–65; and Harold Wolman, "Local Economic Development Policy: What Explains the Divergence between Policy Analysis and Political Behavior?" *Journal of Urban Affairs* 10, no. 1 (1988), 19–28.

[11] Meltsner, *Policy Analysts in the Bureaucracy*, p. 81.

First let us examine the general process of defining a problem. Consider the situation where a client is concerned because it appears that "the poor pay more for health care." How would we define this potential problem? We suggest the following steps:[12]

1. Think about the problem.
2. Delineate the boundaries of the problem.
3. Develop a fact base.
4. List goals and objectives.
5. Identify the policy envelope.
6. Display potential costs and benefits.
7. Review the problem statement.

1. Think about the Problem. Bardach has demonstrated that we usually know more about a problem than we realize.[13] We need to structure our thoughts to assemble what we know and to catalog available data. The result of this first step should be as precise and complete a statement of the empirical situation as means permit. Since a problem implies that something is not as it should be, the values underlying the problem definition must be made explicit. How the values of the client, the analyst, the affected publics, and other groups shaped the problem should be made clear. Whether the values are explicitly stated or implied will depend on the problem, the analyst, and the client.

In the "poor pay more for health care" example, the client's implied value is that the poor should pay no more than other groups for health care, and perhaps less, depending upon how "more" is defined. Quickly collect empirical data to determine how much households in a range of income categories pay for selected types of health care. From this determine (on a per-capita or perhousehold basis) whether the annual amount paid for health care (in absolute dollars and as a percentage of income) varies among income groups.

2. Delineate the Boundaries of the Problem. Specify the problem's location, the length of time it has existed, and historical events that have shaped the problem. We must be aware of the connection of the problem under analysis to other problems. As these other problems are resolved or as they worsen, our analysis can be affected.

In the health-care example, is the apparent problem restricted to the metropolitan area or is it a statewide or nationwide phenomenon? Is it a recent or long-standing problem? The problem may have arisen only recently because of

---

[12] See also Peter B. Checkland, "Formulating Problems for Systems Analysis," in *Handbook of Systems Analysis: Overview of Uses, Procedures, Applications, and Practice*, ed. Hugh J. Miser and Edward S. Quade (New York: North Holland, 1985), pp. 151–70; and Edward Lumsdaine and Monika Lumsdaine, *Creative Problem Solving* (New York: McGraw-Hill, 1990), pp. 79–100.

[13] Eugene Bardach, "Gathering Data for Policy Research," *Journal of Urban Analysis* 2, no. 1 (April 1974), 117–44.

an increase in the unemployment rate, leaving many without income and health-insurance coverage and reducing expenditures on health care.

3. Develop a Fact Base. Problem definition requires some basic information. Back-of-the-envelope calculations can help to generate information about the problem. Consult multiple sources of data and use several estimating techniques. Verify data and compare them with other established facts and benchmarks. The facts to collect can be derived from the problem statement.

In the "poor pay more" example, facts that should become part of our analytic base would include information about the key words and phrases: *poor, pay more,* and *health care.* At a minimum, *poor* suggests the need for data about the measurement of poverty, numbers of families, individuals, and households in various income categories. *Pay more* suggests the need to know how health care is defined and paid for and how much is paid by various income groups, including cash payments and direct versus third-party payments. It might even suggest the need for facts about differences in life span as a measure of *paying more. Health care* implies facts about expenditures on drugs, doctor's care, dental care, reactive versus preventive expenditures, inpatient versus outpatient care, and so on. With such a long list, the analyst could quickly become buried in data. Methods presented later can help with this pitfall. Developing these facts may generate insights about values and problem boundaries.

4. List Goals and Objectives. Acceptability of possible solutions will depend on the goals and objectives of the respective actors. Some goals and objectives may have to be stated tentatively and revised as the analysis progresses. Others will have to be deduced. Nonetheless, a general goals statement and list of objectives must be prepared, or we run the risk that the problem will be ill-defined. The objectives must be stated so they can be measured, and the measures for each objective must be specified. In the current example, the goal may be to maintain the health of society. Objectives may be to improve access (enable people to purchase health care), to improve health care quality, to reduce the cost of health care, or to reduce the financial impact on lower-income groups of purchasing health care. Measures might include increases in visits for preventive care, a reduction in wages lost because of illness, a reduction in annual household expenditures on drugs and hospitalization, or a reduction in low-income household expenditures on health care and health insurance.

5. Identify the Policy Envelope. The policy envelope, the range of variables considered in a problem, will affect the alternatives eventually examined. Sometimes the policy envelope is prescribed by the client, sometimes it is determined by the setting in which the analyst is working, and other times it is defined by time and resources available. The analyst will also receive important clues about the size of the policy envelope from the community, attentive groups, and other actors. The analyst must locate the leverage points where policy can be affected, as well as the relevant decision makers. If these policy-sensitive variables are not included in the envelope, the superior policy may not be identified, and if identified, may not be implementable.

In the health-care case, variables to be considered might include patient or household payments, but they may also include third-party payments. Will both inpatient and outpatient services be covered? Will hospital management efficiency be considered? The practices of consumers, insurers, and physicians could be included in the envelope. Other possible actors could include the state insurance board, the American Medical Association, and the media.

6. Display Potential Costs and Benefits. Report in narrative, chart, or tabular form the potential costs and benefits of the problem to the actors and interested parties. Indicate what each actor will gain or lose if the problem is resolved. Here the attention is not on the impact of alternative solutions, but on the range of views about what the problem is and what a theoretical solution would be. The analyst should restate assumptions and analytic limitations at this point so that unintentional biases may be discovered by independent reviewers.

In the current example, the poor may benefit by receiving better health care, by improvement in health, or by financial savings. Physicians and hospitals may benefit by receiving quicker payment for health care, but they may also experience increased case loads. The nonpoor should also be considered. Their access to health care may be reduced if persons not now using the health-care system are encouraged to use it.

7. Review the Problem Statement. Has the problem been stated in a way that will allow for action? Have enough insights been developed to give clues about possible alternatives? Challenge the assumptions you have made.

We assumed that the cost of health care affects its use, and thus the solutions have focused on ways to reduce that burden. But perhaps the benefit of health care is not perceived by various groups. The problem definition might therefore involve an educational component.

Basic methods that are used during problem definition include *back-of-the-envelope calculations* to estimate the size of the problem, *quick decision analysis* to identify key attributes of the problem, *creation of valid operational definitions* to assure that we are measuring what we think we are, *political analysis* so we do not overlook nonquantifiable factors, and the *issue paper* or *first-cut analysis* that identifies the analyses that are needed.

BACK-OF-THE-ENVELOPE CALCULATIONS

When Richard Zeckhauser began his first day as an analyst in the Defense Department, his boss, Alain Enthoven, spoke with him about his highly quantitative college thesis. Zeckhauser recalls the following conversation:

That was good fun. Let's talk about your work here in the Defense Department.
Do you know how to add, subtract, multiply, and divide?
Yes.
Do you understand what marginal analysis is?
Yes.
Good, that and common sense is what you will need.[14]

There is little doubt that the quality of public debate on most issues would be raised considerably by the use of a few simple statistics. As part of the first step in defining problems, "sit and think," simple back-of-the-envelope calculations should be performed. These will help to place boundaries around the problem and indicate both the sign (direction) and magnitude of the problem.

Quantitative information will be part of some problem descriptions. For others, numbers will have to be derived. Mosteller has suggested the following four basic methods for determining unknown numbers:

1. Look up the number in a *reference source.*
2. Collect the number through a *systematic survey* or other investigation.
3. *Guess* the number.
4. Get *experts* to help you guess the number.[15]

Mosteller offers a number of practical examples. Following is a capsule review of his major points, along with our own, about each of the four methods:

Using Reference Sources

1. Check the details of how the numbers were derived. Various sources may use different operational definitions. (See the section on operational definitions in this chapter).
2. Use multiple sources.
3. Avoid, if you can, sources that don't offer operational definitions.

Using Surveys

1. There is often not enough time to develop a new formal survey.
2. However, there are a number of national as well as local surveys done on a regular basis by well-known organizations (e.g., research centers and metropolitan newspapers) that might contain the needed data.

[14] Robert D. Behn and James W. Vaupel, *Quick Analysis for Busy Decision Makers* (New York: Basic Books, 1982), p. 7.

[15] Frederick Mosteller, "Assessing Unknown Numbers: Order of Magnitude Estimation," in *Statistics and Public Policy*, ed. William B. Fairley and Frederick Mosteller (Reading, MA: Addison-Wesley, 1977), pp. 163–64.

Guessing

1. Rates that do not vary much from place to place can sometimes be used to guess an absolute number when used with a base population (e.g., death rates times a population to guess the number of deaths).
2. In some disciplines there are established rules of thumb. These can often be used. However, occasional reexamination of such rules is advisable.
3. One known variable can be used to guess another if a relationship between the two is also known. These relationships are often linear, but not always. Population growth as a function of time and previous growth rates is an example.
4. Boundaries can and should be placed on guesstimates. For example, the maximum number of children now using diapers in the United States cannot be larger than the current U.S. population between the ages of birth to four years.
5. Similar rates borrowed from a phenomenon close to the one under observation may be appropriate.
6. The phenomenon under investigation can be broken down so that separate, different rates can be applied to the subpopulations. Death rates again provide a good example, since they are available for age groupings.
7. Employ triangulation; estimate the unknown quantity using several completely separate approaches and data sources, and compare the results for reasonableness.
8. Estimate totals by summing several components, but be careful to use reasonable ranges for the value of each component because error compounds easily with this method.

Using Experts

1. Consult experts, but be sure they are indeed experts on the particular topic. Most will be honest in evaluating themselves.
2. Beyond the usual means (see "Interviewing" in Chapter 3), there are methods for pooling estimates by experts and perhaps lowering the probable error of the estimate (see "Brainstorming" in Chapter 6).

Once base data have been found, develop back-of-the-envelope calculations using ordinary mathematical operations—usually adding, subtracting, dividing, or multiplying and perhaps, on rare occasions, raising to a power or converting to a logarithm.

Back-of-the-envelope calculations can help answer basic policy questions such as the following:

1. How many persons or households are affected by this problem?
2. How much does a service cost per unit delivered?
3. At the current rate how long will it take before the resource is expended?
4. How many clients can be served with a given budget?
5. Will staff increases be required by a new regulation?
6. What is the likely magnitude of the impact of a project on the city's budget?
7. How many additional households in the state would fall below the poverty line if the income measure were increased $1,000?
8. How many calls per night should a new crisis-intervention hotline expect?

9. By the year 2010, given existing trends, how many persons will be eligible for a given program?

The back-of-the-envelope calculation method amounts to establishing some of the key dimensions of the problem and checking numerical estimates against known reference points. This can best be explained through examples.

In the early 1970s Singer performed checks on the estimate that New York City heroin addicts stole $2 to $5 billion of private property per year. He did this in a number of simple ways, checking the consistency of the results, and found that the total was probably about one-tenth of the widely accepted estimate. However, the "mythical number" had gained credibility over time and was being used by numerous groups and individuals working on the heroin problem. Singer's simple methods included:

1. Checking the logic of the original estimating technique (number of estimated addicts times required cash per day)
2. Checking the likelihood of there being the estimated number of addicts used in item 1
3. Checking the definition of "addicts" in item 1
4. Verifying whether all defined as "addicts" would require the cash per day originally estimated
5. Checking whether addicts might have other sources of cash
6. Checking what proportion of all stolen property the $2 to $5 billion represented
7. Analyzing all types of stealing versus types of addict stealing
8. Checking the demographics of the addict population against known New York City demographics to see if the size of the estimated addict population was possible or probable.[16]

Thirteen years after Singer examined the heroin addict estimate, Reuter revisited the problem and found that again the estimates of the number of addicts and the number of crimes committed were questionably high. He attributed this to both estimating techniques that are sufficiently complex so that it takes a great deal of effort to uncover their shortcomings, and a strong interest in keeping the number high but none in keeping it accurate. He believes that mythical numbers are routinely produced by government agencies as a result of demands that government officials know more than they actually do.[17]

Both Singer and Reuter make the point that commonly accepted baseline data should be checked by analysts before they begin to work on a problem. For example, the number of compulsive gamblers cited in several official documents in the late 1960s and early 1970s was found by Reuter to have been based on a late-night phone call to a Gamblers Anonymous hotline by a government official

---

[16] Max Singer, "The Vitality of Mythical Numbers," *The Public Interest* 23 (Spring 1971), 3–9.

[17] Peter Reuter, "The (Continued) Vitality of Mythical Numbers," *The Public Interest* 75 (Spring 1984), 136.

who needed a number to plug into a table.[18] Many accepted standards are simply wrong, and it takes only a few hours to verify standards and avoid an erroneous analysis.

Another classic example of the use of back-of-the-envelope calculations is provided by Downs in his analysis of the cost to urban households of highway and renewal projects.[19] His goal was to estimate uncompensated costs imposed by these two federal programs and then to suggest policies that would compensate deserving households. To do this he first developed a list of 22 different types of losses covering such items as losses due to the taking of real property, seeking alternative housing, moving costs, increased costs of traveling to work, and losses in property value due to adverse effects of completed projects. He then developed seven tests to decide whether a specific loss should be compensated. Finally, for those losses that should be compensated, he estimated the size of the population affected and the magnitude of the loss. He concluded:

> . . . *present practices in urban areas regarding residential households displaced by highways and urban renewal projects will unfairly impose uncompensated costs of at least $156.5 to $230.2 million per year (in 1968 dollars) upon approximately 237,200 displaced persons and at least another 237,200 non-displaced persons.* In my opinion, this represents injustice on a massive scale. It amounts to an uncompensated loss averaging from $812 to $1,194 per household for each of the estimated 192,800 households involved. The median income of these households is probably around $4,000 per year. Therefore, *the average uncompensated loss which each is compelled to suffer amounts to confiscation of from 20 to 30 percent of one year's income.*[20]

The Singer, Reuter, and Downs articles provide examples of the insights we gain from using common sense, care with operational definitions, employment of readily available numerical data, and simple mathematical operations. The most sophisticated analysis provides little insight if our baseline data and standards are inaccurate.

QUICK DECISION ANALYSIS

Behn and Vaupel have classified policy analysis into "researched analysis" and "quick analysis."[21] We have made similar distinctions, as discussed in Chapter 1. Behn and Vaupel have also discussed the tools of "quick decision analysis," which we refer to here.[22] Since they devote an entire book to the development of this particular analytical skill, it is obvious that we cannot cover the technique in the

---

[18] Ibid., p. 145.

[19] Anthony Downs, *Urban Problems and Prospects* (Chicago: Markham, 1970), pp. 192–227.

[20] Ibid., p. 223.

[21] Robert D. Behn and James W. Vaupel, "Quick Analysis," *Policy Studies Journal* (Spring 1978), 328.

[22] Behn and Vaupel, *Quick Analysis for Busy Decision Makers.*

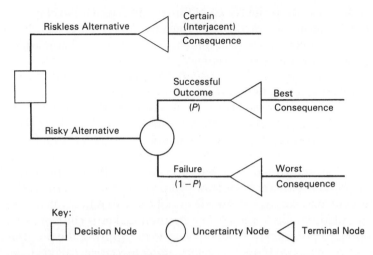

Figure 4-1   The Basic Decision Sapling

Source: From *Quick Analysis for Busy Decision Makers* by Robert D. Behn and James W. Vaupel. © 1982 by Basic Books, Inc., Publishers, p. 41. Reprinted by permission of the publisher.

same depth. After you have learned the essence of performing quick decision analysis, you can expand your skills by working through the Behn and Vaupel text from which the following definition of quick decision analysis is taken:

> Quick analysis uses decision "saplings" (simple decision trees with only a few branches to capture the essence of the decision dilemma), subjective probabilities and preferences. For example, the decision sapling [shown in Figure 4-1] . . . describes the most basic decision dilemma involving uncertainty. There are only two alternatives, one of which is substantially more risky than the other, and there are only two possible outcomes for the risky alternative. The dilemma is whether to gamble on winning the best consequence by choosing the risky alternative, or to avoid the chance of getting the worst consequence by selecting the certain consequence of the riskless alternative. Not only can this decision sapling help resolve a wide variety of decision problems, but it is an essential component of the decision trees for all other dilemmas that involve uncertainty.[23]

Reading Figure 4-1 from left to right, the decision maker must decide between the risky and riskless alternatives. The riskless alternative has a known, middle-of-the-road consequence. The risky alternative has two possible outcomes, one better than and one worse than the riskless alternative outcome. The decision maker must estimate the probabilities of the best outcome and the worst outcome (1 − the probability of the best outcome) to decide whether to pursue the risky or riskless alternative. This thought process and the sketching of decision trees can be very useful in basic policy analysis.

An example of the usefulness of quick decision analysis is provided by a

[23] Behn and Vaupel, "Quick Analysis," p. 328.

proposed policy to abate property taxes for certain types of development in the declining central business district of a large city. (See Figure 4-2.) People who try to solve this problem are struck initially by the need to know which of the following possible outcomes will occur:

- Outcome 1: Do nothing but get development anyway.
- Outcome 2: Do nothing and get no development.
- Outcome 3: Abate taxes and get development.
- Outcome 4: Abate taxes but get no development.

The problem shown here is a bit more complex than Behn and Vaupel's simple sapling because there are at least two possible outcomes for each alternative. Reading the decision tree from left to right, the first item encountered, the rectangle, is called the *decision node*. The decision maker is confronted with two choices: approve a program to abate taxes or do not approve the program. From the rectangle emanate two branches, each leading to a circle, called an *uncertainty node*, to which are attached two *outcome branches*. For each of the two possible decisions, abate taxes or do not abate taxes, there are two uncertain events, get

Figure 4-2 Shall We Abate Taxes to Encourage Downtown Development?

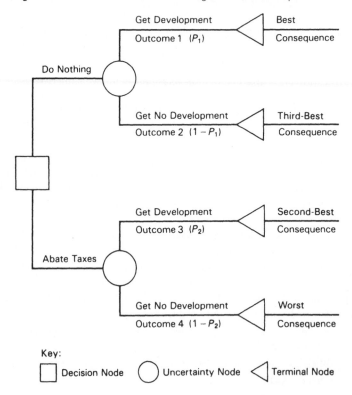

development or get no development. The probability of each of these events is shown in parentheses on the outcome branch. For each of the two choices the two probabilities must add up to 1.0 (certainty).

If we decide to not abate taxes, two outcomes with two probabilities are possible:

- Development will occur (P_1).
- Development will not occur ($1 - P_1$).

If we decide to abate taxes two outcomes with two probabilities are possible:

- Development will occur (P_2).
- Development will not occur ($1 - P_2$).

In reality, there are hundreds of possible outcomes, given that various amounts of development can occur whether or not the tax abatement program is approved. However, for simplicity's sake we will act as if only four outcomes were possible. Each of the outcome branches has a triangular *terminal node* and a *consequence branch*.

Since abating property taxes is a very real cost to the city, the best consequence is to get the same amount of new development without abating taxes. The worst consequence is to have abated taxes and have gotten no development. The other two states lie somewhere in between, with abating taxes and getting development as shown in Figure 4-2 apparently worth more (second-best consequence) than doing nothing and getting nothing (third-best consequence).

There are two major uncertainties in this decision tree: What are the odds of getting development, given you've chosen to either adopt or not adopt the policy? There are also four possible outcomes for which you need to assess someone's preferences. Once these factors are specified, decision analysis helps us make the best choice, consistent with someone's beliefs about the uncertainties and preferences for the outcomes. Unfortunately, the odds of getting development if either action or inaction is decided upon are unknown, as are the values that can be placed on any of the four outcomes. Some analysts might be tempted to focus on the apparently dominant question of whether abating taxes would indeed encourage development (P_2), to the exclusion of other important analyses. Adoption of the best policy might hinge on this uncertainty, but it might not. Even if the policy promoted the desired development, we must ask what the benefits to the city would be and whether they would outweigh the costs of implementing the program. This major question deserves considerable attention. For example, if the values on the four outcomes were different from those shown in Figure 4-2, with doing nothing and getting nothing the second-best instead of the third-best outcome (see Figure 4-3), the abate/get development uncertainty would be moot. Doing nothing provides two possible outcomes, both of which are preferable to the action outcomes.

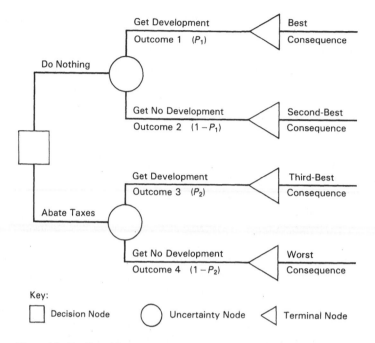

Key:

☐ Decision Node ◯ Uncertainty Node ◁ Terminal Node

Figure 4-3 Ranking of Consequence Associated with Four Separate Tax Abatement Policy Outcomes Are Changed

What is shown here is that it is preferable to do nothing and get nothing (second-best consequence) rather than to abate taxes and get development (third-best consequence). One possible explanation for this is that in the second case (Figure 4-3) the benefits achieved from the development would be outweighed by the costs of the tax abatement program. Were we engaged in this analysis in the real world, it would be important to estimate the costs and benefits associated with each of the four outcomes. What we show in Figures 4-2 and 4-3 are unquantified outcomes. The four consequences are simply shown in preferential order.

This example shows that all uncertainties demand attention, not just the one surrounding whether or not abating taxes will cause development to occur. Experience shows, though, that many people, when confronted with this particular problem, get completely absorbed in the causality question: Does the policy cause investors to develop something? In policy planning we are often confronted with uncertainty about whether a policy or program will cause a certain effect, but good analysts will spend an appropriate amount of time on such a question and then move on to other important uncertainties. They make best guesses or assumptions and then forge ahead with the remainder of the inquiry. They often find that the original uncertainty, which at first appeared to dominate, becomes unimportant. Presuming only 25 hours are available to examine this problem, here is a suggested work plan:

First, gather and analyze the experiences of other cities on the two uncertainties—P_1, if we do nothing how likely is it that development will happen anyway, and P_2, if we abate taxes how likely is it that we will get development? Then develop a best guess as to their probability of occurrence in this case. Quickly interview a local developer or two. Spend no more than eight hours on this task. Second, spend most of the remaining time refining the values of the four possible outcomes. This will involve:

1. Valuing the benefits of development for outcome 1
2. Valuing the possible opportunity costs for outcome 2
3. Valuing the benefits of development and the costs of abatement for outcome 3
4. Valuing the costs of abatement for outcome 4

At this point it might be possible to use some elements of decision analysis to make a recommendation to the client, but that isn't the main goal of using quick decision analysis in problem definition. The real objective is to structure the policy problem so it can be more fully analyzed. Here, by using the techniques of decision analysis, we have exposed a number of questions needing investigation. In addition to the probability that the proposed abatement program will cause development to happen, these questions include:

1. The value of the benefits of development if it happens
2. The cost of the abatement program
3. The opportunity cost of doing nothing
4. The probability that development may happen even if the program is not undertaken

When thinking about a policy problem we should assess whether the key characteristics of the problem can be structured into a decision-analysis framework. Often they can be, and then quick analysis can help to identify critical components of the problems and strengths and weaknesses in alternatives. Decision problems should be broken into their component parts: subdecisions, uncertainties, outcomes, and consequences. Having simplified the problem, you can then attempt to put values on the uncertainties and the preferences the client might have for the outcomes (often costs and benefits). Behn and Vaupel also suggest a last step, which is "rethink" by using sensitivity analysis.[24] (See Chapter 7.)

CREATION OF VALID OPERATIONAL DEFINITIONS

One of our principles of analysis is to "say it with numbers." That is, wherever possible, measure the problem being analyzed or the alternative solutions being assessed so that a portion of the analysis can be done quantitatively. This process

---

[24] Behn and Vaupel, *Quick Analysis for Busy Decision Makers*, pp. 23–24.

of expressing a problem statement or objective in measurable terms is referred to as *creating an operational definition*. Serious problems can arise if the step that turns ideas into measures is not done with care.

The first concern is reliability. Will the measure produce unambiguous data? For example, if tons of trash collected per person-hour is used to judge the efficiency of garbage collection systems, can the measure be used to compare different cities, under different climatic conditions, and with different types of collection routes? If not, the measure will be unreliable.

A second concern is that of fractional measurement. Sometimes a measure only partially conveys the meaning of the original concept. Many of the phenomena we want to measure in policy analysis are complex and multidimensional. Thus, it proves nearly impossible to get a valid sense of any phenomenon with a single statistic. For example, a measure often used in health planning is the ratio of hospital bed-days occupied per some measure of population. To some, fewer occupancy days might indicate a healthier population (over time, or in one area versus another). However, this ignores the questions of whether doctors are prescribing shorter stays or whether people are unable to afford many days in the hospital, whether an illness is defined as an inpatient treatment in some communities and not in others, or whether the age structure of the populations might be considerably different. Finally, what does it mean about individual people and their specific illnesses? Is everyone using the hospital less, or just some groups? Are all groups equally well served? Obviously one measure cannot answer all these questions. If the concept to be measured is the health of the population of an area, many more measures will be required. If a single measure becomes the indicator of progress on an important issue, there is a clear danger that resources will be spent to affect that measure alone, perhaps overlooking better approaches. Many students may have been the victims of the way some colleges measure departmental productivity: "student credit hours delivered." In colleges where such a measure is applied rather mechanistically, administrators may promote policies to raise their departmental student head counts, in some cases seriously compromising many other important educational objectives.

Another dimension of the fractional-measurement problem involves relying too greatly on quantitative measures and ignoring qualitative ones. Measures that can be counted often take precedence because they are easier to explain to the public and the media. Numerical changes are also readily visible. Analysts need to fight the urge to simplify an idea to only its measurable attributes. Our college example serves here as well. In determining a method for allocating resources among college departments, rewarding efficient delivery of student credit hours does not necessarily reward those best meeting the college's educational goals. It focuses on only one means of achieving those goals. It is often easier to measure means pursued than ends achieved. The goals of public policies and programs are usually multifaceted and complex. The first step in resolving this problem is, of course, to recognize it.

The final dimension of the fractional-measurement problem is that of spillovers. It is tempting for policy analysts to deliver to their client recommendations that maximize something for the client's organization, ignoring significant spillovers to other entities. Using federal cost-sharing funds that maximize economic benefits to the client's locale but harm adjacent political entities or the society at large is a common example. Thus, blind pursuit of the goals of clients or a single political or organizational entity can substantially harm other groups. To be responsible and ethical, the policy analyst must share knowledge of harmful or beneficial spillovers when they exist.

Indirect measurement is a third problem in developing operational measures. Because policy analysts usually face time and resource constraints, they are often forced to use existing data sets developed for other purposes. A common secondary data source is the U.S. Census. Often the available secondary data are outdated and don't precisely measure the concepts we have in mind. When this is true, all the problems of fractional measurement can be exacerbated.

Serious problems can arise when the units for which data are reported by the secondary source are substituted for those of real social units. For example, a great deal of data is collected for Census tracts (containing approximately 3,000 to 5,000 people) in each decennial Census. Many urban researchers have been interested in problems of neighborhoods and the potential for organized neighborhoods to prevent certain crimes such as vandalism and rape. Lacking the resources to gather primary data in these organized neighborhoods, researchers have treated Census tracts and groups of tracts as if they were neighborhoods, using the available data to study local problems and policy proposals. However, real neighborhoods often cut across Census-tract boundaries, despite the Census Bureau's attempts to establish tract boundaries that correspond to those of neighborhoods. This mismatch can lead analysts to misdiagnose problems and recommend inappropriate public policy.

A related error is known in the social science literature as the "ecological fallacy."[25] Conclusions should not be, but sometimes are, generalized to measurement units other than the one being studied. For example, Census-tract health or crime statistics do not ordinarily support conclusions about individuals or families. In the classic case of ecological correlation, a study of Census-tract crime rates in Seattle found that tracts with high percentages of Japanese had high crime rates. The researchers concluded that Japanese people were criminals. Quite to the contrary, the Japanese as a group had lower crime rates than nearly every other ethnic group in Seattle, but many Japanese had low incomes and resided in tracts where there was higher-than-average criminal activity. Policy analysts must use data collected for the unit being studied, not substitute aggregate data or data for other units. Often the temptation is to use aggregate geographic data to draw conclusions about individuals. This will sometimes, but

---

[25] W. S. Robinson, "Ecological Correlation and the Behavior of Individuals," *American Sociological Review* 15 (June 1950), 351–57; and David S. Sawicki, "Studies of Aggregated Areal Data: Problems of Statistical Inference," *Land Economics* 49, no. 1 (February 1973), 109–14.

not always, yield correct results. Public policy can usually deal more effectively with problems of real social or political units than with those delineated for ease of data gathering. For example, an effective neighborhood crime-prevention strategy might deal with attributes of the neighborhoods (physical layout, types of police activity, street lighting, organizations) that could be changed through policy, rather than the characteristics of individuals (age, education, income) aggregated as they are in Census-tract statistics.

The need to operationalize definitions—that is, state problems in a way that permits us to identify and measure their component parts—should be evident. The above review suggests that a valid operational definition will:

1. State the concept in unambiguous terms.
2. Give attention to qualitative as well as quantitative measures.
3. Take account of spillovers.
4. Use primary data when possible.
5. Use data collected for the unit of analysis under study.
6. Draw only conclusions warranted by the unit of analysis.
7. Avoid speculating about individual characteristics from group data.
8. Develop policy aimed at real social and political units.

The problem of delivering energy-cost assistance to poor people provides an example of operationalizing a definition. One hypothesis connected to this problem is: "The lower the *household's income*, the larger the proportion of *income* that is *paid* for *fuel*." In order to test the veracity of such a statement, we would first have to agree on the problem, and then agree on a way to measure that idea. In our simple hypothesis, each of the key words needs to be defined and operationalized. We won't do that in detail here, but we will scratch the surface.

First the idea of a *household* must be defined and measured. The idea should be to locate all those persons under one roof sharing the fuel bills of that place. The Census defined *household* as:

> . . . [consisting] of all persons who occupy a housing unit. By definition, the count of households is the same as the count of housing units.[26]

It further defined housing units as:

> . . . a house, apartment, a group of rooms, or a single room occupied or intended for occupancy as separate living quarters. . . . The occupants may be a single family, one person living alone, two or more families living together, and/or other groups of related or unrelated persons who share living arrangements.[27]

---

[26] U.S. Bureau of the Census, *Current Housing Reports H-170-87-21, American Housing Survey for the Atlanta Metropolitan Area in 1987* (Washington, DC: Bureau of the Census, 1990), Appendix A, p. APP-21.

[27] Ibid., p. APP-4.

This seems like a reasonable definition for our purposes, and using it would perhaps allow us to use a secondary data source to derive the total number of households in certain income classes. For our purposes, families that have doubled up, or singles living together, are as important as single families or individuals. We simply want to know who is sharing the cost for fuel in a household. Thus, the Census definition seems appropriate.

Next is the word *income*, modified by the term *household*. Again, the idea is to include the pooled ability of the persons in the household to pay for fuel. Yearly income, especially if not averaged, may not be a perfect indicator. Total wealth has some advantages as a measure of ability to pay. However, it may be that certain kinds of wealth, like the value of the home people occupy, cannot be easily converted to cash in order to pay for fuel. In addition, there is probably no easily available source of data on wealth. Again, it proves convenient to adopt the Census definition. It is as follows: the yearly total of:

> . . . the amounts reported for wage and salary income, interest on dividends, Social Security or railroad retirement income, public assistance or welfare payments, alimony or child support, and all other money income. The figure represents the amount of income received before deductions for personal income taxes, Social Security, union dues, bond purchases, health insurance premiums, Medicare deductions, etc.[28]

The next terms to be explored are *paid* and *fuel*. The idea is, of course, that money to pay for household energy needs should be made available to households in proportion to the difficulty they have in paying large fuel bills. The program was created in the belief that, in addition to paying the same high unit price for fuel as the rest of the population from their lower incomes, a disproportionately large number of poor people live in poorly insulated houses with inefficient heating systems, using the most expensive fuel, which is often oil. In rural areas, some people may substitute other fuels. Some households may be able to obtain wood for little or no cash payment by cutting and hauling it themselves. In both urban and rural areas inadequate heating is often replaced or supplemented by electric space heaters or, despite the danger, by leaving the gas oven on. Disregarding for the moment the availability of data, we suggest the following as an operational definition of *paid for fuel*: "The sum of all monies paid for all forms of energy in one calendar year that can be verified by receipt, less $300." The $300 will roughly cover the cost of energy not used for heating. We have done nothing about the substitution of personal labor for fuel payments, implicitly assuming that this arrangement is rare, an assumption worth questioning in some rural areas where wood is a common fuel.

This very brief example gives the idea of how to operationalize indicators. Many policy problems are more complex than our single hypothesis above. However, in every case the analyst should avoid ambiguity, use multiple measures

[28] Ibid., p. APP-16.

to define a complex concept, use qualitative as well as quantitative measures, employ primary data whenever possible, and be cautious when using secondary data.

POLITICAL ANALYSIS

Consideration of political factors was identified earlier as a distinctive element of policy analysis. Explicitly examining political issues in the process of identifying and analyzing alternatives to policy problems distinguishes policy analysis from other forms of systematic analysis. Yet there has been limited success in translating existing political science theories into methodological advice or policy guidance.[29] Moreover, political analysis has been most closely linked with policy implementation rather than policy formulation. After we know what we (the organization, our superior, our client, and so on) want, we figure out a way to get it. Coplin and O'Leary, in their guide to understanding political problems, define a political problem as "one in which you must get some other people to act or stop acting in a certain way in order to achieve a goal important to you."[30] The advice they give for devising a political game plan appears to assume that the proper policy has been identified and we need to figure out how to reach it.

Meltsner maintains that the timing and location of political analysis depend on the situation:

> One approach would be to conceive of analysis as a two-step process: (1) supply an answer based on quantitative and economic reasoning, and (2) then modify that answer using political considerations. . . .
>
> Another approach, more difficult but also probably more effective, is to introduce politics at each stage of policy analysis. The analyst would consider political feasibility in the selection of a policy problem, in the definition of that problem, in the identification of alternatives, and in the recommendation of preferred alternatives.[31]

In the first approach, politics is one of the criteria used to select the preferred alternative. But in the second approach, which Meltsner calls "an iterative procedure," there is "a continuing interplay between means and ends, as new information is introduced into the process."[32]

We prefer the second approach, which considers political factors throughout the policy analysis process, but this may not always be possible, especially for

---

[29] Peter J. May, "Politics and Policy Analysis," *Political Science Quarterly* 101, no. 1 (Spring 1986), 110.

[30] William D. Coplin and Michael K. O'Leary, *Everyman's Prince: A Guide to Understanding Your Political Problems*, rev. ed. (North Scituate, MA: Duxbury Press, 1972), p. 3.

[31] Arnold J. Meltsner, "Political Feasibility and Policy Analysis," *Public Administration Review* 32, no. 6 (November/December 1972), 865.

[32] Ibid., p. 865.

beginning analysts who have little political experience or for certain narrowly defined problems. Whenever possible, political factors should be part of problem definition, criteria selection, and alternatives generation, evaluation, and display.[33]

Several things are necessary if political factors are to be incorporated into the policy analysis process. Analysts must look at political issues as an integral part of the policy process, learn terminology to communicate about these political factors, and use consistent methods to report, display, and analyze political issues. Recognizing the importance of political influences means not so much recognizing that designing and implementing policy involves politics, for we presume that students of planning and public policy realize the political nature of the policy process and do not hold a politics-is-evil attitude. Rather, because we so strongly desire to identify the technically superior alternative, and we become so engrossed in calculating economic costs and benefits, we may postpone the political analysis. Instead, we need to recognize explicitly the political aspects of the technical analysis. While seeking out numerical information and calculating economic costs and benefits, we are working with information that can yield political insights, if we know what to look for and if we have the right perspective. A strict numerical analysis will have to be grounded in client and decision-maker values, goals, and objectives, if it is to yield useful results; and these values, goals, and objectives tell a great amount about political positions and relationships.

Explicit recognition and consideration of decision-maker values is essential to successful planning and analysis. Innes has discussed the often-documented failure of decision makers to use information developed through planning and policy analysis, attributing this failure to the tendency of planners and analysts to view the production of information as separate from the political process. She suggests that a better approach is to emphasize the subjective meaning of problems and to recognize that knowledge developed interactively with the knowledge users is likely to have more impact on decisions.[34] Whenever possible, therefore, involve the client or decision maker in the production of information and knowledge. Be certain that their views, values, and priorities can be addressed by the types of data collected, analyses performed, and information generated.

During problem definition, when the scope of the analysis is being determined, and when the problem is being reduced to a manageable size through back-of-the-envelope calculations, ask questions about the political history of the problem, the technical and political objectives of the analysis, and the political variables that will affect the definition of policy alternatives. The analyst must ask whether this is a technical or political problem or whether the problem contains both components. Is the political analysis intended to get the public to

---

[33] For the importance of building on political decision making in strategic planning, see John M. Bryson, *Strategic Planning for Public and Nonprofit Organizations: A Guide to Strengthening and Sustaining Organizational Achievement* (San Francisco: Jossey-Bass, 1988), pp. 66–70.

[34] Judith Innes, "Knowledge and Action: Making the Link," *Journal of Planning Education and Research* 6, no. 2 (Winter 1987), 86–92.

recognize the problem, to convince our client or superior to accept the analysis, or is it to garner votes from the legislature or council? Different purposes will require different political analyses. If we want the public to recognize the problem, we might concentrate on ways to cause important public groups to increase their stakes in the problem. If we want our superior to accept the analysis, we might focus on office or agency politics. If we want to obtain a majority vote for a technical solution, we might think of alternative means for introducing the policy and timing its introduction.

A terminology for discussing political analysis has developed, and Meltsner provides guidance by suggesting that political problems should be analyzed in terms of the *actors* involved, their *motivations* and *beliefs*, the *resources* they hold, their effectiveness in using the resources, and the *sites* at which decisions will be made.[35] Answering the following questions will help to clarify political problems.

Actors.   Who are the individuals or groups usually concerned about this type of problem, and who might reasonably be expected to become involved in the current problem?

Motivations.   What are the motives, needs, desires, goals, and objectives of the actors? What do they want? What will it take to satisfy the various actors?

Beliefs.   What does each key actor believe about the problem? What are the attitudes and values held by the various participants? What do they see as desirable means and ends? What will they accept?

Resources.   What does each actor have that can be used to get what is wanted? Resources are often monetary but can take the form of management skills or a sense of timing. Some individuals and groups are better able to use their resources than others. Which actors are most able and likely to get what they want?

Sites.   Where will decisions be made? By whom? When? Sites can be identified from legislative intent, administrative procedure, or past conflicts. Sometimes decisions are broken apart and are made at several sites.

Leung has proposed a systematic way to recognize the subjective nature of value judgments and policy options in policymaking before, during, and after a policy is implemented.[36] He suggests that answers be sought for the following: *What* is being pursued by the policy actor, is it being pursued *effectively*, at what *cost*, and will the policy initiative be *accepted* and successfully implemented? And

[35] Meltsner, "Political Feasibility and Policy Analysis," pp. 859–67.

[36] Hok Lin Leung, *Towards a Subjective Approach to Policy Planning & Evaluation: Common-Sense Structured* (Winnipeg, Canada: Ronald P. Frye, 1985).

May suggests that political strategists should be concerned with identifying windows of opportunity, estimating their size, and working to expand them.[37]

Gather the information with which to complete the checklists quickly. Specify the central actors and sites so that the analysis can be reduced to a manageable size. Do not discard unused information and do not ignore peripheral actors. As events unfold, peripheral actors may become involved, and apparently irrelevant data may become useful. In addition to the checklists, tables that display issues and decision trees can be used for coding and classifying political data to reveal the basic components of the problem, the relative positions of actors, and the sequence of potential problems.

An example will serve to illustrate how political considerations can be incorporated into policy analysis. One of the authors was involved as a citizen in the preparation and passing of a program and budget for a community development (CD) program. In this case example, the bulk of community development funds had been spent on physical improvements (rather than on social services) in two target areas. Funds had gone to housing rehabilitation, street and sidewalk reconstruction, and lighting installation, as well as clean-up, paint-up, and several self-help programs run by community organizations. The annual community development budget was developed by a citizen commission, with technical support from city staff and with input from several dozen public hearings that took place over an eight-month period.

The commission developed a list of needed projects that exceeded by ten times the annual CD budget. Thus, priorities had to be set through a combination of technical (staff input) and political (citizen input at neighborhood meetings) means. Each of several past years had seen the commission's proposed program and budget approved by the city council after only light scrutiny and polite debate between Republican and Democratic council members. The commission's priorities and proposed budget had been accepted with little question until recently, when a council member suggested an alternative budget to fund projects that would benefit persons in her ward and would use virtually the entire community development budget allocation. During preparation of the CD budget, the commission countered these proposals with technical arguments: the alternative projects would absorb all of the CD budget, they were not cost-effective, and they would benefit only a small portion of the target-area population. Although commission members and staff believed that the proposed program and budget were technically superior, the commission chair and CD department director defined the problem as essentially a political one: how to get enough council votes to pass the proposed budget before the deadline for submission of the budget to the federal government, before the CD commission chair's term would expire, and before the CD director took a position elsewhere.

Sensing that the council would not be convinced on the technical argument

[37] Peter J. May, "Politics and Policy Analysis," *Political Science Quarterly* 101, no. 1 (Spring 1986), 117.

alone (the council member who had proposed modifications to the budget was a member of the 5-to-2 majority), the CD director and CD commission chair analyzed alternative ways to present the program to the council and how to maximize the chance of council approval.

In this case, the policy analysts (the CD director and commission chair) saw the target areas and the citizen commission as their clients and concentrated on ways to cause the citizens in the target area to recognize their stake in the problem, to have the commission take a political stance, to develop political support, and to decide what evidence to use and when to make a move. The CD director and chair used two quick methods to collect and analyze these political data: an issue table and a decision tree.

An issue table can be used to classify and correlate data from the political checklists. For the problem-definition stage of the process, the table would include a list of actors and problem components. The importance of problem components to actors can be coded in the cells of the table. The CD budget problem was tabulated by identifying actors, listing the issues important to each, and estimating the relative importance of issues, as in Table 4-1. At this stage, high, middle, or low values might be assigned for relative importance, or outcomes of issues might be listed as desired or not desired. Notes may be added to the table to clarify ambiguous points. Later, during the comparison of alternatives, additional information will be entered into the table. At this point, the tabulation helps to organize our thoughts, clarify the issues, and specify the actors.

Basic decision analysis can also be helpful in defining the political aspects of the problem. Using the decision-tree approach, various sequences of events

Table 4-1 CD Budget Allocation Issue Table

	ISSUES/PROBLEM COMPONENTS				
Actors	Target CD Funds	Spread CD Funds	Make Neighborhood Improvements	Keep Commission's Status	Get Budget in on Time
CD commission	+	−	+	+	+
CD chair	+	−	+	+	+
CD director	+	−	+	+	+
Target-area residents	+	−	+	0	0
Republicans	−	+	+	0	0
Democrats	−	+	+	0	0
Mayor	−	+	+	+	+
Council member	+	−	+	0	0

KEY:
+ Desired
− Not desired
0 Not relevant

Note: The importance of the issues might be indicated by a numerical scale.

of the problem. Using the decision-tree approach, various sequences of events and constraints at each step can be shown. Probabilities of events can be estimated and likely outcomes can be assessed. The CD director and commission chair devised the decision tree shown in Figure 4-4 to help them think about how the CD budget problem could be defined and how the consequences of various decisions could be assessed. They reasoned that if the commission revised the budget (substituted the council member's projects without objection), the budget would almost certainly be approved by the council, but the commission would relinquish its strong role in preparing the CD budget, and it might be difficult to get people to serve on the commission in the future. If the commission took its proposed (unrevised) budget to the council, there would be a major debate and perhaps the budget would be rejected. If the budget were to be rejected, the council itself could modify the budget, or it could return the budget to the commission with a request for revision. In the former case an alternative budget would be submitted on time for federal funding, but the commission would relinquish its leading role in budget development. In the latter case the budget would be delayed and funding might be lost. If the council accepted the commission's unrevised budget, there would be a chance that the mayor would veto it. If he vetoed the budget, its submission would be delayed. If he did not veto it, the commission's unrevised budget would be submitted on time, resulting in the best outcome.

The political thinking of the CD director and commission chair is shown in Figure 4-4. They reasoned that if the public and media became interested in the topic, the council would lean toward accepting the commission's unrevised budget. So they assigned a 60% probability to council acceptance of the budget. They felt that the mayor was not likely to veto the commission's budget, since that would slow preparation of the general city budget, which he wanted to move ahead. They assigned a 20% probability to a veto by the mayor. If the council rejected the commission's budget, it might also modify the budget to suit itself. The director and chair reasoned that there was less than a 50-50 chance that the council would go this far because of the negative impact such treatment of a citizen commission would have. A 40% probability was assigned to council modification of the rejected commission budget. Thus, there were five possible outcomes with five probabilities:

If the commission were to revise the budget, the council would certainly accept it ($P_1 = 1.0$).

If the commission were not to revise the budget, four outcomes were possible:

- Council would accept ($P_2 = .6$) and the mayor would not veto ($P_3 = .8$). The probability of this compound event is $P_2 \times P_3 = .48$
- Council would accept ($P_2 = .6$) and the mayor would veto ($1 - P_3 = .2$). The probability of this compound event is $P_2 \times (1 - P_3) = .12$
- Council would reject ($1 - P_2 = .4$) and the council would return the same budget ($P_4 = .6$). The probability of this compound event is $(1 - P_2) \times P_4 = .24$

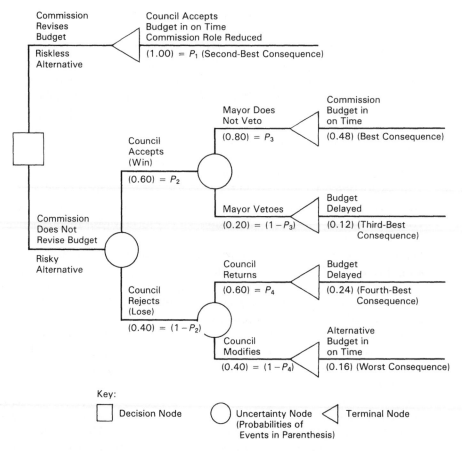

Figure 4-4 A Decision Tree: To Revise or Not to Revise the Community Development Budget

- Council would reject $(1 - P_2 = .4)$ and the council would modify the budget to suit itself $(1 - P_4 = .4)$. The probability of this compound event is $(1 - P_2) \times (1 - P_4) = .16$

Having developed the decision tree, the CD director and commission chair needed to determine whether they preferred the sure alternative of revising the budget and having the council accept it over the risky alternative that had four possible outcomes, each with its own probability and value. They chose to take a chance on the risky alternative. Their reasoning boiled down to a decision that a near 50% chance (0.48) of the best consequence was better than the sure (1.0) outcome of revising the budget and having the council accept it. When working with problems of this type, analysts go back and forth between the valuing of consequences and weighing their probabilities. The vehicle for doing this is called the *preference probability*.[38]

Deciding to submit the unrevised budget, the CD director and commission chair were left to observe whether their estimates of the probabilities led them to the correct decision. Of course, the director and chair were aware that their probabilities might have been wrong. If their estimates of council acceptance of 0.6, or of 0.8 for the mayor not vetoing the budget were too high, the joint probability of the unrevised budget being accepted would have been lower than 0.48. As it turned out, the commission's budget was approved after a long and acrimonious battle on the council floor. Without political decision analysis the director and chair might have decided to take the unrevised budget to council anyway, but the decision tree made them think more formally and systematically about possible actors, decision sites, and consequences.

It is hard to think of policy problems (other than simple textbook examples) that do not have political aspects or ramifications. Some problems are more political than others, and thus the importance of political feasibility analysis will vary. We suggest that a political analysis should be conducted as each problem is defined. If no political issues are discovered (we would be surprised), the search for the best technical solution can proceed without constraints.

We urge the beginning analyst to be cautious about political analysis. At first, the analyst may only be able to recognize the political problems and leave them to the client to handle. As the analyst's skills develop, the client may come to trust the analyst's political insights. It is important to remember that political officials and decision makers take pride in their political astuteness and may not appreciate political advice from a neophyte. Moreover, political feasibility analysis is not an exact science and should not be viewed as predictive. May warns us never to expect more than a partial feasibility calculus.[39] Nonetheless, beginning analysts should conduct political analyses, even if only for personal consumption. We close this section with a list of tips for political analysis:

1. Determine whether the obvious problem is only a symptom of a larger controversy.
2. Make sure you look for underlying issues and related problems.
3. Check your sources of information. Much political data are anecdotal, second-hand, and vague. Use several sources if possible, and question the validity of sensational data.
4. Take advantage of internal review. Does your account of the political situation ring true to other analysts? Do they interpret past events in the same way?

---

[38] We will not discuss in this book a method for establishing how to value consequences. Behn and Vaupel explain this in detail. They use a system of weighing preferences for a certain percentage chance of one outcome against another percentage chance of a competing outcome—thus the term *preference probability*. See Behn and Vaupel, *Quick Analysis for Busy Decision Makers*.

[39] May, "Politics and Policy Analysis," p. 121.

5. Remember that political data are only part of the fact base. Do not let this aspect of analysis displace other important components.

THE ISSUE PAPER VERSUS FIRST-CUT ANALYSIS

The State and Local Finances Project developed a systematic approach to problem definition called the *issue paper*.[40] In a sense the issue paper is a feasibility study of whether or not to do "researched analysis." It provides the basis for more detailed analysis but is developed from readily available data and information. It touches briefly on each step in the entire process of policy analysis. However, the issue paper usually devotes little space to those steps that engage researchers the most—for example, evaluating policies. Although basic policy analysis is also done quickly, it is conducted with the intention of delivering a usable recommendation to the client. It may, and indeed should, contain a section suggesting to the client the possibilities for in-depth study, including a timetable, resources needed, and the benefits to be derived from the additional investment. Thus, basic analysis goes beyond the issue paper, which is intentionally only a feasibility study. Researched analysis differs from both the issue paper and basic analysis, since each step in the policy analysis process is done in depth. The term *researched policy analysis* implies that those steps that employ traditional research methods are likely to receive more attention than those that require approaches such as political feasibility analysis or scenario writing.

We feel that the issue paper has few advantages, that basic policy analysis as described here is preferable. Since there is often only the time or inclination to complete one analysis, every attempt should be made to use it to give advice about the substance of the problem, not just about whether to study it further. This view is consistent with our belief that policy analysis can be done at many levels, and that a continuum of time and resources can be devoted to the analysis, yielding increasing levels of detail and accuracy. The benefits derived from such investments are not necessarily linear, and careful thought will reveal this to the analyst. Figure 4-5 illustrates what three examples might look like if one actually were able to forecast the benefits and costs of various levels of analysis.

In the linear example (A), the benefits received are, in the range shown, constantly proportional to the investment made. For example, the analyst is searching the client files of a social service agency for cases exhibiting the problem under consideration. Each hour spent yields about three relevant cases. In the geometric example (C), benefits are received at a constantly changing rate. An example of this might be person-hours invested in searching for alternative solutions. At first, more hours spent searching produce more good alternatives and increase the value of the analysis. Eventually, however, the best alternatives have been identified, and

[40] State and Local Finances Project, *A First Step to Analysis: The Issue Paper,* PPB Note 11 (Washington, DC: George Washington University, July 1968). For a format for an issue paper see Checkland, "Formulating Problems for Systems Analysis," pp. 168–69.

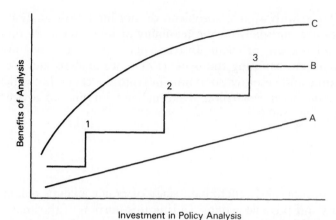

Figure 4-5 The Benefits of Analysis Received per Unit of Investment in Analysis for Three Separate Programs

spending more time does not increase the benefits very much. In the step-function example (B), a range of possible investments in analysis may all generate the same level of benefits. For example, a large amount of survey data has been gathered, but unless it can be computerized, will not benefit the analysis at all. At point 1 all data have been entered on a computer and listed. To reap additional benefits beyond this point, additional programming is needed to allow the data to be manipulated as necessary to do the analysis. When this is completed at point 2 a variety of descriptive material becomes available and sheds some light on the problem. Another investment is then required in analytical time and resources until point 3 is reached, where many detailed observations can be made about the problem based on the survey.

This last example illustrates three steps in a researched analysis, but we might also describe an example where the first step was basic analysis and subsequent steps were researched analysis. For curve B, points 1, 2, and 3 are the best choices in time and effort for ending the analysis. Why invest at all for no gain, or invest more for little additional benefit? For A and C the decision of where to stop is more difficult. For A the answer is probably to choose that level that gives enough information for your purpose but is within the budget. For C it is important to note the changing rate of benefit gain for investment cost and to choose a point, within the budget, where marginal gain becomes less than marginal cost (where information begins to cost more than it is worth). Time limitations also often constrain the decision. The analysis payoff for many policy problems resembles the step function B. For experienced analysts, decisions about the scale of analysis are not usually difficult to make, because the points in analysis at which benefits (knowledge) will increase dramatically are fairly evident, although the prediction of benefits may be qualitative rather than quantitative.[41]

[41] Stuart S. Nagel has presented a decision-analysis approach to this same question. See Stuart S. Nagel, *Policy Evaluation: Making Optimum Decisions* (New York: Praeger, 1982), pp. 32–36.

When first faced with a policy problem, do not limit your analysis to an issue paper, concentrating solely on the feasibility of investing more time and resources into studying the problem. Instead, perform basic policy analysis, which includes a section assessing the benefits of more analysis and a recommended level of time and resource commitment from the client, but which also goes further and contains an evaluation of alternative solutions and advice based on analysis done to that point.

SUMMARY

The problem-verification and redefinition stage of policy analysis delimits the range of problems and possible actions. During this portion of the analysis the interrelationship between how the problem is defined, who is concerned about the issue, what factors should be considered in the analysis, and ideas about possible solutions will begin to be clarified. Good analysts think ahead, scan the environment in order to anticipate problems, collect relevant data on strategic issues, and prepare memos on emerging topics. Beginning analysts should watch for and investigate potential issues before they are identified by clients. Policy problems must be important to relevant groups, precisely stated, formulated so data about them can be collected objectively, and contain measurable concepts and variables. Back-of-the-envelope calculations and decision analysis can be used to define a problem quickly and to identify its relevant components. Political analysis can be used to reveal important nonquantitative issues and potential implementation problems early in the policy development process so that these factors can be fully considered throughout the analysis. Having defined the problem, the next step in the policy analysis process is to establish the evaluation criteria that will be used in the process of deciding among competing policy options.

GLOSSARY

Back-of-the-Envelope Calculations simple ways to estimate numbers that are important to defining the direction and magnitude of a problem. Also methods for establishing some of the key dimensions of the problem and checking numerical estimates against known reference points.

Consequence Branch the result of a decision sequence, measured in some way.

Decision Node the point in a decision tree that indicates the decision maker's initial choice.

Decision Tree a graphic representation of the critical parts of a decision, including subdeci-sions, uncertainties, outcomes, and consequences.

Ecological Fallacy an error in logic through which conclusions are generalized to measurement units other than the ones being studied.

Fractional Measurement an issue of problem definition that means failing to capture an entire concept with the operational definition. Types of fractional measurement include using a single measure to stand for a complex issue or relying too greatly on quantitative measures and ignoring qualitative ones, and ignoring spillovers to those outside the client's constituency.

Indirect Measurement an issue of problem definition in which statistics gathered for another use are applied, although their operational definition does not really match the concept under the current circumstances.

Issue Paper a feasibility study of whether to do researched analysis. Differs from basic policy analysis in that the latter is conducted with the intention of delivering a usable recommendation *on the problem* rather than a recommendation about the usefulness of further study.

Outcome one possible result of decisions and uncertainty.

Policy Envelope the range of variables that constrains a problem definition.

Political Analysis the portion of problem definition in which actors, their motivations and beliefs, their resources, and the various decision sites are systematically scrutinized in order to understand what characteristics a successful solution must have.

Quick Decision Analysis an analytical technique and decision-making tool that can help to identify critical components of problems, and strengths and weaknesses of alternative solutions.

Reliability of Measures an issue in problem definition that measures the extent to which a single measure can be used to compare a concept under different circumstances.

Terminal Node the point in a decision tree that identifies the end of the preceding decision sequence. Attached to the terminal node is a consequence branch.

Uncertainty Node the point in a decision tree at which the outcome is determined by forces the decision maker does not control and can only estimate. This estimate usually takes the form of a "probability" or likelihood of occurrence.

Values general beliefs about the relative utility, merit, or worth of goods, objects, services, or actions.

EXERCISES

1. Revise the problem definition you wrote for the teen-age auto accidents problem in Chapter 2, using the ideas discussed in this chapter. Attempt in this definition to delimit the extent of the problem and possible actions. Specify more clearly who is concerned, what factors should be considered in the analysis, how widespread the problem is, and its political dimensions. Be sure to develop valid operational definitions of the problem.

2. Read the opinion piece by Michael Kinsley. Define the drinking and driving problem as one simply concocted by adults.

Revenge Of the Grown-Ups

Michael Kinsley

Vetoing the highway bill broke President Reagan's heart, because he was so eager to end the 55 mph speed limit. This issue is wildly popular with the general population and regarded by many conservatives as a matter of principle: burdensome government vs. human freedom.

Meanwhile, though, the Reagan administration pursues another popular campaign to force states to raise their minimum drinking ages to 21, for the avowed purpose of increasing highway safety. Using the same mechanism that enforces the speed limit—withholding of federal highway funds—a 1984 law gave states until last Sept. 30 to outlaw teen-age drinking. Forty-two met the deadline, in a dramatic reversal of the lower-drinking-age trend of the previous decade.

The best estimate is that raising the speed limit will cost about 700 lives a year, plus injuries. That doesn't mean it shouldn't be done. Although no one would sacrifice those 700 lives if we knew in advance whose they were, the social trade-off of anonymous human lives for human freedom or even mere human convenience is an inevitable part of life. If you doubt this, what about lowering the speed limit to 45 or 35? That would save even more lives. Most people have decided that shaving a few minutes off highway trips is worth the risk, and they're not crazy to think so.

But what, then, of the trade-off in the case of teen-age drinking? The best studies suggest that raising the drinking age reduces fatalities among 18- to 20-year-olds by about 7 percent, which would be something like 360 lives a year. There is no good evidence that banning drink for 18-year-olds has any effect on drinking by younger teens. And there is some evidence that raising the drinking age *increases* highway deaths among people in their early twenties. A certain type, it appears, is going to kill himself when he starts drinking, whenever that is.

So. Raising the speed limit will cost perhaps twice as many lives as raising the drinking age will save. You might argue that teen lives are more precious. But in fact, the only reason this particular social trade-off is so popular is that in one case the burden is being imposed on a small minority of the population.

Wasn't anyone around here ever a teen-ager? It's absurd to expect people not to let alcohol pass their lips in college, and even more absurd if they're already out in the productive work force or serving their country in the military. The vast majority of teen-agers do not drink and drive. Nor do they drink to excess. (Or if they do once or twice, so what?) Yet they are being denied, or at least there is an attempt to deny them, one of the pleasures of life—a pleasure adults would never deny themselves.

All across the policy landscape these days we see the spectacle of grown-ups alarmed that teen-agers might be enjoying themselves too much—drinking, using drugs, listening to dirty rock lyrics, having sex. Other issues are more genuinely difficult than the drinking-age question. Yet why is it that every politician in need of an easy issue dreams up something new for adults to impose on kids? If it's not some conservative demanding high school drug tests, it's some liberal wanting to bring back the draft.

Teen-age sex has become a national obsession. Or rather, it has risen out of the national subconscious to become a political obsession. The unattractive relish with which some people have seized on AIDS as a reason to crusade for chastity suggests that they might be secretly disappointed if a cure were found tomorrow.

It's almost as if there's an element of vengeance here. Vengeance for what? Among older people, perhaps, vengeance for the 1960s. Among many of today's parents, who were teens themselves in the 1960s, vengeance for being young while we are young no longer. Baby boomers, with our huge demographic weight, can push the other generations around. Two decades ago we terrorized our elders. Now we terrorize our youngers.

Poor kids. The grotesque lyrics quoted with alarm in Tipper Gore's "Raising PG Kids in an X-Rated Society" (handbook of the alarmist movement over rock songs) strike me as an almost pathetic attempt to shock a generation of parents who were old hands at the disgust-the-old-folks game before these pups were even born. Those parents would like today's teen-agers to avail themselves of the many opportunities for good, clean fun—which weren't sufficient for them a generation ago.

3.   Pressure groups opposing the increase in the legal drinking age to 21 argued that the increase in the legal drinking age would cause high school and under-age college students to shift the location of their drinking from bars to private homes, dorm rooms, and automobiles. Is this a valid argument? Examine this issue in the context of the statement that: "All solutions breed new problems."

4.   To many persons living in large metropolitan areas, commuting to work can be frustrating. They view traffic congestion as a serious problem. To others, congestion is a natural consequence of human behavior and not something to worry about. Using ideas discussed in this chapter, explore the concept of traffic congestion as a problem that may or may not need attention. In other words, define it from a number of different perspectives.

5.   Some time ago a significant movement of people and jobs began to take place. The general pattern of the move was characterized as being from the snowbelt states to the sunbelt states. To many, the possible continuation of this movement through the 1990s is a serious problem. Develop three well-articulated problem statements—one for a snow-belt city mayor, another for the president of the United States, and a third for a citizen action group that is, if nothing else, pragmatic—it suggests a solution.

6.   Read your local newspaper carefully for a week, searching for a local problem that seems to be on everyone's mind. Seek out a public official who seems to have opinions about the problem and its solution, and engage this person in a discussion about the problem. Before having that meeting be sure to review this chapter, especially the sections on "identifying and defining problems," "developing the problem statement," and "political analysis." Try to explore some of the points made in this chapter in your discussion—not directly, but subtly. Write up the results of your discussion, referring to concepts discussed in this chapter.

7.   Every so often a school or school district will decide to enact a dress code for students. (See the article "On Dress Code's First Day, Ties Aplenty.") Usually both strong support and strong opposition are generated. Is the way students dress a problem? Should a dress code include hair length as well as clothes? What about the rule of wearing no gold? What problems would a dress code resolve?

On Dress Code's First Day, Ties Aplenty

They didn't have to, but almost all the senior boys at Boys and Girls High School wore neckties to school yesterday.

Yesterday was Dress for Success Day at the Brooklyn school, the first day of the legally unenforceable but enthusiastically received dress code declared last week by their principal, Frank Mickens.

At an assembly, 400 seniors chanted "Go Mickens! Go Mickens! Go Mickens!" and gave the principal a standing ovation when he told them, "You have set a higher standard not only for young people in this city, but for young people across the country."

Brian Johnson, a senior, was wearing a pink tie. "I think a lot of the kids are looking for more direction, more leadership," he said. Students feel tremendous peer pressure "to wear the right kind of clothes and keep up with whatever you have to be with the in crowd," he added.

School board policy prohibits mandatory dress codes. But Mr. Mickens says the policy will raise the self-esteem of his students, many of whom cope with the temptations of drugs on the Bedford-Stuyvesant streets outside the school. He has already banned hats and jewelry.

Mr. Mickens asked senior boys to wear ties and dress shirts on Fridays. The dress code will be extended to all grades by February. Eventually it will be in effect every day of the week. A code for girls is planned for next year.

Ties From Baltimore

Mr. Mickens's plans drew attention around the country, and a dozen packages of donated shirts and ties were heaped on the stage. "These are less than a quarter of the boxes of shirts and ties people from Baltimore and San Francisco, Maine, Connecticut and right here in Brooklyn have sent to you," he said.

The donations included shirts and ties from the New York Jets and Remington Apparel and an offer from Victor Kiam, owner of Remington Products, to buy a tie for every city pupil, he said. The offers will insure that "no student will fail to meet the code simply because he can't afford to" Mr. Mickens said.

Another senior, Scott Gold, said peer pressure would help the code. "When the juniors see the seniors are doing it, they'll want to be down," he explained, using the slang term for in fashion.

One student in a hooded sweatshirt said he would not follow the dress code "because everyone should have the right to wear whatever they want to."

"It's not what you have on here," he said, then tapped his temple, "but what you have up here that counts."

But Mr. Gold said he liked the plan because "it's what Mr. Mickens wants and because it makes us feel special."

"I have friends who go to other schools and they've been laughing at me a little bit," he said, "but I think deep inside, they wish they went to Boys and Girls."

8.   Movies are rated as a guide for potential viewers. The movie-rating scheme has been revised numerous times over the decades. What problem(s) does the movie-rating system address? If you conclude that the current system addresses one or more problems, how could the rating system be improved? What problems would likely be generated if the rating system were eliminated?

9.   Ben J. Wattenberg and Richard M. Scammon wrote "Black Progress and Liberal Rhetoric," and it was published in the April 1973 issue of *Commentary* (55, no. 4). Letters to the editor poured in and were published in subsequent issues. The authors were arguing that the black population of the United States had made significant progress under President Johnson's Great Society programs, and that criticism by liberals of the lack of progress was misguided and only served to undermine the liberal cause. The authors offer a battery of statistics to show progress had indeed taken place. Put yourself back in 1973 and write a 20-page, double-spaced, typed analysis that includes the following:

(a)   An attempt to describe the authors' overall concept of "progress."

(b)   A list of the key (at least six) dimensions to that concept (i.e., "moving into the middle class").

(c)   A critique, for each dimension, of the measures used to operationalize the concept. Here you should be very specific about the adequacy, reliability, and validity of their statistics.

(d)   Your own concept of "progress."

(e)   Dimensions of your own concept.

(f)   Specific statistics that would measure your dimensions. Here you should pay particular attention to the availability of data and the difficulty of generating them if they are unavailable.

10.   Identify a local problem in which improvement looks like decline. Verify, define, and detail the problem.

11.   Newspaper and television coverage of missing children has heightened America's interest in and concern for child kidnapping. Supermarkets now sell do-it-yourself fingerprint kits, child kidnapping insurance is available, and parents are forming networks of "safe houses" where children can find protection from threatening strangers. Various

sources have reported that 50,000 children are kidnapped each year. Is this an accurate estimate? Where did it originate? Conduct your own back-of-the-envelope calculation to estimate the number of children kidnapped each year. Specify your definition of child kidnapping. Use several methods to derive estimates of the number of children kidnapped each year. Defend your most likely estimate.

12. In fewer than two working hours for each, using back-of-the-envelope calculation methods and very specific operational definitions, attempt to measure:

(a) The number of unemployed minority teenagers in the city of Boston at the present time

(b) The number of homeless people in Seattle, Washington, at the present time

(c) The number of families in California who own second homes, used primarily for vacations

(d) The number of smokers versus nonsmokers in the city of Atlanta

Document your calculations in a written form that will allow the reader to follow every step of your work. Should you find official estimates of the sizes of these subpopulations, be sure to investigate thoroughly how the estimates were derived.

13. An express transit system (transitway) is proposed for construction paralleling for 12 miles the major freeway access to the downtown of a large metropolitan area. The proposal is in response to a complaint that there is traffic congestion for both autos and buses on the existing freeway during the peak hours. This two-lane bus-only freeway is projected to relieve this congestion. Here are some data:

Present one-way peak traffic volume	10,000	passengers per hour
Present modal split	2.5%	passengers on bus
	97.5%	passengers in autos
Maximum freeway capacity without delay	5,250	auto lengths per hour
Ratio of bus to auto vehicle lengths	1.6	autos per bus
Maximum one-way transitway capacity without delay	1,000	auto lengths per hour
Present occupancy rates	1.3	persons per auto
	50	persons per bus

(a) Perform back-of-the-envelope calculations on these data and comment about the dimensions of the existing problem and the way it has been defined.

(b) Explore alternative problem definitions.

(c) What data would you need next to identify the magnitude of this problem for your locale?

14. A city is attempting to rehabilitate much of its decaying sewer system. The Environmental Protection Agency (EPA) has offered the city two basic strategies. The first is 55% federal funding for conventional treatment facilities. Although this funding is not certain (all big-city projects get scored and ranked), it is far more certain than the alternative. The alternative is a new experimental program to which the city can apply. The city's planners and engineers feel that the types of technology that can be employed here are far superior and cheaper to the city in the long run than conventional treatment works. The decision dilemma is that, because this is an experimental program, federal funding is less likely. The four possible outcomes and their probabilities are as follows:

- Submit conventional proposal/EPA approves: $P = 0.9$
- Submit conventional proposal/EPA disapproves: $P = 0.1$

    • Submit experimental proposal/EPA approves: $P = 0.4$
    • Submit experimental proposal/EPA disapproves: $P = 0.6$

The value for each of these outcomes has not been exactly quantified. However, it is clear that EPA disapproval of either proposal is worse than EPA approval of either. The city prefers approval of the experimental program over the conventional one. Disapproval of the conventional program proposal seems to be the worst possible outcome. Draw a diagram of the city's decision dilemma.

15. It has been proposed that a city become codeveloper of an office building with a private real estate firm. Through this mechanism the city hopes to encourage more in-city office activity rather than have the activity develop in the suburbs. It is proposed that the city use for the project a vacant parcel of land it owns, and that it use its tax-exempt status to float bonds to pay for 50% of the project. In return, the city will receive the property taxes generated by the building, and the private developer will pay back the full cost of the bonds over a 20-year period. If, however, the office development fails, the city assumes payment of the bonds. Diagram this decision dilemma with all decision, uncertainty, and terminal nodes.

16. A city is considering hosting a future Summer Olympics. The decision to go ahead with putting together a proposal has been left in the hands of the mayor, who asks for your advice. You do some preliminary analysis and come up with the following points: To do nothing at this time will involve no cost to the city, but obviously there will be no gain. Putting together a viable bid for the games will cost the city $500,000 in staff time and expenses. Should the city lose its bid, there will be no further costs. Should the city win, the outcomes can vary, but they can be summarized by writing a most optimistic and a most pessimistic scenario. The most optimistic appears to cost the city $100 million more (beyond the $500,000) but returns to it $135 million in revenues. The most pessimistic costs the city $75 million more and returns $65 million. The probability of getting the optimistic is 0.6 and of getting the pessimistic is 0.4 or $(1.0 - 0.6)$. The probability of getting the Olympics is 0.3. Diagram this decision dilemma.

17. Think about several decisions facing you at the present time. They could be trivial, like which shoes to wear to an upcoming party, or important, like whether or not to marry or purchase a home. Choose one of these situations, and diagram it with all decision, uncertainty, and terminal nodes.

18. A city wishes to provide subsidized loans to poorer homeowners whose houses are *badly deteriorated*. Develop a detailed operational definition for the concept of a *badly deteriorated home* that will be functional in this situation.

19. A state wishes to provide monies to a limited number of its cities to help them attract and retain jobs. It wishes to identify 5% of the cities in the state as most in need. The term used to describe these cities has been *economically depressed*. Develop an operational definition for *economically depressed* cities in this context.

20. There have been numerous attempts to rate the cities in the United States in terms of their acceptability as places to live. Most of these attempts use 10 or 12 dimensions of a city and sum the results for each of the dimensions into an overall score for each city. Invariably, one of the dimensions used involves climate. In this context, develop an operational definition for *pleasant climate* that could be used to rank the cities.

21. For Exercises 18, 19, and 20 above, find a source of data that would permit you to measure your operational definition for the analytic unit being employed (i.e., houses, cities, and cities again).

22. For decades there has been a continuing dispute about the extent of poverty in the United States. Define *poverty* and develop some preliminary statistical data documenting the existence of poverty, given your definition, in the United States at present.

23. Working together with an instructor or a colleague who is also using this book, identify a problem that seems to be confronting one of your local governments. Following closely our description of a first-cut analysis, write one on the problem you chose.

24. You are familiar with the information contained in the following paragraph because of your position as an analyst for the Ambrosia County Board of Commissioners. Develop a one-page problem statement, using the principles contained in Chapter 4. Do not attempt a lengthy political analysis, as you do not have enough information. Your first-cut analysis will be used to convince the commission chair of a need for commission action.

Ambrosia County is constructing a major new sewage treatment plant. Ambrosia County has the ability to collect taxes on real property to finance public capital improvements. So far, $21 million in federal funds and $8.4 million in state funds have been committed to the project. Ambrosia County can float bond issues for water and sewer projects by passing two resolutions, 30 days apart, to this effect. The bond sale must occur no sooner than 30 days following the second resolution. Ambrosia County would probably have to pay at least 14% interest on 20-year general-obligation bonds floated before the end of the year. The sewerage project has been under way for about 18 months. For the first six months—the planning phase—billings were running about $70,000 a month. During the design phase, lasting about five months, billings were about $28,000 a month for professional design services. Although minor expenditures continue to be charged to the planning and design accounts, most of the billings for the past seven months have been for construction. The billings ran like this: month 1, $1.4 million; month 2, $1.82 million; month 3, $2.66 million; month 4, $3.78 million; month 5, $3.92 million; month 6, $4.34 million; month 7, $4.76 million. It is now July. The local matching funds available in Ambrosia County's budget last year amounted to $7 million. Taxes are due January 1, and after they are collected are invested in a way so as to be readily available for withdrawals needed to pay contractors, but still earning interest until needed. This year $16.8 million was budgeted, again available January 1. The federal and state funds are also accessible as needed. The project was originally intended to take 36 months to complete but has been running substantially ahead of schedule since the construction phase began. When the planning phase was completed, the total cost of the project was estimated to cost $75.6 million in uninflated dollars. Inflation has been running at about 12% a year. Next year's budget has not yet been set but will be decided in November, and tax dollars will again be available January 1.

Chapter Five

Establishing Evaluation Criteria

We outlined the importance of establishing evaluation criteria in our discussion of the policy analysis process. Analysts use evaluation criteria to compare alternatives and judge which will be acceptable to relevant constituencies. By stating the evaluation criteria before comparing alternatives, the analyst establishes rules to follow and reduces the temptation to rationalize favorite options. How does the analyst work with decision makers to identify and establish evaluation criteria, and how is their achievement measured? These are the subjects of this chapter.

Criteria are what we use to guide making a decision. They can be "measures, rules, and standards . . . all those attributes, objectives, or goals which have been judged relevant in a given decision situation by a particular decision maker" (individual or group).[1] To recapitulate what we've said earlier about the policy analysis process and the place of criteria in that process, we begin by defining the problem and determining the general goals and more specific, measurable objectives of our client. Once we know what is desired, we seek alternative ways of attaining the goals and objectives. The consequences of selecting each of the various alternatives are then estimated. These impacts might include financial costs and benefits, political consequences, legal issues, and so on. *Criteria* are used to help us compare the alternatives. Quade defines a criterion as the standard by

[1] Milan Zeleny, *Multiple Criteria Decision Making* (New York: McGraw-Hill, 1982), p. 17.

which we can rank the alternatives in order of preference, using the information uncovered about their impacts.[2] *Measures* are used to operationalize the criteria. To *operationalize* means to make more specific for the sake of consistency. "The (operational) definition should be sufficiently precise that all persons using the procedure will achieve the same results."[3] Notice that these terms move from the more abstract and client oriented to the more practical and analyst oriented. In order, they are goals, objectives, evaluation criteria, and measures. Although not all policy analysts and planners distinguish a unique meaning for each of these terms, we feel it is helpful to think of these terms hierarchically. In Chapter 4 we discussed the process of "identifying the problem." This process is intimately connected with the process of developing evaluation criteria. Especially relevant is the discussion of creating valid operational definitions, because that is exactly what we do when we create measures for evaluation criteria. First, let us briefly define the four terms, and then illustrate the definitions with an example.

Goals.   Formally and broadly worded statements about what we desire to achieve in the long run.

Objectives.   More focused and concretely worded statements about end states, most usually with a time dimension and a client population specified.

Criteria.   Specific statements about the dimensions of the objectives that will be used to evaluate alternative policies or programs. Important dimensions include cost, benefit, effectiveness, risk, political viability, administrative ease, legality, uncertainty, equity, and timing.

Measures.   Tangible, if not quantitative, operational definitions of criteria. Each criterion should have multiple measures associated with it. Measures can be used comparatively over time on the same problem, or over space, comparing different places with the same problem, in order to judge how close alternatives come to satisfying stated criteria.

As an example, we will use the problem of water pollution in the rivers of a metropolitan area. The *goal,* often stated by public officials, is to "clean up our rivers and make them safe and usable." One *objective* could be to make the segment of the Challoochee River from the county line north to Beaver Dam fit for fishing for nongame fish (bullheads, carp, and sunfish). One group of *criteria* addressing this objective would relate to effectiveness: Would the program actually make it possible for those fish to survive in that environment? Changes to

[2] Edward S. Quade, *Analysis for Public Decisions*, 2nd ed. (New York: Elsevier Scientific, 1982), p. 31.
[3] Hubert M. Blalock, Jr., *Social Statistics*, 2nd ed. rev. (New York: McGraw-Hill, 1979), p. 12.

water quality, the amount and variation of flow, and other uses of the water and stream banks might be relevant. One *measure* of effectiveness in altering water quality might be the level of dissolved oxygen present in this particular river segment—for example, 5 milligrams per liter might be chosen as a minimum necessary to permit these types of fish to survive.

The process of establishing goals, objectives, criteria, and measures is essential if we are to judge whether a proposed program or policy is worth undertaking and whether it is preferable to another proposal. Whether the analyst works in isolation on this process or interacts with the client is an important and often-asked question.

THE PROCESS OF ESTABLISHING EVALUATION CRITERIA

Clearly it is not sufficient for the analyst to devise a list of criteria and determine their relative importance. These activities must be undertaken in concert with groups and individuals involved in the decision process. A number of technical methods for dealing with multiple and conflicting criteria have been devised, and we will discuss them later. The first step, though, is to define and establish acceptable and useful criteria. The role of the analyst includes helping the decision maker to clarify what is sought and to define the objectives so that alternatives can be designed. If the objectives have not been specified properly, the alternatives designed will be inappropriate and the recommended alternative will not solve the real problem.

In practice, however, decision makers may not be willing to establish clear evaluation criteria. They may not wish to define such terms as *equity* or *efficiency*, and they may not want the analyst to predict how much unemployment would be reduced by a favored program or the relationship between the benefits from two competing programs. The reasons are obvious. Politicians must serve the interests of diverse groups; they do not want to support the program favored by one group at the risk of alienating another group. They know from experience that programs are rarely implemented as designed and that outcomes are seldom as projected, and they do not want to be tied to one solution or program. As times change, and as the needs of constituencies change, politicians want to be able to respond without being committed to old ideas.

These desires often manifest themselves in two ways. The first is that often the political process fosters the development of purposefully vague, singular objectives: "the economic development of city X," for example. The second is that often a proposed policy or program has several objectives, the objectives each have several related criteria, and each of the criteria has several associated measures.

Braybrooke and Lindblom[4] called the first problem the "naive criteria"

---

[4]David Braybrooke and Charles E. Lindblom, *A Strategy of Decision* (New York: Free Press, 1963), pp. 6–8.

evaluation method. Although they quickly dismiss the method, unfortunately it can still be found in practice. They object to the approach because it involves merely announcing general values such as "security" and "employment" that are supposed to lead to recommendations. They also object to merely postulating measures for these values—for example, reducing unemployment to a certain level. They predict that this results in unexpected and significant conflicts among the stated criteria and the surfacing of other relevant criteria. Braybrooke and Lindblom further criticize this method because it gives no clue to the source, history, or relevance of the values presented. They argue that to succeed, such a method would have to anticipate difficulties, beginning with conflicting values and differences of opinion. Ranking the criteria to produce a set of "naive priorities" considers the conflicting-values problem but helps little when gains in one area have to be traded off against losses in another area, or when gains on a lower-ranked criterion could be had if gains on a higher-ranked criterion were forgone. The ranking also does not help in deciding among policies that offer different combinations of benefits or that meet criteria to different degrees.[5]

The second common problem analysts have with politicians is their unwillingness to discard multiple, conflicting objectives.[6] Analysts in the public sector may be employed by one body to serve the needs of another group, for example, the community development planner employed by the planning department but assigned to work for a specific neighborhood. Such a person may have to wrestle with the objectives of several groups: the city agency, the neighborhood, and professional planners and analysts. In this case, the objectives of a given program might include physically improving residences in the neighborhood, improving the agency's visibility in the neighborhood, expending program funds on schedule, minimizing cost overruns, and changing neighbors' attitudes toward their physical surroundings. For each of these objectives a set of criteria and multiple measures would have to be designed.

Is it appropriate for the analyst to step in and decide among competing objectives, criteria, or measures? The politician-planner with senior standing would more likely be able to do so than a technician-planner with junior standing. But beyond whether it is possible, is it ethical? In Chapter 2 we discussed the issue of ethics in analysis and found that ethical decisions were not always easy to specify and make, and moreover, what is viewed as ethical evolves over time. The American Institute of Certified Planners has a Code of Ethics and Professional Conduct that is similar to that of other professions. Over the years the code has been revised and updated. In the 1977 version, the code stated that planners are experts who "attempt to provide public . . . decision makers with the best possible information, analysis, and recommendations to promote the

---

[5] Ibid., pp. 6–8.

[6] For methodological help in this area, see Edward S. Quade, "Objectives, Constraints, and Alternatives," in *Handbook of Systems Analysis: Overview of Uses, Procedures, Applications, and Practice*, ed. Hugh J. Miser and Edward S. Quade (New York: North Holland, 1985), pp. 171–89.

public welfare."[7] According to Howe and Kaufman, "Such a definition would argue that planners should avoid taking upon themselves the right to define the goals that guide the definition and solution of problems, or trying to openly and actively get their own particular views adopted in the political system. They should have a restrictive view of the scope of planning."[8] Note however, that this view refers to general goals. The more specific criteria and measures are generally considered well within the analyst's legitimate sphere of influence. Additionally, Howe and Kaufman point out that the majority of professional planners they surveyed violate this code often in practice. In fact, one of the cornerstones of the profession has been its historic concern with social responsibility. Thus, when social concerns are present, most planners opt for a more political than simply technical role. In fact, the profession has been drifting away from its technician-only role model for years. Only about 30% of the respondents to the Howe and Kaufman survey describe their roles that way.[9]

Recent personal interviews have also revealed that planners act in more than technical ways, are involved in political and ethical issues, and take positions on competing objectives.[10] Moreover, the current AICP code recognizes this conflict between serving the client and serving the public interest: "A planner owes diligent, creative, independent and competent performance of work in pursuit of the client's or employer's interest. Such performance should be consistent with the planner's faithful service to the public interest."[11] Your decisions regarding competing objectives will surely be shaped by personal as well as professional ethics.

Braybrooke and Lindblom also argue that the more sophisticated concepts from economics that purport to solve the problem of multiple objectives, such as the rational-deductive ideal and the welfare function, cannot be realized and are not helpful.[12] They criticize these methods because they require information that cannot be obtained, cannot cope with real-world political problems, and confuse individual and social preferences—problems that we have discussed in earlier chapters. The early works of Simon,[13] March and Simon,[14] Braybrooke

[7] American Institute of Planners, *Planning Policies* (Washington, DC: Author, 1977), p. 2.

[8] Elizabeth Howe and Jerome Kaufman, "The Ethics of Contemporary American Planners," *Journal of the American Planning Association* 45, no. 3 (July 1979), 253.

[9] Ibid., p. 253.

[10] Jerome L. Kaufman, "Hamelethics in Planning: To Do or Not to Do," *Business and Professional Ethics Journal* 6, no. 2 (1989), 66–77.

[11] American Institute of Certified Planners, "AICP Code of Ethics and Professional Conduct," *1990/91 Roster* (Washington, DC: Author, 1990), p. iv.

[12] Braybrooke and Lindblom, *A Strategy of Decision*, pp. 9–16.

[13] Herbert A. Simon, *Administrative Behavior: A Study of Decision-Making Processes in Administrative Organizations*, 3rd ed. (New York: Free Press, 1976; 1st ed., New York: Macmillan, 1947). Although the first edition of *Administration Behavior* was published in 1947, the book was essentially completed in 1942 (1976, p. ix).

[14] James G. March and Herbert A. Simon, *Organizations* (New York: Wiley, 1958).

and Lindblom,[15] then Wildavsky,[16] and Rondinelli,[17] and later Alexander,[18] and Formaini[19] largely discredited the rational-deductive ideal. In Chapter 8 we will discuss methods that seek with varying degrees of success to overcome the problem of multiple objectives, criteria, and measures.

Because decision makers do not wish to establish clear evaluation criteria does not mean that they necessarily want to be free to change directions from week to week. Rather, they want to be able to head in a general direction, to aim toward a goal, but use a variety of ways to get there. You may have to initiate the analysis with only a vague idea of what is sought, clarifying the details of the alternatives as the analysis progresses. Arriving near the target, not necessarily on it, is often acceptable to the decision maker. Analysts and evaluators, on the other hand, would like to have specific criteria against which to measure progress toward goals and objectives.

How does the analyst discover criteria? What types of criteria should be considered? How do we know when the relevant criteria have been discovered? There is, of course, no formula that can be applied here; defining criteria is learned by doing, by interacting with clients, and by working through the analysis. New criteria will be discovered as old criteria are examined.

Except in the case where one is acting as a citizen-analyst, the primary source of program objectives and evaluation criteria is one's client or employer. However, clients may need help expressing these objectives and criteria, and even where the client has stated explicit criteria, the analyst may feel it is necessary to introduce additional objectives and criteria or revise existing ones.

How does the analyst know when all relevant criteria have been identified? Experience helps, but several types of criteria apply in virtually all policy analyses. We discuss these below, but first we need to cover a number of underlying economic concepts that we hope even the reader with a background in economics will review.

SEVERAL IMPORTANT ECONOMIC CONCEPTS

A number of concepts that appear repeatedly in policy analysis are drawn from the field of microeconomics. These concepts need to become an integral part of the analyst's thought process and vocabulary. We introduce the concepts here

[15] Braybrooke and Lindblom, *A Strategy of Decision.*

[16] Aaron Wildavsky, "If Planning Is Everything, Maybe It's Nothing," *Policy Sciences* 4, no. 2 (June 1973), 127–53.

[17] Dennis A. Rondinelli, "Urban Planning as Policy Analysis: Management of Urban Change," *Journal of the American Institute of Planners* 39, no. 1 (January 1973), 13.

[18] Ernest R. Alexander, "After Rationality, What? A Review of Responses to Paradigm Breakdown," *Journal of the American Planning Association* 50, no. 1 (Winter 1984), 62–69.

[19] Robert Formaini, *The Myth of Scientific Public Policy* (New Brunswick, NJ: Transaction Books, 1990).

with the advice that the student who plans to pursue the study of policy analysis should take courses in the economics of policy analysis. Apgar and Brown have prepared a useful introduction to the topic.[20]

The Free-Market Model

Many prescriptions for change as well as analytical models used by economists rely on the concept of the free, or perfect, market. It is when markets fail to achieve public objectives that governments enter to provide basic goods or services or to tax or regulate private interests. It is essential, then, for the student of policy planning to understand the concept of a free market and the factors that can cause these perfect conditions to deteriorate and require governmental intervention.

An assumption of the perfect-market model is that, by trading, people move incrementally toward greater welfare for everyone. This happens every time a trade makes one person better off and no person worse off. This is called the *Pareto criterion*. Under perfect conditions, say economists, free competition using a price system will produce a condition in which no one can be made better off without someone being made worse off. This is called the *Pareto optimum*. The concept can be illustrated using producers or consumers: two producers, one digging clams and another making shovels, or two consumers, one favoring wine and another cheese. It should be obvious that at a very basic level both can be made better off through exchange. MacRae and Wilde illustrate this concept in a useful way by noting an example developed by Buchanan:

> In their dormitory the living conditions are identical for both roommates and therefore a matter for joint decision, unless a decision rule such as that of seniority is somehow imposed. If one person wishes the room temperature to be 75° and the other prefers 65°, one or both will be unhappy with the outcome regardless of the ultimate thermometer reading. Similarly, the two roommates might have different preferred times for turning out the lights at night. In such circumstances it becomes possible for the students to set up a "market" for temperatures and lights-out times and thereby to trade off these two goods according to their relative importance for each person. As Buchanan describes the result,
>
> *By simultaneously considering two variables rather than each variable separately, the possibility of mutual agreement between the two parties is enhanced and there is less need for reliance on arbitrary decision rules. The results are more efficient than under such rules, in that the preferences of the parties are more fully satisfied.*[21]

[20] William C. Apgar and H. James Brown, *Microeconomics and Public Policy* (Glenview, IL: Scott, Foresman, 1987); see also Lee S. Friedman, *Microeconomic Policy Analysis* (New York: McGraw-Hill, 1984).

[21] James M. Buchanan, *The Demand and Supply of Public Goods* (Chicago: Rand McNally, 1968), pp. 102–108, quoted in Duncan MacRae, Jr., and James A. Wilde, *Policy Analysis for Public Decisions* (North Scituate, MA: Duxbury Press, 1979), p. 160; but for a criticism of the Pareto criterion see David C. Paris and James F. Reynolds, *The Logic of Policy Inquiry* (New York: Longman, 1983), pp. 79–109.

This last phrase of Buchanan's is important because it reveals the weight that economists place on the ability of a system to satisfy the preferences of participants. This quality is most clearly evident in economists' use of the term *efficiency*. "An economic system responsible for deciding which goods and services will be produced will be judged to be more or less 'efficient' depending on how closely this allocation of resources corresponds to the preferences of consumers and producers."[22] Although perfect competition in a free market may yield the most efficient allocation of a society's resources, it won't necessarily yield an allocation that all will judge as equitable. Obviously, in order to participate in exchanges in the marketplace, an individual must have resources to exchange.

Some knowledge of the workings of the free-market model, and of the dynamics of supply and demand, is necessary for policy planners and analysts. This is so because they must be able to identify when free markets fail and government intervention is necessary, and because as a supplier of goods and services itself, the public sector needs to be able to judge the efficiency of its policies. There are numerous reasons why the free market can fail as a device for the optimal expression of consumer preferences and allocation of society's resources. By far the most important condition for a free market is the existence of pure competition. It must not be possible for any one actor or small group to cause changes in the market (e.g., prices or supply of products) through its actions. Monopolies are such actors. However, other conditions of the market may also cause less than ideally competitive situations. Rules and regulations in force to protect consumers and producers, such as labor unions, patents, or professional licensing procedures, can have market-distorting effects. Connected to the concept of pure competition is the requirement that complete information must be available to those in the market or considering entering it. Such information obviously includes prices of commodities but may also include other conditions about the marketplace. If complete information is not available to all producers and consumers, then the market mechanism can fail.

A fourth reason for market failure is the cost of transactions. As indicated in Buchanan's example, free trade is the central mechanism of a free market. But as the example also shows, there is effort involved in those exchanges. If the problem were expanded beyond the roommates to the entire dormitory, the exchanges could become extremely time-consuming. The gain in efficiency would be weighed against the cost of time involved in transactions. However, the ideal model presumes no transaction costs. A fifth reason why the market may fail is its inability to stop those who have not paid for a good from using it, preventing the price system from allocating resources efficiently. National defense is the classic example of this kind of public good, but there are many other examples of public goods or services from which nonpayers cannot be excluded, yet are essential and that individuals cannot buy independently. A last reason for the failure of markets is that of externalities: exchanges that affect others

[22] MacRae and Wilde, *Policy Analysis for Public Decisions*, p. 160.

than the producer and consumer directly involved. Externalities can be either negative or positive. This is such an important topic that we'll discuss it separately in a later section.

Costs

The concept of cost is central to policy analysis. Economists view costs as resources employed. Nearly every public action that can be imagined involves the use of resources. Those resources, be they tax dollars or other types of resources, must usually be diverted from other uses. Thus, it has been argued that the term *opportunity cost* be substituted for the simpler term *cost* in policy analysis.[23] Clearly, the results of analysis might be very different if some of the major resources to be employed were currently idle. According to Bickner,[24] a common pitfall in policy analysis is "ignoring costs altogether"—for example, forsaking cost for some very desirable goal: "Price is no object." More subtle dangers include counting only a portion of total program costs. Several common errors are made. The first is to identify program costs as synonymous with cash outlays—what government pays directly for the endeavor. This is seldom the only cost connected with a program. A second error is to identify and count only those costs that are monetarizable. Most public actions involve costs that are not monetarizable, and some that are not tangible. However, these costs may still be very important. Long-run costs also are often ignored.

Another pitfall is to ignore costs when they fall to people or governments outside the client's concern. A very common example of this is when analysts count only the local government's costs as the total cost of the project and weigh them against the total benefit accruing to the local unit of government. Cost-sharing from other levels of government could even make building pyramids look desirable if a local government counted only its own costs. If our actions have effects that fall outside our client's purview, be they benefits or costs, they should not be ignored. Closely connected to this idea is the one that ascribes equal value to each dollar of cost (or benefit) no matter what its origin. This is a question of equity: Is a dollar of impact on one group equal to a dollar on another?[25] Many people presume that the actual cost of a proposal is a fact that merely needs to be established, whereas benefits or effects are much more complex and difficult concepts to measure. In fact, there is seldom a clear single answer to what a proposal's costs are, or an easy method for establishing them. Three other cost-related issues, discussed below, are *marginal costs, sunk costs*, and *opportunity costs.*

For any proposal the analyst must first measure all direct costs. Included

---

[23] Apgar and Brown, *Microeconomics and Public Policy*, p. 4.

[24] Robert E. Bickner, "Pitfalls in the Analysis of Costs," in *Pitfalls of Analysis*, ed. Giandomenico Majone and Edward S. Quade (New York: Wiley, 1980), p. 57.

[25] For an approach to showing differential impact, see Michael J. Frost, *How to Use Cost Benefit Analysis in Project Appraisal*, 2nd ed. (New York: Wiley, 1975), chap. 8.

are one-time fixed costs, borrowing costs, and operating and maintenance costs. These should be aggregated for the duration of the program, which is usually the time frame chosen to analyze the proposal. For many types of evaluations the analyst will also wish to measure indirect costs, that is, the costs connected to the impact of the proposal (e.g., building a parking garage may cause increased downtown traffic and its attendant costs). These indirect costs include those to be experienced by our client or governmental unit and its population, as well as those to be felt by other governments or populations. These may or may not be tangible or monetarizable.

A final warning about the concept of costs is in order. Because some costs are easily identified and monetarizable, policy analysts are attracted to them as an item worthy of much analytical time, and indeed they are. But don't forget the larger picture, which includes answering these questions: Is this an effective proposal, what are its impacts, on whom, and is it feasible? Planning and policy analysis must go far beyond cost analysis if it is to yield rich information for decision makers.

Benefits

Benefits are really the flip side of costs. In fact, sometimes they are referred to as negative costs (cost savings). Benefits may be associated, but not necessarily, with the goals of a proposal—the impacts the client wanted to achieve. Many of the observations we will make about costs apply equally well to benefits. Benefits can be direct and indirect, tangible or not, monetarizable or not, ascribable to the client's governmental unit or not, and short term or long term. Many benefits are easily measured because they have a value in the marketplace. That is, the benefit is a good or service that is generally bought and sold and whose price can be relatively easily established, presuming a market without major distortions. (See the discussion of "the free-market model.")

A method for establishing the value of benefits (or costs) when market prices are unavailable or distorted is through the use of *shadow prices*. Shadow prices are usually derived by establishing the value of the benefits in another context, a context that is viewed as a perfectly competitive market. An example is provided by a benefit whose market price is distorted by a type of tax. The *shadow* or *accounting price* of the good would be its economic value free of the distortion caused by taxation. Shadow-pricing techniques have been used, for example, to establish the value of publicly provided recreational benefits that have no established market value.

A critical issue in establishing the benefits of a public action is, of course, forecasting the impact of the action with a level of certainty. But even if that can be done, the task of valuing those impacts remains.[26] The same is true of costs.

---

[26] On the problem of valuation, see Winston Harrington, "Valuing the Environment," *Journal of Policy Analysis and Management* 7, no. 4 (Fall 1988), 722–26.

Standing

During the past several years, Whittington and MacRae have raised the issue of standing in cost-benefit analysis. *Standing*, in this context, refers to who is to be considered when costs and benefits are computed. That is, who has the right to be included in the set of individuals or groups whose changes in welfare or utility are counted when the pros and cons of alternatives are estimated?[27]

While the issue of who has standing is a crucial assumption that must be made by analysts, it has seldom been discussed explicitly. The usual assumption is that all persons within a country's boundaries are to be included in a cost-benefit analysis, if they have at least some rights of citizenship. For example, the costs and benefits to children are counted even though they do not have the right to vote. Some economists have argued that under this conceptualization, the costs and benefits to citizens of other countries ought *not* to be counted. This definition, based on inclusion because of citizenship, was generally accepted and did not cause much concern in the analytic community until recently. In some cases the definition even made marginal projects feasible by spreading the benefits and costs across large numbers of citizens.[28]

As the range of issues addressed by planners and analysts has expanded, the question of whose welfare or utility should be counted also has been more widely considered. Moreover, President Reagan's Executive Order 12291 expanded the use of cost-benefit criteria to include all major regulations, and this also increased the number of problems in which the issue of standing arises.[29] Some typical issue areas include the following:[30]

- Should fetuses have standing in a study of increased eligibility of recipients of Aid to Families with Dependent Children to receive subsidized abortions?
- Should the benefits that children of illegal aliens receive from education be considered in a social cost-benefit analysis of educational policy?
- If a proposed project in the United States will have a polluting effect on Canada, should those effects be counted?
- If the criterion is the ability to vote, then what about the gains to criminals from crimes? Can standing be withheld from convicted criminals?

---

[27] Dale Whittington and Duncan MacRae, Jr., "The Issue of Standing in Cost-Benefit Analysis," *Journal of Policy Analysis and Management* 5, no. 4 (Summer 1986), 669. This is also an issue in program evaluation; see Egon G. Guba and Yvonna S. Lincoln, "The Countenances of Fourth-Generation Evaluation: Description, Judgment, and Negotiation," in *The Politics of Program Evaluation*, ed. Dennis J. Palumbo (Newbury Park, CA: Sage, 1987), pp. 202–34.

[28] Whittington and MacRae, "Issue of Standing in Cost-Benefit Analysis," pp. 666–67.

[29] Duncan MacRae, Jr., and Dale Whittington, "Assessing Preferences in Cost-Benefit Analysis: Reflections on Rural Water Supply Evaluation in Haiti," *Journal of Policy Analysis and Management* 7, no. 2 (Winter 1988), 246.

[30] Whittington and MacRae, "Issue of Standing in Cost-Benefit Analysis," pp. 667–68, 674; and William N. Trumbull, "Who Has Standing in Cost-Benefit Analysis?" *Journal of Policy Analysis and Management* 9, no. 2 (Spring 1990), 202.

- Should gains to the poor be weighted more heavily than gains to the rich, so that a premium is placed on projects that benefit the poor at the expense of the rich?
- In the case of future generations, should the benefits and costs to as yet unborn persons be considered in the evaluation of a program to develop alternative power sources?

In policy analysis, the question of standing can be interpreted in at least four ways. At the level of the greatest individual involvement, it means the right to represent one's own preferences; that is, to be part of the decision-making process. A second and broader interpretation is the right to have one's preferences included in a utilitarian aggregation of welfare in which preferences are inferred from demand data or surveys, or estimated in other ways in which the preferences of individuals can be evaluated numerically, even if the individuals do not personally express them. A third concept is an even more inclusive consideration of the preferences of persons who may at present not be able to express their preferences, such as infants and future generations. A fourth notion of standing is the right to have one's preferences represented by someone else even if the person represented does not participate in selecting who is to represent him or her; for example, the inclusion of children's demand in parents' willingness to pay for a good or service.[31]

There is no clear answer to the issue of standing, although at least three have been proposed.

Trumbull believes that we should determine standing by applying the potential Pareto-optimal principle, which says that the policy must have the potential to make at least someone better off without making any one else worse off. He argues that the application of the potential Pareto principle requires that questions regarding standing be answered in specific ways, and that ethical deliberations are not necessary for conducting a cost-benefit analysis.[32]

In contrast, Whittington and MacRae say that rather than the principles of cost-benefit analysis determining who has standing, it should be the political and philosophical positions that underpin the issues that bear upon the decision. Also involved is the question of how competent the decision makers are to understand and use the concepts.[33]

Zerbe argues that the issue is really one of rights. That is, the issue is whose rights are uncertain at the margin. Zerbe holds that we cannot separate standing from the legal context.[34] He believes that the answers to standing will come from

---

[31] Whittington and MacRae, "Issue of Standing in Cost-Benefit Analysis," pp. 669–70.

[32] Trumbull, "Who Has Standing in Cost-Benefit Analysis?" pp. 201–18; and William N. Trumbull, "Reply to Whittington and MacRae," *Journal of Policy Analysis and Management* 9, no. 4 (Fall 1990), 548–50.

[33] Dale Whittington and Duncan MacRae, Jr., "Comment: Judgements about Who Has Standing in Cost-Benefit Analysis," *Journal of Policy Analysis and Management* 9, no. 4 (Fall 1990), 536.

[34] Richard O. Zerbe, Jr., "Does Benefit Cost Analysis Stand Alone? Rights and Standing," *Journal of Policy Analysis and Management* 10, no. 1 (Winter 1991), 96–105.

the legal and political systems, and that data from analysts can be used to describe the results of alternative assumptions about rights.

Trumbull believes that cost-benefit analysis is meant to direct resources to more highly valued uses and that this is simply a restatement of the potential Pareto principle. He thinks that most people agree that a project that shifts resources according to the potential Pareto principle would be preferable to one that shifted resources to a less valued project, as long as the former is no worse in all other relevant respects.[35] Trumbull lays out five principles for deciding what preferences have standing: Affected parties must have a willingness to pay, the perspective must be *ex ante* or forward-looking, the results of cost-benefit analysis must be evaluated within the context of other concerns, the evaluation has to be consistent with physical and social constraints, and the preferences of all who are affected must be counted.[36]

Following these principles, Trumbull has argued that cost-benefit analysis must accord standing to future generations and citizens of other countries, that certain individuals should not be given less than full standing in order to count for the distributional consequences of a project, and that preferences from a subset of the population cannot be used to determine costs and benefits. But he denies standing to current recipients of the benefits of existing programs, presumably because of the sunk-cost argument, and also to criminals, because the rules of the game are meant to circumscribe the behavior of criminals. He also holds that constraints that will continue to exist cannot be ignored because this would overvalue benefits to society.[37]

Economists who apply the strict potential Pareto principle say essentially that analysts are advisers who pass along this information to decision makers.[38] As we have argued in this book, this is too narrow a view of policy analysis. Single-criterion policy-evaluation methods have been shown to have limited usefulness, and even many multiobjective approaches fail to highlight the moral and ethical issues that are always part of policy analysis. The philosophical arguments about why some preferences should be included and others should be ignored have to be part of the calculus.[39]

Zerbe states that the outcome of cost-benefit analysis will normally depend upon who has the initial right and who therefore needs to attempt to bribe whom to give up the right.[40] Under this model, the existing system of rights sets the basis for the judgment. This allows us, for example, to answer the question about the illicit gains of the thief. Society and the courts are in agreement on the existing pattern of rights that says the thief has no rights to illicit gains.

---

[35] Trumbull, "Reply to Whittington and MacRae," p. 548.

[36] Trumbull, "Who Has Standing in Cost-Benefit Analysis?" p. 216.

[37] Ibid., pp. 204, 206, 216; and Trumbull, "Reply to Whittington and MacRae," p. 549.

[38] This point is also held by Whittington and MacRae, "Judgements about Who Has Standing," p. 537.

[39] MacRae and Whittington, "Assessing Preferences in Cost-Benefit Analysis," pp. 258–59.

[40] Zerbe, "Does Benefit Cost Analysis Stand Alone?" p. 97.

After the give-and-take among authors, they all agree to one degree or another that cost-benefit analysis is only one ingredient for arriving at a recommendation. We believe that determining standing involves judgment, not simply applying the potential Pareto principle. The issue is indeed more than a cost-benefit or economic calculation. It involves issues of ethics, rights, law, public discussion and debate, and politics. Moreover, in many cases the courts will decide who has standing.

In our minds, the final decision regarding who has standing is often contextual. Therefore, we recommend that when there is doubt, the analysis should be conducted both ways. The analyst should demonstrate to what extent the issue of standing affects the outcome of the analysis.

We recommend that the analyst conduct a sensitivity analysis, clearly state the assumptions, display the results, and discuss them thoroughly. It could be that the costs and benefits to the group or groups whose standing is in question are so small that the decision is not affected by whether they are included. On the other hand, standing could be a key variable, for example, if you are dealing with an environmental issue or a decision that involves children or persons with limited mental abilities.

The last word has not been written on standing, so it will be necessary to remain alert to the literature.

Externalities

An *externality* is a phenomenon or effect to which the market assigns no value, positive or negative, but that has a societal cost or benefit. For example, if a producer of bread pays the same price to wrap it in plastic or paper, the market price of the wrapping does not reflect the fact that the paper, being organic, likely can be manufactured with fewer environmental consequences and disposed of more cheaply than the plastic. Neither the bread manufacturer nor the customers pay for this, but city taxpayers will in increased environmental pollution and landfill costs. Externalities can be generated by both producers and consumers, and they can be positive and negative. A solution to this problem must be imposed by a unit of government. It can either require paper wrapping through regulation, encourage the manufacturer to use paper by granting inducements, or punish the producer with a higher tax on plastic wrapping material. Other examples of negative externalities include a noisy airport, a building left to deteriorate, and smoking in a public place. Positive externalities are a bit less obvious, but a good example is the responsible corporation that builds a handsome headquarters and opens the adjacent gardens to the public; neighbors who invest in the appearance of their property; and a very successful retail cheese store that, by being present, provides more business for the nearby wine emporium.

The goal of public policy is often to add the price of externalities into the market price. Examples might include requiring those who produce negative externalities to compensate those harmed, taxing those who are beneficiaries of positive externalities, taxing those who produce the negative externalities, and rewarding those who produce positive externalities. The principles of marginal economics can be used to decide on the correct amount of compensation to bring about the most efficient solution. In assessing these charges, government forces those who produce negative effects on others to bear the costs, thus using market forces to encourage producers to avoid these costs, sometimes in innovative ways that bring widespread social benefits.

Elasticity

The concept of *elasticity* is important to policy analysts because governments often consider the provision of goods and services to individuals and speculate about what their response levels will be at different prices. An example is the pricing of municipal water to encourage conservation while attempting to maximize the return to the publicly owned provider. Additionally, governments are often on the giving or receiving end of grants or subsidies intended to serve to induce them to engage in some kind of activity. The *price elasticity of demand* for a good or service is a measure of the kind of response that can be expected from a consumer, given a change in price. Specifically, it is the percentage change in the quantity of a given item purchased, divided by the percentage change in price of the same item. For most goods and services the price elasticity is negative: As the price rises, the volume purchased goes down. Economics textbooks often define price elasticity as the absolute value of the percentage change in consumption divided by the absolute value of the percentage change in price. This always results in a positive value, which makes it impossible to identify instances in which price and consumption changes are positively correlated. To avoid this confusion, we follow the approach of Apgar and Brown and compute elasticity using data unaltered by an absolute value conversion.[41]

Although the price elasticity of demand for most goods and services will be negative, the magnitude of the change can vary. If the percentage change in price is greater than the percentage change in quantity sold, then the commodity is said to be *price inelastic*; whereas if the percentage change in quantity sold is greater than that in price, then the commodity is said to be *price elastic*. When the changes are equivalent, the commodity is said to have unit elasticity. Thus, if elasticity is -0.3, demand for the item is not very responsive; whereas if elasticity is -3.0, demand is very responsive. It is also possible to have perfect elasticity, where an unlimited number may be sold at a given price; and also perfect inelasticity, where no matter what the price, only a limited quantity can be sold. It is important to specify the range of prices and volumes for which particular elasticities hold, since elasticity can vary with the magnitudes of price and volume.

[41] Apgar and Brown, *Microeconomics and Public Policy*, pp. 123–24.

Several other factors have important effects on a commodity's elasticity. These are the time period of analysis, the volume of a commodity, the number of possible consumers available in that time period, the availability of substitutes, and the size of the item in the consumer's budget. All things being equal, elasticity will increase with additional consumers or volumes of the commodity, the more substitutes, the longer the time period, and the larger the item is in the consumer's budget.

Another type of elasticity is *income elasticity*, the ratio of the percentage change in the quantity of a good or service demanded to the percentage change in consumer income. The measure shows whether consumers spend a greater or lesser share of their income on a particular good or service as income rises or falls. Potatoes are the classic low elasticity commodity, and luxury items, such as foreign travel, the high elasticity example.

It is often essential to be able to estimate the response of a hypothetical consumer, be it an individual or governmental unit, to an offer of a public good or service at a certain price. Most cities might not undertake repair of their failing sewer systems if the federal government offered to share only 10% of the cost, but if the federal share were 75%, most cities probably would. The pricing of public goods and services in order to achieve public objectives has become an important activity, and analysts must be capable of forecasting a market response.

Marginal Analysis

An important economic concept in policy analysis is the notion of *marginality*. It must be used in thinking about both the benefits and costs of public actions, but we will illustrate it here with costs. In order to produce a public action or program, a number of inputs are ordinarily used, labor and materials being two obvious ones. For any action, we can divide the costs into those that are fixed and those that are variable. *Fixed costs* do not vary with the scale of the public action, at least in the short run. An example might be the administrative cost connected with a proposed program to preserve agricultural land. For purposes of illustration we'll presume that the administrative cost of the program is fixed, at say $49,000 per year, whether 2,000 or 2 million acres of land are involved. In the short run the cost is fixed. *Variable costs* vary with the level of output. An example would be the cost of labor associated with solid-waste collection. To collect more waste, most programs would require more labor. The unit price of labor might remain constant over the range of the effort proposed; it might become cheaper (economies of scale) or more expensive (diseconomies of scale), or it might be cheaper at some points and more expensive at others.

When thinking of distributing the cost of a new program, planners can consider average and marginal costs. *Average costs* are simply total costs divided by total output, for example, $350 per ton of solid waste collected. A major pitfall for policy analysts is the use of average costs in analyzing decisions that involve additions to, or expansions of, existing programs. Marginal costs are generally more appropriate.

The *marginal cost* is incurred by the production of an additional unit of output. If, in our agricultural-land-preservation program, the total cost (fixed plus variable) of preserving 2 million acres is $560,000, and of preserving 2.1 million acres is $567,000, then the marginal cost of the additional 100,000 acres is $7,000, or 7 cents per acre. This is not the same as either of the average costs ($560,000/2 million acres = 28 cents per acre, or $567,000/2.1 million acres = 27 cents per acre). Marginal costs usually decline with additional output, but they need not necessarily do so.

In policy analysis and planning we wish to evaluate our client's world *with* the program and *without* the program. If our analysis is directed at a program expansion, the relevant cost is the marginal cost of expanding output from one level to another. Similarly, if implementing a project involves employing resources that are already built, their cost can be ignored. These are called *sunk costs*. A classic example of sunk costs can be illustrated by a proposal to expand access to an area of a city by widening the existing highway and using an existing bridge. The cost of the bridge, even if it were financed with bonds and not yet fully paid for, should not be part of the cost of the proposal. That cost is sunk. It would exist whether or not we went ahead with our improved-access program. Thus, the worlds with the program and without the program would both contain the bridge. There is no difference. Another example of sunk costs, or costs previously incurred, is that of land clearance for a development project. Presume a city spent $2 million to purchase and clear a downtown parcel. Let's say they then have only two proposals before them: do nothing and receive no benefits, or build a municipal parking garage for $4 million and receive $5 million in benefits. It would be an error to add sunk costs to the $4 million and assert total costs as $6 million and total benefits as $5 million and choose to do nothing. Had analysts estimated these costs before the $2 million was spent, their advice should have been to do nothing. But now that the cost is sunk and there is a fresh decision before them, the net benefit is $5 − $4 million = $1 million, and the advice should be to go ahead (all other things equal). There have been instances where the rule of not counting sunk costs has been abused so as to argue for poor projects. If proponents of a program completed a sizable part of it before the feasibility analysis was done, and then ignored these expenditures (treated them as sunk costs in the analysis), the results could be misleading. Much of the debate on the completion of the Tennessee Tombigbee Dam focused on whether to count sunk costs.

On any proposal we are most interested in the marginal cost of implementing the program. On only limited occasions will this be synonymous with the total cost, which would allow the use of average costs in analysis. Another use for the concept of marginal analysis is in decisions about the scale of a program. For private firms, the rule of marginality states that output should be produced to the point where marginal cost equals marginal revenue. This will maximize

Table 5-1 Costs and Revenues for the Private Parking Firm (in thousands of dollars)

Size of Lot (No. of Autos)	Total Revenue	Marginal Revenue	Total Cost	Average Cost per 100 Autos	Marginal Cost per 100 Autos	Profit
100	2,800	—	2,940	2,940	2,940	−140
200	4,200	1,400	4,200	2,100	1,260	0
300	5,600	1,400	5,320	1,773	1,120	+280
400	7,000	1,400	6,720	1,680	1,400	+280
500	8,400	1,400	8,680	1,736	1,960	−280
600	9,800	1,400	11,200	1,867	2,520	−1,400

Table 5-2 Costs and Benefits for the City (in thousands of dollars)

Size of Lot (No. of Autos)	Total Benefits	Marginal Benefits	Total Cost	Average Cost per 100 Autos	Marginal Cost per 100 Autos	Social Welfare
100	4,760	—	2,940	2,940	2,940	+1,820
200	6,720	1,960	4,200	2,100	1,260	+2,520
300	8,680	1,960	5,320	1,773	1,120	+3,360
400	10,640	1,960	6,720	1,680	1,400	+3,920
500	12,600	1,960	8,680	1,736	1,960	+3,920
600	14,560	1,960	11,200	1,867	2,520	+3,360

the firm's profits. For the public sector, the rule states that output should be produced to the point where marginal cost equals marginal (societal) benefit. This will maximize the benefit to society.

Using the municipal parking garage example, let's analyze several scale levels of the proposal as if the decision maker were a private parking firm, and then reanalyze as if the decision maker were a city. Table 5-1 presents the data as they look to the firm, Table 5-2 as they look to the city.[42] Note the major difference is that in addition to the revenues the firm generates, the city evidently experiences $560,000 more in marginal revenue/benefits (positive externalities) for every size of garage. Using the marginality rule to maximize its profit, the private firm would build a garage that accommodates 400 autos (marginal cost = marginal revenue = $1.4 million). The city would maximize social benefit by building a garage that accommodates 500 autos (marginal cost = marginal benefit = $1.96 million). If the marginal costs exceed marginal revenues (or benefits), the producer could increase profits (social welfare) by producing less output. This is confirmed by the last column of our two tables.

As can be seen, eventually a point is reached where additional parking spaces will contribute less to total benefits than the preceding spaces. This is called the *law of diminishing returns*. Closely allied to this concept is the idea of

[42] This explanation is based on ibid., pp. 69–70.

economies and *diseconomies of scale*. The basic difference between them is that diminishing or increasing returns occur in the short run when the levels of some inputs are fixed, whereas economies and diseconomies of scale are said to occur in the long run where the levels of all variables can be increased or decreased.

In the short-run example above, perhaps concrete was in short supply, and the premium paid to get enough for a garage accommodating more than 500 cars wasn't justified by the revenue forecasts. Were we able to expand our analysis to consider waiting for the completion of a new concrete plant in town, we might eventually find the project viable at a much larger scale, with marginal costs equaling marginal benefits for perhaps an 800-car garage. If this is true, we are missing a chance at economies of scale. Diseconomies of scale occur when larger size causes increasing marginal costs. For example, at some point a larger garage will require elevators instead of stairs, and a second entrance and exit ramp. The two ideas, economies of scale and increasing returns, and diseconomies of scale and decreasing returns, are indeed related. The central point is that as long as marginal benefit is greater than marginal cost, enlarging the scale of the project will yield net benefits and it should be done. Net benefits are at a maximum at the point where it stops being profitable to make the project larger.

Equity

Economic evaluation criteria are normally directed at efficiency concepts: How can we get more for society or, more particularly, for the governmental unit that is our client? However, a most important question, often raised, is "get more for whom?" In many instances programs that prove to be very efficient also prove to be very inequitable. The two criteria are seldom both maximized in the same program. The project that brings the greatest amount of development to the city may have its greatest impact on the already well off. The program that provides employment for the unskilled may have limited payoffs for the local economy. Some might contend that the affairs of government are by definition questions of equity—questions of efficiency are best left to the private sector. These observers are likely to note that government must care for the unemployed, persons with disabilities, and the homeless, but it should not also try to be a developer, entertainer, and profit-making service provider. Even if local governments accepted this circumscribed role, questions of efficiency would still arise. How can we most efficiently provide transportation for the poor elderly?[43]

Equity refers to the distribution of goods and services among individual members or subgroups (e.g., the elderly, disabled, female heads of households, etc.) of a society. It can refer to the existing distribution, the status quo, or the distribution that a proposed policy or program will produce. Equity questions

[43] For a key book on equity planning, see Norman Krumholz and John Forester, *Making Equity Planning Work: Leadership in the Public Sector* (Philadelphia: Temple University Press, 1990).

arise not only on the consumption side of public policy ("Who benefits?"), but also on the production side ("Who pays?"). There is no clear right answer to what an appropriate distribution of goods and services to society's members should be. Unlike efficiency questions, which, despite a host of conceptual and mechanical problems, often do have a right answer—for example, "This type of garbage collection is the cheapest"—equity questions do not. The discipline of economics indirectly raises equity questions by detailing the ways actors are connected with efficiency questions pertaining to the same programs. Equity questions are in the domain of philosophy, sociology, psychology, politics, and ethics. The basic principle related to equal and nondiscriminatory treatment, then, is that people should be treated similarly except when there is good reason that they should be treated with differentiation.[44] Defining what constitutes good reason is the dilemma, and involves issues of values. There are several definitions that can help to guide our discussion of equity.

Authors have differentiated between the concepts of horizontal and vertical equity. *Horizontal equity* has been defined as "the equal treatment of equals." The concept is particularly important when analyzing the provision of public goods and services: Does a proposed program provide uniform costs and benefits to similar classes of people? For example, are all families of four whose income is $12,000–$14,000 per year able to participate in the proposed rent-subsidy program? *Vertical equity* concerns questions of the distribution of goods and services to those in unequal circumstances. Clearly, vertical equity provides the much more difficult set of sociopolitical questions. In the example above, how should a family of 14 with $12,000–$14,000 of income be treated, or a family of four with $18,000 of income?

These examples raise some other important points about equity. The first is how the population should be subdivided in order to analyze equity questions. We usually begin by defining the population of our local government—a region, city, or neighborhood. To begin, it undoubtedly does not have the same racial, age, income, sex, and ethnic composition as the United States as a whole. Thus equity questions can be raised vis-à-vis our local government and the country as a whole. The questions can be raised in light of a proposed policy or program or simply about the status quo. But eventually the proposed policy or program will raise equity questions internal to the local government. Short of analyzing the impact of a proposal on each and every individual in the area, how should subgroups be delineated? One clear answer is that the nature of the program often helps to delineate subgroups. Mass-transit programs often raise questions of those with no automobile versus those who have one, rush-hour travelers versus those who can and do avoid peak travel times, single-auto commuters versus car poolers, the handicapped versus those having no handicap, and so on. Housing programs raise questions about owners versus renters, about differential wealth as well as income, and about household size. Housing often raises

[44] Vernon Van Dyke, *Equality and Public Policy* (Chicago: Nelson-Hall, 1990).

questions about race, too, because of long-standing concerns about residential integration.

This last point raises yet another one. Legislation at the state and federal levels and a variety of court decisions have delineated subgroups in American society who have been discriminated against—in housing, in education, in transportation, and in land use. These substantive areas are the foci of local governments. Thus, there are subgroups that over the years have become the natural subjects of equity questions.

Establishing appropriate subgroups for analyzing equity questions connected to local policy problems is made more difficult by having to resolve disputes over definitions. For example, all homeowners are taxed to run public schools. But many homeowners have no children. Some are elderly. What are the horizontal classes here? At first glance, all homeowners would seem to be one class and renters another. But the elderly may want a further refinement. One popular solution to these difficult problems is to employ user fees to pay for services—those persons who want the service must pay for it. But user fees are clearly not always appropriate. In our example, using as a tax base only those families who have children would undoubtedly bankrupt the school system. And, more important, there are assumed to be large positive externalities associated with having an educated population. Everyone benefits.

Another important question surrounds the role that local governments should be expected to play in matters of social equity. If a local government is rather poor and its population is also poor, should it be expected to fund and administer programs aimed at providing, say, health and social services to the poor? Or should these be state or even federal responsibilities? In the United States what we have at this time is a mixture of programs financed and/or administered by federal, state, and local governments and sometimes mandated for local governments by the state or federal government. These local governments are required to provide services of certain kinds without state or federal financial support. In recent years, many programs with equity objectives that were considered a federal responsibility in the 1970s have been returned to local governments.

Another type of equity concern to policy analysts and planners at the local level is *transitional equity*. Issues of transitional equity arise when a new policy, plan, or regulation creates different, perhaps unfair, situations for specific individuals or classes of individuals. The classic issue of transitional equity for local planners involves the imposition of new land-use regulations and their effect on existing property owners. In some instances property owners might be compensated by governments if the value of their land is reduced by a governmental action or if their land is taken by government for a public purpose.

A final type of equity concern is *intergenerational equity*. Questions of intergenerational equity arise when proposed policies or programs appear to have long-run costs or benefits. Programs that set aside conservancy districts or subsidize the restoration of historic areas are cases in point. Should current taxpayers subsidize the lifestyles of future generations, or can we expect that future generations will be relatively so much better off than us that they should pay for their own lifestyles? That, of course, is only part of the question, since greater income and wealth in the future may be unable to reproduce what can be conserved at the moment. Clear intergenerational equity questions surround national health and income insurance programs. How much have individuals supported national insurance in their lifetimes, and how much should they be allowed to receive in their later years? How much should the younger working population have to pay to support the older nonworking population? Although not a question directly affecting local governments, the poor elderly often confront the social welfare system of local governments as a last resort.

Elsewhere in this book we suggest ways of analyzing the impact of proposed policies and programs on specific subgroups of citizens. In this section on concepts from economics, we want to emphasize that although programs directed at equity objectives may be more properly funded by higher levels of government, programs at the local level often pose important equity questions. Questions can arise about who should pay for programs and who should be able to use them. These questions are as important as whether a program is efficient in an economic sense. In fact, sometimes there will be conscious decisions made in program design, trading off some efficiency objectives for some equity ones.

COMMONLY EMPLOYED EVALUATION CRITERIA

It is essential to define specific objectives once the goals of a program or policy have been identified. Then evaluation criteria can be developed for each objective, and multiple measures of each criterion can be devised. The types of criteria employed depend on the nature of the problem, the objectives, and alternative policies or programs under review. Evaluation criteria are essential to measuring achievement of any objective.

Numerous authors have suggested categories of criteria.[45] We will use Bardach's typology to organize our review of commonly applied evaluation criteria. He identified "four main constraints which bear on the objective of designing a policy that will work as intended: technical feasibility, political viability, economic and financial possibility, and administrative operability."[46] We believe that most

---

[45] Quade, *Analysis for Public Decisions,* p. 95; MacRae and Wilde, *Policy Analysis for Public Decisions*, pp. 54–56; Harry Hatry, Louis Blair, Donald Fisk, and Wayne Kimmel, *Program Analysis for State and Local Governments* (Washington, DC: Urban Institute, 1976), p. 49; Theodore H. Poister, *Public Program Analysis: Applied Research Methods* (Baltimore: University Park Press, 1978), pp. 9–145; William N. Dunn, *Public Policy Analysis: An Introduction* (Englewood Cliffs, NJ: Prentice Hall, 1981), pp. 232–39; and David L. Weimer and Aidan R. Vining, *Policy Analysis: Concepts and Practice* (Englewood Cliffs, NJ: Prentice Hall, 1989), pp. 198–200.

[46] Eugene Bardach, *The Skill Factor in Politics: Repealing the Mental Commitment Laws in California* (Berkeley and Los Angeles: University of California Press, 1972), p. 216. See also Hok Lin Leung, *Towards a Subjective Approach to Policy Planning & Evaluation: Common-Sense Structured* (Winnipeg, Canada: Ronald P. Frye, 1985), pp. xi–xii.

major criteria fall into these four broad categories, and that for each policy problem the analyst should identify relevant criteria in each category. The categories can be briefly described as follows:

Technical feasibility criteria measure whether policy or program outcomes achieve their purpose. They address the basic question of whether the alternative will work in a technical sense. Will the bridge carry the expected traffic? Will the water be treated to the quality level sought? Will the vehicle obtain the minimum miles-per-gallon fuel rating? Although this criterion appears straightforward, evaluating it is often a complex process. Whenever human behavior is involved, we are never absolutely sure that a policy or program will have its intended effect.

Economic and financial possibility criteria measure, first, what the programs cost, and second, what they produce as benefits. Benefits can be direct or indirect, short- and long-term, quantifiable or not. They can have mostly fiscal implications for the client—that is, impacts felt on profits and losses for private clients and revenue or debt for public clients. Or the policies can have mostly economic implications for the client; that is, they can have impacts on the economy of the geographic area. Many policies and programs have both fiscal and economic impacts, and these need to be evaluated with both types of criteria.

Political viability criteria measure policy or program outcomes in terms of impact on relevant power groups such as decision makers, legislators, administrators, citizen coalitions, neighborhood groups, unions, and other political alliances. The central question is whether one or more alternatives will be acceptable or can be made acceptable to the relevant groups. Measurements in this category are often subjective and less quantifiable. Political insight, understanding of organizational and administrative preferences and procedures, and knowledge of the motivation of actors enable these criteria to be used.

Administrative operability criteria measure how possible it is to actually implement the proposed policy or program within the political, social and, most important, administrative context. Is the staffing available, will employees cooperate in delivering the service, do we have the physical facilities necessary, can it be done on time?

We now discuss several common evaluative criteria associated with each of these four categories.

Technical Feasibility

The two principal criteria that fall under this category are effectiveness and adequacy. The criterion of *effectiveness* focuses on whether the proposed policy or program will have, or has had, its intended effect. To what degree does the proposed action accomplish the objectives set forth? Can changes in the real world be traced back to the program, or are they the result of other factors? At times, the effectiveness of a program is reasonably concrete, and measures of it are easily developed. For example, the effectiveness of solid-waste collection services is measured quite directly. A team of analysts from the Urban Institute developed 15 specific measures of the effectiveness of solid-waste collection services, which they grouped into the following categories: "pleasing aesthetics, clean streets, health and safety, minimum citizen inconvenience, and general citizen satisfaction."[47] The measures themselves are designed so that local officials can easily collect, process, and interpret the data. On the other hand, in the Housing Allowance Demand Experiment, in order to judge whether the program was meeting its principal objective of increasing the supply of affordable housing, a complex experiment was designed. It involved drawing samples of poor households in two cities, assigning them to one of 24 categories (including one control group), offering them a variety of plans for subsidizing their housing, and periodically inspecting their housing and interviewing them for four years. The effectiveness criteria themselves were quite complex. These two examples barely hint at the complexity of assessing effectiveness for our purposes, because, as we have stated, this book focuses on judging policies and programs before they are implemented. This means that we must often forecast program impacts, not just measure them after they occur.

The most direct and quick method available for estimating impacts is, of course, to find how the proposed policy or program has worked elsewhere. However, the contexts within which programs or policies are implemented can vary a good deal and have an important effect on program outcomes. Thus, outcomes in other contexts are not always perfect indicators of future outcomes in our case. The types of effectiveness criteria employed and the methods used for evaluating them *ex-ante* are, in part, derived from *ex-post* evaluation methods. (Chapter 9 covers these concepts and methods.)

Several important dimensions of effectiveness criteria are whether the program or policy effects are direct or indirect, long-term or short-term, quantifiable or not, and adequate or inadequate. A program or policy impact is said to be *direct* if it addresses a stated objective of the program and *indirect* if it creates an impact not associated with a stated objective. Thus, if the objective of building a downtown riverfront mall was to create recreational opportunities for downtown workers, and the values of adjacent properties were raised as a result, this latter impact would be deemed an indirect effect. Had both effects been identified as policy objectives, then both would be considered direct effects. It is indeed a thin line that separates the two.

Categorizing impacts into long term and short term is a policy-specific activity. That is, the definition of what constitutes a long-term impact will vary from program to program. As a general rule, *long-term* impacts are those experi-

---

[47] Harry P. Hatry, Louis H. Blair, Donald M. Fisk, John M. Greiner, John R. Hall, Jr., and Philip S. Schoenman, *How Effective Are Your Community Services: Procedures for Monitoring the Effectiveness of Municipal Services* (Washington, DC: Urban Institute and International City Management Association, 1977); and Harry P. Hatry, Mark Fall, Thomas O. Singer, and E. Blaine Liner, *Monitoring the Outcomes of Economic Development Programs: A Manual* (Washington, DC: Urban Institute, 1990).

enced sometime in the future and thus require discounting to value accurately. *Short-term* impacts are immediate and often direct and mitigatable. The long-term impact of our riverfront park may be increased land values, but the short-term effect during the construction phase may be decreased values.

Some effectiveness criteria can be measured *quantitatively*. The rest will have to be described in other ways. The park provides quantifiable land-value effects but largely nonquantifiable aesthetic effects for the workers who gather there. Often quantifiables such as land values are used as measures of nonquantifiable impacts such as improved aesthetics. However, the danger of double counting is ever present.

Finally, an effect may be adequate or inadequate; that is, the policy or program may not be able to resolve fully the stated problem or fulfill the stated objective. For example, funding may not be available to serve each household that meets the program's eligibility criteria. The program guidelines might then be revised to reflect a more restrictive operational objective, such as serving only the most needy households. *Adequacy* measures how far toward a solution we can proceed with resources available. Even an effective program may fall short of its objectives or solve only part of a larger problem.

Economic and Financial Possibility

A major reason why the discipline of economics has achieved prominence in policy analysis is that it deals with measurable concepts. Analysts and decision makers alike prefer "hard" analysis and information that can be communicated in quantitative terms.[48]

Three concepts are prominent in any discussion of economic evaluation criteria: tangible versus intangible criteria, monetarizable versus nonmonetarizable criteria, and direct versus indirect cost-benefit criteria. These three descriptors will be used to discuss the more popular economic evaluation criteria in use in policy analysis. We begin with a brief description of each.

In general, *tangible* costs and benefits are those that can somehow be counted. *Monetarizable* costs and benefits go even further because they can be counted in monetary (i.e., dollar) terms, since we can somehow judge their value in the marketplace. So, for example, the amount of refuse collected in one week's time by one three-person crew is definitely tangible. It can be measured by weight and by volume. It is certainly possible to measure many of the costs connected with collecting the refuse, and it might even be possible, though not necessarily desirable, to measure the benefits of collection. This might be done by observing what other cities are willing to pay a crew to collect a comparable amount of

---

[48] There are many pitfalls in using quantitative measures when evaluating policies and plans. For more on this topic see Formaini, *Myth of Scientific Public Policy*, pp. 39–65; Judith Innes, *Social Indicators and Public Policy: Interactive Processes of Design and Application* (Amsterdam: Elsevier Scientific, 1975); and David C. Paris and James F. Reynolds, *The Logic of Policy Inquiry* (New York: Longman, 1983), pp. 110–65.

refuse in a week's time. More globally, the benefits of collection would include the public health, convenience, and aesthetic benefits of such a service. Whereas the former measure of benefits is even monetarizable, this latter concept is, at least partially, intangible. Recall that earlier in this chapter we described an economic technique called shadow pricing, which is sometimes used to monetarize inherently nonmonetarizable, if not intangible, costs and/or benefits.

If all costs and benefits of a proposed policy are monetarizable (a rare occurrence), then several different types of evaluations can be made. First, the proposed policy can be evaluated alone for economic feasibility. Using some measure—for example, a rate of return—decision makers can determine whether undertaking the project is desirable. Second, the proposed policy can be evaluated against other totally monetarized policies, and the most desirable one can be chosen using either the difference between, or the ratio of, monetarized benefits and costs. This second type of monetarized evaluation can be subdivided into evaluation between programs or policies with the same goals (e.g., increasing the supply of single-family rental housing) and evaluation between programs or policies with different goals (e.g., guns versus butter). Although the latter type of evaluation was deemed feasible in the early 1960s when President Johnson issued an Executive Order requiring such analysis within the federal government, the idea fell into disrepute until revived by President Reagan. The main reason for not undertaking such an evaluation of policies with different goals is that most programs or policies are not entirely monetarizable. Thus, holding the prime goal of the proposal constant at least allows for more legitimate comparison.

In addition to whether a proposed policy's costs and benefits are tangible, and further, monetarizable, an additional characteristic is whether they are *direct* or *indirect*. Often the question of whether the benefits are direct or indirect can be answered by legislative intent: What did decision makers have in mind? It is possible to propose policies that have multiple objectives and then use these several objectives in measuring direct benefits. The classic example is the dam project whose major stated goal is the generation of electrical power, but that also generates substantial recreational benefits. The decision of whether to classify recreation as well as electricity as a direct benefit is initially made by those decision makers supporting the proposal. But it also should be the focus of public discussion. Whether to count only direct benefits or to include direct and indirect benefits is then a matter of public policy. Similarly, proposed projects, programs, plans, or policies can have direct and indirect costs. Direct costs obviously include outlays by the "owner," usually a unit of government, for the project. These can be one-time or recurring investment costs as well as operating and maintenance costs. However, projects can have indirect costs as well, such as negative impacts (e.g., loss of land devoted to agriculture in the dam example), which may be experienced by the unit of government, its citizens, or even parties outside the governmental unit. Another cost that may be of concern is *opportunity cost*. This is the difference between the value of the goods and services to be used in the proposed project and their value if they were used in some alternative way. An example would be a parcel of land the city owns that could be auctioned off for $700,000 but is instead used as the site for a park. The opportunity cost of the land is $700,000 in this case.

Whether that cost is counted depends on how the analysis is being done. Is the project being analyzed alone (e.g., for feasibility) or against others, including possibly the auction alternative? In general, all costs, direct and indirect, must be considered in policy analysis. Below are possible evaluation criteria drawn from the discipline of economics.

Change in net worth measures all changes in assets and liabilities of the appropriate governmental unit and its subunits: businesses, citizens, and so on. The concept can be measured somewhat narrowly, using, for example, the gross regional product of an area as a measure of flows of assets and liabilities. Or it can be measured more broadly to include changes in stocks of, for example, human capital (e.g., total level of education of the population) and nonhuman resources (e.g., forests, mines, etc.). In any case, the concept is the change in net worth of some area delineated in space, usually one corresponding with the unit of government of concern. This is a useful concept for policy analysts, although in practice, projecting changes in net worth caused by proposed policies takes a good deal of time, and the tools used, such as input-output techniques, and income and product accounting, are those of researched analysis. Since changes in net worth must necessarily deal with monetarized stocks and flows, programs or policies that have major nonmonetarizable or intangible components would not be adequately analyzed using this concept. Measuring changes in net worth is particularly appropriate for evaluating policies whose major impact will be on the economy of the region—for example, a proposed state tax on industrial machines and equipment.

Economic efficiency asks that the benefits to be gained in the use of resources (costs) be maximized—the result being the maximization of satisfaction by society. The concepts of *efficiency* and *effectiveness* are related but should not be confused. Maximum efficiency may not occur at the same point where effectiveness is achieved. It may be higher or lower. For example, assume you need to provide daily hot meals to 500 people. Any food-service provider who can do that will be effective. The food-service provider who can do that for the lowest price provides the most cost-effective alternative. One food-service provider may offer a much cheaper price per meal—but only if you purchase at least 1,000 meals a day. This last alternative is more efficient (has a lower unit price) but not effective, since it can't satisfy your basic objective. Effectiveness, on the other hand, is often dichotomous, rather than being a continuous variable like efficiency. The program either is effective or it isn't. Under these circumstances one can search for the cheapest effective alternative (or most cost-effective alternative), but the most efficient alternative may be totally different. Efficiency is measured in dollars (costs) per unit of output (benefit)—for example, cost per unit of energy produced, or cost per gallon of sewage treated. The ratio can also be inverted to compute, for example, houses inspected per thousand dollars of agency funds. Ratios such as these can only be used to compare alternatives that produce different quantities of the same benefit.

Cost-benefit analysis is a more versatile tool for measuring efficiency. It may be used to produce several distinct measures. The first is *economic feasibility*. Feasibility is achieved whenever the present (discounted) value of the benefits exceeds the present (discounted) value of the costs. Using this as a decision criterion, you would undertake any affordable project with discounted benefits larger than discounted costs. This operationalizes the idea that whenever discounted benefits exceed discounted costs, resources would be profitably invested in the proposal. The key here, of course, is the return that could be achieved by other investments. Since most program's funds are obtained from taxes, one definition of taxpayers' opportunity cost would be the current after-tax return being received by taxpayers from other investments. This rate is called the discount rate. (See "Discounting" in Chapter 7.)

A problem with this first measure is that public resources are always limited, and it is likely that many more programs than could be funded would pass the feasibility test. Of course, this does depend on the discount rate used, and if it were to be set very high, it is possible that this would effectively pare the list to an affordable set of projects. Another measure, again using discounted benefits and costs, is the *ratio of discounted benefits to discounted costs.* Using this measure, we would approve programs or policies with the highest ratios, approving them in descending order of ratios until our budget limit was reached. This measure has a weakness in that proposals with higher ratios may not be those that maximize net benefits. Since economic efficiency dictates that we maximize benefits minus costs incurred, analysts have come to rely more on a third measure, *discounted benefits minus discounted costs.*

Discounted benefits minus discounted costs is called the *net present value* of a proposed program. To be sure, it is difficult to compare several programs aimed at the same objective or several programs aimed at entirely different objectives, or even to judge the feasibility of a single program. In every instance, however, the program with the highest net present value will be most efficient, and only those for which this value is greater than zero will be worth undertaking. Since the concept of net present value is such an important idea, it is discussed further in Chapter 7.

Profitability is a criterion many local governments use to evaluate proposed projects and policies. In its narrowest sense profitability is defined as the difference between monetarized revenues and monetarized costs to a government. For some entities, *cost-revenue analysis* is an important tool for judging the merits of a proposed project or policy. It might be used to evaluate changes in zoning requirements to allow condominium development on the lakefront, or to evaluate constructing and operating a municipal parking garage, because net cash-flow effects, which are all this criterion measures, are of great importance. The method discounts and forecasts future revenues and costs and measures the project's profitability considering the governmental unit's fiscal position. It asks the question: "Does the city find the garage profitable?" Obviously all items in the computations would be monetarized. When the decision concerns a type of physical development, especially residential, the cost-revenue analysis is called *fiscal impact analysis*.[49]

Cost effectiveness is an appropriate criterion when the goal is to accomplish a certain task at minimum cost. It may not be easy or even desirable to measure the benefits of such a project or program. Rather, a cost-effectiveness analysis seeks to identify the alternative that achieves the objective but minimizes cost. This, of course, assumes that all the alternatives that are being compared can readily be determined to meet, or fail to meet, the objective(s), eliminating from further consideration any that do not. Furthermore, it assumes that any additional benefits, beyond meeting the objective, or any nonmonetarizable costs, are insignificant. If they are not, some measure of economic efficiency will have to be used instead, allowing the measurement of supplementary benefits and costs. A principal advantage of cost-effectiveness analysis is that both costs and benefits need not be monetarized—typically only costs are. Cost-effectiveness analysis has often been used to evaluate alternatives for collecting solid waste, where the effectiveness of the alternatives is presumed to be the same. That is, a certain amount of trash is collected, at a given level of convenience to residents, with comparable aesthetic results. Given that presumption, the analyst can now seek the alternative that minimizes cost. Cost-effectiveness analysis makes no assumption about the profitability, feasibility, or economic efficiency of a program. Rather, it requires a given minimum of benefits from the program (effectiveness) and attempts to find the alternative that provides them most cheaply.

The criteria discussed here certainly do not exhaust the list of possible evaluation criteria drawn from economics. They do, however, constitute the most common criteria employed to judge the efficacy of public actions. Since most involve numerical calculation in some way, they tend to dominate decision making both analytically and philosophically.

Political Viability

Policy is developed in the political arena and must survive the political test. Some observers even argue that since all policy is eventually normative, it will be based on political considerations regardless of the results of scientific analysis.[50] If a policy will not be supported by decision makers, officials, or voters, then it

---

[49] Robert W. Burchell and David Listokin, *The Fiscal Impact Handbook: Estimating Local Costs and Revenues of Land Development* (New Brunswick, NJ: Rutgers University, Center for Urban Policy Research, 1978); Arthur C. Nelson, ed., *Development Impact Fees: Policy Rationale, Practice, Theory, and Issues* (Chicago: Planners Press, 1988); and James C. Nicholas, Arthur C. Nelson, and Julian C. Juergensmeyer, *A Practitioner's Guide to Development Impact Fees* (Chicago: Planners Press, 1991).

[50] Formaini, *Myth of Scientific Public Policy,* p. 96.

has little chance of being adopted or, if adopted, implemented. Consequently, alternatives must be subjected to political assessment. Which are acceptable to various power groups? What concessions will have to be made to gain support for each option? What resources do decision makers hold that could be used if necessary? What trade-offs are acceptable in order to secure agreement on the alternative? Political criteria, then, deal with the acceptability of alternatives to decision makers, public officials, influential citizens and groups, and other sources of power. Since the actions of an analyst could affect political viability, political criteria should not be used to decide whether to pursue a certain objective, but rather to indicate which of several alternatives can be implemented with the least political opposition or what efforts might be taken by the client to make an alternative politically viable. We are concerned with the eventual feasibility of implementation and the constraints associated with policy options under consideration.[51]

Political criteria deal with the beliefs and motivations of actors. What do the actors believe about the problem, and what do they need or want? What are their base positions, the nonnegotiable points? What political obligations exist because of past agreements or coalitions? Do such obligations suggest relevant criteria?[52] Laws, rules, and regulations that specify the bounds on acceptable alternatives result from the political process. We may work to change laws, but these requirements are often accepted in the short run, especially in quick analysis.

Making judgments about what is politically feasible can be a dangerous business, for what is not feasible today may be feasible tomorrow, and if judged infeasible, potentially important options may be given short shrift. Instead of establishing political criteria to decide what will and what will not fly, Meltsner suggests that analysts develop the ability to anticipate when clients will be open to new suggestions and when political conditions are receptive to a policy change.[53] Political criteria that should be considered in virtually every analysis include acceptability, appropriateness, responsiveness, legality, and equity.

Acceptability refers both to the determination of whether a policy is acceptable to actors in the political process and to the determination of whether clients and other actors are receptive to new policies. In the first sense we may ask which of several policies are acceptable to relevant actors or which of several policies are most favored. In quick analysis for one-time activities, we typically are faced with evaluating policies on the basis of which will most likely be acceptable to key actors, the attentive public, public officials, and lawmakers. However, when

---

[51] Alan Walter Steiss and George A. Daneke, *Performance Administration* (Lexington, MA: D.C. Heath, 1980), pp. 194–99.

[52] Criteria often derive from political obligations. See MacRae and Wilde, *Policy Analysis for Public Decisions,* p. 52; and Robert T. Nakamura and Frank Smallwood, *The Politics of Policy Implementation* (New York: St. Martin's Press, 1980), pp. 31–45.

[53] Arnold J. Meltsner, *Policy Analysts in the Bureaucracy* (Berkeley and Los Angeles: University of California Press, 1976), p. 277.

working with clients over time or when working on the same problem for some time, we may be able to identify when our client, the public, or other actors will be receptive to new ideas. The skilled analyst will surely take advantage of these opportunities to include new policies for evaluation.

Appropriateness is related to acceptability in that it addresses the issue of whether policy objectives mesh with the values of the community or society. Should we be pursuing the stated objective? This is essentially an ethical question and involves issues of human values, rights, redistribution, and similar considerations. The criterion of appropriateness should be addressed early in the analysis, but we may be able to address it completely only by examining the full collection of criteria as they balance one another.

Responsiveness is related to acceptability and appropriateness and involves the target group's perception of whether the policy or program will meet its needs. Will the program be operated in a way that will be responsive to the needs of citizens? A policy might be efficient and effective but not what the target population needs or wants. For example, a curfew might be enforced in an effective, efficient, and equitable manner, but teen-agers and parents may desire recreation facilities rather than the curfew.

Legal criteria can be considered within the category of political criteria, since laws can be made and changed through political action. At the outset of the analysis we might investigate existing laws, rules, and regulations that may affect the design of alternatives. If we identify desirable policies that are not supported by current laws, typically we do not eliminate them from consideration but identify the laws that would have to be changed and the political problems in doing so.[54]

Equity as a political criterion arises when the differential impact of a policy change is important.[55] As we mentioned earlier, policy changes seldom affect all parties equally, and there is little likelihood that we can devise policies without externalities. Since policy changes are often intended to modify existing discrepancies, the question becomes one of whether certain groups or individuals will experience a disproportionate share of the burden or will receive windfall benefits. How are the benefits of the policy distributed among relevant groups, and how are the costs borne by these and other groups? The issue is one of a fair distribution rather than merely an equal distribution, with fairness related to the

---

[54] Robert A. Heineman, William T. Bluhm, Steven A. Peterson, and Edward N. Kearny, *The World of the Policy Analyst: Rationality, Values, and Politics* (Chatham, NJ: Chatham House, 1990), p. 42.

[55] Equity is relatively little used in practice as a criterion, although a number of writers have discussed its relationship to the impact of costs and benefits. See Braybrooke and Lindblom, *Strategy of Decision*, pp. 169–99; Michael Carley, *Rational Techniques in Policy Analysis* (London: Heinemann, 1980), pp. 78–80; George C. Edwards and Ira Sharkansky, *The Policy Predicament: Making and Implementing Public Policy* (San Francisco: W. H. Freeman, 1978), pp. 198–206; MacRae and Wilde, *Policy Analysis for Public Decisions*, pp. 64–70; Edith Stokey and Richard Zeckhauser, *A Primer for Policy Analysis* (New York: Norton, 1978), pp. 281–86; and Weimer and Vining, *Policy Analysis*, pp. 190–93.

need for a program or service. What constitutes fairness involves moral and ethical issues, and there is not always a clear-cut answer. Sometimes equity is defined as a redistribution of income, the right to a minimum level of service, or payment for services in relation to ability to pay.

Few programs or policies have equity, or fair distribution of costs and benefits, as their primary goal. Many programs, however, do have equity as an important secondary goal. A program to subsidize the building of single-family rental housing would be an example. Although the vast majority of policies, plans, and programs at all levels of government have no explicit equity intentions, all have equity implications, and these need to be analyzed. Most public actions require resources in order to be implemented. Who pays for these actions or gives up some resources is an equity question. And public actions invariably generate costs as well as benefits. To whom do these costs and benefits accrue?

Traditional efficiency, profitability, and feasibility criteria from economics ignore equity considerations. It is presumed that the benefits of a project or program that passes the economic test will generate benefits to someone and that the recipient of these benefits could compensate those who paid for the program or experienced costs as a result of the program. The key word here is *could*. There are few examples of public policies that have been designed explicitly to tax those who win and compensate those who lose. One example is the policy of compensation to residents in the paths of planned highways. Some of these highways are built because they show themselves to be economically efficient— they produce an excess of benefits over costs for the society as a whole. However, it has been shown that residents in the paths of such highways suffer large, and traditionally uncompensated, costs.[56] Some states have now instituted policies that in effect, tax the winners of these highway construction projects (highway users and taxpayers) and compensate the losers (residents and businesses in the path). The equity of the program is partly assessed by gauging how costs and benefits accrue to affected subgroups. For example, the direct benefits from highways go to those who use them: the owners of cars and trucks who travel over them. The program may tax all citizens, however, including those without cars and those who own cars but never use the highway. Ignoring the argument for the moment that all of society benefits from highway construction through increased business activity, it seems clear that the incidence of benefits and tax is not the same. The equity provisions of the program are obviously not perfect.

The first check for equity is, of course, to see whether the net effect of program or policy costs and benefits (and mitigation measures aimed at redistributing costs and benefits) is zero for the affected populations. In fact, there are usually net benefits because the project probably also passed some type of efficiency test. But, in addition, there are other common tests for fairness. The most common are checks for fairness of distribution of costs and benefits by (1) residential location, (2) income class, (3) race and ethnicity, (4) age, (5) sex, (6)

---

[56] Anthony Downs, *Urban Problems and Prospects* (Chicago: Markham, 1970).

family status, (7) homeownership status, and (8) current versus future generations.

Specify political viability criteria before identifying and evaluating alternatives, so the alternatives can reflect important political factors and be more likely to succeed. Although we stress the importance of saying it with numbers whenever possible, we also believe that the systematic analysis of qualitative information is an essential part of quick, basic analysis.

Administrative Operability

If a technically feasible, economically possible, and politically viable policy cannot be implemented, if the administrative talent and delivery systems are not available, then the superiority of the policy must be called into question. Is the existing administrative system capable of delivering the policy or program? How much control does the client have? What other groups and individuals must be relied upon? Can bottlenecks and opposition be avoided? What are the major organizational limitations? Are there alternative methods of implementation? Steiss and Daneke have made the point this way: "All too often, however, policy makers assume that if they can design it, someone can implement and manage it. . . . Many public policies are adopted with absolutely no knowledge of the particular actions that will be necessary to implement them."[57] The problem, they point out, is that this shifts the responsibility for authentic policymaking to administrators, who may follow the path of least resistance. Specific criteria to consider in evaluating administrative operability include authority, institutional commitment, capability, and organizational support.

Authority to implement a policy, to turn it into a program, is often a critical criterion. Does the implementing group or agency have clear authority to make necessary changes, to require cooperation from other groups, to determine priorities? In Chapter 8 we discuss the importance of implementation analysis as a way to assure that the agreed-upon policy will be put in place. However, it is important to raise questions of implementation authority early in the analytic process, both to avoid settling on an alternative that no one can implement and to identify changes that will be needed in order to establish implementation authority for potentially superior alternatives.

Institutional commitment from both above and below is important. Not only top administrators, but office and field staff as well, must be committed to policy implementation. Most policies require change in staff behavior, and without it the many seemingly small actions necessary to implement a policy may not be carried out. By stating institutional commitment as a criterion, we again both avoid choosing a totally unrealistic policy and focus attention on organizational changes needed to implement preferred alternatives.

Capability, both staff and financial, is essential to policy implementation.

---

[57] Steiss and Daneke, *Performance Administration*, p. 193.

Can the implementing organization do what it is being asked? Do the administrators and staff have the necessary skills to put the policy into effect? Does the implementing agency have the financial capacity to do what will be demanded of it? Policies that appeared superior have failed because technical and financial requirements exceeded staff and organizational capability. Thus, this criterion is essential for identifying both what is possible under existing conditions and what changes are needed to facilitate implementation.

Organizational support is also an important criterion because it is not sufficient to have only the authority to implement a policy and the commitment of key personnel. It is also necessary to have sufficient equipment, physical facilities, and other support services. Will they be available? If not available now, how likely is it that they will be available when the policy is put into effect?

SUMMARY

This chapter discussed the concept of the criterion as a means to judge whether alternatives are meeting objectives. Several important economic concepts, including externalities, elasticity, and marginality, were reviewed as a basis for understanding commonly applied quantitative criteria. Evaluation criteria were grouped into four categories—technical feasibility, economic and financial possibility, political viability, and administrative operability. We suggested that for all policy problems, the analyst seek criteria in these categories. We focused attention on economic and financial possibility, since they are often at the heart of public policy problems. In our zeal to quantify, however, we should not overlook other types of criteria.

What makes a good criterion? MacRae and Wilde advise us that criteria should be "*clear*, so that they can be used in quantitative analysis; *consistent*, so that you can reconcile various values and disvalues with one another; and *general*, so that they will allow you to compare a wide range of policy alternatives."[58] Hatry and others suggest that good effectiveness measures (criteria) should provide *important* information that justifies difficulties in collecting the data, be *valid, accurate* indicators of the concept, provide *unique* information not available through another measure, be *timely*, be *available* without violating privacy and confidentiality requirements, be available *within cost constraints*, and as a group provide *complete* information.[59]

The next chapter deals with the process of identifying alternatives that later will be evaluated in terms of the types of criteria discussed above. We should point out again that the policy analysis process is iterative, and that criteria specified early in the process may be modified later as we learn more through our efforts to design and evaluate alternative policies.

[58] MacRae and Wilde, *Policy Analysis for Public Decisions,* p. 46.
[59] Hatry et al., *Program Analysis for State and Local Governments,* p. 49.

GLOSSARY

Adequacy an evaluation criterion. Measures whether the policy or program *fully* meets stated objectives. For example, although a nutrition program is improving the diet of low-income pregnant women, it is not *adequate*, if, for example, not all women in this category are being helped.

Administrative Operability an evaluation criterion. Measures how possible the alternative will be to implement.

Average Cost total cost divided by the total units of output.

Cost-Benefit Analysis a tool for measuring the relative efficiency of a range of alternatives.

Cost-Effectiveness Analysis a tool for finding the alternative that accomplishes the specified goal at the lowest cost. Differs from cost-benefit analysis, which may be used to compare alternatives that have very different goals.

Cost-Revenue Analysis sometimes called a fiscal impact analysis. A tool for evaluating the profitability of a proposed action. Only monetarized revenues and costs to the entity undertaking the action are considered.

Criteria the plural of criterion. Specific statements, rules, or standards about the dimensions of the objectives that will be used to evaluate alternatives, and make a decision.

Direct Costs resources that must be committed to implement the policy or program. This includes borrowing costs, one-time fixed costs, and operation and maintenance costs.

Direct Impact an effect of a policy or program that addresses a stated objective of that policy or program.

Economic and Financial Possibility an evaluation criterion. Measures the cost of the alternative and the value of the benefits it will produce.

Economic Efficiency that allocation of resources that most closely corresponds to consumer's and producer's preferences. As an evaluation criterion, maximizing benefits for the use of a given amount of resources (costs).

Economies and Diseconomies of Scale the consequence that, as greater quantities of a commodity are produced, marginal costs may go up (diseconomies) or down (economies).

Effectiveness an evaluation criterion. Measures whether the policy or program has its intended effect. For example, whether a nutrition program is improving the diet of low-income pregnant women. See also *Adequacy*, which is not always distinguished from effectiveness.

Equity refers to the distribution of goods and services among individual members or subgroups and involves questions of who benefits and who pays.

Externality an effect, consequence, or phenomenon to which a free market assigns no value, positive or negative, but that has a societal cost or benefit. For example, a producer saves money by burning cheap but dirty fuel. The consumers also get a cheaper product as a result. The externality of polluted air imposes costs (lower home values, poorer health, an unattractive environment) on nearby residents, who are not paid by the market for the disadvantages they suffer. Externalities can be imposed on others by producers or consumers and can be positive or negative.

Fixed Costs those costs that do not vary with the level of output.

Goals formally and broadly worded statements about what we desire to achieve for the public good in the long run.

Income Elasticity the ratio of the percentage change in the quantity of a good or service demanded to the percentage change in consumer income. Goods with low income elasticity are purchased in similar quantities no matter what the purchaser's income is, whereas goods or services with high elasticities are those that households purchase more of when they have higher incomes.

Indirect Costs the costs associated with impacts or consequences of a policy or program (e.g., loss of tax revenues when a commercial building is bought by the city and converted into a community center).

Indirect Impact an effect of a policy or program that is not associated with one of its stated objectives.

Intangible Costs or Benefits costs or benefits

which cannot be measured in recognized units (pain and suffering, amenity, loss of confidence, etc.). See also *Opportunity Costs* and *Tangible Costs or Benefits*.

Law of Diminishing Returns the observation that most phenomena eventually reach a point at which the last dollar spent produces fewer benefits than the dollar that preceded it.

Marginal Analysis a comparision of the cost incurred by the production of one additional unit of output at different levels of production (1,001 units instead of 1,000 or 5,001 instead of 5,000) with the benefits derived from producing one additional unit at each different level of production. The result is a best scale (level of production) for the policy or program, defined as that level at which marginal costs equal marginal benefits.

Marginal Cost the cost incurred by the production of an additional unit of output.

Measures tangible, though not necessarily quantitative, operational definitions of criteria. Each criterion should have multiple measures associated with it. Comparison of the same measure for different alternatives, or for a single phenomenon over time, enables the analyst to judge degrees of difference or change and progress toward goal attainment.

Monetarizable Costs or Benefits costs or benefits that can be expressed in dollars. See also *Opportunity Costs*.

Net Present Value the discounted benefits of a policy or program less its discounted costs.

Objectives more focused and concretely worded statements than goals. Objectives also deal with end states, most usually with a specified time dimension and client population.

Operationalize to make more specific for the sake of consistency. An operational definition should be sufficiently precise so that all persons using it will achieve the same results.

Opportunity Costs the resources diverted from other uses to make a given policy or program possible. These include those resources that can be expressed in dollars (monetarizable costs), nonmonetarizable but tangible costs (such as increased numbers of accidents), and intangible costs (such as delays in delivering regular services due to staff having additional responsibilities under the new program).

Pareto Criterion a trade of goods, currency, or services that makes at least one person better off and no one worse off.

Pareto Optimality the theoretical end state reached by a free-market price system under perfect conditions in which no one can be made better off without making someone else worse off.

Political Viability a criterion for evaluating alternatives. Measures whether the alternative is acceptable or can be made acceptable to relevant groups.

Price Elasticity of Demand a measure of the response from consumers if the price of a good or service changes—specifically, the percentage change in the number of units sold, divided by the percentage change in price. When the percentage change in price is greater than the percentage change in units sold, the commodity is said to be price inelastic. When the percentage of units sold is greater than the percentage change in price, the commodity is said to be price elastic or to have high price elasticity. Perfect elasticity means that an unlimited number may be sold at a given price. Perfect inelasticity means that only a given number will be sold, no matter what the price.

Public Goods goods and services that are by their nature necessary and available to everyone, whether or not they have helped to pay for them (national defense is the classic example).

Shadow Pricing a method of establishing the monetary value of benefits or costs when market prices are unavailable or distorted. These are usually obtained by finding a competitive market in which that benefit or cost does exist. For example, the shadow prices of publicly provided recreation facilities might be obtained by researching how much it would cost to purchase private memberships in clubs offering the same types of facilities—tennis courts, for example.

Standing refers to who is to be considered when costs and benefits are computed. That is, who has the right to be included in the set of individuals or groups whose changes in welfare or utility are counted when the pros and cons of alternatives are estimated.

Sunk Costs resources that have already been committed before the decision on the new policy or program is considered. These can be ignored in computing the cost of the policy, as they have already been spent and there is no way to take them back.

Tangible Costs or Benefits costs or benefits that can be measured in some type of recognized unit. See also *Opportunity Costs* and *Intangible Costs or Benefits*. These may or may not be monetarizable.

Technical Feasibility a criterion for evaluating alternatives. Measures whether the alternative will actually produce the desired result—meeting the major objectives.

Variable Costs costs that vary with the level of output.

EXERCISES

1. Refine and expand the evaluation criteria you developed for the teen-age driver problem in Chapter 2. Include criteria in at least the following categories:

   (a) Cost

   (b) Efficiency

   (c) Effectiveness

   (d) Morbidity and mortality rates

   (e) Political feasibility

   (f) Administrative ease

   (g) Equity

   (h) Technical feasibility

2. Identify which groups should have standing and which should not in each of the following examples. Use your imagination and mention as many affected parties as conceivable.

   (a) A program to give sterile needles to heroin users, some of whom are pregnant

   (b) A policy to require air bags on the passenger side of all new automobiles by 1995

   (c) A program to teach English as a second language in the school system in a town in southern Texas

   (d) A policy forbidding smoking in all restaurants in your city

   (e) A program to subsidize the building of residence halls for Olympic athletes on a university campus in the host city

3. Many cities employ private businesses to provide services to citizens. One service often provided by private companies is solid-waste collection. In choosing among companies bidding on a five-year contract to collect your city's solid waste, what criteria might you employ to evaluate the bids? Specifically, what measures of these criteria would you expect to use?

4. Providing spare parts and tools to the government is a big business, and apparently a profitable one. In recent years, however, there have been accusations that the prices of spare parts have been greatly inflated by some suppliers, with the government paying hundreds of dollars each for single hammers, screwdrivers, wrenches, and similar items. Although a number of committees and commissions have examined this issue, reports of such abuses continue to surface. Stopping this spare-parts abuse is apparently a complicated undertaking. You will not be asked to solve this problem, but if you were to be assigned this task, what criteria should be used for judging alternatives? Identify, describe, and justify the technical, economic, political, and administrative criteria you believe should be used in such an analysis.

5.   Ambrosia County is seeking a consultant to serve as financial advisor while they plan for a bond issue to finance a portion of the remainder of their new sewage treatment plant. In their request for proposals, they asked for the following information:

(a) Describe your firm's experience as a financial adviser or senior manager for tax-exempt public utility issuers, particularly for water and sewer issues.

(b) Identify the members of your firm who would participate in this project, describe their experience, and specify their exact role and availability to Ambrosia County.

(c) Describe the technical, analytic, and computer resources you expect to use for the development of the Ambrosia County financial plan, and specify how you intend to use these resources.

(d) Describe any innovations you have developed or refined for tax-exempt utility issuers, particularly in the water and sewer area, by briefly outlining the problem, your solution, and the results.

(e) Outline your scope of services and a tentative plan of action you would recommend for Ambrosia County's first issues.

(f) Assuming issues of around $30 million next year, estimate your fee to perform the financial advisory services outlined.

(g) Provide a list of public utility clients, together with names and telephone numbers of references for each.

Propose ten evaluation criteria that the staff who developed the above questions should use in evaluating the written proposals. The same questions should also serve as the basic outline for questioning of the proposers' references and their project teams during interviews. Each criterion should be expressed as a short phrase, further explained in a short paragraph.

6.   Carefully review back issues of your local newspaper for a one- or two-week period and choose a spending issue currently being debated—an issue that involves a go/no-go decision. Then choose a public official who is actively involved in the debate. Set up an interview with that person and attempt to learn what he or she feels the principal goal of the proposed program is. In addition, see if this public official will identify secondary goals and objectives and can detail for you the measures he or she feels are appropriate to evaluating whether the goals of the program will be met. Summarize the discussion in a paper not to exceed six pages.

7.   Many believe that governments should become involved only when the free market fails. Why might local governments involve themselves in the following activities? What could be the rationale?

(a) Zoning of land uses

(b) Provision of water

(c) Construction and maintenance of roads

(d) Construction and maintenance of airports

(e) Subsidization of house rent for low-income people

(f) Police protection

(g) Fire protection

(h) Using their tax-exempt status to subsidize the construction of a downtown mall

(i) Deferment of taxes on a new industry for five years

(j) Solid-waste collection

(k) Provision of solid-waste containers to families

(l) Provision of tennis courts and swimming pools

Discuss the activity in some detail and how the service, if it is to be provided, should be allocated among citizens (i.e., only to some, to all, only to those who pay, etc.).

8.   Identify the average costs, marginal costs, sunk costs, intangibles, tangibles, monetarizables, nonmonetarizables and externalities in the following situation. Some items may be described by more than one of the above terms.

A county wishes to encourage more commuters to use mass transit. Many individuals still persist in driving to work alone in their automobiles despite the heavy congestion. One proposal is to add two additional (directional) lanes to the existing major freeway corridor at a cost of $168 million. The existing freeway was built at a cost of $210 million in the 1970s. The total cost of the freeway would then be $378 million. Presume that 2.7 million commutation trips per year would be made on this expanded freeway.

9.   Give examples of each of the following concepts by describing a proposed local government service or project. You may use an example to illustrate more than one concept.

(a)   Average cost
(b)   Marginal cost
(c)   Sunk cost
(d)   Increasing return
(e)   Diminishing return
(f)   Economy of scale
(g)   Diseconomy of scale
(h)   Intangible benefit
(i)   Intangible cost
(j)   Tangible benefit
(k)   Tangible cost
(l)   Monetarizable benefit
(m)   Monetarizable cost
(n)   Nonmonetarizable benefit
(o)   Nonmonetarizable cost
(p)   Negative producer externality
(q)   Positive producer externality
(r)   Negative consumer externality
(s)   Positive consumer externality
(t)   Fixed cost
(u)   Variable cost

10.   The budget for the library system of a large city has been slashed. Preliminary analysis indicates that the best way to administer the cut is to close two underutilized branch libraries or to eliminate bookmobile services. You are to head the team that will analyze these options and make recommendations on which to choose. First, develop some broad concepts that can be used to evaluate the performance of the library system as a whole, the branches, and the bookmobile program. Next, develop very specific statistical indicators that can be used to evaluate the branches against the bookmobile. These indicators must employ readily available data, not data that would need to be gathered using elaborate, formal research techniques.

11.   Discuss at some length the equity questions posed by the following proposed actions:

(a)   A city wants to use its power of eminent domain to purchase an abandoned downtown hotel and turn it into a publicly owned and operated automobile parking structure with low monthly fees.

(b) A housing subsidy program is proposed to help families who are just short of being able to purchase their own homes. To be eligible to participate in the program, individuals must have at least $7,000 in equity and an annual income of $20,000–$30,000. The program will be locally financed.

(c) A proposal is made to make local governments entirely responsible for unemployment compensation.

(d) The city council is considering outlawing smoking in all city-owned public buildings.

(e) Most cities pay for solid-waste collection through the property tax.

(f) In some cities the elderly are given a tax credit on their property tax bill. The objective is to allow them to continue to own their own home.

(g) Freeways are invariably opposed by residents in whose neighborhoods the road is to be located. Those favoring such roads are ordinarily those who will use it frequently for trips to work, shopping, or play but whose neighborhood is distant from the freeway.

(h) A city along the seacoast wishes to purchase a 100-acre tract along the water, which it plans to maintain as an undeveloped area.

(i) A city has identified three possible sites for its future solid-waste disposal area. All are equal in every way except in terms of equity criteria.

(j) To induce manufacturing firms to move to within its city's limits, the common council has passed a bill that permits the city to provide free sewer and water infrastructure and to abate property taxes for the first five years of operation of the firm.

12. How would you measure the effectiveness of public policies or programs designed to address the following goals?

(a) Reduce street crime in particular neighborhoods.

(b) Provide job training for unemployed youths.

(c) Reduce traffic congestion during the rush hours.

(d) Increase retail activity in a city's downtown.

(e) Reduce racial segregation of residences.

(f) Reduce the use of illegal drugs.

(g) Reduce the exposure of school children to radon gas.

(h) Improve the quality of garbage collection.

(i) Clean up the downtown river and make it swimmable again.

(j) Reduce the pollutants from auto emissions.

13. For each of the goals listed in Exercise 12, describe a possible policy, program, or project that might address the issue. Describe each in no more than 100 words.

14. For each of the policies, programs, or projects you described in Exercise 13, list some possible measure of efficiency that could be used to judge its success.

15. The state develops its budget every two years, and each time, the issue of budget cutting within the university system raises its head. As on many previous occasions, the legislators have singled out the small, rural, two-year campuses as possible targets for closing. They have issued a directive that reads as follows: "A cost-benefit analysis shall be performed on each two-year campus, and on the two-year system as a whole to determine whether or not some or all of these campuses should be permanently closed."

Your first task as chief of an analytic staff of eight people is to develop a memorandum to the chair of the appropriate legislative committee, responding to the request. That memorandum will be your first attempt to sketch a six-month work program for your staff. Since *cost-benefit* is simply a catch phrase to most legislators, you will be able to outline a fairly broad approach to evaluation. In developing your memorandum, be sure to touch on at least the following points (these points make for a minimum response—you should hit other key issues):

(a) Explain what a strictly defined cost-benefit analysis is, and either accept or reject doing what has been mandated (be tactful). In so doing discuss the criteria for decision making you think the legislators should use and how these are typically explored by cost-benefit analysis.

(b) Presuming all two-year campuses cannot be studied at the same level of detail, develop criteria for identifying "high-priority" and "low-priority" (for evaluation purposes) campuses.

(c) Detail a list of "output indicators" that you want your staff to develop for each campus—in other words, a uniform data set that can be used in comparing campuses on a set of "critical decision variables."

(d) Together with item (c) above offer a description of the methods to be employed in gathering the necessary data and then analyzing them.

(e) Describe, on some timetable (total time is six months), what kinds of output (written reports, or whatever) your staff will be providing to the legislative committee and what kind of information you'll want back from the legislators. In other words, describe the nature of the interaction between your staff and the committee.

(f) All evaluations of this kind face the tough challenge of intangibles. Name some key ones and discuss your approach to including them in the analysis.

(g) Discuss secondary effects the analysis will face.

(h) Discuss major uncertainties the analysis will face.

(i) Discuss the notion of *opportunity cost* in this context.

(j) Discuss the notion of *sunk costs* in this context and how they will be handled in the evaluation process.

(k) Discuss the major equity issues at stake.

(l) Discuss the role of university policy making and goal setting in this process.

(m) Several legislators insist that your committee come up with a grand index. This they feel will take the heat off them. They'll simply adopt your "bottom line." Please address this issue.

Chapter Six

Identifying Alternatives

The policy analysis process revolves around choices. Reasonable people may wish to attain different ends, and they may support different means to the same end. Evaluation criteria measure the extent to which competing policies achieve an agreed-upon goal, and they help us select the preferred alternative from among those under consideration. This chapter presents the ways to identify alternative policies. First, general sources of alternatives are discussed. Then specific, quickly applied methods of identifying policy options and modifying existing solutions are presented. We conclude by mentioning the major pitfalls likely to be encountered in the process of specifying alternatives.

Because an alternative cannot be selected if it is not in the set of options being considered, and because generating alternatives is a creative challenge, many analyses derail at this step in the process. Potential alternatives may be constrained prematurely by short-sighted analysts or clients because they appear politically unacceptable, too expensive, or so novel that no one believes they will be accepted. The ideal is to consider all possible options, but this is seldom feasible, even in extensively researched analysis. Instead, we seek to generate enough alternatives so there will be a choice among several good ones, but not to evaluate in detail many marginal alternatives. If options could be fully evaluated as they were thought of, analysts would know when they had devised an acceptable option and could stop their search. But the challenge of alternatives generation is that unlikely options can sometimes succeed because they encounter less political opposition, have lower benefits but dramatically lower costs than other options, or make use of a new technology. Consequently, be expansive when generating alternatives. Create as many as possible and eliminate the unpromising ones in a systematic way so you know what conditions might support reconsidering those previously dismissed.

A common error in generating alternatives is creating so-called solutions that do not squarely address the problem. This may occur because the problem is imperfectly or incompletely defined, the objectives have not been clearly identified, or the analyst has a bias toward a particular solution. It may even result from analytic sloppiness. No matter the reason, if the alternatives or possible solutions that are analyzed do not truly address the problem, then the entire process of analyzing alternatives is a wasted exercise.

To create feasible alternatives, the problem we are trying to solve must be correctly identified and its various components must be specified. (See Chapter 4.) Furthermore, if we are to evaluate alternatives or possible solutions, we must also identify relevant judgment criteria. Although in practice the analyst moves back and forth between evaluating alternatives, designing alternatives, and specifying criteria, we have argued that the policy analysis process should begin with problem definition and the specification of criteria. Having completed these steps, alternatives can be crafted. We believe that this sequence will help the analyst avoid locking in on favored alternatives that do not relate to the problem or that cannot satisfy the evaluation criteria.

In recent years writers have noted that the alternatives design stage has been sorely neglected in the policy process.[1] One reason is the assumption that alternative policies exist and that they merely need to be found and evaluated. Having examined the process by which alternatives were generated in three cases—U.S. Vietnam policy, the site for a third London airport, and budget cuts at the University of Wisconsin—Alexander argues that "the creative process appears to be a blend of invention and discovery (or adoption), the proportions of which might vary with the characteristics of the problem and the decision environment."[2] An effective design process, in Alexander's thinking, would combine high levels of both creativity and searching. But the fact remains that most alternatives are found, adapted, or remodeled from other experiences, and few are created or invented. Our intention here is to describe both the many ways in which alternatives can be found and the methods analysts might use in attempting to devise new alternatives.

---

[1] The following sources provide an excellent overview of the relative lack of research on designing alternatives. Ernest R. Alexander, "The Design of Alternatives in Organizational Contexts: A Pilot Study," *Administrative Science Quarterly* 42, no. 3 (September 1979), 382–404; Ernest R. Alexander, "Design in the Decision-Making Process," *Policy Sciences* 14, no. 3 (June 1982), 279–92; and Peter J. May, "Hints for Crafting Alternative Policies," *Policy Analysis* 7, no. 2 (Spring 1981), 227–44.

[2] Alexander, "Design of Alternatives," p. 384.

A number of writers have argued that a problem solver needs to consider many alternatives, and that these should be real alternatives, not merely weak options that are knocked over to impress one's client or boss. A study of physicians diagnosing a difficult illness showed that the physician who considered the most possible hypotheses, who considered the most alternatives, who postponed judgment until enough facts were accumulated, and who did not dismiss negative evidence, made the correct diagnosis.[3] On the other hand, the number of alternatives that can be seriously considered is limited.[4] Brightman cites research indicating that problem solvers are capable of evaluating between four and seven hypotheses at the same time.[5]

Although the analyst (or client) may reduce the number of alternatives to be examined in detail, many options ought to be considered at the outset. Osborn, an expert on imagination and creativity, argued for the consideration of many alternatives, citing the numerous alternatives examined by various inventors and problem solvers before they found the right one. Osborn asserted that quantity breeds quality in creative effort. He held that the more ideas considered, the more likely some would be good ideas. He also felt that the best ideas seldom came first in the search process.[6]

> ... for invention *or* discovery, we should always swing our searchlight here, there and everywhere. The more alternatives we uncover, the more likely we are to find what we seek—and this is often found in the obvious. A pencil will make any such hunt more fruitful. If we jot down one alternative after another, the very jotting-down steps up our creative power; and each alternative we list is likely to light up another alternative. . . .[7]

MacRae and Wilde, contemporary writers on policy analysis, also argue that a wide variety of alternatives should be considered initially, so that the analyst is less likely to overlook important options, and so that more options will be available during the compromise stage when policy recommendations are made politically feasible.[8]

How important is the degree of difference between alternatives devised by the analyst and the status quo? Braybrooke and Lindblom believe that considering only incremental change restricts variety, but that dramatically different alternatives are often politically irrelevant, and that the analyst often fails to have

[3] Harvey J. Brightman, *Problem Solving: A Logical and Creative Approach* (Atlanta: Georgia State University Business Press, 1980), pp. 132–37.

[4] Arnold J. Meltsner, *Policy Analysts in the Bureaucracy* (Berkeley and Los Angeles: University of California Press, 1976), p. 135.

[5] Brightman, *Problem Solving*, p. 136.

[6] Alex Osborn, *Your Creative Power: How to Use Imagination* (New York: Scribner's, 1949), pp. 146–48.

[7] Ibid., pp. 50–51.

[8] Duncan MacRae, Jr., and James A. Wilde, *Policy Analysis for Public Decisions* (North Scituate, MA: Duxbury Press, 1979), p. 97.

the information or ability to evaluate such alternatives.[9] Moreover, Hall argues that policymakers are more likely to be receptive to ideas that are consistent with prevailing views and concepts than those that challenge prevailing paradigms.[10] We also need to remember that it is more likely that *demand* will cause policymakers to embrace new ideas rather than the persuasiveness of our intellectual arguments,[11] and one policy study seldom influences policy outcomes.[12] Consequently, our advice is to consider policies that require only incremental changes from the status quo *but also* to include options that may at present appear radically different, even unacceptable, to obtain an idea of what may be possible under changed circumstances.

What are the characteristics of a good alternative? Walker has summarized the criteria that a number of analysts say decision makers consider when selecting among alternatives. Thus, the following should be considered in the design stage:[13]

- Cost—Can we afford the option and will it be cost-effective?
- Stability—Will the objectives be sustained despite disturbances encountered in normal operations?
- Reliability—What is the probability the option will be operating at any given time?
- Invulnerability—Will the alternative continue to perform if one of its parts fails or is damaged?
- Flexibility—Can the alternative serve more than one purpose?
- Riskiness—Does the alternative have a high chance for failure?
- Communicability—Is the option easy to understand by those not involved in the analysis?
- Merit—Does the alternative have face validity; that is, does it appear to address the problem?
- Simplicity—Is the alternative easy to implement?
- Compatibility—Does the option comport with existing norms and procedures?
- Reversibility—How difficult will it be to return to the prior conditions if the option fails?

[9] David Braybrooke and Charles E. Lindblom, *A Strategy of Decision* (New York: Free Press, 1963), pp. 83–90.

[10] Peter A. Hall, "Policy Paradigms, Experts, and the State: The Case of Macroeconomic Policy-Making in Britain," in *Social Scientists, Policy, and the State,* ed. Stephen Brooks and Alain-G. Gagnon (New York: Praeger, 1990), p. 73.

[11] Stephen Brooks, "The Market for Social Scientific Knowledge: The Case of Free Trade in Canada," in *Social Scientists, Policy, and the State,* ed. Stephen Brooks and Alain-G. Gagnon (New York: Praeger, 1990), pp. 92–93; but on the relationship between supply (advice) and demand (consent), see Peter deLeon, *Advice and Consent: The Development of the Policy Sciences* (New York: Russell Sage Foundation, 1988).

[12] Carol H. Weiss, "The Uneasy Partnership Endures: Social Science and Government," in *Social Scientists, Policy, and the State,* ed. Stephen Brooks and Alain-G. Gagnon (New York: Praeger, 1990), p. 101.

[13] Adapted from Warren E. Walker, "Generating and Screening Alternatives," in *Handbook of Systems Analysis: Craft Issues and Procedural Choices,* ed. Hugh J. Miser and Edward S. Quade (Chichester, Eng.: Wiley, 1988), pp. 221–22.

- Robustness—To what extent can the alternative succeed in widely different future environments?

The question remains, however, as to how an analyst actually identifies or creates alternatives. In Chapter 2 we suggested a number of principles to guide analytic thinking. Several of these principles are particularly relevant when devising alternatives. First, focus on the central decision criterion. If you are able to determine the criterion on which the decision will be made, this will help you narrow the space within which to search for alternatives. Second, think about the types of policy actions that can be taken. Governments can take direct and indirect actions and they can pursue monetary or nonmonetary policies. Table 1-1 suggested that governments can either provide or purchase a good or service directly, tax or subsidize to indirectly create a desired outcome, prohibit or require an action, or inform or implore persons to act in certain ways. Policies that fall into more than one category are also possible, and generic policies must be modified to fit particular situations. Nonetheless, it is helpful to keep this classification scheme in mind when thinking about possible policies. In Chapter 2 we also reminded the analyst to avoid the temptation to apply familiar solutions without question. In the following sections we discuss processes for searching for alternatives and ways to create them.

SOURCES OF ALTERNATIVES

Where does the analyst obtain alternatives? How are they generated, discovered, or created? We have already indicated that the no-action alternative, retaining the status quo, should always be considered, and that it is needed as a baseline alternative in cost-benefit analysis, for example. Additional alternatives can be derived from the experience of others with related problems, research findings from these cases, analogy to similar problems, the experience or insights of experts, requirements of authority, the beliefs of participants, legal prescriptions, technical knowledge, and so on. A planning consultant searching for ways to increase business along a small in-town shopping strip could talk with public planners and consultants in this and other cities and with proprietors of businesses in successful in-town shopping areas to learn what they consider reasons for their successes and failures (experience of others). Successful suburban malls might also be studied (analogy). The analyst could also seek out scholars or developers known for their work in commercial redevelopment (use of experts). Another approach would be to find out what types of policies or physical changes might make the business eligible for grants, loans, special tax benefits, or public provision of capital facilities or in-kind services (requirements of authority). Naturally the analyst would want to know what the business owners' own ideas are (beliefs of participants) and what could be done under local ordinances and regulations (legal prescriptions). Familiarity with modern retailing may suggest how a new technology such as targeted advertising via cable television might help the area's businesses (technical knowledge).

Weimer and Vining believe there are basically four sources for alternatives: existing policy proposals, generic solutions, modified generic solutions, and custom-made solutions.[14] Athey also argues that alternatives can be derived in four ways: Keep the existing system, modify the existing system, use a prepackaged design, or create a new system design.[15] The existing system is analyzed as a benchmark, as a way to gain understanding about the present system, as a source of clues about new alternatives, and in order to know how to respond to defenders of the existing system. For example, existing policy might be changed to minimize the negative aspects of the present system. This approach recognizes that it is often difficult to change the existing structure and that since the system worked in the past a slightly different system might meet today's needs.

Prepackaged designs, or generic solutions, in Athey's schema, include buying an existing solution from an organization, using the solution of others as a starting point, and seeking advice from experts. However, Majone has cautioned against accepting without question textbook solutions, citing as an example survey results that show the percentage of professional economists who believe in the superiority of effluent charges is much smaller than one would expect from their near unanimous endorsement in environmental textbooks.[16] New system designs include idealized designs, parallel situations, and morphological approaches. The idealized approach begins by assuming no restrictions, then constraints are added to see how much each lowers the effectiveness of the ideal. The parallel-situation approach involves searching in other fields for analogies that suggest solutions, and the morphological approach involves identifying the basic components of subsystem forms and determining possible combinations of the basic components. We will describe these approaches in more detail later.

Dunn has also presented a range of ways in which to identify alternatives, including obtaining them from experts and authority, using scientific methods, examining parallel cases, and using analogy. He also identifies the beliefs and values of affected groups and ethical systems (ideas offered by social critics and philosophers) as sources of alternatives.[17] This group of alternatives could also encompass alternatives that respond to political requirements.

Yet another view of how to find alternatives is presented by Brightman, who believes that some alternatives are waiting to be found while others must be designed. He suggests that searching for existing alternatives includes the passive approach, in which we wait for alternatives to be proposed for the problem we

---

[14] David L. Weimer and Aidan R. Vining, *Policy Analysis: Concepts and Practice* (Englewood Cliffs, NJ: Prentice Hall, 1989), p. 200.

[15] Thomas H. Athey, *Systematic Systems Approach* (Englewood Cliffs, NJ: Prentice Hall, 1982), pp. 69–79.

[16] Giandomenico Majone, *Evidence, Argument, and Persuasion in the Policy Process* (New Haven: Yale University Press, 1989), p. 141.

[17] William N. Dunn, *Public Policy Analysis: An Introduction* (Englewood Cliffs, NJ: Prentice Hall, 1981), pp. 145–46.

face, the search-generation approach, in which we let others know we are looking for alternatives, the neighborhood approach, in which we examine incremental changes, the historical or analogical search for solutions to similar problems, and the divergence search for truly different alternatives.[18] Brightman suggests that new alternatives can be designed in two ways. Either ready-made alternatives are modified, or alternatives are derived from a statement of objectives and a consideration of constraints.[19] Brightman notes that our view of a problem, and the alternatives we then examine, are hampered by our disciplinary training. After developing depth in a field, he believes, we begin to focus selectively on aspects of the problem. To counteract this tendency, he advises us to view the problem as others see it, to redefine the problem, and to think about the assumptions we have made.[20] This again suggests the iterative nature of policy analysis, and the link between problem definition and possible solutions. Brightman illustrates this need by asking the reader to solve several perceptual problems, and until the reader looks at the problem in a certain way (such as through the eyes of a child) the solution cannot be seen.

It is important to recognize that alternatives are selected in a political and administrative context and that their effectiveness will be related to that context. Majone notes that the selection of policy alternatives is not a technical problem that can be safely delegated to experts: "It raises institutional, social, and moral issues that must be clarified through a process of public deliberation and resolved by political means."[21]

Advice about the process of identifying alternatives can take the beginning analyst only so far. We learn best by doing, and the case studies in this book will help you learn how to devise alternatives. However, we believe that the search for alternatives can be made more productive through a two-step process. First, the analyst should identify a wide range of possible alternatives. Having identified generic and specific options used or proposed elsewhere, types or categories of options, and possible ways to modify the status quo, the analyst should refine, modify, alter, adapt, reconstruct, and otherwise invent alternatives that will respond to the nuances of the specific policy problem being analyzed. The first step is basically a search process. The second step requires creative manipulation. Below we first present numerous ways of locating existing alternatives; then we present a method for creating new alternatives.

SEARCHING FOR ALTERNATIVES

In addition to the general processes described above, there are several specific methods for identifying potential alternatives. Sometimes alternatives are derived through "researched" methods; that is, formal research projects are under-

---

[18] Brightman, *Problem Solving*, pp. 185–86.
[19] Ibid., pp. 187–88.
[20] Ibid., pp. 74–83.
[21] Majone, *Evidence, Argument, and Persuasion*, p. 143.

Researched analysis and experimentation	Passive collection and classification
No-action analysis	Development of typologies
Quick surveys	Analogy, metaphor, and synectics
Literature review	Brainstorming
Comparison of real-world experiences	Comparison with an ideal

Figure 6-1 Methods of Identifying Alternatives

taken to determine the pros and cons of possible options, often in various settings. Instead of this approach, we want to be able to identify alternatives quickly, and this requires that we use approaches other than researched methods. These methods (listed in Figure 6-1) include no-action analysis, literature reviews, quick surveys, the use of analogy and metaphor, brainstorming, and examination of ideal solutions. No-action analysis investigates the status quo to see whether time might resolve the problem and to provide a base against which to measure other alternatives. Literature reviews can reveal successful solutions used elsewhere. Quick surveys can generate similar information. Analogy and metaphor help us identify alternatives by looking at similar problems and solutions. Brainstorming involves various techniques to help us ferret out ideas and options that are not obvious. The examination of ideal or extreme solutions helps us to identify the range of possibilities and causes us to think more expansively.

Researched Analysis and Experimentation

Because we are focusing on basic, quick analysis, we will not discuss researched methods for identifying alternatives, except to note that useful researched methods exist for those situations where time is available. Among the more commonly used researched methods is survey research, where the attitudes, opinions, and beliefs of affected parties are probed to uncover suggestions about and preferences for various actions. Survey research methods might also be used to collect data about possible alternatives from other analysts and from experts.

Comparative analysis, discussed below as a quick method, could be used as a researched method if, for example, we were to collect data from numerous jurisdictions about policies for a particular problem and then compare these data to determine the effectiveness of alternatives in different settings. Evaluation research can also be used to detect possible alternatives. For example, experimental designs using preprogram and postprogram data for treatment and control groups could be used to help determine which alternatives are more effective and to suggest modifications in alternatives that would make them more effective in various settings. Moreover, the ability to manage large amounts of computer-based data to observe and explore patterns not previously obvious can lead to fortunate, unanticipated, and sometimes unrelated discoveries. The use of fluoride to control tooth decay was one alternative identified through such a pattern recognition process. And space satellite photography and surveying techniques promise advances in natural resource preservation, weather prediction, and agricultural planning.[22] Such approaches are clearly beyond the effort and time limits imposed by basic analysis, but data from such analyses can become input to basic analysis. Most basic analysis will have to rely on such methods as no-action analysis, literature reviews, experience elsewhere, the use of analogy and metaphor, brainstorming, and the analysis of the ideal—methods that can be carried out quickly.

No-Action (Status Quo) Analysis

Alternatives are sought because the client, some authority, a community group, or other body has perceived that a problem exists and an alternative policy or action can ameliorate the problem. To decide which alternative to adopt, an evaluation is conducted to estimate how effective various proposals might be in changing the status quo. We want to know what the situation would be like with this remedial action and what it would be like without the action. In order to be able to make such a judgment, we have to invest as much time in analyzing the no-action alternative as in analyzing the action alternatives.[23] Developing a detailed no-action alternative and forecasting its results provides a benchmark against which the results of all action alternatives can be measured. In practice, unfortunately, little time is usually spent on a serious analysis of no action. Rather, the no-action alternative is described simply as the obviously unacceptable status quo—an option so weak that almost any action will appear preferable.

Creating a useful baseline alternative is a compelling reason to develop a no-action analysis, but there are other reasons as well. First, potential budget reductions and budget reallocations call for careful analysis of the alternative of doing nothing. Trade-offs must be clear, since immediate savings may have to be exchanged for greater future costs if doing nothing is the alternative selected. Second, no-action analysis can help clarify project objectives. Third, it can underline the need (or lack of need) for action. Fourth, no-action analysis provides a framework for linking project-specific planning to a comprehensive or strategic plan. Finally, accepting the possibility that no action could be the best solution acknowledges the difficulties inherent in problem definition, and the possibility that the problem does not have an optimal solution.

The no-action alternative rarely involves doing absolutely nothing. Thus, it is seldom true that the no-action alternative has no direct costs. Transportation planning has developed the best-articulated concept of no action: minimum maintenance. The no-action alternative for a transportation problem cannot

---

[22] Richard Hofferbert, *The Reach and Grasp of Policy Analysis: Comparative Views of the Craft* (Tuscaloosa: University of Alabama Press, 1990), pp. 41–56.

[23] Amy Helling, Michael Matichich, and David Sawicki, "The No-Action Alternative: A Tool for Comprehensive Planning and Policy Analysis," *Environmental Impact Assessment Review* 2, no. 2 (June 1982), 141–58.

increase traffic capacity or upgrade service, and it must include the completion of projects under development and the continuation of existing transportation policies such as reasonable maintenance.[24]

The rationale for using what is, in effect, a reasonable-maintenance policy as a benchmark to which other alternatives can be compared includes the ease with which future service and operational characteristics and maintenance costs can be predicted; the assumption that a minimum level of service and safety must be maintained; and the belief that extrapolation of current conditions into the future will be generally more reliable and valid than a benchmark of no investment whatsoever. Thus, the supply of transportation facilities and services is held constant while other parts of the system—population, land use, and economic activity—are allowed to vary. Comparisons are then made among the impacts of a variety of action alternatives and this no-action alternative.

While this reasonable-maintenance definition can be usefully applied to projects in functional policy areas other than transportation, it does have problems. The line between no action and limited action, or maintenance, is unclear. Straying over this line may defeat the purpose of no action as a true benchmark and cause problems in the evaluation. A second pitfall is that in some instances developing the impact data for a maintenance or limited-action option could be more difficult than determining it for no action at all or for immediate disinvestment.

When evaluating plans or programs before they are implemented, it is necessary to assess what changes are a direct result of the proposed action. These "impacts" are defined as the difference between two states: the future with the proposed action and a second, baseline reference state. There are a number of alternative reference states.[25] These include:

1. The original state existing before the action was taken, commonly referred to as the current situation or existing conditions.
2. The state that would evolve in the absence of the plan or program. This is the no-action alternative.
3. Some goal or target state.
4. The ideal state.

It is the second of these that provides the advantages of a benchmark for analysis, since it matches exactly the scenarios of the action alternatives, absent only the proposed action. In all other aspects, the two states are identical, with the effects of the proposed alternative isolated. In practice, the first reference state, existing conditions, is often used because data on the current situation can be obtained more easily than for a future state. However, changes in population

[24] J. S. Lane, L. R. Grenzeback, T. J. Martin, and S. C. Lockwood, *The No-Action Alternative: Impact Assessment Guidelines*, National Cooperative Highway Research Program, Report No. 217 (Washington, DC: National Research Council, December 1979).

[25] Donald M. McAllister, *Evaluation in Environmental Planning: Assessing Environmental, Social, Economic, and Political Tradeoffs* (Cambridge, MA: MIT Press, 1980).

and patterns of development, for example, will occur whether or not a plan or public works program is implemented, and these changes cannot be distinguished from those attributable to the proposal when existing conditions are used as a reference state. The third and fourth possible reference states above suffer from the same weakness. Therefore, we recommend using the no-action alternative as the reference state.

The action alternative(s) should be subdivided in a manner that allows description of the effects of taking action on some elements and no action on some others. For example, the proposal might be subdivided so that information would be available to describe what would happen if all but the most expensive, or least cost-effective, element were implemented, or if a particularly objectionable element were shelved. An action alternative thus becomes more flexible and less of an all-or-nothing proposition. Segmenting also identifies the effects and linkages of subelements of the proposed action, allowing them to be placed in rough priority of importance. It can also lead to refined recommendations for action on parts of the proposal that meet truly critical needs or have noteworthy benefits, while eliminating portions that offer less compelling reasons for action.

Similar arguments can be advanced for segmenting the alternatives in time: proposing no action for a period followed by action. For example, an alternative under which no action lasted three years might show few adverse impacts, whereas no action for ten years might show conditions deteriorating unacceptably. The analysis may reveal several critical points rather than a continuous, smooth decline. Because it will take time to implement the proposed action, it may be important to work backward from a critical threshold, such as an expected massive failure of an existing sewage treatment system, to make sure action is taken before the threshold is crossed. Such critical points can be identified by comparing the results of action and no-action alternatives for several future dates rather than for only a single design year.

Quick Surveys

From a very practical standpoint it is a good idea to let other analysts and friends know you are working on a new problem, for they may have suggestions about alternatives or will remain alert for ideas to pass on to you. Analysts develop a network of friends to call upon, to test ideas on, and with whom to share new ideas. Classmates can form the basis of this network. When faced with a new problem, try these contacts for relevant ideas. One of the first steps in generating alternatives is to get in touch with people in this network. A more formal approach might include a systematic telephone survey of other analysts and experts in the field to generate ideas and to develop lists of possible sources and other people to contact.[26] This quick survey can also yield a list of suggested

---

[26] On the use of experts, see Olaf Helmer, "Using Expert Judgment," in *Handbook of Systems Analysis: Craft Issues and Procedural Choices*, ed. Hugh J. Miser and Edward S. Quade (Chichester, Eng.: Wiley, 1988), pp. 87–119.

alternatives, analysts who have dealt with similar problems, other locales or organizations that have experienced similar problems, relevant literature, and other types of advice and counsel. The quick-survey approach might also involve recording and classifying alternatives suggested at public meetings, public hearings, and those in editorials, letters to the editor, and the like. Since the point of this data collection is to obtain as many ideas as possible, not to determine the prevalence of various opinions, representativeness of samples is not an issue. For more detail on quick data collection, refer back to Chapter 3.

Literature Review

It would be a mistake to overlook the literature as a source of alternatives. Books and journals in the fields of planning and policy analysis may contain cases that will illuminate the search for alternatives. The literature of the substantive field in which the problem is located (e.g., housing, education, water quality) should also be examined as a source of alternatives used elsewhere (both successes and failures) and proposed policies that may not have been tried. Remember that "documents lead to people and people lead to documents."

Comparison of Real-World Experiences

While searching for alternatives through a quick survey or literature review, analysts uncover both policy ideas and real-world experience. We believe it is important to separate from this list a special list of real-world alternatives and to compare types of alternatives used in settings similar to yours. The alternative alone may be a valuable idea, but its relative usefulness is enhanced if we can determine why it was adopted, what other alternatives were discarded, whether the alternative was modified after implementation, who supported and who opposed it, and how it has fared. Obtaining this information on more than a few real-world alternatives can become a large research project, an undertaking much beyond basic, quick analysis. However, an iterative approach might be used. A quick first cut could be made to identify similar cases, follow-ups could be made on the more similar cases, and details about the most relevant cases could be obtained at an even later stage of analysis. The purpose of the comparative analysis of real-world experiences is not to identify the one best alternative but to generate a list of possible options that experience has shown can be implemented. It is not unusual to find that many apparently good alternatives fall flat when no way can be found to implement them. Consequently, a few alternatives drawn from real-world experience should be among those selected for further analysis.

Passive Collection and Classification

To this point we have discussed the search for alternatives as if it were essentially an active pursuit of elusive concepts or new ideas. This is not always the case. In his study of policy analysts at the federal level, Meltsner reports that preferences often exist before the analysis, and that analysts are not always free to consider all alternatives or devise new ones. Sometimes they can seize on an already developed idea when its time arrives.[27] Proposals will come from clients or superiors, from advocates of various positions, and from organizations and other interest groups. Besides actively seeking alternatives, the analyst should systematically record and classify alternatives suggested by others. Past positions taken by affected groups might also be examined. Alternatives derived from these sources may be suitable in their original form or may be modified. A little humility, in the form of admitting that someone else has a good idea, can lead to good alternatives.

Development of Typologies

If problems can be grouped into types or classes, parallels become clearer. Thinking about the types of individuals, groups, or organizations affected by a potential policy can help us identify alternatives. For example, possible alternative ways of providing recreation opportunities were identified by developing a typology of recreation users (e.g., day trippers, overnighters, campers, motelers, etc.) and then conceptualizing alternatives to respond to their various needs. In analyzing the heroin problem, Moore developed a typology of users in order to understand the problem and possible policies for addressing it.[28] Developing typologies is essentially a list-making approach where we first identify affected groups, then identify their probable reactions to each alternative, and then develop specific means of making promising alternatives more acceptable to them.

Analogy, Metaphor, and Synectics

A possible solution to a problem might be found by examining how analogous problems were solved in the past. Such approaches have been titled *analogy*, *metaphor*, or *simile*, using terms from the study of literature. The distinctions among these terms do not appear to have been carried over into policy analysis. All are used to mean searching for solutions by looking at similar situations.

Analogy, metaphor, and simile have been used in problem solving both to define problems and to help the problem solvers identify possible solutions or alternatives. Supporters of this method argue that we often fail to find a solution to a problem because we do not recognize that our seemingly new problem is really an old problem. In thinking about possible solutions, attributes of the problem are listed and then analogies to the attributes are identified. The idea is that we can relate what we know about one problem and its solution to other problems and their solutions. The analogy may be drawn from an area quite

---

[27] Meltsner, *Policy Analysts*, pp. 130–40.

[28] Mark H. Moore, "Anatomy of the Heroin Problem: An Exercise in Problem Definition," *Policy Analysis* 2, no. 2 (Fall 1976), 639–62.

different from that of the problem. Its purpose is to cause the problem solvers to begin thinking of possibilities so that these ideas may generate other ideas.

Using analogies to solve problems is the basis for *synectics*, a technique developed since the mid 1940s by Gordon. The synectics process is intended to provide the problem solver new perspectives on a problem and to suggest possible solutions. Synectics brings individuals together in a problem-stating/problem-solving group so that the chance of finding a solution is increased.[29] The synectic process involves both "making the strange familiar" and "making the familiar strange." The first of these we do in any problem-solving setting where we attempt to define and understand the problem. But synectics experts argue that making the strange familiar, if used alone, will yield superficial solutions. In order to get a new viewpoint, they believe, we must view the problem in a new way, because most problems are not new. The new viewpoint, however, can bring about a new solution.[30] Synectics uses four types of analogy to take a new look at familiar problems: personal analogy, direct analogy, symbolic analogy, and fantasy analogy.[31]

Personal analogy involves placing one's self into the problem situation and attempting to identify with the problem. For example, to improve on ship or submarine designs, analysts have imagined themselves as fish or other marine life. Chemists have attempted to identify with molecules in action. Policy analysts may imagine themselves as defendants or proponents. This technique requires a loss of self, something which many of us are unable to do easily. Novices need to be led through this method in order to be comfortable and confident with this type of role playing.

Direct analogy involves searching for solutions among solutions to other problems. Ways to package food products might be used to provide ideas about ways to make an energy-efficient entrance to a home. The ways that animals cope with the cold might also suggest ways for conserving energy.

Symbolic analogy uses objective and impersonal images to describe a problem. Symbolic analogy is qualitative rather than quantitative and is generated by association. The analyst tries to imagine solutions that are aesthetically satisfying rather than technologically accurate. A rope trick was once used as the symbolic solution for a type of jacking mechanism that would fit into a small box.

Fantasy analogies allow the analyst to work like a writer or painter and describe the world in an ideal form. In a similar way, a physicist could pretend that the laws of physics do not hold and design a solution to a problem. When the laws are brought back into the picture, the physicist may have found aberrations in the laws that lead to a solution to the problem. In the process of inventing a vaporproof closure for space suits, fantasy analogy was used to devise an alternative by conceptualizing the zipper as a trained insect pulling a thread

[29] W. J. J. Gordon, *Synectics* (New York: Harper & Row, 1961), pp. 3–7.
[30] Ibid., p. 34.
[31] Ibid., pp. 35–36.

between two springs that push rubber lips together.[32] The final alternative is, of course, seldom like the fantasy analogy. The fantasy analogy is useful in the early stage of analysis for stimulating thinking and for suggesting possible options.

Analogy and metaphor have been used to help understand or model urban processes and to help understand problems and alternatives quite different from the subject of the analogy. We have already mentioned the analogy of the cows grazing on the commons, in which their owners ignore the costs that the cows impose on others who share ownership of the commons. One of the many problems explained by this analogy is that of car owners who use a common expressway and ignore the cost that their use imposes on others.[33]

There is no guarantee that analogies will result in the right alternatives. May has pointed out that when using analogy, policymakers have tended to seize upon the first analogy that comes to mind; they do not continue to search, and they do not pause to analyze the case, test its fitness, or ask how it might be misleading. Furthermore, he argues, they see a trend running toward the present and assume it will continue into the future. May believes, however, that policymakers could use history more discriminatingly and seek alternative analogies to understand whether a moral observed in one case is a principle exemplified in many other cases. He also points out that instead of extending a trend line, policymakers could seek to understand whether the forces that produced the trend will continue into the future.[34]

Brainstorming

Brainstorming can be used to conceptualize possible solutions to problems. Osborn developed the brainstorming technique from the late 1930s through the 1950s as a way to generate ideas, although he notes that a similar procedure was used in India for more than 400 years by Hindu teachers working with religious groups.[35]

The modern brainstorming session is a creative conference for producing a checklist of ideas leading to a problem solution. Brainstorming ranges from informal, quick meetings among staff members working on a problem to more structured meetings of staff, experts, and consultants. Most of us use the term *brainstorm* very loosely to refer to any group discussion of a problem and its possible solutions. The group might be comprised on the spur of the moment of persons assigned to work on a problem plus others in the office who are assumed to have some insight into the problem. However, Osborn's technique

[32] Ibid., pp. 48–51.

[33] Edith Stokey and Richard Zeckhauser, *A Primer for Policy Analysis* (New York: Norton, 1978), p. 11.

[34] Ernest R. May, *"Lessons" of the Past: The Use and Misuse of History in American Foreign Policy* (New York: Oxford University Press, 1973), pp. xi–xii.

[35] Alex F. Osborn, *Applied Imagination: Principles and Procedures of Creative Problem-Solving*, 3rd ed. (New York: Scribner's, 1963), p. 151.

is more formalized, with participants being chosen for their demonstrated expertise in the problem area. The meeting process is also more structured. Ideas are developed in a first-phase brainstorming session where criticism and evaluation are kept to a minimum, and ideas are evaluated in a follow-up session. Possible problem solutions are then ranked and packaged into a problem solution. Osborn emphasized that a true brainstorming session must follow the deferment-of-judgment principle; that is, ideas should be evaluated after the idea-generation phase in order not to throw cold water on good ideas or to shut out good ideas because people who could offer them feel they might be criticized.[36]

Brainstorming's supporters argue that it is a superior way to generate ideas, and that a properly conducted brainstorming session can produce many more good ideas in less time than a typical conference. Research results apparently support this contention.[37] A number of reasons have been given for the higher productivity of brainstorming sessions, including the chain-reaction effect (ideas from one person will trigger ideas in others), the impact of rivalry (suggestions by one person can be improved by another, and competition will make participants work harder), and positive reinforcement (ideas are rewarded and criticism is held to a minimum). Osborn provided a set of basic rules to follow for brainstorming sessions:[38]

1. *Criticism is ruled out.* Adverse judgment of ideas must be withheld until later.
2. *"Free-wheeling" is welcomed.* The wilder the idea, the better; it is easier to tame down than to think up.
3. *Quantity is wanted.* The greater the number of ideas, the more likelihood of useful ideas.
4. *Combination and improvement are sought.* In addition to contributing ideas of their own, participants should suggest how ideas of others can be turned into better ideas, or how two or more ideas can be joined into still another idea.

Other guidelines include working as a large group, not dividing into little groups; keeping a written record of all ideas suggested; encouraging people to contribute ideas even if they think their ideas are worthless; and focusing on a specific problem so that thoughts can be directed. Before we present specific steps for conducting a brainstorming session, we should point out that the method has been criticized. Others have argued that deferred judgment does not always result in better solutions, that individuals find it hard not to criticize one another's ideas, and that brainstorming does more harm than good.[39] Osborn, the developer of the method, recognized that brainstorming has drawbacks, and he argued that brainstorming should be a supplement to other methods of problem

---

[36] Ibid., p. 152.

[37] Ibid., pp. 152–53.

[38] Ibid., p. 156; but see also Edward and Monika Lumsdaine, *Creative Problem Solving* (New York: McGraw-Hill, 1990), pp. 101–36.

[39] Brightman, *Problem Solving*, p. 91.

solving. Osborn warned against failing to define the problem accurately, failing to encourage participants when initial ideas were not very good, failing subsequently to evaluate and criticize the ideas, overselling the technique, and failing to follow brainstorming procedures.[40]

Over the years, individuals and groups using brainstorming have found that a group of 4 to 12 people works best, that an odd-numbered group may be necessary for decision making but not for idea generating, that ideas produced by brainstorming should be screened at a later session by persons other than those who generated them, and that the panel should consist of a leader, an associate leader, five core members, and five guests. The core members serve as pacesetters with above-average facility in generating ideas, and the members of the group should be rotated. Experience suggests that the group should be comprised of peers, since superiors can discourage free participation by subordinates. The leader begins the session by spelling out the charge, calling for suggestions, and keeping the session moving. One idea at a time should be offered, and "hitchhike" ideas (modifications of ideas already offered) should be taken before going on to other ideas in order to make best use of the power of association. Ideas should be recorded by a secretary and numbered, but not associated with individuals. The pace of idea suggesting should be quick. Sessions may be as short as 15 minutes or as long as 45 minutes.[41] A day or two after the session, participants might be recontacted to see if they have useful afterthoughts.

A follow-up session is used to categorize and refine the brainstorm ideas. The list of ideas is categorized and screened by all or part of the brainstorm panel. Sometimes it is evaluated by others. The final evaluation should be done by those directly responsible for the problem.[42] The evaluators, or final screeners, play an important role in deciding which ideas are pursued. They must avoid dismissing eccentric ideas, and they must confirm the value of promising ideas.

In addition to verbal brainstorming, written brainstorming or "brainwriting" has been used with larger groups of people and with people who cannot meet in the same location. The Lumsdaines describe a number of brainwriting techniques ranging from the "gallery method," where ideas are written on large posters and then the participants circulate among them to add their own ideas, to the Japanese "Ringii" process, in which an idea is submitted to members of an organization who add to or modify the idea. The original idea is then reworked by its proponent or an independent panel. Yet other possibilities include electronic brainstorming via electronic mail (the high-tech equivalent of posting ideas on the office bulletin board for comment) to interactive brainstorming that combines silent idea writing with the verbal sharing of ideas and force-fitting techniques that cause the mind to take creative leaps.[43]

---

[40] Osborn, *Applied Imagination*, pp. 191–92.

[41] Ibid., pp. 166–79.

[42] Ibid., pp. 197–203.

[43] Lumsdaine and Lumsdaine, *Creative Problem Solving*, pp. 112–20.

In quick analysis, brainstorming sessions to generate alternatives might include a staff meeting with people from other departments, a session with a citizen group, board, or commission, or even a session designed to make good use of expensive consultants.

Comparison with an Ideal

Writers about problem solving hold that problems need to be defined broadly, especially when innovation is sought and we do not know what we're seeking. In these cases they argue that the problem should be stated all-inclusively so that even the remotest possibility is not precluded—so that we do not precondition our mind to a narrow range of possibilities.[44] Put another way, it is often useful to conceptualize what the ideal alternative would be, even if that ideal is beyond reach. Once the ideal has been described, constraints can be added to see if an acceptable alternative remains. It may even be possible to find ways to eliminate the constraints so that the ideal can be realized. Even if removing constraints is not possible, simply thinking about the ideal may trigger good ideas. It may help us devise other alternatives that approach the ideal and better define our preferences. Arrow's axiom of the independence of irrelevant alternatives states that a choice made from a given set of alternatives depends only on the ordering of the alternatives in that set, meaning that only *available* alternatives have a bearing on the choice to be made.[45] Zeleny argues to the contrary that unattainable or irrelevant alternatives do influence our preferences. In this regard he asks:

> When the electorate chose between Reagan and Carter, was the fact that Ford did not run irrelevant? Is it true that Kennedy, although finally not a candidate but always a potential candidate or at least a point of reference, had no effect on the choice between Reagan and Carter? Do not people choose among the available so as to emulate as closely as possible the preferred nonavailable? Or to move as far away as possible from the one considered mediocre?[46]

Zeleny goes on to cite research that shows when subjects were given a choice among attractive but imperfect alternatives, their choice was influenced by whether, prior to the decision, they were shown a "perfect" or "mediocre" alternative that was not available to them.[47]

We argue that the "ideal" alternative can be a useful concept in identifying alternatives. Its value is not so much in stating a goal to be attained, but rather in causing us to think about alternative means to move toward the ideal. The

---

[44] Osborn, *Applied Imagination*, p. 92

[45] Kenneth J. Arrow, *Social Choice and Individual Values*, 2nd ed. (New York: Wiley, 1964), pp. 26–28.

[46] Milan Zeleny, *Multiple Criteria Decision Making* (New York: McGraw-Hill, 1982), p. 135. See also Stokey and Zeckhauser, *Primer for Policy Analysis*, pp. 287–90.

[47] Zeleny, *Multiple Criteria Decision Making*, pp. 135–37.

ideal has been suggested as a paradigm that should compete with the traditional concept of optimality, and advanced methods have been devised, such as compromise programming, to help analysts determine the best solution to a problem by examining the distance from the ideal. This method is too involved to discuss here, but the concept of the ideal should not be overlooked.

CREATING ALTERNATIVES

After compiling the list of possible options from among the alternatives suggested by others, those used in different locales, or those uncovered through the use of analogy or brainstorming, we still have to combine or fine-tune those alternatives to make them applicable to our problem, relevant in today's world, and responsive to policy constraints. The individual variables making up the alternatives will most likely have to be modified to produce a relevant alternative that squarely addresses the problem. Unfortunately, the literature does not provide a great amount of guidance when it comes to *creating* alternatives—except to tell us to be creative.[48] Most alternatives, however, appear to be adapted from other settings rather than being created.[49]

Alexander formalized a method for solving complex problems for which no prototype exists by "decomposing" problems into their component parts, analyzing the patterns of interactions among the components, and then recomposing the parts into a solution.[50] A computer-based researched method, this approach is intended to aid the designer in systematically structuring physical design problems. It has been used to solve problems of community mental health facilities design, highway route location, and office distribution and organization.[51] Its technical requirements, however, are beyond those of basic, quick analysis.

The morphological approach, taken from the science of form and structure, has also been used to create alternatives for complex problems with multiple objectives. Each of the system components is defined, and the possible forms it could take are identified. The subsystem forms are then combined in all possible ways to determine potential full-systems designs.[52] This approach has been likened to the process of ordering from a menu, where one item is selected from

---

[48] May, "Hints for Crafting Alternative Policies."

[49] Alexander, "Design in the Decision-Making Process," p. 282.

[50] Christopher Alexander, *Notes on the Synthesis of Form* (Cambridge, MA: Harvard University Press, 1964).

[51] Donald M. Koenig and Charles Rusch, *Design for Mental Health Services at the Community Level* (Berkeley: University of California, Architectural Experimental Laboratory, 1965); Marvin L. Manheim, *Highway Route Location as a Hierarchically-Structured Sequential Decision Process* (Cambridge, MA: MIT, Civil Engineering Systems Laboratory, 1964); Richardson, Severns, Scheeler & Associates, *Functional Relationships Study* (Champaign, IL: Author, 1969).

[52] Fritz Zwicky, *Discovery, Invention, Research Through the Morphological Approach* (New York: Macmillan, 1969).

those available in each of several categories.[53] While this may be a useful way for designing alternatives when component parts are known, identifying those components remains a difficult undertaking. One popular way in which components as well as complete alternatives are identified is by investigating comparable situations, as we mentioned earlier.

Feasible Manipulations

May has proposed a method for creating alternatives that resembles the morphological and decomposition approaches. He suggests that an early examination of "feasible manipulations" can be undertaken to address aspects of the policy problem.[54] Alternatives are then devised by combining the manipulated variables into coherent strategies, and these strategies are revised as the problem is redefined and the evaluation criteria shift. May's advice is drawn from his belief that the analyst can determine the variables in a problem that can be manipulated, and that this requires a sense both of what *can* be done and *should* be done. After the analyst has figured out what variables can be manipulated, and how much each variable can be manipulated, the possible actions can be packaged into sets of competing *strategies*. May uses the word *strategies* rather than *alternatives*, since he believes it captures the sense that competing policies involve manipulations of the same set of policy variables. He notes that "In forming feasible packages of actions, one must be able to conceptualize how different levels of variables fit together. . . . Typically, different combinations of levels of policy variables must be combined in order to obtain what are acceptable strategies in terms of a number of relevant criteria."[55]

May illustrates the process of establishing feasible manipulations with an example of the ways in which prison officials can reduce idle time among prisoners to help quell prisoner motives for rioting. First he identified the kinds of activities that prisoners can engage in, requirements, benefits, scheduling of activities, and the type of supervisory staff. Table 6-1 presents the range of feasible manipulations. Table 6-2 shows May's recombination of the various levels of policy variables into alternative strategies. In the process of trial-and-error combinations, May found that the type of staffing could be eliminated from consideration in further packaging strategies. In addition to the status quo, May devised an "incentives" strategy that provided rewards to prisoners for participation, a "disincentives" strategy that required some participation by all prisoners but punishment for nonparticipation, and a "forced participation" strategy that mandated a given amount of participation.[56]

Patton took a similar approach to defining alternatives in his quick analysis

[53] Athey, *Systematic Systems Approach,* pp. 74–76.
[54] May, "Hints for Crafting Alternative Policies," p. 235.
[55] Ibid., p. 240.
[56] Ibid., pp. 235–42.

Table 6-1   May's Feasible Manipulations

Policy Variable	RANGE OF MANIPULATION		
	Limited	Moderate	Wide
Range of prisoner activities	Institutional industries and support activities	Institutional industries; support activities; limited vocational education	Institutional industries; support activities; vocational and academic education; structured recreation programs
Participation requirements	Mandatory participation of 10 hours per day	Mandatory minimum participation of 4 hours per day	Voluntary participation
Participation benefits	No pay; punishment for non-participation	Nominal pay for some activities	Pay and parole considerations
Scheduling of activities	Concurrent 10-hour day availability	Staggered, 12-hour day availability	Multiple offerings, 16-hour day availability
Staffing	Guards supervise activities	Paraprofessionals supervise activities	Prisoners supervise activities

Source: Peter J. May, "Hints for Crafting Alternative Policies," *Policy Analysis* 7, no. 2 (Spring 1981), 237.

Table 6-2   May's Recombination of Policy Variables

	Status Quo	Incentives	Disincentives	Forced Participation
Range of prisoner activities	Moderate	Wide	Moderate	Limited
Participation requirements	Voluntary participation	Voluntary participation	Mandatory participation of 4 hours per day	Mandatory participation of 10 hours per day
Participation benefits	Nominal pay for some activities	Pay and parole considerations	Punishment for nonparticipation	Nominal pay
Scheduling of activities	Concurrent	Multiple offerings	Concurrent	Staggered

Source: Peter J. May, "Hints for Crafting Alternative Policies," *Policy Analysis* 7, no. 2 (Spring 1981), 241.

of early-retirement options for the University of California system.[57] Being required to develop a report on the costs and benefits of early-retirement policies in a seven-day period, he first defined the problem as primarily an issue of budgetary stringencies. He then examined experience in business and industry, identified the policy variables that had been manipulated in these settings, figured out how much each could be manipulated in the university setting, and packaged the manipulable variables into competing alternatives or strategies.

[57]Carl V. Patton, "A Seven-Day Project: Early Faculty Retirement Alternatives," *Policy Analysis* 1, no. 4 (Fall 1975), 731–53.

Patton's strategies to encourage faculty members to retire early included incentive annuities based on the faculty member's own earnings history, early annuities based on the average earnings of the faculty member's peers, and early annuities combined with partial employment (Table 6-3). The effectiveness of the alternatives was gauged by computing the impact on faculty members of various ages with a range of years of service in terms of funds freed, number of early retirements generated, increase in the size of the early-retirement annuity, and relationship of the early-retirement annuity to preretirement salary. In later work, more alternatives were devised in the same way, and other evaluation criteria, including political, legal, and administrative feasibility, were considered, but the relative effectiveness of the alternatives remained the same.[58]

Modifying Existing Solutions

Although the analyst may be able to identify a long list of possible alternatives, many may need changing to be workable. Osborn, whom we cited earlier, spent a great amount of his career teaching people how to be more creative. In helping people to learn how to solve problems, Osborn devised a number of ways to modify existing solutions in order to generate new ones, including magnifying, minifying, combining, and rearranging existing options.[59] We have modified his categories to produce the following ways of creating policy options.

Magnify	Make larger, higher, longer. Add resources. Apply more often. Duplicate. Multiply. Exaggerate. Add new components.
Minify	Make smaller, shorter, narrower, lower, lighter. Miniaturize. Omit, remove, split apart. Understate.
Substitute	Switch components. Switch order. Use different materials. Change location. Change the sponsor.
Combine	Blend two approaches. Combine units. Combine purposes. Combine sponsors.
Rearrange	Reverse. Invert. Change sequence. Speed up. Slow down. Randomize. Place in a pattern.

Not only might existing options be made larger or smaller, or be combined, substituted, or rearranged, but they can be placed in a different location, or their timing, financing, or organization may be varied as well.

Location	Single location versus multiple locations. Scattered sites, nodes, linear arrangement. Permanent versus temporary. Mobile, rotating, dense, sparse, mixed, or segregated. Layered or juxtapositioned. Below ground, above ground. Adaptive reuse.

[58] Carl V. Patton, *Academia in Transition: Early Retirement or Mid-Career Change* (Cambridge, MA: Abt Books, 1979).

[59] Osborn, *Applied Imagination*, pp. 286–87.

Table 6-3 Results of Patton's Feasible Manipulations of Early-Retirement Options

Early Retirement Frees Some Funds but Usually Not Enough for the Hiring of a Replacement

		FUNDS FREED BY EACH ALTERNATIVE				
Age Group	Years of Service	Alternative 1 (Individual-Based Annuity)	Alternative 2 (Group-Based Annuity)			Alternative 3 (Partial Employment Plus Annuity)[a]
		Average[b]	Low third[c]	Mid third[d]	High third[e]	Average[b]
51–55	11–15	$3,407	$ −1,735	$3,407	$8,553	$2,567
51–55	16–20	972	−3,820	972	5,805	1,208
51–55	21+	−1,682	−6,187	−1,682	2,783	−1,939
56–60	11–15	8,326	2,650	8,326	14,002	3,312
56–60	16–20	5,903	475	5,903	11,332	1,985
56–60	21+	3,400	−1,820	3,400	8,350	588
61–65	11–15	15,188	8,901	15,188	21,423	5,556
61–65	16–20	12,967	10,139	12,967	19,047	4,449
61–65	21+	10,883	4,898	10,883	16,412	4,593

[a] Early retiree reemployed at one-half time.
[b] Average amount of funds freed by retiring a person within the age-service group.
[c] Funds freed by retiring a person whose salary is in the lowest third for the age-service group.
[d] Funds freed by retiring a person earning the mean salary for the age-service group.
[e] Funds freed by retiring a person whose salary is in the top third for the age-service group.

Early Retirement Under These Options Produces Larger Annuities Than Regular Early Retirement

		EARLY RETIREMENT INCOME AS PERCENTAGE OF NORMAL EARLY ANNUITY INCOME				
Age Group	Years of Service	Alternative 1 (Individual-Based Annuity)	Alternative 2 (Group-Based Annuity)			Alternative 3 (Partial Employment Plus Annuity)[a]
		Average[b]	Low third[c]	Mid third[d]	High third[e]	Average[b]
56–60	11–15	216%	270%	216%	180%	309%
56–60	16–20	192	240	192	159	251
56–60	21+	174	217	174	148	208
61–65	11–15	131	163	131	109	264
61–65	16–20	122	135	122	102	219
61–65	21+	116	145	116	100	173

[a] Early retiree reemployed at one-half time.
[b] Benefits to all early retirees within the age-service group.
[c] Benefits to an early retiree whose salary is in the lowest third for the age-service group.
[d] Benefits to an early retiree earning the mean salary for the age-service group.
[e] Benefits to an early retiree whose salary is in the highest third for the age-service group.

Source: Carl V. Patton, "A Seven-Day Project: Early Faculty Retirement Alternatives," *Policy Analysis* 1, no. 4 (Fall 1975), 743, 746.

Timing   Accelerate, lag, stagger, sequence, make concurrent. Accomplish in the shortest amount of time, stretch out over the longest feasible period. Time sharing.

Financing   Provide or purchase. Institute a tax or user fee. Subsidize. Use marginal or average cost pricing. Charge according to ability to pay or benefit derived. Copayment, deductible, partially subsidized, fully subsidized.

Organization   Centralize, decentralize. Provide as general purpose, special purpose. Mandate, regulate. Prohibit. Leave to individual decisions, with or without an incentive. Enforce, do not enforce. Inform. Implore.

Potential alternatives might also be modified or adapted by reconsidering how they might be implemented. The location of decisions, influence points, and how risk is handled can be varied to reveal potential alternatives.

Decision   Existing organization or individual, new organization or indi-
sites   vidual. Elected or appointed. Technical or political. Advisory or binding. Appealable or not.

Influence   Pressure from users, providers, intermediaries. Other benefi-
points   ciaries, those harmed.

Risk   Encourage adoption through guarantees, insurance, or reme-
management   dial correction after-the-fact.

Having identified the policy variables that can be manipulated, and having determined in what way, and to what extent, the variables can be manipulated, we must recombine them into competing alternatives (or strategies in May's conceptualization). This is no easy task, and the menu approach is not likely to work. "Only through an iterative process of trying a combination of manipulations, assessing that combination, then repackaging in light of the assessment can one begin to formulate a reasonable set of alternatives."[60] Since analysts are limited in their ability to compare many strategies, those that differ on relatively unimportant variables should be combined. By repackaging and recombining the policy elements, we can identify combinations that are better than others and that more completely satisfy evaluation criteria.

We have said that as many reasonable alternatives as possible need to be identified. While agreeing with this principle, Walker has argued, however, that alternatives need to be screened in order to narrow the range that will need to be examined in detail. A good screening process, he says, should not miss capturing any very good alternatives while reducing the number of alternatives to be evaluated later.[61] He suggests that during the alternatives identification stage we

---

[60] May, "Hints for Crafting Alternative Policies," p. 240.

[61] Warren E. Walker, "Generating and Screening Alternatives," in *Handbook of Systems Analysis: Craft Issues and Procedural Choices*, ed. Hugh J. Miser and Edward S. Quade (Chichester, Eng.: Wiley, 1988), pp. 229–30.

can eliminate from further consideration those alternatives that will not be able to be implemented for technical, economic, administrative, or organizational reasons, those that are politically unacceptable, and those that are dominated on all important measures by other alternatives. He notes, however, that the analyst might want to consider what steps might be taken to eliminate some of these obstacles so that in the longer term these alternatives might become feasible. Nagel has further argued that policy analysts have an obligation to show what would be required to make a second- or third-place alternative the preferred one.[62] We agree with this suggestion.

Both methods of searching for or identifying alternatives and methods for creating or devising alternatives have been presented. However, the distinction between search and creativity is not absolutely clear. Brainstorming, for example, might result in the assembly of a wide range of solutions that have been tried elsewhere but that might work in the present setting, or it might result in the creation of a new alternative.

Our emphasis in generating alternatives has been on search methods. This focus reflects our belief that relevant alternatives are devised by combining search and creativity in an interactive process. From our point of view, Alexander hit the nail on the head in his discussions of creativity. He wrote that true creativity which produces a genuine innovation that goes beyond routine imitation "is a process that, while far from random, defies prediction or predetermination," that design is likely "a mix of search and creativity, and that creativity itself includes at least some, if not a good deal of, information retrieval, processing and transformation," and that "there is probably at least a residue of inexplicable, extra-rational creativity in addressing novel problems, nonroutine situations, or in developing highly innovative and unprecedented solutions."[63]

Unfortunately our knowledge of extra-rational creative methods lags behind our knowledge of search methods, and we must rely upon what we know best. The hope is that policy analysis will be conducted in organizations with environments that will stimulate creativity, and that our knowledge of how to create alternatives will be enhanced.

PITFALLS TO AVOID

We introduced the topic of identifying alternatives by discussing the importance of generating many alternatives, postponing selection of the preferred alternative, thinking expansively, and conducting a continuous search for possible alternatives. Whether identifying alternatives or defining the problem is more difficult is a moot point. Both are difficult, important tasks, and if either is

---

[62] Stuart S. Nagel, "Introduction," in *Confronting Values in Policy Analysis: The Politics of Criteria,* ed. Frank Fischer and John Forester (Newbury Park, CA: Sage, 1987), p. 9.
[63] Alexander, "Design in the Decision-Making Process," p. 287.

mishandled we are not likely to solve the problem. Repeating what we said at the outset: If good, technically feasible alternatives are not included among the alternatives to be evaluated, or if the problem was defined incorrectly, then the most brilliant, technically superior analysis of alternatives is a waste of time. There is no way to guarantee that we have indeed identified good, solid, sound, appropriate alternatives, but we can improve our chances by avoiding a number of pitfalls, including the following:

Relying Too Heavily on Past Experiences.   In order to understand policy issues, analysts try to identify those parts of problems that resemble other problems from the past, and they explore options used in the past. Relying too heavily on the past, however, can cause us to classify problems incorrectly because of a desire to make them fit existing mental models, to adapt solutions used before because they are familiar rather than relevant, and to miss new possibilities because we have narrowed our view too soon.

Failing to Record Ideas and Insights as They Occur.   During brainstorming sessions ideas often come quickly, and it takes both effort and diligence to record all ideas and insights, especially since some may not seem particularly relevant at the time. At other times we may fail to record ideas because of inconvenience or because we think we will recall them later. Record such ideas as soon as they are generated, even if only to put down a few words, to avoid losing the ideas.

Locking in on a Problem Definition Too Soon.   We indicated earlier that problem definition is an iterative process, that a problem may not be fully defined until we have revealed hidden dimensions during the process of specifying criteria and identifying alternatives. If we conclude too soon that we have indeed identified *the* problem (or *the* goal for that matter), we may specify the problem incorrectly and in turn fail to identify relevant, possibly optimal alternatives. Examining alternatives generation in three cases, Alexander reports:

> In none of these cases, then, do we observe the free interplay between ends and means, between goal definition and alternatives design, that is prescribed for rational decision making. Rather, goal or problem definition was foreclosed, and design was preempted by perceptual, ideological, or organizational considerations which became the most limiting constraint on the ultimate range of possible solutions.[64]

Forming a Preference Too Early.   All analysts have biases toward certain types of solutions—for example, preferences for a market solution rather than a regulatory solution, or for centralization over decentralization. If we fall victim to our preferences early in the analysis, we will likely rule out or fail to consider possible alternatives.[65]

[64] Alexander, "Design of Alternatives," p. 397.
[65] Alexander, "Design in the Decision-Making Process," p. 282.

Criticizing Ideas as They Are Offered.   In brainstorming sessions participants are urged not to criticize ideas, because criticism can choke off new ideas. This same practice should carry over into other aspects of identifying alternatives, for criticism can discourage people from presenting potentially useful ideas. This criticism can be direct (actively voicing disapproval or scorn) or indirect (ignoring or failing to recognize suggestions), but either approach is likely to reduce greatly the chance that good alternatives will be discovered.

Ruling Out Alternatives through Pre-evaluation.   Sometimes alternatives are dismissed before they can be formally evaluated because they do not square with the beliefs of participants,[66] they were never part of the initial set considered due to major cultural constraints,[67] or the analyst fears the option may generate criticism.[68] This early-elimination process (pre-evaluation), then, gives dominance to one criterion rather than permitting a complete analysis with the full range of applicable criteria.

Failing to Reconsider Dismissed Alternatives as Conditions Change.   We have repeatedly stressed the iterative nature of policy analysis and the need to shift back and forth between problem definition and the creation and evaluation of alternatives. This iterative approach is necessary because problems and alternatives may not be fully defined without reference to one another, but it is also important because conditions may change during analysis, and alternatives dismissed early in the process may become relevant later.

SUMMARY

We have discussed the need for alternatives, the general sources for ideas about alternatives, and numerous ways to identify alternatives. We have also noted that real alternatives, not throwaway ones, are necessary. Alternatives are also generated by working through the analysis and will emerge as the problem is defined and refined. The analyst must begin writing as soon as possible. Everything that is known about the topic should be written down early. This will generate other ideas. Information and ideas should be added as they come to mind. The analysis should be a series of approximations, and early closure on a preferred alternative should be avoided. Osborn even warns us not to go to the library first, because that may cause us to fall into the rut created in the past.[69] He also cautions that too good a memory may block creative thinking because it

[66] Alexander, "Design of Alternatives," p. 398.

[67] Amos Rapoport, *Human Aspects of Urban Form: Towards a Man-Environment Approach to Urban Form and Design* (Oxford: Pergamon Press, 1977), p. 16; see also Amos Rapoport, *History and Precedent in Environmental Design* (New York: Plenum Press, 1990), esp. pp. 460–67.

[68] Meltsner, *Policy Analysts,* p. 136.

[69] Osborn, *Applied Imagination,* p. 134.

will cause us to throw out good ideas, since we too easily remember problems of the past.[70] Furthermore, we ought to react positively to a new idea, to think up as many positive reasons as possible for the new idea, because there will be many people eager to tell us why the alternative will not work.[71]

Forget quality initially and generate as many alternatives as possible. Start early and write down as many options as you can. Pick a place to work, set a deadline, team up with someone, give yourself a quota, keep searching, develop lists, and keep notes. Do not rule out your own creativity as a source of alternatives. Our experiences, travel, reading, and professional practice should be generating a stockpile of good ideas waiting to be used. Keep up with policy and planning literature. Know where to search for information about various types of problems. Read the footnotes and references of important articles. Collect key reports and publications ahead of time. Develop contacts. Share your information, attend conferences, and meet other analysts. Keep a list of names and telephone numbers of people working in your subject area. Practice.

Above all, do not give short shrift to the process of identifying alternatives, for this step may well be the most critical in the policy analysis process. As we noted earlier, the most careful, systematic, and high-quality evaluation of alternatives will not be able to reveal the best alternative if that alternative is not among those identified for evaluation. Alexander's study of alternatives generation in several organizations, where he has examined the linkage between problem definition, alternatives generation, and alternatives evaluation, illustrates the critical place of alternatives development in policy analysis. He points out the important fact that the policy finally selected may be determined more by the process of identifying alternatives than by the process of alternatives evaluation. Referring to the cases he examined, Alexander notes that the "process of limiting alternatives by inhibiting their design, by 'blending' options, and by their early informal elimination, seems to be the most powerful factor in deciding which options were evaluated, and in affecting the ultimate outcomes."[72]

Our final advice, then, is for the analyst to engage in a systematic, careful search for relevant alternatives, to develop an inventory of generic options that can be modified to fit the current problem, to use systematic design methods where possible to generate new alternatives, and to be aware that political and bureaucratic processes may act to eliminate relevant, possibly optimal alternatives before they can be formally evaluated. You should also take actions to retain, reconsider, and revive alternatives that have been dismissed without adequate evaluation.

---

[70] Ibid., p. 54.
[71] Ibid., p. 91.
[72] Alexander, "Design of Alternatives," p. 402.

GLOSSARY

Advocacy Search Process consideration of policies proposed by interested groups and individuals.

Analogy the examination of how similar problems were resolved in the past to identify possible alternatives for current problems. Also referred to as the use of metaphor or simile.

Brainstorming a formal group process technique for generating ideas in which ideas from one person are intended to trigger ideas from another. Positive reinforcement is encouraged and criticism is held to a minimum.

Brainwriting a form of written brainstorming used with larger groups of people and with people who cannot meet in the same location.

Development of Typologies grouping of problems into classes or types so we can understand them through our ability to see parallels in problems and their solutions—for example, identifying types of commuters and then conceptualizing alternatives to respond to their various needs.

Feasible Manipulations an approach to creating alternatives through the manipulation of variables into coherent strategies.

Metaphor see *Analogy*.

Morphological Approach generating alternatives by identifying the basic components of the system and the forms each could take. These are then combined in all possible ways to create alternatives for the entire system.

No-Action Alternative the state that would evolve in the absence of an action alternative (plan, program, policy) for the future. This is not the same as the status quo. The no-action alternative can often be defined as reasonable maintenance or extrapolation of current trends and policies.

Simile see *Analogy*.

Synectics a technique that brings people together to provide problem solvers new perspectives on problems to increase the chance that a solution will be found. Synectics uses analogy to take a new look at familiar problems.

EXERCISES

1. Refine and expand the alternative policies identified in the teen-age driver problem in Chapter 2. Be sure to identify alternatives in each of these categories:
   - (a) Age limitations
   - (b) Alcohol and drug consumption
   - (c) Automotive equipment
   - (d) Educational programs
   - (e) Licensing requirements
   - (f) Licensing restrictions
   - (g) Taxation devices
   - (h) Parental roles
   - (i) Peer actions
   - (j) General law enforcement
   - (k) Traffic enforcement

2. Most cities today are concerned about the number of homeless people who congregate in downtown commercial and tourist areas. Describe the concern as a mayor might see it. Then identify five alternative policies for dealing with this concern.

3. Propose ten one-sentence alternatives for solving each of the following problems. Do not worry about constraints or externalities. Propose alternatives that are as different from one another as possible, and all of which address the stated problems.

    (*a*)   My front yard is a mixture of grass and weeds. I want to get rid of the weeds.

    (*b*)   Pedestrians cross the streets wherever they please in downtown, endangering themselves and causing traffic problems.

    (*c*)   The city of Metropolis is short of water every summer, and every summer the shortage gets more severe.

4.   Find out how ten universities regulate on-campus parking for resident students who have their own automobiles. Classify these real alternatives.

5.   Consider a local problem that has been resolved recently. Reconstruct a list of alternatives that were considered. Expand the list to include 20 alternatives that could have been considered as well.

6.   Identify a current problem for your locality. Identify at least five groups with a stake in the issue. Identify the preferred alternative for each group.

7.   Using an important, current local problem as the subject, conduct a quick survey and literature review to determine the alternatives considered by similar cities. If you cannot think of a good topic, investigate the alternatives considered by cities that have adopted ordinances to regulate the burning of leaves.

8.   Select a problem. Identify five similar problems and list the ways they were solved. Modify those five solutions as solutions to five other current problems.

9.   Using a current issue that has been reported in your local paper, develop a set of other possible solutions through passive collection and classification. That is, examine past articles, editorials, and letters to the editor to construct a list of alternatives suggested by various groups.

10.   Using the information collected for Exercise 9, generate a list of your own alternatives. Identify the ideal solution. List the constraints. Beginning with the ideal, generate alternatives that recognize the existence of the constraints. Discuss the ways in which the ideal is reduced in desirability by the constraints.

11.   Distinguish between the use of the word *brainstorming* in common day-to-day language and its use in a policy analysis sense.

12.   Conduct a brainstorming session. Think up ways to reduce the time it takes to bring a defendant to trial.

13.   Conduct a brainstorming session. Think up ways to reduce littering on your college campus or in a downtown park.

14.   Use analogy to generate ways to create energy-efficient entrances to an apartment building. Build this analogy on the ways in which food products are packaged and stored.

15.   Develop a typology of local urban park users; then devise at least six ways to meet these needs.

16.   Using the feasible-manipulations approach, develop alternatives for reducing truancy levels among high school students. First identify the policy variables involved and the degree to which they can be manipulated. Then experiment with the various ways in which these policy variables can be recombined and packaged into new alternatives.

17.   Following Osborn's approach to modifying existing solutions, generate new alternatives for the problem situations listed below. For each, attempt to magnify, minify, substitute, combine, rearrange, and so on.

    (*a*)   Housing for the elderly

    (*b*)   Handicapped access to public transit

    (*c*)   Airport noise abatement

    (*d*)   Library book theft

    (*e*)   Litter at the beach

Chapter Seven

Evaluating Alternative Policies

In this book we are primarily interested in analyzing policies, programs, and projects before they are undertaken—*ex-ante* evaluation. More work has been done, however, in *ex-post* evaluation, or evaluation after implementation, much of it analyzing human services programs funded or run by the federal government. The U.S. government alone has spent nearly a billion dollars a year for program evaluation, and this expenditure underwrote the development of the field of ex-post human services program evaluation. The processes and the methods of ex-post evaluation are becoming standardized, and we provide a review of ex-post evaluation methods along with a discussion of program monitoring in Chapter 9. Our focus in this chapter is on evaluating public actions before they are implemented.

If evaluating policies after they are implemented is difficult and has created a whole new field of endeavor, what can be said of evaluating programs before they are implemented? First, the activity is more difficult because it necessarily involves projecting future states with and without the proposed policy or program. This requires somehow forecasting the effects of the proposed action. Second, there has not been an investment in ex-ante evaluation comparable to that in ex-post evaluation, nor have the many policies and programs of state and local governments that are the focus of this book received much attention.

The principal activity in ex-ante evaluation, then, is predicting the future with the public action, and the future without the public action. As shown in the section on "No-Action (Status Quo) Analysis" in Chapter 6, it is essential to have a baseline state (no-action) to which the effects of an action alternative can be compared. Prediction of future states of the world is tricky. Not only do we need to be concerned about what types of methods are appropriate to use, but the question of what to forecast is important. What is forecasted depends very much on how the problem is defined (Chapter 4) and what is to be evaluated.

Thus, another central concern in ex-ante evaluation is deciding what to evaluate, and therefore what to forecast. The principal question of ex-ante evaluation is whether the proposed policy will work: Will it meet the desired objectives? The second question is whether it will do so in an efficient, equitable, and politically viable manner. (See Chapter 5 on evaluation criteria.) The basic methods discussed in this chapter address these two concerns: the *forecasting* of project or policy impacts and the *evaluation* of the technical, economic, and political importance of those impacts.

The first topic, forecasting, is divided into three sections: extrapolative, theoretical, and intuitive forecasting techniques. The second topic, the evaluation of predicted outcomes, includes discounting, measuring efficiency, sensitivity analysis, allocation formulas, quick decision analysis, and political analysis.

A key question at this and other stages of the policy analysis process is the relationship between the analyst and the client. How far should the analyst go in making critical decisions for the client? Since many of the steps in the policy analysis process strongly influence the alternative chosen, it is evident that all analyses combine objective analysis and subjective choice.[1] This is especially true in the evaluation phase. How can the information be presented to clients so that their values and opinions are used in evaluating alternative policies? To what degree have viable alternatives been eliminated on the basis of the analyst's subjective preferences? What does this mean about alternatives development and rejection conducted before the client begins to evaluate? These questions are central to selecting appropriate forecasting and evaluation methods.

FORECASTING METHODS

We will discuss three types of forecasting methods. The first, *extrapolation*, is the simplest and most straightforward. The basic assumption is that a simple extension of what has occurred is a good approximation of what will occur. This assumption is sometimes useful in developing baseline data for the no-action alternative. It is much less useful in assessing the future impacts of an action program or policy unless there has been previous experience with such an action. However, if historical data for a similar policy are available, using them to predict

---

[1] Giandomenico Majone, *Evidence, Argument, and Persuasion in the Policy Process* (New Haven: Yale University Press, 1989), p. 28.

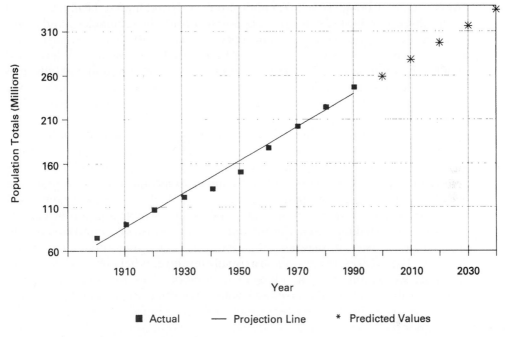

Figure 7-1   U.S. Population Totals, 1900–2040

what will happen to the proposed policy in the new context is largely an exercise in extrapolation. A common example of the use of extrapolation techniques is provided by simple population projections. In Figure 7-1 the past total population of the United States is plotted on a simple graph and a straight line fitted through these points. For example, future population totals for the years 2000 through 2040 can be extrapolated by extending the straight line into the future and reading the extrapolated values from the ordinate for those years.

Using *theoretical models* is another basic method for forecasting the effects of proposed policies. In this book we like to think of model making as a generic activity that is done daily by most people rather than as a specialized activity of social scientists.[2] We encourage students to develop their own models for use in predicting the outcomes of proposed policies. A model specifies the linkages between variables under consideration and allows us to predict the outcomes of a policy action. A model is nothing more than informed speculation about individual and collective human behavior, or more generally, the behavior of some system, whether human or nonhuman. If, for example, the policy under consideration is the institution of new police beat patrols in high-crime areas, and a model is chosen as the forecasting technique, then we will want to model how

[2]Charles A. Lave and James G. March, *An Introduction to Models in the Social Sciences* (New York: Harper & Row, 1975).

future neighborhood crime prevention would respond both to beat patrols and to the absence of beat patrols. We might first consult the criminology and policy analysis literature to see if others have looked at this problem before (perhaps even experimented with foot patrols and measured the results) and developed models. In addition to searching the literature, the analyst should seek information from colleagues in other cities and states on policies and programs that have been tried in their locales.[3] (Recall the sections in Chapter 3 on methods of data collection.)

Intuitive prediction techniques are undoubtedly the most common forecasting method. At their worst they are nothing more than people's stereotypes of human behavior—for example, that welfare causes recipients to become lazy and unmotivated. At their best the techniques can include a formal appraisal of what a group of experts in a particular subject area think the effects of a proposed policy will be. Of course, care should be taken to assemble a group of experts who have no vested interest in the outcome of the forecast, or if interested parties are going to be used, an analysis of their interests vis-à-vis their prediction should be done. The quickest predictions are usually intuitive. When time and resources are short, we rely on our own judgment and that of a handful of key informants to predict the outcome of a proposed policy. We will discuss ways to make that seat-of-the-pants method somewhat more reliable and legitimate.

Extrapolative Techniques

Extrapolative techniques have many virtues. They are simple and cheap to use and are often more accurate than sophisticated methods.[4] The underlying assumptions are that the patterns that existed in the past will continue into the future, and that those patterns are regular and can be measured. To be useful, measurements of trends must be precise and must use valid operational definitions of the subject at hand.[5] The most reliable type of prediction is persistence prediction—that is, predicting that things will continue pretty much as they are. For example, if it is raining today, the easiest and most reliable prediction without additional information would be that it will rain tomorrow.

Phenomena described with numbers can be forecast with extrapolation techniques. As is evident in the modeling example that follows, extrapolation

[3]You might consider joining organizations that provide a means to share data among other analysts, such as the Council of Governors' Policy Advisors, located in Washington, DC; the Planners' Advisory Service, located in Chicago; or the Council of State Governments, located in Lexington, KY.

[4]Andrew M. Isserman, "The Accuracy of Population Projections for Sub-County Areas," *Journal of the American Institute of Planners* 43, no. 3 (July 1977), 247–59; and William J. Drummond and David S. Sawicki, "GTEXTRAP: Multiple Region Population Projection Using Extrapolation Software," in *Spreadsheet Models for Urban and Regional Development*, ed. Richard Brail and Richard Klosterman (New Brunswick, NJ: Rutgers University Center for Urban Policy Research, forthcoming).

[5]William N. Dunn, *Public Policy Analysis: An Introduction* (Englewood Cliffs, NJ: Prentice Hall, 1981), p. 151.

can also be used more generally to allow experience from one circumstance to be used as a base for predicting the consequences of a policy alternative in another. In this section, however, we concentrate on numerical extrapolation.

The key to making extrapolative forecasts is having a good base of data and understanding the pattern within it. (See also the section in Chapter 3 on basic data analysis.) A useful rule is to plot the data first. There is no substitute for a preliminary visual check of the data. Because population forecasts are often at the center of local planning and policy issues, we will illustrate our points with a population forecast. We begin with Figure 7-1, which shows a plot of the actual total population of the United States for the years 1900–1990. Remember that by convention we plot the phenomenon under study, or dependent variable, on the Y axis (the ordinate) and time, the independent variable, on the X axis (the abscissa).

Having plotted the historical population data, we must first ask if the basic assumptions underlying the extrapolation are correct in this case. First, will past patterns hold in the future? The answer is not clear. There are two distinctly modern trends affecting the United States' population total: a worldwide slow-down in economic growth, and a declining birthrate. If the patterns vary, we must ask if they are regular and measurable. Among the most common regular variations in patterns over time are seasonal and cyclical fluctuations. For example, construction activity declines in the winter, particularly in the North. Similarly, construction activity declines in periods of recession. Population growth also slows in times of economic recession and depression. This information may be of little use for forecasting if we don't know what economic activity level to predict. The United States' economy may or may not move from its current state to future ones in the same way it has done in the past.

In plotting any set of historical data, we must make several important decisions that will probably affect the results of the extrapolation. The first is the selection of a time period. Figure 7-1 employs the 1900–1990 historical data, but different results would probably be obtained if we plotted earlier years. Another decision to be made is whether to plot the actual population count or to plot the population change over the time period. The best approach is to plot everything if you have the time. You are looking for a pattern, and as you recall from the section on using charts and graphs for analysis, you begin with a hypothesis. If your hypothesis is that population is growing linearly (same absolute number per time period) and you are correct, plotting absolute numbers will produce a pattern—a straight line. If your hypothesis is that population is growing geometrically (same percentage change per time period), you should plot percentage changes. This would also produce a straight line were your hypothesis true. Since linear patterns are easier to extrapolate, we often use logarithms to turn exponential data into linear data. This is discussed below and illustrated later in Figure 7-6.

Once the data are plotted, the next step is to extrapolate to future years. Examining the population data for the United States, we might argue that, except for the depression period 1930–40, the population appears to be growing along a reasonably straight line. We can attempt to extrapolate these data by drawing a line through the points with a ruler. Such an attempt is shown in Figure 7-1. Note that the assumption of a constant rate of increase does not seem appropriate when these population data are presented as percentage-change data as in Figure 7-2. There is no readily discernible pattern of percentage change. If we attempted to draw a line through these data, it would be approximately horizontal, meaning our best prediction for the future would be the average of past changes for the period plotted. Since not all of our assumptions are appropriate, we would not extrapolate the percentage-change data. Drawing a line though the absolute numbers, as shown in Figure 7-1, and extending the line to the years 2000, 2010, 2020, 2030, and 2040 yields forecast U.S. populations of approximately 255 million, 275 million, 295 million, 315 million, and 335 million, respectively.

To forecast populations in the same way, but with a bit more precision, we could calculate a mathematical formula that describes a line that fits through those data points. Since we have made the assumption of linearity, we can use

Figure 7-2 U.S. Population Changes, 1900–1990

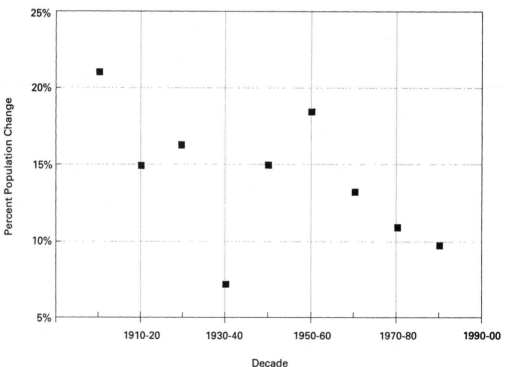

correlation and regression techniques based on the formula for a straight line, which is:

$$Y = a + bX$$

where a = the point where the regression line intersects the Y axis

b = the slope of the line; that is, the increase in Y for a unit increase in X

For Figure 7-1, visual inspection shows a to be approximately 48 million persons—determined by extending the extrapolation line back to the Y axis (1890). Rough calculations show b to be approximately 19 million persons per decade—determined by dividing the sum of the population increases each decade between 1900 and 1990 by nine (the number of decades).[6] Knowing the values of a and b, we can compute Y (the population) for any X (year). The formula we use to do this follows, with the earlier notation (symbolism) changed slightly.

The form of the equation will look like this:

$$P_{t+n} = P_t + b(n)$$

where P_{t+n} = population in year $t + n$

t = a time index (here it is decades, but it could be years)

P_t = population in year t

b = average growth increment per unit of time

n = number of units of time (in years, decades, etc.)

To use this formula to project population for a future period, 1890 serves as time period zero ($n = 0$), 1900 is time period one ($n = 1$), 1910 is time period two, and so on. The hypothetical population for 1890 as determined by the regression equation was 48,334,667, so we used that figure for a, and we mathematically determined b to be 1,911,979 when the time period is years and 19,119,790 when the time period is decades. Thus, for the relevant range of our data the formula will be:

---

[6] In practice, the values of X and Y are seldom located exactly on the regression line (i.e., there will not be a perfect correlation). Also, the values of a and b may not be able to be determined by inspection. The following formulas are used:

$$b = \frac{N \Sigma XY - (\Sigma X)(\Sigma Y)}{N \Sigma X^2 - (\Sigma X)^2}$$

$$a = \frac{\Sigma Y - b \Sigma X}{N}$$

$$P_{1890 + n} = 48,334,667 + 19,119,790 \ (n)$$

where n = number of decades since 1890

So, the population forecast for 2000 would be:

$$P_{2000} = 48,334,667 + 19,119,790 \ (11)$$
$$= 258,652,333 \text{ persons}$$

Likewise, the population forecast for the year 2010 would be:

$$P_{2010} = 48,334,667 + 19,119,790 \ (12)$$
$$= 277,772,121 \text{ persons}$$

These precisely extrapolated figures are very close to those derived by simply using a ruler to draw a line through the points. The projections are close because in drawing the line through the points we have followed the same rule that regression analysis uses: The line must pass through the scatter of points in such a way as to minimize the variation of observed cases around this line. This produces the "best fit" of the line through the points.

Numerous situations that require policy analysis, and therefore forecasting, do not appear to involve linear phenomena. Three examples of such patterns are catastrophic change, long-term growth, and long-term decline. The first describes situations experiencing sudden and sharp discontinuities. For example, Figures 7-3 and 7-4 show historic data points for the population of Wisconsin and percentage change. Three decades are outstanding for their irregularity. The first is the 1930–40 time period. This minor "catastrophe" of significantly lower population growth than over the rest of the time period is consistent with the U.S. pattern. Both Wisconsin and the United States as a whole experienced a small 7% change. This slow increase in population from 1930 to 1940 has been explained as the result of an economic depression. In the most recent decades, 1970–80 and 1980–90, Wisconsin experienced a much lower growth rate than the country as a whole. Reasons include the population movement that took place from snowbelt to sunbelt cities and the failure of midwestern state economies to keep pace with the economy of the United States. The question facing the forecaster today is whether Wisconsin will continue its course of decline relative to the United States as a whole or whether it will resume a more normal share of the country's growth. Was the 1970–90 period part of a long-run pattern, or was it a drastic discontinuity? If considered a discontinuity, more sophisticated forecasting methods would be appropriate.[7]

[7]T. J. Cartwright, "Planning and Chaos Theory," *Journal of the American Planning Association* 57, no. 1 (Winter 1991), 44–56; and C. A. Isnard and E. C. Zeeman, "Some Models from Catastrophe Theory in the Social Sciences," in *The Use of Models in the Social Sciences,* ed. Lyndhurst Collins (Boulder, CO: Westview Press, 1976), pp. 44–100.

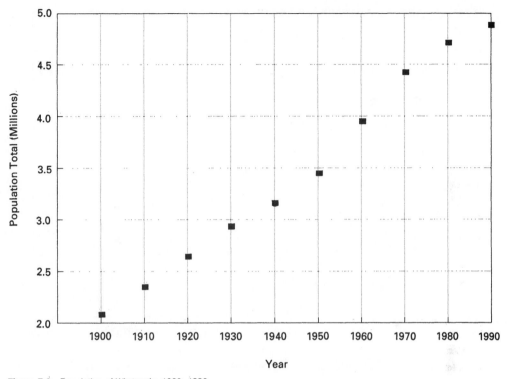

Figure 7-3 Population of Wisconsin, 1900–1990

Figures 7-5 and 7-6 illustrate how nonlinear data can on occasion be transposed into linear logarithmic data, extrapolated linearly and retransposed. The population of a suburb has been growing at a rapid exponential rate, approximately 26% per decade. Plotted normally, the pattern is curvilinear (Figure 7-5). However, when the population values are transformed into their common logarithms and plotted, they form a straight line (Figure 7-6). Either regression analysis or the simple ruler technique can be used to extrapolate the logarithmic data to future years.

Logarithms to base 10 are simple to use because they rely on raising the base 10 to an integral power. For example, $10^0 = 1$, $10^1 = 10$, $10^2 = 100$, $10^3 = 1,000$, and so on. Thus, the number 956 must have a logarithm that falls somewhere between 2 and 3 or between 2.0000 and 3.0000, obviously closer to 3.0000. Each integral exponent of 10 is called an *order of magnitude*, here the 2 or the 3. The decimal value is called the *mantissa* of the logarithm. For 10, 100, and 1,000 the mantissas are zero. Appendix 7–1 provides a table of common logarithms. Here are some numbers and their logarithms:

log 10   = 1.0000

log 20   = 1.3010

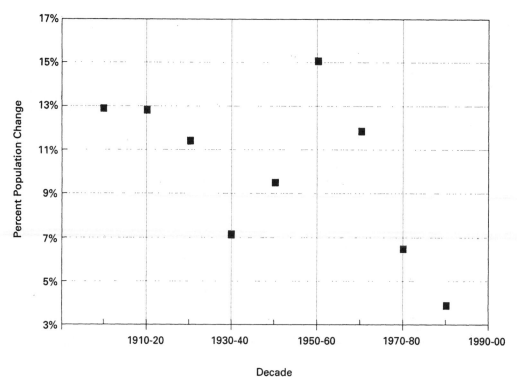

Figure 7-4   Wisconsin Population Changes, 1900–1990

log 40   = 1.6021
log 400   = 2.6021
log 4,000   = 3.6021
log 10,000   = 4.0000
log 100,000   = 5.0000

Note that as the number grows by factors of ten from 40 to 400 to 4,000, the order of magnitude of the logarithm grows by 1, from 1 to 2 to 3. In the example in Figure 7-6 the logarithm grows by 0.1000 each decade. This linear growth in the logarithm means there is a geometric growth in the actual population total. Thus, the log for the projected year 2000 population would be 4.9000 + 0.1000 = 5.0000. A log of 5 then converts to a population of 100,000 as the year 2000 forecast.

The use of logs, of course, does not always involve quantities that are so obvious. Sometimes we need to use a process of finding antilogs. The antilog of a log is the corresponding number. For example, 10,000 is the antilog of the log 4.0000. To ascertain the antilog, we first establish the order of magnitude. For

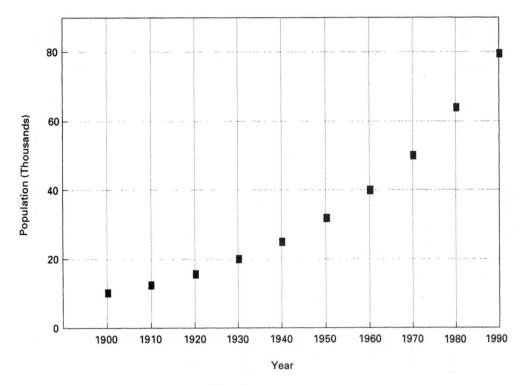

Figure 7-5   Population of a Growing Suburb, 1900–1990

the log 3.4829, for example, we establish first that the antilog must be somewhere between 1,000 (log 3.0000) and 10,000 (log 4.0000). (The order of magnitude is 3, since the number is greater than log 3 but not greater than log 4). Next, we look up the mantissa in a table of logs; in this case the mantissa is .4829 for which the antilog is 3.04. Then we adjust the antilog by the appropriate order of magnitude (3). The antilog of the log 3.4829 is therefore 3,040 (moving the decimal of the antilog 3.04 three places to the right). To find antilogs that do not appear exactly in the table, we interpolate. For example, the log .4833 falls between .4829 and .4843. It is 4/14 of the distance from 3.04 to 3.05, or 3.042857. Thus, the antilog of 5.4833 is 304,285.7 (moving the decimal of the antilog 3.042857 five places to the right).

Simple extrapolation methods can be made more sophisticated. For example, in population forecasting we might be interested in comparing a ratio of one area's historic population total to another; for example, Wisconsin's to the United States' and extrapolating the relationship to obtain a Wisconsin total. This technique is often used because forecasts for larger units are usually more sophisticated and less subject to variation. This ratio technique could be further extended to extrapolate the rate with which the smaller unit's share of the larger unit's total population would change, instead of assuming a static ratio. There

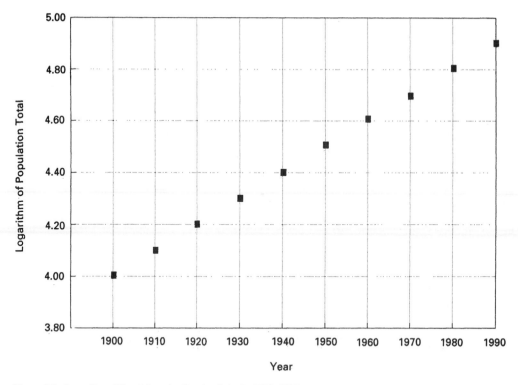

Figure 7-6 Logarithm of Population of a Growing Suburb, 1900–1990

are numerous ways to make extrapolation techniques more precise and sophisticated,[8] but the underlying assumptions remain: There has to be a clear pattern in the data and the belief that the pattern will continue into the forecasted future.

Theoretical Forecasting Techniques: Modeling

Virtually all rational decisions are made on the basis of some model, some construct of how a subsystem of the world functions. Some of these models have become highly developed, tested, and standardized. An example would be the law of gravity. If we wanted to estimate how long it would take for something falling from 40 stories to hit the ground, we could guess, but would do far better to recall Newton's law of gravitation, which states that two material bodies of mass M_1 and M_2 are mutually attracted with a force of magnitude F given by the formula:

$$F = G\frac{M_1 M_2}{R^2}$$

[8] Donald P. Pittenger, *Projecting State and Local Populations* (Cambridge, MA: Ballinger, 1976).

where R = distance between the bodies

             G = a universal proportionality constant called the *constant of gravitation*

Once we understand this model, we know that bodies near the earth's surface fall to the surface at a rate of acceleration of 32.2 feet/second². Thus, in the first second, a body falls 32.2 feet; in the second, 64.4 feet; in the third, 128.8 feet, and so on. To estimate the time it takes a body to fall 40 stories we need to first calculate the elevation, say 40 stories × 10 feet per story = 400 feet, and then solve the following two equations:

distance = velocity × time $(d = vt)$

velocity = acceleration × time $(v = at)$

Substituting (at) for v, we get $d = (at)t$, which we solve:

$$400 \text{ feet} = \left(\frac{32.2 \text{ feet}}{\text{second}^2}t\right)t$$

$$400 \text{ feet} = \frac{32.2 \text{ feet } t^2}{\text{second}^2}$$

$$\frac{400 \text{ feet}}{32.2 \text{ feet}} = \frac{t^2}{\text{second}^2}$$

$$400 \text{ seconds}^2 = 32.2t^2$$

$$20 \text{ seconds} = \sqrt{32.2}t$$

$$t = \frac{20 \text{ seconds}}{\sqrt{32.2}}$$

$$t = 3.5245 \text{ seconds}$$

It appears that it will take about 3½ seconds for an object to fall 40 stories. Once this first calculation is made, if we have time we can begin to think of the other factors that might affect this process: wind resistance from updrafts near the building, downdrafts that might speed the fall, the shape and density of the falling body, and even further refinements to the 32.2 feet/second² constant, which is affected slightly by latitudinal location.

Existing research into the law of gravity is a great aid to our ability to estimate the time it would take the falling object to reach the ground. Similarly, we rely on models of human behavior that affect what we expect the results of different public policies to be—models that describe complex human behavior patterns (e.g., welfare support and motivation). There are also empirical models that reduce the problem to calculations, and nonempirical models that do not quantify the phenomenon under scrutiny, perhaps because it is too complex. One of the first activities in defining a policy problem is to identify any models that portray the problem in a way that permits sound analysis and also leaves it open to change through policy. Thus, the student or practitioner of policy analysis should be familiar with the most important formal models that have been described in our field. Some of these models will be used to calculate a quantifiable answer. Others will serve primarily as explanatory theories about behavior. An example of the latter type might be the laws of supply and demand and the associated concepts of marginal-cost pricing and elasticity. We wouldn't often need to use these conceptual models to calculate numerical answers, but they provide a theoretical explanation of behavior that informs our approach to problem definition and analysis. Finally, we must be able to seek sources of data and information and develop our own simple and practical models of the problem we are facing.

Let us say that you are employed as a policy analyst for the mayor's office in a large Great Lakes port city. The director of the port has advanced the idea that the city should build a new grain elevator at the port to attract new business as corn production in the Midwest increases. The mayor would like to honor the director's request to build the elevator, but like most cities, this one is in a difficult fiscal position, and the elevator would cost over $40 million. As you begin to define the issue, some models appear immediately relevant. We can only describe briefly what the models would be like and how you would use them. To begin with, two grain elevators already exist in the port. They are privately owned, and their equipment is outdated. Part of the need, says the director, is to prevent trucks and trains carrying grain to the port from being delayed in unloading, since time is money. There are competing ports on the Great Lakes and the Mississippi River, and farmers make a rational economic choice of destination by observing the market price offered at each elevator, transportation distance, cost, and time. The key to the success of this new elevator appears to be that portion of the grain production it could capture from other ports and from the two elevators in the same port, and at what price. As a policy analyst for the city, you see little advantage in causing the two existing elevators to fail financially. Several models seem appropriate immediately. Some you will use only for their explanatory value because of time constraints and lack of data. However, you may be able to run some data through one or two others that will give you more insight into this policy issue. A brief description of a few appropriate models follows.

Will the new elevator capture enough grain at a high enough selling price to farmers to attract them, and yet low enough to generate a profit? To answer this question we'd need to look at historic corn production in this region, the distance corn must be transported to alternative ports, and the conditions in those ports that allow their elevators to set their prices. A model could be developed to predict what volume of grain our port could capture at varying price differences with other ports. Accessibility and, of course, prices paid to farmers would be major factors. A logical unit of analysis might be corn output by county. We would be interested in the feasibility of each county's corn crop being shipped through our elevator. The model might begin like this:

- County X corn production in tons $= C_x$.
- County X distance from our port and others in miles $= D_0, D_1, D_2$, etc.
- Ports' price paid per ton $= P_0, P_1, P_2$, etc.
- Other costs incurred by farmers as a function of the transport mode, elevator quality, etc., at each port $= OC_0, OC_1, OC_2$, etc.

Each farmer will attempt to maximize profit, subject of course to a variety of real-world considerations, which for the moment we will ignore. For simplicity we will treat each county as if it had only one farmer, who made a single decision and attempted to maximize profit. By calculating the distances from all relevant counties to all ports and by determining the other costs to farmers of using the alternative ports (OC), we can then develop a computer program that will apportion corn production by county to ports, given transport costs per unit of distance (which itself could be varied), varying differential prices paid among ports, and profit maximization for each corn-producing county. This model should answer the question of how high a price our elevators would have to pay relative to other ports to get certain volume levels. This model was developed using basic concepts of supply, demand, and price from our knowledge of economics.

An even more central question is what the benefits of this project are to the city, and, if they vary by volume of corn processed, how much corn would need to be processed to break even. Ignoring for the moment secondary benefits to the city such as increased use of rail transport, and secondary costs such as increased use of the street and highway systems, we can concentrate on simple fiscal impact. The major costs are building and maintaining the elevator and possibly losing business (and therefore taxes and fees) on the two existing elevators. The major benefits are revenues from the elevator should it be city owned. Planning and policy analysis has a formal model to handle this question called the *discounted-cost model*. Discounting will be described later in this chapter.

As a part of the answer to the question of what benefits the city would receive from such a project, we need to determine how the two privately owned existing elevators will react to the building of a publicly owned elevator. Will they go out of business or raise their offering price to regional corn producers? What effect would such moves have on the question our first model addressed: How much Great Lakes grain activity can our port attract? Clearly there is interaction between our models. Again a formal model exists that can address this question. Although there would usually not be enough time to use it in quick analysis, we must understand it conceptually. The model is derived from game theory, which is simply a method for analyzing decision making in conflict situations. The individual decision unit (in our case one of the three elevators in our port, or our three elevators versus all other Great Lakes elevators) is not in complete control of other decision units. What price we set may well have an impact on what prices other elevators set, and in turn on which farmers use which elevators. The essence of game theory is that each different decision unit may have different goals and objectives, but their fates are intertwined. Principles from game theory can help us predict what will happen when each grain elevator sets a price and grain suppliers begin to react.

Yet another model of direct relevance to this problem involves the ability of the grain elevator operators, be they private or public parties, to sell the grain for more than they paid the farmers for it. In our example, the market for this corn lies in eastern Europe. Some of our competing ports sell largely to South America. Historically corn sales from our port have been tied to a variety of policies affecting international trade and the current value of the dollar. To be able to project its marketability in the future we will need to examine the past history of international corn sales, especially to eastern Europe.

Although there may be dozens of other models applicable to this typical policy issue, we will end the example with one that is simple but important. As we begin to define the problem, reviewing the array of critical questions and applicable models, it has become apparent that the building of a new grain elevator in the port is a risky venture. A simple probability model can help us understand this conceptually. For this project to be successful, enough corn must be produced, and we must be able to offer a price sufficiently higher than other ports so that our other two elevators don't cause the city to have losses greater than its investment, and so that we can buy enough grain. To do that we must have good markets for the grain at still higher prices. These events are not entirely independent, but if they were, and if each had a good chance of being true, say 80%, our chance of their all being true is still rather low. The probability of (1) enough grain, (2) at a competitive price, (3) that doesn't undercut our other elevators, and (4) sold at prices that allow a good profit margin is probably well under 50%. Using 0.8 probabilities (for 80% chance) for each event, we get $(0.8)(0.8)(0.8)(0.8) = 0.41$, or a 41% chance. The project is risky. None of the four events is certain. The weather may be bad, or there may be civil strife in Poland. We are not sure of the outcome. In addition, the amount of risk is uncertain; that is, we are unable to say for sure that the probability of each is exactly 80%. Thus, we have both risk and uncertainty present.[9]

With this understanding we begin to devise alternatives to reduce the risk for the city without losing the possible benefits. Some initial suggestions to accomplish this include building the elevator, but leasing it in a long-term contract with a grain cooperative; using industrial revenue bonds to build it; using state, interstate, and maybe even federal monies in the project, since the benefits appear widespread; getting long-term contractual commitments from farmers, the federal agriculture department, or the importing countries, or all three.

This example shows that models are used in evaluating policies to forecast outcomes. The models can help to organize our thinking, or we can actually run data through them and obtain projections. The models can be our own or someone else's. Models are useful because they help to "focus judgment"[10]—that

[9] Ruth P. Mack, *Planning on Uncertainty: Decision Making in Business and Government Administration* (New York: Wiley-Interscience, 1971), p. 29.

[10] Edward S. Quade, *Analysis for Public Decisions*, 2nd ed. (New York: Elsevier Scientific, 1982), p. 144.

is, they help us as individuals and team members to strip away the nonessentials of a problem and focus on a few key variables. Good models don't necessarily simulate a complex reality but rather generate rich information about the consequences of action or no-action policies. As shown in our example, developing a model can help the policy analyst focus on the key factors in the problem and on relationships among these key factors. Once this is done, hypotheses about the consequences of action can be tested by "running the model" conceptually or empirically. A model is useful in evaluating a policy if it yields information about the consequences of the policy, and if it does this more efficiently than other approaches. If this is true, the cost of the modeling activity is justified. To make a model truly relevant, decision makers themselves should participate in creating, testing, and running it. A number of model-building exercises are provided at the end of this chapter.

Intuitive Forecasting Techniques

Dunn uses the term *retroductive* to describe the type of reasoning process used in intuitive forecasting.[11] A future state is first described, and then retroductive logic is used to find data and assumptions consistent with the forecasted end state. Modeling, on the other hand, uses deductive logic and theories to develop predictions. Extrapolation uses inductive logic and historical data to develop predictions. Intuitive forecasting techniques are the ones most often employed in policy analysis. For a primitive forecast, the analyst simply queries a few persons about their view of the future, given the hypothetical adoption of an action alternative. These persons should also be asked to predict the future with no change from present policies—in other words, given the hypothetical adoption of the no-action alternative. Sophisticated methodologies have been developed to make intuitive forecasting more accurate, richer in detail, and more legitimate, so that it carries some weight in a policy context. For the most part, these more sophisticated methods—Delphi, cross-impact analysis, and feasibility assessment—take too much time and too many resources to be used as basic methods. A true Delphi, for example, involves relatively strict controls on the methods of interviewing and reinterviewing panelists and summarizing the results.[12]

Policy analysts can adopt some important principles from these researched methods to use when time and resources are limited. To be sure, the most important objective of creating these researched intuitive techniques, legitimizing the conclusions in a political context, must be speeded up or short-circuited when a quick approach is adopted. There are several ways to mitigate this problem, but none can address it fully. Interviewing forecasters who are respected either for their knowledge on this particular subject or for their general knowledge

[11] Dunn, *Public Policy Analysis*, p. 195.

[12] Harold A. Linstone and Murray Turoff, eds., *The Delphi Method: Techniques and Applications* (Reading, MA: Addison-Wesley, 1975); Harold Sackman, *Delphi Critique* (Lexington, MA: D.C. Heath, 1975).

and wisdom, and then divulging their names, is the most direct means of dealing with the question of legitimacy. Should there be a general consensus among those questioned, then some mention of this will also lend credence to the forecast, particularly if the participants are regarded as politically and ideologically diverse. Several principles from the Delphi process that can be adopted for use in a quick intuitive forecast include selection of knowledgeable participants, independence and anonymity of participants in the first stage, reinterviewing and revising of initial forecasts with individual participants after disclosure of preliminary results, and developing a consensual forecast.

These straightforward principles are probably best illustrated with an example. In Chapter 4 we described the policy problem of whether or not to abate city property taxes to encourage redevelopment of a specific area within the central city of a large declining region. An important question was whether or not abating these taxes would, in fact, encourage development. Another was whether redevelopment might happen without abatement; that is, under the no-action strategy. Using intuitive forecasting techniques, we can attempt to estimate the probabilities of each outcome, given the actions of abating taxes or doing nothing.

The first principle is to choose knowledgeable persons to interview. In our case this would include planning professionals in other cities that had abated taxes and experienced the results, as well as developers and business leaders in those cities. A comparable set of persons would also be interviewed in the subject city. They could provide the local contextual factors as well as probabilities based on those factors. In addition, persons with expertise in the area of real estate finance and marketing, especially those who may have studied this particular question more broadly, should be interviewed. With limited time we might interview no more than ten persons. It goes without saying that the questionnaire itself should be very well organized, pointed at the central questions, and consistently administered, probably by one person. (See the section on interviewing in Chapter 3.)

The second principle is anonymity. Our ten persons should be interviewed independently of one another and their anonymity preserved, at least initially. Once the first round of interviewing is complete, the results should be compiled and the participants informed of the results, with inconsistencies in the assumptions, data, and logic highlighted. This could be summarized in writing, but with time short it is more likely to be communicated orally. Next, our ten experts would be asked to comment on these findings and revise their forecasts if they felt they should. This information would be compiled into a final forecast, hoping that a consensus had developed. In our example, this intuitive forecasting process would probably take about 20 to 30 hours of time. Although this lacks the rigor of the actual Delphi process, it applies some important principles from that methodology and accomplishes some of the objectives of formal intuitive forecasting while remaining quick and basic in nature.

There are several other intuitive forecasting techniques. One of them, scenario writing, is used a great deal in policy analysis. We describe this method later in this chapter. Two other methods are cross-impact analysis and feasibility assessment. The latter is discussed in several contexts in this book, including this chapter as well as Chapter 6. The reason that this technique, or variants of it, appears so often is that considering the feasibility of a policy or program is an integral part of the policy analysis process. Checks for feasibility should not be consigned to one step in the analytic process for a go/no-go decision. Rather, the whole notion of feasibility needs to be made part of problem definition, alternatives generation, and evaluation.[13] Cross-impact analysis is really an extension of Delphi techniques. It addresses Delphi's lack of a mechanism for discovering mutually exclusive or conflicting outcomes. Thus, some outcomes forecast by Delphi could be impossible to obtain simultaneously: for example, full employment *and* a low rate of inflation. Cross-impact analysis addresses this problem directly by analyzing conditional probabilities—for example, the likelihood that inflation will be low if full employment is achieved. It examines the "interactions of forecasted items."[14]

For complex policy problems, the use of cross-impact analysis involves a computer and fairly elaborate data that are not easily generated. Intuitive forecasts are required of both the conditional and unconditional probabilities of future events. Thus, cross-impact analysis is a researched method, not a quick method. Like Delphi, though, there are principles that can be used even under time and resource constraints. The most important of these is the need for a check of the logical consistency of intuitive forecasts. Some outcomes may preclude others or make them highly unlikely. The analyst should seek these inconsistencies when developing the first-round consensus and present them openly to participants in the second round. However, the formalizing of intuitive forecasting techniques is hampered tremendously by the need to find consensus. As Dunn points out, the messy and ill-structured policy problems that require intuitive forecasting rather than other, more structured types are exactly the types of problems in which attitudes, values, and facts will differ.[15] Thus, agreement that a specific policy intervention will result in a single set of forecasted events is also unlikely.

EVALUATION METHODS

At the beginning of this chapter we noted that in order to evaluate proposed programs or policies we first had to project their future impacts. The first part of the chapter reviewed basic projection methods. This second part of the chapter

[13] Robert D. Behn, "Policy Analysis and Policy Politics," *Policy Analysis* 7, no. 2 (Spring 1981), 199–226.

[14] T. J. Gordon and M. Hayward, "Initial Experiments with the Cross-Impact Matrix Method of Forecasting," *Futures* 1, no. 2 (1968), 101; and Olaf Helmer, "Using Expert Judgment," in *Handbook of Systems Analysis: Craft Issues and Procedural Choices*, ed. Hugh J. Miser and Edward S. Quade (Chichester, Eng.: Wiley, 1988), pp. 107–113.

[15] Dunn, *Public Policy Analysis*, p. 206.

discusses several basic methods for evaluating programs, once their impacts have been forecast. We consider discounting, which permits comparisons between current and future impacts, accounting for the time value of money. We also examine how to measure efficiency, as well as sensitivity analysis, which permits comparisons among alternatives while varying the values of key variables, thus attempting to deal with the uncertainty surrounding future events. The creation and testing of allocation formulas using sensitivity techniques has become an important subset of sensitivity analysis in policy work, so discussion of allocation formulas and their development is included here. Finally, we revisit quick decision analysis, which we introduced in Chapter 4 as a tool to structure our thinking. Here we show how, in limited circumstances, it can also be used actually to evaluate policies and programs.

Discounting

In this chapter we presume that the criteria for choosing an alternative policy, plan, or project have been established, and it is time to evaluate the proposals using these criteria. Many public policies have impacts that will be felt for many years, and some evaluation criteria, such as minimizing costs or maximizing net benefits, must necessarily be measured in the future as well as the present. Most public bodies, like individuals, have a preference for benefits sooner rather than later, particularly when those benefits come in the form of cash or can be measured in dollar equivalents. Simply put, a dollar today is worth more than a dollar next year. The preference can be strong or weak, usually depending on what could be done with the money if one had it now (opportunity cost). We would have a strong preference if a dollar's worth of benefits today were worth only 60 cents to us if we didn't receive them until next year, or a very weak preference if a dollar's worth of benefits today were worth 98 cents to us if we receive them next year. When we look forward in time from the present, we say that our money gains interest using some interest rate. When looking backward from some future time, we discount money's value using some discount rate. This preference for having money or benefits sooner results from several factors, including the opportunity cost (e.g., interest), the risk of waiting, and inflation. Most analysts agree that the issues of risk and uncertainty should not enter a discounting analysis but should be handled separately. It is conceptually easier to work with interest and discount rates that are risk free. The issue of inflation will be discussed later.

So, waiting one year to receive $100 makes the discounted, or present, value of that $100 worth less than $100. What is the present value of $100 received a year from now? Or, conversely, what is $100 received now worth a year from now? It depends on what investment opportunities are available. If, for example, $100 could be invested risk free at an 8% interest rate, the $100 received today would be worth $108 ($100 × 108%) a year from now. And $100 received next year would be worth only $92.59 today ($100 ÷ 108%). If the discount rate were even higher, say 12%, the respective values would be $112 and $89.29. The mathematical expression of this phenomenon is the *compound-interest formula*, where:

$$S_{t+1} = S_t + (S_t \times r) = S_t(1 + r)$$

The value one year from now, at time $t + 1$, is equal to the value now (S_t), in time t, plus the year's interest ($S_t \times r$). When we work backward in time, r is called the *discount rate*, which is used below to discount future value (S_{t+1}) to present value (S_t):

$$S_t = \frac{S_{t+1}}{1 + r}$$

As you will see later, the interest rate and discount rate for public sector projects need not be the same number.

Since many projects are evaluated by assessing their costs and benefits over some long time period, it is essential to understand both the mechanics of discounting and the major assumptions that underlie its use. Many projects will be characterized by a series of benefits (B) and costs (C) over time:

$$B_t + B_{t+1} + B_{t+2} + B_{t+3} + \ldots + B_n$$

and

$$C_t + C_{t+1} + C_{t+2} + C_{t+3} + \ldots + C_n$$

On occasion it is simply easier to speak about *annual net benefits*, which are really yearly benefits minus yearly costs:

$$(B_t - C_t) + (B_{t+1} - C_{t+1}) + (B_{t+2} - C_{t+2}) + (B_{t+3} - C_{t+3}) + \ldots + (B_n - C_n)$$

Any one of these yearly figures could be negative as well as positive. A typical public investment project ordinarily shows higher costs than benefits in the early years and higher benefits than costs in later years—or negative net benefits early and positive net benefits later. The one instance when you would not wish to compute net annual benefits before discounting would be if you wished to calculate a benefit-cost ratio. To do that, benefits and costs must be discounted separately. We will show this below.

The most commonly encountered measure of the efficiency of a public investment project is its present worth, or net present value (NPV). NPV is the sum of all discounted benefits and discounted costs for the duration of the project. Thus:

$$\text{NPV} = (B_t - C_t) + \frac{B_{t+1} - C_{t+1}}{(1 + r)^1} + \frac{B_{t+2} - C_{t+2}}{(1 + r)^2} + \ldots + \frac{B_n - C_n}{(1 + r)^n}$$

Let us illustrate the discounting procedure with an example. A project costs $15,000 to implement immediately (we won't discount, and we will call this time zero). The project returns $4,000 per year in benefits every year thereafter for the next five years and has only one remaining cost, a maintenance charge of $1,223 in year three. The pattern of costs and benefits is shown in Table 7-1.

Using, for example, a 4% discount rate, we can compute the net present value several ways. We will do it first by treating the cost and benefit streams separately, computing the discount factors using the formula $1/(1 + r)^n$, which yields a discount factor of .9615 for year one and .9246 for year two; for example, $1/(1 + .04)^1$ and $1/(1 + .04)^2$.

Discounted benefits (DB)
$= 0(1.0) + 4,000(.9615) + 4,000(.9246) + 4,000(.8890) + 4,000(.8548) + 4,000(.8219)$
$= 4,000(4.4518) = \$17,807.20$

Discounted costs (DC)
$= -15,000(1.0) + 0(.9615) + 0(.9246) + (-1,223)(.8890) + 0(.8548) + 0(.8219)$
$= -15,000 + (-1,223)(.8890) = -15,000 + (-1,087.25) = -\$16,087.25$

Net present value thus is the simple sum of discounted benefits and costs. Note that for bookkeeping purposes, costs are expressed negatively. This convention can be helpful with larger problems that involve more extensive sets of figures.

$$\text{NPV} = \text{DB} + \text{DC} = \$17,807.20 + (-\$16,087.25)$$
$$= +\$1,719.95$$

Another method used to compute net present value first calculates the net annual benefits (benefits minus costs) and then discounts this number. In our example above this would be:

$$\text{NPV} = (0 - 15,000)(1.0) + (4,000 - 0)(.9615)$$
$$+ (4,000 - 0)(.9246) + (4,000 - 1,223)(.8890)$$
$$+ (4,000 - 0)(.8548) + (4,000 - 0)(.8219)$$

Table 7-1 Basic Data for the Discounting Example

	YEAR					
	0	1	2	3	4	5
Benefits	0	$4,000	$4,000	$4,000	$4,000	$4,000
Costs	$15,000	0	0	$1,223	0	0
Discount rate (r)	4%	4%	4%	4%	4%	4%
Discount factor $1/(1 + r)^n$	1.0	.9615	.9246	.8890	.8548	.8219

Note: See Appendices 7-2 and 7-3 for discount factors.

$$= -15,000 + 4,000(.9615) + 4,000(.9246) + 2,777(.8890) + 4,000(.8548)$$
$$+ 4,000(.8219)$$
$$= -15,000 + 3,846.00 + 3,698.40 + 2,468.75 + 3,419.20 + 3,287.60$$
$$= -15,000 + 16,719.95 = +\$1,719.95$$

Although the two methods resulted in the same answer in this case, differences could result because of rounding. Retain four significant digits on the discount factors and round only after the final result has been tallied. Modern pocket calculators and microcomputers have made the process of discounting costs and benefits fairly easy. Where the calculator has an operation that compounds interest, a routine can be devised fairly easily to compute NPV. Should a sophisticated pocket calculator or microcomputer not be available, you can also use tables of discount factors. The tables take two forms. The simplest one answers the question: "What is the value to me at the present time of $1 given to me n years in the future if the discount rate is $r\%$?" The matrix of years versus discount rates appears as Appendix 7-2. Note that for our problem we would look up years 1, 2, 3, 4, and 5 for a discount rate of 4% and get .9615, .9246, .8890, .8548, and .8219, as we did earlier by using the formula $1/(1 + r)^n$ where r is the discount rate and n the year of benefit (or cost). The second type of table answers the question: "What is the value to me at the present time of $1 given to me each year for n years in the future if the discount rate is $r\%$?" Because our problem contained an annual amount, a $4,000 benefit every year after year 0, we could use this second type of table. The matrix of years versus discount rates appears as Appendix 7-3. Note that for our problem we would look up five years and a discount rate of 4% and obtain a discount factor of 4.4518. The formula for deriving this second table is as follows:

present value $\quad=$ discount factor $\times$ annual dollar benefit (or cost)

$$\text{discount factor} \quad = \frac{1 - \dfrac{1}{(1 + r)^n}}{r}$$

where

$r =$ the discount rate
$n =$ the number of years over which benefits are received and payments made

In our example above, this is

$$B = \frac{1 - \dfrac{1}{(1 + .04)^5}}{.04} = \frac{1 - .82193}{.04} = \frac{.17807}{.04} = 4.4518$$

The experienced analyst will use the tables in Appendices 7-2 and 7-3 to compute net present values for extensive problems. But beware of three common pitfalls:

1. Always check your results intuitively to catch mathematical errors. For example, a $4,000 annuity for five years discounted at any rate (other than 0%) must always be worth less than $20,000.
2. Be very careful to use arithmetic signs consistently. For example, record costs consistently as negative numbers, and *add* them (as negatives) to benefits to get NPV. Or treat them as positive numbers consistently, subtracting them from benefits to get NPV.
3. If the final desired measure of efficiency is the benefit-cost ratio, then benefits and costs will have to be discounted separately. You may not derive annual net benefits and then discount. The benefit-cost ratio should be used in only a few special cases. For virtually all policy analyses, net present value is the correct measure to use, as shown below.[16]

Three Measures of Efficiency

Three related but significantly different measures are used to weigh alternative proposals: net present value (also known as discounted net benefits), the benefit-cost ratio, and the internal rate of return. Net present value was illustrated above. The benefit-cost ratio is simply the ratio of discounted benefits to discounted costs. In our example above, using a 4% discount rate, the ratio would be:

$$\frac{DB}{DC} = \frac{4,000(.9615 + .9246 + .8890 + .8548 + .8219)}{15,000 + 1,223(.8890)}$$

$$= \frac{17,807.20}{16,087.25} = 1.11$$

Projects that have the highest benefit-cost ratios are not necessarily those that deliver the highest net present value. The scale of the project enters into the calculus, and the conclusion depends on whether one is trying to decide between several projects or simply to ask whether a single project is efficient. The most efficient projects have the highest ratios, but often we would want to maximize net benefits (present value). When choosing projects from among a large group of alternatives, a single criterion is seldom used. However, we would theoretically choose the set of projects that yields the highest net present value without exceeding the budget.

Cost-benefit analysis has been criticized because it has dominated regulatory policy, pushed aside the management of risk, and negated the government's role in managing risk. Tolchin has further argued: "Although cost-benefit analysis can be useful in determining the most cost-effective alternative among competing regulatory devices, it should be removed as a dominant policy tool for being

[16] Edith Stokey and Richard Zeckhauser, *A Primer for Policy Analysis* (New York: Norton, 1978), p. 146.

inadequate, inequitable, and subject to excessive political distortion in its application."[17]

Byrne criticizes cost-benefit analysis because it is based on what he believes
are two flawed premises, that the basic dilemma of today is how to arrive at
rational solutions to complex social problems and that cost-benefit analysis can
provide nonnormative solutions to normative social problems. He states: "Cost-
benefit analysis is not neutral, does not offer nonnormative solutions, and cannot
rationalize social problems without considerable violence to our understanding
of these problems."[18]

Another decision criterion used in the past has been to choose the project
with the highest internal rate of return, which is the discount rate at which
discounted benefits equal discounted costs. Three conditions must hold if the
NPV and internal rate of return are to lead to choosing the same projects: There
can be no budgetary limitations, projects must not preclude one another, and
streams of net returns must first be negative and then positive.[19] There may be
more than one rate of return for projects that experience costs as well as benefits
in advanced years. There are two ways to compute the internal rate of return.
The first is to approach it, with successive iterations, using discount rates from
the tables. The second is to write a mathematical equation and solve for r, the
discount rate. In our example, the 4% used earlier proves to be close (DB =
$17,807; DC = $16,087), but we will need to value costs slightly higher and
benefits slightly lower if they are to be equivalent. To do that, given the pattern
of benefits and costs over time, it appears we'll have to try a higher discount rate
for the costs to be larger. Let's try 10%:

$$DB = 4,000(3.7908) \qquad = \$15,163$$
$$DC = 15,000 + 1,223(.7513) = \$15,919$$

On this try we used Appendix 7-2 for the discounted cost ($1,223 in year three)
and Appendix 7-3 for the discounted benefit stream ($4,000 for each of five
years). This proves to be very close, but the discounted costs are now a bit high.

So we'll go down to 6% and try:

$$DB = 4,000(4.2124) \qquad = \$16,850$$
$$DC = 15,000 + 1,223(.8396) = \$16,027$$

---

[17] Susan J. Tolchin, "The Political Uses of Evaluation Research: Cost-benefit Analysis and the
Cotton Dust Standard," in *The Politics of Program Evaluation*, ed. Dennis J. Palumbo (Newbury
Park, CA: Sage, 1987), p. 266.

[18] John Byrne, "Policy Science and the Administrative State: The Political Economy of Cost-
Benefit Analysis," in *Confronting Values in Policy Analysis: The Politics of Criteria*, ed. Frank
Fischer and John Forester (Newbury Park, CA: Sage, 1987), p. 90.

[19] Stokey and Zeckhauser, *Primer for Policy Analysis*, p. 167.

Now the discounted costs are a bit too low. The solution lies between 10% and 6%. Now, again using the tables and trying 8%:

$$DB = 4,000(3.9927) = \$15,971$$

$$DC = 15,000 + 1,223(.7938) = \$15,971$$

Since the discounted benefits are equal to the discounted costs, we can say that the internal rate of return is 8%. The summary of our trials is shown in Table 7-2. We can solve for the rate of return algebraically, or use a packaged computer program, rather than using trial and error and the discount tables. However, the algebraic solutions can be complex when the problem involves a long time period.

Another criterion of the past was to go ahead with a project if it yielded an internal rate of return greater than the discount rate. This criterion has fallen into disfavor because the discount rate is not an objective fact; it is chosen to approximate the time preference for money of the decision-making unit. When a governmental unit sets a discount rate, it is more a political decision than a matter of finance or economics. Low rates encourage much more governmental activity; high rates usually cause project proposals to be rejected.

Many economists have written about the use of the discount rate. One major group believes that it should approximate the opportunity cost of private capital (after tax), because it is taxpayers who are providing the money to implement public projects. Another group believes that each governmental unit should use the interest rate it pays to borrow money (bonds) for its discount rate.

Selection of discount rates also affects how the analyst weighs intergenerational equity. Low rates encourage the development of projects with long-term benefits: Note the difference in impact between a 2% rate and a 10% rate on a benefit (or cost) received 20 years from now, .6730 and .1486, respectively. (See Appendix 7-2 for the discount rates.) Thus, one might argue for the use of low discount rates to make investments now for future generations. Others argue that, at the rate the standard of living has been growing in the past several decades, future generations will be much richer than present ones. To use low discount rates, then, robs from the poorer present generations to benefit the richer, future ones. At present, a number of governmental units have adopted a standard discount rate that they require each of their offices to use. For

Table 7-2 Determining the Internal Rate of Return

Discount Rate	Discounted Benefits	Discounted Costs
4%	$17,807	$16,087
10%	$15,163	$15,919
6%	$16,850	$16,027
8%	$15,971	$15,971

example, the Environmental Protection Agency once used a 7.625% discount rate when reviewing all proposed local sewage collection and treatment system improvements. Local governments had to adopt this figure if they were to receive federal funds for their projects. However, in the future, we can probably expect that different discount rates will be used by the same governmental unit for different types of projects—for example, recreation versus job creation—and we may even begin to see different rates for different time periods of a single proposed project. Formaini, among others, has argued that our preference for a discount rate may change over time and that a static rate may well invalidate the analysis.[20]

Since the decision of which discount rate to use is a political one, and since a half percent difference in the rate can change which program, if any, is recommended as most efficient, some answer needs to be found for analysts searching for the most appropriate rate to use. *Sensitivity analysis* is a solution to the problem. The analyst should test a variety of discount rates to see if the basic recommendation changes with different rates. The analyst can also seek that rate at which decision makers will be indifferent to the choice. The topic of sensitivity analysis, illustrated with discount rates, is covered in the next section.

Inflation is often a major issue. Some have argued that when inflation is high, the discount rate should be raised to include it. There are several responses to this. The first is that the rate governments have to pay for their bonds already incorporates a market response to inflation.[21] Future costs and benefits are not inflated for computational purposes. But this answer is too simple. The typical public project or program is characterized by large initial investment costs and long payback periods. If projects are analyzed using higher discount rates reflecting inflation, but future benefits are not similarly inflated, then projects analyzed in inflationary times are more likely to be rejected. A partial solution to this problem is to inflate future costs and benefits to their projected market value in the year they are paid or received. If this is done, analysts will get different go/no-go decisions or choices among alternatives than if they ignore inflation. The following example proves the point.

Presume a project with $6,000 of immediate costs yields two years of benefits, $3,000 in the first year and $4,000 in the second. The net present value is first computed presuming no inflation, no change in the 10% discount rate, and no attempt to deal with inflation:

$$\text{NPV} = -6{,}000 + \frac{3{,}000}{(1.10)^1} + \frac{4{,}000}{(1.10)^2} = +\$33$$

Then, presuming 2% annual inflation on all items, we adjust the discount rate by 2%, bringing it to 12%, and get:

---

[20] Robert Formaini, *The Myth of Scientific Public Policy* (New Brunswick, NJ: Transaction Books, 1990), p. 50.
[21] Stokey and Zeckhauser, *Primer for Policy Analysis*, p. 174.

$$\text{NPV} = -6{,}000 + \frac{3{,}000}{(1.12)^1} + \frac{4{,}000}{(1.12)^2} = -\$133$$

Finally, presuming we adjust the value of the benefits to their current market value at the time they are received, at the 2% inflation rate, we have:

$$\text{NPV} = -6{,}000 + \frac{3{,}000(1.02)^1}{(1.12)^1} + \frac{4{,}000(1.02)^2}{(1.12)^2}$$
$$= -6{,}000 + 2{,}732 + 3{,}318$$
$$= +\$50$$

This example shows that including inflation in the discount rate and/or the value of future costs and benefits makes a great deal of difference if net present value is to be the primary decision criterion. Whether or not inflation is taken into account, and how it is, can affect whether or not we decide to select the alternative and, further, which alternative proves preferable.

Most policy analysts and planners agree that using the net present value criterion is preferable in most instances to using the internal rate of return or the benefit-cost ratio. Unfortunately, the internal rate of return can sometimes have two valid mathematical solutions. It also has at its center the discount rate whose value is arguable and must be decided politically. The benefit-cost ratio is fine for finding the project that is most efficient, but doesn't work when there is a budget constraint and a number of projects must be chosen together to maximize net benefits (net present value). In addition, it is possible to bolster the benefit-cost ratio by shifting certain types of benefits (from the numerator), classifying them as cost savings (putting them in the denominator). The only real disadvantage of the net present value criterion is that it favors large projects. The solution is, of course, to use no one measure alone, but to use a variety of criteria for evaluating programs.

Sensitivity Analysis

Seldom is one alternative clearly superior under all circumstances. Changing valuations of decision criteria, different perceptions and attitudes about risk and uncertainty, and different beliefs in "the facts" of the case will often produce preferences for different alternatives. Policy analysts must be confident that they can give useful advice to decision makers despite all of these variables. To do this their advice should be conditional, based on what decision makers value and believe. The analyst's mission is to clarify the issues and lay out the consequences of a variety of alternatives, so the one that most closely matches the decision maker's values and opinions can be selected. Philosophically this is a very different attitude from the one that has the analyst advocating a proposal. This former view of the analyst's role is based on several assumptions. The first is that decision makers are bright and motivated to use the methods of analysis that we, as analysts, can deliver. This is certainly not always the case.[22] The second is that we are able to communicate the results of our work in a way that is usable by decision makers. This is also a critical assumption that is not always met in practice. The third is that decision makers are open, at least somewhat, to the results of analysis: They don't view it as merely eyewash.

Like other basic methods of policy analysis we have described, sensitivity analysis is best learned by doing. Practically any problem, alternative, value, variable, or assumption can be subjected to sensitivity analysis. We recommend establishing a reasonable range of values for every variable relevant to a particular policy problem. To develop these ranges, ascertain decision makers' decision criteria as well as critical uncertainties and risks. Then, whenever you apply an analytic technique to evaluate alternatives (e.g., finding the net present value), test both ends of the range of values for every variable that you suspect might be critically sensitive. Critical sensitivities are those that, when varied, change the nature of the recommendation. For example, if in testing two proposals, A and B, using two different discount rates, say 8% and 12%, the net present value of A is greater at 8%, but the net present value of B is greater at 12%, then the discount rate is a sensitive variable. If testing the discount rate through a reasonable range of values always showed the same alternative had the higher NPV, then the discount rate would not be considered sensitive for this particular evaluation criterion, NPV. It might, however, prove sensitive for other possible evaluation criteria. Experienced analysts begin to develop an idea of the sensitive factors in a policy problem fairly early in the analytic process. We illustrate several types of sensitivity analyses in this section with a simple project appraisal. Remember that the principle of sensitivity analysis has much broader application than can be demonstrated with a simple example.

Let us consider a typical project: A tunnel has been proposed as a replacement for a ferry service that now operates largely to carry suburban commuters to and from work in the central city, which is cut off from the outskirts by a major river. The costs of this tunnel construction project are estimated at $64 million with an annual maintenance charge of $20,000 per year. Every ten years after construction an additional $500,000 charge will be required. Some fear construction cost overruns on the order of 50%. The life of the tunnel is conservatively estimated at 50 years. In terms of benefits from the new tunnel, it is to replace a ferry that would require $500,000 a year to operate, maintain, and insure (because it is quite old). For our example we will ignore the idea of purchasing a new ferry. The tunnel saves commuters a good deal of time over the old ferry crossing. It is estimated that each working day 5,000 commuters will be saved a half-hour delay, and this has been priced as worth $8 per commuter hour and $1.50 in operation and maintenance for each of the 3,000 vehicles involved. However, there has been much debate about the value of

[22] Peter Szanton, *Not Well Advised* (New York: Russell Sage Foundation, 1981).

commuters' time. The governmental unit involved recently floated bonds at an 8% interest rate, so most parties have agreed to use that rate as the appropriate discount rate for evaluating the project.

Although an analysis of this problem could be complex and interesting, our purpose here is limited to demonstrating sensitivity analysis, so we will concentrate on major questions. Let's presume that it has been decided that the principal decision criterion is efficiency, and that the measure selected is the net present value. Therefore, we will begin our analysis with a computation of the net present value of the project at an 8% discount rate. The project looks like this:

Costs: $64 M (plus possible 50% cost overrun) + $20,000 per year + $500,000 in years 10, 20, 30, 40, 50

Benefits: $.5 M per year cost savings, plus cost savings each working day (5 days/week × 50 weeks = 250 working days):

5,000 commuters × ½ hour time saved × $8/hour = $20,000 per day

3,000 vehicles × $1.50 saved on operation and maintenance = $4,500 per day

= $6.625 M per year in cost savings
  [$500,000 + ($20,000 + $4,500) × 250 days/year]

At 8% the difference between a 40- and 50-year project life is negligible (see Appendix 7-2: discount factor of $r = .0460$ at 40 years and $r = .0213$ at 50 years). We will use 50 years because it is the expected life of the structure. So, using these assumptions, we'll compute the net present value:

$$\begin{aligned}
NPV &= \$6.625\,M(12.2355) - \$64.0\,M - \$20,000(12.2355) \\
&\quad - \$.5\,M(.4632 + .2145 + .0994 + .0460 + .0213) \\
&= \$6.625\,M(12.2355) - \$64.0\,M - \$244,710 - \$.5\,M(.8444) \\
&= \$81,060,187 - \$64,000,000 - \$244,710 - \$422,200 \\
&= +\,\$16,393,277
\end{aligned}$$

Using the discount tables in Appendices 7-2 and 7-3, we can compute NPV, as above, trying other discount rates. The results are shown in Table 7-3. We can

Table 7-3 Using Sensitivity Analysis to Test the Effect of the Discount Rate

Discount Rate	Discounted Benefits	Discounted Costs	NPV
0%	$306.25 M	$67.50 M	+$238.75 M
6%	$104.42 M	$64.91 M	+$ 39.51 M
8%	$ 81.06 M	$64.67 M	+$ 16.39 M
10%	$ 65.65 M	$64.51 M	+$ 1.14 M
11%	$ 59.90 M	$64.45 M	−$ 4.55 M
12%	$ 55.02 M	$64.42 M	−$ 9.40 M

see, incidentally, that the internal rate of return lies somewhere between 10% and 11%. Although we have purposely made this project simple, there are a few other variables to consider for sensitivity. Project lives of under 20 years would not provide enough benefits to make the project feasible (NPV would be less than $0), and the tunnel is obviously more durable than that. As we discussed earlier, a 40-year project life would produce a result very similar to the one we derived. Besides the discount rate, then, the value of commuters' time, the risk of cost overruns, and the uncertainty about traffic levels in the future remain as possibly sensitive items. Since the choice of a discount rate has proven sensitive, the implications of each rate should be discussed openly with decision makers.

Now, using an 8% discount rate as the basis, we can rerun the analysis with varying values placed on commuters' time. The results are shown in Table 7-4. As can be seen from this analysis, the value placed on commuters' time is critically sensitive: changes in it change the outcome of the analysis. When commuters' time is said to be worth nothing, the project's NPV is a large loss, − $44.3 million, owing to benefits being much lower. At the original value employed, $8 per hour or $4 per half-hour, the project's NPV was + $16.39 million. The table shows that the project becomes feasible (the NPV is greater than zero) when commuters' time becomes worth about $5.80 per hour. At $5 per hour it isn't feasible, and at $6 per hour it just becomes feasible (NPV = + $1.6 million).

In attempting to find the value of commuters' time that causes the project to become feasible, we conducted a *break-even analysis*. This can be done by altering one variable at a time, which we have done here, or by altering more than one at a time. We can use break-even analysis to decide whether a single project is feasible, as above, or we can use it to compare several projects, setting the value of a variable at a point where we are indifferent between two alternative proposals. This kind of analysis is helpful for communicating with decision makers about their values. For example, decision makers can be told that if they favor building the tunnel and accept the critical assumptions such as the 8%

Table 7-4   Testing the Sensitivity
of Commuters' Time

Value of Commuters' Time per Hour	NPV
$ 0 per hour	− $44.28 M
$ 1 per hour	− $36.63 M
$ 2 per hour	− $28.98 M
$ 3 per hour	− $21.34 M
$ 4 per hour	− $13.68 M
$ 5 per hour	− $ 6.04 M
$ 6 per hour	+ $ 1.60 M
$ 7 per hour	+ $ 9.25 M
$ 8 per hour	+ $16.39 M
$16 per hour	+ $78.08 M

discount rate and the 50-year project life, then they are, in effect, assigning a value of at least $5.80 per hour to commuters' time. Discussion can then focus on that particular variable and public opinion about it.

Contingency analysis is another type of sensitivity analysis. In contingency analysis some basic assumption or part of the environment of the problem or solution is varied. In our problem, the potential cost overrun provides a perfect opportunity for contingency analysis. If the overrun really happened, would the project still be feasible? In our example we can change the cost of the project to $96 million, indicating the 50% overrun. Our net present value, holding all other values constant and using an 8% discount rate, is:

$$\text{NPV} = \text{discounted benefits} - \text{discounted project costs} - \text{discounted operating costs}$$
$$= \$6.625\ \text{M}(12.2355) - \$96\ \text{M} - \$20,000(12.2355) - \$.5\ \text{M}(.8444)$$
$$= \$81.06\ \text{M} - \$96\ \text{M} - \$.245\ \text{M} - \$.422\ \text{M} = -\$15.6\ \text{M}$$

Under these circumstances the project becomes infeasible (NPV is less than $0). The point at which cost overruns cause the project to become infeasible can be calculated with the following equation:

$$\text{NPV} = 0 = -\$64 \times y\% \text{ cost overrun} + \$81.06 - \$.245 - \$.422 \text{ (in millions)}$$
$$64y = 81.06 - .667$$
$$y = 1.26 \text{ or a } 26\% \text{ cost overrun}$$

Essentially we are computing the amount that the estimated project cost could increase to offset the amount by which discounted benefits exceed discounted costs. Thus, a cost overrun of about 26% would cause discounted costs to be greater than discounted benefits and make the project infeasible. More detailed analysis could now be focused on the likelihood of such an overrun in this case.

Yet another type of sensitivity analysis is *a fortiori* analysis. Here every effort is made to prove the favored alternative to be the less attractive one. In our example the tunnel is the favored alternative: It has survived as a proposal through many initial screenings. We can see that the factors working against its feasibility are higher discount rates, lower values for commuters' time, shorter project horizons, and cost overruns. A fortiori analysis establishes the likelihood that each and any of these factors might have a value that would make the project infeasible. What, for example, is the likelihood of the 26% cost overrun or of the tunnel lasting only, say, 20 years instead of 50? The likelihood that these events would occur independently or in combination must be assessed.

Using researched analysis techniques, the analyst could use a computer to assign likely expected values and ranges for all variables, and then, using programmed statistical techniques, allow the computer to assign values to all variables in a number of different experimental runs. This simulates the idea of uncertainty in the real world. This statistical process is called *Monte Carlo sampling.* If there are a sufficient number of runs, and the project looks feasible in a majority of those runs, then the project is deemed feasible. This technique can be done only with computing equipment, but sensitivity testing as discussed here can be done without a computer.

Most policy problems can be reduced to three to five sensitive variables. In fact, they must be reduced to a few critical variables to do basic policy analysis. Then, using a hand calculator or microcomputer, you can perform analyses like those described here. If more time and resources become available later, then more elaborate researched analysis can be performed. For most policy problems the kind of sensitivity analysis described here will prove adequate.

In summary, sensitivity analysis includes four steps:

1. List all the variables relevant to the policy problem.
2. Establish a range of likely values for each.
3. Holding all others constant, test the range of values for one variable to see if any one (or all) decision criteria are affected. This establishes the sensitive variables.
4. Lastly, test the sensitive variables using break-even, contingency, and a fortiori concepts as appropriate.

Allocation Formulas

All levels of government use formulas to allocate resources to subunits of government and to assign project scores to determine funding priority. The techniques used to develop such formulas, mostly simple arithmetic, are so common that they have gone largely unnoticed by policy analysts. Moreover, the results of their use, the actual allocations, are often of vital importance to the units of government involved.[23] Since the techniques of sensitivity analysis are useful in analyzing allocation formulas, we include a discussion of this topic here. We first describe some general problems encountered in the development and administration of such formulas and then describe a specific formula used to allocate state and federal water-pollution abatement construction grant money in Wisconsin. The abbreviated description is intended simply to provide a concrete example of an allocation formula in use for those who have not been exposed to the idea. Another example is provided by the "Emergency Aid for Home Fuel" case (Chapter 14).

The process used to develop an allocation formula should be no different from the one followed in the entire policy analysis process. An essential first step is to establish exactly what the goals and objectives of the program or policy are and to operationalize the objectives. In the example that follows, it was essential for the state to decide what the specific objectives of the water-pollution abatement program were and how the performance of each proposed project on each

---

[23] As an example see Ernest R. Alexander, "Sensitivity Analysis in Complex Decision Models," *Journal of the American Planning Association* 55, no. 3 (Summer 1989), 323–33.

objective was going to be measured.[24] The characteristics of each project, such as number of people served, are aggregated into an overall score that can be used for ranking projects for possible funding. We discuss only the most common methods of aggregating and the usual pitfalls associated with each. One overriding principle applies when developing allocation formulas: The factors used in the formula need to be theoretically connected to the needs the program is addressing. Following are the five most common methods of developing allocation formulas.

1. Add or subtract the values of each characteristic of each project to obtain a project score. Table 7-5 shows some hypothetical data for discussion purposes, using this simple summation approach and only two project characteristics. In this example Project 1's score would be $3.0 + 18.0 = 21.0$; 2's would be $1.8 + 53.0 = 54.8$, and N's would be $2.5 + 45.0 = 47.5$. Presuming that the high score wins, Project 2 would win highest priority of the three projects. Ordinarily, of course, more than two project characteristics would be used.

One obvious problem with such a scoring system is that those characteristics with higher average scores get weighted more heavily in the formula. In our example, because of the units chosen, miles of shoreline affected is far more important than population served. When large-valued variables also exhibit a large range of values for projects, as miles of shoreline affected does, the problem is exacerbated. All things equal, projects that score well on shoreline are going to be ranked highest. Sometimes this is the intention of the formula designers, but certainly not always. There are dozens of ways to manipulate the original values of the characteristics either to amplify or to reduce the weights between characteristics: transformation to logs, conversion to percentages, division or multiplication by a constant, and so on. Clearly, expressing population served in thousands rather than millions would have shifted the emphasis rather dramatically. Values of characteristics that contribute to project viability or need are most commonly added, and those that detract are subtracted.

2. Multiply or divide the values of each characteristic of each project to obtain a project score. As a simple example we will multiply the two characteristics in Table 7-5. The projects' scores then become:

> For Project 1: $3.0 \times 18.0 = 54.0$
> For Project 2: $1.8 \times 53.0 = 95.4$
> For Project N: $2.5 \times 45.0 = 112.5$

The operations of multiplication and division imply that the relationship between factors is such that increases in one factor, in effect, cause changes in the valuation of the whole project. Should this be true, multiplying (or conversely, dividing) is appropriate. In our example, the combination of multiplying seems to say

---

[24] For an overview of policy indicators, see Duncan MacRae, Jr., *Policy Indicators: Links between Social Science and Public Debate* (Chapel Hill: University of North Carolina Press, 1985).

Table 7-5 Simple Addition of Project Scores as an Allocation Formula

	Population Served (in millions)	Miles of Shoreline Affected
Project 1	3.0	18.0
Project 2	1.8	53.0
•	•	•
•	•	•
•	•	•
Project N	2.5	45.0
Range of values	0.8–3.5	6.0–87.0
Mean of values	2.6	51.2
Standard deviation of values	0.2	21.0
Variance of values	0.04	441.0
Number of projects	300	300

that giving more people access to more shoreline is disproportionately better than simply having one or the other (simple addition).

3. Normalize scores for each characteristic; then add or subtract as in method 1. This is the most popular method for altering the raw-score weighting system. The sum of values for each characteristic is first totaled. For example, a total of (2.6 × 300) possible points exist for population served. Each project's score for that characteristic is then divided by the total, so that each project's score is a percentage of the total, which is of course 100%. In our example, for population served, the scores would be normalized to:

$$\text{For Project 1:} \frac{3.0}{2.6 \times 300} = 0.00385$$

$$\text{For Project 2:} \frac{1.8}{2.6 \times 300} = 0.00231$$

$$\text{For Project } N: \frac{2.5}{2.6 \times 300} = 0.00321$$

An attribute of this kind of "normalized" scoring system is that those characteristics with very little variance in the scores—for example, a mean with most values huddled closely around it—will contribute little to differentiating project priorities. This may or may not be the intention of the formula designer. In our example, population exhibits a small amount of variance. In effect, then, this characteristic is the same for most projects. A way of coping with differential variance of the characteristics is to ignore the fact that we have interval data and to treat them as merely ordinal data. Thus, the projects would be ordered from largest to smallest population and assigned values, in order, from 300 to 1. We may wish, for example, not to distinguish among those projects whose population affected is between .08 and 2.7 million people, but to separate this group from those projects scoring above 2.7 million. This may be a result of the pressing need for recreation areas near very large cities. In this case, the data may be better expressed in binary form, with those having values from 0.8 to 2.7 million set equal to zero and those having values greater than 2.7 million set equal to one. In other words, if the population served by the project is 2.7 million or fewer, the project would not be approved.

4. Normalize scores for each characteristic, then multiply and/or divide as in method 3. Two problems discussed previously affect this method. First, despite normalization, characteristics with high variation on their scores can dominate any formula. For example, if, after normalization, characteristic A has a range of 0.05 to 0.07 and characteristic B a range of 0.01 to 0.10 among all projects, it is likely that a project's priority will be based on characteristic B. Projects with even the highest score on A, 0.07, would need at least a 0.05 on B to compete with projects that scored the least on A, 0.05, but scored a 0.07 on B. Thus, all projects scoring above 0.07 on B would beat all projects with the highest scores on A by definition. This may or may not be a desirable result.

The second possible problem is that the multiplication or division of scores implies a certain synergism among the factors, that a good score on both (or more than two) characteristics is preferable to a great score on one and a low score on another. Thus, presuming a large number of projects that score a total of ten points on two characteristics, the one that will rate highest will be the one with scores of two fives. Again, it may be desirable to make projects with balanced scores the winners, but it may not be. The analyst simply must be aware how the method affects the results.

5. Create a weighting system for the characteristics, either from inherent attributes of the characteristics (e.g., orders of magnitude) or by explicit assertion (e.g., overall score = 2 × characteristic A + 0.5 × characteristic B). This popular method of formula development best demonstrates a central problem with all of the methods mentioned: the arbitrary nature of any allocation formula. There are several key criteria for judging the adequacy of an allocation formula. One is pragmatic: Does it allocate funds or choose projects in a politically feasible and sensible way? The other is normative: Does the formula operationalize the program's goals and objectives? Often in order to achieve success on the former criterion, tremendous sacrifices are made in the integrity of the latter. As previously noted, each weight in a weighting scheme (including equal weights to all factors) should be supported with theoretical constructs.

An example of the process of establishing the goals of a program and, in effect, analyzing the program's intended results is provided by a State of Wisconsin process for ranking local water-pollution abatement projects for state and federal funding. In Wisconsin there were over 500 local pollution-abatement projects competing for state and federal funds. The Environmental Protection Agency (EPA) required that the state include four considerations in its ranking formula: (1) the severity of the pollution problems, (2) the population affected, (3) the need for preserving high-quality waters, and (4) national priorities. States, then, had wide discretion in administering their grant programs. Wisconsin's formula had six components, one of which was a compound measure.

The overall objective set by the Wisconsin Department of Natural Resources (WDNR) was "to abate the most pollution per (state and federal) dollar spent." Attainment of this goal is, of course, very difficult to measure; and that difficulty is compounded by the need to judge it before awarding the funds for implementing the project. Development of a single measure of pollution abatement that could be used on all projects, like pounds of phosphorus removed, was impossible. There are many measures of pollution: phosphorus levels, suspended solids, biological oxygen demand, the presence of specific chemical and biological elements, and even temperature. Pollutions in sediments can also be a serious source of pollution when disturbed. Another critical issue is the efficiency of abatement. Should the state use resources to maintain clean water, make marginal changes to waters almost up to standards, or clean up the dirtiest water? Finally there is a question that combines efficiency and equity questions: Should project dollars be concentrated where people are concentrated, in the most urban parts of the state? Or is it fairer to raise water quality uniformly over the state so that each individual is equally protected? In general, the federal government had emphasized compliance with minimum water-quality standards. But in Wisconsin this would mean very little activity in rural areas with generally higher water quality. Quite obviously political, if not equity, considerations entered into the development of the WDNR's funding formula. For the moment we will ignore these, however, and continue to analyze this situation in the context of a technical goal-setting and evaluation process. A complex process of citizen involvement and professional consulting resulted in the following ranking system:

Project's Priority Score = River Basin Score +

Health Hazard Score +

Assimilative Capacity Factor Score +

Nutrient Control Score +

Population Score +

Project Category Score

Each one of these six factors had a different possible range. For example, river basins scored from nearly 0 to 7.4, populations from 2.0 to 6.0, and project categories from 2.0 to 18.0. Thus, the formula factors weighed differently in the project's overall score. Some of the six factors themselves were quite complex. For example, the River Basin Score was developed as a general characterization of the water quality and population of an area. The formula used to compute the River Basin Score was:

$$P_P + \frac{1}{10}P_{WQ} + 10P_T + 10P_W + P_{PAB}$$

- P_P is the log of the population of the area per square mile. It is intended to give the sense of the population affected, but its range is limited in two ways: the use of logs instead of the actual numbers, and the use of density instead of the actual population of the area affected.
- P_{WQ} is a water-quality index that reflects only one dimension, dissolved oxygen.
- P_T is the number of trout streams per square mile for the river basin within which the project is located.
- P_W is the miles of state or federally designated wild rivers per square mile. P_T and P_W are directed at the preservation of high-quality waters.
- P_{PAB} is 0.5 if the EPA considers the segment to be part of a "Priority Accomplishment Basin," and 0 if it does not.

The five factors are not given equal weight. Whereas the range of P_{PAB} is from 0 to 0.5, the ranges of $10P_T$ and $10P_W$ are from 0 to very large numbers. Also, the factor, P_P includes a factor, "Population Score," that is used as a separate component. The River Basin Score tends to give priority to rural areas over urban ones, and to the preservation of cleaner waters over improving degraded waters. Of course, the range of this River Basin factor is narrow, from 0 to 7.4. It is the Project Category Score that has the largest range and contributes most to the overall ranking of a particular project.

This allocation formula is overly complex because it includes all objectives and has unclear priorities. But even the smallest office can analyze the results of such allocation formulas with a microcomputer. In this case, it was essential for the Milwaukee Metropolitan Sewerage District, among many other public and private bodies, to review the proposed formula and comment on its adequacy. A university team, acting as consultants to several state legislators who represented Milwaukee, analyzed the proposed formula, noting especially how Milwaukee projects were faring. This is a very typical assignment for a policy analyst working with a client—that is, determining what factors are causing the client's projects to rank high or low, and noting how changes in the funding formula could alter the priority position of the client's projects. Under more ideal circumstances the formula would be based on a consistent set of objectives for the program as a whole, and the analyst's comments would be more appropriately directed at the adequacy of the formula in measuring those objectives. But, in practice, these formulas are often used as devices to diffuse political opposition, and the analyst must be on guard.

We offer a number of guidelines for the development of such formulas.

1. Develop the program or policy's objectives first. They should be clear, unambiguous, and not conflicting.
2. Keep the formula simple. With a limited number of clearly stated objectives it should be possible to develop simple operational measures of these objectives. (See Chapter 4.)
3. Be certain that data are readily available for all units of analysis for these measures (in this case water-pollution abatement projects).

4. Use simple methods to combine measures. That is, arithmetic procedures and weighting systems should be simple, clear, theoretically defensible, and, of course, must work mathematically to allocate the total correctly.

In the WDNR's case, an alternative funding formula could have been developed to address more directly the idea of efficiency. It would have been possible, for example, to characterize the extensiveness and current degree of human activity adjacent to the water body. Then rough measures of benefit could be derived by combining measures of water-quality improvement (e.g., grade 5 to grade 3) and extent of impact (e.g., miles of shore and/or adjacent population). Thus, hypothetically we might compare Project A, which cost $10 million in state and federal money, raised water quality from grade 5 to grade 3, and directly affected 11 miles of river used for recreational purposes, with Project B, which cost $5 million, raised water quality one grade, and affected 20 miles of river. One scoring system might look like this:

$$\text{Project A's score} = \frac{2 \text{ grades} \times 11 \text{ miles}}{\$10 \text{ million}} = \frac{22}{10} = 2.2$$

$$\text{Project B's score} = \frac{1 \text{ grade} \times 20 \text{ miles}}{\$5 \text{ million}} = \frac{20}{5} = 4.0$$

This is an extremely simple approach, but it does directly address the notion of efficiency, which was the DNR's main goal. As with any measurement system, operational definitions of terms such as *impact on a water body* and *grades of water-quality improvement* would need to be clearly defined and easily measured. Once the formula is developed, extensive sensitivity tests need to be performed to see if the allocation of project priorities appears rational, equitable, and politically feasible.

Quick Decision Analysis Revisited

In Chapter 4 we showed how decision analysis could be used to structure our thinking about problems; it can be used to decide what the key issues are and what further information we should gather and analyze. We used the example of a policy of abating property taxes to encourage downtown redevelopment. We did not specify, though, how this method could be used to evaluate alternative policies. We do that in this section.

Let us return to our tax-abatement problem. The decision diagram of Figure 4-2 is repeated in Figure 7-7. Remember, there are two vital pieces of information we need: the costs and benefits of each of the four possible outcomes and the likelihood that, given the choice of a policy, one of two outcomes would happen, development or no development. To these two items we can now add two more: the attitude toward risk and uncertainty of the decision makers, and their personal valuation of our predicted outcomes. Let's presume that the

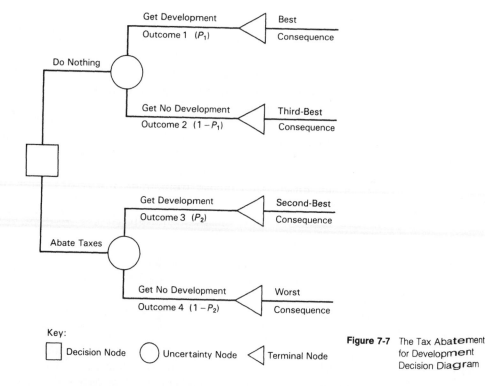

Key:

☐ Decision Node   ◯ Uncertainty Node   ◁ Terminal Node

Figure 7-7 The Tax Abatement for Development Decision Diagram

likelihood of development and its consequences have now been studied in more depth than suggested in Chapter 4. We are now able to value, in terms of costs and benefits to the city, each of the four possible outcomes. Keeping our example simple, and ignoring discounting, let's say the picture looks like the case presented in Table 7-6.

The costs and benefits which appear in Table 7-6 are, of course, the best estimates of the analysts, given their assessment of the consequences of each outcome. You can see that they have refined their initial values from simply ranking them from best to worst (see Chapter 4) to +$75 million, $0, +$200 million, −$200 million. In the case presented in Figure 4-3, the choice was clear—do nothing—because in each case that policy produced outcomes preferable to the abate-taxes policy outcomes. But now it appears that it might be possible to make the city better off by adopting the abatement policy: There is a chance of a $200 million net benefit. Of course we can imagine that for each policy, abate or not, there is a continuum of possible development outcomes from none to a great deal. However, for purposes of our example, we have summarized these as most likely success and failure outcomes for each of the two policies, go and no go, and the likely occurrence of each. Because we include all possible outcomes in these two categories for each policy, the probabilities for the two outcomes will have to add to 1.0 for each policy. In the terminology of decision

Table 7-6 The Costs and Benefits of Different Possible Outcomes of a Policy to Abate Taxes for Downtown Development (in millions of dollars)

Costs and Benefits of the Outcome	Outcome 1 Do Nothing/ Get Development	Outcome 2 Do Nothing/ Get No Development	Outcome 3 Abate Taxes/ Get Development	Outcome 4 Abate Taxes/ Get No Development
Increased property tax receipts	+$100	$0	+$900	$ 0
Decreased property tax receipts (taxes abated)	$ 0	$0	−$600	−$200
Increased public service costs	−$ 25	$0	−$100	$ 0
Net benefit (+) or loss (−) to city	+$ 75	$0	+$200	−$200

analysis the outcomes must be *mutually exclusive* (no overlap) and *collectively exhaustive* (no other possible outcomes). Let us now assume that, having assessed economic conditions, the positions of various possible developers, and the outcomes of the adoption of comparable policies in other cities, the analysts have decided that the probabilities for outcomes look like those shown in Figure 7-8.

Presuming for the moment that decision makers accept the analyst's valuation of outcomes, +$75 million, $0, +$200 million, and −$200 million, we must next consider the decision makers' attitudes about risk to evaluate which is the best policy to adopt. Calculating the *expected value* of an outcome, by multiplying the probability of its occurrence by its worth (e.g., in dollars) if it did come about, is a way of comparing outcomes that have different degrees of risk and different payoffs using a common measure. If decision makers were always willing to select the alternative with the highest expected value, a method that would maximize long-run benefits if it were based on accurate numbers, they would be called *risk neutral*. This is, incidentally, seldom the case.

Figure 7-8 Probabilities for Tax-Abatement Outcomes

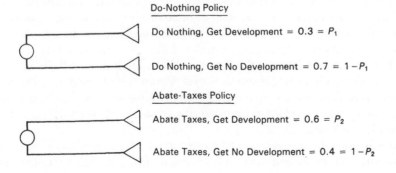

Do-Nothing Policy

Do Nothing, Get Development = 0.3 = P_1

Do Nothing, Get No Development = 0.7 = $1 - P_1$

Abate-Taxes Policy

Abate Taxes, Get Development = 0.6 = P_2

Abate Taxes, Get No Development = 0.4 = $1 - P_2$

For doing nothing, the expected value is a 0.3 chance at $+$75$ million and a 0.7 chance at $0. Multiplying gives us the expected value for doing nothing:

$$0.3 \times (+\$75 \text{ M}) + 0.7 \times (\$0) = +\$22.5 \text{ M}$$

For adopting the policy the expected value is:

$$0.6 \times (+\$200 \text{ M}) + 0.4 \times (-\$200 \text{ M}) = +\$40.0 \text{ M}$$

Thus, if decision makers were risk neutral, they would adopt the policy of abating taxes because it has a higher expected value than doing nothing. Before discussing other attitudes about risk, let us review what we have done to be able to come to this decision point.

First, we laid out the dimensions of the problem and captured them in a decision diagram. Although there was a continuum of possible outcomes for each policy, we identified the most likely outcome for each. We then assessed the value of these possible outcomes by looking at existing property tax records and forecasting levels of potential development. Next we estimated the probabilities of occurrence of each of the outcomes for each of the policies. Finally, we calculated the expected values of each of the two policies. Each one of these steps, of course, could require a major research project. But we are suggesting that analysis like this can be done even in very short periods of time. One simply does as well as possible with the information available.

Decision makers might be risk neutral if they could ignore special interests. If the expected-value criterion were consistently used to select policies, society as a whole would be better off in the long run. However, some projects could have substantial positive or negative consequences for individual groups or persons. In our redevelopment-policy question, downtown business interests could certainly be affected by the decision. Even if special interests were not a factor, disappointing results in the short run from a few projects might put a politician out of office well before the overall long-run benefit of many more projects was appreciated. Thus, it may be the unusual elected decision maker who ignores short-run implications, such as the potential disaster of a failed project or the differential impact on selected subgroups of the population. Only the exceptional leader will select what will, in the long run, be the best decision criterion for all projects and all citizens. See Chapter 5 for a more extensive discussion of these issues.

The point behind our inclusion of decision analysis as a basic method of policy analysis and planning is not, however, that it will be used to select alternative policies. Rather, we are suggesting that decision analysis can be a powerful tool in structuring our approach to analyzing problems where uncertainty about the possible outcomes exists.

As we review let's analyze another policy that often faces city governments, and this time add the idea of sensitivity testing to decision analysis. Let's presume

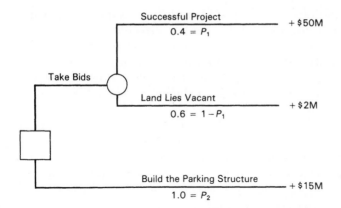

Successful Project
0.4 = P_1 + $50M

Take Bids

Land Lies Vacant
0.6 = 1 − P_1 + $2M

Build the Parking Structure   + $15M
1.0 = P_2

Figure 7-9 To Sell or Not to Sell Land to the Highest Bidder

the city council is facing a decision about whether to sell a vacant parcel of downtown land to the highest bidder or to redevelop the parcel itself as a municipal parking garage. The success of the garage alternative appears to be certain. A need for parking in this area has been demonstrated in the latest study of downtown traffic and circulation, and a detailed analysis of existing fee systems has helped to establish the long-term income potential of this structure. The success of the proposal to sell the land looks far less certain. In the recent past some successful bidders have allowed land to lie vacant for years, but others have completed projects, such as a new 30-story office complex. Although the range of possible outcomes is great, the city's planners feel that the most likely consequences and their payoffs are as shown in Figure 7-9.

Figure 7-9 presents a standard decision dilemma with the parking structure outcome lying between the two possible outcomes of selling the land to the highest bidder. The initial analytic effort should be spent on verifying the planners' estimates of the possible payoffs from the alternatives. Were the parking studies adequate? What discount rates were used? What costs and benefits were included for each alternative? What project time frame was used? Were opportunity costs considered? Sensitivity analysis would allow us to develop a range of payoffs for each alternative, depending on the values of the more sensitive variables.

The next concern involves the probabilities placed on the outcomes themselves. The parking-structure payoff, $15 million, has been deemed virtually certain. But the results of selling the property are uncertain. If we used the planners' estimates of probability along with these estimates of payoffs, and the risk-neutral expected-value decision criterion, we would choose to put the land up for bid. The expected values of each choice are as follows:

Take bids:
($50 M × 0.4) + ($2 M × 0.6) = $21.2 M

Build the garage:
($15 M × 1.0) = $15.0 M

Sensitivity testing could be used not only to examine the likely magnitudes of the payoffs, but also to explore whether the policy choice changes, given different outcome probabilities. For example, what probability (P) makes the risk-neutral decision maker indifferent between policy options? That is, what probability makes the expected payoffs of the two actions equal? This can be expressed mathematically as a sure $15 million (i.e., $15 million $\times$ 1.0) set equal to an unknown probability (P) of taking a bid and having a successful project pay $50 million (expected value $50 million $\times$ P) and taking a bid and having the land lie vacant [payoff $2 million and probability $(1 - P)$ yields expected value $2 million $(1 - P)$]. The probabilities of the two possible outcomes from taking bids must add to 1.0. Thus, $P + (1 - P) = 1.0$. The break-even equation then becomes:

$$\$15.0 \text{ M} \times 1.0 = \$50 \text{ M} \times P + \$2 \text{ M} \times (1.0 - P)$$

$$15 = 50P + 2 - 2P$$

$$13 = 48P$$

$$P = \frac{13}{48} = 0.27$$

The results of the equation tell us that if the odds of a successful project were deemed to be less than 27%, the criterion of expected value would lead us to choose the certain alternative—building the municipal parking garage. If the odds were more than 27%, we would put the land up for bid. At 27% we would be indifferent between the two options.

If politicians are not risk neutral, what rules do guide their decisions? Many are risk averse. That is, they value avoiding risk more than gaining benefits. This is especially true when the stakes are high. Large projects and highly visible policies are likely to be unambiguously associated with the politician's public record. There is an entire literature (utility theory) on individual attitudes toward payoff and risk. As policy analysts and planners, we are particularly interested in these attitudes among public decision makers. This is especially complex because these people represent their own self-interest *and* the interest of particular subgroups or the general welfare. Knowing that, however, should not prevent us from using what we do know to structure and evaluate policies and programs in the framework of a decision analysis.

Preferences of citizens, politicians, and officials can influence the policy eventually adopted, even when these preferences are inconsistent with economic rationality. We need to be able to derive these preferences in order to incorporate them into the decision process. To this point in our discussion of selecting among alternatives we have essentially been concerned with the selection of the preferred alternative using technical, economic, or ethical criteria. Such a preferred alternative may not be politically viable, however. If an alternative cannot be implemented, then it is not the preferred alternative.

POLITICAL ANALYSIS

Political analysis has several meanings. In one sense political analysis refers to the acceptability of the alternatives to the political system. How will politicians, decision makers, and voters respond to our client's preferred alternative? This question cannot be answered in isolation, however, since our client (as well as ourselves) is part of the political process and can affect the outcome of policy decisions. Political analysis, therefore, has at least three meanings in policy analysis and planning. There is the analysis we do to help clients discover preferences. There is the analysis of how the political system will respond to the preferred alternative. Finally, there is the analysis of the actions we and our client might take to cause the preferred alternative to be politically acceptable to other participants in the decision and implementation process. This latter type of policy analysis is political persuasion.[25] We may have to persuade analysts, decision makers, politicians, voters, elected officials, and others to see things as we do and to support a particular option.

This raises the question, however, of whether initial alternatives should be selected or screened out on the basis of political acceptability. At the outset of analysis there may be several alternatives that are clearly not viable for a variety of reasons: They demand astronomical resources, they run counter to moral and ethical values, they are illegal, they violate civil liberties, and so on. This may rule out some alternatives. But most often at the outset of analysis we should consider as wide a range of alternatives as possible, determine those that are technically feasible, and then estimate whether they are politically viable or how they might be made so. On the one hand we do not want to rule out possible alternatives at the beginning of analysis, but on the other hand we do not want to select an alternative that is doomed from the outset. MacRae and Wilde, in their discussion of ethics in analysis, provide an answer to this dilemma in their advice to would-be citizen analysts:

> As a citizen you are free to choose your own values or criteria in terms of which to compare prospective policies. At the same time, however, you are engaging in a collective choice with fellow members of a political community, and if you want to have your policy choices enacted you may wish either to draw values from that community or to persuade your fellow citizens to choose in terms of values you propose. You are therefore making your choice of values not in isolation from your fellow citizens, but in interaction with them.[26]

The analyst working for an organization or decision maker must also draw values from the community or else persuade others to agree. We tried to indicate

---

[25] Majone, *Evidence, Argument, and Persuasion*, pp. 78–81.

[26] Duncan MacRae, Jr., and James A. Wilde, *Policy Analysis for Public Decisions* (North Scituate, MA: Duxbury Press, 1979), p. 56.

this earlier when we discussed problem definition, the identification of criteria, and the selection of alternatives. All of this is done in light of values held by one's client, the community, and relevant groups and organizations. In these early stages the relative power of groups and individuals may affect the way a problem is defined, the options that are identified, and the selection criteria that are agreed upon. Political factors are again considered when alternatives are compared, and steps can be taken to assure that a wide range of political factors is considered. A number of writers and analysts have provided checklists, outlines, and other suggestions for political analysis, but even the beginning analyst will have developed a good feel for political issues after having carefully defined the policy problem, identified relevant evaluation criteria, and searched for alternatives.

Political Feasibility Analysis

During the problem-definition phase the analyst will have determined both the technical and political goals and objectives of the client and will have determined whether the problem is technical, political, or both. Analysts should also determine the nature of any political analysis that needs to be conducted—that is, whether it is needed to cause the public to recognize the problem, to have the client accept the analysis, or to garner votes from the legislature or council. By the stage in the analysis where we are displaying and comparing alternatives, we should have a good idea of the particular type of political analysis required. If we need public recognition of the problem, we may concentrate on ways to bring the matter to the attention of key organizational leaders. If we need to have certain groups support the alternative, we may concentrate on areas of mutual interest and benefit. If we want to obtain a majority vote for a technical solution, we might concentrate on alternative means of introducing the policy and the location and timing of the introduction.

Meltsner is one of the few people who has provided guidance to the process of political feasibility analysis by suggesting that political problems should be analyzed in terms of the *actors* involved, their *beliefs and motivations*, the *resources* they hold, their *effectiveness* in using these resources, and the *sites* at which decisions will be made.[27] During the problem-definition stage this information might be compiled as checklists so that central actors and decision sites are considered; as decision trees so that the interrelation of actors, decision sites, and sequence of events is revealed; and as scorecards or impact tables so that the relative

---

[27] Arnold J. Meltsner, "Political Feasibility and Policy Analysis," *Public Administrative Review* 32, no. 6 (November/December 1972), 859–67; and Arnold J. Meltsner, *Rules for Rulers: The Politics of Advice* (Philadelphia: Temple University Press, 1990); see also Hok Lin Leung, *Towards a Subjective Approach to Policy Planning & Evaluation: Common-Sense Structured* (Winnipeg, Canada: Ronald P. Frye, 1985); but also see Peter J. May, "Politics and Policy Analysis," *Political Science Quarterly* 101, no. 1 (Spring 1986), 109–25; and David J. Webber, "Analyzing Political Feasibility: Political Scientists' Unique Contribution to Policy Analysis," *Policy Studies Journal* 14, no. 4 (June 1986), 545–53.

importance of issues to actors and the preferences of actors for various alternatives can be specified. If such a scorecard is prepared during the problem-definition stage, it can be expanded during the comparison of alternatives to reveal possible political problems, potential supporters and opponents, areas of compromise, new alternatives that might be considered, existing alternatives that might be modified to gain supporters, and steps to take to enhance opportunities for implementation.

In the political analysis phase we expand the analysis conducted during the problem-definition stage by reconsidering and elaborating on the questions about actors, beliefs, resources, effectiveness, and decision sites. We attempt to collect the following information:

Actors. Who are the individuals or groups concerned about this problem who might reasonably be expected to support or oppose the alternative?

1. Modify the list of concerned and potential actors and organizations.
2. Identify individuals or groups not likely to be involved but who might be affected if one of the alternatives is adopted.

Beliefs and Motivations. What does each actor believe about the problem and possible solutions? What do the actors need or want?

1. Restate each actor's beliefs.
2. Restate each actor's goals and objectives.
3. Identify what each actor can and will do to obtain these goals.
4. Identify their nonnegotiable positions.

Resources. What does each actor have that can be used to get what is wanted? List resources that fall into at least the following categories.

1. Power, influence, or authority to control events, to modify procedures, and to affect the actions of other actors.
2. Financial resources to support analysis, litigation, and communication.

Effectiveness. Some individuals and groups are better able to use their resources than others. Which actors are most able and likely to get what they want?

1. Rank the actors in terms of their ability to mobilize and use their resources.
2. Focus attention on the key actors.

Sites. By whom or in what organizations will decisions be made? When? Sites can be identified from legislative intent, administrative procedure, and past conflicts. Sometimes decisions are broken down and are made at several sites.

1. Identify windows of opportunity.
2. List the traditional sites.
3. Identify the sequences of decision sites.
4. Identify sites that fall outside the formal or informal rules of the process.
5. Identify possible veto sites.
6. Identify actors who are the gatekeepers, who control or have superior influence at one or more sites.
7. Draw a diagram that links the sites and shows the typical or standard progression through sites.

Answers to questions such as those above, which can be detailed and complicated, are not likely to be found without research. The complete list cannot be answered in quick analysis, but the analyst must develop the skill to focus on the questions most relevant to the particular case, with the list triggering these thought processes. Some of this information may have been collected during earlier phases of analysis. The careful analyst will keep notes during analysis and keep in mind from the outset the need for political information.

The questions asked during this phase of analysis include who will support and who will oppose the various options, which alternatives will be easier to implement, and what types of additional analysis might be needed. The political information specified above can be used to help answer these questions. Meltsner suggests that the analyst construct a political map to show how the major actors are linked to the alternatives being considered.[28]

May has suggested that in political mapping we should distinguish between perceptual maps and position maps. Perceptual political maps involve efforts to describe how policy features are perceived by relevant interest groups, actors, and decision makers, while position political maps involve describing the support, opposition, and influence of these same groups and individuals.[29] Using the mapping concept, the policy options should be portrayed according to how they are perceived by major actors, decision makers, and interest groups. The actors, decision makers, and interest groups should be categorized as supporters, opponents, and those undecided for each option. Areas of consensus, compromise, and coalition should be identified. Using these perceptual descriptions, the analyst can design political strategies for altering perceptual maps of the policy options by modifying policy features, addressing misperceptions, or manipulating other variables. Using the position maps, and considering past decisions of actors in various settings, the analyst can estimate the likely outcomes or potential for success and failure for each alternative. This analysis can also provide insights into which elements of the options would be most usefully stressed and how the options might best be implemented. If the analysis indicates that no option is likely to be supported, the political analysis may provide information about the

---

[28] Meltsner, "Political Feasibility and Policy Analysis," p. 863.
[29] May, "Politics and Policy Analysis," pp. 122–24.

characteristics of new, technically feasible options that could obtain political support. For example, insights can be gained into new types of funding arrangements that might make an alternative more acceptable, different organizational structures that might make opponents more supportive of a particular option, or particular trade-offs that might gain the support of key actors.

This discussion of political analysis has assumed that the client seeks political advice from the analyst and that the analyst will provide this advice as part of the comparison of alternatives. Sometimes, however, the client may be highly skilled in politics, and political advice, especially from a beginning analyst, may seem presumptuous. In these cases the analyst must develop a clear understanding of the client's needs and desires. But even in cases where the client will perform the political analysis, the analyst or planner should collect and display political factors along with the technical and economic factors that bear on the alternatives. We recommend that even new analysts present political factors in a scorecard format. As you become more experienced, both in analysis and in working with a particular client, the political analysis can become a more prominent part of the display and comparison of alternatives.

Beyond the argument that the political arena is where the action is, there are several other reasons for including political analysis as part of the comparison of alternatives, even though we cannot produce precise data. Meltsner has noted that there is usually error in the other parts of the analysis, reminding us that economic data can be wrong, that the choice of discount rates may be arbitrary, and that externalities that cannot be measured are often ignored. He further argues that our political estimates will not necessarily preempt the client's political judgment. Most clients will view themselves as political experts and will reanalyze the scorecard data or work their own way through a decision tree. Meltsner concludes by asking us to recall that the purpose of analysis is to develop our understanding of complex problems, to work toward resolving them, that all problems won't be solved, and that the analyst will be wrong some of the time.[30] In practice political facts change frequently. Some anticipated consequences may not occur. Unanticipated ones will arise. Predictions of policy consequences are often wrong.[31] The policy analyst who engages in political analysis should be prepared to modify alternatives, to reconsider attitudes about favored options, and to recognize that even if favored alternatives are adopted and implemented, the results may not be those expected.

Coplin and O'Leary have developed a structured method for analyzing political problems. Their method, called PRINCE (*PR*obe, *IN*teract, *C*alculate, *E*xecute), involves constructing tables that show the positions that actors hold on issues, the power that actors have to get what they want, the importance of

---

[30]Meltsner, "Political Feasibility and Policy Analysis," p. 866.
[31]George C. Edwards and Ira Sharkansky, *The Policy Predicament: Making and Implementing Public Policy* (San Francisco: W. H. Freeman, 1978), pp. 170–75.

issues to actors, and potential interactions among actors.[32] The PRINCE method requires that the analyst make numerical estimates about the strength of positions, relative power among actors, degree of importance of issues, and so on. In this regard the system encounters some of the problems of quantifying criteria in evaluating alternatives. Making estimates of relative strength and importance is not easy, and making such estimates quickly is even more difficult. Such methods also are essentially researched methods that require substantial time for data collection. Thus, we will not cover them in detail here. However, methods such as PRINCE can be used to organize our thinking about political issues, to help us display issues and concerns, and to aid in communicating with decision makers. When we act as citizen-analysts, PRINCE may be directly useful for helping us obtain our political ends. Whether we can use PRINCE to derive advice for our clients again depends on our experience, our relationship with our client, and the complexity of the issues. On-the-job training and actual experience in the political process are essential before a policy analyst or policy planner can make political recommendations, and not everyone can do a good job of it then.

Methods such as PRINCE, the goals-achievement matrix, the planning balance sheet, and the Goeller scorecard tend to make the evaluation of alternatives and political analysis appear scientific. Estimating preference values, power functions, and other numerical indices must be done cautiously. Most such numbers are rough approximations, and modifications of certain critical values could overstate or underestimate the importance of a particular issue. Remember, the values used in these tables are estimates derived from our understanding of political factors. How confident can a beginning analyst be about such things as the relative power of actors, the salience of issues to actors, potential alliances, and so on? Because of these concerns, we fall back on our recommendation for a scorecard analysis that permits the client or decision maker to determine relative weights of key variables. All but the most experienced and trusted analyst will be overruled or second-guessed by the client or decision maker, anyway.

When the purpose of analysis includes drawing up a plan to intervene in the political process, to heighten salience, to redistribute power, to build coalitions—actions most likely beyond our definition of quick analysis—data from methods such as PRINCE can provide insights into how these battles might be fought, who might be potential allies, what strategies might be used, and so on. Short of this, however, the political information we have been collecting can be used in implementation analysis—that is, it can be used to examine possible ways in which to implement a preferred policy or program.

---

[32] William D. Coplin and Michael K. O'Leary, *Everyman's Prince: A Guide to Understanding Your Political Problems*, rev. ed. (North Scituate, MA: Duxbury Press, 1972); see also William D. Coplin and Michael K. O'Leary, *Public Policy Skills* (Croton-on-Hudson, NY: Policy Studies Associates, 1988), pp. 172–202.

Implementation Analysis

In our conceptualization of the policy analysis process, we focus mainly on identifying and evaluating alternative policies, and less on the specific steps necessary to implement a policy. The actual steps involved in implementation, will be, of course, specific to the particular alternative selected. This is not to say, however, that implementation is unimportant. To the contrary, we believe that not only must an alternative be selected that promises to resolve the issues identified, but as we said earlier, the alternative must also be able to be implemented, and implementation has to be considered at other parts of the policy analysis process.[33]

But practice has shown that not all policies are designed with implementation in mind, and implementation is sometimes begun before the policy is fully adopted.[34] Experience has shown that the top-down bureaucratic approach to implementation has not always met with success, nor has turning over implementation to the service deliverers through a strictly bottom-up approach involving "street-level" bureaucrats and clients.[35] One response to this dilemma was the concept of backward mapping, in which the desired behavior at the delivery point is specified and then actions are devised to change the behavior at each level in the organization so that the policy can be achieved.[36] Younis and Davidson, among others, suggest a policy-action continuum that recognizes the link between policy and implementation and the need to consider implementation feasibility during the policy design stage, as well as interaction and negotiation among actors as policy is implemented.[37] Early implementation studies, in fact, drew wrong conclusions because they used a definition of implementation that was often too narrow.[38]

---

[33] See John Forester, "Anticipating Implementation: Normative Practices in Planning and Policy Analysis," in *Confronting Values in Policy Analysis: The Politics of Criteria*, ed. Frank Fischer and John Forester (Newbury Park, CA: Sage, 1987), pp. 153–73; and Dennis J. Palumbo and Donald J. Calista, "Introduction: The Relation of Implementation Research to Policy Outcomes," in *Implementation and the Policy Process: Opening Up the Black Box*, ed. Dennis J. Palumbo and Donald J. Calista (New York: Greenwood Press, 1990), pp. xi–xviii.

[34] Carl P. Carlucci, "Acquisition: The Missing Link in the Implementation of Technology," in *Implementation and the Policy Process: Opening Up the Black Box*, ed. Dennis J. Palumbo and Donald J. Calista (New York: Greenwood Press, 1990), p. 150.

[35] For an overview, see Palumbo and Calista, *Implementation and the Policy Process*.

[36] Richard F. Elmore, "Backward Mapping: Implementation Research and Policy Decisions," in *Studying Implementation: Methodological and Administrative Issues*, ed. Walter Williams (Chatham, NJ: Chatham House, 1982), pp. 18–35.

[37] Talib Younis and Ian Davidson, "The Study of Implementation," in *Implementation in Public Policy*, ed. Talib Younis (Aldershot, Eng.: Dartmouth, 1990), pp. 9–10; and Robert T. Nakamura and Frank Smallwood, *The Politics of Policy Implementation* (New York: St. Martin's Press, 1980).

[38] Dennis J. Palumbo and Donald J. Calista, "Opening Up the Black Box: Implementation and the Policy Process," in *Implementation and the Policy Process: Opening Up the Black Box*, ed. Dennis J. Palumbo and Donald J. Calista (New York: Greenwood Press, 1990), p. 5.

Even a widely accepted policy may run into trouble while being implemented. A number of agencies, departments, and bureaucrats must interact to place even a small policy into operation,[39] and often these details are ignored or glossed over during policy analysis. It is often assumed that, once the policy has been adopted, it will be implemented effectively, but this can be a dangerous assumption. Instead, anticipating implementation pitfalls must be part of the policy analysis process. Moreover, it has been said that policies often change during implementation,[40] that much of public policy is actually made during the implementation process,[41] and that implementers (i.e., administrators, private agencies, interest groups, consultants, state and local governments, legislative and executive staffs, and target groups) shape policy at every stage of the policymaking process.[42]

Implementing an agreed-upon policy, even when the decision comes from the highest authority, is not easy. Edwards and Sharkansky provide a number of examples in which high-ranking officials order a policy decision to be implemented but nothing happens. They, too, argue that policymakers should use the likelihood of implementation as one of the criteria for evaluating policy alternatives.[43] They also point out that few policies are self-executing and that most policies, even simple ones, require a great deal of effort to be implemented.

Analysts need to be careful not to become enamored with their proposals before evaluating their chances for successful implementation.

> . . . the tendency to equate the desirable with the feasible is always strong, especially in politics [but] . . . accepting too readily that something is impossible can impede progress in public policy no less than in science and technology. Experience shows that with sufficient determination and imagination it is often possible to remove or relax many constraints, or to use them creatively to discover new possibilities.[44]

Nakamura and Smallwood make an important distinction between policymakers and policy implementers. They assert that policymakers usually do not implement policy themselves, but rely on implementers and intermediaries to carry out their policies.[45] They have even conceptualized three policy environments—one in which the policy is formed, one in which the policy is implemented, and one in which the policy is evaluated. Because they see these different environments, they place great importance on the directives and instructions

[39] Bruce F. Goeller, "A Framework for Evaluating Success in Systems Analysis," in *Handbook of Systems Analysis: Craft Issues and Procedural Choices*, ed. Hugh J. Miser and Edward S. Quade (Chichester, Eng.: Wiley, 1988), pp. 577–78.

[40] Younis and Davidson, "Study of Implementation," p. 4.

[41] Dennis J. Palumbo, *Public Policy in America: Government in Action* (San Diego: Harcourt Brace Jovanovich, 1988), pp. 92, 103–06.

[42] Palumbo and Calista, "Opening Up the Black Box," pp. 6–10.

[43] Edwards and Sharkansky, *Policy Predicament*, p. 292.

[44] Majone, *Evidence, Argument, and Persuasion*, pp. 69–70.

[45] Nakamura and Smallwood, *Politics of Policy Implementation*.

that policymakers in the first environment pass on to the implementers in the second environment. This is consistent with the argument by Edwards and Sharkansky that "the first requirement for effective implementation is that those responsible for carrying out a decision must know what they are supposed to do."[46]

These writers appear to agree with Pressman and Wildavsky who point out that the odds are against new policies being implemented, and it is a wonder that any new policies *are* implemented.[47] The process of implementation itself involves so many actors, so many sets of instructions and different groups and organizations, and so much information, that the decision maker cannot simply assume implementation decisions will be carried out.[48] Meltsner and Bellavita have also studied the importance of effective communications within an organization as a key ingredient in successful policy implementation. They point out the need for the organization to anticipate and decide what to work on and what to set aside, to encourage participation from people who have first-hand experience, and to take specific actions to help people do their jobs better.[49]

Steiss and Daneke have addressed implementation analysis, pointing out that it is a mistake to regard the implementation of policies as purely management functions that are beyond the purview of the policy analyst.[50] They are concerned because too often policymakers assume that because they can design a policy, someone else can implement it, and because too often public policies are adopted with no knowledge of what will be necessary to carry them out.[51] Steiss and Daneke hold that implementation feasibility should be assessed before policies are selected, and they provide a method for determining whether such an analysis is needed. They suggest that each alternative should be analyzed in terms of the *degree of consensus* among the individuals or groups involved in or affected by the program and the *magnitude of change* that the alternative represents. They provide the guideline that "programs having high consensus/low change present few problems in implementation; whereas those with low consensus/high change present many difficulties. Alternatives evidencing high consensus/high change or low consensus/low change may require further assessment of implementation feasibility, at the discretion of the manager or analyst."[52]

[46] Edwards and Sharkansky, *Policy Predicament*, p. 295.

[47] Jeffrey L. Pressman and Aaron Wildavsky, *Implementation* (Berkeley: University of California Press, 1973).

[48] Herbert Kaufman, *Administrative Feedback: Monitoring Subordinates' Behavior* (Washington, DC: Brookings Institution, 1973); and Edwards and Sharkansky, *Policy Predicament*, pp. 292–321.

[49] Arnold J. Meltsner and Christopher Bellavita, *The Policy Organization* (Beverly Hills: Sage, 1983).

[50] Alan Walter Steiss and George A. Daneke, *Performance Administration* (Lexington, MA: D.C. Heath, 1980).

[51] For a pithy example, see Rolfe Tomlinson, Edward S. Quade, and Hugh J. Miser, "Implementation," in *Handbook of Systems Analysis: Overview of Uses, Procedures, Applications, and Practice*, ed. Hugh J. Miser and Edward S. Quade (New York: North Holland, 1985), pp. 253–54.

[52] Steiss and Daneke, *Performance Administration*, p. 194.

The nature of government policy is the most useful factor in estimating magnitude of change, according to Steiss and Daneke. They also believe that incremental policies require the least change, and that nonincremental programs (designed to introduce new programs) require much more change and therefore will be more difficult to implement. Degree of consensus, they suggest, can be based on an evaluation of the attitudes of the actors we have been considering, including the target group, political leaders, administrators and bureaucrats, community and interest groups, and other concerned parties such as evaluators and analysts.[53]

While in the short run the rules of the implementation game are set, policy actors can attempt to change the rules to their favor. Majone argues that policy actors can change feasibility conditions through institutional change. Over time, rules for debating issues, setting agendas, and reaching and implementing decisions can be changed.[54]

Systematic approaches to analyzing implementation feasibility are still under development. However, Hatry and others provide a checklist of a dozen factors that should be considered in assessing the feasibility of implementing alternatives. Their points include such items as the number of agencies involved, threats to officials and jobs and groups, changes in behavior of government employees, availability of funds, legal issues, and level of public support.[55]

Another checklist, provided by Nakamura and Smallwood, includes questions about the political climate (key actors, their beliefs and resources), the resource base (leverage or inducements to move actors), mobilization potential (sources of opposition, support, and compromise), and assessment indicators (criteria for measuring success).[56]

Bardach views the implementation process as a set of games in which many actors maneuver to get what they want, using such well-known games as spending more to get more, foiling monitoring mechanisms, renegotiating goals after programs begin, and adding new elements to existing popular programs. Recognizing this, he has suggested steps the policy analyst can take to design policies that have a better chance to be implemented:

1. Ensure that the social, economic, and political theory behind the policy is reasonable and sophisticated.
2. Select an administrative strategy that relies on actual or simulated markets rather than on bureaucratic processes.
3. Identify program elements and those who might provide them.
4. Identify relevant actors and the games they play.

---

[53] Ibid.

[54] Majone, *Evidence, Argument, and Persuasion,* pp. 95–98.

[55] Harry Hatry, Louis Blair, Donald Fisk, and Wayne Kimmel, *Program Analysis for State and Local Governments* (Washington, DC: Urban Institute, 1976), pp. 100–101.

[56] Nakamura and Smallwood, *Politics of Policy Implementation,* p. 177; see also Majone, *Evidence, Argument, and Persuasion,* p. 100.

5. Identify facilitative and retracking mechanisms.
6. Determine how to phase in a program so as to maximize support.[57]

Although Bardach provides this guidance, he also warns that good implementation alone cannot offset the effects of bad policy, and that since the implementation process "is relatively unstructured, and its evaluation is very sensitive to the errors in political judgment and defects in skill . . . implementation analysis [should] be handled as art rather than as science."[58] Like Bardach, Levin concludes that in the cases he has studied the conditions contributing to effective implementation are idiosyncratic rather than generalizable.[59] Levin was, however, able to identify that within limits, strong leadership, a favorable context such as a crisis, and private interest groups make useful contributions to effective implementation. His analysis suggests that there is no formula that guarantees effective implementation, and that the conditions that permit effective implementation often cannot or should not be replicated. For example, leadership talent is scarce and costly, client groups may not be strong, and a crisis may be difficult to summon on cue. Rather than try to orchestrate these conditions in order to put a difficult-to-implement policy in place, Levin suggests moving toward policies that are more self-administering and self-executing.[60] These tentative findings suggest that much more needs to be learned about what makes a successful policy and that policy analysis, political analysis, and policy evaluation must be linked.

Noting that most of the implementation literature rejects a unidimensional approach to implementation, Ingram has proposed using a broad framework for such studies. She suggests that we view implementation as a seamless web of policy formulation, implementation, and outcome. Depending on the characteristics of the policy being implemented, she believes two types of implementation challenges emerge: The implementing agency must have the will, competence, skill, or resources to carry out implementation, and the agency must be able to succeed at constituency politics. Ingram has developed a flexible framework for analyzing implementation that recognizes components such as negotiation and information costs, clarity of goals and procedures, the level at which decisions are made, the type of evaluation criteria used, and the types of variables affecting implementation.[61]

Winter developed a model of the implementation process in which he

---

[57] Eugene Bardach, "On Designing Implementable Programs," in *Pitfalls of Analysis*, ed. Giandomenico Majone and Edward S. Quade (Chichester, Eng.: Wiley, 1980), pp. 143–54.

[58] Bardach, "On Designing Implementable Programs," p. 156.

[59] Martin A. Levin, "Conditions Contributing to Effective Implementation and Their Limits," in *Research in Public Policy Analysis and Management: Basic Theory, Methods and Perspectives*, Vol. 1, ed. John P. Crecine (Greenwich, CT: JAI Press, 1981), pp. 65–67.

[60] Ibid., pp. 68–108.

[61] Helen Ingram, "Implementation: A Review and a Suggested Framework," in *Public Administration: The State of the Discipline*, ed. Naomi B. Lynn and Aaron Wildavsky (Chatham, NJ: Chatham House, 1990), pp. 475–77.

identified four key variables affecting implementation results: the policy formation process, organizational implementation behavior, the coping behavior of street-level bureaucrats, and target-group response and changes in society.[62] He states that their relative importance varies according to the type of policy being implemented, noting that the role of the street-level bureaucracy is probably most important in human and social services and the target-group response is probably more important in the implementation of regulatory policies. Both Ingram and Winter note, however, that some work needs to be done before a set of rules can be prescribed.

Assessing implementation feasibility involves projecting essentially the same set of political and organizational factors as was done for political analysis. In fact, implementation analysis, we would argue, is merely one of the factors that ought to be considered in estimating political viability. Steiss and Daneke tell us to examine political, social, and organizational constraints, including issues such as who wins and loses, who supports or opposes the option, how agencies responded to similar proposals in the past, how the proposal will be affected by changes in economic conditions, what sources of funds are available to support the program, the extent to which relevant organizations are prepared and able to accept the option, how they performed in the past, and community climate and disposition toward new ideas.[63]

While we argue that implementation feasibility ought to be one of the factors considered in the political analysis section of the scorecard analysis, we also recognize that the beginning analyst alone may not be able to identify all the impacts and consequences. Again it may be best for the novice to attempt to identify implementation problems, constraints, and opportunities related to each alternative, to display these factors in the scorecard, and to allow the client to value their importance. In any event, the results of implementation analysis can be used to identify problems and uncertainties that might be encountered during program implementation, so at least they will not come as complete surprises.

Brightman has suggested that the worst-case scenario approach be used to evaluate the implementation feasibility of apparently successful alternatives, under the assumption that "every solution breeds new problems."[64] By systematically considering worst-case scenarios, he argues, we may decide that the best course of action involves too great a risk. Rather than leaving the scenario in narrative form, Brightman puts it into the form of a worst-case matrix or adverse-consequences worksheet. For each alternative, Brightman lists all the problems and errors that can occur during implementation and assigns values ranging from 0 to 100 to reflect their seriousness and probabilities that reflect the chance

[62] Søren Winter, "Integrating Implementation Research," in *Implementation and the Policy Process: Opening Up the Black Box,* ed. Dennis J. Palumbo and Donald J. Calista (New York: Greenwood Press, 1990), p. 31.

[63] Steiss and Daneke, *Performance Administration,* pp. 194–99.

[64] Brightman, *Problem Solving,* p. 50.

of the problem occurring. A worst-case score is obtained for each alternative by weighting the degree of seriousness for each potential problem by the probability value and then summing the scores. The higher the score, the greater the implementation risk.[65] This information may cause us to decide not to implement the preferred alternative, or it may alert us to problems that will have to be resolved so that we can prepare a contingency plan for addressing them during implementation.

Scenario Writing

Scenario writing is a technique that may be used both in the process of evaluating alternatives and as a means for presenting the results of policy analyses. Scripts are written to analyze what the likely results would be if various alternatives were to be adopted. In the evaluation step, the analyst writes scenarios for personal use, or for the use of the client, as an aid in thinking about the pros and cons of various alternatives.

Weimer and Vining distinguish between forward-mapping and backward-mapping versions of scenario writing. In forward mapping the analyst specifies the chain of behaviors that link a policy to a desired outcome. In backward mapping the analyst begins by looking at the behavior to be changed to ferret out those interventions or alternatives that could alter the behavior.[66] Forward mapping, therefore, is most useful for identifying implementation problems, whereas backward mapping is more useful for identifying feasible alternatives.

Usually scenarios focus on the political and qualitative components of the policy analysis process, but more generally they can be used to describe future states of the world in which one or more alternatives are being implemented.[67]

Scenarios can also be used for the presentation of analyses, to show why certain alternatives are rejected and why a particular one is superior, and to show the steps needed to get an alternative adopted. Such a script can be presented to a client as part of the analytic report. Sometimes it might serve as the full report. Although only one scenario might be presented as the final product, the analyst will usually work through several versions. One scenario might be an *optimistic* one in which the preferred alternative is eventually accepted. Another might be the *worst-case* scenario in which the proposal loses badly and actions are taken to cut one's losses. Another version might be the *midrange* scenario in which the proposal is delayed or is even defeated but the client ends up in a better position from which to pursue the proposal in the future. Other scenarios might explain the consequences of each alternative under economic growth, decline, or a con-

[65] Ibid., pp. 50–51.

[66] David L. Weimer and Aidan R. Vining, *Policy Analysis: Concepts and Practice* (Englewood Cliffs, NJ: Prentice Hall, 1989), pp. 311–15.

[67] Olaf Helmer, *Social Technology* (New York: Basic Books, 1966); and Larry Hirshhorn, "Scenario Writing: A Developmental Approach," *Journal of the American Planning Association* 46, no. 2 (April 1980), 172–83.

tinuation of current conditions. A scenario can be written either as an individual script for the political fate of a preferred technically superior option, or as part of a battery of scenarios in order to compare the political feasibility of a final group of equivalent alternatives. The scenarios can also be written to compare different combinations of alternatives, such as high-risk/high-gain options with low-risk/low-gain options, short-term versus long-term options, and so on.

The political data collected earlier in the analytic process are used in the writing of the scenario. First, summarize the general policy area and set the stage for the alternative being analyzed. The alternative should be described in detail, and the relevant actors, key interest groups, and areas of compromise discussed earlier should also be described. Next, the scenarios should be written. Usually it is easiest to begin with the optimistic scenario.

The optimistic scenario describes a process of positioning, negotiation, and bargaining that concludes with the policy being adopted after relatively few compromises. This scenario depicts the intricacies of the policy process, explores the various routes through the process, involves virtually all of the relevant actors, explores their beliefs, motivations, and resources, and predicts an expected outcome under normal circumstances.

Scenarios that modify the optimistic scenario can also be devised to help us understand what actions we might have to take if we encounter strong opposition, if the time frame for implementation is shortened, or if the implementation process stalls and strong leadership is needed. However, before expanding on the optimistic scenario, it may be useful to compose the worst-case or bail-out scenario.

In the worst-case scenario, the proposal loses in the worst possible manner, except that the client is forewarned and is able to bail out before the crash. The idea behind this scenario is to think systematically about all of the things that might go wrong, to develop insights into the warning signals of these potential dangers, and to gain ideas about what such a catastrophe would look like in order to identify the actions that the client can take to reduce losses, once the danger signs have been identified.

These two scenarios should anchor the ends of the political spectrum with the best and worst cases. Next, several middle-range scenarios can provide useful information about other possible outcomes, such as situations in which decisions are delayed, proposals are sidetracked, temporary setbacks occur, or the policy is defeated, but in a less than catastrophic way, with the result that valuable information is gained that can be used in a later attempt to have the policy adopted. These scenarios cause us to consider yet other ways in which our proposals can be delayed, who might attempt to delay them, and the resources they hold. Information generated here can be useful when we develop versions of the optimistic scenario that involve major negotiations, bargaining, or other strategies. Middle-range scenarios can suggest ways in which to modify the optimistic scenario to account for minor problems and pitfalls and to identify ways to reduce the number of concessions that have to be made to gain a successful conclusion for the optimistic scenario.

Scenarios therefore help the analyst think about political problems and pitfalls in a realistic way. Political factors, like raw numbers, need to be analyzed, interpreted, and presented in a meaningful way to the users of the analysis. The scenario is one such method. Moreover, scenarios can help to identify politically viable alternatives, provide information about modifications to make alternatives more acceptable, and highlight potential implementation issues by bringing into consideration uncertainties and potential side effects.

UNCERTAINTY

Identifying the extent of uncertainty in an analysis, even if that uncertainty cannot be stated in quantitative terms, will provide the client useful information about the risk of selecting an alternative. The client or decision maker may decide that too much risk is involved to adopt one of the alternatives, or that so much uncertainty surrounds the analysis that more information should be collected. It may even suggest the need for a pilot project before a final decision is made.[68]

Dror has distinguished between quantitative and qualitative uncertainty. By quantitative uncertainty he means situations where the various possible futures are known, but their probabilities of occurring are unknown. Qualitative uncertainty refers to situations in which the shape of possible futures is unknown.[69] Most attempts to deal with uncertainty have focused on quantitative uncertainty.

Although few analyses have specifically identified the uncertainties they contain, several writers and practitioners have suggested that when faced with uncertainty, the analyst should consider one or more of the following options:[70]

- Delay action until better information is available.
- Map out certainties, risks, uncertainties, and missing information.
- Collect more information in an attempt to reduce the uncertainty.
- Estimate costs and benefits with a range of values rather than with a single value.
- Develop a set of alternatives that recognizes possible future states at various points in time.
- Adopt redundant alternatives or modify an existing alternative to obtain more flexibility.
- Compromise by selecting an acceptable, although not necessarily optimum, alternative.

[68] Hatry et al., *Program Analysis*, pp. 94–95.

[69] Yehezkel Dror, "Uncertainty: Coping with It and with Political Feasibility," in *Handbook of Systems Analysis: Craft Issues and Procedural Choices,* ed. Hugh J. Miser and Edward S. Quade (Chichester, Eng.: Wiley, 1988), p. 249.

[70] Dror, "Uncertainty," pp. 247–81; Hatry et al., *Program Analysis*, pp. 93–94; and Brita Schwarz, Kenneth C. Bowen, Istvan Kiss, and Edward S. Quade, "Guidance for Decision," in *Handbook of Systems Analysis: Overview of Uses, Procedures, Applications, and Practice,* ed. Hugh J. Miser and Edward S. Quade (New York: North Holland, 1985), p. 240.

- Select the alternative that will give the best result under the worst expected conditions.
- Explicitly consider the consequences of low-probability but high-impact contingencies.
- Use decision theory to select the alternative with the best likely outcome based on estimates of the probabilities that various events will occur.
- Use sensitivity analysis to examine the possible effects of changes in assumptions.
- Provide at least qualitative statements that identify the major uncertainties and risks.

Schwarz and colleagues suggest that a general rule for dealing with uncertainty might be similar to that taken by the U.S. military, which once had the following approach:

> Any attempt to determine a unique best solution to a problem involving a large number of uncertain factors, some of which may be under the influence of other decision makers, is doomed to failure. The aim instead should be to search out or design alternatives that perform well or even close to the best for what appears to be the most likely set of consequences, and from such alternatives, whenever it can be done, select the one that gives some sort of reasonable satisfactory performance under the more likely and even most pessimistic circumstances.[71]

Even when great care has been taken to address uncertainty, less than desirable outcomes sometimes do occur. Identifying such unintended consequences or side effects is obviously easier said than done, and policy texts contain numerous examples of unintended consequences that are obvious to us—after the fact. But identifying unintended consequences before implementation remains an art. Perhaps relatively little can be done to anticipate them.

> One step policymakers can take to avoid unintended consequences is to look beyond a program's objectives when assessing it. . . . [T]here are many "effects" of programs which are not expressed in their objectives. Aside from this, probably the most we can hope for is that policymakers be sensitive to the possibility of unintended consequences and be willing to suggest refinements in their programs to avoid or repair the worst of those consequences.[72]

In practice, the least that the beginning analyst should do is to include simple, unweighted descriptions of political concerns, implementation issues, and unintended consequences in the analysis. Analysts who have more highly developed working relationships with their clients might assist the client in weighting the decision criteria and spelling out the more likely impacts and consequences in the form of scenarios.

---

[71] Schwarz et al., "Guidance for Decision," pp. 240–41; see also Dror, "Uncertainty," pp. 247–81.

[72] Edwards and Sharkansky, *Policy Predicament*, p. 185.

SUMMARY

In this chapter we presented methods for evaluating proposed policies or projects to decide which, if any, alternatives should be implemented. We noted that it is difficult to perform this type of evaluation because it necessarily involves projecting the future impacts of the proposed actions. Thus, we began the chapter with a discussion of the three types of basic forecasting methods: extrapolative, modeling, and intuitive. We then described several basic methods for evaluating alternative proposals once their consequences had been forecast. These basic methods included discounting, measuring efficiency, sensitivity analysis, and quick decision analysis. We also discussed the derivation and testing of allocation formulas, which have become important tasks for policy analysts in recent times. We also covered political feasibility analysis, implementation analysis, and scenario writing as methods for evaluating policy alternatives, as well as how to deal with uncertainty.

Although this chapter concentrated heavily on numerical analysis, it is important to note that quantitative evaluation is not free of values.[73] For example, forecasting involves selecting relevant time periods and appropriate projection models, cost-benefit analysis involves selecting an appropriate discount rate, and creating allocation formulas involves selecting relevant and politically acceptable project characteristics and determining weighting schemes.

The beginning analyst must determine whether it is best simply to describe political factors or whether an analysis and recommendation is desired. Beginners are likely to relinquish this role to the client or decision maker, or perhaps to a senior analyst. But even in these cases, the analyst should display political factors in the policy presentation. This process alone will help the analyst develop an understanding of implementation problems and possibilities.

The scenario approach was presented as a method that can be used to both analyze and display issues. The scenario approach involves writing scripts that detail the pros and cons of various alternatives. For a beginning analyst the scenario may be most valuable for personal consumption—as a way to determine whether all options have been considered and to test the internal consistency of one's own thinking. More experienced individuals can use scenarios to estimate consequences of political decisions, to generate recommendations for the client, and to present the results of the analysis in an interesting and thought-provoking way.

All analyses include uncertainties and unintended side effects, and even broadly supported alternatives may not be implemented as expected. These possibilities must be explained to the client. No matter how careful and diligent

[73] Robert A. Heineman, William T. Bluhm, Steven A. Peterson, and Edward N. Kearny, *The World of the Policy Analyst: Rationality, Values, and Politics* (Chatham, NJ: Chatham House, 1990), pp. 45–49; and Duncan MacRae, Jr., *Policy Indicators: Links between Social Science and Public Debate* (Chapel Hill: University of North Carolina Press, 1985), pp. 293–325.

the analyst is, errors in prediction will occur, new information will be discovered late in the analytical process, participants will change their positions, and so on. Analyses must therefore be revised as new data become available, and successive approximations of possible outcomes must be made. However, there is seldom enough time, money, and information to permit the analyst to conduct the perfect analysis. Therefore, the beginning analyst, as well as the seasoned veteran, must do the best possible job in the time available with the resources and information at hand.

In Chapter 8 we review methods of displaying alternatives that communicate the results of the analysis to the client. And in Chapter 9 we discuss monitoring programs and policies as they are being implemented, and evaluating them after they are in place.

GLOSSARY

A Fortiori Analysis   testing the sensitivity of project outcomes to changes in values of variables, making every effort to prove the favored alternative is less attractive than another.

Annual Net Benefits   yearly benefits minus yearly costs.

Benefit-Cost Ratio   the ratio of discounted benefits to discounted costs. The alternative with the highest benefit-cost ratio does not necessarily have the highest net present value.

Break-Even Analysis   discovering which values for one or more important variables cause the net present value to change from negative to positive (no-go changes to go) or cause decision makers to be indifferent as to which of two alternatives is chosen. This helps to focus on whether the values assigned to those variables are acceptable.

Cross-Impact Analysis   an inductive forecasting technique that ensures, as the Delphi technique does not, that predicted outcomes will not be mutually exclusive or conflicting.

Delphi Technique   a refined form of inductive forecasting. Some characteristics of the Delphi process that are applicable to quick, basic analysis include selection of knowledgeable participants, independence and anonymity of participants in the first stage, reinterviewing and revising of initial forecasts with individual participants after disclosure of preliminary results, and developing a consensual forecast.

Discount Rate   the rate estimated to approximate the time preference for money of the decision-making unit. Or the rate at which a benefit declines in value if the decision-making body cannot have it now, but must postpone receiving it. This preference for having benefits sooner results from several factors: opportunity cost (lost interest, profit from an investment, etc.), the risk that if one waits one may not receive the benefit, and inflation. However, most analysis should consider risk separately—that is, use a riskless discount rate. This generally makes the analysis easier to do and to understand.

Ex-Ante Evaluation   the analysis of policies, programs, and projects before they are undertaken.

Expected Value   probability multiplied by the value of the outcome.

Ex-Post Evaluation   evaluation after implementation.

Extrapolative Forecasting   a method of prediction that assumes that the patterns that existed in the past will continue into the future, and that those patterns are regular and can be measured.

Independent Probabilities   the concept, important for decision analysis, that the likelihood of two events occurring is unrelated. If one occurs, it does not make the other any more or less likely to happen, and vice versa.

Inductive Forecasting   a set of methods in which the future state is predicted (by persons who have some knowledge that makes them likely to do this accurately), and then data and assumptions necessary to achieve this outcome are deduced.

Interest Rate   (often the same as the discount rate, but not always) the rate that the market will pay to have benefits now instead of later. Thus, it reflects the same factors as the discount rate but is applied from now into the future rather than backward to the present from some future time. Also note that it is set by market forces (affected by government monetary policy, etc.), whereas a discount rate is selected for the purpose of analysis.

Internal Rate of Return   the discount rate at which discounted benefits equal discounted costs. Choosing the project with the highest internal rate of return will yield the same alternative as net present value if (1) there are no budgetary limitations, (2) projects do not preclude one another, and (3) all alternatives have streams of net returns that are first negative and then positive.

Modeling   see *Theoretical Forecasting*.

Net Present Value   the discounted future value (first discount costs and benefits separately, then find the net value of the two streams), using whatever discount rate has been determined appropriate in this case. A common rule for selecting the most efficient alternative is to choose the alternative with the highest present value that is still within the budget.

PRINCE   an acronym for PRobe, INteract, Calculate, Execute. This is a structured method for analyzing political problems developed by Coplin and O'Leary.

Ratio Forecasting Technique   a type of extrapolative forecasting in which the relevant measure (say, total population) in a small unit is compared to that in a larger unit in the form of a ratio (the first number divided by the second) for several points in time. The ratio is then extrapolated into the future.

Scenario Writing   a method useful both for evaluating alternatives and for presenting the results of analysis. Scenarios are scripts of what might happen under different alternatives. They describe in narrative form the unfolding of events, reactions of key actors, and consequences—including measurable costs and benefits as well as intangible changes. The worst-case scenario is a commonly used concept.

Sensitivity Analysis   a process used to discover which assumptions are critical (or sensitive) to the analysis. This is done by testing a number of plausible values for each important variable. Critical sensitivities are those that, when varied, change the nature of the recommendation.

Theoretical Forecasting   modeling, or using a construct of how some subsystem of the world functions to predict how things will happen in the future. There are empirical models, which reduce the problem to calculations, and nonempirical models, which do not quantify the problem under scrutiny.

EXERCISES

1.   Refine and expand the evaluation of alternatives you conducted for the teen-age driver problem in Chapter 2, using the concepts discussed in this chapter. Be sure that you discuss the fiscal and political costs and benefits of the various alternatives. Identify the preferred alternative and specify what steps would be necessary to implement it. What unintended consequences might result from the implementation of your preferred alternative?

2.   Develop a simple model that will predict for your state the property loss resulting from accidents by teen-age drivers over the next ten-year period. Also develop a simple model that will predict for your state the loss of lives to teen-age drivers and their passengers over the next ten-year period. Specify the uncertainties in these predictions.

3.   Population data are displayed below for a hypothetical city, state, and region. First plot the data; then extrapolate the year 2020 population of each. In plotting, be sure to

plot for all three areas: population totals, absolute changes, and proportions of smaller areas to larger. Make a conscious decision about which years to use as the base for extrapolation. Use both a ruler on graph paper and a mathematical technique and compare the results of the two approaches.

	POPULATION		
Year	City	State	Multistate Region
1910	375,000	3,750,000	15,000,000
1920	675,000	4,500,000	18,000,000
1930	1,050,000	5,250,000	21,000,000
1940	1,500,000	6,000,000	24,000,000
1950	2,025,000	6,750,000	27,000,000
1960	2,625,000	7,500,000	30,000,000
1970	3,300,000	8,250,000	33,000,000
1980	4,050,000	9,000,000	36,000,000
1990	4,875,000	9,750,000	39,000,000

4. Assume that the federal government has done some very sophisticated projections to the year 2020 for this multistate region, and they appear as follows: 2000—42,900,000; 2010—49,335,000; 2020—59,202,000. Revise the extrapolations you developed in Exercise 3 above.

5. Would it be appropriate to use linear regression to fit a line through the population data shown below? Would you need to convert any data to logarithms?

Year	Population
1810	5,000
1820	5,400
1830	6,300
1840	7,000
1850	7,500
1860	7,800
1870	8,500
1880	10,000
1890	11,000
1900	11,500
1910	13,000
1920	15,500
1930	16,000
1940	18,000
1950	19,000
1960	20,500
1970	23,000
1980	25,500
1990	27,800

6. Would it be appropriate to use linear regression to fit a line through the following population data? Would you need to convert any data to logarithms?

Year	Population
1910	50,000
1920	55,200
1930	57,600
1940	64,700
1950	70,100
1960	75,400
1970	79,800
1980	84,900
1990	90,300

Exercises 7 through 10: Several situations are described below where having a simple model could be very helpful in making some preliminary policy decisions. Using only your imagination and whatever knowledge you may have of the problem described, develop a model that could aid in analyzing various policies about the situation. Name the key variables in your model and their relationships to one another. Then discuss very specifically the kinds of data that would be needed to operationalize your simple model, and where you might expect to obtain such data.

7.   City planning departments often face the problem of trying to predict what subareas will develop next, and with what kind of development. Generate a simple model that will predict the locations and types of development that can be anticipated in the 50 subareas of the region within the next 20 years.

8.   Many cities in the United States are facing rapid changes in the size and age composition of their school-age populations. Develop a simple model that would predict the enrollments in their public kindergarten through sixth-grade elementary schools ten years from now.

9.   The transportation authority in a major metropolitan area will soon open a new line to the airport. Develop a model that will predict for them the number of riders on this line that they should expect during the second year of operation.

10.   It has been recently discovered that an adhesive that contained asbestos was widely used in laying flooring, especially linoleum, in private homes. When this glue is exposed and disturbed, especially by sanding, a serious health hazard is created. Develop a simple model that predicts how many houses in your city, with what kind of characteristics, have this problem.

11.   Develop a simple model that will forecast the number of additional deaths from traffic accidents in the nation if the speed limit were raised to 70 mph.

12.   If the speed limit were raised to 70 mph, there would be expected benefits in terms of time saved and expected costs in terms of lives lost. Discuss who would be expected to experience the costs and who would experience the benefits.

13.   In the mid-1970s government experts predicted that the number of highway fatalities would rise from 40,000 in 1975 to more than 70,000 by 1985. Instead of going up, total highway fatalities remained the same. Develop a model that would explain this phenomenon. What uncertainties did the government analysts face when they made their predictions in 1975?

14.   The reader is undoubtedly a member of several organizations, one or more at work and several outside of work. Many may be students and thus members of an academic discipline, and thus also members of a university, school, college, program, and/or department. Use intuitive forecasting techniques to assess the future size of one of those organi-

zations. Before making a final choice of organization, please read Exercise 15. Take about 20 hours to complete this problem and follow roughly the following procedure:

(a) Define the organization. What is its current membership size and organizational structure? Choose one of modest size—not, for example, the Roman Catholic Church in the United States.

(b) Choose at least three people who would be considered experts on the history of your chosen organization and its probable future membership size. Choose those whom you can readily interview in person.

(c) Develop a well-organized but concise questionnaire to be used during your interviews, and have an instructor or a colleague criticize the questionnaire before attempting to use it. The central objective of the interview will be to forecast the future size of the organization 10 and 20 years hence. A secondary objective will be to predict what factors will cause that outcome.

(d) Conduct a first round of interviews with the chosen experts. Maintain confidentiality and tell them of your procedure.

(e) Analyze the results of the first round of interviews and write a 500-word report of your findings.

(f) Send copies of the draft report to your interviewees and conduct a very brief follow-up interview with each, perhaps by telephone, to see if they would like to modify their forecasts in light of your report.

(g) Rewrite your report into final form.

15.   For the organization you chose in Exercise 14, gather historic membership data. Use some type of extrapolation technique to predict membership size 10 and 20 years hence.

16.   For the organization you chose in Exercises 14 and 15, use the information gained in solving those problems to develop a simple model of how the membership of the organization grows. Using that model, predict the future size of the organization 10 and 20 years hence.

17.   Some school districts and state legislatures are considering (and some have passed) laws decreeing that students who leave school before age 18, students who can't pass a minimum competency test, and students who don't make satisfactory progress in school either are not issued a driver's license or lose their current driver's licenses. What are the likely impacts of such a policy? Pay particular attention to the ostensible objective of such a policy—to make sure that students stay in school until they graduate. Using the modified Delphi process described in Exercise 14, choose experts in education, school administration, law enforcement, and youth guidance to assess the likely impact of such a policy on the schools in your state. Address specifically the details of such a policy; for example, defining what constitutes dropping out of school, minimum competency, and satisfactory progress. Do all of this in 20 hours or less.

18.   The news media across the nation have addressed the issue of radon gas leaking into homes. How widespread is the problem? How many homes across the nation are likely to have this problem? Should there be a federal policy to have all homes inspected for radon? What about self-inspection? Estimate the maximum amount that a radon test kit for home use should cost if an effective and efficient self-inspection program were to be established.

19.   Many high school districts are considering policies that require student athletes to maintain a certain grade-point average (e.g., C, C+, or B) if they are to be permitted to play sports. What are the likely impacts of such a policy? Pay particular attention to the ostensible objective of such a policy—to make sure that all students learn as much as possible in high school. Using the modified Delphi process described in Exercise 14, choose experts in education, school administration, athletics, and youth guidance to assess

the likely impact of such a policy in your local school district. Do all of this in 20 hours or less.

20. In this set of practice problems you will derive the actual numbers in the discounting tables given to you in Appendices 7-2 and 7-3. The Table in Appendix 7-2 answers the question "What is the value to me at the present time of $1 given to me n years in the future if the discount rate is r%?"

 (a) Derive the discount factors for the following discount rate/future year combinations and check your work in the table:

   (1) 10%, year 2
   (2) 5%, year 5
   (3) 15%, year 10
   (4) 7%, year 4
   (5) 1%, year 15
   What kind of a general pattern do you see here?

 (b) The table in Appendix 7-3 answers the question "What is the value to me at the present time of $1 given to me each year for n years in the future if the discount rate is r%?" Derive the discount factors for the following discount rate/annuity combinations, and check your work in the table:

   (1) 10%, $1 for 3 years
   (2) 5%, $1 for 5 years
   (3) 3%, $1 for 10 years
   (4) 1%, $1 for 6 years
   (5) 20%, $1 for 5 years
   What kind of a general pattern do you see here?

21. Using only the discounting factors in Appendix 7-2, compute the net present value of the following four projects (benefits and costs are in thousands of dollars):

 (a)

Years	0	1	2	3	4	5
Benefits	0	200	300	400	500	600
Costs	1,000	100	100	100	100	100

   discount rate = 5%

 (b) Same project as (a), but use a 10% discount rate.

 (c)

Years	0	1	2	3	4	5
Benefits	0	20,000	25,000	30,000	40,000	10,000
Costs	60,000	0	0	0	0	20,000

   discount rate = 7%

 (d) Same project as (c), but use a 15% discount rate.

22. Using only the discounting factors in Appendix 7-3, compute the net present value of the following four projects (benefits and costs are in thousands of dollars):

 (a)

Years	0	1	2	3	4 through 20
Benefits	0	2,000	2,000	2,000	2,000 per year
Costs	0	1,000	1,000	1,000	1,000 per year

   discount rate = 5%

 (b) Same project as (a), but use a 15% discount rate.

(c)   Years   0   1   2   3   4 through 25
      Benefits   0   900   900   900   900 per year
      Costs   700   700   700   700   700 per year
              discount rate = 7%

(d)   Same project as (c), but use a 15% discount rate.

23.   Using a combination of Appendices 7-2 and 7-3, compute net present values for the following projects (benefits and costs are in thousands of dollars):

(a)   Years   0   1   2   3   4 through 20
      Benefits   0   100   100   100   100 per year
      Costs   1,500   (with 200 maintenance in years 5, 10, 15, and 20)
              discount rate = 5%

(b)   Same project as (a), but use a 10% discount rate.

(c)   Years   0   1   2   3   4 through 40
      Benefits   0   100   200   300   300 per year
      Costs   5,000   (with 100 maintenance cost in years 10, 20, 30, and 40)
              discount rate = 2%

(d)   Same project as (c), but use an 8% discount rate.

24.   For each of the four projects in Exercises 21 through 23 compute an internal rate of return.

25.   A city of 500,000 set in a major metropolitan region of well over a million is considering building a new stadium to replace its aging facility. The facility is used primarily for professional football and baseball games. The costs of the new stadium as well as the costs of updating and maintaining the old one are:

- Alternative 1 costs (maintain the old stadium):
     Year 0: $16 million
     Years 1–20: $6 million per year maintenance costs
- Alternative 2 costs (build a new stadium):
     Year 0: $50 million
     Years 1–20: $4 million per year maintenance costs

It is anticipated that the building of a new stadium will cause more activity to take place there. All things equal, the professional football and baseball teams are expected to increase their revenues 10% and 20%, respectively. It is also expected that the site of the city's two free annual musical concerts will be changed from a downtown park to the new stadium, and that some events like very large summer rock concerts previously scheduled for the city-owned convention center will be held in the new stadium. Net revenues to the city of each of these events are shown below:

- *Last Year's Net Revenue Sources*
     Football contract $2.4 M
     Baseball contract $3.6 M
     Two free concerts   −$0.4 M
     Convention center bookings:
        Blind Ambition Tour $0.4 M
        Ala Mode Concert $0.2 M
- *Future Net Revenue Source*
     New activity to city (estimate) $2.0 M

Bonds were issued recently to generate funds to construct a municipal swimming pool. The bonds sold for 8%. Discuss whether you would advise building the new stadium on pure efficiency (fiscal impact) criteria. If you find the project should not be recommended, suggest new contracts with the professional football and baseball teams that would cause your recommendation to change.

26.   In the discussion of sensitivity analysis in this chapter a proposed tunnel is used as an example. Assume that another possible alternative has been suggested—purchasing a new ferry. The purchase price is $15 million and the annual operation, maintenance, and insurance charge is estimated to be $200,000. The service provided by the new ferry is better than that provided by the old one, and thus only half of the savings on commuter time and vehicle operation and maintenance is realized by building the tunnel over buying the new ferry ($3,312,500 per year). Which is the preferable alternative? Specify the uncertainties.

27.   The planning director in a city of 354,870 has decided to use an allocation formula to dispense the next five years' housing assistance budget. The goal of the project is to provide subsidized low-interest loans to encourage home ownership among those unable to afford conventional home loans. The director asks that you use some recently published statistics on the city's ten major subareas to allocate the program monies. A major objective is to allocate the monies in a fair way over the entire city—but according to need somehow defined and measured. Your formula will set up target budgets for each city subarea. The subarea data are provided in the table titled "1990 statistics—City Subareas." Develop an allocation formula and use it to budget the $3 million. Write a very brief memo to the director explaining your formula, displaying the five-year budgets for each subarea, and discussing why you feel it fulfills the program's stated goals.

28.   At the end of Chapter 4 you were asked to diagram the decision facing a city submitting an application to the EPA. Given the probabilities of each of the four outcomes, discuss the magnitude of the differences in outcomes that would justify choosing the experimental program. As part of your discussion, review what the attitude toward risk and uncertainty by the city administration might be as they make this important decision.

29.   At the end of Chapter 4 you were asked to diagram a decision to develop an office building. Using only your imagination, invent some numbers for the possible payoffs and probabilities. Finally, using your invented numbers, make a recommendation to the city on what action to take in this case. Explain how in the real world you might actually attempt to find the data that would be needed to make a decision.

30.   At the end of Chapter 4 you were asked to diagram a decision that needed to be made by a city mayor with respect to submitting a bid to host a future Olympics. On the basis of the decision diagram you developed, what decision do you recommend the mayor should make? What does your recommendation presume about the mayor's preference for risk? Carry that problem a bit further. What is the break-even probability of the Olympics being successful if the predicted costs and benefits remain the same? Presume that further analysis alters the predicted costs and benefits of the most positive and most negative scenarios to the following: $120 million costs, $145 million benefits for the optimistic; $80 million costs, $60 million benefits for the pessimistic. What is the break-even probability of the Olympics being successful, given these predicted outcomes?

31.   Construct a political analysis that describes the interrelationships among actors in one of the stories found on page 1 of today's newspaper.

32.   Conduct a quick political analysis of the possible adoption of a statewide income tax (or income tax increase) that would replace the local property tax.

33.   If your college or university is on a semester system, conduct a quick political analysis of moving to the quarter system. If your college or university is on the quarter system,

1990 Statistics—City Subareas

	1	2	3	4	5	6	7	8	9	10	Total
Total population	54,573	29,043	27,958	58,990	38,773	21,143	37,486	23,337	46,877	16,690	354,870
Total no. housing units	21,570	11,085	8,710	16,854	14,631	8,491	14,308	9,525	21,021	6,322	132,518
No. households renter-occupied	5,393	2,882	3,919	10,787	12,144	2,717	3,577	1,619	2,523	1,454	47,015
No. households owner-occupied	16,178	8,203	4,790	6,068	2,487	5,774	10,731	7,906	18,499	4,868	85,503
Average house value	$57,540	$91,000	$62,580	$60,620	$32,200	$36,540	$33,880	$105,840	$143,220	$78,540	$72,429
Standard deviation	$14,759	$15,883	$21,942	$20,051	$16,493	$18,026	$17,717	$22,218	$25,053	$23,503	$21,899
Average monthly rent paid	$265	$249	$169	$179	$165	$315	$274	$420	$434	$339	$289
Standard deviation	$68	$43	$59	$64	$73	$130	$126	$88	$76	$101	$82
Average household income	$34,971	$36,697	$19,996	$15,519	$10,991	$29,723	$31,361	$65,145	$85,093	$42,993	$34,954
Standard deviation	$13,988	$11,879	$10,798	$9,008	$5,796	$11,889	$12,545	$20,458	$29,837	$17,197	$13,973
No. households in poverty	6,358	3,965	6,139	12,683	12,717	4,329	6,542	683	12	832	54,260
Renters	3,243	2,062	4,359	11,415	11,502	2,511	3,336	294	11	408	39,139
Owners	3,115	1,903	1,780	1,268	1,215	1,818	3,206	389	1	424	15,120
No. households minority headed	3,074	1,065	3,146	446	53	4,447	4,321	102	11	408	17,072
No. households female headed	1,675	544	1,230	396	78	3,986	5,379	88	145	231	13,752

conduct an analysis of moving to the semester system. Use Meltsner's approach of identifying actors, beliefs, motivations, resources, effectiveness, and sites.

34. Identify the steps necessary to implement even a simple policy. Either identify a local policy or spell out the steps to implement a local policy to ban overnight parking on city streets or to implement a leaf-burning prohibition.

35. An exercise in Chapter 4 asked you to develop a problem statement for the Chair of the Ambrosia County Board of Commissioners. Now write two scenarios for the Board using the same information: What would happen if they took no action, and what would happen if they decided to float a $15 million bond issue as rapidly as possible?

36. Develop optimistic, midrange, and worst-case scenarios that describe the state of women's rights ten years from today.

37. Using the women's-rights case, perform a sensitivity analysis to estimate how the midrange scenario outcome will change if major assumptions upon which the analysis is based are changed.

38. It has been said that "every solution breeds new problems." Assuming this is true, write a worst-case scenario that describes the complications that could occur during the implementation of the above no-parking or no-leaf-burning ordinances.

39. Write a worst-case scenario for the implementation of a curfew for teen-agers in your town. If a curfew exists, write the worst-case implementation scenario for tightening the curfew by one hour.

Appendix 7-1   Common Logarithms of Numbers 1.00–9.99

	0.00	0.01	0.02	0.03	0.04	0.05	0.06	0.07	0.08	0.09
1.00	0.0000	0.0043	0.0086	0.0128	0.0170	0.0212	0.0253	0.0294	0.0334	0.0374
1.10	0.0414	0.0453	0.0492	0.0531	0.0569	0.0607	0.0645	0.0682	0.0719	0.0755
1.20	0.0792	0.0828	0.0864	0.0899	0.0934	0.0969	0.1004	0.1038	0.1072	0.1106
1.30	0.1139	0.1173	0.1206	0.1239	0.1271	0.1303	0.1335	0.1367	0.1399	0.1430
1.40	0.1461	0.1492	0.1523	0.1553	0.1584	0.1614	0.1644	0.1673	0.1703	0.1732
1.50	0.1761	0.1790	0.1818	0.1847	0.1875	0.1903	0.1931	0.1959	0.1987	0.2014
1.60	0.2041	0.2068	0.2095	0.2122	0.2148	0.2175	0.2201	0.2227	0.2253	0.2279
1.70	0.2304	0.2330	0.2355	0.2380	0.2405	0.2430	0.2455	0.2480	0.2504	0.2529
1.80	0.2553	0.2577	0.2601	0.2625	0.2648	0.2672	0.2695	0.2718	0.2742	0.2765
1.90	0.2788	0.2810	0.2833	0.2856	0.2878	0.2900	0.2923	0.2945	0.2967	0.2989
2.00	0.3010	0.3032	0.3054	0.3075	0.3096	0.3118	0.3139	0.3160	0.3181	0.3201
2.10	0.3222	0.3243	0.3263	0.3284	0.3304	0.3324	0.3345	0.3365	0.3385	0.3404
2.20	0.3424	0.3444	0.3464	0.3483	0.3502	0.3522	0.3541	0.3560	0.3579	0.3598
2.30	0.3617	0.3636	0.3655	0.3674	0.3692	0.3711	0.3729	0.3747	0.3766	0.3784
2.40	0.3802	0.3820	0.3838	0.3856	0.3874	0.3892	0.3909	0.3927	0.3945	0.3962
2.50	0.3979	0.3997	0.4014	0.4031	0.4048	0.4065	0.4082	0.4099	0.4116	0.4133
2.60	0.4150	0.4166	0.4183	0.4200	0.4216	0.4232	0.4249	0.4265	0.4281	0.4298
2.70	0.4314	0.4330	0.4346	0.4362	0.4378	0.4393	0.4409	0.4425	0.4440	0.4456
2.80	0.4472	0.4487	0.4502	0.4518	0.4533	0.4548	0.4564	0.4579	0.4594	0.4609
2.90	0.4624	0.4639	0.4654	0.4669	0.4683	0.4698	0.4713	0.4728	0.4742	0.4757
3.00	0.4771	0.4786	0.4800	0.4814	0.4829	0.4843	0.4857	0.4871	0.4886	0.4900
3.10	0.4914	0.4928	0.4942	0.4955	0.4969	0.4983	0.4997	0.5011	0.5024	0.5038
3.20	0.5051	0.5065	0.5079	0.5092	0.5105	0.5119	0.5132	0.5145	0.5159	0.5172
3.30	0.5185	0.5198	0.5211	0.5224	0.5237	0.5250	0.5263	0.5276	0.5289	0.5302

Appendix 7-1 (continued)

	0.00	0.01	0.02	0.03	0.04	0.05	0.06	0.07	0.08	0.09
3.40	0.5315	0.5328	0.5340	0.5353	0.5366	0.5378	0.5391	0.5403	0.5416	0.5428
3.50	0.5441	0.5453	0.5465	0.5478	0.5490	0.5502	0.5514	0.5527	0.5539	0.5551
3.60	0.5563	0.5575	0.5587	0.5599	0.5611	0.5623	0.5635	0.5647	0.5658	0.5670
3.70	0.5682	0.5694	0.5705	0.5717	0.5729	0.5740	0.5752	0.5763	0.5775	0.5786
3.80	0.5798	0.5809	0.5821	0.5832	0.5843	0.5855	0.5866	0.5877	0.5888	0.5899
3.90	0.5911	0.5922	0.5933	0.5944	0.5955	0.5966	0.5977	0.5988	0.5999	0.6010
4.00	0.6021	0.6031	0.6042	0.6053	0.6064	0.6075	0.6085	0.6096	0.6107	0.6117
4.10	0.6128	0.6138	0.6149	0.6160	0.6170	0.6180	0.6191	0.6201	0.6212	0.6222
4.20	0.6232	0.6243	0.6253	0.6263	0.6274	0.6284	0.6294	0.6304	0.6314	0.6325
4.30	0.6335	0.6345	0.6355	0.6365	0.6375	0.6385	0.6395	0.6405	0.6415	0.6425
4.40	0.6435	0.6444	0.6454	0.6464	0.6474	0.6484	0.6493	0.6503	0.6513	0.6522
4.50	0.6532	0.6542	0.6551	0.6561	0.6571	0.6580	0.6590	0.6599	0.6609	0.6618
4.60	0.6628	0.6637	0.6646	0.6656	0.6665	0.6675	0.6684	0.6693	0.6702	0.6712
4.70	0.6721	0.6730	0.6739	0.6749	0.6758	0.6767	0.6776	0.6785	0.6794	0.6803
4.80	0.6812	0.6821	0.6830	0.6839	0.6848	0.6857	0.6866	0.6875	0.6884	0.6893
4.90	0.6902	0.6911	0.6920	0.6928	0.6937	0.6946	0.6955	0.6964	0.6972	0.6981
5.00	0.6990	0.6998	0.7007	0.7016	0.7024	0.7033	0.7042	0.7050	0.7059	0.7067
5.10	0.7076	0.7084	0.7093	0.7101	0.7110	0.7118	0.7126	0.7135	0.7143	0.7152
5.20	0.7160	0.7168	0.7177	0.7185	0.7193	0.7202	0.7210	0.7218	0.7226	0.7235
5.30	0.7243	0.7251	0.7259	0.7267	0.7275	0.7284	0.7292	0.7300	0.7308	0.7316
5.40	0.7324	0.7332	0.7340	0.7348	0.7356	0.7364	0.7372	0.7380	0.7388	0.7396
5.50	0.7404	0.7412	0.7419	0.7427	0.7435	0.7443	0.7451	0.7459	0.7466	0.7474
5.60	0.7482	0.7490	0.7497	0.7505	0.7513	0.7520	0.7528	0.7536	0.7543	0.7551
5.70	0.7559	0.7566	0.7574	0.7582	0.7589	0.7597	0.7604	0.7612	0.7619	0.7627
5.80	0.7634	0.7642	0.7649	0.7657	0.7664	0.7672	0.7679	0.7686	0.7694	0.7701
5.90	0.7709	0.7716	0.7723	0.7731	0.7738	0.7745	0.7752	0.7760	0.7767	0.7774
6.00	0.7782	0.7789	0.7796	0.7803	0.7810	0.7818	0.7825	0.7832	0.7839	0.7846
6.10	0.7853	0.7860	0.7868	0.7875	0.7882	0.7889	0.7896	0.7903	0.7910	0.7917
6.20	0.7924	0.7931	0.7938	0.7945	0.7952	0.7959	0.7966	0.7973	0.7980	0.7987
6.30	0.7993	0.8000	0.8007	0.8014	0.8021	0.8028	0.8035	0.8041	0.8048	0.8055
6.40	0.8062	0.8069	0.8075	0.8082	0.8089	0.8096	0.8102	0.8109	0.8116	0.8122
6.50	0.8129	0.8136	0.8142	0.8149	0.8156	0.8162	0.8169	0.8176	0.8182	0.8189
6.60	0.8195	0.8202	0.8209	0.8215	0.8222	0.8228	0.8235	0.8241	0.8248	0.8254
6.70	0.8261	0.8267	0.8274	0.8280	0.8287	0.8293	0.8299	0.8306	0.8312	0.8319
6.80	0.8325	0.8331	0.8338	0.8344	0.8351	0.8357	0.8363	0.8370	0.8376	0.8382
6.90	0.8388	0.8395	0.8401	0.8407	0.8414	0.8420	0.8426	0.8432	0.8439	0.8445
7.00	0.8451	0.8457	0.8463	0.8470	0.8476	0.8482	0.8488	0.8494	0.8500	0.8506
7.10	0.8513	0.8519	0.8525	0.8531	0.8537	0.8543	0.8549	0.8555	0.8561	0.8567
7.20	0.8573	0.8579	0.8585	0.8591	0.8597	0.8603	0.8609	0.8615	0.8621	0.8627
7.30	0.8633	0.8639	0.8645	0.8651	0.8657	0.8663	0.8669	0.8675	0.8681	0.8686
7.40	0.8692	0.8698	0.8704	0.8710	0.8716	0.8722	0.8727	0.8733	0.8739	0.8745
7.50	0.8751	0.8756	0.8762	0.8768	0.8774	0.8779	0.8785	0.8791	0.8797	0.8802
7.60	0.8808	0.8814	0.8820	0.8825	0.8831	0.8837	0.8842	0.8848	0.8854	0.8859
7.70	0.8865	0.8871	0.8876	0.8882	0.8887	0.8893	0.8899	0.8904	0.8910	0.8915
7.80	0.8921	0.8927	0.8932	0.8938	0.8943	0.8949	0.8954	0.8960	0.8965	0.8971
7.90	0.8976	0.8982	0.8987	0.8993	0.8998	0.9004	0.9009	0.9015	0.9020	0.9025

Appendix 7-1   (continued)

	0.00	0.01	0.02	0.03	0.04	0.05	0.06	0.07	0.08	0.09
8.00	0.9031	0.9036	0.9042	0.9047	0.9053	0.9058	0.9063	0.9069	0.9074	0.9079
8.10	0.9085	0.9090	0.9096	0.9101	0.9106	0.9112	0.9117	0.9122	0.9128	0.9133
8.20	0.9138	0.9143	0.9149	0.9154	0.9159	0.9165	0.9170	0.9175	0.9180	0.9186
8.30	0.9191	0.9196	0.9201	0.9206	0.9212	0.9217	0.9222	0.9227	0.9232	0.9238
8.40	0.9243	0.9248	0.9253	0.9258	0.9263	0.9269	0.9274	0.9279	0.9284	0.9289
8.50	0.9294	0.9299	0.9304	0.9309	0.9315	0.9320	0.9325	0.9330	0.9335	0.9340
8.60	0.9345	0.9350	0.9355	0.9360	0.9365	0.9370	0.9375	0.9380	0.9385	0.9390
8.70	0.9395	0.9400	0.9405	0.9410	0.9415	0.9420	0.9425	0.9430	0.9435	0.9440
8.80	0.9445	0.9450	0.9455	0.9460	0.9465	0.9469	0.9474	0.9479	0.9484	0.9489
8.90	0.9494	0.9499	0.9504	0.9509	0.9513	0.9518	0.9523	0.9528	0.9533	0.9538
9.00	0.9542	0.9547	0.9552	0.9557	0.9562	0.9566	0.9571	0.9576	0.9581	0.9586
9.10	0.9590	0.9595	0.9600	0.9605	0.9609	0.9614	0.9619	0.9624	0.9628	0.9633
9.20	0.9638	0.9643	0.9647	0.9652	0.9657	0.9661	0.9666	0.9671	0.9675	0.9680
9.30	0.9685	0.9689	0.9694	0.9699	0.9703	0.9708	0.9713	0.9717	0.9722	0.9727
9.40	0.9731	0.9736	0.9741	0.9745	0.9750	0.9754	0.9759	0.9763	0.9768	0.9773
9.50	0.9777	0.9782	0.9786	0.9791	0.9795	0.9800	0.9805	0.9809	0.9814	0.9818
9.60	0.9823	0.9827	0.9832	0.9836	0.9841	0.9845	0.9850	0.9854	0.9859	0.9863
9.70	0.9868	0.9872	0.9877	0.9881	0.9886	0.9890	0.9894	0.9899	0.9903	0.9908
9.80	0.9912	0.9917	0.9921	0.9926	0.9930	0.9934	0.9939	0.9943	0.9948	0.9952
9.90	0.9956	0.9961	0.9965	0.9969	0.9974	0.9978	0.9983	0.9987	0.9991	0.9996

Numbers are read by adding the value at the top of the column (example: .03) to the number in the far left row (example: 2.20). The sum (2.23) is the number. The corresponding logarithm is read as the entry in the matrix (0.3483). Thus the log of 8.64 is 0.9365. The antilog of 0.9759 is 9.46. Interpolation is used to calculate numbers and logs not shown in this table.

Appendix 7-2 Present Value of $1

DISCOUNT RATE

Year	1%	2%	3%	4%	5%	6%	7%	8%	9%	10%	12%	15%	20%	25%	30%	40%	50%
1	0.9901	0.9804	0.9709	0.9615	0.9524	0.9434	0.9346	0.9259	0.9174	0.9091	0.8929	0.8696	0.8333	0.8000	0.7692	0.7143	0.6667
2	0.9803	0.9612	0.9426	0.9246	0.9070	0.8900	0.8734	0.8573	0.8417	0.8264	0.7972	0.7561	0.6944	0.6400	0.5917	0.5102	0.4444
3	0.9706	0.9423	0.9151	0.8890	0.8638	0.8396	0.8163	0.7938	0.7722	0.7513	0.7118	0.6575	0.5787	0.5120	0.4552	0.3644	0.2963
4	0.9610	0.9238	0.8885	0.8548	0.8227	0.7921	0.7629	0.7350	0.7084	0.6830	0.6355	0.5718	0.4823	0.4096	0.3501	0.2603	0.1975
5	0.9515	0.9057	0.8626	0.8219	0.7835	0.7473	0.7130	0.6806	0.6499	0.6209	0.5674	0.4972	0.4019	0.3277	0.2693	0.1859	0.1317
6	0.9420	0.8880	0.8375	0.7903	0.7462	0.7050	0.6663	0.6302	0.5963	0.5645	0.5066	0.4323	0.3349	0.2621	0.2072	0.1328	0.0878
7	0.9327	0.8706	0.8131	0.7599	0.7107	0.6651	0.6227	0.5835	0.5470	0.5132	0.4523	0.3759	0.2791	0.2097	0.1594	0.0949	0.0585
8	0.9235	0.8535	0.7894	0.7307	0.6768	0.6274	0.5820	0.5403	0.5019	0.4665	0.4039	0.3269	0.2326	0.1678	0.1226	0.0678	0.0390
9	0.9143	0.8368	0.7664	0.7026	0.6446	0.5919	0.5439	0.5002	0.4604	0.4241	0.3606	0.2843	0.1938	0.1342	0.0943	0.0484	0.0260
10	0.9053	0.8203	0.7441	0.6756	0.6139	0.5584	0.5083	0.4632	0.4224	0.3855	0.3220	0.2472	0.1615	0.1074	0.0725	0.0346	0.0173
11	0.8963	0.8043	0.7224	0.6496	0.5847	0.5268	0.4751	0.4289	0.3875	0.3505	0.2875	0.2149	0.1346	0.0859	0.0558	0.0247	0.0116
12	0.8874	0.7885	0.7014	0.6246	0.5568	0.4970	0.4440	0.3971	0.3555	0.3186	0.2567	0.1869	0.1122	0.0687	0.0429	0.0176	0.0077
13	0.8787	0.7730	0.6810	0.6006	0.5303	0.4688	0.4150	0.3677	0.3262	0.2897	0.2292	0.1625	0.0935	0.0550	0.0330	0.0126	0.0051
14	0.8700	0.7579	0.6611	0.5775	0.5051	0.4423	0.3878	0.3405	0.2992	0.2633	0.2046	0.1413	0.0779	0.0440	0.0254	0.0090	0.0034
15	0.8613	0.7430	0.6419	0.5553	0.4810	0.4173	0.3624	0.3152	0.2745	0.2394	0.1827	0.1229	0.0649	0.0352	0.0195	0.0064	0.0023
16	0.8528	0.7284	0.6232	0.5339	0.4581	0.3936	0.3387	0.2919	0.2519	0.2176	0.1631	0.1069	0.0541	0.0281	0.0150	0.0046	0.0015
17	0.8444	0.7142	0.6050	0.5134	0.4363	0.3714	0.3166	0.2703	0.2311	0.1978	0.1456	0.0929	0.0451	0.0225	0.0116	0.0033	0.0010
18	0.8360	0.7002	0.5874	0.4936	0.4155	0.3503	0.2959	0.2502	0.2120	0.1799	0.1300	0.0808	0.0376	0.0180	0.0089	0.0023	0.0007
19	0.8277	0.6864	0.5703	0.4746	0.3957	0.3305	0.2765	0.2317	0.1945	0.1635	0.1161	0.0703	0.0313	0.0144	0.0068	0.0017	0.0005
20	0.8195	0.6730	0.5537	0.4564	0.3769	0.3118	0.2584	0.2145	0.1784	0.1486	0.1037	0.0611	0.0261	0.0115	0.0053	0.0012	0.0003
21	0.8114	0.6598	0.5375	0.4388	0.3589	0.2942	0.2415	0.1987	0.1637	0.1351	0.0926	0.0531	0.0217	0.0092	0.0040	0.0009	0.0002
22	0.8034	0.6468	0.5219	0.4220	0.3418	0.2775	0.2257	0.1839	0.1502	0.1228	0.0826	0.0462	0.0181	0.0074	0.0031	0.0006	0.0001
23	0.7954	0.6342	0.5067	0.4057	0.3256	0.2618	0.2109	0.1703	0.1378	0.1117	0.0738	0.0402	0.0151	0.0059	0.0024	0.0004	0.0001
24	0.7876	0.6217	0.4919	0.3901	0.3101	0.2470	0.1971	0.1577	0.1264	0.1015	0.0659	0.0349	0.0126	0.0047	0.0018	0.0003	0.0001
25	0.7798	0.6095	0.4776	0.3751	0.2953	0.2330	0.1842	0.1460	0.1160	0.0923	0.0588	0.0304	0.0105	0.0038	0.0014	0.0002	0.0000
30	0.7419	0.5521	0.4120	0.3083	0.2314	0.1741	0.1314	0.0994	0.0754	0.0573	0.0334	0.0151	0.0042	0.0012	0.0004	0.0000	0.0000
40	0.6717	0.4529	0.3066	0.2083	0.1420	0.0972	0.0668	0.0460	0.0318	0.0221	0.0107	0.0037	0.0007	0.0001	0.0000	0.0000	0.0000
50	0.6080	0.3715	0.2281	0.1407	0.0872	0.0543	0.0339	0.0213	0.0134	0.0085	0.0035	0.0009	0.0001	0.0000	0.0000	0.0000	0.0000

The numbers in this table answer the question: "What is the value today of $1 given to me in the year n, if the discount rate employed is r%?"

Appendix 7-3   Present Value of $1 Received Annually for n Years

DISCOUNT RATE

Year	1%	2%	3%	4%	5%	6%	7%	8%	9%	10%	12%	15%	20%	25%	30%	40%	50%
1	0.9901	0.9804	0.9709	0.9615	0.9524	0.9434	0.9346	0.9259	0.9174	0.9091	0.8929	0.8696	0.8333	0.8000	0.7692	0.7143	0.6667
2	1.9704	1.9416	1.9135	1.8861	1.8594	1.8334	1.8080	1.7833	1.7591	1.7355	1.6901	1.6257	1.5278	1.4400	1.3609	1.2245	1.1111
3	2.9410	2.8839	2.8286	2.7751	2.7232	2.6730	2.6243	2.5771	2.5313	2.4869	2.4018	2.2832	2.1065	1.9520	1.8161	1.5889	1.4074
4	3.9020	3.8077	3.7171	3.6299	3.5460	3.4651	3.3872	3.3121	3.2397	3.1699	3.0373	2.8550	2.5887	2.3616	2.1662	1.8492	1.6049
5	4.8534	4.7135	4.5797	4.4518	4.3295	4.2124	4.1002	3.9927	3.8897	3.7908	3.6048	3.3522	2.9906	2.6893	2.4356	2.0352	1.7366
6	5.7955	5.6014	5.4172	5.2421	5.0757	4.9173	4.7665	4.6229	4.4859	4.3553	4.1114	3.7845	3.3255	2.9514	2.6427	2.1680	1.8244
7	6.7282	6.4720	6.2303	6.0021	5.7864	5.5824	5.3893	5.2064	5.0330	4.8684	4.5638	4.1604	3.6046	3.1611	2.8021	2.2628	1.8829
8	7.6517	7.3255	7.0197	6.7327	6.4632	6.2098	5.9713	5.7466	5.5348	5.3349	4.9676	4.4873	3.8372	3.3289	2.9247	2.3306	1.9220
9	8.5660	8.1622	7.7861	7.4353	7.1078	6.8017	6.5152	6.2469	5.9952	5.7590	5.3282	4.7716	4.0310	3.4631	3.0190	2.3790	1.9480
10	9.4713	8.9826	8.5302	8.1109	7.7217	7.3601	7.0236	6.7101	6.4177	6.1446	5.6502	5.0188	4.1925	3.5705	3.0915	2.4136	1.9653
11	10.3676	9.7868	9.2526	8.7605	8.3064	7.8869	7.4987	7.1390	6.8052	6.4951	5.9377	5.2337	4.3271	3.6564	3.1473	2.4383	1.9769
12	11.2551	10.5753	9.9540	9.3851	8.8633	8.3838	7.9427	7.5361	7.1607	6.8137	6.1944	5.4206	4.4392	3.7251	3.1903	2.4559	1.9846
13	12.1337	11.3484	10.6350	9.9856	9.3936	8.8527	8.3577	7.9038	7.4869	7.1034	6.4235	5.5831	4.5327	3.7801	3.2233	2.4685	1.9897
14	13.0037	12.1062	11.2961	10.5631	9.8986	9.2950	8.7455	8.2442	7.7862	7.3667	6.6282	5.7245	4.6106	3.8241	3.2487	2.4775	1.9931
15	13.8651	12.8493	11.9379	11.1184	10.3797	9.7122	9.1079	8.5595	8.0607	7.6061	6.8109	5.8474	4.6755	3.8593	3.2682	2.4839	1.9954
16	14.7179	13.5777	12.5611	11.6523	10.8378	10.1059	9.4466	8.8514	8.3126	7.8237	6.9740	5.9542	4.7296	3.8874	3.2832	2.4885	1.9970
17	15.5623	14.2919	13.1661	12.1657	11.2741	10.4773	9.7632	9.1216	8.5436	8.0216	7.1196	6.0472	4.7746	3.9099	3.2948	2.4918	1.9980
18	16.3983	14.9920	13.7535	12.6593	11.6896	10.8276	10.0591	9.3719	8.7556	8.2014	7.2497	6.1280	4.8122	3.9279	3.3037	2.4941	1.9986
19	17.2260	15.6785	14.3238	13.1339	12.0853	11.1581	10.3356	9.6036	8.9501	8.3649	7.3658	6.1982	4.8435	3.9424	3.3105	2.4958	1.9991
20	18.0456	16.3514	14.8775	13.5903	12.4622	11.4699	10.5940	9.8181	9.1285	8.5136	7.4694	6.2593	4.8696	3.9539	3.3158	2.4970	1.9994
21	18.8570	17.0112	15.4150	14.0292	12.8212	11.7641	10.8355	10.0168	9.2922	8.6487	7.5620	6.3125	4.8913	3.9631	3.3198	2.4979	1.9996
22	19.6604	17.6580	15.9369	14.4511	13.1630	12.0416	11.0612	10.2007	9.4424	8.7715	7.6446	6.3587	4.9094	3.9705	3.3230	2.4985	1.9997
23	20.4558	18.2922	16.4436	14.8568	13.4886	12.3034	11.2722	10.3711	9.5802	8.8832	7.7184	6.3988	4.9245	3.9764	3.3254	2.4989	1.9998
24	21.2434	18.9139	16.9355	15.2470	13.7986	12.5504	11.4693	10.5288	9.7066	8.9847	7.7843	6.4338	4.9371	3.9811	3.3272	2.4992	1.9999
25	22.0232	19.5235	17.4131	15.6221	14.0939	12.7834	11.6536	10.6748	9.8226	9.0770	7.8431	6.4641	4.9476	3.9849	3.3286	2.4994	1.9999
30	25.8077	22.3965	19.6004	17.2920	15.3725	13.7648	12.4090	11.2578	10.2737	9.4269	8.0552	6.5660	4.9789	3.9950	3.3321	2.4999	2.0000
40	32.8347	27.3555	23.1148	19.7928	17.1591	15.0463	13.3317	11.9246	10.7574	9.7791	8.2438	6.6418	4.9966	3.9995	3.3332	2.5000	2.0000
50	39.1961	31.4236	25.7298	21.4822	18.2559	15.7619	13.8007	12.2335	10.9617	9.9148	8.3045	6.6605	4.9995	3.9999	3.3333	2.5000	2.0000

The numbers in this table answer the question: "What is the value today of $1 given to me each year for n years, if the discount rate employed is r%?"

Chapter Eight

Displaying Alternatives
and
Distinguishing among Them

The evaluation techniques described in Chapter 7 provide a great amount of information about the relative efficiency of policies under consideration. But very seldom do the results of these methods alone provide enough information to determine which is the best policy. Calculating the probable net present value of alternative policies alone, for example, will not necessarily reveal the superior policy, because most policy decisions involve several decision criteria other than cost, including political viability, administrative ease, and legal feasibility. Moreover, there are often important elements of many decisions that are very difficult to convert to dollar or other numerical values.

This chapter presents ways to display alternatives so that decision makers can select a preferred alternative from among them. First, we discuss the limitations of relying strictly on technical analyses for selecting an alternative and the need to present technical evaluations as simply as possible. Next we discuss the conflicts between individual and collective rationality as they complicate the process of selecting a preferred alternative. The related problem of considering multiple criteria in decision processes is then examined. These issues provide the groundwork for a presentation of several basic comparison methods that can be used to relate quantitative and qualitative factors when deciding among competing options. The issue of whether to weight criteria is also discussed. The central message of this chapter is that quantitative analysis alone is usually not sufficient, that technical and economic analyses do not speak for themselves, and that quantitative and qualitative analyses can result in conflicting conclusions that must be compared with one another in a consistent, logical way in order to make decisions possible.

By this point in the book we hope that the reader has developed a healthy skepticism about the possibility of identifying a single, correct policy that is acceptable to all involved and affected groups and individuals. Seldom is this possible because groups, individuals, analysts, decision makers, and other stakeholders have conflicting objectives and values. The purpose of the policy analysis process, as we have illustrated, is to identify the option that can most efficiently and effectively resolve a problem, that is politically viable, and that can be implemented. It is obvious that the superior technical solution that is politically unacceptable or impossible to implement is not the best alternative. The policy analysis process, then, must include a step that integrates technical and political considerations, that recognizes and deals with the problem of multiple criteria, and that relates quantitative and qualitative data. These concerns are addressed in this chapter.

PROBLEMS IN SELECTING THE BEST POLICY

We have defined the policy analysis process as being the technical, economic, and political evaluation of alternative policies prior to their implementation. The policies under consideration are examined to determine the extent to which each satisfies certain evaluation criteria. Examples of such criteria include the following: Which option will provide the greatest net benefit? Which provides the greatest benefit for a fixed dollar amount invested? Which will incur the least political resistance? Which provides the best technical solution? For some relatively simple problems, technical or economic information may point to a preferred solution. In most analyses, however, this will not be the case. For example, the best technical solution may be politically unacceptable. The least costly solution may have undesirable side effects. Alternatives that satisfy criteria important to one group may not satisfy criteria important to another group. Individual decision makers may find that no one solution satisfies all criteria. How, then, are decisions to be made? How does the analyst balance the conflicts in the analysis? What decision aids can be provided? Conflicting data must be displayed and interpreted in a coherent manner so that informed decisions can be reached. Above all, it is important to remember that if the decision maker cannot understand the analysis, or has to decipher formulas, printouts, and complex tables, the analysis will likely have little impact. Although analysts are often called on to make oral presentations, most policy analyses are presented in writing. Analysts rarely have the opportunity to explain detailed concepts or complicated tables. The written report usually has to stand on its own.

Edwards and Sharkansky have addressed many of the problems involved in assessing alternatives and selecting the preferred one.[1] They argue that the analyst will encounter not only technical problems but political opposition and unintended consequences as well. Furthermore, they point out that even the measurement of benefits and costs is open to political manipulation, and that equity must be considered because some people benefit more than others. It would be convenient if there were techniques that facilitated easy measurement, analysis, and resolution of these problems, but no such method exists and no single technique is likely to be devised. Efficiency alone, measured through quantitative analysis such as discounting, cost-benefit analysis, and decision analysis, cannot be used to select the preferred alternative. Policy problems must be examined from other viewpoints as well in order to arrive at a judgment of impact and acceptability that will stand up when challenged, often long after the decision has been made. Our position is that after the numbers have been produced, the results must be displayed in a logical and consistent manner and the alternatives must be compared against one another in light of the relative importance of the decision criteria to decision makers and relevant groups. Each alternative must be examined to determine how fully it meets decision makers' goals, how efficiently it meets those goals, whether it is equitable, and whether it has unintended consequences.

Depending upon the relationship with the client, the analyst might present the results as a sequential enumeration and evaluation of alternatives or might make a strong argument for the preferred alternative. When either approach is taken, the outcome of the technical/economic evaluation must be related to evaluation criteria. If the criteria are ranked or weighted, either by using the preferences of the client or by assuming preferences based on prior actions of the client, a preferred alternative may possibly be selected.

Multiple advocacy has been proposed as a way of organizing expert advice on a topic to bring competing ideas and viewpoints together rather than relying on the analysis and recommendations from advisers who share the viewpoint of the client. This process of debate and persuasion systematically exposes the policymaker to arguments made by the advocates themselves. It is said to ensure that all interested parties are represented in true adversarial roles in a structured and balanced debate.[2]

In order for clients and decision makers to select among alternatives, it is usually necessary to display the results graphically as well as in narrative form. Often a matrix or spreadsheet is used to permit comparisons. Sometimes the results of the analysis are presented in scenarios. Each scenario presents a concise description of one alternative, an accounting of its costs and benefits, and an identification of who benefits, who loses, and how easy or difficult it will be to implement the alternative.

---

[1] George C. Edwards and Ira Sharkansky, *The Policy Predicament: Making and Implementing Policy* (San Francisco: W. H. Freeman, 1978), pp. 170–206.

[2] Giandomenico Majone, *Evidence, Argument, and Persuasion in the Policy Process* (New Haven: Yale University Press, 1989), p. 40.

The analyst should resist the temptation to display all the technical work, although many hours or weeks may have gone into its production. In many cases, simple graphics may be sufficient to carry the argument. The major challenge is the size and diversity of the audience. With many divergent viewpoints represented at the decision-making table, capturing the essence of the decision's multiple dimensions in an acceptable way will be difficult.

CONFLICT BETWEEN INDIVIDUAL AND COLLECTIVE RATIONALITY

The conflict between individual rationality—the decision made when only one person is involved in making a decision, and collective rationality, the resulting decision when several people are involved in making a decision—presents problems in policy analysis and planning. The conflict between individual and collective rationality, as it affects analyzing alternatives, has been discussed by many writers. You have probably heard of the "prisoner's dilemma." Two suspects are held in separate cells. The prosecuting attorney does not have enough evidence to convict on the charge unless one or both of the suspects confess. There is enough evidence to convict both of lesser crimes. The prosecutor separately tells each that if both confess to the more serious crime, a reduced sentence will be recommended for both. If neither confesses, both will be tried for the lesser crime. If one confesses, the one who did not confess will be prosecuted and the other will be given probation. The prisoners are not allowed to communicate. This scenario provides an example where individual and collective rationality are in opposition. There is an individual rational decision for each person when neither knows what the other will decide and a different rational decision if the two could decide on a collective response. Individually, both would decide to confess. Collectively, neither would decide to confess. Both reason that they would be better off confessing, because if they don't, and the other person does, they will be convicted of the serious crime. Thus, they decide to suboptimize and each take a moderate but certain sentence rather than try to optimize but run the risk of incurring a stiff sentence.

The problem of conflicting preferences has been taken beyond the two-person situation and has been shown to exist for larger groups. In the "paradox of voting," individuals can be shown to have mutually exclusive preferences for one of three options, but when the results of the individual voting are tallied, there is no preferred alternative. The paradox is usually described by examining the individual and collective preferences of three rational committee members for three options.[3] Abel prefers option A to B and B to C and, therefore, because of transitivity prefers A to C. Baker prefers B to C and C to A and, therefore,

---

[3] For substantive examples, see William N. Dunn, *Public Policy Analysis: An Introduction* (Englewood Cliffs, NJ: Prentice Hall, 1981), pp. 227–30; and Edward S. Quade, *Analysis for Public Decisions*, 2nd ed. (New York: Elsevier Scientific, 1982), pp. 91–92.

Table 8-1 The Paradox of Voting

Individual Members	Preferences	Rank
Abel	A over B	A
	B over C	B
	A over C	C
Baker	B over C	B
	C over A	C
	B over A	A
Charlie	C over A	C
	A over B	A
	C over B	B
Group values	A over B (Abel and Charlie)	
	B over C (Abel and Baker)	
	C over A (Baker and Charlie)	

B to A. Charlie prefers C to A and A to B and, therefore, C to B. These individual preferences are shown in Table 8-1.

When the individual preferences of the committee members are summed to produce the group preference shown in Table 8-1, we find that option A is preferred over B by a margin of two to one (by Abel and Charlie), and B is preferred over C also by two to one (by Abel and Baker). Following the ruling of transitivity, we would therefore expect the group to prefer A over C. However, the summation of individual choices shows a group preference of C to A by two to one (by Baker and Charlie). The result of aggregating individual preferences thus results in a cyclical set of preferences where the group prefers A to B, B to C, and C to A. Arrow based his "impossibility theorem" on this conflict between individual and collective preference. It illustrates the point that it is impossible, when preferences are transitive, to aggregate individual preferences through majority voting to produce a collective decision that will be optimal for all individuals.[4]

Both the prisoner's dilemma and the paradox of voting illustrate the need to find ways to make group decisions that take into account conflicting objectives and the divergent preferences of affected and involved parties. Potential methods are presented later in this chapter, but yet another factor that can confound the policy decision process must be recognized: the problem of multiple criteria.

[4] Kenneth J. Arrow, *Social Choice and Individual Values,* 2nd ed. (New York: Wiley, 1963).

THE PROBLEM OF MULTIPLE CRITERIA

In public problem solving, analysts discover conflict among objectives and among criteria. We discussed earlier the possibility that decision makers might support conflicting objectives, and the prisoner's dilemma suggests that individuals do not always make optimal decisions. In addition to revealing the conflicts among objectives and among the criteria used to measure achievement, analysis will reveal objectives not considered earlier. As alternatives are examined, the analyst may discover that there is no dominant alternative, as illustrated in the paradox of voting, that there is no objective agreed upon by all interested parties, and that objectives preferred by affected groups are in conflict. When faced with this problem, analysts typically take one of several approaches to comparing alternatives. They may try to compare alternatives by transforming the costs and benefits to dollar terms and then evaluating them using this common denominator. They may alternatively seek to define a so-called higher-level objective, a more general one that people can agree upon. This might be derived through voting or through conflict-resolving techniques. The analyst might get the client to agree on minimum levels of attainment for all but the most important objective, which would then be maximized. The analyst might get the client to rank objectives and then determine which alternative satisfies the top objective. Alternatively, the analyst may decide not to attempt to optimize but rather to "satisfice"[5]—that is, select a solution that may not be the best, but one that is good enough and that can be agreed upon. Perhaps the majority of policy solutions, especially quick solutions, are arrived at through satisficing. In fact, optimizing when there are conflicting or multiple goals often is extremely difficult. In some cases there may be no way to combine or add up the various impacts.

Cost-benefit analysis, which requires us to translate costs and benefits into dollar terms, has the potential for dealing with problems that have conflicting objectives. The use of the dollar as a common denominator should permit the comparison or trading off of conflicting objectives, and even the compensation of persons who might be hurt by the alternative or its side effects. Problems arise here because some costs cannot be estimated, and some people may feel that the alternative is so objectionable that no amount of money can compensate them. Thus, results of such an analysis cannot always balance out the conflicting objectives.

The general economic rule for deciding among competing options is that of selecting the one with the greatest net benefit. We would select project S that

[5] Herbert A. Simon, "A Behavioral Model of Rational Choice," *Quarterly Journal of Economics* 69 (February 1955), 99–118; and Herbert A. Simon, *Administrative Behavior*, 3rd ed. (New York: Free Press, 1976), pp. xxviii, 38–41; see also Edward S. Quade, "Objectives, Constraints, and Alternatives," in *Handbook of Systems Analysis: Overview of Uses, Procedures, Applications, and Practice*, ed. Hugh J. Miser and Edward S. Quade (New York: North Holland, 1985), pp. 171–89.

cost $10 million and yielded $11 million ($1 million net benefit) over project P that cost $10 thousand and yielded $20,000 ($10,000 net benefit). We would make this decision if we did not have a budget constraint and the projects were mutually exclusive. Our decision would be different if we could spend the $10 million on 100 P projects ($10 million net benefit) or if we could do both P and S. When alternatives are similar in scale, the net-benefit rule applies; when they differ in size, a cost-benefit or cost-effectiveness ratio may be useful.

Economic analyses can be helpful to decision makers, despite the problems cited above. The value of net benefits, the ratio of benefits to costs, and the minimum cost for achieving a given output are all useful evaluation criteria to the person faced with a policy decision. Yet there are preferences and decision criteria that go beyond these economic factors. That is, the dollar is a good common denominator, but everything that is important in a decision cannot usually be reduced to dollars. In some cases, one option will dominate all others— that is, will be superior on all criteria. But this happens only rarely. In portfolio analysis, securities (or projects) are selected using the joint criteria of expected returns and risk. The returns for alternative investments are plotted against risk, and the preferred portfolio is the one with the larger expected return and lower risk. The method of graphing portfolio returns reveals those options that are dominated by other portfolios. In this way, inferior or dominated solutions can be ruled out.[6]

We also must recognize the potential for *suboptimization*, which results when problems are broken into components that are then solved and are later recombined. An optimum solution may be found for each part, but the summation of solutions may result in an alternative that is not as good as we could devise if all the component problems could have been solved simultaneously. Suboptimization presents problems in selecting criteria that are consistent among component problems, but on the other hand, this may be the only way in which some problems in complex political settings can be solved.

Krone points out that secondary evaluation criteria are often used because they are considered to be positively correlated with, and more easily measured than, the primary criterion.[7] He warns, however, that poor evaluation methods may allow the secondary criteria to assume the role of primary criteria. For example, input data such as library volumes acquired may become acceptable as system output measures. Thus, such criteria must be clearly identified, and the decision maker must be satisfied that they are indeed positively correlated with the primary criterion.

Even in business, profit maximization is seldom the only criterion used. Business executives also consider the firm's goodwill, public responsibility, the reputation of the brand name, personnel development, employee attitudes, long-

[6] Milan Zeleny, *Multiple Criteria Decision Making* (New York: McGraw-Hill, 1982), pp. 50–55.

[7] Robert M. Krone, *Systems Analysis and Policy Sciences: Theory and Practice* (New York: Wiley, 1980), pp. 48–51.

range goals, and legal constraints.[8] Zeleny argues that a single criterion is typically used under conditions of extreme time pressure, emergency, or crisis to simplify, speed up, or control the decision process. In these cases when only one criterion exists, measurement and search are all that are needed to select the preferred option. When faced with multiple criteria, even when measurement is perfect and the search for solutions is efficient, Zeleny believes there is need for a process that will result in the making of a decision.[9]

What can analysts do when faced with a multiple-criteria problem? First, we must recognize that the condition exists and not simply attempt to optimize one objective. Second, we must consider the various ways in which the attributes might be compared, including the pros and cons of each method. Third, we must be aware of whether the decision maker is seeking an ordering of alternatives or a reporting of the pros and cons of each. Finally, we should compare the alternatives in a way that illuminates the quantitative and qualitative differences among them.

SEVERAL METHODS OF DEALING WITH MULTIPLE CRITERIA

Faced with the need to select among alternatives quickly, analysts have devised a number of comparison techniques. Some of the methods attempt to summarize the pros and cons of the options into a single value. Others try to incorporate quantitative and qualitative information into a scorecard or matrix. Variations of these methods incorporate weighting schemes that attempt to give more consideration to certain criteria. Some of the schemes are relatively simple; others are more complex. Some are intended for use by an analyst-decision maker team; others are intended to be used with larger groups and incorporate citizen input. In this section we present many of the commonly used methods, beginning with several simple comparison methods that have technical shortcomings. We review these methods so that the reader is aware of their limitations. Next we review two methods that are used to reveal nondominated or superior alternatives. These methods are useful when at least one criterion can be stated quantitatively and the other criteria can be traded off against the quantifiable criterion. We then present matrix or scorecard display systems that are useful for comparing complicated alternatives that must satisfy a number of criteria.

BASIC COMPARISON METHODS

People have long sought ways to simplify the process of deciding between or among alternatives when no answer appears obvious. When Benjamin Franklin was asked for advice in this area, he proposed a basic method that is followed

---

[8]Thomas H. Athey, *Systematic Systems Approach* (Englewood Cliffs, NJ: Prentice Hall, 1982), p. 108; and Zeleny, *Multiple Criteria Decision Making*, p. 84.

[9]Zeleny, *Multiple Criteria Decision Making*, pp. 74–75.

today. When asked for help by his friend Joseph Priestley, who was trying to decide whether to accept a new job, Benjamin Franklin replied as follows:

> In affairs of so much importance to you, wherein you ask my advice. I cannot, for want of sufficient premises, counsel you what to determine: but, if you please, I will tell you how.
>
> When these difficult cases occur, they are difficult, chiefly, because, while we have them under consideration, all the reasons pros and cons are not present to the mind at the same time. Hence the various purposes or inclinations that alternatively prevail, and the uncertainty that perplexes us.
>
> To get this over, my way is to divide half of a sheet of paper by a line, into two columns: writing over the one 'pro' and over the other 'con.' Then, during three or four days' consideration, I put down under the different heads, short hints of the different motives that at different times occur to me for or against the measure.
>
> When I have got these together in one view, I endeavour to estimate their respective weights, and, where I find two (one on each side) that seem equal, I strike them both out. If I find a reason 'pro' equal to some two reasons 'con' I strike out the three reasons. If I judge some two reasons 'con,' equal to some three reasons 'pro' I strike out the five: and thus proceeding, I find, at length, where the balance lies: and if, after a day or two of further consideration, nothing new that is of importance occurs on either side, I come to a determination accordingly.
>
> And, though the weight of reasons cannot be taken with algebraic quantities, yet, when each is thus considered separately and comparatively, and the whole lies before me, I think I can judge better, and am less liable to make a rash step: in fact, I have found great advantage from this kind of equation in what may be called *moral or prudential algebra.*
>
> Wishing sincerely that you may determine for the best, I am ever, my dear friend,
>
> Yours most affectionately,
Benjamin Franklin[10]

Franklin's approach would be applicable in situations where we have a limited number of options, where an individual will make the decision, where outcomes of options are relatively certain, and where preferences are known. Although Franklin's approach compared only two alternatives, it could be extended to compare more than two alternatives by making successive comparisons, but we would risk encountering the paradox of voting. Franklin suggested comparing the various pros and cons of each alternative, but since determining the relative preferences of clients or decision makers can be difficult, analysts often first determine the possible outcomes of policies under consideration and then compare the outcomes. Stokey and Zeckhauser have described some of the more common ways in which these comparisons are made, including paired comparisons, satisficing, lexicographic ordering, searching for nondominated alternatives, and the equivalent-alternatives method.[11] To these we add McKenna's standard-alternative method. In summary, the methods are:

[10] Benjamin Franklin quoted in Harvey J. Brightman, *Problem Solving: A Logical and Creative Approach* (Atlanta: Georgia State University Business Press, 1980), pp. 194–95.

[11] Edith Stokey and Richard Zeckhauser, *A Primer for Policy Analysis* (New York: Norton, 1978), pp. 123–33.

Paired Comparisons

Alternatives might be compared in pairs. The process begins by comparing two options. The superior of the two is compared to a third, and the superior of these two is compared to a fourth, and so on. Although widely used, this method is cumbersome when there are many options to compare, and it does not result in a ranking of alternatives, merely the identification of the surviving alternative. This method has an intuitive appeal to some people because by comparing the full alternatives, we do not use summary measures or examine only key components of the alternatives. On the other hand, this approach may cause us to overlook important considerations that might be revealed if we focused on individual variables.

Satisficing

Satisficing is a rule-of-thumb way to make a satisfactory, but not necessarily best choice. Satisfactory levels are defined for criteria. Then a selection is made among the options that attain at least these levels for all criteria. If none of the options is at least satisfactory on all criteria, we may decide to reduce our requirements. On the other hand, several options may more than meet our criteria, so we may increase the requirements. The key to satisficing lies on one's knowledge of what level of achievement will really be adequate for a given criterion, and whether a better alternative might be found if the search is continued. Usually the search stops after the first satisfactory alternative is identified.

Lexicographic Ordering

Lexicographic ordering is a version of satisficing in which alternatives are ranked, one criterion at a time, starting with the most important criterion. If two or more alternatives are tied for the highest ranking on the most important criterion, then they are compared on the second criterion. The surviving alternatives are compared on the third most important criterion, and so on. This method is appealing because of its simplicity but requires agreement by participants on the ordering of criteria and the assumption of no interaction effects when considering two or more criteria simultaneously.

Nondominated-Alternatives Method

The nondominated-alternatives approach involves measuring each alternative on each criterion. All alternatives are then ranked for how well they satisfy each criterion. Those alternatives that are dominated by other alternatives, meaning those that are inferior to at least one other option on at least one criterion, are eliminated. An alternative dominates another if it is superior on at least one criterion and no worse on all the rest. One Pareto-optimal nondominated alternative that is superior on all measures may be identified, or two or more

Table 8-2   Recreation Building Suitability Rankings

| | RANK | |
Proposed Building	Suitability for Athletics	Suitability for Crafts
I	4	4
II	1	2
III	3	5
IV	2	1
V	5	3

Note: 1 is the best score; 5 is the worst.

Source: Edith Stokey and Richard Zeckhauser, *A Primer for Policy Analysis* (New York: Norton, 1978), p. 126.

options that are equally satisfying may be revealed. These alternatives can be further investigated using other means.[12]

Searching for a nondominated alternative, while it may not identify *the* preferred option, can be a very helpful method when we are faced with a long list of possible options, when preferences can be ordered but not quantified on an interval scale, when options must be compared on both quantitative and qualitative scales, and when we are pressed for time. Stokey and Zeckhauser give a useful example of a choice among five proposed recreation buildings on two criteria—suitability for athletics and suitability for crafts.[13] The building suitabilities are ranked in Table 8-2.

Table 8-2 shows that buildings II and IV are preferred to I, III, and V in terms of both suitability for athletics and suitability for crafts. Buildings I, III, and V are therefore "dominated" alternatives; that is, other alternatives are preferred on both criteria. These results can be graphed as shown in Figure 8-1 to help describe the analysis.[14] Neither II nor IV is dominated, and since we have not defined strength of preference, and we have assumed suitability for athletics and suitability for crafts to be equally important, we have no way to decide between these two options. If we added a third criterion, say, suitability for community meetings, it might help us select one of these alternatives over the other. But as long as the selection is based on a limited number of ordered criteria, we should use this method to display results and to aid in decision making, rather than to find the optimum solution. For example, adding a third criterion, suitability for community meetings, might generate Table 8-3.

One interpretation of Table 8-3 might be that IV is the nondominated alternative because it is superior for both crafts and meetings. However, this

[12] Ibid., pp. 126–27.

[13] Ibid.

[14] The scale is set in numerical descending order so that superior values are at the top and right edges of the graph. See Chapter 3 for a discussion of this convention.

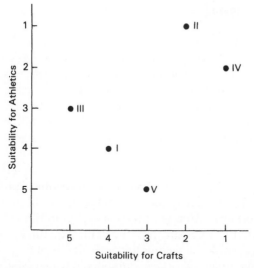

Note: 1 is the best score; 5 is the worst.

Figure 8-1 Graph of Suitability Rankings

Source: Edith Stokey and Richard Zeckhauser, *A Primer for Policy Analysis* (New York: Norton, 1978), p. 127.

display may also cause a discussion of the relative preference for the criteria, which might lead to the conclusion that suitability for athletics is the most important criterion, and that other decision methods should be used. However, the nondominated solution approach can be very helpful in quick analysis to reduce the number of alternatives that must be considered. Advanced mathematical methods for finding nondominated alternatives are available.[15]

Table 8-3 Adding a Third Suitability Measure

| Proposed Building | RANK | | |
	Suitability for Athletics	Suitability for Crafts	Suitability for Meetings
I	4	4	3
II	1	2	2
III	3	5	5
IV	2	1	1
V	5	3	4

Note: 1 is the best score; 5 is the worst.

[15] Zeleny, *Multiple Criteria Decision Making.*

Equivalent-Alternatives Method

When we are faced with several options and several criteria, inspection alone will not permit us to identify the superior alternative. However, the dominance approach can permit us to reduce the number of alternatives so that we can then compare equivalent alternatives (EA) to help us identify the superior option. Stokey and Zeckhauser show how equivalent alternatives can be compared to rule out some options.[16] First, each alternative is ranked on each criterion and displayed in tabular form. Ties are given the same ranking. Dominated alternatives are excluded through the process described earlier. It may be possible to unambiguously rule out several options, but we will likely be left with two or more nondominated options. Stokey and Zeckhauser have illustrated how the options can be compared if we are able to measure achievement of one criterion in quantitative terms. The other criteria are then converted to the same unit of measurement for each alternative by asking how much of its quantifiable benefits under the first criterion you would be willing to trade off for improvements in how well it met other criteria. Obviously these numbers may be negative as well as positive. This conversion is performed for all criteria for each alternative. These quantities are then summed for each alternative, and the alternative with the largest quantified benefit is the superior one.[17] This comparison method requires that at least one criterion be measured in quantitative terms, preferably in dollars, but other quantitative measures such as accident rates, units of production, or unemployment rates could be used. The method does require that the client or decision maker be willing to make trade-offs between the quantifiable criterion and other criteria.

A popular example used by several authors will illustrate how this method works.[18] Assume, like Benjamin Franklin's friend, that we are evaluating employment prospects. We will want to consider a number of characteristics of the possible positions, including salary, location or climate, commuting time, the cost of living, the nature of the job, potential colleagues, and so on. Each prospective job could be rated on each of these variables, using an ordinal measure. Using several of the characteristics to illustrate the method, we begin with Table 8-4, which ranks the options. In this example, the jobs are clearly ordered on each criterion, but there could be ties in which case the jobs are given the same ranking on that criterion.

This matrix permits us to identify the dominated alternatives. Job 2 dominates Job 1 and Job 4, and Job 3 dominates 1 and 4. Since neither 2 nor 3 dominates the other, the domination approach alone cannot guide us to selecting

---

[16] Stokey and Zeckhauser, *Primer for Policy Analysis*, pp. 127–30.

[17] Ibid., pp. 128–30.

[18] The example is a composite of that given in Stokey and Zeckhauser, *Primer for Policy Analysis*, pp. 127–30, and in Christopher K. McKenna, *Quantitative Methods for Public Decision Making* (New York: McGraw-Hill, 1980), pp. 115–17, with the graphic displays based on Stokey and Zeckhauser.

Table 8-4 Ranking of Prospective Jobs

	PROSPECTIVE JOBS			
Criteria	1	2	3	4
Salary	C	B	A	D
Climate	D	A	B	C
Commute time	C	B	A	D
Nature of job	D	A	B	C

Note: A is the best score; D is the worst.

Source: Adapted from Edith Stockey and Richard Zeckhauser,
A Primer for Policy Analysis (New York: Norton, 1978), p. 127.

displays the pros and cons of the undominated options. For each criterion we give a numerical value if possible. Where not possible, we write a statement that describes the characteristics of the criterion. We produce a table such as Table 8-5.

Franklin's advice to Priestley was to cross off equivalent pros and cons and combinations of pros and cons. Here we take a similar approach to equating the two options (jobs in this case) until one, in essence, has more pros than the other. But rather than equating pros and cons, we will equate the values of the various criteria to one criterion—in this case, salary, since it can be measured in dollars.

We begin by equating the two jobs on the first two criteria by asking how much of the $42,000 salary of Job 3 we would give up for 40 more days of sunshine. Assume that we would give up $3,000 for 40 days of sunshine. This would give us a new Job, 3[a], that is equivalent to Job 3 because our trading off of sunshine for salary made the two jobs equal. This procedure gives us a new table of job attributes as shown in Table 8-6.

This trading-off process is continued with the third criterion, commuting time, which is superior for Job 3[a]. Thus, we ask how much of the salary of Job 2 we would be willing to give up to make the commuting time to both jobs equal. At the $36,000 salary this might approximate $700 in time alone, not counting

Table 8-5 Initial Comparison of Undominated Options

	PROSPECTIVE JOBS	
Criteria	2	3
Salary	$36,000	$42,000
Climate (days of sunshine)	240	200
Commute time (minutes)	30	20
Nature of job	Very interesting (VI)	Interesting (I)
	Good advancement (GA)	Poor advancement (PA)

Table 8-6 Climate Equated

	PROSPECTIVE JOBS	
Criteria	2	3[a]
Salary	$36,000	$39,000
Climate (days of sunshine)	240	240
Commute time (minutes)	30	20
Nature of job	VI, GA	I, PA

bus fare or gasoline costs, but let's call this total amount $700. Thus, we get Job 2[a], which is equivalent to Job 2. We next construct a new table as in Table 8-7.

We then move to the last criterion, the nature of the job, where we again ask the question: How much of the salary of Job 3[a] would we be willing to give up to make the nature of the two jobs equivalent? We may decide that we would be willing to give up $4,500 of Job 3[a] in order to have the nature of 3[a] equivalent to Job 2[a]. At this point the answer is obvious, but Table 8-8 shows the final table that compares the new Job 3[b] with Job 2[a].

All criteria except salary are now equalized. By trading off between the jobs we have created a new Job 3[b] which is equivalent to the original Job 3, and a new Job 2[a], which is equivalent to the original Job 2. Now, except for salary, Jobs 2[a] and 3[b] are equivalent. By inspection we can see that Job 2[a] dominates Job 3[b] because of salary. It is probably clear to you that in the last trade-off step we needed only determine that a very interesting job with good advancement possibilities was worth more than $3,700 in salary to decide that Job 2 was the superior position. In other words, we decided that the better climate and the better nature of Job 2 were worth more than $6,000 in salary and a shorter commute. In a simple example we may have been able to decide this intuitively, but the process shown here makes us clearly state our preferences and will work for more complicated alternatives with longer lists of criteria.

Table 8-7 Climate and Commuting Time Equated

	PROSPECTIVE JOBS	
Criteria	2[a]	3[a]
Salary	$35,300	$39,000
Climate (days of sunshine)	240	240
Commute time (minutes)	20	20
Nature of job	VI, GA	I, PA

Table 8-8   All Criteria except Salary Equated

	PROSPECTIVE JOBS	
Criteria	2[a]	3[b]
Salary	$35,300	$34,500
Climate (days of sunshine)	240	240
Commute time (minutes)	20	20
Nature of job	VI, GA	VI, GA

Standard-Alternative Method

McKenna suggests a similar trade-off method that involves comparing alternatives under consideration to a standard alternative (SA).[19] To use the trade-off approach, all meaningful criteria must be part of the analysis. McKenna gives the following process:

1. Construct a "standard" alternative *C* with characteristics for all but one criterion.
2. Trade off *A* against *C* to determine what value for the missing criterion would make the decision maker indifferent between *A* and *C*.
3. Trade off *B* against *C* to determine what value for the missing criterion would make the decision maker indifferent between *B* and *C*.
4. The more favorable value inserted in *C* corresponds to the preferred alternative, either *A* or *B*.[20]

We will use the same data to illustrate this approach as were used for the equivalent-alternatives method. The notation system has been changed to avoid confusion with the earlier example. Table 8-9 contrasts Jobs A and B with Job C, the standard alternative, which we constructed from experience as a realistic alternative.

Jobs A and B are traded off against the standard alternative. First, trade off Job A and then Job B. Considering Job A, how much in salary are 10 extra days of sunshine worth? Using the same value scheme as for the EA method, we determine that this is $750. Thus, we have two job descriptions shown in Table 8-10 where $750 is added to Job A to make Job A[a]. Job B is compared to the standard alternative in the same way, where the 30 fewer days of sunshine reduce the value of Job B by $2,250, to $39,750.

Next we trade off commute time. The five-minute differences between Jobs A and B and the standard alternative are each worth $350, using the same value system as in the EA example. Thus, we are indifferent between Job A[a] and Job

[19] McKenna, *Quantitative Methods for Public Decision Making*, pp. 115–17.
[20] Ibid., p. 116.

Table 8-9 Jobs A and B Contrasted with a Standard Alternative

Criteria	PROSPECTIVE JOBS		STANDARD ALT.
	A	B	C
Salary	$36,000	$42,000	—
Climate (days of sunshine)	240	200	230
Commute time (minutes)	30	20	25
Nature of job	VI, GA	I, PA	I, GA

A^b and Job B^a and Job B^b in Table 8-11. (We have subtracted the $350 from Job A^a to produce Job A^b, and we have added $350 to Job B^a to produce Job B^b.)

Finally, we trade off the nature of the job. We derive the equivalences shown in Table 8-12, assuming $2,250 is the difference between VI, GA and I, GA, and between I, PA and I, GA.

Since Job A has a higher salary when traded off against the standard alternative, we prefer Job A (version A^c) to Job B (version B^c)—the same result as with the equivalent-alternatives method.

The standard-alternative approach appeals to some because two less-than-satisfactory alternatives are compared to a preferred alternative, whereas in the equivalent-alternatives approach they were being compared to each other. However, to us it seems more straightforward to compare the two alternatives to each other. The standard-alternative approach is useful, on the other hand, when we are comparing several alternatives. It is easier to compare each to a standard than to compare them among one another.

The equivalent-alternatives method can be used for a number of planning and policy analysis applications, when we can narrow down the range of alternatives to several nondominated options, when at least one criterion can be stated in quantifiable terms, and when the client or decision maker is willing and able to trade off the remaining criteria against the quantifiable one. We recommend that the equivalent-alternatives approach be added to the analyst's package of quickly used basic methods of policy analysis and planning.

Table 8-10 Climate Compared to the Standard Alternative

Criteria	PROSPECTIVE JOBS			
	A	A^a	B	B^b
Salary	$36,000	$36,750	$42,000	$39,750
Climate (days of sunshine)	240	230	200	230
Commute time (minutes)	30	30	20	20
Nature of job	VI, GA	VI, GA	I, PA	I, PA

Table 8-11 Climate Compared to the Standard Alternative

Criteria	PROSPECTIVE JOBS			
	A[a]	A[b]	B[a]	B[b]
Salary	$36,750	$36,400	$39,750	$40,100
Climate (days of sunshine)	230	230	230	230
Commute time (minutes)	30	25	20	25
Nature of job	VI, GA	VI, GA	I, PA	I, PA

Table 8-12 All Criteria except Salary Equated to the Standard Alternative

Criteria	PROSPECTIVE JOBS			
	A[b]	A[c]	B[b]	B[c]
Salary	$36,400	$38,650	$40,100	$37,850
Climate (days of sunshine)	230	230	230	230
Commute time (minutes)	25	25	25	25
Nature of job	VI, GA	I, GA	I, PA	I, GA

Other, more complicated methods of comparing alternatives with multiple attributes, methods that go beyond quick analysis, include the determination of the objective function of the decision maker and various methods for determining priorities. The *objective function* is a mathematical description of the weights assigned to each criterion, and it permits an equation to be developed that maximizes or minimizes the combination of values. Specifying the objective function proves difficult for many analyses. If we rely on decision makers for the objective function, we may ignore preferences of other groups in society. Work is being conducted on improving this method, but it goes beyond basic analysis. Computer programs are available to help decision makers consider alternative policies and relative weights of criteria.[21] The greatest problem with all of these methods is that they are easily demonstrated for a single decision maker with an identifiable value system, but difficult to use when trying to make collective policy decisions.

MATRIX (SCORECARD) DISPLAY SYSTEMS

Planners and analysts have been trying to deal with the multiattribute or multiple-criterion problem because they have needed to compare the positive and negative attributes of alternatives without summarizing them all in one measurement. Typically, proposals were developed to respond to a community problem after

---

[21] Zeleny, *Multiple Criteria Decision Making*, pp. 449–51; and Stuart S. Nagel, "Projecting Trends in Public Policy," in *Policy Theory and Policy Evaluation: Concepts, Knowledge, Causes and Norms*, ed. Stuart S. Nagel (New York: Greenwood Press, 1990), pp. 180–88.

the problem was defined, community or organizational goals were stated, and criteria were specified so that achievement or lack of achievement of the goal could be measured. Planners and analysts recognized that some alternatives might go farther than others toward satisfying some criteria. A checklist approach has been used, then, to indicate the extent to which alternatives satisfy criteria. The alternatives are listed along one axis of a matrix. The criteria are listed along the other axis. Each cell of the matrix contains a description of the extent to which the alternative satisfies the criterion. In the checklist approach, satisfaction is indicated on an ordinal basis through subjective, professional judgments. Achievement scores, from 1 to 3, 1 to 5, 1 to 10, or 1 to 100, are assigned based on the analyst's assessment of the extent to which the alternative meets a given criterion. The scores for each alternative are then summed, and the alternative with the highest score is assumed to be the preferred option. The implied assumption here is that the criteria are all equal. Many analysts and writers have criticized this approach, and it has been generally recognized as a less-than-satisfactory method because of its subjectivity. Variations of this approach, where the criteria are weighted to somehow reflect community or societal values, have been used, but the basic criticism remains. On what basis are the rankings made? If we are working for one decision maker, that person may be willing and able to specify the relative importance of criteria. Specifying community preferences for criteria is much more difficult. We may be able to obtain some idea of relative preferences through revealed preferences (e.g., willingness to pay for certain products) or through opinion surveys. However, these approaches are often less than satisfactory and give ambiguous results.[22]

Although they have problems, we are interested in matrix display methods because of the frequent criticism of other methods, especially those that produce a single summary value. Such methods may cause important information to be lost, suppress vital information, obscure decisions about assumptions and weights given to criteria, force the analyst's values on the decision maker, and may not be useful to groups of decision makers.[23] Aggregate methods are useful as initial screening devices and in helping individuals or small groups with similar preferences to select among options. The disaggregated approach may be more useful for public-sector problems where different groups hold different values and where political factors may loom large.

Goeller Scorecard

Various matrix systems have been used to display the pros and cons of options. One such method is the *Goeller scorecard*.[24] The Goeller scorecard de-

---

[22] A detailed discussion of these problems can be found in Nathaniel Litchfield, Peter Kettle, and Michael Whitbread, *Evaluation in the Planning Process* (Oxford: Pergamon Press, 1975).

[23] Quade, *Analysis for Public Decisions*, pp. 217–19.

[24] Bruce F. Goeller et al., *Protecting an Estuary from Floods—A Policy Analysis of the Oosterschelde* (Santa Monica: Rand Corporation, 1977), cited in Quade, *Analysis for Public Decisions*, pp. 218–19.

scribes the impacts for each alternative in "natural" units—that is, in monetary terms, time, physical units, other quantified terms, or in qualitative terms. Each row of the scorecard represents one impact and each column represents an alternative. What is known about the impact of each alternative is shown in the respective cells in numerical or written form. A column shows all the impacts for an alternative. A row shows each alternative's value for a given criterion. Shading, colors, or other notation can be used to indicate the extent to which the alternatives meet each criterion. For example, darker tones could indicate the more beneficial impacts, and lighter tones could indicate negative impacts. The scorecard in Figure 8-2 is summarized from an evaluation of early retirement options for university faculty members.[25] The scorecard presents both quantitative and qualitative information from the perspective of the university.

The scorecard display can be used to present a variety of impacts, both quantitative and qualitative, and allows the client or decision maker to assign weights to the various criteria as he or she believes appropriate. In the case of the retirement options, the analysis was intended for use by various decision makers in different settings: individual faculty members, faculty governance groups, and administrators at universities across the country. The scorecard method allowed these individuals and groups to apply their own weights to the numerous criteria. Supporters of the scorecard method argue that it is easier for a group of decision makers to agree on the same alternative than on weights for the individual criteria. Even if they individually weight the criteria differently, they may be able to arrive at overall agreement. In fact, this has been the case at universities where early retirement options have been adopted, although faculty members and administrators weight the criteria differently. Faculty members, for example, give greater weight to the retirement income level, and administrators give greater weight to the amount of funds freed.

Alternative-Consequence Matrix

Brightman's *alternative-consequence matrix* is another scorecard method that can be useful.[26] Alternatives are listed on one axis, criteria or objectives on the other. The consequences or pros and cons are shown in the cells, but somewhat differently from the Goeller scorecard. Brightman would have us measure the consequences in each cell by assigning them a grade of either pass or fail or a numerical score. Major criteria, or what he calls *musts*, are measured on a pass or fail scale. If an alternative meets a *must* criterion, it is given a pass; if it does not meet the *must* criterion, it is given a fail. Only the alternatives that pass all the *must* criteria are considered further. Thus, we have another way to identify and eliminate inferior alternatives. The superior alternatives are then examined to the extent that they satisfy the *want* criteria. These criteria are measured on

---

[25] Carl V. Patton, *Academia in Transition: Early Retirement or Mid-Career Change* (Cambridge, MA: Abt Books, 1979).

[26] Brightman, *Problem Solving*, pp. 195–99.

SELECTED EARLY-RETIREMENT OPTIONS*

Selected Criteria	Group-Based Annuity	Individual-Based Annuity	Partial-Employment-Individual Annuity
Funds Freed to the University	$9,076	$10,343	$7,927
Employee Replacement Rate	0.61	0.69	0.53
Retirement Income Level	$24,380	$27,784	$30,200
Administrative Feasibility	Benefit schedule encourages lower-valued persons to retire	Problems estimating number of voluntary retirements	Reemployment may be cumbersome
Legal Feasibility	Precedent exists	Precedent exists	Precedent exists
Political Feasibility	Lower-paid given larger benefits	Individuals concerned about reemployment	Employee remains on payroll

[a] For an average-salaried employee aged 60 with 30 years service.

Key: � Best □ Intermediate ⌐ ⌐ Worst

Source: Carl V. Patton, *Academia in Transition: Early Retirement or Mid-Career Change* (Cambridge, MA: Abt Books, 1979).

Figure 8-2 Scorecard Evaluation of Selected Early-Retirement Options

at least an ordinal scale. We prefer to use an interval scale (e.g., using dollars, acres, or time) if possible, but an ordinal scale (rank-ordering) can also provide very useful information, as we saw in the Goeller scorecard approach.

OTHER MATRIX METHODS

Several matrix methods have been devised with the intent of quantifying the extent to which criteria are fulfilled, rather than simply ranking achievement or displaying quantitative and qualitative data in the cells of the matrix. These methods typically require so much data and time to prepare that they fall into the category of researched methods. Furthermore, questions exist about the accuracy of the technical analyses accompanying the systems. We do not recommend these methods for quick, basic analysis, but we summarize them below so that the reader is aware that they exist and can be aware of their pros and cons.

Goals-Achievement Matrix

Hill has developed the *goals-achievement matrix* (GAM) as an extension of the methods that attempt to determine the extent to which alternative plans achieve predetermined goals, objectives, or criteria.[27] The GAM extends the checklist approach by attempting to quantify the extent to which the criteria are fulfilled, rather than simply ranking them. In the GAM approach, criteria are established prior to the design of options and before analysis. Both quantitative and qualitative criteria are established, the ways in which the criteria will be measured are specified, the criteria are ranked or weighted in terms of their relative importance before analysis is undertaken, and the importance of each criterion to various groups is ranked. These rankings are presented in numerical terms as much as possible. The extent to which each alternative meets each criterion is estimated, and these values are then weighted by the relative importance of the criteria and the weight of the relevant groups and are displayed in the matrix. Then the values for each criterion are summed for each alternative to obtain the overall goals-achievement level for each alternative.[28] The goals-achievement matrix has been suggested as a useful evaluation method because it is rational, possesses internal consistency, and is comprehensible to citizens, professionals, and politicians.[29] Our concern with such a method is that it requires the mathematical ranking of criteria and the assigning of mathematical weights to the values of certain groups. It is not clear how this might be done when more than one decision maker is involved.

---

[27] Morris Hill, "A Goals-Achievement Matrix for Evaluating Alternative Plans," *Journal of the American Institute of Planners* 34, no. 1 (January 1968), 19–29. See Donald Miller, "Project Location Analysis Using the Goals Achievement Method of Evaluation," *Journal of the American Planning Association* 46, no. 2 (April 1980), 195–208, for an example of an application of this method.

[28] Hill, "Goals-Achievement Matrix," pp. 19–29.

[29] F. Stuart Chapin, Jr., and Edward J. Kaiser, *Urban Land Use Planning*, 3rd ed. (Urbana: University of Illinois Press, 1979), p. 614.

Variations on GAM

McKenna provides one of several variations on the goals-achievement approach.[30] His method compares alternatives and criteria (or objectives). The approach requires that both the relative utility of each objective be stated and that the probability that each alternative will achieve each objective be estimated. The approach assumes that a utility value can be determined for each objective, the more important the objective the higher the utility value, and that the utility value of achieving two objectives is the sum of the individual utility values.[31] Determining the relative utility of the objective (ranking the criteria) might be the result of a citizen participation process. The cells in the table are the probabilities that each alternative will achieve each objective. The expected effectiveness of each alternative is determined by weighting the individual probabilities by the relative utility of each objective. The alternatives are then compared, and the one with the highest effectiveness is selected. Like the GAM this method requires us to rank the criteria (determine the relative utility of the objectives). Furthermore, we must estimate the probabilities that alternatives will meet objectives, rather than estimate the quantitative or qualitative impact of each alternative on the criteria. One possible advantage of this approach is its incorporation of nonquantifiable objectives, but nonquantifiable objectives can be incorporated in other methods that do not require the prior ranking of criteria.

Planning Balance Sheet

A similar approach, the *planning balance sheet* (PBS) has been developed by Litchfield and others, growing out of benefit-cost analysis, but adapted to specify the incidence of costs and benefits on groups that will be affected.[32] PBS analysis first specifies the groups involved in each alternative, both producers and consumers. Producer/operators are listed on one axis, and consumers are listed on the other. The "transactions" between the groups are shown in the body of the matrix, with the intention of presenting a comprehensive set of social accounts.[33] The "transactions" include not only goods and services, but other outputs or impacts and related costs and benefits stated in quantifiable terms whenever possible. Where this is not possible, nonquantifiable items are listed so the decision maker can consider them in the final analysis. The planning balance sheet has been called effective because it has its base in welfare economics, is internally consistent, and provides a systematic basis for evaluation.[34] The PBS approach, in contrast to GAM, does not use a weighting system nor does it require the

---

[30] McKenna, *Quantitative Methods for Public Decision Making*, pp. 118–25.

[31] Ibid., p. 118.

[32] Litchfield et al., *Evaluation in the Planning Process*.

[33] Ibid., p. 61.

[34] Chapin and Kaiser, *Urban Land Use Planning*, p. 66.

ranking of objectives. The approach requires cost-benefit skills and may be somewhat difficult for lay persons to understand.

The originators of GAM and PBS have debated the relative usefulness of their methods, and that argument need not be repeated here.[35] The two methods do highlight the arguments surrounding the ranking of objectives and weighting of criteria. The major differences seem to be that GAM attempts to determine whether alternatives satisfy certain criteria determined in advance, and PBS attempts to determine the impact of alternatives on the welfare of those affected.[36] Both GAM and PBS require substantial data and are not very useful for quick analysis. They do, however, indicate the importance of methods that respond to the need to recognize multiple objectives and trade-offs between alternatives.

Which Matrix Method Should Be Used?

We believe the beginning analyst will find matrix and scorecard methods very valuable for displaying and comparing alternatives. We also believe that the Goeller scorecard method is especially useful for displaying and comparing alternatives when more than a single decision maker will be involved in comparing and evaluating the alternatives, and when qualitative information is part of the analysis. Recall that the equivalent-alternatives approach has been recommended when a single client or decision maker is willing to trade off alternatives in relation to at least one quantifiable alternative. The EA method requires agreement on trade-offs, where the Goeller scorecard allows various decision makers to assign their own values and weights to the criteria. In practice, the EA method is difficult to carry out with groups because of the problem of getting people to agree on trade-offs. The scorecard method is less problematic. In either case, however, it is not necessary to rank or weight criteria before analysis, as is required for the GAM approach. As difficult as it is to get groups of people to trade off among alternatives in the EA method, it is even more difficult to get them to agree on the weighting of criteria before the impacts are identified.

WEIGHTS, RATING SYSTEMS, AND INDEX NUMBERS

The issue of weighting criteria has been referred to several times before. We return to it here because some analysts feel they can improve on the scorecard method by weighting the criteria. After the analyst has quantified and qualified the impacts of the alternatives, there may appear to be a need for a number or statistic that can be used to summarize or aggregate the work. Proponents of aggregation argue that a disaggregated analysis is merely useless documentation

---

[35] Hill, "Goals-Achievement Matrix;" and Litchfield et al., *Evaluation in the Planning Process.*
[36] Litchfield et al., *Evaluation in the Planning Process*, p. 96.

and that aggregation and value weighting are at least implicit in every analysis and therefore ought to be made explicit and be exposed to debate.[37] Those who do not support aggregation argue that it hides or loses important information, may obscure the strengths and weaknesses of alternatives, and too often reflects the values of the analyst and not those of the persons affected by the decisions.[38] This group argues that value weighting is a political process best left to politicians.

The dilemma in the weighting argument is that people (and perhaps especially decision makers) often do value certain attributes or criteria more than others. For example, when searching for a job we may talk about the importance of advancement or friendly colleagues, but take the highest-paying job. When we buy a car we may talk about the importance of fuel efficiency or buying domestic, but have the desire to buy a high-status or imported car. The decision maker faces the same dilemma. It is not unusual for such a person to speak about the importance of protecting wilderness and then support rezoning a conservation area to permit construction of a plant that promises to provide new jobs. A decision maker might be concerned about minority views but vote with the majority to assure reelection.

Quade argues that if decision makers are willing to spend the time, they could, with the help of analysts, devise a set of criteria weights. However, he believes that it would be better to have decision makers spend their time weighing the pros and cons of the actual impacts rather than determining criteria weights.[39] In a similar vein, let us assume for a minute that a method for ranking criteria is available. The danger before us would be that we might devote most of our time to the details of this quantification system at the risk of obtaining precise rankings for the wrong criteria. Before involving decision makers in ranking either alternatives or consequences, we should be sure we have done our best to assist them in defining the right criteria in the first place! Perhaps the underlying tenet of quick, basic analysis—demonstrated by the discussion of weighting of criteria—is that it is better to be roughly right than precisely wrong, or as Coleman has put it: *"For policy research, results that are with high certainty approximately correct are more valuable than results which are more elegantly derived but possibly grossly incorrect."*[40]

Dimock provides the following anecdote as a warning against placing too much importance on weighting:

> During the early New Deal period I heard of an instance which illustrates the dangers of too great a reliance on quantitative analysis. A planning division sought to determine the best location for a new community to be established under a rural

[37] Michael Carley, *Rational Techniques in Policy Analysis* (London: Heinemann, 1980), p. 75.

[38] Ibid.

[39] Quade, *Analysis for Public Decisions*, p. 102.

[40] James S. Coleman, "Problems of Conceptualization and Measurement in Studying Policy Impacts," in *Public Policy Evaluation*, ed. Kenneth M. Dolbeare (Beverly Hills: Sage, 1975), p. 23.

resettlement program. Factors such as employment opportunities, climate, terrain, and transportation facilities were appropriately weighted, and when the totals for the various possible sites were added up, one of them was way out ahead of the others with a rating of 95 out of a hundred possible points. The site, however, was on the banks of a large river, and the 5 minus points related to seasonal flooding. In the first flood season the whole town was carried down the river.[41]

Almost all analysis eventually reaches a point beyond which there is little value in additional information. This is similarly true of quantification. Regularly ask yourself how useful more information would be to a decision maker, and whether more quantification truly will improve a decision. A number of experiments have shown that people make decisions that are inconsistent with principles of economic rationality, selecting a lower- over a higher-valued economic outcome. The answer to the apparent inconsistency is not that people are irrational or ignorant, but that an individual's choice depends on the context in which it is made.[42] For example, in an experiment, two groups were presented factually identical but differently worded dilemmas.[43] One group was told that an outbreak of flu would most likely kill 600 people, and that the government could choose between two programs. Program A would save 200 people. Program B had a one-third probability of saving all 600 and a two-thirds probability of saving no one. Given this description, 72% of the group chose program A, following the theory of rational choice for certainty over risk.

When a second group was told that under program A 400 would die and under B there would be a one-third probability that no one would die and a two-thirds probability that all 600 would die, only 22% chose program A. This suggests that one's choice depends on context. Tversky, who conducted this experiment, concluded that people are more averse to loss than they are attracted to gain, and that when choices are presented in terms of loss they will chose the risk rather than certainty.[44]

SUMMARY

Technical and economic analyses do not speak for themselves. Alternatives must be presented, displayed, and compared in a way that enables decision makers to identify differences among them and to decide which alternative is superior. We offered a number of ways to present and compare alternatives in this chapter, rejecting simple comparison methods because they failed to recognize the impor-

[41] Marshall E. Dimock, *A Philosophy of Administration: Toward Creative Growth* (New York: Harper & Row, 1958), p. 143.

[42] Zeleny, *Multiple Criteria Decision Making*, p. 465.

[43] "Women and Smoking, Boys and Mathematics," *Chronicle of Higher Education*, December 7, 1983, 8.

[44] Ibid., p. 8.

tance of multiple criteria in policy analysis and planning. We discussed several ways to evaluate potential alternatives in terms of their ability to satisfy multiple criteria. A major question regarding these methods is whether the relative importance of the criteria should be recognized and, if so, how this should be incorporated into the analysis. We discussed the extent to which criteria should be summarized in a single statistic for each alternative and presented arguments by proponents for aggregated analysis and by proponents for disaggregated analysis. Our preference is for the scorecard method, which displays the extent to which each criterion is met by the various alternatives. The scorecard presents the data in their natural units—quantified where possible, but using written descriptions where necessary—permitting the decision maker to weigh the relative importance of each criterion.

Along with the scorecard method we recommend the use of scenarios for describing the pros and cons of competing alternatives. In Chapter 7 we described the use of scenarios to both analyze alternatives and to present the results of policy analyses. Scenarios can be used to discuss the pros and cons of the alternatives and to show why one alternative ought to be rejected and another ought to be adopted. They can also be used to describe the political actions that will need to be taken in order to make a technically superior alternative politically viable. The scenarios can be written to compare different combinations of alternatives, such as high-risk/high-gain options with low-risk/low-gain options. In some instances the client may desire the analyst to make a strong argument for a preferred option. In this case the scorecard analysis, augmented by a strong scenario, may be used to argue for a preferred option. For beginning analysts, the scorecard alone, or accompanied with an essentially descriptive scenario, may be best.

In Chapter 9, the last chapter in the methods section of this book, we discuss monitoring programs and policies as they are being implemented, and evaluating them after they are in place. The chapters to this point in the book have dealt essentially with the techniques and methods used in deciding which alternative is superior from some point of view, prior to its adoption. In many instances, once an alternative is adopted, the planner or policy analyst may drop out of the picture and some operating agency may take over the implementation and evaluation processes. In other cases, the planner or policy analyst will remain involved in monitoring policies after they are put in place to see that they are not inadvertently modified. The planner or policy analyst may also be involved in evaluating implemented policies to determine whether they have had the intended effect and to produce information that can be used in future policy analyses. Chapter 9 thus presents the final step in the policy analysis process— policy monitoring, evaluation, and feedback.

GLOSSARY

Alternatives-Consequence Matrix a matrix method of selecting among alternatives. Like the Goeller scorecard, criteria are displayed along the vertical axis, and alternatives along the horizontal axis. Each cell in the matrix is filled in with a pass or fail determination (for major criteria) or a numerical ranking (for minor criteria). Any alternative that fails on any major criterion is unacceptable. Those that pass on all major criteria are ranked based on their scores on minor criteria.

Collective Rationality the choice reached by a group of two or more rational people, each acting in their own self-interest, and each having a say in the decision.

Dominant Alternative an alternative that is superior to others on all criteria.

Dominated Alternative an alternative that is inferior to at least one other option on at least one criterion.

Equivalent-Alternatives Method a method of selecting among alternatives in which the values of the pros and cons are determined by estimating how much of a quantifiable benefit of one alternative you would be willing to trade for an improvement in how well it meets another criterion. When all benefits and disadvantages of the alternatives have been traded off against one another, the alternative with the largest quantified benefit is presumed to be superior.

Goals-Achievement Matrix a researched method of selecting among alternatives. This method requires valuing the extent to which each alternative meets each criterion and the relative importance of the different criteria to various groups.

Goeller Scorecard a matrix method of selecting among alternatives. Each criterion (row) is measured in its natural units for each alternative (column).

Individual Rationality the choice a rational individual would make if he or she were the only person involved in the decision.

Kenneth Arrow's Impossibility Theorem the theorem that it is impossible to aggregate individual preferences through majority voting to produce a collective decision that will be optimal for all individuals when preferences are transitive.

Lexicographic Ordering a method for selecting among alternatives—a version of satisficing. Alternatives are ranked, one criterion at a time, starting with the most important. If two or more alternatives are tied for the highest ranking on the most important criterion, then they are compared using the second criterion. If some are still tied, they are compared using the third most important criterion until only one alternative is left. This approach requires general agreement on the relative importance of different criteria and assumes that there are no interactive effects when two or more attributes occur together.

Nondominated-Alternatives Method a method for selecting among alternatives that involves measuring how well each alternative satisfies each criterion. Those alternatives that are dominated by other alternatives, meaning those that are inferior to at least one other option on at least one criterion, are eliminated. One Pareto-optimal nondominated alternative that is superior on all measures may be identified, or two or more options that are equally satisfying may be revealed.

Objective Function a mathematical description of the weights assigned to each criterion, permitting an equation to be developed that maximizes or minimizes the combination of values.

Paired Comparisons a method for selecting among alternatives in which two alternatives are compared, the best of these is then compared to a third, the best of this pair is then compared to a fourth, and so on. This leads to a choice, but not to a ranking of those not chosen.

Planning Balance Sheet a researched method of selecting among alternatives that specifies the groups involved in all alternatives—producers and consumers—on the two axes of a matrix. The "transactions" between these groups are then shown in the body of the matrix. These include not only goods and services but other impacts, costs, and benefits, stated in quantifiable terms whenever possible.

Satisficing a term coined by Simon to mean selecting a solution that may not be the best,

but that is good enough, and that can be agreed upon. Usually the search stops after the first satisfactory alternative is identified.
Standard-Alternative Method   a method of se- lecting among alternatives that resembles the equivalent-alternatives method, but com- pares each alternative under consideration to a single, standard alternative.

EXERCISES

1.   Using the information presented in this chapter, devise a means for displaying and selecting among the alternatives developed for the teen-age driver exercise in Chapter 2 (and refined in the following chapters). Be sure this system allows the trading off or comparison of fiscal and political costs and benefits, and individual and collective values.

2.   Why is a single criterion unlikely to yield useful results in most real-world policy analyses?

3.   Use the nondominated-alternatives approach to compare the relative suitability of the four highway routes summarized below. Recognizing that this is a simplified example, comment on the pros and cons of the method.

	RANK	
Proposed Route	Suitability for Commuting to Employment Centers	Suitability for Access to Recreation Centers
I	2	3
II	3	1
III	4	2
IV	1	4

Note: 1 is the best score; 4 is the worst score.

4.   Adding a third criterion—least number of households affected by highway noise generated—what conclusion can be drawn? Devise a way to make a policy recommenda- tion using the three criteria provided.

	RANK
Proposed Route	Least Number of Households Affected by Highway Noise Generated
I	1
II	4
III	2
IV	3

Note: 1 is the least number affected; 4 is the greatest number affected.

5. Demonstrate that the same result would be obtained by using either the equivalent-alternatives method or the standard-alternative method for the two jobs described below. Which is the preferred job?

Criteria	Job A	Job B
Salary	$33,000	$39,000
Climate (days of sun)	220	200
Commute time (minutes)	40	20
Job characteristics	VI, GA	I, PA

6. Evaluate the same information using the Goeller scorecard approach.

7. Write a scenario that presents the rationale for selecting the superior job in the example above.

8. Use the display methods described in this chapter, or devise your own, to help analyze the following decisions, both in quantitative and qualitative terms:

   (a) Where to live: residence house, apartment, with or without a roommate, etc.

   (b) What car to buy: domestic or imported, with or without an advanced sound system, air conditioning or not, etc.

   (c) Whether to take a year off to study abroad

9. In Chapter 4 you were asked to develop a problem statement for the chair of the Ambrosia County Board of Commissioners. In Chapter 7 you were asked to develop two scenarios for the commissioners. Now summarize your scenarios for the Ambrosia County Board of Commissioners in a Goeller scorecard. Revise your scenario to advocate for your preferred alternative.

10. Describe and defend your position on the value of weights, rating systems, and index numbers in the system of comparing alternatives.

Chapter Nine

Monitoring and Evaluating Implemented Policies

As in the other steps of the policy analysis process, in this final step, monitoring and evaluation, there are connections between formal research methods and the quick methods we describe. But here the relationship comes full circle. Suppose, for example, that you are working for a state government, and that the question before you is whether the state should permit horse racing and gambling on the races. The main objectives stated by the proponents of this program are to raise revenue for the state that would run the operation and to stimulate the state's tourism industry. You are confronted with an ex-ante evaluation problem like the ones we discussed in earlier chapters, and you are instructed to complete your preliminary analysis within a month. You can use a number of methods, but the first that should come to mind is a trip to the library to see if anyone has published either the results of an ex-post study of the fiscal implications of horse racing or the results of an ex-ante study of the expected impacts of horse racing. These data would become inputs to your ex-ante analysis. In either case, the evaluation could have been a very comprehensive and detailed researched analysis using primary data, or it could have been one like you have been assigned—one that had to be completed quickly, essentially using available information.

We hope this makes it clear that both researched and quick ex-post and ex-ante evaluations conducted elsewhere can be used in the quick ex-ante analyses we described in previous chapters. To be able to use these evaluations in ex-ante

362

analysis you must understand the principles of both quick and researched ex-post and ex-ante analysis.

Analysts are also called on to conduct quick ex-post analyses; that is, to conduct analyses of operating programs, to determine whether they are producing the desired results, to recommend whether they ought to be modified, and even to determine whether resources should be shifted to other programs. Often these ex-post analyses must be conducted quickly using available data, but even quick analyses should be designed so that their outcomes can be evaluated in rigorous, reliable ways.

In this concluding chapter of the methods section of this book we discuss the place of monitoring and evaluation in the policy analysis process, review the arguments surrounding alternative approaches to ex-post evaluation, present an overview of basic ex-post evaluation methods that can be used in quick analysis, and provide guidelines for conducting evaluations quickly. We will be drawing from researched methods that were developed for the formal evaluation of programs rather than for basic analysis. But these researched methods include concepts and principles that are relevant to anyone attempting to evaluate a policy before or after it has been implemented—and they apply to quick as well as researched evaluations.

Knowledge of researched evaluation methods can help the analyst design a quick ex-post or ex-ante analysis using valid, reliable methods of evaluation. It can also provide an understanding of how to construct a researched evaluation should the quick analysis recommend one. Furthermore, knowledge of appropriate approaches to ex-post evaluation can help us determine the merit of other analysts' evaluation results that we may wish to incorporate into our own ex-ante analyses.

Monitoring and evaluation are essential steps in the policy and planning process for many reasons. As we have indicated, the policy analysis process does not stop with the implementation of the apparently superior policy. Even after a policy has been implemented, doubt may remain as to whether the proper problem was identified, whether an important aspect of the problem was overlooked, or whether the policy conclusion or recommendation might have been different had better, more recent data been available. In quick analysis some policy variables may have to be omitted; existing conditions, impacts, outcomes and possible side effects can only be estimated; and recommendations must be derived under conditions of uncertainty. In addition, recommendations may not be implemented properly.

These concerns require us to monitor and evaluate policies and programs to see that the correct alternative is implemented, to assure that it does not haphazardly change form, and to determine whether it is having the desired impact, whether it should be redesigned or modified, or whether it should be terminated. Such a monitoring process should also produce information that can be used in designing better alternatives for future policy analyses.

Monitoring and evaluation efforts often show us that a program is not working. As part of the feedback process, this information—which is as important as positive information—provides evidence about what will *not* work. Brightman points out that successful problem solvers do not close their eyes to negative evidence, but instead use this information to narrow the range of potential solutions they consider the next time they face the problem.[1] In order to improve our ability to do quick analysis, we need to follow up on the results of our work to learn why policies fail as well as succeed.

Goeller has pointed out that success is often difficult to define and measure because various parties have different goals and perspectives. He believes that rather than using one criterion, analysts should distinguish among three types of success: analytic success, utilization success, and outcome success.[2] *Analytic success* refers to how the study was conducted and presented. *Utilization success* refers to how the study was used by decision makers. *Outcome success* refers to the impact the policy had on the problem or target group. Goeller also points out that there is a hierarchy among these types of success, and that analytic success is the foundation for utilization and outcome success. If the analytic study was of poor quality, then the utilization of the study results is likely to produce little outcome success. In this chapter we focus primarily on outcome success, although we realize that the policy study must be both conducted properly and implemented as designed.

In Chapter 2 we discussed the characteristics of a good policy analysis. We held that a good analysis addresses an important problem in a logical, valid, replicable manner, and provides information that can be used by decision makers in adopting economically viable, technically feasible, ethical, and politically acceptable policies that will resolve public issues. Miser and Quade have discussed indicators of quality in analysis, which we summarize below as a useful overview of the characteristics of a successful analysis.[3]

1. A substantial effort devoted to formulating the problem
2. An exhaustive search for alternatives
3. Explicit recognition and careful treatment of uncertainties
4. Substantial testing for sensitivity
5. Clear statements of assumptions, boundaries, and constraints
6. Data scrutinized for accuracy and relevance before being transformed into information and evidence
7. Appropriate models selected and developed
8. Models verified and tested for validity

[1] Harvey J. Brightman, *Problem Solving: A Logical and Creative Approach* (Atlanta: Georgia State University Business Press, 1980), pp. 136–37.

[2] Bruce F. Goeller, "A Framework for Evaluating Success in Systems Analysis," in *Handbook of Systems Analysis: Craft Issues and Procedural Choices*, ed. Hugh J. Miser and Edward S. Quade (Chichester, Eng.: Wiley, 1988), pp. 586–613.

[3] Hugh J. Miser and Edward S. Quade, "Toward Quality Control," in *Handbook of Systems Analysis: Craft Issues and Procedural Choices*, ed. Hugh J. Miser and Edward S. Quade (Chichester, Eng.: Wiley, 1988), p. 649.

9. Subjective judgments made explicit and justified
10. Adequate attention to the interests of others, including the general public, in recommendations
11. Reports written so the findings can be used in further thinking about the problem
12. At least a preliminary implementation plan
13. Explicit recognition of the environment, future generations, and interest groups that might be negatively affected
14. Attention to questions of equity and ways to compensate losers
15. Consistency with moral standards and the public welfare
16. Alternatives investigated for political and organizational feasibility
17. An effort to discover hidden costs that might later plague the implementers
18. Frequent communication between the analysis team and the client/sponsor and staffs
19. Extensive documentation and justification of the work

Assuming that a policy analysis was conducted properly and was sufficiently convincing that it was implemented, there is still the possibility that the policy will fail. It is important to understand the types of policy failures so as to do what is possible to guard against them.

TYPES OF POLICY FAILURES

Policies or programs fail because either the program could not be implemented as designed (program failure), or the program was run as designed but did not produce the desired results (theory failure).[4] For example, if a controlled substance abuse program is implemented as designed, is staffed as expected, and attracts the target group sought, but does not reduce substance abuse among participants, this would be termed a theory failure. If the attempt failed because the program was not structured as designed, was not staffed as planned, and did not attract the right participants, this would be termed a program failure. Policy or program evaluation tends to look primarily at theory failure, but it is often worthwhile to consider the possibility that the policy or program could not be implemented as envisioned.

We cannot assume policies will be carried out as designed. There are many places within an organization where instructions can go astray,[5] and top officials must take steps to help guarantee that policies are implemented properly. These actions include assuring that the policy is unambiguously stated, that instructions for administration are clearly and consistently communicated, that trained and

---

[4] Carol H. Weiss, *Evaluation Research: Methods for Assessing Program Effectiveness* (Englewood Cliffs, NJ: Prentice Hall, 1972), p. 38; and Giandomenico Majone, *Evidence, Argument, and Persuasion in the Policy Process* (New Haven: Yale University Press, 1989), p. 72.

[5] Herbert Kaufman, *Administrative Feedback: Monitoring Subordinates' Behavior* (Washington, DC: Brookings Institution, 1973).

informed staff are available and have the authority and incentive to execute the policy, and that staff actions are reviewed.[6] Implemented policies may also be quite different from those designed because of lack of communication,[7] changes in the problem situation, or political forces.[8] Zeleny attributes this type of failure to the tendency to view decision making and implementation as two separate processes. Drawing from Drucker's study of Japanese decision making, Zeleny suggests a process of formulating alternatives, reassessing goals and objectives, and involving the people who will implement the final decision in the decision-creating process. This potentially time-consuming work aims at gaining a consensus on a decision so that fewer people have to be convinced to implement it. Zeleny believes there is little advantage in making fast, efficient, optimal decisions that require such enormous effort to implement that they become obsolete or suboptimal before they are put in place.[9] The political process is a fact of life for planners and policy analysts, and the actors in that process must be part of the policy cycle if policies are to be successfully implemented.

The connection between policy evaluation and implementation has been recognized by various policy analysts. In the words of Browne and Wildavsky:

> In the world of action, implementation and evaluation are often carried on by the same people—public officials. They act and observe, observe and act, combining program execution with intelligence about consequences, so as to reinforce or alter behavior. Doing well or doing badly, hardly conscious of the analytic distinctions involved, participants in the policy process act simultaneously as evaluators of the programs they implement and implementors of the programs they evaluate.[10]

Browne and Wildavsky warn, however, against mixing evaluation and implementation analysis, suggesting that the conceptual distinction between evaluation and implementation be maintained to "protect against the absorption of analysis into action to the detriment of both."[11] They note that evaluators have tried to become implementers, which is both good, because evaluation becomes more relevant, and bad, because it becomes less knowledgeable. When evaluation becomes indistinguishable from implementation, they argue, the broad vision of the evaluator is sacrificed. By specifying the domain of implementation, the distinctiveness and integrity of evaluation are preserved. They further hold

---

[6]George C. Edwards and Ira Sharkansky, *The Policy Predicament: Making and Implementing Public Policy* (San Francisco: W. H. Freeman, 1978), pp. 293–321.

[7]Hok Lin Leung, *Towards a Subjective Approach to Policy Planning & Evaluation: Common-Sense Structured* (Winnipeg, Canada: Ronald P. Frye, 1985), pp. 21–22.

[8]Dennis J. Palumbo, "Politics and Evaluation," in *The Politics of Program Evaluation*, ed. Dennis J. Palumbo (Newbury Park, CA: Sage, 1987), p. 35.

[9]Milan Zeleny, *Multiple Criteria Decision Making* (New York: McGraw-Hill, 1982), pp. 478–79.

[10]Angela Browne and Aaron Wildavsky, "What Should Evaluation Mean to Implementation?" in *The Politics of Program Evaluation*, ed. Dennis J. Palumbo (Newbury Park, CA: Sage, 1987), p. 166.

[11]Ibid., p. 169.

that evaluation is concerned with the causes of outcomes, while implementation focuses on utilizing causal knowledge to alter outcomes.

The relationship between policy evaluation and policy termination must also not be overlooked. The fear is not only that bad programs will be continued because they are not evaluated, but also that good programs will be terminated without evaluation.

In a review of termination activities, de Leon focused on the evaluation and termination stages of policy analysis, concluding that neither stage makes much sense without the other. He noted that policy termination may be complete or partial, that even complete terminations may be temporary, and that programs may have "multiple deaths and rebirths."[12] Terminating a program is difficult, although easier than terminating policies or organizations.[13] Sometimes technical limitations prevent analysts from obtaining sufficient evidence to justify termination, and bureaucratic entities use a variety of strategies to survive, including building coalitions, redefining program goals, and opposing evaluation. Numerous programs slated for termination have been able to survive one attack after another, and until recently, very few evaluations resulted in the termination of government programs.[14]

Criteria that often play a key role in terminating a program include whether it exceeds financial capabilities, whether it detracts from governmental efficiency, and whether it differs from prevailing values and political ideologies, with the latter playing an increasingly strong role.[15] Although good programs may be terminated for political reasons, and bad ones may be continued, persuasive analysis and policy evaluation can help to prevent this from happening.[16]

Clearly the full policy analysis process includes both the examination of possible alternatives before the fact (ex-ante evaluation) and the evaluation of implemented policies (ex-post evaluation). If we are serious about policy evaluation, then we will also want to take steps to assure that the policy implemented is the one that was designed, and that it is modified only as a result of ex-post evaluation. If a policy is only partially implemented, it cannot be judged a success or failure until we know why it was not implemented.[17]

---

[12] Peter de Leon, "Policy Evaluation and Program Termination," *Policy Studies Review* 2, no. 4 (May 1983), 631–47.

[13] Peter de Leon, "Policy Termination as a Political Phenomenon," in *The Politics of Program Evaluation*, ed. Dennis J. Palumbo (Newbury Park, CA: Sage, 1987), p. 188.

[14] Robert T. Nakamoura and Frank Smallwood, *The Politics of Policy Implementation* (New York: St. Martin's Press, 1980), pp. 67–84.

[15] de Leon, "Policy Evaluation and Program Termination," pp. 634–42; de Leon, "Policy Termination as a Political Phenomenon," pp. 191–93; and Marilyn L. Ray, "Policy Evaluation and the Argumentation Process," in *Policy Theory and Policy Evaluation*, ed. Stuart S. Nagel (New York: Greenwood Press, 1990), pp. 61–73.

[16] de Leon, "Policy Evaluation and Program Termination," pp. 640–41.

[17] Dennis J. Palumbo and Donald J. Calista, "Opening Up the Black Box: Implementation and the Policy Process," in *Implementation and the Policy Process: Opening Up the Black Box*, ed. Dennis J. Palumbo and Donald J. Calista (New York: Greenwood Press, 1990), pp. 11–12.

THE POLICY EVALUATION CONTINUUM

Policy evaluation is not simply an activity that takes place at the end of the policy cycle; it should be considered from the beginning. We are the first to admit, however, that policy evaluation is often not considered until late in the policy cycle—if at all. This is especially true for small-scale projects, when resources are limited, and when time is running out. Even in these cases, though, policies should be designed with implementation and evaluation in mind, and aids to policy evaluation should be built into the policy evaluation continuum, which begins with ex-ante policy analysis and runs through ex-post policy evaluation (Table 9-1).[18]

Ex-ante policy analysis involves the identification and clarification of policy problems, the specification of criteria that are used in examining the pros and cons of alternatives, the identification of a range of potential alternatives, the quantitative and qualitative analysis of these alternatives to estimate the extent to which they will meet the criteria, the comparison of the relative benefits and costs of the alternatives, possibly including a recommendation for a preferred alternative, *and the specification of the steps necessary for implementing and evaluating the policy.*

Policy maintenance includes the set of activities undertaken to ensure that the policy or program is implemented as designed. Such efforts involve maintaining the integrity of the policy as it passes out of the decision maker's hands into operating agencies or bureaus. The purpose of policy maintenance is not to prevent necessary changes from being made, but to prevent haphazard changes from occurring and to record other purposeful changes in order that they are recognized and can be considered during the evaluation of the program.

Policy monitoring is the process of recording changes in key variables after policy or program implementation. Policy monitoring determines whether any changes occurred as a result of the implemented policy. Although policy monitoring sounds relatively straightforward, it requires that key variables be identified, that quick ways to measure changes in these variables be devised, and that this process remain free of biases from program supporters or detractors.

Ex-post policy evaluation, in the most general sense, involves the examination of the extent to which policy objectives were achieved. This requires relating the quantitative and qualitative information derived during policy monitoring to program goals, objectives, and criteria and deciding whether the policy should be continued because it is achieving its objectives, should be modified in order to move toward achieving its objectives, or should be terminated because of a lack of effect or unintended negative consequences.

Although ex-post evaluations typically are researched efforts after a program has been under way for some time, analysts are also asked for quick evaluations without warning. There may be no time to assemble primary data,

---

[18] For a more detailed discussion see Carl V. Patton, "Policy Analysis with Implementation in Mind," in *Strategic Perspectives on Planning Practice,* ed. Barry Checkoway (Lexington, MA: Lexington Books, 1986).

Table 9-1   The Policy Analysis—Policy Evaluation Continuum

Ex-ante policy analysis	The preprogram quantitative and qualitative analysis of problems, decision criteria, alternatives, pros, cons, and expected outcomes of implemented policies, and steps necessary for implementation and evaluation.
Policy maintenance	The analysis of the policy or program as implemented to assure that it was implemented as designed and does not change unintentionally during implementation.
Policy monitoring	The recording of changes after the policy or program is implemented.
Ex-post policy evaluation	The quantitative and qualitative analysis of whether the policy objectives were achieved and whether the policy should be continued, modified, or terminated.

but instead the analyst may have to produce recommendations for a new budget, help a client kill or save a policy at the next council meeting, or uncover evidence that a program is having some impact so that it may be extended long enough for a formal, researched evaluation to be conducted.

To respond to these needs, we will discuss the types of evaluation frameworks that might be used during the policy-monitoring stage, identify sources of evaluation data, outline the technical and political problems inherent in policy monitoring and evaluation, and discuss ways to improve the chances for successful policy evaluation.

Predicting the consequences of policies before they are implemented is a difficult task, and measuring the impact of programs after they have been implemented sounds much simpler. Unfortunately even this task is complicated by measurement difficulties, political opposition, and unintended consequences.[19] Nonetheless, policy evaluation can be used to reduce the uncertainty surrounding policy decisions[20] and thus aid in the implementation of policy, if we link policy analysis, implementation, and evaluation.

TYPES OF EX-POST EVALUATION

The beginnings of a formalized, scientific approach to the evaluation of planning and policy problems can be traced back to the 1930s,[21] but the major growth period for the field came after World War II as a result of the linking of national

---

[19] Edwards and Sharkansky, *Policy Predicament*, pp. 170–210; and Majone, *Evidence, Argument, and Persuasion*, pp. 175–83.

[20] Alan Walter Steiss and George A. Daneke, *Performance Administration* (Lexington, MA: D.C. Heath, 1980), pp. 225–48.

[21] A. Stephen Stephan, "Prospects and Possibilities: The New Deal and The New Social Research," *Social Forces* 13 (May 1935), reprinted in *Readings in Evaluation Research*, 2nd ed., ed. Francis G. Caro (New York: Russell Sage Foundation, 1977), pp. 40–53.

policymaking and budgeting powers with efforts to overcome domestic social problems. This action generated both scholarly and applied interest in and organizational and financial support for evaluation research. Although the impetus for formal evaluation came from the federal level, and that effort may have peaked,[22] efforts continue at the local level.[23] The methods for evaluating policies or programs have generated much debate. Our purpose is not to discuss this in detail but rather to provide a quick overview so that the analyst can acquire basic skills and avoid common mistakes.

Evaluation continued to expand during the 1960s and developed into a field with its specialized literature, professional organizations, and debate over appropriate methods. Early work in the field followed primarily the quantitative, experimental design approach espoused by such writers as Campbell and Stanley, and Suchman.[24] They emphasized the use of randomly selected treatment and control groups and before and after measures of quantitative indicators such as test scores, skill levels, and productivity rates. The quantitative formal experimental research design approach was also the dominant approach of evaluators in the early 1970s.[25] At the same time, however, other researchers began to question the value of using only the quantitative approach.[26]

By the mid- to late-1970s a number of evaluators were making arguments for the qualitative or subjective historical case-study approach.[27] This approach focuses on the way the policy or program operates and how participants view the program. The purposes of this approach are to develop an understanding

[22] Richard Hofferbert, *The Reach and Grasp of Policy Analysis: Comparative Views of the Craft* (Tuscaloosa: University of Alabama Press, 1990), pp. 4–11.

[23] Michael Quinn Patton, *Practical Evaluation* (Beverly Hills: Sage, 1982), pp. 22–23; and Harry P. Hatry, Mark Fall, Thomas O. Singer, and E. Blaine Liner, *Monitoring the Outcomes of Economic Development Programs: A Manual* (Washington, DC: Urban Institute, 1990).

[24] Donald T. Campbell and Julian C. Stanley, *Experimental and Quasi-Experimental Designs for Research* (Chicago: Rand McNally, 1966); and Edward A. Suchman, *Evaluative Research: Principles and Practice in Public Service and Social Action Programs* (New York: Russell Sage Foundation, 1967). It should be noted that these individuals had written on the topic during the 1950s. For example, see Donald T. Campbell, "Factors Relevant to the Validity of Experiments in Social Settings," *Psychological Bulletin* 54, no. 4 (July 1957), 297–312; and Edward A. Suchman, "The Principles of Research Design," in *An Introduction to Social Research*, ed. John T. Doby, Edward A. Suchman, John C. McKinney, Roy G. Francis, and John P. Dean (Harrisburg, PA: Stackpole, 1954), pp. 253–70.

[25] Peter H. Rossi and Walter Williams, *Evaluating Social Programs: Theory, Practice and Politics* (New York: Seminar Press, 1972); and Carol H. Weiss, *Evaluation Research: Methods for Assessing Program Effectiveness* (Englewood Cliffs, NJ: Prentice Hall, 1972).

[26] Robert S. Weiss and Martin Rein, "The Evaluation of Broad-Aim Programs: Difficulties in Experimental Design and an Alternative," in *Evaluating Action Programs: Readings in Social Action and Education*, ed. Carol H. Weiss (Boston: Allyn & Bacon, 1972), pp. 236–49; and Irwin Deutscher, "Toward Avoiding the Goal Trap in Evaluation Research," in *Readings in Evaluation Research*, 2nd ed., ed. Francis G. Caro (New York: Russell Sage Foundation, 1977), pp. 221–38.

[27] Egon G. Guba, *Toward a Methodology of Naturalistic Inquiry in Educational Evaluation* (Los Angeles: Center for the Study of Evaluation, UCLA Graduate School of Education, 1978); Egon G. Guba and Yvonna S. Lincoln, *Effective Evaluation* (San Francisco: Jossey-Bass, 1981); Robert E. Stake, "The Case Study Method in Social Inquiry," *Educational Researcher* 7, no. 2 (February 1978), 5–8; Robert E. Stake, ed., *Evaluating the Arts in Education* (Columbus, OH: Charles E. Merrill, 1975); and Michael Quinn Patton, *Qualitative Evaluation Methods* (Beverly Hills: Sage, 1980).

of what is valued by participants; to present the diverse views of involved parties; and to describe as clearly and completely as possible the community system before the program, the exact nature of the intervention, how this program performed, and the new system that resulted. Usually the client is left to weigh the pros and cons of the various aspects of the program.

Both approaches (as well as others) became accepted in the field, with the appropriate choice depending on the situation. Nonetheless, evaluators continued to argue for the importance of their particular approach, with the debate focusing on the quantitative, experimental approach[28] versus the qualitative approach.[29] Looking back, the debate seems a little overdrawn, as it has been shown that valid evaluations can result from a variety of approaches.[30] House maintains that "any approach can be appropriate or inappropriate depending upon the circumstances of its application and the corresponding validity of the assumptions on which it is based."[31] Furthermore, during the 1970s the authors were conducting successful evaluations that called for a variety of approaches, including qualitative case studies, cost-benefit analysis with social-political impact components, quasi-experimental methods that incorporated qualitative, quantitative, and cost data, and even laboratory experiments.[32] We held then, as we do now, that we should apply the most useful tools to the problem, rather than have our knowledge of particular approaches lock us into using only those methods. Consequently, we believe the analyst should have an idea of the variety of evaluation methods available.

During the 1980s, the evaluation debate turned to questions of evaluator neutrality, the explicit recognition of the impact of values on evaluation, the involvement of stakeholders in collaborative evaluations, and the political nature of the evaluation process.

Palumbo has argued, in fact, that "Evaluators may want to be neutral and objective, but their results will be used politically, no matter how scientific they try to be."[33] He goes on to say that they should not try to be neutral and objective because science is not value free and researchers are both observers and partici-

[28] Thomas D. Cook and Donald T. Campbell, *Quasi-Experimentation: Design and Analysis Issues for Field Settings* (Chicago: Rand McNally, 1979); and Peter H. Rossi and Howard E. Freeman, *Evaluation: A Systematic Approach* (Beverly Hills: Sage, 1982).

[29] Guba, *Toward a Methodology of Naturalistic Inquiry*; and Michael Quinn Patton, *Creative Evaluation* (Beverly Hills: Sage, 1981).

[30] Ross F. Conner, ed. *Methodological Advances in Evaluation Research* (Beverly Hills: Sage, 1981), p. 9.

[31] Ernest R. House, *Evaluating with Validity* (Beverly Hills: Sage, 1980), p. 225.

[32] Carl V. Patton, "Selecting Special Students: Who Decides?" *Teachers College Record* 78, no. 1 (September 1976), 102–24; Carl V. Patton, Barry N. Checkoway, Tschango J. Kim, Kenneth B. Kurtz, Michael C. Romanos, Joy Schaad, and Kenneth E. Stabler, *Townsite Management Study: Special Report D-81* (Champaign, IL: Department of the Army, Construction Engineering Research Laboratory, 1977); Carl V. Patton, William C. Lienesch, and James R. Anderson, "Busing the Rural Elderly," *Traffic Quarterly* 29, no. 1 (January 1975), 81–97; and James R. Anderson, Carl V. Patton, and William C. Lienesch, "Simulation in Planning Urban Social Policy," *Simulation* 25, no. 1 (July 1975), 17–21.

[33] Palumbo, "Politics and Evaluation," p. 27.

pants. While he argues that values in general, and political values in particular, are inescapable in evaluation research, he believes that researchers should not produce whatever data they need to support their own preconceived values or those of the program administrator.[34]

Weiss has also noted the political and value-laden nature of evaluation and the fact that evaluators cannot help but get involved in the political issues that surround every evaluation. But she is quick to state that professional ethics demand that once involved in the study, the evaluator should conduct the study with objectivity. Moreover, her view of the political nature of evaluation is a positive one that recognizes that the programs being evaluated have legislative sponsors, staff, and client support, and are part of the political decision process in the competition for resources.[35]

The 1980s also saw a continuation of the concern that evaluation should be relevant and its results should be used,[36] and in order to increase the chance that it will be used, *stakeholders* should be involved in the designing and execution of evaluations. Some writers have questioned this assumption, and stakeholders themselves may prefer to leave the evaluation to experts because of past experiences.[37]

Guba and Lincoln have conceptualized this evaluation history as involving four generations, with the first generation being focused on *measurement*, the second on *description*, the third on *judgment*, and the fourth on *negotiation*. In the first generation the evaluator served as a *technician*, in the second as a *describer*, and in the third as a *judge*. The fourth generation of evaluation retains these roles and adds several others: *"collaborator, learner/teacher, reality shaper, and mediator and change agent."*[38] The modes of evaluation used in this fourth generation model focus on the claims, concerns, and issues espoused by a range of *stakeholder* audiences who are involved with the evaluation. They also recognize and respond to value pluralism, with the consequence that the various stakeholder groups may draw different conclusions from looking at the same facts. As a result, the evaluator must be concerned with fairness or equity so that no group is given an unfair preference in the evaluation.

If we accept the concepts of value pluralism and fairness, then fair judgments are said to be possible only through negotiation, which must be based on collaboration. The collaborative nature of this fourth-generation evaluation is

---

[34] Ibid., p. 29.

[35] Carol H. Weiss, "Where Politics and Evaluation Research Meet," in *The Politics of Program Evaluation*, ed. Dennis J. Palumbo (Newbury Park, CA: Sage, 1987), pp. 47–70.

[36] Michael Quinn Patton, *Utilization-Focused Evaluation*, 2nd ed. (Newbury Park, CA: Sage, 1986).

[37] Michael Quinn Patton, "Evaluation's Political Inherency: Practical Implications for Design and Use," in *The Politics of Program Evaluation*, ed. Dennis J. Palumbo (Newbury Park, CA: Sage, 1987), pp. 117–20.

[38] Egon G. Guba and Yvonna S. Lincoln, "The Countenances of Fourth-Generation Evaluation: Description, Judgment, and Negotiation," in *The Politics of Program Evaluation*, ed. Dennis J. Palumbo (Newbury Park, CA: Sage, 1987), p. 220.

intended to allow stakeholders to provide input into all aspects of an evaluation, but in doing so, the evaluator gives up some control. This means that the fourth-generation evaluator must not only be skilled technically, but must also understand diversity, respect divergent opinions, be able to tolerate ambiguity, have sound social, political and interpersonal skills, avoid being used by others, and be willing to change.[39]

We expect that the future will see a continuation and expansion of the argument that stakeholders should be involved in evaluations in order to improve the chance for utilization, that issues of fairness and equity will be expected to be addressed in evaluation studies, that the evaluator will need to play the various roles of collaborator, teacher, and mediator, that the political nature of evaluation will expand, and that policies will need to be evaluated from alternative perspectives in relation to multiple objectives. Because of the increased social and political demands on evaluators, we believe that the skilled analyst must understand the range of evaluation methods available.[40]

Evaluation approaches used in recent decades have been categorized by several writers, with more than 100 types of evaluation approaches having been identified.[41] House provides one of the more useful systems, grouping evaluation approaches into eight types and analyzing them by audience, points of consensus, methodology, outcome, and questions addressed (Table 9-2). The systems analysis approach seeks to measure output and relate it to variations in programs. The behavioral-objectives approach (also called the goal-based approach) seeks to determine whether the program achieved its stated goals. The decision-making approach (or utilization approach) is intended to provide information that the client or decision maker can use to decide whether the program is effective. The goal-free method seeks to identify all program impacts, not only those intended. The art-criticism approach judges programs against the values of experts. The professional-review method (accreditation approach) measures program achievement by professional standards. The quasi-legal model uses the competing-attorney approach to debate whether a program should be continued or terminated. Finally, the case-study approach attempts to describe program operation as understood by participants.[42]

Anyone who undertakes researched evaluation should review the extensive literature. We provide below an introduction to that literature for those doing quick analysis, recognizing that one or more courses on the topic would be

---

[39] Ibid., pp. 223–24.

[40] See also Stuart S. Nagel, "Projecting Trends in Public Policy," in *Policy Theory and Policy Evaluation: Concepts, Knowledge, Causes and Norms*, ed. Stuart S. Nagel (New York: Greenwood Press, 1990), pp. 194–202.

[41] Patton, *Creative Evaluation*.

[42] House, *Evaluating with Validity*, pp. 15–43. For an overview see Dennis J. Palumbo, *Public Policy in America: Government in Action* (San Diego: Harcourt Brace Jovanovich, 1988), pp. 121–55; and Browne and Wildavsky, "What Should Evaluation Mean to Implementation?" pp. 149–66.

Table 9-2 House's Evaluation Taxonomy

Model	Major Audiences or Reference Groups	Assumes Consensus on	Methodology	Outcome	Typical Questions
Systems analysis	Economists, managers	Goals, known cause and effect, quantified variables	PPBS[a], linear programming, planned variation, cost-benefit analysis	Efficiency	Are the expected effects achieved? Can the effects be achieved more economically? What are the *most* efficient programs?
Behavioral objectives	Managers, psychologists	Prespecified objectives, quantified outcome variables	Behavioral objectives, achievement tests	Productivity, accountability	Is the program achieving the objectives? Is the program producing?
Decision-making	Decision-makers, especially administrators	General goals, criteria	Surveys, questionnaires, interviews, natural variation	Effectiveness, quality control	Is the program effective? What parts are effective?
Goal-free	Consumers	Consequences, criteria	Bias control, logical analysis, modus operandi	Consumer choice, social utility	What are *all* the effects?
Art criticism	Connoisseurs, consumers	Critics, standards	Critical review	Improved standards, heightened awareness	Would a critic approve this program? Is the audience's appreciation increased?
Professional review	Professionals, public	Criteria, panel procedures	Review by panel, self study	Professional acceptance	How would professionals rate this program?
Quasi-legal	Jury	Procedures and judges	Quasi-legal procedures	Resolution	What are the arguments for and against the program?
Case study	Client, practitioners	Negotiations, activities	Case studies, interviews, observations	Understanding diversity	What does the program look like to different people?

Source: Ernest R. House, Figure 1: A Taxonomy of Major Evaluation Approaches, p. 23 in *Evaluating with Validity*, by Ernest R. House. Copyright © 1980 by Sage Publications, Inc. Reprinted by permission of Sage Publications, Inc.

[a] Planning, Programming and Budgeting Systems.

required to develop a professional grasp of the theory, methods, and practice. The evaluation literature now includes a number of classic works, numerous anthologies and readers, and several specialized journals. Furthermore, evaluation research is covered on a regular basis by planning, policy studies, management, and public administration journals. The analyst beginning work in policy monitoring and evaluation can gain a good grasp of the basic issues and principles by reading such primers as *Evaluation Research, Practical Program Evaluation for State and Local Government Officials,* and *Evaluation: Promise and Performance.*[43] These paperbacks provide an overview of the purposes of evaluation, a description of basic evaluation methods, and a discussion of the problems inherent in conducting and using evaluation research.

A number of anthologies and reviews also cover basic evaluation topics such as methods of inquiry, evaluation designs, data collection and analysis, case examples, and utilization of findings.[44] In addition to journals such as *Evaluation and Change,* and *Evaluation Review,* the analyst should examine the *Journal of the American Planning Association,* the *Journal of Policy Analysis and Management,* the *Policy Studies Journal, Policy Studies Review, Public Administration Review,* and the *Policy Studies Review Annual.* Since much of the practical evaluation carried out at local levels is not published, and is otherwise not easy to locate, you will also need to establish contact with other analysts who can help you obtain unpublished evaluation results.

Many organizations responsible for operating or overseeing programs say they conduct evaluations regularly, but these evaluations typically involve such methods as interviews of program managers about program performance, examination of program statistics, application of professional standards, and review of citizen complaints. The main limitations of such efforts are the failure to provide information about the program's effects on the community or citizens; the attention to input data, such as dollars spent or labor expended, rather than output indicators; the haphazard way in which data are collected; limited staff

---

[43] Weiss, *Evaluation Research;* Harry Hatry, Richard E. Winnie, and Donald M. Fisk, *Practical Program Evaluation for State and Local Government Officials,* 2nd ed. (Washington, DC: Urban Institute, 1981); and Joseph S. Wholey, *Evaluation: Promise and Performance* (Washington, DC: Urban Institute, 1979). Other useful primers and reference books include David Nachmias, *Public Policy Evaluation: Approaches and Methods* (New York: St. Martin's Press, 1979); Lynn Lyons Morris, Carol Taylor Fitz-Gibbon, and Marlene E. Henerson, *Program Evaluation Kit,* 8 vols. (Beverly Hills: Sage, 1978); and Hatry et al., *Monitoring the Outcomes of Economic Development Programs.*

[44] Such works would include Francis G. Caro, ed., *Readings in Evaluation Research,* 2nd ed. (New York: Russell Sage Foundation, 1977); Carol H. Weiss, *Evaluating Action Programs: Readings in Social Action and Education* (Boston: Allyn & Bacon, 1972); David Nachmias, ed., *The Practice of Policy Evaluation* (New York: St. Martin's Press, 1980); Elmer L. Struening and Marcia Guttentag, eds., *Handbook of Evaluation Research,* 2 vols. (Beverly Hills: Sage 1975); Clark C. Abt, ed., *Evaluation of Social Programs* (Beverly Hills: Sage, 1976); Thomas D. Cook and Charles S. Reichardt, eds., *Qualitative and Quantitative Methods in Evaluation Research* (Beverly Hills: Sage, 1979); Stuart S. Nagel, ed., *Policy Theory and Policy Evaluation* (New York: Greenwood Press, 1990); Dennis J. Palumbo, ed., *The Politics of Program Evaluation* (Beverly Hills, CA: Sage, 1987); and Patton, *Utilization-Focused Evaluation.*

time given to the evaluation; and the focus on only a portion of a program's operation, typically the part that is most easily measured.[45] Simple before-and-after comparisons or the comparison of actual performance with planned performance may leave doubt about whether the policy, program, or treatment actually caused any or all of the changes observed. This concern has led to the use of experimental approaches in which a policy is applied to one group and withheld from another. The experimental (treatment) and control (nontreatment) groups are compared both before and after. Since real-world experimentation is difficult (e.g., it may be difficult to withhold a policy from part of the population), quasi-experimental evaluation approaches have been designed. These quasi-experimental designs incorporate many of the useful features of experimental design into policy evaluation. They attempt to use the treatment–no treatment and before-and-after comparison concepts. Cost-based approaches can also be incorporated into these experimental and quasi-experimental designs (Figure 9-1). We will briefly review the pros and cons of these often-used approaches.

Before-and-After Comparisons

Perhaps the most widely used evaluation method, the before-and-after approach, involves comparing conditions (of people or locales) before a policy or program is implemented and after it has had a chance to make an impact. Although steps might be taken to identify program objectives and relevant evaluation criteria and to collect data prior to program implementation (rather than to reconstruct the data or rely on data collected for other purposes), this method requires that we assume that any differences between before-and-after data are a result of the policy or program.

This approach can be modified somewhat to compare actual postprogram data with the no-action alternative as it was projected before implementing the program. This variation still fails to identify unanticipated consequences of no action and requires us to assume that the trend extrapolation reflects what would indeed have occurred.

With-and-Without Comparisons

In an attempt to identify what changes might have been brought about by a program, the before-and-after comparison approach has been modified to include comparison of relevant criteria in the locale *with* the program to a locale *without* the program, both before and after implementation. The obvious limitations here are the selection of appropriate comparison locales or groups and the assumption that changes observed in the target locale can be attributed to the policy or program. While the use of a comparison community shows awareness

[45] Hatry et al., *Practical Program Evaluation*, pp. 8–9.

Figure 9-1 Basic Evaluation Approaches

Before-and-after comparisons	Experimental (controlled) models
With-and-without comparisons	Quasi-experimental models
Actual-versus-planned performance comparisons	Cost-oriented approaches

of the need for a control group, the expense of such comparison groups, without other aspects of the experimental design approach, may not be worth the cost.

Actual-versus-Planned Performance Comparisons

This approach compares actual postprogram data to targets set in prior periods, usually before implementation of the program. The analyst sets specific goals and targets for preestablished evaluation criteria for known time periods, and obtains data on the performance that actually occurs. Finally, the analyst compares actual performance to target performance, and seeks plausible explanations for differences that might have been brought about by program and nonprogram factors. In practice, this approach has been modified to involve comparison of actual program performance with implied rather than explicit targets. Targets can be set each year for one or more years in advance, and annual evaluations can be made of programs that have existed for a number of years (where preprogram data may not have much relevance). Although this method may be helpful in revealing year-to-year and other short-term changes, it does not allow us to determine the extent to which changes can be attributed to the policy or program.

These types of designs, which do not have equivalent experimental and control groups or pretests and posttests to help measure and determine the causes of change in key criteria, present a variety of interpretation problems, referred to as problems of internal and external validity. *Internal validity* refers to the ability to determine whether unequivocal conclusions can be drawn about the experiment itself, and *external validity* refers to the ability to generalize from the experiment to other settings.[46] In general, internal-validity problems for the simple evaluation designs described above include the inability to determine whether observed changes occurred because of the program or because of nonexperimental events. Such events include learning by or maturing of participants, improved scoring on a posttest as a result of taking a pretest, changes in measurements or procedures, sampling errors, false conclusions drawn from statistical tests, use of treatment and comparison groups that are not equivalent, dropping out of participants, and uneven growth or maturation of experimental and

---

[46] For a more detailed discussion of internal and external validity see Cook and Campbell, *Quasi-Experimentation*, pp. 37–91; but also see Conner, *Methodological Advances in Evaluation Research*.

comparison groups. Any of these conditions may call into question conclusions about the particular experiment or evaluation, including its application to other settings. When research results are replicated in various settings, they tend to acquire greater credibility or external validity. It is important to be aware, however, that repetition is not replication. The republishing of a single analysis in different contexts, for example, adds nothing to its validity. Consequently, analysts must distinguish between similar experiments that have been replicated in a number of settings and research results that are merely reprinted in numerous sources.[47]

Experimental Models

To overcome the limitations of simple before-and-after comparisons, the experimental-design approach, using the concepts of equivalent control and experimental groups and preprogram and postprogram measurements, has been adopted. The experimental-design approach typically makes comparisons among individuals in randomly selected groups, some of whom are served by the program and some of whom are not served by it or are served in some other way. Comparison groups must be specified before program implementation, and the groups are made similar through random selection and assignment.

The evaluator identifies program objectives and corresponding evaluation criteria and takes the following steps:

1. Selects control and experimental (treatment or target) groups, usually by random assignment or probability sample. Measures the preprogram status (conditions) of each group using the selected evaluation criteria.
2. Applies the program to the target group, but not to the control group. Monitors the operation of the program to prevent outside events from having a distorting impact. Makes adjustments to eliminate or reduce outside influences as necessary.
3. Measures target- and control-group statuses after the program has had an opportunity to effect changes. Compares these to preprogram status levels. If changes exist in the target group but not in the control group, and if, after careful examination, no outside factors are found to have caused the change it is assumed that the program did in fact account for the observed change in the target group.

The basic pretest, posttest, control-group experimental design is diagrammed in Table 9-3. Before-program and after-program conditions are shown for both control and treatment groups, with the Ts and Cs indicating observations or measurements for the treatment and control groups, respectively, and the subscripts 1 and 2 indicating, respectively, preprogram and postprogram measurements. Random selection is used to assign participants to both the treatment and control groups. If the program has an effect, this can be detected in postprogram differences between the treatment- and control-group scores.

[47]John M. Quigley, "Does Rent Control Cause Homelessness? Taking the Claims Seriously," *Journal of Policy Analysis and Management* 9, no. 1 (Winter 1990), 89–93.

Assume that a program was devised to increase reading comprehension among students. Students are randomly assigned to treatment (T) and control (C) groups. The before program scores for the groups, T_1 and C_1, should be similar. If the program is a success, the postprogram score for the treatment group, T_2, should be higher than the postprogram score for the control group, C_2, assuming that the experiment was conducted properly. This design controls for the major internal-validity problems discussed earlier, but problems of external validity remain, including the possibility that the pretest increases the subject's sensitivity to the treatment, or that the subjects participated because of a predisposition that causes them to be more receptive to the program. These threats to external validity can be reduced through the use of more advanced experimental designs, but such designs are difficult to move from the laboratory to the field. The pure experimental-design method is not very useful in quick analysis. Thus quasi-experimental designs should be considered.

Quasi-Experimental Models

Quasi-experimental designs are useful for real-world evaluations when a true experiment cannot be conducted—when we cannot randomly assign persons to treatment and control groups, when we cannot control the administration of the program or policy or restrict the policy to a treatment group or when programs are not directed at individuals. The term *quasi-experimental* unfortunately implies to some persons that there is something wrong or second-rate about the design. Quite to the contrary, quasi-experimental approaches seek to maintain the logic of full experimentation but without the procedures, hardware, techniques, or control of the laboratory. Cook and Campbell's *Quasi-Experimenta-*

Table 9-3   Pretest, Posttest, Control-Group Evaluation Design

	INDICATORS	
	Before-Program Status	After-Program Status
Treatment Group	T_1	T_2
Control Group	C_1	C_2

Key: T_1 = value of indicator for treatment group before program is implemented.
T_2 = value of indicator for treatment group after program is implemented.
C_1 = value of indicator for control group before program is implemented.
C_2 = value of indicator for control group after program is implemented.

Note: Participants are assigned to treatment and control groups by random selection.

tion provides an extensive coverage of this approach and the design options available, including a description of appropriate statistical tests for the designs.[48] There are two basic designs that planners and analysts should find very useful: the nonequivalent control group and the interrupted time-series designs. The *nonequivalent control-group design* involves the comparison of a treatment group and a similar (but not randomly selected) group before and after the policy or program is implemented. The *interrupted time-series design* involves the comparison of a treatment group several times both before and after the policy or program is implemented.

Nonequivalent Control-Group Design. The nonequivalent control-group design (Table 9-4) is read in the same way as the experimental design, with the *T*s and *C*s indicating observations or measurements for the treatment and control groups, respectively, and the subscripts 1 and 2 indicating, respectively, preprogram and postprogram measurements. The dashed line indicates that the control group is logically selected so as to be similar, but not necessarily equivalent, to the treatment group. In short, a group, locale, or other entity is given a program, and both before- and after-program observations are made of relevant variables. Before-and-after observations are also made for the same criteria for a similar group that does not receive the program.

The pretest (before) and posttest (after) observations are compared to judge whether there are pre- and postprogram differences and to what extent the change can be attributed to the policy or program. A variety of possible differences might occur, but if there were no external influences on the treatment and control groups, the groups were similar before the treatment, and the policy or program had an effect, the posttest score for the target group should show an increase or decrease compared with the control group. This design, therefore, allows us to narrow the range of explanations for any changes observed. The pretest and posttest allow us to measure change over time for both target and control groups, and the use of a control group helps us judge whether change in the treatment group resulted from the policy or program or whether it simply reflected a change taking place among similar groups, perhaps being caused by external (nonpolicy) factors.

This design controls for many of the internal threats to validity, but is still not perfect. Differences observed after program implementation may result because the two groups were really not similar, because the members of one group developed more quickly than members of the other group, because nontreatment events affected one group and not the other, or because a control group with extreme pretest scores was selected. Before using such a design, the analyst should establish a strong theory to guide the evaluation and develop an understanding of plausible results.

---

[48]Cook and Campbell, *Quasi-Experimentation,* pp. 95–293.

Table 9-4   Nonequivalent Control-Group Evaluation Design

	INDICATORS	
	Before-Program Status	After-Program Status
Treatment Group	T_1	T_2
Control Group	C_1	C_2

Key: T_1 = value of indicator for treatment group before program is implemented.
T_2 = value of indicator for treatment group after program is implemented.
C_1 = value of indicator for control group before program is implemented.
C_2 = value of indicator for control group after program is implemented.

Note: The dashed line indicates that the treatment and control groups are not equivalent.

The nonequivalent control group design can be modified in a number of ways. For example, it can be adjusted statistically for not being able to collect pretest and posttest scores with the same instrument. Adding one or more additional pretests appears to be the best use of resources in improving the nonequivalent control-group design. This allows us to determine whether the two groups were changing in similar or different ways that might affect the postprogram scores, to develop better estimates of the preprogram scores, and to permit better statistical analysis of gain scores. We could take separate samples for the preprogram and postprogram measures to eliminate the chance that the pretest affects either the posttest score or the test taker's receptivity to the treatment. This improvement requires great caution in design, sampling, and interpretation.[49]

The principles underlying the nonequivalent control-group design can be useful in quick analysis. Suppose we are asked to evaluate quickly the impact of a program established a year ago in our locale to encourage more teens to use the library. The city council is threatening to cut this item from the municipal library's budget under the argument that the back-to-basics movement across the country has caused library use among teens to increase in all cities. You have been asked to present an analysis for next week's council meeting. One can envision an evaluation that would compare library use for the case city before and after the teen library-use program was established with similar data for comparison cities without such a program. This design would allow us to determine whether increases observed locally were also being experienced elsewhere.

[49] Ibid., pp. 115–17.

Since the evaluation is being assigned after the fact, the analyst will have to identify a number of comparable cities and collect teen-use data for earlier periods—in effect, approximating a nonequivalent control-group evaluation. Of course, the analyst will have to select comparison cities that are indeed similar and must make this selection clear to all, so that the results are not biased. Certainly the approach would not be to collect data from comparable cities and then to use data only from the cities that would make the local program appear successful.

Interrupted Time-Series Design.   We introduced the idea of using time-series data to help interpret the nonequivalent control-group design, but the time-series approach can be used as a quasi-experimental design itself. The interrupted time-series design involves periodic tests, measurements, or observations of a relevant variable for our group or locale at equally spaced intervals, with the introduction of a policy, program, or treatment at a predetermined interval. The time-series data are examined to determine whether the introduction of the policy had an effect. This approach is depicted in Table 9-5. The effect of the treatment might be measured as change in the level or direction of the observed variable. For example, before the treatment the data might have depicted a level trend, and following the treatment a similar, but higher- or lower-level trend might be discerned, indicating that the treatment had an effect. For example, consider a truancy-reduction program. Before the program the truancy rate might have been six students per hundred, but after the new truancy-prevention program is instituted the rate might fall to three students per hundred. Other results are possible, including an increase or stabilization in a rate.

In practice, time-series analyses are complicated because the trend data are not always smooth. Impacts may be delayed rather than instantaneous, may vary by season, or may decay over time as the treatment wears off. On rare occasions the impact may even increase over time. To complicate matters, the combination of effects must be interpreted. For example, a policy may induce a change in a rate that is delayed and decays over time.

The interrupted time-series design contains several threats to internal validity. The most obvious problem is that the design does not control for history. Since there is no equivalent control group, the possibility exists that changes observed were not induced by the policy or program but by an external event or nonprogram-related change. Because the time-series data are collected over a relatively long period, there is a chance that the way records are kept during the data-collection period may change. There is also the chance that the policy or program may cause participants to drop out, with the result that the remaining participants may constitute a group with different characteristics, and thus different posttest scores, from what the full group would have had. Time-series data may also be affected by seasonal or cyclical trends, which could lead to false interpretations.

Steps can be taken to reduce these threats to internal validity. Using a

Table 9-5 Interrupted Time-Series Evaluation Design

	INDICATORS	
	Before-Program Status	After-Program Status
One Group	$B_1\ B_2\ B_3\ B_4$	$A_1\ A_2\ A_3\ A_4$

Key: B_1 through B_4 = values of indicator for the group for observation periods before the program is implemented.

A_1 through A_4 = values of indicator for the group for observation periods after the program is implemented.

no-treatment control group helps to identify possible effects of history, and shortening the time intervals between observations enhances interpretations. Carefully monitoring record-keeping procedures throughout the experiment will reveal if differences occur simply because of bookkeeping changes. Including a supplemental study to determine the effect on groups or persons present during the full term of the experiment will avoid the threat of self-selection. Finally, collecting data for longer time series will help to identify cyclical variation.

The interrupted time-series approach can also be used in quick analysis. Suppose this time that you have been assigned the task of determining whether last year's parking-meter-violation fine increase actually reduced the number of violations or simply chased users out of the central business district, as some council members have argued. To address this problem, monthly data on parking-meter revenues and violations could be assembled for a year's period prior to the fine increase and for the year since the increase. These data could be plotted as a time series to see whether monthly meter revenues changed over this two-year period and whether parking-meter violations increased or declined. Of course, these time-series data could be supplemented with other information such as data from user surveys and interviews, if time and resources were available.

The time-series design can be modified in a variety of ways to address the needs of different programs or to respond to data availability. In addition to adding a no-treatment control group, the approach could be modified to test the withdrawal of a treatment after a period of observation. Treatments could be introduced, removed, reintroduced, removed, and so on, or the treatment could be switched back and forth between two groups, each serving as the other's control.

To produce an accurate evaluation, it is essential to select the most appropriate quasi-experimental design. Research has shown that different quasi-experimental designs can generate for the same situation results that vary greatly in the magnitude of estimated effects. In addition, Schwartz and Zorn argue that statistical controls should be added to quasi-experimental evaluation designs to permit the detection of smaller effects.[50]

Generalizing from Quasi-Experimental Designs

The purposes of policy evaluation include not only determining whether the policy or program worked in the case under study, but also estimating whether it will work under other circumstances. As we mentioned earlier, problems with the design of an experiment that make it inappropriate to generalize results across populations, settings, and times are called problems of *external validity*. The issue of what external validity is, how it is measured, and how threats to external validity can be reduced is important and should be examined in detail before an experiment is conducted; thus, the following is intended only to introduce the topic.

It is inappropriate to generalize from experimental results when there is the possibility of interaction effects between the treatment and history, selection, or setting. Something outside of the experiment might happen during its course to affect the impact of the treatment, the participants might be selected in such a way that those involved in the experiment are more or less receptive to the treatment than normal, or the setting of the experiment may result in an exaggerated response to the treatment. For example, the collapse of a hotel walkway might make building inspectors in a pilot program do a better job of inspecting structures. An experiment in computer-based learning might attract volunteers from a pool of computer aficionados who would be predisposed to the treatment. And experiments conducted in university towns might meet with better (or worse) success than those conducted in nonuniversity towns. These threats can be reduced by replicating the experiments at different times using various groups in a variety of settings. Cook and Campbell state:

> Indeed, a strong case can be made that external validity is enhanced more by many heterogeneous small experiments than by one or two large experiments. . . . Many small-scale experiments with local control and choice of measures is in many ways preferable to giant national experiments with a promised standardization that is neither feasible nor even desirable. . . .[51]

Deriving policy recommendations from quasi-experimental designs requires caution, but interpretations are usually less ambiguous than those drawn from other types of data. Disagreement often centers on the question of what is evaluated: Are ends (events or program outcomes) or means (concepts or inputs) measured? Agreement on both the dependent and independent variables must

---

[50]Seymour I. Schwartz and Peter M. Zorn, "A Critique of Quasiexperimental and Statistical Controls for Measuring Program Effects: Applications to Urban Growth Control," *Journal of Policy Analysis and Management* 7, no. 3 (Spring 1988), 491–505.

[51]Cook and Campbell, *Quasi-Experimentation*, p. 80.

also be reached, for in policy evaluation we are seeking to measure the relationship between the independent and dependent variables because we are searching for causality.

To establish causality we must first establish that a time order exists between events—that is, that a change occurs in a valid indicator after the policy is implemented. Second, we must find that there is covariation or association between the variables—that is, as one variable changes so does the other, either in the same or opposite direction. And finally, we must be able to say that this association cannot be explained by another factor. In addition, there must be a theoretical or substantive justification for the relationship. Theory is an essential ingredient of the experimental-design approach as well as of policy analysis in general. Policies are adopted because we expect them to bring about certain changes. Assumptions and observations lead us to develop theories that describe the relationships among variables and specify policies to change or enhance these relationships. After the policy changes are made, we collect data to measure change in the variables and thus confirm or reject our theories.

Cost-Oriented Evaluation Approaches

Cost-benefit and cost-effectiveness analysis methods were described in Chapter 7 as applied to ex-ante analysis. The same methods can be used in ex-post analysis, and there will be comparatively fewer data limitations and other restrictions. But in order for us to conduct a valid ex-post cost-benefit or cost-effectiveness study, the program must have been in operation long enough to have had an impact, and the program must be able to be measured in quantitative terms. The quasi-experimental design approaches to evaluation discussed above measured outcomes as scores, rates, or similar indicators. But since policy impact is also measured in dollar terms, cost-based approaches should be included as measures in the quasi-experimental design approach.

The cost-oriented evaluation approach assumes that government agencies and other institutions have finite budgets with which to approach any given problem, and that the solution may have to be limited by such constraints regardless of the size or importance of the problem. As discussed in Chapter 7, there are two primary types of cost-oriented evaluation methods:

Cost-benefit analysis compares outcome to input with both stated in monetary values. Valuations can be made on such dimensions as rates of return on investment, net differences between discounted costs and benefits, and benefit-to-cost ratios.

Cost-effectiveness analysis identifies ways of achieving objectives at minimal costs. Instead of assigning monetary values to different objectives (as in cost-benefit analysis), this type of evaluation compares the costs of different ways of obtaining the same, measurable objective.

Having measured policy or program impact, we will want to estimate the cost or net benefit of the change in status detected. Following the principles of cost-benefit analysis discussed for ex-ante analysis, the analyst seeks to measure both tangible and intangible benefits and direct and indirect costs. One approach would be to convert these costs and benefits to dollars, and, using the methods presented in Chapter 7, discount these costs and benefits back to a common date, usually the program start-up date. Another approach would be to convert costs and benefits to current dollars. These figures can then be used to estimate the costs and benefits of changes observed during the time of the program.

The analyst should not forget the earlier discussion of ex-ante cost-benefit analysis, including problems of measuring intangible benefits, measuring both direct and indirect costs, and considering distributional questions such as who gained and who lost as a result of the program. Remember, the program with the largest expected net benefit may not be chosen for implementation during ex-ante analysis because of political factors. Likewise, discovery of a high net benefit as part of an ex-post evaluation does not necessarily guarantee continuation of a program. For these reasons, assumptions underlying cost-based evaluations should be stated clearly, and the cost analysis should be combined with other types of analyses. It might be most usefully displayed as part of a Goeller scorecard. Since ex-post cost analyses are most often used to help determine costs for alternative future levels of service, a sensitivity analysis might also be part of the data displayed for decision makers.

Remember, cost data and impact data must be considered together. If the program has had no impact, cost data may only provide an indication of funds that might possibly be spent on another programmatic approach. If the program has had an impact, the cost-benefit data help us decide whether the impact was worth the cost and whether an alternative level of funding for future years might be more efficient.

WHICH METHOD SHOULD BE USED?

The analyst conducting an ex-post evaluation must select an evaluation approach from among a wide range of possible methods. Should a quantitative or qualitative approach be taken? Would a quasi-experimental design be appropriate, or would a case study be better? As we have discussed throughout this book, select the method that fits the problem best and that can be carried out in the time available.

We believe that a successful program must achieve its goals and that organizational survival or client satisfaction alone is not sufficient. For example, if an after-school enrichment program was implemented with the goal of increasing participant reading skill levels but did not do so, the fact that participants gained new friends and improved their self-image in the process would not qualify the program as a success. This is not to suggest that qualitative, political, or case-study data should not be part of the analysis, or that the evaluation of process is unimportant, but that these data should be used in an evaluation design that permits us to measure success or failure of primary policy or program purposes. Clearly evaluation can measure process or product, but we believe that in most instances product will be more important.[52]

What we measure depends to a great extent on the perspective of the evaluation client. Although the common argument is that we should measure outcomes rather than inputs because we are interested in program results, program inputs may be relevant to the politician. The politician is interested in inputs such as dollars and jobs.[53]

The specific data to be collected for policy evaluation will depend on the evaluation criteria established, the client's orientation and biases, and the type of evaluation design adopted. Typically we seek preprogram and postprogram data that will be comparable, accurate, complete, and as inexpensive as possible. Data sources and cautions cited earlier apply again here. Hatry and colleagues, and Weiss as well, provide lists of principal sources of evaluation data that include the following.[54]

1. Government records
2. Institutional records
3. Financial records
4. Documents (minutes, newspaper accounts, transcripts)
5. Feedback from program clientele
6. Diary records of staff and users
7. Observation and other nonreactive measurements
8. Physical evidence such as usage, wear and tear
9. Ratings by peers, staff, or experts
10. Interviews
11. Questionnaires
12. Tests of many varieties (e.g., attitudes, values, preferences, beliefs, knowledge, skill, simulated life situations, etc.)
13. Clinical examinations

We discussed data sources and data collection in Chapter 3 and therefore will not elaborate on the process here.

---

[52] Hofferbert has argued, however, that the American policy evaluation industry has tended to underemphasize the process model of evaluation as a management tool. See Hofferbert, *Reach and Grasp of Policy Analysis*, p. 19.

[53] Robert D. Behn, "Policy Analysis and Policy Politics," *Policy Analysis* 7, no. 2 (Spring 1981), 206.

[54] Hatry et al., *Practical Program Evaluation*, pp. 58–71; and Weiss, *Evaluation Research*, pp. 53–59.

PRINCIPLES OF QUICK EVALUATION

We have depicted the process of monitoring and evaluating policies as a technically and politically complex undertaking that involves much more than post-program accounting and interviewing of program managers. In doing so we identified the various components of policy monitoring and evaluation and explained the basic methods of evaluation. We also indicated the value of the quasi-experimental approach to evaluation design, but we do not wish to oversell its advantages.

In practice, the evaluation of public policy through the experimental approach has met with political and technical difficulties, and the results of experiments sometimes have been equivocal. For example, in determining whether educational performance contracting (paying teachers in relation to student achievement) increases student learning, and in determining whether special funding for teacher training, teacher aides and curriculum improvements reduces racial segregation and discrimination,[55] results were not definitive. Nonetheless, the experimental approach responds to many of the key issues, concerns, and problems of policy evaluation and keeps before us the need to identify program or policy *goals*, develop indicators of goal *achievement*, collect data on *treatment and control* groups, and *compare* these data in terms of goal achievement. But in a nonlaboratory applied setting we find that program goals and objectives are not always stated clearly, that programs and policies contain many elements that are not easily separated, that programs achieve objectives other than those stated, that control and treatment groups are difficult to establish, and that program staff are sometimes reluctant to participate in evaluations of their efforts. Furthermore, it would not be difficult to document that relatively few competent, comprehensive evaluations of public policies or programs have been carried out, especially within state and local governments,[56] and that of those conducted, few ever resulted in program modification or termination.[57]

Although in recent years there has been an increasing demand for program evaluation, opposition to evaluation is always strong. Evaluations are postponed or rejected for a variety of reasons. Foremost among them, we would argue, is the desire to avoid having one's performance graded. Evaluations can be controversial, and even when they do not result in program modification or

[55] Edward M. Gramlich and Patricia P. Koshel, "Is Real-World Experimentation Possible? The Case of Educational Performance Contracting," *Policy Analysis* 1, no. 3 (Summer 1975), 511–30; and Henry Acland, "Are Randomized Experiments the Cadillacs of Design?" *Policy Analysis* 5, no. 2 (Spring 1979), 223–41. See also Leslie L. Roos, Jr., Noralou P. Roos, and Barbara McKinley, "Implementing Randomization," *Policy Analysis* 3, no. 4 (Fall 1977), 547–59.

[56] Hatry et al., *Practical Program Evaluation*, p. 11; and Weiss, *Evaluating Action Programs*.

[57] Robert D. Behn, "How to Terminate a Public Policy: A Dozen Hints for the Would-be Terminator," *Policy Analysis* 4, no. 3 (Summer 1978), 393–414; and Walter J. Jones, "Can Evaluations Influence Programs? The Case of Compensatory Education," *Journal of Policy Analysis and Management* 2, no. 2 (Winter 1983), 174–84.

termination, they can have negative consequences for program personnel, public officials, and politicians. Moreover, evaluations can be expensive. Although the benefits of evaluation may outweigh costs, the benefits may not be as clearly perceived as costs. In addition, evaluations can be hampered by a lack of skilled evaluation personnel or the use of existing staff not trained in evaluation. Beyond all of this, there remains the belief held by some, perhaps many, program administrators that their programs are too complex, multifaceted, or important to be subjected to evaluation. Such persons may also reject evaluation results because they have an ideological commitment to the program, they fear that constituents will not accept or support proposed changes, or because change will cost too much.

Policy evaluation efforts often face an uphill battle, from gaining agreement to undertake the evaluation, through planning and conducting the evaluation, to using the results. Much can go wrong during the process of evaluation, and Hatry has identified pitfalls that might be encountered in program evaluation and a number of tips for evaluators.[58] Rather than summarize Hatry's work, we refer the reader to it and present below principles for planning and conducting quick evaluations and getting clients to use the results.

Determine the Focus of the Evaluation.   Decide whether an evaluation is likely to help improve program performance—that is, determine whether the client really wants an evaluation, whether cooperation will be forthcoming, whether adequate funding and staffing are available, and whether there is enough time in which to conduct the evaluation and for the results to have an impact. Most important of all, be sure that the questions being asked are ones that clients and politicians care about and want to have answered, and that the client knows what to do with the results. Lawrence and Cook point out the importance of designing program evaluations with assistance from "stakeholders" and have begun to suggest how to obtain that help.[59] Basically, quick evaluations will be successful to the extent that clients and analysts are realistic about what information can be produced in a time-constrained evaluation. Be sure you know how much time you have to conduct the evaluation.

Try to Become Involved as Early as Possible.   Often the evaluation is begun after the program is under way. Where possible, design the evaluation before the start of the program, identify acceptable evaluation criteria, establish a time-

---

[58] Harry P. Hatry, "Pitfalls of Evaluation," in *Pitfalls of Analysis*, ed. Giandomenico Majone and Edward S. Quade (Chichester, Eng.: Wiley, 1980), pp. 158–78; and Harry P. Hatry, "Program Evaluation," in *Handbook of Systems Analysis: Craft Issues and Procedural Choices*, ed. Hugh J. Miser and Edward S. Quade (Chichester, Eng.: Wiley, 1988), pp. 421–62. See also Rae W. Archibald and Joseph P. Newhouse, "Social Experimentation: Some Whys and Hows," in *Handbook of Systems Analysis: Craft Issues and Procedural Choices*, ed. Hugh J. Miser and Edward S. Quade (Chichester, Eng.: Wiley, 1988), pp. 173–214.

[59] John E. S. Lawrence and Thomas J. Cook, "Designing Program Evaluation with the Help of Stakeholders," *Journal of Policy Analysis and Management* 2, no. 1 (Fall 1982), 120–23.

table for evaluation, specify other protocols, and explain what can be realistically expected from a quick evaluation.

Decide What Data Will Be Produced. Quick evaluations usually cannot produce information for all interested parties. Therefore, analysts must decide who are the primary users, what information they need, and what can be feasibly collected. Policymakers and clients seek information about continuing or dropping a program. Program directors want to know how to modify the program to make it operate better. Program staff might be interested in technical aspects to make their jobs easier, and consumers seek to know whether they are receiving full value from their tax dollar. A comprehensive evaluation may address all of the above; a quick analysis may be able to cover only a few.

Determine What Change Is Being Measured. If policy evaluation is incorporated as part of the policy analysis process, program goals should be clear, specific, and measurable. When policy evaluation is conducted separately from the policy analysis process, or is added late in the process, analysts must work with program staff to define such goals and objectives, define such statements by themselves, or proceed with an open-ended evaluation. Unfortunately programs often begin without statements of objectives, and program bureaucrats may refuse to approve a statement of objectives needed by an evaluation team. In quick evaluations there is often little time available in which to gain a consensus on what is to be measured. Furthermore, since policies are devised in the public arena, they are often stated in such a way as to appeal to many segments of the public and to avoid offending certain groups. As a result, many policies have vague goals that cannot be measured easily.

When faced with vague or unspecified goals, the evaluator can use a number of clues to determine the intent of policy directives, such as the legal imperative of the policy as written, the legislative history of the policy, or the understanding of the policy by interest groups. Be aware that this process typically produces different definitions, none of which will be acceptable to all participants.

Identify What Policy Action or Intervention Is Being Evaluated. Failure to unambiguously identify the treatment or policy action being evaluated will present problems in outcome measurement. Design the quick evaluation to focus precisely on what has been changed or introduced. This is necessary in order both to develop an adequate measure of program effect and to be able to replicate the policy elsewhere if deemed desirable.

Use Multiple Methods of Measurement. Policy evaluation procedures should be designed to measure a variety of effects, including those upon the individuals or groups served, the broader public, the participating agencies, and the larger system. Include as many measurements in quick analysis as possible. Impact on the population served might be measured through elite interviews or questionnaires, analysis of agency records, or observation. Impact on the public might be measured through quick surveys. Impact on providing or cooperating agencies might be gauged through worker reactions or change in agency output. The impact on the larger system might also be gauged in this way. However, don't collect more data than you need or can analyze in the time available. Be sure to avoid the use of biased samples and other erroneous data.

A key policy evaluation question is: "What measures success?"[60] or "What is enough?" Although we strive to measure changes in outcome measures (the dependent variables), often only input data (the independent variables) are available. Examine both the component parts and the overall impact. Resist the temptation to measure only input data, since we are striving to identify both what caused the effect *and* what the outcomes were. Be sure to adjust for any changes in data-collection methods that may occur during the evaluation period.

Design the Evaluation so It Can Respond to Program Modifications.

Unlike laboratory-based experiments, quick evaluations take place in action settings where the program may change over time, especially when the evaluation is intended to provide information for in-course corrections. Rather than eschew evaluation in these settings, the program might be evaluated by phase, using periodic measurements, and these measurements should be coordinated with clear and unambiguous changes in the program. In addition, those parts of the program that do remain unchanged can be continuously evaluated for the duration of the study.

Policy evaluation has been criticized by people who have argued that a good, conclusive evaluation cannot be conducted if the program is modified during evaluation. On the contrary, we hold that a good evaluation would involve modification of the program if it were found wanting during evaluation.

Design the Evaluation to Provide In-Course as Well as Final Evaluations.

Policy evaluation has been criticized because it has occasionally been used to postpone decisions, to avoid or transfer the responsibility for program shortcomings, to serve purposes of public relations, or simply to fulfill grant requirements. Like formal evaluations, quick evaluation may not result in a definitive decision. The program may continue by default. For this reason, the quick evaluation should be designed to provide information that could be used to make marginal improvements to on-going programs. Designing an evaluation so that only final results are useful overlooks an opportunity to benefit current program users.

Involve Program Staff in the Evaluation.

Program staff may argue against data collection efforts because their job is to serve people rather than fill out

---

[60] Majone has stated that the greatest problems of public accountability are associated with the choice of criteria by which to measure success. Majone, *Evidence, Argument, and Persuasion,* p. 182.

forms. They may also resist needed changes in record-keeping systems. There may even be problems of status rivalry between the evaluation staff and agency or program staff. Some of these problems can be overcome by involving the agency staff in the design of the evaluation, by rewarding participants, by providing useful feedback to agency staff, by designing the evaluation to minimize disruptions, and by comparing programs to their stated goals rather than to other programs.[61] How much of this can be done during quick analysis will vary from one evaluation to another. Be sure, however, not to have people evaluate their own work.

Recognize the Politics of Evaluation. Because evaluations can be threatening, those to be evaluated may attempt to influence the evaluation, to block or escape it, to call it into question, or to thwart data collection efforts.[62] Political considerations often override scientific objectivity. Furthermore, evaluations usually require the cooperation of several organizations and staff who may not see their value. Beyond this, elected officials most often make the final policy evaluation decision. Failing to recognize those factors makes it harder to implement policy evaluation results.[63] Frankly, there is often little the beginning analyst can do about this except understand it.

Make Your Preliminary Findings Available. It is difficult to make changes in operating programs under the best of circumstances, particularly when many individuals are involved. One way to gain the staff's support is to keep them informed, warn them early about possible changes, and invite their responses to initial findings.

Give a Clear Presentation. The way in which evaluation findings are reported is important. Report assumptions and limitations, present alternative explanations for observed outcomes, and separate fact from opinion. Discuss substantive importance as well as statistical significance. A good presentation must be clear and unambiguous if it is to have an impact. It should help make a decision, not merely report a grade. Make sure the results are available in time to be useful. The best, most convincing presentation cannot overcome a bad evaluation design. Thus, we close by repeating that a quick evaluation scheme should contain the following components:

1. A definition of the end (goals/objectives) to be achieved
2. Specification of the policy, program, or actions intended to achieve the end
3. A method for observing and measuring the change or outcome

---

[61] Patton suggests using a task force to help make major decisions about the evaluation approach and to involve stakeholders in the process. Patton, *Practical Evaluation*, pp. 55–98.

[62] Nakamura and Smallwood, *Politics of Policy Implementation*, pp. 74–79.

[63] Edie N. Goldenberg, "The Three Faces of Evaluation," *Journal of Policy Analysis and Management* 2, no. 4 (Summer 1983), 515–25.

4. A method for comparing the outcome against the desired end
5. A way to modify the policy in order that changes can be made in response to the observations

SUMMARY

Policy monitoring, evaluation, and feedback are part of the final step in the policy analysis process—if the policy problem was correctly defined, if appropriate selection criteria were determined, if realistic alternatives were devised, if the evaluation of alternatives resulted in the identification of technically feasible alternatives, if the comparison of feasible alternatives resulted in the selection of a technically superior and politically viable alternative, and if that alternative was implemented properly. Of course, this is a great deal to expect, and most policy analyses involve false starts, modifications along the way, ambiguous results, and equivocal conclusions. But the policy analysis process is supposed to recognize and respond to these difficulties by generating feedback, by permitting successive approximations, by dealing explicitly with uncertainties and political factors, and by building a base upon which to construct future analyses. The challenge is not only to do well with what we already know, but to learn from practice and from our mistakes, to deepen our understanding of how policy is made, analyzed, and implemented, and to improve our ability to conduct quick, clear, and useful analyses when they are needed and while the results can make a difference.

We are cautioned that because value-neutral research is not possible or desirable, evaluations will not produce an ostensibly correct finding:

> . . . they will take a political position about the desirability of various goals, whether *directly*, by judging that the goals are worthwhile, or *indirectly*, by concluding that the goals are being achieved efficiently. Evaluation, therefore, becomes a part of the goal-setting process in organizations (i.e., legislatures, administrative agencies, nonprofit private groups, profit-making organizations), a process that is unquestionably political.[64]

In addition to doing the best we can with what we have to answer ambiguous questions by competing interests, evaluators must also deal explicitly with political considerations in the context of "concerns for use, practicalities, rigor, integrity, accuracy, fairness and credibility."[65]

This chapter presented methods for evaluating policies after they are in place. We presented the rationale for policy monitoring and evaluation, discussed the reasons why policies fail, and reviewed the types of ex-post evaluation methods in use. We focused on the principles of experimental design, with the argument that these principles can help us conduct useful evaluations. We concluded

---

[64] Palumbo, "Politics and Evaluation," p. 32.
[65] Patton, "Evaluation's Political Inherency," p. 143.

the chapter with a discussion of quick evaluation principles. We recognize that this chapter is not a substitute for a course in evaluation research and that our readers may not be called on to conduct full-fledged researched evaluations. However, you may have to apply these principles to quick analyses and use existing or reconstructed data. Above all, policy evaluation should not be seen as an afterthought but rather should be planned for in the earliest steps of the analytic process.

Policy monitoring and evaluation completes the policy cycle—at least it represents the end of one pass through the cycle—and this chapter concludes our discussion of policy analysis methods. The chapters that follow present case studies that can be addressed by the methods presented in the first part of this book. The cases vary by topic and length and are intended to be solved by using quick, basic methods. Most take between 15 and 25 hours to solve.[66]

The seven cases are intended for learning purposes only. Some names and facts have been changed to avoid disclosing confidential information, but this does not lessen the educational value of the cases. The cases are not intended to represent either effective or ineffective administration, nor are they meant to be statements of agency policy.

GLOSSARY

Art-Criticism Approach an evaluation approach that judges programs against the values of experts.

Case-Study Approach an evaluation method that attempts to describe program operation as understood by participants.

Decision-Making Approach an evaluation method designed to provide information that the client can use to decide if the program is effective.

Experimental Design in general terms, this involves an experimental group, to which the policy or program is applied, and a control group, to which it is not. Individual members of these groups should be similar in respects that might influence the results. To both groups a pretest is administered before the experimental group experiences the policy

or program, and a posttest is administered after they experience it. If changes are experienced by the experimental group and not the control group, and if they are not explained by some other factor, then these changes are said to be the result of the policy or program.

External Validity the ability to generalize from the experiment to other settings.

Goal-Based Approach (also called the behavioral objectives approach) an evaluation made in terms of perceived achievement of the desired outcomes. This approach seeks to identify whether the program achieved its stated objectives.

Goal-Free Method an evaluation approach that seeks to identify all program impacts, not only those intended.

---

[66] For additional cases, see Frank Fischer and John Forester, *Confronting Values in Policy Analysis: The Politics of Criteria* (Beverly Hills, CA: Sage, 1987), chaps. 10, 11, 12; George M. Guess and Paul G. Farnham, *Cases in Public Policy Analysis* (New York: Longman, 1989); Lawrence E. Lynn, Jr., *Designing Public Policy: A Casebook on the Role of Policy Analysis* (Santa Monica: Goodyear, 1980); Dennis J. Palumbo, *Public Policy in America: Government in Action* (San Diego: Harcourt Brace Jovanovich, 1988), chaps. 6–10; David L. Weimer and Aidan R. Vining, *Policy Analysis: Concepts and Practice* (Englewood Cliffs, NJ: Prentice Hall, 1989), chaps. 9–12.

Internal Validity the ability to determine whether unequivocal conclusions can be drawn about the experiment itself.

Interrupted Time-Series Design a method of evaluation that involves periodic tests, measurements, or observations of a relevant variable for the experimental group at equally spaced intervals, with the introduction of a policy, program, or treatment at a predetermined interval.

Nonequivalent Control-Group Design a design that resembles the pure experimental design, except that it permits some differences between the control and experimental groups if the differences are not thought to be theoretically important to the policy or program being evaluated. These differences may be measured during the pretesting to give an indication of how significant they should appear in the posttest.

Policy Maintenance the set of activities undertaken to assure that the policy or program is implemented as designed.

Policy Monitoring the process of recording changes in key variables after policy or program implementation.

Professional-Review Method (accreditation approach) an evaluation method that measures program achievement by professional standards.

Quasi-Experimental Approach methods of ex-post evaluation that seek to maintain the logic of full experimentation, but without the procedures, hardware, techniques, or control of the laboratory. Two such approaches that are useful to planners and analysts are the nonequivalent control-group design and the interrupted time-series design.

Quasi-Legal Model an evaluation approach that has competing sides debate whether the program should be continued or terminated.

Systems Model an evaluation that assumes that the policy or program sponsor has multiple goals, some implicit, and that achieving some of these might make it worth continuing the policy.

EXERCISES

1. Devise an evaluation scheme for your preferred solution to the teen-age accident problem of Chapter 2. Use at least one of the quasi-experimental designs discussed in this chapter.

2. Although quick analysis does not normally enable us to use the true experimental-design evaluation approach, a number of principles from experimental design provide insight into the steps necessary to assure a valid interpretation of policy outcomes. What are these principles, and how can they be applied to policy analysis in field settings?

3. A curfew was established in Ourtown and an evaluation of the effectiveness of the curfew was conducted. Preprogram and postprogram delinquency rate data were collected for both Ourtown and Yourtown, a comparison city in the same county that did not and does not have a curfew. Consider the data below, intended to determine the impact of the curfew in Ourtown upon juvenile delinquency rates.

THE QUASI-EXPERIMENTAL DESIGN		
	Before-curfew Delinquency Status	After-curfew Delinquency Status
Ourtown	O_1	O_2
Yourtown	Y_1	Y_2

O_1 = juvenile delinquency rate in Ourtown for the month of August last year
O_2 = juvenile delinquency rate in Ourtown for the month of October last year
Y_1 = juvenile delinquency rate in Yourtown for the month of August last year
Y_2 = juvenile delinquency rate in Yourtown for the month of October last year

The curfew for juveniles was implemented in Ourtown effective September 1, last year. Assume no curfew in Yourtown and no prior curfew in either city.

Delinquency rates:
$O_1 = 0.050, O_2 = 0.040$
$Y_1 = 0.025, Y_2 = 0.020$

(a) What can you conclude from this evaluation? How did you arrive at this conclusion? What comparisons did you make? What other factors did you consider?

(b) What major validity problems (if any) exist in this evaluation design?

(c) What policy recommendations would you give to the mayor and police chief of Ourtown?

4. Library-use data were collected before and during a local media campaign intended to increase the rate of library book borrowing (and an assumed readership of borrowed books). Consider the data below and develop a policy recommendation to the library board. Assume no substantial population change during the two-year period and no other programs aimed at increasing library use.

(a) What can you conclude from this evaluation?

(b) What major validity problems (if any) exist in this design?

(c) What policy recommendations would you give to the library board?

(d) How could the design be improved?

(e) What other monitoring information would be useful in such a design?

BOOK BORROWING FROM THE OURTOWN MAIN LIBRARY AND ALL BRANCHES FOR SELECTED MONTHS (IN THOUSANDS)

Before Media Campaign						Media Campaign Begun	During Media Campaign					
Jan.	Mar.	May	July	Sept.	Nov.		Jan.	Mar.	May	July	Sept.	Nov.
14	12	10	8	14	13		14	12	11	9	14	14

---

5. A few years ago the last of the 50 states raised its minimum legal drinking age to 21. Develop an evaluation scheme that could have been employed to measure the impact of raising your state's legal drinking age to 21 on the teen-age death rate from automobile accidents.

6. Not having devised an evaluation scheme when your state's minimum legal drinking age was raised to 21, how could you now determine whether the increase in the age had an impact on the teen-age death rate from automobile accidents?

7. Select a local program that has recently come under attack and has been reported in your local paper. Assume that you are called on to evaluate this program after the fact. For this specific program, identify the evaluation problems you would likely encounter.

8.   Much concern has been expressed in recent years about street people, bag ladies, and other homeless people. Assume your local government decided to launch a program to provide these people basic medical services. How would you monitor the effects of such a program, especially in ligkt of the transient nature of this population?

9.   The governor is concerned that state funds are often spent on community develop-ment with little idea of whether the programs are having an effect. With the federal government cutting back and the state picking up more of these expenses, the governor is growing even more concerned. He wants to be sure that what the state does pay will make a difference. He feels that simply allocating funds on the basis of population size or some similar criterion may not be very effective. The governor believes we should adopt a program-evaluation strategy to see whether community development efforts will make a difference. He needs your advice about this.

Prepare a memo that lays out how to conduct such an evaluation. Use a problem or issue with which you are familiar and that either is or could be funded in full or in part by the state.

Discuss at least the following:

- (a)   The more useful evaluation designs available
- (b)   How these designs could be set up
- (c)   How the outcomes of these evaluations would be interpreted
- (d)   What information would be needed to decide whether to continue or terminate the program

10.   A local government will soon shift from municipally provided ambulance service to privately provided service, based on the results of a policy analysis. Assume that the analysis was correct. Design an approach to monitoring and evaluating the impact of the policy. Include in this design at least a specification of the variables to be observed, an identification of the ways in which changes will be measured, and a statement of the decision rules that will be used to draw a conclusion. Develop a time line that displays the steps in the process and the responsibilities of actors involved.

11.   A mini-bus system is being established to provide free transportation to essential services for older persons in a rural seven-county area. One bus will serve each county on a demand-responsive basis. The bus system is funded from general revenues in each county, and the consortium is coordinated by a director located in the office of the county supervisor in the central and most heavily populated county. Devise an evaluation framework to measure the impact of the bus service on the mobility and lives of older persons in this seven-county area.

12.   Assume you are the director of the bus service in the seven-county region. You fear that the evaluation will generate negative results. You decide to do your best to thwart the evaluation. What could you do to invalidate the evaluation? Discuss as many actions as you can.

Chapter Ten

Downtown Development[1]

INTRODUCTION

You are the senior policy analyst for a city of over a half million in a metropolitan area of over 2 million that is growing rather rapidly. It is a sunbelt city experiencing the typical problems associated with the exploding growth of the suburbs with commercial, retail, and industrial activity as well as residential growth, and the concomitant stagnation of the central city.

You work closely with the mayor on many development issues. The one facing you this time is what to do with a parcel of land located in the downtown area. Currently, there are two proposals on the table. The first is to put the piece of land out at auction and sell it for the best price, but at a minimum of $1.4 million. The second proposal is for the city to build a city-owned, and perhaps operated, garage on the site. Both positions have support on the common council. You have just returned to your office after a rather lively meeting with the mayor, the president of the common council, and the city's budget director. You sit at your desk and organize the notes that you took at that meeting. It was decided at the meeting that everyone present preferred taking action within the

[1] The idea for this case was provided by Graeme M. Taylor's case, "Downtown Parking Authority (A)," HBS Case Services (Boston: Harvard Business School), Case #8-112-069.

next several weeks. There is an outside possibility that they are willing to delay, but the burden rests on you for making a recommendation on that strategy. If you can convince them that delay would add significantly to the knowledge base that would bring about a good decision, then the mayor is willing to go along with the delay. There seem to be three possible actions. First, build the parking garage. Second, put the land out for bid. And, third, delay for some period of time while a study is undertaken of several key questions.

THE ASSIGNMENT

You have been asked by the mayor to develop a memorandum with a one-page executive summary. The memorandum should explore the three alternatives: build the parking garage; put the land out for bid; or, if you should find compelling reasons, delay and commission a special study of key factors. Please limit your memorandum to no more than 15 double-spaced typed pages and place highly quantitative material in appendices.

BACKGROUND INFORMATION

The site itself is five acres in size. It is located in an area of the city undergoing modest redevelopment. It is close to a major freeway interchange, as well as several important downtown cultural, shopping, and business sites. The lot contains a burned-out building that would have to be removed at a cost of approximately $280,000. The city has just built another parking garage seven miles away. It is eight stories high, can hold 800 cars, and it was built for $9.8 million. The city, with a lot of federal and state aid, has invested heavily in a mass-transit system within the past 20 years. There is a major strategic question that has been unanswered by city government at this point, and that is whether to support full access of automobiles to downtown or to make access more difficult, thus encouraging the use of mass transit. The city's current deficit for operating the mass-transit system is $2.8 million a year. Several studies have been done that shed

some light on the demand for parking in the city. One was a study of downtown workers; another, a market study done by a private parking company; a third, an independent study of traffic done by the regional planning commission.

From these three studies, the following facts emerge: Monday through Friday, 80,000 automobiles enter the downtown area with an average of 1.5 people per vehicle. Of the 80,000, 50,000 are commuting to work, 15,000 to shop, and another 15,000 on business trips. Another 40,000 persons a day enter by mass transit, paying on the average $1.70 per round trip. Of these 40,000, 30,000 are going to work, 8,000 to shop, and 2,000 are on business. The market study done for the private parking firm concluded that there is a need for 7,000 more spaces in the downtown area at current prices. That is, if the parking firm is willing to charge current prices, an additional 7,000 spaces per day would be filled. At present, 22,000 spaces are provided in the downtown area, 12,000 by private vendors and 10,000 by the city government. Current prices for parking and usage patterns follow. Typically in the downtown, the price structure is $2.80 for the first hour, $1.40 for the second hour, and $0.70 per hour for every hour thereafter to a $7.00 maximum per day. Lots in the area of the proposed parking garage are utilized at near capacity between 7:30 A.M. and 6:00 P.M. Eighty percent of these parkers are all-day parkers. The lots run at 30% capacity between 6:00 P.M. and midnight. On Saturday, these lots run at 50% capacity between 7:00 A.M. and 6:00 P.M. with 30% being all-day parkers. They run at 75% capacity between 6:00 P.M. and midnight. On Sunday, these lots run at 20% capacity between 7:00 A.M. and midnight, half of these being all-day parkers.

The budget director has made available data on the operation of other city-owned parking garages. The typical parking garage with a capacity for 800 automobiles costs about $900,000 a year to operate and maintain. In addition to revenue from parking, the typical garage generates $280,000 per year in rent from retail businesses on the first floor. Revenues by structure are not available. Obviously they vary depending on the location of the structure

and the pricing policies and usage rates. One of the studies showed that one-half of all mass-transit users own automobiles available for the trip they were on, but that they preferred using mass transit given the current driving and parking situation in downtown.

Some members of the downtown business association have lobbied the mayor vigorously in favor of building the downtown parking garage. They contend that each space generates at least $42,000 a year in increased retail activity. The city, they say, stands to gain some amount for its own coffers from this, since it imposes a 4.5% sales tax.

The market for office space is less clear. Like many cities its size, this one has lost a great deal of activity to the suburbs. At present, the real boom in both residence and office space is in the outer suburbs, not in the city. However, the city has held its own, especially in office development. The most recent high-rise office building constructed in the downtown was built two years ago and is experiencing a 15% vacancy rate. Last year it contributed $1.05 million to the city in property taxes. Given the location of this site, clearly an office building is the most likely development, and office developers are the most likely to bid on the parcel.

Chapter Eleven

Defending against Accusations of Prejudice

INTRODUCTION

You live in a large city in the Midwest. Your city newspaper has just broken a story about a city-funded study that has shown racial discrimination in the operations of many of the city's apartment complexes (see Exhibit 11-1). You have been out of graduate school now for ten years and have been successfully operating your own six-person consulting firm. You work for businesses and government on a variety of urban policy matters. You have become friends with many business and government leaders in the city and have developed a number of contacts in the housing and development industry.

One of those contacts, a lawyer named Jan McGinty, called you last night. McGinty represents one of the largest developers of rental housing in the midwestern United States, Lynn Jewels. Unfortunately for Jewels, a local fair-housing advocacy group called Square Deal Housing, has threatened a lawsuit.

THE ASSIGNMENT

McGinty has asked that you deliver a memo on fair-share housing and how Jewels is meeting the intent of the terms. You are to submit the memo to McGinty within two weeks. And two days later you are to present your findings to both McGinty and Jewels as well as their senior staff members. You will have 15 minutes to present your findings and will then be asked to field questions.

Be sure to put any detailed numerical analysis in appendices and limit your memo to verbal and simple arithmetic analysis and conclusions.

BACKGROUND INFORMATION

The case is ironic to Jewels because he has been a leader in the civil rights movement since the mid-1950s and has many powerful black friends in the city. The basis of Square Deal's accusation is twofold.

First, some of their members, black and white, posing as potential renters visited one of Jewels' units (Prestige One). The black potential renters were treated quite differently from the white ones (for examples see Exhibit 11-II). Jewels quickly conducted an internal investigation and found that the manager of Prestige One is indeed guilty of prejudice and racial stereotyping. The manager claims that white renters are far more affluent, stay longer, pay rent on time, and don't damage property. The manager steers blacks away and is generally more receptive to whites and Asians. Jewels is surprised. This situation sullies a hard-won reputation. Jewels begins an internal audit of all properties and hires several management consultants to help deal with related personnel problems. McGinty will represent Jewels legally on this matter, and *you are not to be directly involved.*

A second accusation is the subject of your assignment. Square Deal Housing claims that Jewels' apartment units don't contain their "fair share" of the metropolitan area's black tenants. Vaguely citing some population and housing data, it says this is true of individual apartment complexes as well as the overall holdings. In

fact, Square Deal claims that Jewels' rental practices contribute significantly to racial segregation in the metropolitan area.

Jewels explains that the housing profile is simply a result of natural market forces—the housing is expensive and blacks are disproportionately less able to afford such high rents. You convince yourself that Jewels is sincere and is a person who wants to "do the right thing." But Jewels hasn't been very involved in the management portion of the business for a long time and may have people on the staff that aren't as well motivated. In any event, you agree to analyze the situation and "pull no punches."

During your meeting with Jewels you agree to do the following:

- Develop some definitions of "fair share" that will work in this context

- Measure the current circumstance of Jewels' rental patterns (of each of the eight major apartment complexes) and see how they perform against the definition of "fair share" (are they "fair"?)

- Develop a defense for Jewels that can be used in negotiations with Square Deal Housing, or used in court if it comes to that

- Suggest strategies to Jewels for portraying the situation to outsiders in the best light possible, while at the same time suggesting ways to improve the statistical performance of the apartment units—in other words, suggest where management could best concentrate their integration efforts

THE DATA AND DATA PROBLEMS

1. You suggested that current rental fees by amount (in $5 categories) be tabulated by race of renter for each apartment complex. One of your assistants worked with Jewels' people and developed that information. Your assistant included the Census tract within which each resided as well. That information is provided for all eight complexes in Exhibit 11-III.

2. Rental housing costs have been escalating and they play havoc with older data. You sent one of your student interns to check on this and look at inflation in the consumer price index (CPI) in the metropolitan area's rental housing since March 1971. That information is provided in Exhibit 11-IV. (Remember: You are in the case world, and the date is May 18, 1990. Do not attempt to get later actual CPI data. In the case, the last available CPI datum is June 1987.)

3. Metropolitan area housing data are stale. The major available data sources are the 1980 Census, and the sample in the 1982 American Housing Survey. The 1987 American Housing Survey for this area will be issued soon on computer tape, but is not yet available. The 1980 Census and 1982 metropolitan data are available in Exhibit 11-V.

4. You asked an intern to get the latest data possible on the percentages of households and population by race for the tracts and county within which the apartment units are located (tracts 2, 4, and 6, all in county 5); the 7-county region; and the 15-county Metropolitan Statistical Area. That information is available in Exhibit 11-VI.

LEARNING OBJECTIVES

The objectives include, but are not limited to the following:

1. Practicing advocacy for a position with which, and for a client with whom, you are not entirely comfortable
2. Taking great care with operational definitions
3. Practicing sound data analysis
4. Using secondary data sources to their best advantage
5. Learning to write with clarity, organization, and precision
6. Learning to use supporting documentation effectively
7. Learning to work on a mountain of data with severe time constraints
8. Becoming more competent with a microcomputer

EXHIBITS

Exhibit 11-I   Racial Bias Found in Study of Apartments

May 15, 1990

Blacks trying to rent an apartment can expect to encounter race discrimination at nearly one-third of the city's apartment complexes, according to a city-funded study. Roughly 30 of 100 apartment complexes in the study were found to give "preferential treatment" to whites over blacks who sought information on apartment availability and price.

The city used federal housing funds to pay for the study, which was conducted during late

Exhibit 11-I   (continued)

1989 by Square Deal Housing, a private nonprofit agency that investigates complaints of housing discrimination. The agency based its findings on the responses given by apartment managers or employees to black and white men and women who posed as prospective tenants.

"There's no doubt about it—there is a clear pattern of discrimination in the rental housing market," said Alex Pendergrass, executive director of Square Deal Housing. "We found clear preferential treatment shown to whites over blacks, all over the city." Pendergrass said the test results may lead to lawsuits against owners of apartment complexes where discrimination was discovered. The agency has won similar lawsuits against apartment complexes in the past. Square Deal Housing would not release the names or exact addresses of the complexes until officials decide on lawsuits.

Representatives of the city's apartment owners and managers were quick to take issue with the testing results. "That definitely sounds too high," said S. T. Farfly, executive officer of the Apartment Owners and Managers Association, a trade organization. "It pretty much goes against everything we're trying to do. Our goal is to provide affordable housing to everyone."

"I'm really shocked," said Shawn Jobs, president of Jobs Properties, Inc. "I just can't imagine that happening in the city. Not today, in 1990."

City Council President Chris Bologna expects that the apartment complexes where discrimination was found will be contacted to see how they plan to address the problem. "Fair housing is the very moral fabric of this community," Bologna said. "Discrimination anywhere, but especially there, is something that we must not condone. It cannot be tolerated." A spokesperson for Mayor Evenhand said the mayor would not comment until the staff has had a chance to fully review the study.

Racial discrimination in housing was outlawed by President Kennedy's executive order in 1963, although it was not until 1968 that the Fair Housing Act was formally created. Testing for discrimination was upheld by the U.S. Supreme Court and frequently carried out by advocacy groups or governments across the country.

The methodology used by Square Deal

Housing is a common one: Individual testers visit the targeted apartment complex and say they are looking for rental housing. One is black, the other white; both seek the same kind of apartment. They visit the complex within minutes of each other. Afterward, the visits are compared.

In one October test, black and white female testers visited an apartment complex in Waterdown Park 10 minutes apart. Although the black tester's income was higher than the white tester's, the black tester was told no units were available at the time. She was told an apartment might be available in the future, but she was not told when. The white tester, on the other hand, was shown three apartments, and she was told all three were available that day.

"There's no doubt that this is discrimination, and it is absolutely against the law," Pendergrass said. "This kind of discrimination seriously decreases your housing opportunities, and the quality of housing available to you, if you're a minority person seeking housing. You're greatly disadvantaged by it."

In the city study, the discrimination found was dispersed about equally between the northern and southern parts of the city. Of the 31 apartment complexes found to discriminate on the basis of race, 17 were in the northern part of the city and 14 were in the southern portion.

The recent testing echoes patterns found by the U.S. Department of Housing and Urban Development (HUD) in 1989. In that study, 119 metro area apartment complexes were tested, including a number in the suburbs. That study showed that whites received preferential treatment 45% of the time. Blacks were shown preferential treatment 29% of the time, and in 27% of the tests, no discrimination occurred.

Pendergrass said in the testing by the agency, "almost all the discrimination was against blacks." Of the 31 apartment complexes where there was discrimination, "only a couple showed a black preference over the white." Pendergrass said the difference between the two studies shows no improvement in the city. Pendergrass also said the agency expects the discrimination against blacks to be much more widespread outside the inner city.

"It's almost always true, in most major cities across the country, that the suburbs show

Exhibit 11-I (*continued*)

discrimination levels up around 70%. . . . I believe you will still find those figures, or some even higher, if you test outside the inner city today."

Square Deal Housing also reviewed the policies of 22 apartment complexes to determine whether they discriminate on the basis of familial status. A change in federal law effective March 12 states that apartment complexes may not refuse to rent to people because they have children or disabled family members. Seventeen of the 22 complexes tested had written policies stating they did not allow children as residents.

"It would really upset me if this [study] proves to be true," Jobs said. "It would make all of us look very bad. I hope it's not true. If it is, our industry will address it. We'll have to."

This fictional newspaper article was based on an actual newspaper article, and is used here with permission of the source.

Exhibit 11-II   Examples of Housing Discrimination

Here are three examples cited by Square Deal Housing as incidents of discrimination found during its testing.

EXAMPLE 1

Location: Waterdown Park
Date: November 20, 1989

Information given by testers:
Black female, age 34. Annual income of $32,000, with 10 years on job.
White female, age 29. Annual income of $28,000, with five years on job.
Both said they were single, looking for one-bedroom unit for around $600 to $700 per month.

Results:
The black tester was told no units were available at that time but that an apartment for $575 might be available sometime in the future. The white tester was shown three apartments, for $575, $625 and $765, and was told all were available that day.

EXAMPLE 2

Location: Proboscis Woods area
Date: September 18, 1989

Information given by testers:
Black male, age 32. Monthly income of $3,500, with three years on job.
White male, age 30. Monthly income of $2,850, with 1½ years on job.

Both said they were single, without children, looking for one-bedroom unit for around $500 per month.

Results:
The black male was told something might be available in the future but was given no encouragement and no dates of availability, and was told only upon request that it was not known when anything in the price range would be available. The white male was told that though nothing was available that day, something would be available within 14 days. He was asked to fill out an application and was quoted two rental-unit prices in his price range.

EXAMPLE 3

Location: Northridge area
Date: December 13, 1989

Information given by testers:
Black male, 29. Annual income of $38,000.
White female, 26. Annual income of $29,000.
Both drove nice cars and said they were single and were looking for a one-bedroom unit for around $600 to $700 per month.

Results:
The black tester was shown a model and was told no unit was available at that time. The price on a one-bedroom unit was quoted to him as $720 per month plus $170 security deposit. The white tester was told an apartment was available immediately, then shown the unit, and was told a one-bedroom unit would be $635 per month plus $125 deposit.

Exhibit 11-III　Current Rental Rates by Race

Prestige One (Tract 6)

Rent Paid	White	Asian & Other	Black	Total
$375	1	0		1
$400	1	0		1
$430	1	0		1
$435	1	0		1
$440	6	0		6
$445	1	0		1
$450	4	0	1	5
$455	1	0		1
$460	1	1		2
$465	3	0		3
$470	2	0		2
$475	1	0	1	2
$480	1	0		1
$485	0	0	1	1
$490	2	1		3
$495	1	0		1
$500	14	1	1	16
$510	2	0		2
$515	1	0		1
$520	2	0		2
$535	1	0		1
$540	1	1		2
$545	2	0		2
$550	4	1	2	7
$555	2	0		2
$560	19	7	9	35
$565	1	0		1
$570	5	2		7
$575	2	0		2
$580	3	0	1	4
$585	9	1		10
$590	7	1	1	9
$595	1	0		1
$600	2	1		3
$605	1	0		1
$610	21	4	3	28
$615	1	0		1
$625	1	0	1	2
$640	1	0		1
$655	1	0		1
$675	7	2	1	10
$685	1	0		1
$810	1	0		1
$820	2	0		2
$850	1	0	1	2
$865	1	0		1
$875	1	0		1
$890	1	0		1
$925	1	0		1
$930	2	0		2
$950	2	0	3	5
$965	1	0		1
Total	**152**	**23**	**26**	**201**

Prestige Six (Tract 6)

Rent Paid	White	Asian & Other	Black	Total
$375	0	0	1	1
$380	0	0	1	1
$420	1	0		1
$425	11	3	14	28
$450	1	1	1	3
$465	3	2		5
$470	1	0		1
$475	31	3	32	66
$490	5	0	3	8
Total	**53**	**9**	**52**	**114**

Prestige Two (Tract 4)

Rent Paid	White	Asian & Other	Black	Total
$425	1	0		1
$430	0	0		0
$435	1	0		1
$440	4	0		4
$445	1	0		1
$450	5	0		5
$455	9	3		12
$460	5	0	1	6
$465	3	1		4
$470	10	4		14
$475	5	2	2	9
$480	3	0		3
$485	4	0	2	6
$490	4	1		5
$495	0	0		0
$500	1	0		1
$505	1	0		1
$510	0	0	1	1
$515	2	0	1	3
$520	3	1		4
$525	12	0		12
$530	5	2	2	9
$535	4	2	2	8
$540	5	2	3	10
$545	2	0	2	4
$550	12	1	3	16
$555	3	1		4
$560	4	2		6
$565	1	1		2
$570	2	0		2
$575	0	0		0
$580	2	0		2
$585	3	1		4
$590	0	0		0
$595	0	0		0
$600	0	0		0
$605	2	0	1	3
Total	**117**	**26**	**20**	**163**

Prestige Five (Tract 2)

Rent Paid	White	Asian & Other	Black	Total
$250	1	0		1
$255	1	0		1
$260	0	0		0
$265	2	0		2
$270	1	0	1	1
$275	1	0		1
$280	1	0		1
$285	3	0		3
$290	0	0		0
$295	3	0		3
$300	4	1	1	6
$305	7	4	3	14
$310	3	0		3
$315	9	2		11
$320	1	1		2
$325	3	1		4
$330	8	1	3	12
$335	1	0		1
$340	6	2		8
Total	**55**	**12**	**8**	**75**

Prestige Three (Tract 6)

Rent Paid	White	Asian & Other	Black	Total
$225	1	0		1
$275	1	0		1
$285	1	0		1
$305	2	1		3
$310	3	1		4
$315	3	1	1	5
$320	21	1	4	26
$325	18	8	9	35
$330	12	2	4	18
$335	16	2	4	22
$340	8	5	1	14
$345	21	2	6	29
$350	36	7	13	56
$355	24	6	5	35
$360	8	1	4	13
$365	4	1		5
$370	5	2		7
$375	4	0	1	5
$380	5	0	1	6
$385	4	1	2	7
$390	4	1	2	7
$395	2	0	1	3
$400	18	6	5	29
$405	0	0		0
$410	4	2		6
$415	3	1		4
$490	1	0		1
$495	1	0		1
$500	1	0		1
$550	3	1	1	5
Total	**234**	**52**	**64**	**350**

Please note: All rents include costs for water, but not gas or electricity. All Prestige units are heated with gas.

Prestige Eight (Tract 2)

Rent Paid	White	Asian & Other	Black	Total
$240	0	0	1	1
$245	0	0		0
$250	1	0		1
$255	4	1	13	18
$260	0	0		0
$265	0	0		0
$270	5	2	7	14
$275	27	1	32	60
$280	1	0		1
$285	0	0		0
$290	1	1		2
$295	0	0		0
$300	5	2	8	15
$305	2	0		2
$310	2	0	1	3
$315	8	2	14	24
$320	30	1	39	70
$325	0	0	4	4
$330	2	0	1	3
$335	1	0		1
$340	0	0		0
$345	0	0		0
$350	5	1	9	15
Total	**94**	**11**	**129**	**234**

Prestige Four (Tract 2)

Rent Paid	White	Asian & Other	Black	Total
$350	1	0		1
$410	3	0		3
$415	4	1		5
$420	3	0		3
$425	2	0		2
$430	0	0		0
$435	24	6	1	31
$440	0	0		0
$445	0	0		0
$450	1	0		1
$455	0	0		0
$460	0	0		0
$465	0	0		0
$470	1	0		1
$475	23	2		25
$480	1	0		1
$485	7	3		10
$490	5	0		5
$495	21	9	4	34
$500	2	0		2
$505	0	0		0
$510	1	1		2
Total	**99**	**22**	**5**	**126**

Prestige Seven (Tract 4)

Rent Paid	White	Asian & Other	Black	Total
$550	1	0		1
$700	1	0		1
$800	1	0		1
$875	1	0		1
$880	1	0		1
$900	1	1		2
$925	2	0		2
$930	3	0		3
$940	1	0		1
$950	19	0		19
$955	7	2		9
$960	3	1		4
$965	1	0		1
$970	3	0		3
$975	5	0		5
$980	20	5	1	26
$985	1	1		2
$990	1	0		1
$995	4	2		6
$1,000	9	0		9
$1,005	0	0	1	1
$1,010	1	0		1
$1,015	5	1	1	7
$1,020	2	0		2
$1,025	21	11		32
$1,030	3	0		3
$1,035	2	0		2
$1,040	10	1		11
$1,045	0	0		0
$1,050	5	2		7
$1,055	5	0		5
$1,060	0	0		0
$1,065	1	0		1
$1,070	3	1		4
$1,075	1	1		2
$1,080	3	0		3
$1,100	5	1		6
$1,105+	41	2	1	44
Total	**193**	**32**	**4**	**229**

Exhibit 11-IV Consumer Price Index: Rental Housing

Base = 100   July 1983

Jun-72	54.8	Dec-80	84.5
Sep-72	55.1	Feb-81	85.8
Dec-72	55.3	Apr-81	87.4
Mar-73	55.6	Jun-81	88.0
Jun-73	56.2	Aug-81	88.9
Sep-73	56.9	Oct-81	90.1
Dec-73	57.5	Dec-81	91.0
Mar-74	57.9	Feb-82	91.0
Jun-74	58.4	Apr-82	92.4
Sep-74	59.0	Aug-82	93.2
Dec-74	59.7	Jun-82	93.4
Mar-75	60.0	Oct-82	95.6
Jun-75	60.4	Feb-83	96.9
Sep-75	60.7	Dec-82	97.8
Dec-75	61.0	Apr-83	99.5
Mar-76	61.2	Aug-83	100.8
Jun-76	61.5	Oct-83	101.0
Sep-76	61.7	Jun-83	101.5
Dec-76	61.7	Apr-84	103.4
Mar-77	62.3	Feb-84	103.5
Jun-77	63.4	Dec-83	103.7
Sep-77	64.1	Jun-84	106.1
Apr-78	64.4	Aug-84	106.9
Feb-78	64.6	Oct-84	108.3
Dec-77	64.7	Dec-84	109.5
Jun-78	64.8	Feb-85	110.9
Aug-78	64.9	Apr-85	112.6
Oct-78	66.9	Jun-85	114.3
Feb-79	68.9	Aug-85	117.1
Dec-78	69.1	Oct-85	117.2
Apr-79	69.9	Dec-85	119.0
Aug-79	71.4	Feb-86	120.0
Jun-79	72.0	Apr-86	121.5
Oct-79	72.8	Jun-86	122.7
Dec-79	74.0	Aug-86	124.1
Apr-80	74.9	Oct-86	124.6
Feb-80	75.6	Dec-86	125.6
Jun-80	78.0	Feb-87	127.1
Aug-80	80.2	Apr-87	128.7
Oct-80	81.9	Jun-87	130.2

Exhibit 11-V 1982 Annual Housing Survey and 1980 Census Data for Three Categories of Rent, Metropolitan Statistical Area

ANNUAL HOUSING SURVEY 1982			ANNUAL HOUSING SURVEY 1982		
Gross Rent Specified renter occupied	Table A-2 All races	Table A-7 Black	Contract Rent Specified renter occupied	Table A-2 All races	Table A-7 Black
Less than $80	13,000	9,200	Less than $80	21,300	15,900
$80 to $99	3,600	2,700	$80 to $99	7,000	5,300
$100 to $124	4,800	3,000	$100 to $124	8,700	5,900
$125 to $149	7,400	4,300	$125 to $149	10,600	7,200
$150 to $174	7,000	5,900	$150 to $174	13,300	8,900
$175 to $199	10,100	5,700	$175 to $199	11,200	5,700
$200 to $224	13,300	8,000	$200 to $224	15,600	5,700
$225 to $249	12,500	5,400	$225 to $249	16,700	4,600
$250 to $274	14,500	5,300	$250 to $274	22,000	7,000
$275 to $299	17,000	6,200	$275 to $299	27,200	8,100
$300 to $324	24,500	7,100	$300 to $324	21,700	4,600
$325 to $349	21,500	6,700	$325 to $349	20,200	4,600
$350 to $374	17,000	5,100	$350 to $374	15,700	1,500
$375 to $399	19,900	4,200	$375 to $399	12,600	1,300
$400 to $449	28,500	5,200	$400 to $449	14,700	200
$450 to $499	19,200	2,000	$450 to $499	10,900	500
$500 to $549	11,400	500	$500 to $549	5,200	200
$550 to $599	4,400	200	$550 to $599	3,100	400
$600 to $699	7,500	700	$600 to $699	1,700	200
$700 to $749	1,400	200	$700 to $749	400	—
$750 or more	2,600	200	$750 or more	1,300	200
No cash rent	6,200	1,400	No cash rent	6,200	1,400
Median	$328	$248	Median	$279	$178
Total	267,300	89,200	Total	267,300	89,400

Gross Rent Nonsubsidized renter occupied	Table A-2 All races	Table A-7 Black
Less than $80	2,300	1,300
$80 to $99	500	300
$100 to $124	2,600	1,700
$125 to $149	5,300	2,500
$150 to $174	4,800	3,900
$175 to $199	8,200	4,000
$200 to $224	10,700	5,900
$225 to $249	11,200	4,300
$250 to $274	13,100	4,400
$275 to $299	16,300	5,900
$300 to $324	22,800	6,000
$325 to $349	20,900	6,400
$350 to $374	16,600	4,700
$375 to $399	19,300	3,800
$400 to $449	28,500	5,200
$450 to $499	18,900	1,900
$500 to $549	11,400	500
$550 to $599	4,400	200
$600 to $699	7,500	700
$700 to $749	1,400	200
$750 or more	2,600	200
No cash rent	5,700	900
Median	$344	$290
Total	235,000	64,900

Exhibit 11-V (continued)

TABLE A-1, U.S. CENSUS OF HOUSING	
yr round housing units	692,000
occupied	642,600
owner occupied	374,200
white	299,800
black	73,800
renter occupied	268,400
white	176,600
black	89,500

1980 CENSUS OF HOUSING, VOL. 1,
CHARACTERISTICS OF HOUSING UNITS, SMSA, 1980

Gross Rent Specified renter occupied	Table A-2 All races	Table A-7 Black
Less than $50	8,283	7,003
$50 to $59	3,884	2,616
$60 to $79	5,486	3,550
$80 to $99	5,644	3,427
$100 to $119	6,440	4,050
$120 to $149	14,327	8,080
$150 to $169	12,157	5,590
$170 to $199	21,025	9,292
$200 to $249	47,053	16,851
$250 to $299	52,791	14,351
$300 to $349	40,214	7,836
$350 to $399	21,965	3,290
$400 to $499	14,711	1,701
$500 or more	5,793	477
No cash rent	7,586	1,987
Median	$255	$201
Total	267,359	90,101

Contract Rent Specified renter occupied	Table 20 All races	Table 22 Black
Less than $50	13,887	10,593
$50 to $59	5,887	3,726
$60 to $79	11,354	7,353
$80 to $99	10,433	6,802
$100 to $119	12,451	6,508
$120 to $149	20,664	10,394
$150 to $169	18,634	6,890
$170 to $199	25,957	8,352
$200 to $249	51,773	14,236
$250 to $299	44,765	8,304
$300 to $349	22,953	2,161
$350 to $399	10,101	699
$400 to $499	4,878	277
$500 or more	1,993	115
No cash rent	6,625	1,369
Median	$209	$143
Total	262,355	87,779

Exhibit 11-VI Estimates of Population and Households by Race

Estimated 1985 population:	Non-white	Total	Non-white %
County 1	5,947	15,103	39.4%
County 2	1,681	63,272	2.7%
County 3	13,972	169,454	8.2%
County 4	19,848	367,346	5.4%
County 5	150,633	526,203	28.6%
County 6	3,555	61,968	5.7%
County 7	1,912	37,937	5.0%
County 8	193	32,231	0.6%
County 9	334,706	636,073	52.6%
County 10	7,717	228,346	3.4%
County 11	7,732	42,091	18.4%
County 12	9,958	38,571	25.8%
County 13	1,444	29,494	4.9%
County 14	3,966	41,322	9.6%
County 15	7,395	34,441	21.5%
MSA Total	570,659	2,323,852	24.6%

Estimated 1990 population:	Non-white	Total	Non-white %
County 1	6,494	16,539	39.3%
County 2	1,988	74,849	2.7%
County 3	15,540	188,548	8.2%
County 4	23,604	436,972	5.4%
County 5	162,498	569,383	28.5%
County 6	3,979	69,360	5.7%
County 7	2,374	46,831	5.1%
County 8	222	36,518	0.6%
County 9	359,841	682,239	52.7%
County 10	9,792	289,786	3.4%
County 11	8,797	47,875	18.4%
County 12	11,022	42,653	25.8%
County 13	1,608	32,872	4.9%
County 14	4,408	45,896	9.6%
County 15	8,082	37,665	21.5%
MSA Total	620,249	2,617,986	23.7%

Note: In this SMSA "Black" and "Non-white" are nearly synonomous; however, County 5 has a significant (7%) Asian population counted as "Non-white".

SMSA POPULATIONS BY RACE

1980 US Census	Black	Total	% Black
Persons	498,826	2,029,710	24.6%
Households	161,191	770,076	20.9%
Persons/HH	3.09	2.64	
Renters (specified)	89,200	267,300	33.4%
Renters (nonsubsidized)	64,900	235,000	27.6%

% Black households in 7-county region versus the 15-county SMSA, 1980

	Total	Black	% Black
County 2	53,014	3,671	6.9%
County 3	113,311	4,371	3.9%
County 5	181,849	39,092	21.5%
County 6	17,758	738	4.2%
County 9	246,457	103,444	42.0%
County 10	58,142	1,132	1.9%
County 14	12,163	844	6.9%
Total Region	682,694	153,292	22.5%
SMSA	770,076	161,191	20.9%

CENSUS TRACT DATA

Tract	2	4	6
1980 POPULATION			
TOTAL	6,053	6,789	5,113
WHITE	4,031	6,479	4,937
BLACK	1,953	187	150
ASIAN	30	73	12
1980 TOTAL OCCUPIED HOUSING UNITS			
TOTAL	2,708	2,521	1,587
WHITE	2,395	2,396	1,543
BLACK	916	79	37
ASIAN	11	25	0
1980 OWNER-OCCUPIED HOUSING UNITS			
TOTAL	908	1,336	1,376
WHITE	689	1,304	1,354
BLACK	211	11	17
ASIAN	4	10	0
1980 RENTER-OCCUPIED HOUSING UNITS			
TOTAL	1,800	1,185	211
WHITE	1,706	1,092	189
BLACK	705	68	20
ASIAN	7	15	0
1989 POPULATION			
TOTAL	8,364	6,950	6,826
WHITE	4,490	6,426	6,232
NON-WHITE	3,874	524	594
1989 TOTAL OCCUPIED HOUSING UNITS			
TOTAL	3,949	2,975	2,297
WHITE	2,083	2,741	2,145
NON-WHITE	1,866	234	152

Chapter Twelve

Solid-Waste
Collection Methods

INTRODUCTION

A short time ago you became a senior policy analyst in the Office of the Mayor
of a city of over 500,000. Before you were hired, there had been a major controversy over garbage collection when a local newspaper had run a week-long series
on the topic. Reporters had followed garbage workers around and caught some
in taverns, and, in general, not fully engaged in work. The story was complete
with photographs of inactivity. The mayor and public works director defended
the department, saying their loafing was the result of unusually low levels of
demand caused by a snowless spring (garbage collectors are also used as snow
plowers). But to prevent more radical action by an alarmed city council, the
mayor promised to experiment with different methods of collection, and to
report back to the council sometime in the near future. The mayor's delaying
strategy worked, and the controversy subsided.

   The following year there was rather heavy snow in the spring, and the
newspaper decided to reinvestigate. This time they found even more "loafing
on the job." Some council members urged a cut in all crew sizes from four to
three persons; others wanted a hiring freeze placed on the department.

   The mayor again dipped into the well of delay and obfuscation—"the
study." The Department of Public Works (DPW) had never completed its report

on the experiments with other collection methods. However, the mayor scheduled an address to the Common Council in two weeks, at which time the conclusions of the study would be released and a plan of action proposed. Taking the somewhat disjointed results of the experiments (the DPW's staff person in charge had retired months before) and turning out a position paper with the mayor became your task.

THE ASSIGNMENT

This assignment has two parts: numbers and politics. The mayor wants to adopt collection procedures that are cheap, effective, and equitable, but also politically viable. Thus, your analysis should contain those two thrusts. Using the report provided by the retired staff person contained in Exhibit 12-I, develop a detailed planning report that can be released to the press. Second, write a memo to the mayor describing the basic policy options and your analysis of them. For both products you should keep the following hints in mind:

1. Assume a 20-year time period for analysis.
2. Review the design of the experiment and the method used to choose a test area.
3. Discuss the most sensitive variables in terms of choosing the best alternative, and do some sensitivity testing.
4. Discuss uncertainty and risk.
5. Discuss potential problems in implementing your chosen alternative.
6. Discuss equity problems inherent in your analysis.
7. Analyze possible problems caused by inflation.
8. Use discounted annual costs, not total discounted costs, in summarizing your findings.

EXHIBITS

Exhibit 12-I   Draft Report on DPW Solid-Waste Collection Experiments

A Description of the Overall Experiment

Almost two years ago the Office of the Mayor suggested to the DPW commissioner that a wheeled refuse-collection system be evaluated to determine its applicability and economic feasibility in the city. At the outset, it was our recommendation that the entire system of refuse collection be evaluated, from point of origin to point of disposal. It is still our contention that the elimination of solid waste from a community must be done on a systems approach and that, although there exist many elements within this system, each element must be matched with all other elements in the system to obtain optimum efficiency. For certain political reasons, however, our tests were limited to an evaluation of refuse-collection methods (crew sizes and procedures by which they actually collect refuse), types of refuse storage containers (wheeled containers

Exhibit 12-I   (*continued*)

and cans), the locations at which these containers may appear for collection purposes, the work effort on the part of the collectors to service these containers, and a cursory evaluation of two types of collection vehicles used in the collection process. No systematic evaluation has been made of other elements of the refuse-collection system such as transfer stations, all types of collection vehicles, and all types of storage containers (bag system not included). Also, it should be noted that the evaluation herein rendered pertains to the residential (i.e., one and two family) area of the city. No evaluation has been made of the refuse-collection system in the commercial areas or high-density residential areas.

Since the evaluation had to be generalized to the entire city's low-density residential area, since that area varies in many respects from one part of the city to another, and since the cost of experimenting citywide would be prohibitive, it was critical that a pilot area be selected that possessed characteristics paralleling the composition of the city as a whole. These characteristics are as follows:

67.0%   Single-family homes (139,293 units)
33.0%   Duplexes (68,607 units)
31.2%   Dwelling units on alleys (64,950 units)
68.8%   Dwelling units on streets (142,950 units)

Consideration was also given to approximate the proportion of dwelling units with long distances from the point where refuse containers are stored to the location where the collection vehicle would traverse. The pilot area had to be in a contiguous geographic location and represent approximately one week's effort for an existing crew of four collecting in the traditional manner. The actual pilot area selected was a combination of parts of three existing weekly work routes. Because the experiments were to take place in the winter and spring, and because the traditional collection procedure included twice-weekly pickups in spring, once for yard waste (Friday) and once for regular collections (Monday through Thursday), it was necessary to separate these items for total comparability of methods. That was accomplished without problem.

In the collection of data, it was imperative to collect identical data for all types of collection methods. This led to the establishment of a data unit whose meaning would remain constant when applied to various methods of collection that would be used. With this in mind, the basic data unit was defined as the number of dwelling units served per a given amount of time, D.U./.T.

This basic data unit was then applied to the experimental route on a block-by-block basis. This unit of measure is broad enough to include the several functions that were smaller but distinct elements of the various methods of collection (i.e., cart dumping times, walking times, lifting time, etc.). Time-motion data were also collected for most of these smaller units of information, but unless otherwise indicated, these smaller units have been incorporated into the basic measure. A further rationale for the delineation of data units as described above was that the variation in collection method would affect street-access dwelling units and alley-access dwelling units differently. For example, the method of pre-set-out curb collection would affect the time required to collect street-access dwelling units greatly but would not affect alley-access dwelling units at all.

It should also be noted that all methods of collection were implemented twice, once in winter and once in spring, in order to facilitate the averaging of data for each of the particular methods, thereby reducing the degree of influence that an unusual condition might have on the data. Consideration was also given to the effects of other variables such as weather conditions and collection vehicle type. In addition, the factor of the weight of material collected was considered. (See Exhibit 12-II.)

Weight factors are much discussed by those familiar with the solid-waste field. There seems to be some disagreement about their relevancy in terms of costs and collection times. It is our opinion that weights are an important variable that must be taken into account, particularly when speaking in terms of the traditional method of refuse collection; that is, cans. Weights relate directly to the degree of difficulty encountered with collection in the field. When monthly weights are plotted on a graph over a year's period, rough patterns develop showing a relatively light season over the winter months with weights increas-

Exhibit 12-I   (*continued*)

ing rapidly in the spring and reaching a peak in May or June of each year. It was important, then, not only in terms of weights but also in terms of weather conditions, that we implement this experiment in the month of January and then sometime later in the spring in order to experience the widest range of collection weights. Weight figures for the experimental route were found to parallel the weights for the same period during the year citywide. As indicated above, weights are particularly significant when collecting refuse under the can system, where the collector has to lift all weight at least twice. We conclude, however, that collection weights become much less significant when collecting under the Kart system. The Kart is a uniform container that should never have to be physically lifted by the collector. Hydraulics do all the work. If the Kart system were to be fully implemented, the resident should be encouraged to include as much refuse, including yard trash, and so on, in the Kart as possible. It was noticed that the excess bags and yard trash that were found outside the Kart during late May and June did slow the collection effort to some degree.

A Description of Five Trial Methods

During the course of the pilot program, five different methods of collection were tried. The following is a description of each method:

Method 1: The first method used to service the pilot project area was the existing method used throughout single-family and duplex residential areas of the city. The purpose for using this method was to provide control data against which all other methods could be compared. This method employs the use of a rear-loading packer truck, three tote barrels, a truck driver, and three collectors. The crew member assigned the function of driving the truck did not participate in the collection process; however, the driving assignment was rotated from one crew member to another during the day. The collectors would walk on the public sidewalk to the driveway or access walk that led to the location of the refuse cans, then proceed up the walk or drive to the can location. There the cans and/or other containers would be physically emptied into the tote barrel and the tote barrel would be wheeled

on a dolly to the rear of the truck, which would wait on the street. The collector would then detach the tote barrel from the dolly, lift it and dump the contents into the hopper of the truck. If too much refuse existed in the rear yard location for one tote barrel, either a second trip was made by the collector or another collector would get the remaining refuse. Many times this resulted in a delay in the collection effort, since when there was a large load expected at a given dwelling unit, one collector would wait at the front of the driveway and a second collector would signal a waiting crew member if help was needed. Upon completion of the service to the dwelling unit, the collectors would replace the tote barrel on the dolly and walk on the public walk to the next dwelling unit. In the alley portion of the route, the tote barrels would be left on the parkway at the start of the alley and the truck would return to get the tote barrels when the alley portion of the route was complete. (Because of the layout of the pilot route, all the alleys were serviced as a continuous segment.) While servicing the alley segment, the collectors dumped the cans and/or other containers directly into the truck hopper rather than using a tote barrel.

Method 2: This method is exactly the same as Method 1 except that crew size was reduced from four to three.

Method 3: The third method of collection for servicing the pilot area employed the use of a conventional rear-loading packer truck fitted with two electrically activated hydraulic dumpers to empty wheeled refuse containers (Karts). The crew consisted of a driver and two collectors. The Karts were located in the rear yard (usually in the same area cans had been kept) of the dwelling units served by street access and at or near the alley line for dwelling units with alley access. The driver did not participate in the collection process. The collectors would walk from the public walk to the place where the Kart was located (usually in the rear yard). They would then wheel the full Kart out to the street where the truck would be waiting, attach the Kart to the hydraulic dumper, activate the dumper to empty the contents of the Kart into the truck hopper and then lower the Kart back to the street. The

Exhibit 12-I   (*continued*)

collector would then disengage the Kart and replace it on the parkway near the curb. The resident was then responsible for wheeling the empty Kart back to its storage location. It should be noted that in this method, both collectors performed all of the functions (i.e., retrieving, dumping, and replacing Karts). In the alley portion of the route, the collectors would service both sides of the alley at once by wheeling the Kart from its location and, after service, returning the Kart to where it was, unless that location was not near the alley line or if there was a substantial grade difference from the alley line to the backyard location.

Method 4: This method is the same as Method 3 except that before the collectors arrived, the staff brought all Karts to the street or alley line. The purpose of this action was to simulate the effect a pre-set-out condition would have. *Pre-set-out* as referred to in this report means that on the given collection day, the resident would wheel the full refuse Kart to the parkway or alley line where it would be left until processed by the collection crew and then returned by the resident to the storage location. Collection of the pre-set Karts was accomplished by use of the modified rear-loading packer, a driver who did not participate in the collection process, and two collector-equipment operators. Both collectors would service Karts from their pre-set location and after servicing, return them to the same location. Staff labor was not counted as part of this method.

Method 5: The fifth method of collection used to service the pilot area introduced a different type of collection vehicle from the one used in all previous methods. This was a side-loading vehicle with an 18-cubic-yard capacity that could be loaded from either side. The vehicle was capable of being driven from both sides in a standing position. One crew member acted as a driver, the other as collector-equipment operator. They serviced all pre-set Karts.

Equipment Evaluation

Cans: At the onset of the project, all dwelling units in the test area were storing their refuse in cans. Cans ranged in size from 20-gallon ca-

pacity to 55-gallon capacity. They were made of galvanized metal, plastic, or paper (these were the 55-gallon type, probably old industrial tubs). Most were made of metal. Approximately 30% of the metal cans had poorly fitting or no covers at all. In many cases, handles were missing, making them difficult to service. Less than 5% of the residents had storage bins or other types of special structures to house and conceal the cans from view. All but a few new cans or those few which were used only for paper products or packaging material were dirty. All of the above containers were used for refuse storage only, excepts on occasion when a few were used to put out lawn clippings or hedge trimmings.

Tote Barrels and Dollys: The DPW has provided its refuse collectors with two-wheeled dollys that have a removable 55-gallon plastic barrel. The function of this item is to transport the refuse from the cans of street access dwelling units to the truck. This is generally a distance of 100 feet to 120 feet. The dollys have a wheel base of approximately 18 inches and with a heavy load may become unstable when not used on level, hard-surfaced areas such as driveways or sidewalks. The wheels are small and, therefore, present difficulty in wheeling when irregularities in the surface traversed are encountered (i.e., cracked or broken driveways, lawn areas, curbs, etc.). Capacity of the barrel is generally adequate during light seasons in the refuse cycle; however, in the heavier portions of the cycle, a second load is often necessary at a dwelling unit.

Karts: Prior to the deployment of Karts (wheeled refuse containers) into the pilot project area, an evaluation of the three major brands was made by the commissioner of public works and members of the DPW work force while on a tour of southern cities. Only one brand, the "Kartel," met our durability requirements, so it was chosen for these tests.

Trucks: During the course of the experiment two different vehicles were used. They were:

1. Rear-loading packer (Methods 1 through 4): Standard truck with 20-cubic-yard Leach

---

Exhibit 12-I   (*continued*)

push-out body. They cost $112,000 each. In Methods 3 and 4 the truck was modified for dumping Karts at a cost of $7,000. The modification suffered many physical problems during the test period.

2. Side-loading packer (Method 5): Lodal, with 18-cubic-yard capacity. This truck can be loaded from either side and is designed for Karts. They cost $126,000 each.

Description of Cost Sources

A detailed analysis of all items in the budget would reveal that there is a large number of accounts that are either directly connected with refuse collection or indirectly affected by the change in any collection method. Most obvious of all costs in refuse collection is that of labor. Labor cost is actually broken down into wage and fringe areas. In this section the time-data units are converted to costs.

On the tables of time-cost comparison, each method of collection was analyzed to determine what that method would cost if applied to all one- and two-family dwelling units in the city. Time-data units were taken from the data sheets and averaged for each method. All data units for street-access dwelling units were totaled and divided by the total number of street-access dwelling units to establish an average time in minutes to service street-access dwelling units. Data units for alley-access dwelling units were also handled in this manner. The average service time in minutes was then applied to the total number of street-access and alley-access dwelling units in the city. This produced a total number of actual collection minutes necessary to service the one- and two-family dwelling units in the city for the particular method (total crew minutes). The total crew minutes was then divided by 1,950, the number of minutes a department of public works crew works per week under their present contract. The result of this division represents the number of crews necessary to process all one- and two-family dwelling units in the city.

Under the present system and any proposed method, variables such as four-day work weeks, weather, fluctuations in amount of refuse, unforeseen breakdowns, and so on, will cause the need to add extra help to ensure a once-a-week collection. However, since crew number is tied to collection time required, even if the number of crews was doubled, the total collection time remains constant; for example, twice as many crews would each have to work only half as long. Finally, the number of crews or fraction thereof was multiplied by the appropriate annual cost of a crew for the particular method to give total labor cost for collection. Total labor cost as applied here includes the following: actual wage, Social Security, pension fund, medical insurance, life insurance, vacation time, sick leave, injury leave, and miscellaneous holiday time. (Calculated: actual wage × 1.48 = hourly labor cost.)

Costs

Fixed costs are the same for each of the five methods tested. They are:

Commercial collections	$4,439,330
Disposal contract	3,570,000
Compaction operation	589,680
Storeroom	91,000
General administration	630,000
General management	280,000
Brush collection	2,800,000
Leaf collection	1,295,000
Special collections	385,000
Compaction equipment amortization	140,000
Total fixed cost	$14,220,010

Variable costs do vary by method. Each item is discussed separately below.

Karts: All methods except Methods 1 and 2 are based on the use of the Kart system. There are a total of 207,900 dwelling units in the city in single-family and duplex structures. Assuming a need for a reserve of Karts, 215,000 will be purchased at $54.32 each. The manufacture guarantees them as follows:

1. They will last ten years.
2. Defective Karts (new) will be replaced without charge.
3. Other Karts are guaranteed with the following replacement charges:

Exhibit 12-I   (*continued*)

Less than one year old	No charge
1 year to less than 2 years old	$11.20
2 years to less than 3 years old	$22.40
3 years to less than 4 years old	$33.60
4 years to less than 5 years old	$44.80
5 years and older, full charge	$54.32

4. Karts will rise in price no more than the national inflation statistic for the category "oil and oil-related products" as published by the federal government.

   Trucks: It is presumed that the total number of trucks needed includes the number of trucks in the method being examined rounded up to an integer plus about ten backup trucks. Truck life is five years, depreciated straight line with a 10% scrap value at the end of five years. There are two types of trucks. Methods 1 and 2 use the standard truck, purchase price $112,000 each. Methods 3 and 4 use the standard truck retrofitted with $7,000 of hydraulic gear. That gear has no scrap value. Method 5 uses a different type of truck that costs $126,000 each. At present the DPW owns a fleet of 130 standard trucks (26 each 1 year, 2 years, 3 years, 4 years and 5 years old). If a new collection method is adopted, a new strategy of truck purchasing and perhaps retrofitting will be in order. Annual truck mainte-

nance is estimated for each method on a per-truck basis as:

Methods 1 and 2	$7,000 each
Methods 3 and 4	$8,400 each
Method 5	$4,900 each

Public Works Administration: This cost is given on a per-worker basis as $4,060 per crew member per year. It is expected that smaller crews would reduce this expense proportionately.

Supplies and Expenses: $560 per crew member per year. It is expected that smaller crews would reduce this expense proportionately.

Method Labor Cost: In order to determine an approximation of the cost of collecting all single-family and duplex units in the city, we first collected data on two separate week-long tests on each of the five methods. We converted the time-study data to cost data by using the annual number of crews it would take to serve the whole city and multiplying by their particular cost. The results are shown for each method in Exhibit 12-II.

Exhibit 12-II   Time/Cost Comparisons for Solid-Waste Collection Methods

Method 1

Description: Existing method. Backyard pickup, cans, driver plus three collectors.

Weekly Average Performance:

$$\text{total average weight collected (5 days)} = 45,500 \text{ lb per wk}$$
$$730 \text{ street-access units collected in 940 min} = 1.2877 \text{ min/d.u.}$$
$$565 \text{ alley-access units collected in 390 min} = 0.6903 \text{ min/d.u.}$$

City Totals: Using the above performance, we can generate the total time it would take to service the whole residential area of the city:

$$142,950 \text{ street-access units @ } 1.2877 \text{ min/d.u.} = 184,076.7 \text{ total min}$$
$$64,950 \text{ alley-access units @ } 0.6903 \text{ min/d.u.} = 44,834.9 \text{ total min}$$

Exhibit 12-II (continued)

$$\text{total crew* min to serve city/week} = 228,911.6 \text{ min}$$
$$= 3,815.19 \text{ hr}$$

$$\text{*crew: 1 driver @ \$15.08/hr} \times 2,080 \text{ hr/yr} = 31,362.24$$
$$3 \text{ collectors @ \$12.74/hr} \times 2,080 \text{ hr/yr} = 79,497.60$$

Total: $110,859.84/yr

$$\frac{228,911.6 \text{ (total crew min/wk)}}{1950 \text{ (working min/crew/wk)}} = \begin{array}{l} 117.39 \text{ crews} \\ \text{needed to serve city} \end{array}$$

$$117.39 \text{ crews} \times \$110,859.84/\text{crew/yr} = \begin{array}{l} \$13,013,837 \text{ annual labor} \\ \text{cost to serve low-density} \\ \text{residential area of the city} \end{array}$$

Method 2

Description: Backyard pickup, cans, crew size reduced from four to three (one driver and two collectors).

Weekly Average Performance:

$$\text{total average weight collected (5 days)} = 43,750 \text{ lb per wk}$$
$$730 \text{ street-access units collected in 1,000 min} = 1.3699 \text{ min/d.u.}$$
$$565 \text{ alley-access units collected in 430 min} = 0.7611 \text{ min/d.u.}$$

City Totals:

$$142,950 \text{ street-access units @ 1.3699 min/d.u.} = 195,827.2 \text{ total min}$$
$$64,950 \text{ alley-access units @ 0.7611 min/d.u.} = 49,433.4 \text{ total min}$$

$$\text{total crew* min to serve city/wk} = 245,260.6 \text{ min}$$
$$= 4,087.68 \text{ hr}$$

$$\text{*crew: 1 driver @ \$15.08/hr} \times 2,080 \text{ hr/yr} = 31,362.24$$
$$2 \text{ collectors @ \$12.74/hr} \times 2,080 \text{ hr/yr} = 52,998.40$$
Total: $84,360.64/yr

$$\frac{245,260.6 \text{ (total crew min per wk)}}{1950 \text{ (working min/crew wk)}} = \begin{array}{l} 125.77 \text{ crews} \\ \text{needed to serve city} \end{array}$$

$$125.77 \text{ crews} \times \$84,360.64/\text{crew/yr} = \begin{array}{l} \$10,610,038 \text{ annual labor} \\ \text{cost to serve low-density} \\ \text{residential area of the city} \end{array}$$

Method 3

Description: Rear-loading truck retrofitted with hydraulic dumpers. Karts located in the rear yard. Driver and two collectors.

Weekly Average Performance:

$$\text{total average weight collected (5 days):} = 46,700 \text{ lb per wk}$$
$$730 \text{ street-access units collected in 750 min} = 1.0274 \text{ min/d.u.}$$
$$565 \text{ alley-access units collected in 360 min} = 0.6372 \text{ min/d.u.}$$

Exhibit 12-II (continued)

City Totals:

$$142{,}950 \text{ street-access units @ } 1.0274 \text{ min/d.u.} = 146{,}866.8 \text{ total min}$$
$$64{,}950 \text{ alley-access units @ } 0.6372 \text{ min/d.u.} = 41{,}384.1 \text{ total min}$$

$$\text{total crew* min to serve city/wk} = 188{,}250.9 \text{ min}$$
$$= 3{,}137.52 \text{ hr}$$

*crew: (same as Method 2, 1 driver and 2 collectors) = $84,360.64

$$\frac{188{,}250.9 \text{ (total crew min/wk)}}{1950 \text{ (working min/crew/wk)}} = 96.54 \text{ crews}$$
needed to serve city

$$96.54 \text{ crews} \times \$84{,}360.64/\text{crew/yr} = \$8{,}144{,}176 \text{ annual labor}$$
cost to serve low-density
residential area of the city

Method 4

Description: Rear-loading truck retrofitted with hydraulic dumpers. Karts set out to street by residents. Driver and two collectors.

Weekly Average Performance:

$$\text{total average weight collected (5 days)} = 48{,}900 \text{ lb per wk}$$
$$730 \text{ street-access units collected in } 470 \text{ min} = 0.6438 \text{ min/d.u.}$$
$$565 \text{ alley-access units collected in } 265 \text{ min} = 0.4690 \text{ min/d.u.}$$

City Totals:

$$142{,}950 \text{ street-access units @ } 0.6438 \text{ min/d.u.} = 92{,}031.2 \text{ total min}$$
$$64{,}950 \text{ alley-access units @ } 0.4690 \text{ min/d.u.} = 30{,}463.3 \text{ total min}$$

$$\text{total crew* min to serve city/wk} = 122{,}494.5 \text{ min}$$
$$= 2{,}041.6 \text{ hr}$$

*crew: (same as Methods 2 and 3, 1 driver and 2 collectors) = $84,360.64

$$\frac{122{,}494.5 \text{ (total crew min/wk)}}{1950 \text{ (working min/crew/wk)}} = 62.82 \text{ crews}$$
needed to serve city

$$62.82 \text{ crews} \times \$84{,}360.64/\text{crew/yr} = \$5{,}299{,}535 \text{ annual labor}$$
cost to serve low-density
residential area of the city

Method 5

Description: Karts set out to street by residents, side-loading vehicle, driver and one collector.

Weekly Average Performance:

$$\text{total average weight collected (5 days)} = 43{,}200 \text{ lb per wk}$$
$$730 \text{ street-access units collected in } 525 \text{ min} = 0.7192 \text{ min/d.u.}$$
$$565 \text{ alley-access units collected in } 410 \text{ min} = 0.7257 \text{ min/d.u.}$$

Exhibit 12-II (continued)

City Totals:

$$
\begin{array}{rcl}
142{,}950 \text{ street-access units @ } 0.7192 \text{ min/d.u.} &=& 102{,}809.6 \text{ total min} \\
64{,}950 \text{ alley-access units @ } 0.7257 \text{ min/d.u.} &=& 47{,}131.9 \text{ total min} \\
\text{total crew* min to serve city/wk} &=& 149{,}941.5 \text{ min} \\
&=& 2{,}499.0 \text{ hr}
\end{array}
$$

$$
\begin{array}{rcl}
\text{*crew: 1 driver @ } \$15.08/\text{hr} \times 2{,}080 \text{ hr/yr} &=& \$31{,}362.24 \\
\text{1 collector @ } \$12.74/\text{hr} \times 2{,}080 \text{ hr/yr} &=& \$26{,}499.20 \\
\text{Total:} && \$57{,}861.44/\text{yr}
\end{array}
$$

$$
\frac{149{,}941.5 \text{ (total crew min/wk)}}{1950 \text{ (working min/crew/wk)}} = \begin{array}{l} 76.89 \text{ crews} \\ \text{needed to serve city} \end{array}
$$

$$
76.89 \text{ crews} \times \$57{,}861.44/\text{crew/yr} = \begin{array}{l} \$4{,}448{,}966 \text{ annual labor} \\ \text{cost to serve low-density} \\ \text{residential area of the city} \end{array}
$$

Chapter Thirteen

Campus Parking Policies[1]

INTRODUCTION

Over 90% of all U.S. workers receive free parking from their employer. Further-more, over 90% of all U.S. employment centers have more parking spaces than employees, as is typically required by local zoning ordinances and the exigencies of development financing. Universities are unlike most other major employment centers in the United States in that ample, free parking is the exception rather than the rule on both urban and rural campuses. The typical U.S. university has on-campus parking at the rate of only one space for every three students, and one for every two faculty and staff members. Most universities charge students, staff, and faculty at least a modest fee for parking privileges, which can range from as little as $10 per year to as much as $100 per month. Urban campuses tend to have relatively fewer parking spaces and higher parking fees, while suburban and rural campuses tend to have relatively more parking spaces and lower parking fees.

[1] This case was written by Erik Ferguson, assistant professor of city planning at Georgia Tech.

THE ASSIGNMENT

The president of the Georgia Institute of Technology has asked you to examine the parking problem on that campus. You decide to conduct a full-cycle policy analysis, from verifying that a problem exists, through specifying evaluation criteria and reasonable alternatives, to conducting an evaluation of the alternatives that you have selected as most reasonable. All of the basic information you need to conduct your analysis is provided in this case. Suggested additional reading material is listed at the end of the case, which provides an overview of parking pricing and supply control theory, methods, and applications.

There are five key constituencies on campus that must be reasonably well satisfied with any solution you propose to the president. These five key constituencies include the 4,000 resident students, 8,000 commuter students, 2,400 staff, and 1,600 faculty who comprise the Tech community at large, as well as the neighborhoods to the north. Your solution must include short-range pricing strategies and long-range investment strategies to deal with key parking and transportation issues you identify. Your proposed solution is constrained, in that the overall parking and transportation budget must be balanced on an annual basis, regardless of the specifics of who pays how much for which services in any given year.

BACKGROUND INFORMATION

Parking Pricing and Supply at Selected National Universities

The supply of parking spaces varies tremendously from one university to another, but in no case exceeds or even approaches the combined number of students, staff, and faculty on campus (Exhibit 13-I). Annualized parking rates vary considerably as well, both within and across universities. Staff and faculty generally pay about the same rate for parking, while students receive discounted rates at most universities. Some urban campuses have few or no parking spaces set aside exclusively for students. The more conveniently located parking spaces are generally reserved for faculty and administrators. Resident students may face additional parking restrictions; for example, the prohibition of freshmen from

access to campus parking during their first year of residency.

Parking Supply and Demand at Georgia Tech

Georgia Tech is an urban campus, located within a mile of the core of Atlanta's downtown, with 12,000 students and 4,000 faculty and staff (Exhibit 13-II). The university recently undertook an ambitious parking construction program, adding over 1,500 parking spaces in two parking decks, at an average construction cost of $4,000 per parking space. To amortize the bonded debt associated with this construction program, separate, higher parking fees were imposed on the newly built Student Center parking deck. In addition to the annual parking permit fee of $100 per vehicle, a daily charge of $1.50 is assessed against anyone on campus wishing to use the new facility. This parking pricing policy led to considerable dissatisfaction, particularly among students, who apparently prefer to park a mile away from the center of campus and walk or take the Stinger shuttle bus, rather than to pay the $1.50 additional charge for daily access to the more centrally located Student Center parking deck. The result has been parking shortages across campus, except in the Student Center parking deck, which often is far from full, even during periods of peak parking demand. The parking and transportation budget is short more than $100,000 in anticipated revenues, principally because of low utilization of the Student Center parking deck.

There are 9,988 parking spaces on campus, of which 6,600 are scramble spaces, 1,328 are short-term daily spaces, 800 are key-card spaces, 600 are reserved spaces, 500 are restricted spaces, 100 are visitor and short-term hourly spaces, and 60 are handicapped spaces. Scramble spaces are open to anyone who has an annual parking permit. Key-card spaces are restricted in access to those who have key cards to gain access to the lot, but are otherwise open to anyone with an annual parking permit. Reserved spaces are identified with a unique number and are assigned to a specific individual on an annual basis. Of the 6,600 scramble spaces distributed across campus, 5,500 are set aside for students, while 1,100 are set aside for faculty and staff. Short-term daily spaces are all located in the Student Center parking deck, and cost $1.50 per day with an annual parking permit, and $3.00 per day without such a permit. Key-card lots and reserved spaces generally are limited in availability to faculty, staff, and doctoral students, and

are assigned on the basis of seniority, rank, and demonstrated need. Miscellaneous parking spaces with special restrictions include those allocated to family housing, the athletic association, the faculty club, the alumni association, and the student infirmary.

Parking demand varies by location, time of day, day of the week, and on a quarterly or seasonal basis. Virtually every lot is full at some time during any given week, but some lots reach capacity more often than others. Parking restrictions typically are enforced only between the hours of 8:00 A.M. and 5:00 P.M., on weekdays during regular academic quarters, from October through June of each academic year. During other time periods, only traffic regulations are enforced, except that requests from reserved space holders to remove illegally parked cars may be honored at any time, and handicapped spaces are always restricted. About 15,000 annual parking permit applications are processed each year. Of the 15,000 annual parking permits sold, 74% are for first vehicles, 15% for second vehicles, 3% for third and additional vehicles, and 8% for replacement vehicles. Only one vehicle per student, staff, or faculty member is allowed on campus at any given time. Enforcement of this provision of the parking code is principally through the honor system. Additional vehicle permits are provided as a courtesy to multiple vehicle owners, who may need to drive more than one vehicle to campus during the course of any given year. Replacement vehicle permits are provided whenever an existing car is lost, stolen, sold, or destroyed by accident, fire, and so on.

Of the 15,000 annual parking permits sold, 49% go to regular students, 9% to cooperative work exchange students, 20%

to staff members, 20% to faculty members, and 2% to various others. Faculty and staff are more likely than students to register additional vehicles. Students must prove ownership of additional vehicles prior to registration. Fully 76% of all annual parking permits are sold in the fall quarter, with 11% sold in the winter quarter, 8% sold in the spring quarter, and 5% sold in the summer quarter. First vehicle registrations are sold most often in the fall quarter. Second, third, and additional vehicle registrations are sold more often in the winter and spring quarters. Replacement vehicle registrations tend to be sold later in the academic year. Faculty are most likely to register their vehicles in the fall quarter, while cooperative work exchange students are least likely to do so at this time. All annual parking permits are nominally valid from October 1, at the beginning of the academic year, through September 30 of the following year. Parking regulations are only loosely enforced during the month of September, to give new members of the Tech community time to acquire knowledge of parking rules and regulations, and to purchase the requisite permits. Average daily weekday utilization of the Student Center parking deck varies significantly on a monthly basis (Exhibit 13-III).

The Annual Parking and Transportation Budget

The sale of annual parking permits generates about $1.15 million in revenues annually. This constitutes well over half of the entire parking and transportation budget (Exhibit 13-IV). The Student Center parking deck provides $160,000 annually through the collection of daily parking fees. Quarterly transportation fees are assessed against all students at a rate of $9 per quarter, providing another $350,000 per year. Transportation fees are used to cover the operating costs for the Stinger shuttle bus and the Stingerette escort van services, which are used primarily by campus residents. The Georgia Tech police chief has expressed some concern about the high rate of parking violations on campus, particularly among students, who comprise well over 90% of all those cited for parking violations on an annual basis. Despite the fairness and objectivity of the Student Parking Appeals Board, and the fact that over half of all parking tickets issued on campus are never paid, the revenues generated from fines assessed against unregistered and illegally parked cars on campus are quite substantial, contributing over $250,000 to the annual parking budget. The cost of enforcing parking regulations is not insignificant, however.

Parking and transportation expenses at Georgia Tech include $946,000 in parking capital expenses, $725,000 in parking operating expenses, and $350,000 in transportation operating expenses. Parking capital expenses include debt service payments for the retirement of parking deck construction bonds (Exhibit 13-V). Parking operating expenses include parking office management costs and parking enforcement costs. Transportation operating expenses are for campus transit services approved and paid for by student government.

The annual registration fee for first vehicles is $100. Cooperative work-exchange students spend less time on campus, for which they receive a 50% discount off the regular rate. For second, third, additional, and replacement vehicles, the fee is $5, which mainly covers the cost of printing additional parking stickers. The fee for second and additional vehicles is kept artificially low to encourage multiple-vehicle owners to register all of their vehicles. This strategy is intended to avoid some of the costs associated with processing requests for courtesy one-day parking permits, as well as to reduce the number of parking violations which can be dismissed through a formal adjudication process. Key-card lot spaces cost an additional $50, reserved spaces an additional $100 per year. Annual parking permit registration fees for first vehicles are prorated, based on the number of quarters remaining in the academic year at the time the permit is sold. All other parking fees are fixed in price, regardless of when sold.

Parking costs include capital, operating, and maintenance costs. Capital costs are $1,000 per space for surface lots, $4,000 per space for above-ground parking decks, and approximately $20,000 per space for subterranean spaces. These costs are somewhat lower than national averages, reflecting lower factor costs for land and labor in Atlanta, as well as the basic designs employed in parking deck construction at Georgia Tech. On an annual basis, parking capital costs are about $400, and parking operating and maintenance costs about $200, for parking decks at Georgia Tech. This includes all costs associated with periodic resurfacing, adequate liability insurance coverage, maintenance, and all other incidental and indirect costs of parking provision.

Transportation and Mobility at Georgia Tech

The Parking and Transportation Advisory Committee of Georgia Tech recently conducted a survey of students, staff, and faculty on transportation and mobility issues. Overall, 358 of 2,000 surveys distributed across campus were returned, yielding an average 17% response rate. Almost 50% of the faculty and staff surveys were returned, while only about 10% of student surveys were returned. Undergraduate students were particularly unlikely to respond, with a 6% average response rate.

Faculty were most likely to drive alone, to park on campus, and to have used the Student Center parking deck (Exhibit 13-VI). Resident students were most likely to use both the Stinger shuttle bus and the Stingerette escort van services provided on campus. Although residents made up only one-third of the total student body, they made up two-thirds of the users of both the Stinger and the Stingerette services. Faculty tended to be the oldest and best-paid members of the Tech community (Exhibit 13-VII). Staff were much more likely than other groups to be female, and somewhat more likely than faculty to have children living with them in Atlanta. Commuter students were more likely to complain about parking location, while resident students were more concerned with parking pricing and related issues (Exhibit 13-VIII).

The number of students, staff, and faculty will not change appreciably at Georgia Tech over the next decade. The 1996 Summer Olympics will take place in Atlanta, and Tech is scheduled to provide 4,000 dormitory rooms in addition to those already on campus, as well as be the site for the Olympic Village and several sports events.

Off-Campus Issues

Local residents in the Home Park neighborhood north of campus have complained of Georgia Tech students and staff parking on the streets in their neighborhood to avoid Tech's annual parking fees. The City of Atlanta would like Tech to deal with the problem internally; for example, through disciplinary measures. Most homes in Home Park are owned by absentee landlords, including Georgia Tech. Many are occupied by Tech students. Tech would like the city to adopt a neighborhood parking permit program, which city police would have to enforce at city expense. In order for Tech to eliminate the problem internally through incentives, all parking on campus would have to be provided free of charge. This would lead to increased parking demand, however, probably in excess of the existing supply of parking spaces on campus. This would then necessitate an increase in the number of parking spaces on campus, most likely through the construction of additional parking decks. Otherwise, parking demand would spill out on to the local streets again, even with free parking. Monitoring and surveillance of the Home Park area by Tech campus police would likewise entail significant costs.

The President's Mandate

The president of Georgia Tech, a policy analyst by training, recently attended a joint meeting of the Parking Rate Committee and the Transportation and Parking Advisory Committee of Georgia Tech. The president delivered the following critique of current parking pricing policy:

1. Current parking prices do not reflect real opportunity costs or relative values for either surface lots or parking structures.
2. Current parking prices cover only current costs, with no provision for reserves to fund new construction, as needed.

3. Where demand exceeds supply on campus under current parking prices, a priority scheme is used to allocate resources.
4. Reserved spaces for faculty and staff are assigned on an ad hoc basis.[2]

The president suggested basing a revised parking policy on comparisons with experience from other urban campuses around the country. The president recommended developing relative prices first, and then multiplying such relative prices by a fixed term to equate total system revenues with total system costs. The president further identified this case as a classic example of a rational economic pricing problem.

A special task force is being set up at the request of the president to study this problem. The task force will be asked to propose parking pricing and investment criteria and solutions that are equitable to all members of the Tech community and that are efficient from a parking and transportation management perspective. As a member of the president's staff, you have been asked to take the lead on this problem and to develop a report on the subject to the president and the two committees meeting in joint session within two weeks.

GUIDELINES FOR ANALYSIS

1. Develop a simple mathematical model of parking pricing at Georgia Tech.
2. Use the material provided in the case to test your model for accuracy and reliability.
3. Incorporate salient political factors into your analysis.
4. Evaluate the distributional consequences of

---

[2] The president, in fact, was a bit more direct than this. For learning purposes, we have left a little of the preliminary policy analysis done by the president for the student to do as part of the case solution.

parking pricing and investment alternatives using your model.

5. Take a firm position on which parking pricing and investment strategy is best, even though it may be controversial to some or all members of the campus community.

FINAL REPORT

1. Due within two weeks.
2. Use the six-step policy analysis process in its entirety.
3. Prepare a one-page executive summary. Identify in it the problems, criteria, alternatives, and evaluation methods you used.
4. Separate findings from recommendations, and limit your report to no more than 10 to 12 pages in length, typed, double spaced. Place all illustrations, graphics, and tables in a separate appendix.
5. Use subheadings liberally, avoid the use of technical jargon, be succinct, and present relevant data and statistics clearly. Lay out tables that are easy to read, sum to 100%, and so on.

SOURCE MATERIAL

The following readings may assist you in developing a conceptual framework for your analysis. Shoup (1982) provides an overview of pricing theory applied to parking. Surber et al. (1984) describe a case study of parking pricing implementation for a single firm. Mehranian et al. (1987) comparatively analyze two firms in the same location with different parking pricing policies. Feeney (1989) introduces the concept of locational differences as key determinants of parking policy effectiveness. Ferguson (1990) outlines the context of transportation policy in which parking pricing is set, and describes some of the dynamic aspects of parking utilization.

FEENEY, BERNARD. "A Review of the Impact of Parking Policy Measures on Travel Demand." *Transportation Planning and Technology* 13, no. 4 (February 1989), 229–44.

FERGUSON, ERIK. "Transportation Demand Management: Planning, Development and Implementation." *Journal of the American Planning Association* 56, no. 4 (Fall 1990), 442–56.

MEHRANIAN, MARIA, MARTIN WACHS, DONALD SHOUP, and RICHARD PLATKIN. "Parking Cost and Mode Choice among Downtown Workers: A Case Study." *Transportation Research Record* 1130 (1987), 1–5.

SHOUP, DONALD. "Cashing Out Free Parking." *Transportation Quarterly* 36, no. 3 (July 1982), 351–64.

SURBER, MONICA, DONALD SHOUP, and MARTIN WACHS. "Effects of Ending Employer-Paid Parking for Solo Drivers." *Transportation Research Record* 957 (1984), 67–71.

EXHIBITS

Exhibit 13-I   Parking Pricing and Supply at Selected Universities

University	NUMBER			ANNUAL PARKING RATES		
	Students	Faculty/ Staff	Parking Spaces	Faculty	Staff	Students
Auburn University	21,700	4,100	9,200	$30	$20	$15
California State University-Long Beach	33,000	4,000	12,500	$144	$144	$180
Cleveland State University	18,500	1,500	5,000	$252	$252	n/a
Duke University	10,900	6,000	6,200	$120–$200	$120–$200	$50–$75
Florida State University	27,700	5,100	7,900	$53–$150	$53–$150	$10–$28
Georgetown University	12,000	7,000	3,600	$352–$502	$352–502	$177–$376
George Washington University	18,000	4,500	3,000	$900	$900	$1,296
Georgia Institute of Technology	12,000	4,000	10,000	$100–$200	$100–$200	$100
Georgia State University	23,500	2,500	3,200	$200	$200	n/a
Syracuse University	10,000	6,200	4,100	$26–$172	$26–$172	$32–$130
University of California-Irvine	16,400	4,000	8,000	$276–$420	$276–$420	$90–$315
University of Florida	17,400	3,000	17,000	$80–$400	$80–$400	$20–$120
University of Georgia	26,000	5,000	14,000	$72–$120	$66–$114	$9–$15
University of Houston	32,300	4,000	13,300	$70–$140	$70–$140	$10–$70
University of Kentucky	27,000	8,900	16,000	$48–$72	$48–$72	$20–$40
University of North California	26,400	7,000	12,400	$60–$300	$60–$300	$60–$120
University of Pennsylvania	14,000	2,100	9,000	$318–$540	$318–$540	$318–$716
University of Virginia	16,500	6,000	12,300	$48–$180	$48–$180	$30
Wayne State University	32,500	6,952	10,000	$180–$420	$180–$420	n/a

Source: Based on a telephone survey conducted by Georgia Tech in October 1989.

n/a = not applicable.

Exhibit 13-II Georgia Tech Campus

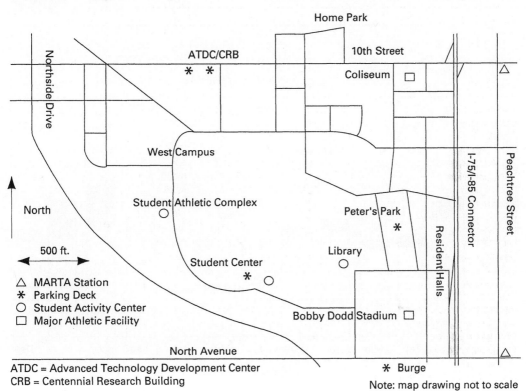

Home Park

ATDC/CRB

10th Street

Coliseum

Northside Drive

West Campus

North

500 ft.

△ MARTA Station
✳ Parking Deck
○ Student Activity Center
□ Major Athletic Facility

Student Athletic Complex

Peter's Park

Library

Student Center

Bobby Dodd Stadium

Resident Halls

I-75/I-85 Connector

Peachtree Street

North Avenue

ATDC = Advanced Technology Development Center
CRB = Centennial Research Building

✳ Burge

Note: map drawing not to scale

Exhibit 13-III   Student Center Parking Deck Utilization

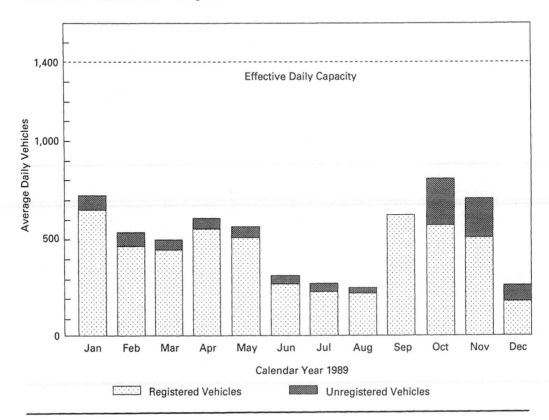

Exhibit 13-IV AY 89–90 Georgia Tech Parking and Transportation Budget (in thousands of dollars)

Budget Line Item	Subtotals	Totals
Parking and transportation revenues by source[a]		
Parking revenues		
Annual vehicle registration permit fees		1,155
Faculty	250	
Staff	225	
Commuter students	400	
Resident students	280	
Keycard parking lot fees		35
Reserved parking space fees		60
Violations (fines and penalties)		250
Daily parking fees (Student Center parking deck)		160
Athletic event parking revenues		35
Miscellaneous parking revenues		25
Total parking revenues		1,720
Quarterly student transportation fees		350
Total projected parking and transportation revenue		2,070
Parking and transportation expenses by source[b]		
Parking costs		
Total capital expenses		946
Peter's parking deck	288	
CRB/ATDC parking decks[c]	108	
Student Center/Burge parking decks	550	
Total operating expenses		725
Personal services	500	
OS & E[d]	100	
Indirect (POD)[e]	41	
Reserve account (5%)	84	
Total parking expenses		1,671
Transportation costs		
Stinger bus operations (private contract)		240
Stingerette escort service (student operated)		75
Reserve account (5%)		35
Total transportation expenses		350
Total parking and transportation expenses		2,021

[a] There is no charge for using the Stinger bus and Stingerette escort van services. As a result, there are no revenues associated with the operation of these services.
[b] These will be approximately the same for all pricing alternatives.
[c] Centennial Research Building/Advanced Technology Development Center.
[d] Office supplies and equipment.
[e] Plant operations department.

Exhibit 13-V Annual Capital Expenditures for Parking

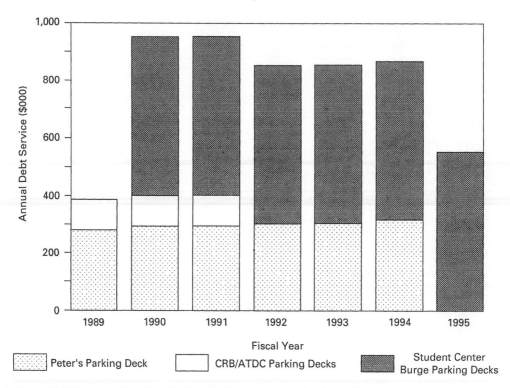

Exhibit 13-VI Travel Behavior by Tech Affiliation

Travel Behavior Characteristics	Resident Students	Commuter Students	Staff Members	Faculty Members
Current mode(s) of travel to Tech[a]				
Drive alone in auto	23%	74%	74%	88%
Share the ride in auto	0%	18%	18%	11%
Walk	91%	18%	4%	3%
Bicycle	5%	11%	0%	1%
MARTA Rapid Rail	0%	8%	7%	6%
MARTA bus	0%	6%	8%	6%
Stinger shuttle bus	28%	6%	1%	0%
Has car available for personal use	77%	91%	89%	97%
Would park on campus, if free	81%	86%	89%	97%
Currently park on campus	30%	75%	84%	91%
Ever parked in Student Center deck	12%	17%	16%	21%
Ever used the Stinger shuttle bus	95%	52%	35%	23%
Ever used the Stingerette escort van	53%	14%	4%	1%

[a] Multiple response possible.

Exhibit 13-VII Demographics by Tech Affiliation

Demographic Characteristics	Resident Students	Commuter Students	Staff Members	Faculty Members
Median 1989 personal income	$5,000	$10,000	$27,000	$52,000
Mean age, in years	21	27	38	43
Male	72%	78%	39%	78%
Female	28%	22%	61%	22%
Married	2%	30%	55%	77%
Not married	98%	70%	45%	23%
With children	2%	9%	49%	45%
Without children	98%	91%	51%	55%

Exhibit 13-VIII Comments on Parking and Transportation by Tech Affiliation

Comments on Parking and Transportation[a]	Resident Students	Commuter Students	Staff Members	Faculty Members
Parking supply is too low for me	23%	34%	28%	22%
Student Center parking deck issues[b]	16%	24%	8%	7%
Parking price is too high for me	23%	18%	20%	11%
Parking price is not fair to me, others	14%	16%	3%	4%
All clearly favorable comments[c]	0%	6%	2%	5%
Need better transportation alternatives	0%	6%	0%	3%
Need better parking code enforcement	5%	5%	6%	4%
Need better campus transit services	14%	4%	3%	4%
Parking supply is too high for others	9%	3%	11%	2%
Need better campus security services	5%	1%	3%	3%
Need better parking amenities[d]	5%	0%	0%	2%
Need better access to MARTA[e]	0%	0%	1%	1%
No response	23%	28%	45%	54%

[a] Based on a completely open-ended question. Multiple response possible.
[b] Mainly price (too high) and availability (too low, at least in terms of being available free of charge).
[c] Such as "the Stinger is really great!" and so on.
[d] Paving of gravel lots near West Campus dorms, and so on.
[e] The nearest MARTA rail station is more than a 1/2 mile walk from the center of campus.

Chapter Fourteen

Emergency Aid for Home Fuel: Developing an Allocation Formula

INTRODUCTION

In the late 1970s a number of agencies within the federal government had become aware of the rising costs of fuel to heat houses of the poor and near-poor in this country. While total winterization (insulation, caulking, weatherstripping and insulating storm windows) may be the most cost-effective long-term solution for minimizing heating bills, it was clear that some individuals might freeze to death waiting for the insulation truck to arrive. Clearly, the needs of some poverty households were so pressing that only immediate counseling and financial aid would save them from discomfort, draft-related illnesses, and, in the case of older persons, the possibility of temperature-related deaths.

Responding to this need, the federal government, through the Community Services Administration (CSA), initiated a program of energy counseling and cash/credit subsidies to poverty households through the Crisis Intervention Program. The program was developed as a response to a number of factors that included the prediction of an extremely severe winter heating season; a growing constituency of voting older persons; the 140% increase in fuel costs over the previous six years; a well-articulated snow belt position on the biased distributional consequences of other federal programs; increasing discontent with the CSA's inability to identify and serve the poor; and finally, the deaths of seven older New York State residents due to utility disconnections. The final legislation contained the following elements: a state-based voucher system to provide up to $250 per household to pay existing or future bills, and an alternative $50 cash payment to households that paid their bills but were now experiencing hardship as a result (the Anderson amendment).

THE ASSIGNMENT[1]

The time is now the 1990s, and there continues to be a national program, but it is administered by the individual 50 states. The states receive funds based on criteria contained in the legislation. (See the letter from CSA Director Olivarez to all governors contained on Exhibit 14-I.) The setting for this case is the State of Wisconsin, which spent about $50 million on the program in 1990.

You are a policy planner on the staff of the county executive of a Wisconsin county. The counties to be staffed are:

- *Milwaukee*: a strictly urban county in the southeastern part of the state, containing the state's largest city, Milwaukee, and its only sizable poor minority population. It is also the site of the University of Wisconsin–Milwaukee.
- *Dane*: a primarily urban county with a rural component located 90 miles west of Milwaukee. The county includes Madison, the state's second largest city, which is the state capital and the site of the University of Wisconsin–Madison.
- *Rusk*: a primarily rural county (one of the least populated), whose largest city is about 4,000. It is located in a cold part of the state, the northwest/central region.

You have been invited by an administrator of the State's Office of Economic Opportunity (OEO), along with the planners for the two other counties, to participate in updating the state's action plan, which has as its central charge the development of a formula to allocate portions of the $50 million on a county-by-county basis. The formula and the resulting plan should be defensible in a number of respects. First, it should provide an efficient distribution of funds to the counties that can use them. All unspent monies must be returned to the state, pooled, and used for weatherization programs. However, a lack of success in getting the money to the poor is likely to be interpreted as a state's noncompliance with the legislation's mandates and could result in a loss of funds in the future. Second, the formula should provide an equitable distribution of funds that responds to the "needs" of each county, somehow defined and measured. Elderly poverty households, as well as the handicapped, are to be served "first and primarily," but there are no national guidelines for implementing this. Third, the plan must win the approval of some of the other 72 counties, many of which are paying close attention to the development of the plan. Specifically, at the

---

[1]The emergency aid program has changed dramatically since it was initiated in the early 1970s, but the lessons from the case remain valid.

meeting to which you have been invited, it will be essential to win at least partial concurrence of the planners from the other two counties represented as well as from the OEO administrator. The administrator, of course, will make the final decision.

THE SPECIFIC TASKS

You are to produce three specific products:

1. A memorandum to be sent to the state OEO administrator (with copies to the planners representing the other two counties) that presents the formula you propose be used to allocate portions of the $50 million to Wisconsin's 72 counties. Be sure to display the dollar allocation that results from your formula for each of the three counties to be represented at the meeting, and the rest of the counties in the state lumped together. Provide a succinct rationale for your formula. This memo should not exceed three double-spaced typed pages.

2. Materials, including index-card notes and poster-sized tables and charts, that will allow you to present the contents of the above memorandum in a succinct way at the meeting with OEO officials. You will be given about ten minutes at the meeting to present your formula and your rationale. You should have this oral presentation carefully planned. There will be a good number of state staff people in attendance.

3. A memorandum of a maximum of 10 double-spaced pages, not including appendices you may wish to add, to be sent to your boss, the county executive, that:

    (a) Develops a needs assessment of your specific county for this program and attempts to quantify that need as well as the data allow.

    (b) Attaches the memo to OEO, and analyzes for your county executive why you have developed the formula you have, and where it may be open to criticism.

    (c) Prepares your county executive for the inevitable telephone calls that will come asking for compromises in the allocation formula. Specifically you need to prepare the executive for selecting the factors on

which ground can be given, those that should not be changed without a fight, and those on which to be indifferent. Again, the executive will want to get as much of the state's $50 million as possible in order to address the county's needs, subject to all the other constraints mentioned above.

    (d) Gives a preliminary plan for how this program can be successfully implemented in your county. This is very preliminary but is essential because it is not clear that once you get your allocation you'll be able to allocate all of it without problems. Once the state gets the $50 million, it will have only one month to spend it. See the program guidelines supplied in Exhibit 14-1. Remember that the elderly are often the most difficult to serve. You have less than 1% of the monies available to provide advertising for this one-month program. Overspending will have to be paid for out of other county funds. Underspending will document your county's evident lack of need and the monies will return to the state, with no guarantee that you will receive them again.

You should develop a written response and strategy that clearly serves your county, but remains politically viable for the rest of the state. A purely parochial plan has an extremely low probability of acceptance. Be especially aware of the characteristics of the other two counties involved in the meeting.

The potential for fraud is extremely high at the service level, and administrative costs for program implementation are negligible.

Above all, time is short. Counties in

Wisconsin have less than two weeks to digest and analyze the latest state plan before it goes to CSA.

SOURCE MATERIAL

A wealth of data is available that characterizes individuals, households, families, and other items for Wisconsin counties and the State of Wisconsin as a whole. Several important sources are listed below. There are many more.

U.S. BUREAU OF THE CENSUS, *County and City Data Book*, 1988. Washington, DC: U.S. Government Printing Office, 1988. Also available on floppy disk.

U.S. BUREAU OF THE CENSUS, *Census of Housing, 1980, Vol. 1, Housing Characteristics for States, Cities, and Counties: Part 51, Wisconsin.* Washington, DC: U.S. Government Printing Office, 1980.

U.S. BUREAU OF THE CENSUS, *Census of Population: 1980 Vol. 1, Characteristics of the Population, Part 51, Wisconsin.* Washington, DC: U.S. Government Printing Office, 1980.

EXHIBITS

Exhibit 14-I   Letter from CSA Director Olivarez to All Governors[2]

Community Services Administration

Washington, DC 20506

MEMORANDUM

TO: ALL GOVERNORS

FROM: G. G. Olivarez, Director

Special Crisis Intervention Program funds are now available for relieving part of the energy cost burden that has fallen most heavily on the poor and near-poor as a result of the recent severe weather and escalating energy prices.

Allocations among the states were made using a formula provided by the Congress. The formula included population-weighted heating degree days, number of elderly persons with incomes no higher than 150% of the poverty guideline (see Attachment 1), number of poor and near-poor households, and the cost of fuel. Since all the outstanding energy/fuel bills of the poor and near-poor cannot be paid with these funds, priority shall be given to eligible elderly persons (age 65 and over).

Because this is an emergency program of very short lifespan, the Community Services Administration will make one grant in each state, preferably to an existing grantee such as the State

Economic Opportunity Office, so as to avoid time-consuming procedures required before new grantees can be funded.

As the Senate report that accompanied the Supplemental Appropriations bill states:

> Governors shall administer this program by utilizing Community Action Agencies and other appropriate State and local public or private agencies. These agencies shall, in allocating emergency assistance funds, give particular consideration to those cases in which emergency assistance can be coordinated with weatherization assistance. Wherever possible, the emergency assistance funds should be allocated so as to contribute to the agency's long-term goal of promoting energy conservation in the homes of low-income and near-poor families and individuals.

[2]This memorandum has been edited and revised to conform to the current version of the case.

Exhibit 14-I *(continued)*

The Senate report calls on governors to "assure that the greatest household needs are met first." For this reason, particular care should be taken to select agencies that will be able to provide effective services to the elderly, to persons not on welfare, and in remote rural areas. Households receiving assistance must have incomes no higher than 150% of the poverty guideline.

As described by Congress, the Special Crisis Intervention Program funds may be used only for (1) payments directly to eligible households and/or (2) payments to utility companies and fuel dealers on behalf of eligible households for energy/fuel supplies. In this connection the Senate report states:

> Governors shall make available to local administering agencies such nonfederal support as the local agencies deem necessary, not to exceed an amount up to 10% of the federal funds to provide for proper certification of the eligibility and need of recipients.

In rare instances where administrative costs may exceed 10%, the state may require the Local Administering Agency to absorb the extra costs. We do not believe it is the intent of Congress to limit the nature of the administrative assistance supplied to the Local Administering Agencies by governors for determination of income and program eligibility to resources not funded by the federal government; rather, that the term *nonfederal support* is intended merely to isolate and safeguard the Special Crisis Intervention Program funds from being spent for administrative costs.

Funds granted to your state but that cannot be effectively obligated for crisis intervention by the expiration date will be reprogrammed, for support of weatherization activities in your state. Reprogrammed funds should be spent in a manner consistent with an approved state emergency energy conservation funding plan for carrying out the Weatherization Program under Section 222(a)(12) of the Economic Opportunity Act of 1964, as amended. Any funds reprogrammed for weatherization would be subject to existing CSA nonfederal share requirements.

Program Design: Two categories of eligible households may be served by the Special Crisis Intervention Program:

1. Those who, because of large unpaid energy/fuel bills, have had their utilities shut off, are threatened with shutoff or are threatened with inability to obtain delivery of heating fuel. For this category, a one-time payment of up to $350 may be made on behalf of the household. Payments must be made directly to utility companies and fuel suppliers.

2. Those who can prove dire financial need at time of application as a result of having paid large energy/fuel bills in whole or in part. A one-time payment of up to $100 may be made directly to eligible households in this category. In addition, a one-time payment, not to exceed the balance of the allowable $350, may be made on behalf of the household as a credit toward future deliveries; these payments must be made directly to utility companies and fuel dealers.

Limitation on Payments: The sum of all payments made to and/or on behalf of any eligible household described in (1) or (2) above may not exceed $350.

No payment made under this program shall be considered income for the purpose of determining eligibility or benefits under any income transfer program including, but not limited to, public assistance, veterans' benefits, food stamps, or Supplemental Security Income.

In submitting the Request For Funds, you will be agreeing to provide administrative support in amounts up to 10% of the amount of the grant as deemed necessary by the local administering agencies.

Your State Funding Plan for the Special Crisis Intervention Program should be in preparation. No funds can actually be released to you until this plan is received and approved. Your state plan should be a brief document that must include but is not limited to the following elements.

1. Allocation of Funds by Substate Area: Please provide both a percentage and dollar amount breakdown by county. (The total dollar allocation for Wisconsin is $50 million.)

Exhibit 14-I (*continued*)

2. Disbursement Mechanism and Safeguards: The plan must include a description of the mechanism by which you propose to disburse the funds to ensure that:

A. No coin or currency will be exchanged;
B. No eligible household will receive assistance in excess of $350;
C. Certification for payment will be made to utilities and fuel dealers only after verification of amounts owed or paid;
D. Certification for payment by the local administering agency will be final and will constitute obligation of funds unless duplication or fraud is evidenced;
E. Local Administering Agencies do not certify assistance in excess of the total sum that you authorize them to obligate;
F. No payments are made under this program to households having access to direct assistance through other supportive service networks, such as welfare, except in cases when such other networks cannot respond in an effective and timely manner;
G. All Local Administering Agencies will notify, inform, contact and, where appropriate, certify eligible households with persons unable to leave their residences due to handicap, infirmity;
H. Households in remote rural areas will receive timely notification of the program and will be provided ample opportunity for full participation.

3. Monitoring: A description of the state's methods that you will require for monitoring of the program at the local level, for initial and immediate investigation of charges involving poor administration of the program, faulty or inadequate certification, failure of energy suppliers to provide relief, and duplication and/or fraud. Specify which agency (agencies) will have this responsibility. Provide the mailing address and telephone number of the contact person in the responsible agency or agencies. Please include a procedure for notifying the appropriate CSA Regional Office of the initiation of an investigation and of the outcome of all such investigations.

4. Certification of Agreements Reached: Completion of a certification, following the enclosed format that agreements have been reached with participating utility companies and fuel suppliers to ensure that in each case where payment is certified:

1. The outstanding bill is reduced by the full amount of the Special Crisis Intervention Program payment;
2. For any remaining balance, the customer is offered a deferred payment arrangement;
3. A reconnection charge, to be paid by the customer, is made only where such a charge is company practice;
4. No security deposit is required to be paid except where such a deposit is required by state law or explicit state regulation; and finally,
5. Reconnection of service is made upon certification for payment and satisfaction of the above requirements.

Review and Approval of State Funding Plans: Review and Approval of State Plans will be limited to making sure that plans include all required elements, and that they are in accord with applicable law and regulations.

Attachment 1 Poverty Guidelines for Wisconsin Households, 1990

	ANNUAL HOUSEHOLD INCOME	
Household Size	100% of Poverty	150% of Poverty
1	$ 5,980	$ 8,970
2	$ 8,020	$12,030
3	$10,060	$15,090
4	$12,100	$18,150
5	$14,140	$21,210
6	$16,180	$24,270
7	$18,220	$27,330
8	$20,260	$30,390
For each person above eight, add:	$ 2,040	$ 3,060

Exhibit 14-II   Internal Memorandum / State OEO[3]

TO: The files
FROM: Chris Baker
          Staff Analyst
RE: Heating fuel disconnections forecasted
          by county

The status of disconnection data:

1. For natural gas and electricity we have for each county the number of actual disconnections reported within the past six months. Most of these disconnections occurred right after the lifting of the winter moratorium. These data are sound.

2. For liquid propane (LP) and fuel oil we had no data, so we ran a survey of seven counties and have extrapolated the results to all counties. This will be explained below.

We recently surveyed seven sample counties to determine the number of households (by county) that have been refused fuel service or are on a cash-only basis. The counties surveyed were Bayfield, Chippewa, Columbia, La Crosse, Marathon, Outagamie, and Ozaukee. One county was selected from each of the seven emergency government divisions in the state. They represent a mix of urban–rural and wealthy–less wealthy counties. The county emergency government director for those counties conducted a telephone survey of all fuel oil and LP dealers in the respective counties. Information collected included:

1. Number of dealers
2. Number of households served
3. Number of households refused service or on a cash-only basis
4. Number of households that are expected to fall into a cash only or no-service offered status within a few weeks

The results are shown in Table 1.
Jan Ericksen and I met to evaluate the data collected and to determine the best way to use it in a statewide extrapolation. We noted a positive correlation, not unexpected, between median

county income and percentage of households disconnected for each county. The survey's average percentage of "nonserviced households by county" came to 5.05%, which is very close to the 4% figure that was supplied to my office when the fuel oil and LP dealers association was queried as to the number of customers who are refused service or are on a cash-only basis.

Since income decreases as the percentage of households refused service increases, we decided to use a sliding factor (range = 2.74% to 7.11%) to forecast oil and LP disconnections by county. We first forecast the percentage disconnections by county and then multiplied that factor times the number of oil and LP customers in that county. Those results are shown in Table 2. Note that the discrepancy in number of customers served in Tables 1 and 2 is accounted for by two facts. First, dealers are reported by county, but their customers may be from several counties. Second, customers in Table 1 are only the customers of the dealers surveyed. And this survey was not of all dealers.

Finally, we added together for each county our projected oil and LP gas disconnections and the actual electricity and natural gas disconnections to get the total number of estimated disconnections. These results are exhibited in Table 3.

Having surveyed many fuel dealers, a few of their insights and opinions are worth noting. These include:

1. Dealers agreed that they experienced much higher than usual numbers of nonpayments this past winter—probably due to weather severity and increasing fuel costs.

2. Some dealers have reservations about the program. Their greatest concern is that once the government agrees to pay past fuel bills, it may deter customer payments in the future. They desire that it be stated plainly that this is one-time assistance.

[3]This is a fictitious memo based on several actual memoranda.

3. Another area that most dealers felt was a great problem was that welfare people who receive a block grant are free to spend it as they see fit. It seems that these people spend their funds for food, shelter, and sundries. Allowances for fuel come last and by then there isn't any money left. The lack of concern could be caused by the fact that these people are aware that no one will be allowed to freeze in Wisconsin. State or federal action may be required to deal with this.

4. The previous administration of fuel funds by Community Action Program (CAP) agencies was brought up often. Most cases where CAP authorized fuel, it was in the amount of 50 gallons. It is not profitable for the oil dealers to deliver such a small amount. Some refuse to deliver, while others do it but at a personal loss.

5. Dealers are concerned that when the $50 million program is announced to pay back bills there will be a storm of applications. They want reassurance that guidelines will be set up.

Table 1   LP—Fuel Oil Survey, 1990

County	Number of Customers Served by Dealers Surveyed	Anticipated Number of Cut-offs	Percentage	County 1989 Median Household Income
Bayfield	3,460	370	10.6	$11,768
Chippewa	13,790	1,539	11.2	15,203
Columbia	11,060	802	7.2	16,385
La Crosse	18,150	107	0.6	15,900
Marathon	19,150	454	2.4	17,344
Outagamie	20,000	300	1.5	19,415
Ozaukee	6,425	127	1.9	25,554

Table 2 Forecasted LP and Fuel Oil Disconnections by County, 1990

Wisconsin County	Median 1979 Household Income	Number of LP and Fuel Oil Customers	Projected Disconnection Rate	Projected Number of Disconnections
Adams	$12,990	2,616	5.44%	142
Ashland	$11,666	3,275	6.06%	199
Barron	$13,421	7,594	5.27%	400
Bayfield	$11,768	942	6.01%	57
Brown	$18,595	11,184	3.80%	425
Buffalo	$13,422	3,573	5.27%	188
Burnett	$11,129	2,836	6.35%	180
Calumet	$20,452	3,816	3.46%	132
Chippewa	$15,203	10,338	4.65%	481
Clark	$12,805	6,814	5.52%	376
Columbia	$16,385	8,651	4.32%	373
Crawford	$12,300	3,379	5.75%	194
Dane	$18,309	38,124	3.86%	1,473
Dodge	$18,126	11,808	3.90%	461
Door	$15,802	4,442	4.48%	199
Douglas	$15,066	7,749	4.69%	364
Dunn	$13,871	6,337	5.10%	323
Eau Claire	$15,300	13,459	4.62%	622
Florence	$11,903	864	5.94%	51
Fond du Lac	$18,159	11,676	3.89%	455
Forest	$11,214	1,256	6.31%	79
Grant	$15,122	10,100	4.68%	472
Green	$16,766	6,271	4.22%	265
Green Lake	$15,057	2,769	4.70%	130
Iowa	$14,350	4,283	4.93%	211
Iron	$ 9,944	1,595	7.11%	113
Jackson	$12,574	3,726	5.62%	210
Jefferson	$18,206	8,583	3.88%	333
Juneau	$12,528	3,845	5.64%	217
Kenosha	$20,084	9,229	3.52%	325
Kewaunee	$16,519	3,434	4.28%	147
La Crosse	$15,900	14,149	4.45%	629
Lafayette	$15,224	3,936	4.65%	183
Langlade	$12,738	3,759	5.55%	209
Lincoln	$14,267	4,251	4.96%	211
Manitowoc	$17,622	7,473	4.01%	300
Marathon	$17,344	14,220	4.08%	580
Marinette	$13,945	5,824	5.07%	295
Marquette	$12,586	2,012	5.62%	113
Menominee	$13,352	370	5.30%	20
Milwaukee	$18,122	83,328	3.90%	3,252
Monroe	$15,095	6,616	4.68%	310
Oconto	$13,463	4,627	5.25%	243
Oneida	$14,521	4,514	4.87%	220
Outagamie	$19,415	17,693	3.64%	644
Ozaukee	$25,554	6,600	2.77%	183
Pepin	$13,902	1,695	5.09%	86
Pierce	$16,801	6,037	4.21%	254
Polk	$14,106	6,428	5.01%	322
Portage	$16,659	6,937	4.25%	294
Price	$11,947	3,996	5.92%	237
Racine	$20,944	16,996	3.38%	574
Richland	$13,229	4,158	5.35%	222
Rock	$19,154	15,929	3.69%	588
Rusk	$11,565	2,828	6.12%	173
St. Croix	$19,568	7,818	3.61%	283
Sauk	$15,507	9,236	4.56%	421
Sawyer	$11,118	2,836	6.36%	180
Shawano	$13,932	7,414	5.08%	376
Sheboygan	$18,719	11,089	3.78%	419
Taylor	$14,217	3,691	4.97%	184
Trempealeau	$13,566	5,857	5.21%	305
Vernon	$12,546	5,930	5.64%	334
Vilas	$12,373	2,943	5.72%	168
Walworth	$17,457	8,047	4.05%	326
Washburn	$12,046	2,928	5.87%	172
Washington	$21,989	9,422	3.22%	303
Waukesha	$25,827	29,058	2.74%	796
Waupaca	$15,286	8,075	4.63%	374
Waushara	$12,734	3,295	5.55%	183
Winnebago	$18,063	13,866	3.92%	543
Wood	$17,482	12,413	4.05%	502
WISCONSIN	$17,680			

Table 3 Total Number of Disconnected Households Estimated by County, 1990

Wisconsin County	Public Service Commission Reported Gas and Electricity Disconnections	Number of LP and Fuel Oil Estimated Disconnections	Total Estimated Disconnections	Wisconsin County	Public Service Commission Reported Gas and Electricity Disconnections	Number of LP and Fuel Oil Estimated Disconnections	Total Estimated Disconnections
Adams	42	142	184	Marinette	80	295	375
Ashland	6	199	205	Marquette	17	113	130
Barron	41	400	441	Menominee	10	20	30
Bayfield	33	57	90	Milwaukee	9,060	3,252	12,312
Brown	292	425	717	Monroe	60	310	370
Buffalo	15	188	203	Oconto	40	243	283
Burnett	0	180	180	Oneida	84	220	304
Calumet	19	132	151	Outagamie	160	644	804
Chippewa	45	481	526	Ozaukee	112	183	295
Clark	38	376	414	Pepin	6	86	92
Columbia	56	373	429	Pierce	29	254	283
Crawford	3	194	197	Polk	45	322	367
Dane	360	1,473	1,833	Portage	72	294	366
Dodge	120	461	581	Price	14	237	251
Door	43	199	242	Racine	278	574	852
Douglas	25	364	389	Richland	7	222	229
Dunn	35	323	358	Rock	100	588	688
Eau Claire	165	622	787	Rusk	18	173	191
Florence	0	51	51	St. Croix	20	283	303
Fond du Lac	75	455	530	Sauk	21	421	442
Forest	23	79	102	Sawyer	42	180	222
Grant	20	472	492	Shawano	29	376	405
Green	33	265	298	Sheboygan	178	419	597
Green Lake	30	130	160	Taylor	5	184	189
Iowa	7	211	218	Trempealeau	26	305	331
Iron	15	113	128	Vernon	6	334	340
Jackson	12	210	222	Vilas	40	168	208
Jefferson	68	333	401	Walworth	300	326	626
Juneau	5	217	222	Washburn	2	172	174
Kenosha	132	325	457	Washington	145	303	448
Kewaunee	26	147	173	Waukesha	192	796	988
La Crosse	185	629	814	Waupaca	32	374	406
Lafayette	6	183	189	Waushara	15	183	198
Langlade	44	209	253	Winnebago	192	543	735
Lincoln	51	211	262	Wood	40	502	542
Manitowoc	105	300	405				
Marathon	148	580	728	WISCONSIN	13,800	25,609	39,409

Exhibit 14-III Estimated Percentages of Types of Fuel Used for Home Heating, by County, State of Wisconsin, 1990

FUEL TYPE	COUNTY			
	Dane	Milwaukee	Rusk	State of Wisconsin
Piped gas	50%	70%	10%	50%
Fuel oil and kerosene	42%	24%	65%	39%
LP gas	4%	1%	15%	6%
Electricity	2%	2%	1%	2%
Coal or coke	—	3%	—	2%
Other, including wood	—	—	9%	1%

Exhibit 14-IV Heating Degree Days by County, State of Wisconsin, Averages for 1951–1980 (Base Temperature 65°)

Adams	7,978	Iowa	7,484	Polk	8,480
Ashland	9,091	Iron	9,169	Portage	7,945
Barron	8,658	Jackson	8,107	Price	9,249
Bayfield	8,764	Jefferson	7,141	Racine	7,142
Brown	8,143	Juneau	8,312	Richland	7,518
Buffalo	7,990	Kenosha	7,090	Rock	6,687
Burnett	9,042	Kewaunee	7,869	Rusk	8,742
Calumet	7,543	La Crosse	7,540	St. Croix	8,093
Chippewa	8,409	Lafayette	7,285	Sauk	7,674
Clark	8,804	Langlade	8,624	Sawyer	9,854
Columbia	7,750	Lincoln	8,765	Shawano	7,953
Crawford	7,016	Manitowoc	7,589	Sheboygan	7,388
Dane	7,423	Marathon	8,565	Taylor	8,911
Dodge	7,166	Marinette	7,963	Trempealeau	7,829
Door	7,898	Marquette	7,811	Vernon	7,601
Douglas	9,305	Menominee	8,200	Vilas	9,100
Dunn	7,913	Milwaukee	7,053	Walworth	6,909
Eau Claire	8,463	Monroe	7,802	Washburn	8,811
Florence	9,527	Oconto	8,024	Washington	7,525
Fond du Lac	7,568	Oneida	9,236	Waukesha	7,240
Forest	8,746	Outagamie	7,753	Waupaca	7,751
Grant	7,229	Ozaukee	7,301	Waushara	8,016
Green	7,365	Pepin	8,115	Winnebago	7,692
Green Lake	7,667	Pierce	8,093	Wood	8,336

State of Wisconsin average   8,039

This table has been adapted from: U.S. Department of Commerce, National Climatic Center, *Climatography of the United States,* No. 81 (by state). "Monthly Normals of Temperature, Precipitation, and Heating and Cooling Degree Days, 1951–80."

Heating degree days are defined in this table as the sum of all days in a year in which heating is required, multiplied by the number of degrees the average temperature was below 65°F. For example: 4 days @ 64 = 4 × 1 = 4 degree days; 6 days @ 63 = 6 × 2 = 12 degree days; 12 days @ −20 = 12 × (65 − (−20)) = 12 × 85 = 1,020 degree days; and so on. Other data sources might use different base temperatures.

Chapter Fifteen

A Tax on Paper Diapers

INTRODUCTION

You are a policy analyst working for a state senator. An environmental coalition, working on problems of solid and hazardous waste, has convinced a key group of state legislators that a tax should be imposed on "wasteful paper products." One of their proposals is a 10% sales tax on paper diapers. They assert that the public subsidizes both the paper industry (through cheap water for production and pollution control as well as underpriced wood supplies) and the consumers of paper diapers (through underpriced solid-waste disposal). The environmentalists say that the total annual cost to U.S. society of paper diapering (were all children to use them) would be $7 billion, and that taxpayers would support nearly $1 billion of that amount through hidden subsidies. They want to eliminate that subsidy, as well as cut down on the volume of waste being brought to the state's landfills. It has been five years since a major landfill was built in this state, and citizen groups have become well mobilized in their efforts to stop their location anywhere near any of the state's urbanized areas. The disposal of solid waste has become a crisis of major proportions.

The state senator for whom you work is a key member of the Congressional Budget and Finance Committee. The senator is fiscally conservative, but open to these types of arguments. Thus, your assignment is to check ("without prejudice") "the legitimacy of the environmentalist's claims," as well as explore "the efficacy of the policy of a 10% sales tax on paper diapers."

First, you should gather some basic data, which are easily available, and develop some back-of-the-envelope calculations, checking the environmentalist's claims for orders of magnitude.

Second, analyze the family as the decision-making unit. See what the three diapering alternatives (home-washed cotton, diaper-service cotton, and paper disposables) would cost them, and find out what the costs and benefits would be for them for each alternative. A publication from a cloth diaper service, Dy-Dee Wash, is particularly helpful and a copy is attached (Dy-Dee Wash cost comparison, Milwaukee, WI, n.d., Exhibit 15-I). The publication was last available in 1985, so the data must be reestimated and/or inflated.

Third, explore the problem from a societal perspective. Use the city and/or county as the decision-making unit and explore the three alternatives and their associated costs and benefits.

Fourth, speculate on the responses to any proposed policy that families, governments, and the two major diaper-related industries might have.

THE ASSIGNMENT

You must submit a briefing memorandum to the senator two weeks from today. Be sure to begin it with the usual one-page executive summary, and give a recommended course of action: Adopt the tax, kill it, or delay and study it some more. If you are going to urge a delay, be sure to spell out exactly how you will use staff time to learn more about the problem and the possible policies that could be adopted. Two weeks from today you must present your findings in person to the senator, and answer any questions. The memorandum should be a maximum of 5,000 words, excluding technical appendices.

UNDERLYING THEMES

Some of the themes that underlie this case are these:

- Much can be done with simple arithmetic, readily available data, and some back-of-the-envelope calculations.
- It is not just international crises that provide the grist for the policy analyst's mill, but often the everyday functioning of societies and individuals. Many policy problems are, indeed, mundane.

- The results of the analysis, if not the approach itself, are highly dependent on who the analyst adopts as the client.
- Important economic concepts underpin many policy problems. Marginality, elasticity, externalities, opportunity cost, and societal benefit, for example, need to be an integral part of the analyst's thought processes. Even the simplest problem, like the one described here, probably contains elements that are amenable to economic analysis.

- There are a number of policy approaches to correcting government failures and market failures, and they all have limitations and collateral consequences that need analysis.

LEARNING OBJECTIVES

The teaching and learning objectives include, but are not limited to, these:

1. Learning to use back-of-the-envelope calculations.
2. Thinking about working for a client, and writing and doing research that can be understood by that client.
3. Confronting a number of economic concepts that always underpin a policy problem like this one. These include marginality, elasticity, externalities, opportunity cost, and societal cost and benefit.
4. Learning to cast one's work in a political context. Who are the actors, and what will their positions be?
5. Exploring the appropriate policy mechanisms for dealing with a market failure of this type. What are the likely impacts of the proposed tax on the major stakeholders, and what might be some alternative, and perhaps superior, policies?
6. Presenting a briefing paper orally in an effective way.

SOURCE MATERIAL

To help you get started, a number of publications are listed below that were generated by using the key word *diaper* on a university library database. They are:

"Battle for Bottom Share." *Fortune*, February 13, 1989, p. 9.

BOUDA, FRANCIS. "Baby Diapers in 1988: Is the Future Really behind Us?" *Nonwovens Industry*, January 1989, p. 26 et passim.

BOUDA, FRANCIS. "The Baby Diaper Market: The Gathering Storm." *Nonwovens Industry*, January 1990, p. 26 et passim.

BOUDA, FRANCIS, and JOHN M. BOUDA. "Adult Incontinence: Positioning for People's Preference." *Nonwovens Industry*, March 1989, p. 46 et passim.

DARCEY, SUE. "States Opt for Recycling as Landfill Problem-Solver." *World Wastes*, October 1988, p. 34 et passim.

DE COURCY HINDS, MICHAEL. "Do Disposable Diapers Ever Go Away?" *New York Times*, December 10, 1988, p. 33.

DUNBAR, FREDERICK C., and MARK P. BERKMAN. "Sanitary Landfills Are Too Cheap!" *Waste Age*, May 1987, p. 91 et passim.

"Environmental Challenge Forces P&G's Hand." *Nonwovens Industry*, July 1989, p. 8.

"Environmental Costs of Keeping Baby Dry." *Science News*, March 4, 1989, p. 141.

FEEDER, BARNABY J. "What's New in Diapers." *New York Times*, March 12, 1989, p. 15.

HADDAD, CLARE. "The European Diaper Scene: New Recipes to Delight or Confuse Mothers." *Nonwovens Industry*, July 1989, p. 28 et passim.

"In Vermont, a Proposal to Ban Disposable Diapers." *New York Times*, December 31, 1989, p. 33.

"It's Diaper City at the Landfill." *U.S. News & World Report*, July 3, 1989, p. 12.

JACOBSEN, MICHAEL. "The Dioxin Debate: It Won't Go Away." *Nonwovens Industry*, March 1989, pp. 56–60.

LEHRBURGER, CARL. "Diapers in the Waste Stream." Philadelphia: National Association of Diaper Services, 1989.

LEHRBURGER, CARL, and RACHEL SNYDER. "The Disposable Diaper Myth: Out of Sight, Out of Mind." *Whole Earth Review*, Fall 1988, pp. 60–67.

MCCARTHY, REBECCA. "Critics Doubt Diapers Are Biodegradable." *Atlanta Journal and Constitution*, November 28, 1989, p. D-4.

"Nebraska Passes Anti-Diaper Legislation." *Nonwovens Industry*, June 1989, p. 8.

NOONAN, ELLEN. "A Diaper Film Review." *Nonwovens Industry*, January 1989, p. 50 et passim.

NOONAN, ELLEN. "Disposing of the Disposables: Defining the Problem." *Nonwovens Industry*, September 1989, p. 22 et passim.

NOONAN, ELLEN. "Disposing of The Disposables: Finding the Solutions." *Nonwovens Industry*, October 1989, p. 21 et passim.

NOONAN, ELLEN. "Disposing of the Disposables: Learning from the Experts." *Nonwovens Industry*, November 1989, pp. 44–47.

SHERMAN, STRATFORD. "Trashing a $150 Billion Business." *Fortune*, August 28, 1989, pp. 90–96.

"This Market Didn't Bottom Out." *Wall Street Journal*, August 30, 1989, p. B-1.

EXHIBIT

Exhibit 15-I Diaper Service Analysis

HOME DELIVERY DIAPER SERVICE		SYNTHETIC DIAPERS		HOME LAUNDERING COSTS PER LOAD	
75 DIAPER SERVICE	$ 8.70	HUGGIES MEDIUM (96)	$ 10.58	PRE-SOAK (BORAX) 1/2 CUP	$ .04
80 DIAPER SERVICE	8.85	HUGGIES MEDIUM (48)	4.38	DETERGENT(IVORY)1CUP	.64
85 DIAPER SERVICE	9.00	HUGGIES NEWBORN (66)	10.58	BLEACH (CLOROX) 1/2 CUP	.04
90 DIAPER SERVICE	9.15	LUVS MEDIUM (96)	10.58	SOFTENER 1/2 CUP	.04
ADDITIONAL DIAPERS ANY QUANTITIES AVAILABLE		LUVS LARGE (32)	10.58	WATER (28 GALLONS)	.03
5 DIAPERS MORE FOR ONLY	15¢	PAMPERS SMALL (66)	10.58	HEAT FOR WATER	.08
SPECIAL rate for 2 in diapers.		PAMPERS MEDIUM (48)	10.58	ELECTRICITY (WASHER)	.02
We also furnish TRAINING PANTS.		PAMPERS LARGE (64)	10.58	ELECTRICITY (DRYER)	.36
		PAMPERS SUPER (32)	3.98	DIAPERS	.37
SURPRISED?				DIAPER PAIL	.02
		Don't forget cost of family car and gasoline the effects on our ecology with a new baby using up close to 400 diapers in a month!		WASHER WEAR	.19

WEEKLY COST (90 DIAPERS)	$ 9.15	AVERAGE WEEKLY COST (90 DIAPERS)	$ 20.05	AVERAGE WEEKLY COST (90 DIAPERS, 4-LOADS)	$ 8.04
				DRYER WEAR	.15
				SEPTIC TANK (TOTAL COST)	?
				WATER SOFTENER UNIT	.03
				TOTAL COST PER LOAD	2.01

Only .10¢ per diaper

WHAT'S IT DOING TO YOUR FOOD BUDGET?

Almost 22¢ per change!

Compare these prices in your area... After comparing the costs above—including your time and labor at home and the high cost of gasoline for travel to the store we sincerely believe that Dy-Dee Wash is the most economical way to diaper your baby!

Don't forget the value of your time, your labor, your health. An uncluttered house. The use of your car. But most important, no amount of home laundering gets diapering as sanitary and clean as we can professionally. You can't even buy the antiseptic we use.

IS IT WORTH IT?

.09 a diaper

cotton

(Notice how the cost of paper/plastic diapers increases as the baby grows.)

Minimum service 4 weeks

Dy-Dee Wash Diaper Service

Chapter Sixteen

Public–Private Development: Underground Atlanta

INTRODUCTION

In 1984, the mayor and common council, along with many other public officials and private citizens, were considering a project that would fully redevelop Underground Atlanta, an area of the city well known to many tourists. Underground Atlanta, once successful, had been closed since 1982 and had been in disrepair sometime before that.

Among the exhibits in this chapter are selected pages from Atlanta's proposal to the U.S. Department of Housing and Urban Development for an Urban Development Action Grant (UDAG). These pages spell out the nature of the project, the project financing, and other important details. Also included is an article from *Atlanta* magazine that provides another description of the situation facing Atlanta public officials.

What follows below is an account of a meeting of several fictitious members of the Atlanta City Council. You are to assume the role of policy analyst for one of these council members, Pepper Adams. You are asked at the end of this brief exchange among three council members to develop an issue paper for council member Adams. Pepper Adams represents a district in the far northside of the city, not near the central business district, and tends to be a fiscal conservative. Thus, Adams is predisposed to oppose this project. Pat Pinestreet represents a downtown district and therefore represents downtown business and convention interests. Maxie Laquest chairs a key committee that will decide whether to go ahead with this project. At this point Laquest is neutral.

THE ASSIGNMENT

Your assignment is to do a preliminary analysis of Underground Atlanta for Pepper Adams, acting as if the decision had not yet been made. Assume that there are no special studies available and all the information that you have at your disposal is encapsulated in that provided here. There is no other information, or at least you can't obtain it for the purpose of writing this analysis.

ISSUES AND ACTORS

Pepper Adams: What bothers me about this project is that the city stands to lose a hell of a lot of money. And what do we have to gain even if it works? I don't think it will work. Atlanta's not like Boston or Baltimore or San Francisco; there is nothing beautiful in our downtown. Our beauty is out in the countryside. There is no water amenity like there is in those three places. Without water, people aren't going to go to this thing.

Pat Pinestreet: We have been doing marvelously in the convention business for some time, but that bubble is going to burst. Once conventioneers have been to Atlanta they realize that the downtown is dead and there is no convenient way to get to the suburban amenities. There is more "there" in Lenox Square or out on the perimeter than there is in downtown Atlanta. Somehow if we want our convention business to thrive, we have got to get something in our downtown area, and we better do it quick. The Rouse Company has a terrific reputation and they believe in this project, so we should believe in it too.

Maxie Laquest: Pat, we've done excellently with our convention business so far. What's led you to believe we're in any kind of trouble? If the objective of this project is to shore up the convention business, why isn't there more of a physical link between the convention area down by International Boulevard and Underground Atlanta, which is many blocks away?

Pat Pinestreet: The truth is, if you ask anyone who's ever visited Atlanta what they remember, they remember Underground Atlanta. That gives us a foot in the door. We've already got something going. That's why this is the perfect project.

Pepper Adams: If this is the perfect project, why don't business interests finance it? If the convention and business communities think it's so terrific, let them put their money in rather than the city putting its money in.

Pat Pinestreet: Let's face it: I'm willing to admit that Underground may not work, or at least may not work at the levels that the optimists think it may. However, we're into a whole new ball game. What we're doing here is providing a public subsidy for a utility. Think of Underground Atlanta like you think of the road system, the parks, the water mains, and the sewer pipes. We are providing utilities and we must provide this subsidy. From the subsidy will come activity, which is what we need in the City of Atlanta.

Maxie Laquest: Do you think that this project is really going to generate that many jobs? The proposal says 3,000, but it's hard for me to believe this will generate 3,000 jobs. They're also the most menial kinds of jobs. It seems to me if we're after creating jobs, we could do it more directly than subsidizing this project.

Pepper Adams: But the real question is, will it work? The project has 220,000 square feet of retail space. The American City Corporation forecasts net revenue per square foot of $600. That's unbelievable! That amount isn't experienced in the best developments of this kind. At that level the project can produce enough revenue to amortize the bonded debt, but at lower levels the city's going to underwrite that project.

Maxie Laquest: I can see it now. Several muggings and a rape and the entire project is washed out and the city is left holding the bag. Pat, how do you respond to that?

Pat Pinestreet: No guts, no glory! Let's face it, the federal government's got a big stake in this too. We're taking advantage of their money, not just our own.

Pepper Adams: (*Turning to a staff analyst*) What I would like you to do is write up for me one of your issue papers. I'm predisposed to try to get the council to delay action on this one, but not to delay for its own sake. I would want to be convinced that delaying would allow us time to get more information. At this point, though, I don't know what information we'd want. I'm not certain what the key questions are here. You'll have to get this paper done quickly because we're having an important meeting on this at this time next week.

EXHIBITS

Underground Atlanta: The Second Coming

Andy Young and his in-house visionaries think a new Underground complex is the answer to downtown's woes. They had better be right.

By DAVID NORDAN

Andy Young was obviously not in doubt on a muggy June morning as he sat back, cool and detached in his City Hall office, surrounded by souvenirs from his African travels, and remonstrated on the massive and risky venture which will almost certainly make or break his reputation as mayor of Atlanta.

It has been from this second-floor vantage point that the city's mayors have launched their schemes and visions since the neo-deco edifice went up in 1929—sometimes only to see them come limping back without a sail or a mast. And, as sure as the sun rises and sets over a yardarm, the $130 million refurbishing, or second coming, of Underground Atlanta will go down in the books either as "Andy's Triumph" or "Andy's Folly."

He was asked about that, indirectly.

"I don't see that there's that much risk involved," Young responded, flicking the wimp of a question away as if it were no more than a slightly annoying fly buzzing about his mayoral head.

Three days after the interview, a not-quite-so convinced Atlanta City Council would neverthe-less vote unanimously to proceed full speed ahead with Young's project—with some key members, notably Finance Committee Chairman Ira Jackson and Economic Development Com-mittee Chairman Robb Pitts, warning even as they voted that they still harbored serious misgiv-ings.

"Everything has had its naysayers," the mayor said, "the same people were against MARTA and the airport expansion. They've been wrong on everything so far, so I don't see why we should pay any attention to them now.

"Look at New Orleans. It was dying and would have collapsed without its Superdome. Even if Underground turns out to be a bad investment, it can end up saving a city. There's no way it can lose money overall." Young's self-assurance is apt testimony to the old saw that an effective leader "may often be wrong but never in doubt."

"There's a dynamic involved," he explained. The dynamic that Mayor Young hopes to rekin-dle symbolically flickered out in March 1982 when Ron Ergene, lonelier than the Maytag repairman, closed the doors to his Wax N' Wicks Candle Shop, turned in his business license, and aban-doned Underground once again to the winos and rats who 15 years earlier had been evicted from their private domain.

Ergene's shop was the last to leave, and the lights finally went out on an experiment that should have worked.

Underground, where the zero mile post sticks up to mark the beginning point of the city in 1838, has remained virtually untouched in a way that is unique to Atlanta and unlike the heart of any other American city. This is because the area has been sealed away under viaducts since the morass of adjacent rail lines had to be covered over. This act of impromptu urban design in the early 1900s in essence made the second story the first story of buildings in that part of town, leaving "under-ground" a vacant cavern.

What you get by walking through the place is a fascinating stroll through the past, through a world that ceased to exist in most cities soon after the advent of the horseless carriage.

The section languished forgotten for a half-century until it was developed with an eye to its

history in the late 1960s. It flourished for almost 10 years. At the height of its popularity in 1973, it hosted 3.5 million visitors and its businesses took in $17 million.

Then in the early 1970s a variety of factors combined to signal its doom. Business was dampened by the recession of that era, the proj-ect was undermanaged, undercapitalized and the quality of concessions undercontrolled.

Ironically, this happened at a time when the city and state decided to lower the drinking age to 18, opening the doors of establishments to a more rowdy clientele and types of entertain-ment—hard rock—which drove away well-heeled locals and tourists in droves.

But the death knell came with the construction of the MARTA lines next to Underground and the MARTA station at Five Points. The work dis-rupted and destroyed some of the most popular attractions. The area fell into a degree of ruin, crime increased, and visitors simply stopped coming.

Underground's Heyday

During the heyday of old Underground, it was a delightful combination of rustic charm and after-dark revelry. Sights and sounds and smells to tease the senses abounded—food of every de-scription, jazz, folk, bluegrass, Gay Nineties oom-pa-pa from corner to corner, Victorian store-fronts restored to their original flashy entice-ments, 40-foot tall, pure marble corner columns gracing the front of a grand, double-doored sa-loon where your grandfather might have spent a stiff-collared Saturday afternoon with his cronies over nickel beer—and probably did if your roots go back that far in Atlanta. . . .

Still, whatever else Lenox Square [a large suburban shopping mall] may be, it is not nor can it ever be what old Underground was. And this reality may prove to be the key rebuttal to de-tractors who insist that Atlanta suburbanites will not forsake their current playgrounds, with all their shopping mall glass and chrome charm, to travel downtown from time to time to take in a new Underground.

For more than any of the modern entertain-ment centers in the newer sections of Atlanta and the suburbs, the old Underground was a people place with a continuing festival atmosphere. It was a party. This, according to the urban planners, is the missing piece in downtown Atlanta, the piece that absolutely must be replaced if the city is to continue to be a $500 million per year convention center.

The out-of-towners will stop coming, the very plausible argument goes, if they are not given something to do besides walk around and look up at the tall buildings.

[Dante] Stephenson [owner of a popular bar in the old Underground] scoffs at suggestions that Atlantans and their suburbanite neighbors won't patronize a new Underground.

"That's bull," he says. "They'll come back—because Underground has a charm nothing in this state or this country has. Water? We don't need water. Rouse even considered building a huge lake down there, but we don't need it. Underground is unique. There's nothing like it anywhere else, and the locals take it for granted. I think they're nuts."

The Future of Downtown

"Underground is critical" to the future of downtown, says longtime Central Atlanta Progress Executive Director Dan Sweat. "With the new airport, the World Congress Center, and MARTA, things will come together. What's missing is something like Underground. We've set the stage, now we have to build on top of it."

Agreement comes from a less expected quarter with the endorsement of super-architect/developer John Portman, whose plans to put up his own big entertainment complex in the area of his Peachtree Center and Regency Hotel were to some extent one-upped by the mayor. Portman had envisioned a more futuristic-type project—along the theme of Epcot Center and Walt Disney World in Florida—and he says he hasn't given up on that idea. But he says he is "very supportive" of the new Underground project.

"I think it's something the city needs," says Portman. "A city is like a business. There comes a time when we have to make capital improvements."

'Suburb Chasing Suburb'

If it costs the taxpayers some money, he suggests, well, so be it. "It's still worth it. I don't think it should be expected to break even, any more than the zoo, City Hall or the auditorium. It will determine whether Atlanta becomes like Los Angeles, with suburb chasing after suburb, or more like San Francisco. Human amenities, that's what makes it.

"As we move forward we have to capitalize and strengthen the heritage we have while moving on into the scientific future. Otherwise we'll remain just the poor ol' South. If you listen to the naysayers, nothing will ever get done."

With the necessary initial focus on such abstruse topics as return per square footage, bond indebtedness viability, market and sales projections, venture capital and the like—in other words, will the damn thing pay for itself or go belly up like the old Underground?—Mayor Young's concept of "a dynamic" has gone largely unexamined.

The mayor and his in-house dreamers—and indeed the tried and tested planners at the Rouse Company, the Columbia, Maryland, based firm which will develop and manage the new Underground—believe the spin-off benefits of the $130 million project will eventually be of far more value to Atlanta than the development itself.

This is what Young means when he talks about "a dynamic."

Sparkling Urban Setting

He says the new Underground—a phantasmagoria of entertainment, restaurants, and specialty shops, softened by fountains and greenery and modernized above ground with office buildings—will spawn an era of rejuvenation in the blighted and abandoned south-central downtown section that will transform it into a sparkling urban setting on a par with the Peachtree Street, Buckhead, and Lenox areas.

There is certainly some risk to Atlanta taxpayers, but, due to a complex financing arrangement, it will be minimal. The city's share of the project cost, even though the city will eventually own all the property, will amount to something over $80 million, furnished by an $80 million, 10% bond issue payable over ten years from Underground tax revenues. Even if the total project makes nothing at all, the total annual cost to Atlanta will be no more than $8 million—Young believes the project will easily pay the whole tab—with the exception of additional costs for security and maintenance.

Initially, Atlanta will contribute about $15

million from its 1% sales tax increase windfall, which the mayor politicked out of the General Assembly last year. Yet this amount is to be reimbursed from another $15 million federal Urban Development grant—if the Reagan administration chooses to approve it.

Joint-Venture Partners

Another $19 million is to be put up by private investors brought together under a syndicate umbrella. The investment is not expected to net any profits for these individuals for a number of years but is to be offered as a tax shelter. Their identities have not been determined, with the exception of black entrepreneur Herman Russell—who will join Rouse as a minority joint-venture partner—and probably the Rouse Company itself. Downtown developer Tom Cousins, who owns the nearby Omni International, is also said to have expressed an interest. But this, again, is unofficial.

The Rouse Company, a 45-year-old firm with three decades of downtown development experience and assets of $1.2 billion, is to manage Underground under contract and under its own philosophy, which is specifically designed for this type of project. Rouse currently is undertaking about 20 other such projects around the country and has enjoyed tremendous success with similar efforts in Baltimore, Boston, and New York, among others.

"Atlanta is a big market," said Vice President for Corporate Affairs Scott Ditch. "It has a large regional market and lots of visitors. In addition, there's not a strong entertainment project downtown. We think there's a strong demand or we wouldn't be in it.

"We also had the skepticism in Baltimore and Boston that people wouldn't come back downtown. But in both cities we get the majority of our visitors from the suburbs," Ditch said. "People close to the situation often don't believe things can change that much. We know they can.

"If you don't do it, what are you going to do? Let downtown go to hell? Be serious. Can you let a city the size of Atlanta go that way? There's more doubting about the potential by Atlantans than people elsewhere."

New Suburbanites

Most of those doubts have centered around arguments that the new breed of Atlanta suburbanites—many of whom rarely if ever set foot in downtown—will drive past their own neighborhood watering holes, as plastic and monolithic as most of them are, to spend their money in the heart of the city, particularly in a section that has long been one of Atlanta's most depressed inner-city areas.

In order for Underground to live up to expectations—11.5 million visitors a year and turning some $80 million in sales by 1989—planners suggest that about 30 percent of its patronage will have to come from the suburbs. Some doubt that they will, and some parrot Dante Stephenson's caustic answer to that objection.

Detractors

Others say they support the concept but point to problems of security, a negative factor that was instrumental in the downfall of old Underground. The city answers that special measures, including large numbers of additional private and city police, will be part of the package. Critics such as Councilman Jackson say it will cost Atlanta a minimum of $2 million a year to provide it.

Even if the place turns out to be safer than a suburban cul-de-sac, there remains the problem of image which plagues this rundown part of downtown. "One or two muggings or rapes, and you can forget Underground," suggested one detractor.

And then there is the most delicate and least discussed question of all—race relations. And it is raised on both sides of the racial spectrum in a biracial city.

"White folks from the suburbs—particularly on the northside where the disposable income is—are going to be about as comfortable down there with blacks on Saturday night as I would be in Forsyth County drinking moonshine with the good ol' boys," said Jackson, who is black.

"Let's face it," said a top official in the Cousins organization, "white people from Cobb County don't rub shoulders with blacks—period."

With the City Council's footdragging vote in early June to proceed with the application for a $15 million federal UDAG grant, it became a foregone conclusion that the project will be built. Most of the criticism has quieted to a murmur. Even among cynics, no one can be found who will wish the project bad luck.

Mayoral Legacies

Every mayor during the past 30 years has left something of his own vision behind in the form of tangible, usually massive, physical projects. William B. Hartsfield built the first modern airport, Ivan Allen brought the stadium to town, Sam Massell laid the groundwork and got MARTA off the drawing boards and onto the rails, Maynard Jackson followed through on that and then presided over the $800 million expansion of the airport to international status.

Each achievement has tied in one way or another with the others, serving more as cornerstones than stepping stones, and contributed to the overall development of the city as a mostly modern, up-to-date transportation-savvy city—

one of the better ones in the country by most measurements.

Andrew Young has no "edifice complex," in the words of a longtime friend and associate, but he has an idea of what he—following his predecessors' example—wants to leave behind.

It was with that in mind that he picked up the Underground torch—Mayor Jackson had flirted with it, asking the Rouse Company to do a feasibility study near the end of his administration in the late 1970s—and proceeded with the idea that it could provide the spark that would result in the completed redevelopment of downtown.

He remains convinced that it's the way to go—perhaps wrong, but never in doubt.

Source: Atlanta Magazine, August 1984, pp. 44–46, 110. (Edited by the authors.)

CITY OF ATLANTA

655 NORTH OMNI INTERNATIONAL ATLANTA, GEORGIA 30335

February 6, 1984

ANDREW YOUNG MAYOR

OFFICE OF ECONOMIC DEVELOPMENT RICHARD STOGNER Chief

M E M O R A N D U M

TO: Council President Marvin Arrington; Members of the Atlanta City Council
FROM: Richard A. Stogner; Chief of Economic Development
SUBJECT: Underground Atlanta Briefing Material

The attached briefing book on the Underground Atlanta Project has been prepared from the material submitted with the UDAG Grant Application on January 31, 1984. The material contains a project summary, a financial sources and uses summary, the financial plan of January 16, 1984, and a set of the project drawings.

Developing the financial plan for the Underground Atlanta Project has been difficult. Urban Renewal projects often involve complicated and difficult financing and this project is no exception. In addition, a great number of alternative financial approaches have been evaluated and discarded. The financial plan, as presented, has undergone considerable evolution and change and represents an investment of over fifteen months of

intensive effort. *The financial plan is a viable one.* It has been developed with an understanding of the risks involved and the rewards to be gained. We have tried to minimize the financial risks to the City.

The plan contains an underwrite on the City's behalf to cover any deficiency that might occur in the debt service on the project bonds. However, it does not contemplate that the City will have to fund any such deficiency.

In the final analysis, any financial plan is only as good as its underlying projections and assumptions. Working with The Rouse Company, we have tried to develop our forecasts and assumptions on a conservative, sound, and reasonable basis. In this regard, the inherent risk is not that the project will not work, it will; but that it will work at a level lower than forecast. The American City Corporation forecast a net revenue per square foot of $600.00. After consultation with The Rouse Company, we are using $400.00 per square foot in our forecast. At this level, the project can produce enough revenue to amortize the bonded debt. At a lower level, the underwrite might be activated. At a higher level, a substantial cash surplus is generated. We believe that the level of risk is acceptable compared with the re-

sults: 3,000 permanent jobs, creation of a major entertainment/retail/dining complex, and revitalization of the South CBD.

RAS: smp

Underground Atlanta Summary[1]

Project Size

- 220,000 square feet retail
  - 114,000 square feet food and entertainment
  - 106,000 square feet specialty retail
- 65,000 square feet office
- 65,000 square feet expansion reserve

Financing

Total	$124,570,000
Project Revenue Bond	$76,982,000
Syndicated Equity	15,334,000
City Sales Tax "Windfall"	12,000,000
CDBG	6,000,000
UDAG	14,254,000
Calculated UDAG Leverage Ratio	4.18 : 1

Community Benefits

- 3,000 jobs
- $880,000 local sales tax receipts
- Support of convention industry
- Spin-off to other retail and similar activities in downtown
- Treatment of "slum and blight"
- Development stimulus in underutilized southern CBD

PART III—
DESCRIPTION OF PROPOSED PROJECT

Section A—Statement of Problems and Objectives

The adopted Economic Development Strategy (EDS) of the City of Atlanta states that "the challenge to local leadership, and the primary purpose of the City of Atlanta's Economic Development Strategy, is to reverse these trends [out-migration of jobs, lack of tax base growth, inadequate job training] by providing meaningful employment opportunities to all Atlantans. Atlanta must retain and expand the number of its jobs by capitalizing wherever possible on the City's economic strengths . . ." (page 14). Specific objectives contained in the EDS that relate directly to the revitalization of Underground At-

lanta include strengthening of Atlanta's downtown and providing increased support for Atlanta's important convention industry. In addition, revitalization of Underground Atlanta is included as a specific, very high priority project in the EDS. At present, revitalization of Underground Atlanta has become Atlanta's *highest* priority development project.

Revitalization of Underground Atlanta will accomplish four important objectives: support of Atlanta's convention industry, enhancement of downtown, provision of jobs, and tax base enhancement. Atlanta is the third largest conven-

---

[1] An excerpt from Atlanta's proposal to the U.S. Department of Housing and Urban Development to receive an Urban Development Action Grant, January 1984.

tion city in the U.S. Atlanta has obtained this status in the last decade and a half. The convention industry is one of the fastest growing industries in the City; many experts attribute as many as 80,000 jobs (directly and indirectly) in the region to this industry. In three of the four basic attributes sought in a convention site—access, convention facilities, and quality and number of hotel rooms—Atlanta is among the nation's leaders. In the fourth attribute—cultural and entertainment opportunities—Atlanta is rated very poorly. To maintain strength in what is becoming a very highly competitive national convention industry (and to maintain jobs and job growth) Atlanta must overcome this weakness via development of a major entertainment center in its downtown.

Downtown Atlanta has enjoyed strong growth over the last two decades. Unfortunately, this growth has been predominantly only in the area of office space. The vast majority of people who use downtown are there only during the working day; downtown is relatively deserted after 6:00 P.M. on workdays and on weekends. Because downtown is relatively deserted at these times, local residents tend to stay away due to a perception of crime and personal danger; the "desertedness" of downtown tends to feed on itself. Existing retail and other commercial businesses downtown suffer because of the lack of use of downtown. The project area itself, as presently constituted, is especially detrimental to downtown and is characterized by deteriorating structures, fire hazards, criminal activity, and economic disuse. It has, in fact, been found to be a slum and blighted area by the City Council. Revitalization of Underground Atlanta as an entertainment center that will attract millions of visitors each year, will significantly address the problem of underuse of downtown Atlanta. Underground Atlanta will attract business not only to itself, but by attracting people to downtown will help overcome the perception of danger downtown and create important spin-off markets for other commercial uses in downtown.

Atlanta has a significant structural problem with un- and under-employment, especially among unskilled people. This problem is disguised in region-wide statistics, but exists in painful reality for the majority of the residents of the southside of the City of Atlanta. The principal reason for the government of the City of Atlanta to be involved in economic development is to help address this problem. The revitalization of Underground Atlanta will produce up to 3,000 private sector jobs. Not only is this a very high number of jobs for a single project to generate, but the majority of these jobs will be in retailing and food services so they will be available to relatively unskilled people.

During the inflationary decade of the '70s, the City of Atlanta, which was highly dependent on property tax, suffered from very low growth in tax revenues. City employment was decreased, primarily in laboring jobs, and services were curtailed. In 1982, to help address dependency on property tax and the revenue effects of inflation, the city substituted a local 1% sales tax for a portion of its property tax. In 1989, the project's *pro forma* year, Underground Atlanta is conservatively expected to produce $880,000 in sales tax revenue alone for the City of Atlanta. This is opposed to an estimated $18,284 in current property tax receipts from the area (estimated from current tax assessments), and $45,000 in estimated current sales tax receipts.

Section B1—Brief Project Description

Underground Atlanta is located in Atlanta's southern central business district—the "Heart of Atlanta." The "Heart of Atlanta" area is generally bounded by Marietta and Decatur Streets on the north, the interstate highway system on the east and south, and the tracks of the Southern Railway to the west. The area has a number of significant impediments to development and many of the existing buildings have been allowed to deteriorate. The southern portion of the area, particularly, consists of underutilized land, surface parking, and a melange of marginal uses. Especially to suburban residents, the area has an image of crime, physical threat, and decline.

Foremost among the physical impediments to investment and growth in the "Heart of Atlanta" is the railroad gulch which separates this area from the remainder of the CBD. Historically, the rail lines which run east and west through downtown created impediments to north–south movement and commerce. Between the turn of the century and the 1920s a system of viaducts was built to overcome this problem from a traffic standpoint. But, the deep scar of the "gulch"—the undeveloped land among the viaducts occupied by the rail lines—remains as an interruption in the continuity of development and continues as a psychological barrier to movement and commerce.

Construction of the viaduct system also created the unique physical setting for Underground Atlanta. The viaducts were built and sealed up against existing buildings. What had been the second floor of these buildings became the main floor; over the years the ground floors were hidden and forgotten.

In the late 1960s, an entertainment complex was created in this area under the viaducts. Property was assembled through a series of leaseholds, and the complex was opened in 1969. At its peak in 1972, Underground Atlanta housed 70 businesses, attracted 3.5 million visitors, and generated sales of $17 million. But, for reasons including general economic recession, lowered drinking age, and disruptive construction of the MARTA fixed rail rapid transit system in the area, Underground declined to a point where its management company ceased operations in 1976. Many who have studied the situation believe the entertainment complex could have survived had it had central control of property and operations, sufficient capital and adequate funds for maintenance, and competent central management, but it did not.

At present, the Underground Atlanta area (bounded generally by Martin Luther King Jr. Drive on the south, the "gulch" on the north, Peachtree Street on the west, and Central Avenue on the east) is a slum and blighted area and an economic drag on the City of Atlanta. It has been made an Urban Redevelopment area by the Council of the City of Atlanta.

The goal of the Underground Atlanta revitalization project is to return the area, both that part above the viaducts and that part below, and its environs, to a standard, habitable, safe, healthy, and productive area. The goal includes returning the area to economic vitality, producing over $88 million in retail sales and 3,000 jobs by 1989.

Underground Atlanta is to be redeveloped as a "festival marketplace," characterized by dining, entertainment, and specialty retail uses, all of high quality. Space in buildings above the viaduct level will be used for professional office space. Redevelopment is to be accomplished through rehabilitation and reuse of existing structures as

the area provides the unique physical setting needed for such a marketplace. Also, the immediate environs of Underground Atlanta must be improved to attract visitors, to assure lasting success, and to encourage further private investment in the remainder of the "Heart of Atlanta."

The core of Underground Atlanta is the two blocks bounded by Alabama, Peachtree, Central, and Martin Luther King Jr. Drive. Here, using powers of eminent domain, the City will acquire property necessary for the project. Then, after disposition to private enterprise, via rehabilitation of existing property (with some new construction necessitated by recent fires) will be created approximately 220,000 square feet of specialty retail, entertainment, and dining uses. Approximately 60% will be entertainment and dining. An additional 65,000 square feet will be redeveloped for office use, and another 65,000 square feet held in reserve for future expansion. A small amount of this retail and entertainment usage will actually be developed in the block immediately to the west where it fronts Alabama Street. This will create a link to Rich's downtown department store. Two parking structures to accommodate 1,100 cars will also be built in these two major blocks.

One of the blocks directly north of this commercial core, the block bounded by Peachtree, Alabama, Pryor, and Wall, is part of the "gulch." To treat the blighting influence of the gulch and to create a major attraction and entrance to the commercial core, the area between the viaducts, approximately 30 to 40 feet above grade, will be bridged over. This bridge will take the form of a plaza platform at the viaduct level with a terrace structure, in the middle of the platform, extending down to grade level into Underground Atlanta.

The block immediately east of the commercial core is to be developed as another main entrance plaza. Presently used primarily as an at-grade parking lot, this land also sites the historic Georgia Railroad Freight Depot, one of the oldest buildings in Atlanta. The depot is to be rehabilitated and used as a museum and meeting room while the remainder of the property is to be used as plaza open space. An at-grade street (supplanted by a viaduct) which runs between this block and the commercial core will be closed to add usable land to this area. This land will be used to site a new building, a Colonnade Market, intended to function as the eastern anchor of the core development.

The total estimated cost of the Underground Atlanta revitalization project is $124,570,000, including all hard and soft costs, land acquisition, and contingencies. Of this total $66,384,000 is attributable to commercial for-profit activity and $57,736,000 is programmed to public improvements, including the two parking structures.

Land for the project is to be acquired by the City of Atlanta using, if necessary, power of eminent domain, or through agreement with public agencies which control some property needed for the project. All property will then be transferred to the Atlanta Downtown Development Authority. The Authority will in turn dispose of the property needed for commercial development to a private corporation, Underground Atlanta, Inc., which will proceed with development. The Authority will retain property needed for public improvements and cause those improvements to proceed. Management agreements will be executed with The Rouse Company for both construction and post-construction operations management.

Financing for the project will be complex. First, the Atlanta Downtown Development Authority will issue a project revenue bond in the amount of $76,982,000. After capitalized interest and other expenses, $7,736,000 will be available; $57,736,000 will be retained by the Authority for noncommercial related expenses and $19,246,000 will be loaned to the private developer. The private developer will syndicate equity in the project of at least $15,334,000. The City will provide an equity infusion with the private portions of the project of $18,000,000 to be provided from a local sales tax "windfall" and CDBG funds. A UDAG loan of $14,254,000 is necessary to complete the funding.

Development Summary

1. *Developer(s)*. Several development and management entities will be involved in the project. These include: the City of Atlanta, the Atlanta Downtown Development Authority, Underground Atlanta, Inc., and The Rouse Company. The private developer will be Underground Atlanta, Inc., a limited partnership.

The City of Atlanta, using its powers of land acquisition and assembly, will acquire all land necessary for the development of the project. The City will then enter a development agreement with The Rouse Company (TRC) under which TRC will be the master development coordinator for the project. The City will also enter into an operations agreement with TRC under which TRC will be the project operator when development is complete.

The City of Atlanta will then transfer all project land and existing improvements to the Atlanta Downtown Development Authority (ADDA) using a warranty deed with a reversion of ownership to the City. The City will also assign its agreements with TRC to ADDA. The City will contract with the ADDA for complete project implementation.

The ADDA will issue project revenue bonds in an amount sufficient to provide useful proceeds of approximately $58 million for use in the project. A portion of these funds will be used to construct all the noncommercial components of the project, the remainder will be lent to the private developer to help finance the commercial aspects of the project. Even though only a portion of the bond proceeds will be lent to the partnership, the partnership will be liable to pay the authority all funds it needs in excess of Debt Service Reserve Fund interest earnings and parking revenues to repay the bonds. Project revenues are the only source available to meet this obligation. The bonds will be underwritten to the bondholders by the City. That is to say, bond payments will be guaranteed to the bondholders by the City in the event project revenues are insufficient to meet payments. However, whenever the City does make such a payment such payment will automatically become a debt to the partnership to be accrued on its books at 9.5% interest until the City is repaid.

The ADDA will transfer land and existing improvements needed for commercial development to the private developer, Underground Atlanta, Inc. The land will be leased, the improvements sold.

The lease will be in an amount sufficient for the Authority to meet its total project bond obligations after income from parking revenues, interest from the debt service reserve fund, and debt, i.e., payments from the partnership. The mortgage will be on a property value of $2,400,000 at 12% interest only, accrued interest and principal due on sale.

The Authority will assign the development

and on-going operation management agreements with The Rouse Company to the partnership.

The Authority will cause all non-commercial aspects of the project to be built using the remainder (after assignment) of the development agreement with The Rouse Company and paying these costs from bond proceeds. The partnership will cause all commercial components of the project to be built using the development agreement with The Rouse Company and paying these costs with funds lent from the Authority, equity, a CDBG loan from the City, and the UDAG loan from the City.

2. *Sources of Funds and Amount to Complete Project.* A complex multiplicity of funds will be used to implement the project.

(a) *Debt Financing* (to the Private Developer)

Source	Amount	Rate/Term
DDA Bond	$76,982,000	9.5%/30 yrs.

Note:

(1) The total amount, $76,982,000, is a bond debt of the Atlanta Downtown Development Authority. While only 25% of the bond proceeds will be directly lent to the private developer, Underground Atlanta, Inc., Underground Atlanta, Inc., will assume full liability for repayment of this obligation.

(2) The Authority will have two other sources of income to apply to this $76,982,000 debt:
- A debt service reserve fund with a present value of $8,247,000.
- Parking revenue—First year income

projection is $630,000. This amount at 9.5% for 30 years has a present value, as bond debt payment, of $6,196,000. After deducting these two values, the partnership is actually liable for repayment of $62,539,000 of the bonds. For UDAG leverage ratio calculation purposes, this amount discounts from 9.5% to 11% to a present value of $41,580,000.

(b) *Equity Investment by Developer*

Source	Amount
Underground Atlanta, Inc.	$15,344,000 (Syndicated)

(c) *UDAG Amount Requested*
$14,254,000

(d) *Other Public Funds*

$12,000,000	City of Atlanta Sales Tax Windfall Funds
6,000,000	City of Atlanta CDBG Funds
$18,000,000	

Note:

(1) Sales Tax Windfall funds are a one time infusion of funds available to local governments in Georgia which institute a local option 1% sales tax.

(2) The $12,000,000 should be viewed as a subsidy infusion to ADDA with the appraised value only due City on sale of project.

(3) The CDBG funds will be lent to the partnership at 8% interest only with principal and accrued interest due upon sale or refinancing. Interest will be allowed to accrue.

3. *Other Funds.* No other funds are involved.

Bibliography

ABT, CLARK C., ed. *Evaluation of Social Programs.* Beverly Hills: Sage, 1976.

ACKOFF, RUSSELL L. *The Art of Problem Solving.* New York: Wiley, 1978.

ACLAND, HENRY. "Are Randomized Experiments the Cadillacs of Design?" *Policy Analysis* 5, no. 2 (Spring 1979), 223–41.

ALEXANDER, CHRISTOPHER. *Notes on the Synthesis of Form.* Cambridge: Harvard University Press, 1964.

ALEXANDER, ERNEST R. "After Rationality, What? A Review of Responses to Paradigm Breakdown." *Journal of the American Planning Association* 50, no. 1 (Winter 1984), 62–69.

———. "Design in the Decision-Making Process." *Policy Sciences* 14, no. 3 (June 1982), 279–92.

———. "The Design of Alternatives in Organizational Contexts: A Pilot Study." *Administrative Science Quarterly* 42, no. 3 (September 1979), 382–404.

———. "Sensitivity Analysis in Complex Decision Models." *Journal of the American Planning Association* 55, no. 3 (Summer 1989), 323–33.

———, ANTHONY JAMES CATANESE, and DAVID S. SAWICKI. *Urban Planning: A Guide to Information Sources.* Volume 2 in the Urban Studies Information Guide Series. Detroit: Gale Research Company, 1979.

ALTERMAN, RACHELLE, and DUNCAN MACRAE, JR. "Planning and Policy Analysis: Converging or Diverging Trends?" *Journal of the American Planning Association* 49, no. 2 (Spring 1983), 200–215.

ALTMAN, STANLEY M. "The Dilemma of Data Rich, Information Poor Service Organizations: Analyzing Operational Data." *Journal of Urban Analysis* 3, no. 1 (April 1976), 61–75.

———. "Teaching Data Analysis to Individuals Entering the Public Service." *Journal of Urban Analysis* 3, no. 2 (October 1976), 211–37.

AMERICAN INSTITUTE OF CERTIFIED PLANNERS."AICP Code of Ethics and Professional Conduct." *1990/91 Roster.* Washington, DC: American Institute of Certified Planners, 1990, p. iv.

AMERICAN INSTITUTE OF PLANNERS. *Planning Policies.* Washington, DC: American Institute of Planners, 1977.

AMY, DOUGLAS. "Can Policy Analysis be Ethical?" In *Confronting Values in Policy Analysis: The Politics of Criteria,* ed. Frank Fischer and John Forester. Newbury Park, CA: Sage, 1987, pp. 45–67.

ANDERSON, JAMES R., CARL V. PATTON, and WILLIAM C. LIENESCH. "Simulation in Planning Urban Social Policy." *Simulation* 25, no. 1 (July 1975), 17–21.

APGAR, WILLIAM C., and H. JAMES BROWN. *Microeco-*

nomics and Public Policy. Glenview, IL: Scott, Foresman, 1987.

ARCHIBALD, RAE W., and JOSEPH P. NEWHOUSE. "Social Experimentation: Some Whys and Hows." In *Handbook of Systems Analysis: Craft Issues and Procedural Choices,* ed. Hugh J. Miser and Edward S. Quade. Chichester, Eng.: Wiley, 1988, pp. 173–214.

ARROW, KENNETH J. *Social Choice and Individual Values,* 2nd ed. New York: Wiley, 1963.

ATHEY, THOMAS H. *Systematic Systems Approach.* Englewood Cliffs, NJ: Prentice Hall, 1982.

BABBIE, EARL R. *Survey Research Methods,* 2nd ed. Belmont, CA: Wadsworth, 1990.

BAILEY, KENNETH D. *Methods of Social Research.* New York: Free Press, 1978.

BANFIELD, EDWARD C. *The Unheavenly City Revisited.* Boston: Little, Brown, 1974.

BARDACH, EUGENE. "On Designing Implementable Programs." In *Pitfalls of Analysis,* ed. Giandomenico Majone and Edward S. Quade. Chichester, Eng.: Wiley, 1980, pp. 138–58.

———. "Gathering Data for Policy Research." *Journal of Urban Analysis* 2, no. 1 (April 1974), 117–44.

———. "Problems of Problem Definition in Policy Analysis." In *Research in Public Policy Analysis and Management,* Vol. 1, ed. John P. Crecine. Greenwich, CT: JAI Press, 1981, pp. 161–71.

———. *The Skill Factor in Politics: Repealing the Mental Commitment Laws in California.* Berkeley and Los Angeles: University of California Press, 1972.

BARRIE, DONALD S., and BOYD C. PAULSON, JR. *Professional Construction Management.* New York: McGraw-Hill, 1978.

BEATLEY, TIMOTHY. "Applying Moral Principles to Growth Management." *Journal of the American Planning Association* 50, no. 4 (Autumn 1984), 459–69.

———. "Environmental Ethics and Planning Theory." *Journal of Planning Literature* 4, no. 1 (Winter 1989), 1–32.

BEHN, ROBERT D. "How to Terminate a Public Policy: A Dozen Hints for the Would-Be Terminator." *Policy Analysis* 4, no. 3 (Summer 1978), 393–414.

———. "Policy Analysis and Policy Politics." *Policy Analysis* 7, no. 2 (Spring 1981), 199–226.

———, and JAMES W. VAUPEL. *Quick Analysis for Busy Decision Makers.* New York: Basic Books, 1982.

BELLAVITA, CHRISTOPHER. "The Hero's Journey in Public Administration." In *How Public Organizations Work: Learning from Experience,* ed. Christopher Bellavita. New York: Praeger, 1990, pp. 43–66.

———, ed. *How Public Organizations Work: Learning from Experience.* New York: Praeger, 1990.

———. "Learning from Experience." In *How Public Organizations Work: Learning from Experience,* ed.

Christopher Bellavita. New York: Praeger, 1990, pp. 209–10.

———. "Preface." In *How Public Organizations Work: Learning from Experience,* ed. Christopher Bellavita. New York: Praeger, 1990, pp. xiii–xvii.

BERELSON, BERNARD, and GARY A. STEINER. *Human Behavior: An Inventory of Scientific Findings.* New York: Harcourt Brace Jovanovich, 1964.

BICKNER, ROBERT E. "Pitfalls in the Analysis of Costs." In *Pitfalls of Analysis,* ed. Giandomenico Majone and Edward S. Quade. Chichester, Eng.: Wiley, 1980, pp. 57–69.

BLALOCK, HUBERT M., JR. *Social Statistics,* 2nd ed., rev. New York: McGraw-Hill, 1979.

BOK, SISSELA. *Lying: Moral Choice in Public and Private Life.* New York: Pantheon Books, 1978.

———. "Whistleblowing and Professional Responsibilities." In *Ethics Teaching in Higher Education,* ed. Daniel Callahan and Sissela Bok. New York: Plenum Press, 1980, pp. 277–95.

BOLAN, RICHARD S. "The Structure of Ethical Choice in Planning Practice." *Journal of Planning Education and Research* 3, no. 1 (Summer 1983), 23–34.

BRACKEN, IAN. *Urban Planning Methods: Research and Policy Analysis.* London: Methuen, 1981.

BRAYBROOKE, DAVID, and CHARLES E. LINDBLOM. *A Strategy of Decision.* New York: Free Press, 1963.

BRIGHTMAN, HARVEY J. *Problem Solving: A Logical and Creative Approach.* Atlanta: Georgia State University Business Press, 1980.

BROOKS, STEPHEN. "The Market for Social Scientific Knowledge: The Case of Free Trade in Canada." In *Social Scientists, Policy, and the State,* ed. Stephen Brooks and Alain-G. Gagnon. New York: Praeger, 1990, pp. 79–94.

———, and ALAIN-G. GAGNON, eds. *Social Scientists, Policy and the State.* New York: Praeger, 1990.

BROWN, PETER G. "Ethics and Education for the Public Service in a Liberal State." *Journal of Policy Analysis and Management* 6, no. 1 (Fall 1986), 56–68.

BROWNE, ANGELA, and AARON WILDAVSKY. "What Should Evaluation Mean to Implementation?" In *The Politics of Program Evaluation,* ed. Dennis J. Palumbo. Newbury Park, CA: Sage, 1987, pp. 146–72.

BRYSON, JOHN M. *Strategic Planning for Public and Nonprofit Organizations: A Guide to Strengthening and Sustaining Organizational Achievement.* San Francisco: Jossey-Bass, 1988.

———, PHILIP BROMILEY, and YOON SOO JUNG. "Influences of Context and Process on Project Planning Success." *Journal of Planning Education and Research* 9, no. 3 (Summer 1990), 183–95.

———, and ROBERT C. EINSWEILER, eds. *Strategic Planning: Threats and Opportunities for Planners.* Chicago: Planners Press, 1988.

BURCHELL, ROBERT W., and DAVID LISTOKIN. *The Fiscal Impact Handbook: Estimating Local Costs and Revenues of Land Development.* New Brunswick, NJ: Rutgers University, Center for Urban Policy Research, 1978.

BYRNE, JOHN. "Policy Science and the Administrative State: The Political Economy of Cost-Benefit Analysis." In *Confronting Values in Policy Analysis: The Politics of Criteria,* ed. Frank Fischer and John Forester. Newbury Park, CA: Sage, 1987, pp. 70–93.

CALLAHAN, DANIEL, and SISSELA BOK, eds. *Ethics Teaching in Higher Education.* New York: Plenum Press, 1980.

CALLAHAN, JOAN C., ed. *Ethical Issues in Professional Life.* New York: Oxford University Press, 1988.

CAMPBELL, DONALD T. "Factors Relevant to the Validity of Experiments in Social Settings." *Psychological Bulletin* 54, no. 4 (July 1957), 297–312.

———, and JULIAN C. STANLEY. *Experimental and Quasi-Experimental Designs for Research.* Chicago: Rand McNally, 1966.

CARLEY, MICHAEL. *Rational Techniques in Policy Analysis.* London: Heinemann, 1980.

CARLUCCI, CARL P. "Acquisition: The Missing Link in the Implementation of Technology." In *Implementation and the Policy Process: Opening Up the Black Box,* ed. Dennis J. Palumbo and Donald J. Calista. New York: Greenwood Press, 1990, pp. 149–60.

CARO, FRANCIS G., ed. *Readings in Evaluation Research,* 2nd ed. New York: Russell Sage Foundation, 1977.

CARTWRIGHT, T. J. "Planning and Chaos Theory." *Journal of the American Planning Association* 57, no. 1 (Winter 1991), 44–56.

CHAPIN, F. STUART, JR., and EDWARD J. KAISER. *Urban Land Use Planning,* 3rd ed. Urbana: University of Illinois Press, 1979.

CHECKLAND, PETER B. "Formulating Problems for Systems Analysis." In *Handbook of Systems Analysis: Overview of Uses, Procedures, Applications, and Practice,* ed. Hugh J. Miser and Edward S. Quade. New York: North Holland, 1985, pp. 151–70.

CHILDRESS, JAMES F., and JOHN MACQUARRIE, eds. *The Westminster Dictionary of Christian Ethics.* Philadelphia: Westminster Press, 1986, p. 122.

CHRONICLE OF HIGHER EDUCATION, "Women and Smoking, Boys and Mathematics," (December 7, 1983, 8.

COLEMAN, JAMES S. "Problems of Conceptualization and Measurement in Studying Policy Impacts." In *Public Policy Evaluation,* ed. Kenneth M. Dolbeare. Beverly Hills: Sage, 1975, pp. 19–40.

CONNOR, ROSS F., ed. *Methodological Advances in Evaluation Research.* Beverly Hills: Sage, 1981.

COOK, THOMAS D., and DONALD T. CAMPBELL. *Quasi-Experimentation: Design and Analysis Issues for Field Settings.* Chicago: Rand McNally, 1979.

———, and CHARLES S. REICHARDT, eds. *Qualitative and Quantitative Methods in Evaluation Research.* Beverly Hills: Sage, 1979.

COOPER, TERRY L. *An Ethic of Citizenship for Public Administration.* Englewood Cliffs, NJ: Prentice Hall, 1991.

———. *The Responsible Administrator: An Approach to Ethics for the Administrative Role,* 3rd ed. San Francisco: Jossey-Bass, 1990.

COPLIN, WILLIAM D., and MICHAEL K. O'LEARY. *Everyman's Prince: A Guide to Understanding Your Political Problems,* rev. ed. North Scituate, MA: Duxbury Press, 1972.

———. *Public Policy Skills.* Croton-on-Hudson, NY: Policy Studies Associates, 1988.

DANDEKAR, HEMALATA C., ed. *The Planner's Use of Information: Techniques for Collection, Organization, and Communication.* Stroudsburg, PA: Hutchinson Ross, 1982.

DAVIS, JAMES A. *Elementary Survey Analysis.* Englewood Cliffs, NJ: Prentice Hall, 1971.

DE LEON, PETER. *Advice and Consent: The Development of the Policy Sciences.* New York: Russell Sage Foundation, 1988.

———. "Policy Evaluation and Program Termination." *Policy Studies Review* 2, no. 4 (May 1983), 631–47.

———. "Policy Termination as a Political Phenomenon." In *The Politics of Program Evaluation,* ed. Dennis J. Palumbo. Newbury Park, CA: Sage, 1987, pp. 173–99.

———. "A Theory of Policy Termination." In *The Policy Cycle,* ed. Judith V. May and Aaron B. Wildavsky. Beverly Hills: Sage, 1978, pp. 279–300.

DEMING, W. EDWARDS. "Making Things Right." In *Statistics: A Guide to the Unknown,* 2nd ed., ed. Judith M. Tanur. San Francisco: Holden-Day, 1978, pp. 279–88.

DEUTSCHER, IRWIN. "Toward Avoiding the Goal Trap in Evaluation Research." In *Readings in Evaluation Research,* 2nd ed., ed. Francis G. Caro. New York: Russell Sage Foundation, 1977, pp. 221–38.

DEXTER, LEWIS ANTHONY. *Elite and Specialized Interviewing.* Evanston, IL: Northwestern University Press, 1970.

DILLMAN, DON A. *Mail and Telephone Surveys: The Total Design Method.* New York: Wiley, 1978.

DIMOCK, MARSHALL E. *A Philosophy of Administration: Toward Creative Growth.* New York: Harper & Row, 1958.

DIXON, WILFRED J., and FRANK J. MASSEY, JR. *Introduction to Statistical Analysis,* 4th ed. New York: McGraw-Hill, 1983.

DOBY, JOHN T., EDWARD A. SUCHMAN, JOHN C. MCKINNEY, ROY G. FRANCIS, and JOHN P. DEAN. *An Introduction to Social Research.* Harrisburg, PA: Stackpole, 1954.

DONAHUE, ANNE MARIE, ed. *Ethics in Politics and Government*. New York: H. W. Wilson, 1989.

DOWNS, ANTHONY. *Urban Problems and Prospects*. Chicago: Markham, 1970.

DROR, YEHEZKEL. "Uncertainty: Coping with It and with Political Feasibility." In *Handbook of Systems Analysis: Craft Issues and Procedural Choices*, ed. Hugh J. Miser and Edward S. Quade. Chichester, Eng.: Wiley, 1988, pp. 247–81.

———. *Ventures in Policy Sciences*. New York: American Elsevier, 1971.

DRUCKER, MARK L. *Urban Decision Making: A Guide to Information Sources*. Detroit: Gale Research Company, 1981.

DRUMMOND, WILLIAM J., and DAVID S. SAWICKI. "GTEXTRAP: Multiple Region Population Projection Using Extrapolation Software." In *Spreadsheet Models for Urban and Regional Development*, ed. Richard Brail and Richard Klosterman. New Brunswick, NJ: Rutgers University, Center for Urban Policy Research, forthcoming.

DUNN, WILLIAM N. "Introduction." In *Values, Ethics, and the Practice of Policy Analysis*, ed. William N. Dunn. Lexington, MA: Lexington Books, 1983, pp. 1–5.

———. *Public Policy Analysis: An Introduction*. Englewood Cliffs, NJ: Prentice Hall, 1981.

———, ed. *Values, Ethics, and the Practice of Policy Analysis*. Lexington, MA: Lexington Books, 1983.

DYE, THOMAS R. *Policy Analysis*. University of Alabama: University of Alabama Press, 1976.

EAGLETON, ANNETTE KOLIS. *Fundamentals of Legal Research for Planners*. St. Louis: Washington University Press, 1978.

EDWARDS, GEORGE C., and IRA SHARKANSKY. *The Policy Predicament: Making and Implementing Public Policy*. San Francisco: W. H. Freeman, 1978.

ELBOW, PETER. *Writing with Power*. New York: Oxford University Press, 1981.

ELMORE, RICHARD F. "Backward Mapping: Implementation Research and Policy Decisions." In *Studying Implementation: Methodological and Administrative Issues*, ed. Walter Williams. Chatham, NJ: Chatham House, 1982, pp. 18–35.

ETZIONI, AMITAI. "Mixed-Scanning: A 'Third' Approach to Decision-Making." *Public Administration Review* 27, no. 5 (December 1967), 385–92.

FAIRLEY, WILLIAM B., and MOSTELLER, FREDERICK, eds. *Statistics and Public Policy*. Reading, MA: Addison-Wesley, 1977.

FINDEISEN, WLADYSLAW, and EDWARD S. QUADE. "The Methodology of Systems Analysis: An Introduction and Overview." In *Handbook of Systems Analysis: Overview of Uses, Procedures, Applications, and Practice*, ed. Hugh J. Miser and Edward S. Quade. New York: North Holland, 1985, pp. 117–49.

FISCHER, FRANK. "Policy Expertise and the 'New Class': A Critique of the Neoconservative Thesis." In *Confronting Values in Policy Analysis: The Politics of Criteria*, ed. Frank Fischer and John Forester. Newbury Park, CA: Sage, 1987, pp. 94–126.

———, and JOHN FORESTER, eds. *Confronting Values in Policy Analysis: The Politics of Criteria*. Beverly Hills: Sage, 1987.

———, and JOHN FORESTER. "Introduction." In *Confronting Values in Policy Analysis: The Politics of Criteria*, ed. Frank Fischer and John Forester. Newbury Park, CA: Sage, 1987, pp. 10–19.

FORESTER, JOHN. "Anticipating Implementation: Normative Practices in Planning and Policy Analysis." In *Confronting Values in Policy Analysis: The Politics of Criteria*, ed. Frank Fischer and John Forester. Newbury Park, CA: Sage, 1987, pp. 153–73.

FORMAINI, ROBERT. *The Myth of Scientific Public Policy*. New Brunswick, NJ: Transaction Books, 1990.

FORTHOFER, RONALD N., and ROBERT G. LEHNEN. *Public Program Analysis: A New Categorical Data Approach*. Belmont, CA: Lifetime Learning Publications, 1981.

FOWLER, FLOYD J., JR. *Survey Research Methods*. Newbury Park, CA: Sage, 1988.

FRANKENA, WILLIAM K. *Ethics*. Englewood Cliffs, NJ: Prentice Hall, 1963.

FREEMAN, LINTON C. *Elementary Applied Statistics: For Students in Behavioral Science*. New York: Wiley, 1965.

FRIEDMAN, LEE S. *Microeconomic Policy Analysis*. New York: McGraw-Hill, 1984.

FROST, MICHAEL J. *How to Use Cost Benefit Analysis in Project Appraisal*, 2nd ed. New York: Wiley, 1975.

GIL, DAVID G. *Unravelling Social Policy: Theory, Analysis, and Political Action towards Social Equity*, 4th ed. Rochester, VT: Schenkman Books, 1990.

GOELLER, BRUCE F. "A Framework for Evaluating Success in Systems Analysis." In *Handbook of Systems Analysis: Craft Issues and Procedural Choices*, ed. Hugh J. Miser and Edward S. Quade. Chichester, Eng.: Wiley, 1988, pp. 567–617.

GOLDENBERG, EDIE N. "The Three Faces of Evaluation." *Journal of Policy Analysis and Management* 2, no. 4 (Summer 1983), 515–25.

GOODMAN, WILLIAM I., and ERIC C. FREUND. *Principles and Practice of Urban Planning*. Washington, DC: International City Managers' Association, 1968.

GORDON, T. J., and H. HAYWARD. "Initial Experiments with the Cross-Impact Matrix Method of Forecasting." *Futures* 1, no. 2 (December 1968), 100–116.

GORDON, W. J. J. *Synectics*. New York: Harper & Row, 1961.

GRAMLICH, EDWARD M., and PATRICIA P. KOSHEL. "Is Real-World Experimentation Possible? The Case of Educational Performance Contracting." *Policy Analysis* 1, no. 3 (Summer 1975), 511–30.

GUBA, EGON G. and YVONNA S. LINCOLN. *Effective Evaluation*. San Francisco: Jossey-Bass, 1981.

——. *Toward a Methodology of Naturalistic Inquiry in Educational Evaluation*. Los Angeles: Center for the Study of Evaluation, UCLA Graduate School of Education, 1978.

——, and YVONNA S. LINCOLN. "The Countenances of Fourth-Generation Evaluation: Description, Judgment, and Negotiation." In *The Politics of Program Evaluation*, ed. Dennis J. Palumbo. Newbury Park, CA: Sage, 1987, pp. 202–34.

GUESS, GEORGE M., and PAUL G. FARNHAM. *Cases in Public Policy Analysis*. New York: Longman, 1989.

HALL, PETER A. "Policy Paradigms, Experts and the State: The Case of Macroeconomic Policy-Making in Britain." In *Social Scientists, Policy, and the State*, ed. Stephen Brooks and Alain-G. Gagnon. New York: Praeger, 1990, pp. 53–78.

HAMBRICK, RALPH S., JR. "Policy Analysis." In *Public Sector Management*, ed. Marcia Lynn Whicker and Todd W. Areson. New York: Praeger, 1990, pp. 99–112.

HARDIN, GARRETT. "The Tragedy of the Commons," *Science* 162 (13 December 1968), 1243–48.

HARRINGTON, WINSTON. "Valuing the Environment." *Journal of Policy Analysis and Management* 7, no. 4 (Fall 1988), 722–26.

HATRY, HARRY P. "Pitfalls of Evaluation." In *Pitfalls of Analysis*, ed. Giandomenico Majone and Edward S. Quade. Chichester, Eng.: Wiley, 1980, pp. 158–78.

——. "Program Evaluation." In *Handbook of Systems Analysis: Craft Issues and Procedural Choices*, ed. Hugh J. Miser and Edward S. Quade. Chichester, Eng.: Wiley 1988, pp. 421–62.

——. LOUIS H. BLAIR, DONALD M. FISK, JOHN M. GREINER, JOHN R. HALL, JR., and PHILIP S. SCHOENMAN. *How Effective Are Your Community Services? Procedures for Monitoring the Effectiveness of Municipal Services*. Washington, DC: Urban Institute and International City Management Association, 1977.

——, LOUIS BLAIR, DONALD FISK, and WAYNE KIMMEL. *Program Analysis for State and Local Governments*. Washington, DC: Urban Institute, 1976.

——, MARK FALL, THOMAS O. SINGER, and E. BLAINE LINER. *Monitoring the Outcomes of Economic Development Programs: A Manual*. Washington, DC: Urban Institute, 1990.

——, RICHARD E. WINNIE, and DONALD M. FISK. *Practical Program Evaluation for State and Local Government Officials*, 2nd ed. Washington, DC: Urban Institute, 1981.

HEINEMAN, ROBERT A., WILLIAM T. BLUHM, STEVEN A. PETERSON, and EDWARD N. KEARNY. *The World of the Policy Analyst: Rationality, Values, and Politics*. Chatham, NJ: Chatham House, 1990.

HELLING, AMY, MICHAEL MATICHICH, and DAVID SA-

WICKI. "The No-Action Alternative: A Tool for Comprehensive Planning and Policy Analysis." *Environmental Impact Assessment Review* 2, no. 2 (June 1982), 141–58.

HELMER, OLAF. *Social Technology*. New York: Basic Books, 1966.

——. "Using Expert Judgment." In *Handbook of Systems Analysis: Craft Issues and Procedural Choices*, ed. Hugh J. Miser and Edward S. Quade. Chichester, Eng.: Wiley, 1988, pp. 87–119.

HENDLER, SUE. "Ethics in Planning: The Views of Students and Practitioners." *Journal of Planning Education and Research* 10, no. 2 (Winter 1991), 99–105.

——. "Professional Codes as Bridges between Planning and Ethics: A Case Study." *Plan Canada* 30, no. 2 (1990), 22–29.

HENRY, GARY T. *Practical Sampling*. Newbury Park, CA: Sage, 1990.

HILL, MORRIS. "A Goals-Achievement Matrix for Evaluating Alternative Plans." *Journal of the American Institute of Planners* 34, no. 1 (January 1968), 19–29.

HILL, PERCY H., ed. *Making Decisions: A Multidisciplinary Introduction*. Reading, MA: Addison-Wesley, 1978.

HIRSCHHORN, LARRY. "Scenario Writing: A Developmental Approach." *Journal of the American Planning Association* 46, no. 2 (April 1980), 172–83.

HOAGLIN, DAVID C., RICHARD J. LIGHT, BUCKNAM McPEEK, FREDERICK MOSTELLER, and MICHAEL A. STOTO. *Data for Decisions: Information Strategies for Policymakers*. Cambridge, MA: Abt Books, 1982.

HOFFERBERT, RICHARD. *The Reach and Grasp of Policy Analysis: Comparative Views of the Craft*. Tuscaloosa: University of Alabama Press, 1990.

HOUSE, ERNEST R. *Evaluating with Validity*. Beverly Hills: Sage, 1980.

HOUSE, PETER W. *The Art of Public Policy Analysis: The Arena of Regulations and Resources*. Beverly Hills: Sage, 1982.

HOWE, ELIZABETH. "Normative Ethics in Planning." *Journal of Planning Literature* 5, no. 2 (November 1990), 123–50.

——, and JEROME KAUFMAN. "Ethics and Professional Practice." In *Values, Ethics, and the Practice of Policy Analysis*, ed. William N. Dunn. Lexington, MA: Lexington Books, 1983, pp. 9–31.

——, and JEROME KAUFMAN. "The Ethics of Contemporary American Planners." *Journal of the American Planning Association* 45, no. 3 (July 1979), 243–55.

HUFF, DARREL. *How to Lie with Statistics*. New York: Norton, 1954.

HYMAN, HERBERT H. *Interviewing in Social Research*. Chicago: University of Chicago Press, 1975.

INGRAM, HELEN. "Implementation: A Review and a Suggested Framework." In *Public Administration:*

The State of the Discipline, ed. Naomi B. Lynn and Aaron Wildavsky. Chatham, NJ: Chatham House, 1990, pp. 462–80.

INNES, JUDITH (DE NEUFVILLE). "Knowledge and Action: Making the Link." *Journal of Planning Education and Research* 6, no. 2 (Winter 1987), 86–92.

———. "The Power of Data Requirements." *Journal of the American Planning Association* 54, no. 3 (Summer 1988), 275–78.

———. *Social Indicators and Public Policy: Interactive Processes of Design and Application.* Amsterdam: Elsevier Scientific, 1975.

ISNARD, C. A., and E. C. ZEEMAN. "Some Models from Catastrophe Theory in the Social Sciences." In *The Use of Models in the Social Sciences*, ed. Lyndhurst Collins. Boulder, CO: Westview Press, 1976.

ISSERMAN, ANDREW M. "The Accuracy of Population Projections for Sub-County Areas." *Journal of the American Institute of Planners* 43, no. 3 (July 1977), 247–59.

JENNINGS, BRUCE. "Interpretation and the Practice of Policy Analysis." In *Confronting Values in Policy Analysis: The Politics of Criteria*, ed. Frank Fischer and John Forester. Newbury Park, CA: Sage, 1987, pp. 128–52.

JONES, CHARLES O. *An Introduction to the Study of Public Policy*, 2nd ed. North Scituate, MA: Duxbury Press, 1977.

JONES, WALTER J. "Can Evaluations Influence Programs? The Case of Compensatory Education." *Journal of Policy Analysis and Management* 2, no. 2 (Winter 1983), 174–84.

KAUFMAN, HERBERT. *Administrative Feedback: Monitoring Subordinates' Behavior.* Washington, DC: Brookings Institution, 1973.

KAUFMAN, JEROME L. "Hamelethics in Planning: To Do or Not to Do." *Business and Professional Ethics Journal* 6, no. 2 (1989), 66–77.

KOBERG, DON, and JIM BAGNALL. *The Universal Traveler.* Los Altos, CA: Wm. Kaufmann, 1974.

KOENIG, DONALD M., and CHARLES RUSCH. *Design for Mental Health Services at the Community Level.* Berkeley: University of California, Architectural Experimental Laboratory, 1965.

KRIEGER, MARTIN H. "The Inner Game of Writing." *Journal of Policy Analysis and Management* 7, no. 2 (Winter 1988), 408–16.

KRISTOL, IRVING. "Where Have All the Answers Gone?" In *Policy Studies Review Annual*, Vol. 4, ed. Bertram H. Raven. Beverly Hills: Sage, 1980, pp. 125–27.

KRONE, ROBERT M. *Systems Analysis and Policy Sciences: Theory and Practice.* New York: Wiley, 1980.

KRUMHOLZ, NORMAN, and JOHN FORESTER. *Making Equity Planning Work: Leadership in the Public Sector.* Philadelphia: Temple University Press, 1990.

LANE, J. S., L. R. GRENZEBACK, T. J. MARTIN, and S. C. LOCKWOOD. *The No-Action Alternative: Impact As-sessment Guidelines.* National Cooperative Highway Research Program, Report 217. Washington, DC: National Research Council, December 1979.

LASSWELL, HAROLD D. "The Policy Orientation." In *The Policy Sciences: Recent Developments in Scope and Methods*, ed. Daniel Lerner and Harold D. Lasswell. Stanford, CA: Stanford University Press, 1951, pp. 3–15.

LAVE, CHARLES A., and JAMES G. MARCH. *An Introduction to Models in the Social Sciences.* New York: Harper & Row, 1975.

LAVRAKAS, PAUL J. *Telephone Survey Methods: Sampling, Selection, and Supervision.* Newbury Park, CA: Sage, 1987.

LAWRENCE, JOHN E. S., and THOMAS J. COOK. "Designing Program Evaluations with the Help of Stakeholders." *Journal of Policy Analysis and Management* 2, no. 1 (Fall 1982), 120–23.

LERNER, DANIEL, and HAROLD D. LASSWELL, eds. *The Policy Sciences: Recent Developments in Scope and Methods.* Stanford, CA: Stanford University Press, 1951.

LEUNG, HOK LIN. *Towards a Subjective Approach to Policy Planning & Evaluation: Common-Sense Structured.* Winnipeg, Canada: Ronald P. Frye, 1985.

LEVIN, MARTIN A. "Conditions Contributing to Effective Implementation and Their Limits." In *Research in Public Policy Analysis and Management: Basic Theory, Methods and Perspectives*, Vol. 1, ed. John P. Crecine. Greenwich, CT: JAI Press, 1981, pp. 65–111.

LEVY, FRANK, ARNOLD J. MELTSNER, and AARON WILDAVSKY. *Urban Outcomes: Schools, Streets, and Libraries.* Berkeley: University of California Press, 1974.

LINDBLOM, CHARLES E. "Policy Analysis." *American Economic Review* 48, no. 3 (June 1958), 298–312.

———. "The Science of 'Muddling Through.'" *Public Administration Review* 19, no. 2 (Spring 1959), 79–88.

———. "Who Needs What Social Research for Policymaking?" *Knowledge: Creation, Diffusion, Utilization* 7, no. 4 (June 1986), 345–66.

LINDER, STEPHEN H., and B. GUY PETERS. "The Design of Instruments for Public Policy." In *Policy Theory and Policy Evaluation: Concepts, Knowledge, Causes and Norms*, ed. Stuart S. Nagel. New York: Greenwood Press, 1990, pp. 103–19.

LINDQUIST, EVERT A. "The Third Community, Policy Inquiry, and Social Scientists." In *Social Scientists, Policy, and the State*, ed. Stephen Brooks and Alain-G. Gagnon. New York: Praeger, 1990, pp. 21–51.

LINEBERRY, ROBERT L. *American Public Policy: What Government Does and What Difference It Makes.* New York: Harper & Row, 1977.

LINNER, JOHN. "Planning and the Political Process: A View from the Trenches." Paper presented at the American Planning Association National Conference, Miami, May 1979.

LINSTONE, HAROLD A., and MURRAY TUROFF, eds. *The Delphi Method: Techniques and Applications.* Reading, MA: Addison-Wesley, 1975.

LITCHFIELD, NATHANIEL, PETER KETTLE, and MICHAEL WHITBREAD. *Evaluation in the Planning Process.* Oxford: Pergamon Press, 1975.

LOWI, THEODORE J. "Four Systems of Policy, Politics and Choice." *Public Administration Review* 32, no. 4 (July/August, 1972), 298–310.

LUKE, TIMOTHY W. "Policy Science and Rational Choice Theory: A Methodological Critique." In *Confronting Values in Policy Analysis: The Politics of Criteria,* ed. Frank Fischer and John Forester. Newbury Park, CA: Sage, 1987, pp. 174–90.

LUMSDAINE, EDWARD, and MONIKA LUMSDAINE. *Creative Problem Solving.* New York: McGraw-Hill, 1990.

LYNCH. THOMAS P. *Policy Analysis in Public Policymaking.* Lexington, MA: Lexington Books, 1975.

LYNN, LAURENCE E., JR. *Designing Public Policy: A Casebook on the Role of Policy Analysis.* Santa Monica: Goodyear, 1980.

———. "Policy Analysis in the Bureaucracy: How New? How Effective?" *Journal of Policy Analysis and Management* 8, no. 3 (Summer 1989), 373–77.

LYNN, NAOMI B., and AARON WILDAVSKY, eds. *Public Administration: The State of the Discipline.* Chatham, NJ: Chatham House, 1990.

MACK, RUTH P. *Planning on Uncertainty: Decision Making in Business and Government Administration.* New York: Wiley-Interscience, 1971.

MACRAE, DUNCAN, JR. "Concepts and Methods of Policy Analysis." *Society* 16, no. 6 (September/October 1979), 17–23.

———. *Policy Indicators: Links between Social Science and Public Debate.* Chapel Hill: University of North Carolina Press, 1985.

———, and DALE WHITTINGTON. "Assessing Preferences in Cost-Benefit Analysis: Reflections on Rural Water Supply Evaluation in Haiti." *Journal of Policy Analysis and Management* 7, no. 2 (Winter 1988), 246–63.

———, and JAMES A. WILDE. *Policy Analysis for Public Decisions.* North Scituate, MA: Duxbury Press, 1979.

MAJONE, GIANDOMENICO. *Evidence, Argument, and Persuasion in the Policy Process.* New Haven: Yale University Press, 1989.

———, and EDWARD S. QUADE, eds. *Pitfalls of Analysis.* Chichester, Eng.: Wiley, 1980.

MANHEIM, MARVIN, L. *Highway Route Location as a Hierarchically-Structured Sequential Decision Process.* Cambridge, MA: MIT, Civil Engineering Systems Laboratory, Research Report R64–15, 1964.

MARCH, JAMES G., and HERBERT A. SIMON. *Organizations.* New York: Wiley, 1958.

MARCUSE, PETER. "Professional Ethics and Beyond: Values in Planning." *Journal of the American Institute of Planners* 42, no. 3 (July 1976), 264–74.

MAY, ERNEST R. *"Lessons" of the Past: The Use and Misuse of History in American Foreign Policy.* New York: Oxford University Press, 1973.

MAY, PETER J. "Hints for Crafting Alternative Policies." *Policy Analysis* 7, no. 2 (Spring 1981), 227–44.

———. "Politics and Policy Analysis." *Political Science Quarterly* 101, no. 1 (Spring 1986), 109–25.

MAZMANIAN, DANIEL A., and PAUL A. SABATIER, eds. *Effective Policy Implementation.* Lexington, MA: Lexington Books, 1981.

MCALLISTER, DONALD M. *Evaluation in Environmental Planning: Assessing Environmental, Social, Economic, and Political Tradeoffs.* Cambridge, MA: MIT Press, 1980.

MCKENNA, CHRISTOPHER K. *Quantitative Methods for Public Decision Making.* New York: McGraw-Hill, 1980.

MEEHAN, EUGENE J. *Ethics for Policymaking: A Methodological Analysis.* New York: Greenwood Press, 1990.

———. *Reasoned Argument in Social Science: Linking Research to Policy.* Westport, CT: Greenwood Press, 1981.

MELTSNER, ARNOLD J. "Bureaucratic Policy Analysts." *Policy Analysis* 1, no. 1 (Winter 1975), 115–31.

———. *Policy Analysts in the Bureaucracy.* Berkeley and Los Angeles: University of California Press, 1976.

———. "Political Feasibility and Policy Analysis." *Public Administration Review* 32, no. 6 (November/December 1972), 859–67.

———. *Rules for Rulers: The Politics of Advice.* Philadelphia: Temple University Press, 1990.

———, and CHRISTOPHER BELLAVITA. *The Policy Organization.* Beverly Hills, CA: Sage, 1983.

MERRIAM, DWIGHT. "Demystifying the Law: A Planner's Guide to Legal Research." *Practicing Planner* (June 1979), 4–7.

MERTON, ROBERT K., MARJORIE FISKE, and PATRICIA L. KENDALL. *The Focused Interview: A Manual of Problems and Procedures.* New York: Free Press, 1956.

MEYERSON, MARTIN, and EDWARD C. BANFIELD. *Politics, Planning, and the Public Interest.* New York: Free Press, 1955.

MILLS, MIRIAM K. *Conflict Resolution and Public Policy.* New York: Greenwood Press, 1990.

MISER, HUGH J., and EDWARD S. QUADE. "Craftsmanship in Analysis." In *Handbook of Systems Analysis: Craft Issues and Procedural Choices,* ed. Hugh J. Miser and Edward S. Quade. Chichester, Eng.: Wiley, 1988, pp. 3–26.

———, eds. *Handbook of Systems Analysis: Craft Issues and Procedural Choices.* Chichester, Eng.: Wiley, 1988.

————, eds. *Handbook of Systems Analysis: Overview of Uses, Procedures, Applications, and Practice*. New York: North-Holland, 1985.

————. "Toward Quality Control." In *Handbook of Systems Analysis: Craft Issues and Procedural Choices*, ed. Hugh J. Miser and Edward S. Quade. Chichester, Eng.: Wiley, 1988, pp. 619–56.

MITROFF, IAN, and JAMES R. EMSHOFF. "On Strategic Assumption-Making." *Academy of Management Review* 4, no. 1 (January 1979), 1–12.

MOORE, GARY T., ed. *Emerging Methods in Environmental Design and Planning*. Cambridge, MA: MIT Press, 1970.

MOORE, MARK H. "Anatomy of the Heroin Problem: An Exercise in Problem Definition." *Policy Analysis* 2, no. 2 (Fall 1976), 639–62.

MORRIS, LYNN, CAROL TAYLOR FITZ-GIBBON, and MARLENE E. HENERSON. *Program Evaluation Kit*, 8 vols. Beverly Hills: Sage, 1978.

MOSTELLER, FREDERICK. "Assessing Unknown Numbers: Order of Magnitude Estimation." In *Statistics and Public Policy*, ed. William B. Fairley and Frederick Mosteller. Reading, MA: Addison-Wesley, 1977, pp. 163–84.

————, WILLIAM H. KRUSKAL, RICHARD S. PIETERS, GERALD R. RISING, RICHARD F. LINK, and MARTHA ZELINKA. *Statistics by Example*, Vols. 1–4. Reading, MA: Addison-Wesley, 1973.

MURIN, WILLIAM J., GERALD MICHAEL GREENFIELD, and JOHN D. BUENKER. *Public Policy: A Guide to Information Sources*. Volume 13 in the American Government and History Information Guide Series. Detroit: Gale Research Company, 1981.

MURPHY, JEROME T. *Getting the Facts: A Fieldwork Guide for Evaluators and Policy Analysts*. Santa Monica: Goodyear, 1980.

NACHMIAS, DAVID, ed. *The Practice of Policy Evaluation*. New York: St. Martin's Press, 1980.

————. *Public Policy Evaluation: Approaches and Methods*. New York: St. Martin's Press, 1979.

NAGEL, STUART S. "Conflicting Evaluations of Policy Studies." In *Public Administration: The State of the Discipline*, ed. Naomi B. Lynn and Aaron Wildavsky. Chatham, NJ: Chatham House, 1990, pp. 421–61.

————. "Introduction: Bridging Theory and Practice in Policy/Program Evaluation." In *Policy Theory and Policy Evaluation: Concepts, Knowledge, Causes and Norms*, ed. Stuart S. Nagel. New York: Greenwood Press, 1990, pp. ix–xxiv.

————. *Policy Evaluation: Making Optimum Decisions*. New York: Praeger, 1982.

————, ed. *Policy Theory and Policy Evaluation: Concepts, Knowledge, Causes and Norms*. New York: Greenwood Press, 1990.

————. "Projecting Trends in Public Policy." In *Policy Theory and Policy Evaluation: Concepts, Knowledge, Causes and Norms*, ed. Stuart S. Nagel. New York: Greenwood Press, 1990, pp. 161–204.

————. "Introduction." In *Confronting Values in Policy Analysis: The Politics of Criteria*, ed. Frank Fischer and John Forester. Newbury Park, CA: Sage, 1987, pp. 7–9.

NAKAMURA, ROBERT T., and FRANK SMALLWOOD. *The Politics of Policy Implementation*. New York: St. Martin's Press, 1980.

NATIONAL ASSOCIATION OF ENVIRONMENTAL PROFESSIONALS. "Code of Ethics and Standards of Practice for Environmental Professionals." Alexandria, VA: National Association of Environmental Professionals, February 1978.

NELSON, ARTHUR C., ed. *Development Impact Fees: Policy Rationale, Practice, Theory, and Issues*. Chicago: Planners Press, 1988.

NICHOLAS, JAMES C., ARTHUR C. NELSON, and JULIAN C. JUERGENSMEYER. *A Practitioner's Guide to Development Impact Fees*. Chicago: Planners Press, 1991.

NISHIKAWA, NANCY I. "Survey Methods for Planners." In Hemalata C. Dandekar, *The Planner's Use of Information: Techniques for Collection, Organization, and Communication*. Stroudsburg, PA: Hutchinson Ross, 1982, pp. 32–55.

NISKANEN, WILLIAM A. "Economists and Politicians." *Journal of Policy Analysis and Management* 5, no. 2 (Winter 1986), 234–44.

O'HARE, MICHAEL. "A Typology of Governmental Action." *Journal of Policy Analysis and Management* 8, no. 4 (Fall 1989), 670–72.

OKUN, ARTHUR M. *Equality and Efficiency: The Big Tradeoff*. Washington, DC: Brookings Institution, 1975.

OSBORN, ALEX F. *Applied Imagination: Principles and Procedures of Creative Problem-Solving*, 3rd rev. ed. New York: Scribner's, 1963.

————. *Your Creative Power: How to Use Imagination*. New York: Scribner's, 1949.

PAGE, G. WILLIAM, and CARL V. PATTON. *Quick Answers to Quantitative Problems: A Pocket Primer*. Boston: Academic Press, 1991.

PALUMBO, DENNIS J. "Politics and Evaluation." *The Politics of Program Evaluation*, ed. Dennis J. Palumbo. Beverly Hills, CA: Sage, 1987, pp. 12–46.

————, ed. *The Politics of Program Evaluation*. Beverly Hills: Sage, 1987.

————. *Public Policy in America: Government in Action*. San Diego: Harcourt Brace Jovanovich, 1988.

————, and DONALD J. CALISTA, eds. *Implementation and the Policy Process: Opening Up the Black Box*. New York: Greenwood Press, 1990.

————, and DONALD J. CALISTA. "Introduction: The Relation of Implementation Research to Policy Outcomes." In *Implementation and the Policy Process: Opening Up the Black Box*, ed. Dennis J. Palumbo and Donald J. Calista. New York: Greenwood Press, 1990, pp. xi–xviii.

————, and DONALD J. CALISTA. "Opening Up the Black Box: Implementation and the Policy Process." In *Implementation and the Policy Process: Opening Up the Black Box*, ed. Dennis J. Palumbo and Donald J. Calista. New York: Greenwood Press, 1990, pp. 3–17.

——, STEPHEN B. FAWCETT, and PAULA WRIGHT. *Evaluating and Optimizing Public Policy.* Lexington, MA: Lexington Books, 1981.

——, and GEORGE A. TAYLOR. *Urban Policy: A Guide to Information Sources.* Volume 6 in the Urban Studies Information Guide Series. Detroit: Gale Research Company, 1979.

PARIS, DAVID C., and JAMES F. REYNOLDS. *The Logic of Policy Inquiry.* New York: Longman, 1983.

PATTON, CARL V. *Academia in Transition: Early Retirement or Mid-Career Change.* Cambridge, MA: Abt Books, 1979.

——. "Information for Planning." In *The Practice of Local Government Planning*, 2nd ed., ed. Frank S. So and Judith Getzels. Washington, DC: International City Management Association, 1988, pp. 472–99.

——. "Jobs and Commercial Office Development: Do New Offices Generate New Jobs?" *Economic Development Quarterly* 2, no. 4 (November 1988), 316–25.

——. "Selecting Special Students: Who Decides?" *Teachers College Record* 78, no. 1 (September 1976), 101–24.

——. "A Seven-Day Project: Early Faculty Retirement Alternatives." *Policy Analysis* 1, no. 4 (Fall 1975), 731–53.

——, BARRY N. CHECKOWAY, TSCHANGO J. KIM, KENNETH B. KURTZ, MICHAEL C. ROMANOS, JOY SCHAAD, and KENNETH E. STABLER. *Townsite Management Study: Special Report D-81.* Champaign, IL: Department of the Army, Construction Engineering Research Laboratory, 1977.

——, WILLIAM C. LIENESCH, and JAMES R. ANDERSON. "Busing the Rural Elderly." *Traffic Quarterly* 29, no. 1 (January 1975), 81–97.

——, and KENNETH E. STABLER. "The Small Town in the Urban Fringe: Conflicts in Attitudes and Values." *Journal of the Community Development Society* 10 no. 1 (Spring 1979), 83–93.

PATTON, MICHAEL QUINN. *Creative Evaluation.* Beverly Hills: Sage, 1981.

——. "Evaluation's Political Inherency: Practical Implications for Design and Use." In *The Politics of Program Evaluation*, ed. Dennis J. Palumbo. Newbury Park, CA: Sage, 1987, pp. 100–145.

——. *Practical Evaluation.* Beverly Hills: Sage, 1982.

——. *Qualitative Evaluation Methods.* Beverly Hills: Sage, 1980.

——. *Utilization-Focused Evaluation*, 2nd ed. Newbury Park, CA: Sage, 1986.

PFLAUM, ANN M. and TIMOTHY J. DELMONT. "External Scanning—A Tool for Planners." In *Strategic Planning: Threats and Opportunities for Planners*, ed.

John M. Bryson and Robert C. Einsweiler. Chicago: Planners Press, 1988, pp. 145–59.

PINKUS, CHARLES E., and ANNE DIXSON. *Solving Local Government Problems: Practical Applications of Operations Research in Cities and Regions.* London: George Allen & Unwin, 1981.

PITTENGER, DONALD B. *Projecting State and Local Populations.* Cambridge, MA: Ballinger, 1976.

POISTER, THEODORE H. *Public Program Analysis: Applied Research Methods.* Baltimore: University Park Press, 1978.

POLYA, G. *How to Solve It.* New York: Doubleday, 1957.

PRESSMAN, JEFFREY L., and AARON B. WILDAVSKY. *Implementation.* Berkeley: University of California Press, 1973.

QUADE, EDWARD S. *Analysis for Public Decisions*, 2nd ed. New York: Elsevier Scientific, 1982.

——. "Objectives, Constraints, and Alternatives." In *Handbook of Systems Analysis: Overview of Uses, Procedures, Applications, and Practice*, ed. Hugh J. Miser and Edward S. Quade. New York: North Holland, 1985, pp. 171–89.

QUIGLEY, JOHN M. "Does Rent Control Cause Homelessness? Taking the Claims Seriously." *Journal of Policy Analysis and Management* 9, no. 1 (Winter 1990), 89–93.

——, and SUZANNE SCOTCHMER. "What Counts? Analysis Counts." *Journal of Policy Analysis and Management* 8, no. 3 (Summer 1989), 483–94.

RAIFFA, HOWARD. *Decision Analysis: Introductory Lectures on Choices under Uncertainty.* Reading, MA: Addison-Wesley, 1968.

RAPOPORT, AMOS. *History and Precedent in Environmental Design.* New York: Plenum Press, 1990.

——. *Human Aspects of Urban Form: Towards a Man-Environment Approach to Urban Form and Design.* Oxford: Pergamon, 1977.

RAY, MARILYN L. "Policy Evaluation and the Argumentation Process." In *Policy Theory and Policy Evaluation*, ed. Stuart S. Nagel. New York: Greenwood Press, 1990, pp. 61–73.

REUTER, PETER. "The (Continued) Vitality of Mythical Numbers." *The Public Interest* 75 (Spring 1984), 135–47.

RICHARDSON, SEVERNS, SCHEELER & ASSOCIATES. *Functional Relationships Study.* Champaign, IL: Richardson, Severns, Scheeler & Associates, 1969.

RING, PETER SMITH. "Strategic Issues: What Are They and from Where Do They Come?" In *Strategic Planning: Threats and Opportunities for Planners*, ed. John M. Bryson and Robert C. Einsweiler. Chicago: Planners Press, 1988, pp. 69–83.

ROBINSON, W. S. "Ecological Correlation and the Behavior of Individuals." *American Sociological Review* 15 (June 1950), 351–57.

ROHR, JOHN A. "Ethics in Public Administration: A State-of-the-Discipline Report." In *Public Adminis-*

tration: The State of the Discipline, ed. Naomi B. Lynn and Aaron Wildavsky. Chatham, NJ: Chatham House, 1990, pp. 97–123.

RONDINELLI, DENNIS A. "Urban Planning as Policy Analysis: Management of Urban Change." *Journal of the American Institute of Planners* 39, no. 1 (January 1973), 13–22.

ROOS, LESLIE L., JR., NORALOU P. ROOS, and BARBARA McKINLEY. "Implementing Randomization." *Policy Analysis* 3, no. 4 (Fall 1977), 547–59.

ROSSI, PETER H., and HOWARD E. FREEMAN. *Evaluation: A Systematic Approach*, 2nd ed. Beverly Hills: Sage, 1982.

——— and WALTER WILLIAMS. *Evaluating Social Programs: Theory, Practice, and Politics*. New York: Seminar Press, 1972.

SAATY, THOMAS L., and LUIS G. VARGAS. *The Logic of Priorities: Applications in Business, Energy, Health, and Transportation*. Boston: Kluwer-Nijhoff, 1982.

SACKMAN, HAROLD. *Delphi Critique*. Lexington, MA: D.C. Heath, 1975.

SAWICKI, DAVID S. "Express Transit Systems Analyzed." *Journal of Transport Economics and Policy* 8, no. 3 (September 1974), 274–93.

———. "Studies of Aggregated Areal Data: Problems of Statistical Inference." *Land Economics* 49, no. 1 (February, 1973), 109–14.

———. "Teaching Policy Analysis in a Graduate Planning Program." *Journal of Planning Education and Research* 1, no. 2 (Winter 1982), 78–85.

SCHMID, CALVIN F., and STANTON E. SCHMID. *Handbook of Graphic Presentation*, 2nd ed. New York: Wiley, 1979.

SCHWARTZ, SEYMOUR I., and PETER M. ZORN. "A Critique of Quasiexperimental and Statistical Controls for Measuring Program Effects: Applications to Urban Growth Control." *Journal of Policy Analysis and Management* 7, no. 3 (Spring 1988), 491–505.

SCHWARZ, BRITA, KENNETH C. BOWEN, ISTVAN KISS, and EDWARD S. QUADE. "Guidance for Decision." In *Handbook of Systems Analysis: Overview of Uses, Procedures, Applications, and Practice*, ed. Hugh J. Miser and Edward S. Quade. New York: North Holland, 1985, pp. 219–47.

SCHWARZ, JOHN E. *America's Hidden Success: A Reassessment of Public Policy from Kennedy to Reagan*, rev. ed. New York: Norton, 1988.

SILLS, DAVID, ed. *International Encyclopedia of the Social Sciences*. New York: Macmillan, 1968.

SIMON, HERBERT A. *Administrative Behavior: A Study of Decision-Making Processes in Administrative Organizations*, 3rd ed. New York: Free Press, 1976.

———. "A Behavioral Model of Rational Choice." *Quarterly Journal of Economics* 69 (February 1955), 99–118.

SINGER, MAX. "The Vitality of Mythical Numbers." *The Public Interest* 23 (Spring 1971), 3–9.

SOCOLOW, ROBERT H. "Failures of Discourse: Obstacles to the Integration of Environmental Values into Natural Resource Policy." In *When Values Conflict: Essays on Environmental Analysis, Discourse, and Decision*, ed. Laurence H. Tribe, Corinne S. Schelling, and John Voss. Cambridge, MA: Ballinger, 1976, pp. 1–33.

SPEAR, MARY ELEANOR. *Charting Statistics*. New York: McGraw-Hill, 1952.

STAKE, ROBERT E. "The Case Study Method in Social Inquiry." *Educational Researcher* 7 no. 2 (February 1978), 5–8.

———, ed. *Evaluating the Arts in Education: A Responsive Approach*. Columbus, OH: Charles E. Merrill, 1975.

STATE AND LOCAL FINANCES PROJECT. *A First Step to Analysis: The Issue Paper*. PPB No 11. Washington, D.C. George Washington University, July, 1968.

STEISS, ALAN WALTER, and GEORGE A. DANEKE. *Performance Administration*. Lexington, MA: D.C. Heath, 1980.

STOKEY, EDITH, and RICHARD ZECKHAUSER. *A Primer for Policy Analysis*. New York: Norton, 1978.

STRUENING, ELMER L., and MARCIA GUTTENTAG, eds. *Handbook of Evaluation Research*, 2 vols. Beverly Hills: Sage, 1975.

STRUNK, WILLIAM, JR., and E. B. WHITE. *The Elements of Style*. New York: Macmillan, 1959.

SUCHMAN, EDWARD A. *Evaluative Research: Principles and Practice in Public Service and Social Action Programs*. New York: Russell Sage Foundation, 1967.

———. "The Principles of Research Design." In John T. Doby et al., *An Introduction to Social Research*. Harrisburg, PA: Stackpole, 1954.

SZANTON, PETER. *Not Well Advised*. New York: Russell Sage Foundation, 1981.

TANUR, JUDITH M., ed. *Statistics: A Guide to the Unknown*, 2nd ed. San Francisco: Holden-Day, 1978.

TEITZ, MICHAEL B. "Policy Evaluation: The Uncertain Guide." Berkeley: University of California, Institute for Urban and Regional Development, Working Paper no. 298, September 1978.

THOMPSON, DENNIS. "Ascribing Responsibility to Advisers in Government." In *Ethical Issues in Professional Life*, ed. Joan C. Callahan. New York: Oxford University Press, 1988, pp. 282–90.

TINBERGEN, JAN. *Economic Policy: Principles and Design*. Amsterdam: North Holland, 1956.

TOLCHIN, SUSAN J. "The Political Uses of Evaluation Research: Cost-Benefit Analysis and the Cotton Dust Standard." In *The Politics of Program Evaluation*, ed. Dennis J. Palumbo. Newbury Park, CA: Sage, 1987, pp. 249–69.

TOMLINSON, ROLFE, EDWARD S. QUADE, and HUGH J. MISER. "Implementation." In *Handbook of Systems Analysis: Overview of Uses, Procedures, Applications, and Practice*, ed. Hugh J. Miser and Edward S. Quade. New York: North Holland, 1985, pp. 249–80.

Tong, Rosemarie. "Ethics and the Policy Analyst: The Problem of Responsibility." In *Confronting Values in Policy Analysis: The Politics of Criteria*, ed. Frank Fischer and John Forester. Newbury Park, CA: Sage, 1987, pp. 192–211.

———. *Ethics in Policy Analysis*. Englewood Cliffs, NJ: Prentice Hall, 1986.

Tribe, Lawrence H., Corinne S. Schelling, and John Voss, eds. *When Values Conflict: Essays on Environmental Analysis, Discourse, and Decision*. Cambridge, MA: Ballinger, 1976.

Trumbull, William N. "Reply to Whittington and MacRae." *Journal of Policy Analysis and Management* 9, no. 4 (Fall 1990), 548–50.

———. "Who Has Standing in Cost-Benefit Analysis?" *Journal of Policy Analysis and Management* 9, no. 2 (Spring 1990), 201–18.

Tufte, Edward R. *Data Analysis for Politics and Policy*. Englewood Cliffs, NJ: Prentice Hall, 1974.

———. *Envisioning Information*. Cheshire, CT: Graphics Press, 1990.

———. *The Quantitative Analysis of Social Problems*. Reading, MA: Addison-Wesley, 1970.

———. *The Visual Display of Quantitative Information*. Cheshire, CT: Graphics Press, 1983.

Tukey, John W. *Exploratory Data Analysis*. Reading, MA: Addison-Wesley, 1977.

Ukeles, Jacob B. "Policy Analysis: Myth or Reality?" *Public Administration Review* 37, no. 3 (May/June 1977), 223–28.

U.S. Bureau of the Census. *Census of Population*. Washington, DC: Bureau of the Census, 1990.

———. *Current Housing Report H-170-87-21, American Housing Survey for the Atlanta Metropolitan Area in 1987*. Washington, DC: Bureau of the Census, 1990.

Van Dyke, Vernon. *Equality and Public Policy*. Chicago: Nelson-Hall, 1990.

Vasu, Michael L., Debra W. Stewart, and G. David Garson. *Organizational Behavior and Public Management*, 2nd ed. New York: Marcel Dekker, 1990.

Wachs, Martin, ed. *Ethics in Planning*. New Brunswick, NJ: Center for Urban Policy Research, 1985.

———. "Introduction." In *Ethics in Planning*, ed. Martin Wachs. New Brunswick, NJ: Center for Urban Policy Research, 1985, pp. xiii–xxi.

Walker, Warren E. "Generating and Screening Alternatives." In *Handbook of Systems Analysis: Craft Issues and Procedural Choices*, ed. Hugh J. Miser and Edward S. Quade. Chichester, Eng.: Wiley, 1988, pp. 217–46.

Webb, Eugene J., Donald F. Campbell, Richard D. Schwartz, and Lee Sechrest. *Unobtrusive Measures: Nonreactive Research in the Social Sciences*. Chicago: Rand McNally, 1966.

Webber, David J. "Analyzing Political Feasibility: Political Scientists' Unique Contribution to Policy Analysis." *Policy Studies Journal* 14, no. 4 (June 1986), 545–53.

Weimer, David L., and Aidan R. Vining. *Policy Analysis: Concepts and Practice*. Englewood Cliffs, NJ: Prentice Hall, 1989.

Weiss, Carol H., ed. *Evaluating Action Programs: Readings in Social Action and Education*. Boston: Allyn & Bacon, 1972.

———. *Evaluation Research: Methods for Assessing Program Effectiveness*. Englewood Cliffs, NJ: Prentice Hall, 1972.

———. "The Uneasy Partnership Endures: Social Science and Government." In *Social Scientists, Policy, and the State*, ed. Stephen Brooks and Alain-G. Gagnon. New York: Praeger, 1990, pp. 97–111.

———. "Where Politics and Evaluation Research Meet." In *The Politics of Program Evaluation*, ed. Dennis J. Palumbo. Newbury Park, CA: Sage, 1987, pp. 47–70.

Weiss, Robert S., and Martin Rein. "The Evaluation of Broad-Aim Programs: Difficulties in Experimental Design and an Alternative." In *Evaluating Action Programs: Readings in Social Action and Education*, ed. Carol H. Weiss. Boston: Allyn & Bacon, 1972, pp. 236–49.

Whicker, Marcia Lynn, and Todd W. Areson, eds. *Public Sector Management*. New York: Praeger, 1990.

Whittick, Arnold, ed. *Encyclopedia of Urban Planning*. New York: McGraw-Hill, 1974.

Whittington, Dale, and Duncan MacRae, Jr. "Comment: Judgements about Who Has Standing in Cost-Benefit Analysis." *Journal of Policy Analysis and Management* 9 no. 4 (Fall 1990), 536–47.

———. "The Issue of Standing in Cost-Benefit Analysis." *Journal of Policy Analysis and Management* 5, no. 4 (Summer 1986), 665–82.

Wholey, Joseph S. *Evaluation: Promise and Performance*. Washington, D.C. Urban Institute, 1979.

Wildavsky, Aaron. *Budgeting: A Comparative Theory of Budgetary Processes*. Boston: Little, Brown, 1975.

———. "If Planning Is Everything, Maybe It's Nothing." *Policy Sciences* 4, no. 2 (June 1973), 127–53.

———. *The Politics of the Budgetary Process*, 2nd ed. Boston: Little, Brown, 1974.

———. *Speaking Truth to Power: The Art and Craft of Policy Analysis*. Boston: Little, Brown, 1979.

———. "Ubiquitous Anomie: Public Service in an Era of Ideological Dissensus." *Public Administration Review* 48, no. 4 (July/August 1988), 753–55.

Williams, Walter. *Social Policy Research and Analysis: The Experience in the Federal Social Agencies*. New York: American Elsevier, 1971.

———, ed. *Studying Implementation: Methodological and Administrative Issues*. Chatham, NJ: Chatham House, 1982.

Winter, Søren. "Integrating Implementation Research." In *Implementation and the Policy Process: Opening Up the Black Box*, ed. Dennis J. Palumbo and Donald J. Calista. New York: Greenwood Press, 1990, pp. 19–38.

WITZLING, LAWRENCE P., and ROBERT C. GREENSTREET. *Presenting Statistics: A Manager's Guide to the Persuasive Use of Statistics*. New York: Wiley, 1989.

WOLMAN, HAROLD. "Local Economic Development Policy: What Explains the Divergence between Policy Analysis and Political Behavior?" *Journal of Urban Affairs* 10, no. 1 (1988), 19–28.

YOUNIS, TALIB, ed. *Implementation in Public Policy*. Aldershot, Eng.: Dartmouth, 1990.

———, and IAN DAVIDSON. "The Study of Implementation." In *Implementation in Public Policy*, ed. Talib Younis. Aldershot, Eng.: Dartmouth, 1990, pp. 3–14.

ZELENY, MILAN. *Multiple Criteria Decision Making*. New York: McGraw-Hill, 1982.

ZERBE, RICHARD O., JR. "Does Benefit Cost Analysis Stand Alone? Rights and Standing." *Journal of Policy Analysis and Management* 10, no. 1 (Winter 1991), 96–105.

ZWICKY, FRITZ. *Discovery, Invention, Research through the Morphological Approach*. New York: Macmillan, 1969.

Index

Abating taxes example, 274
Abstracts, data from, 85–86
Accounting (shadow) price, 195, 221
Act-deontology, 36, 37, 66
Actors, political analysis in terms of, 170, 302–3
Actual-versus-planned performance comparisons, pros and cons, 377–78
Act-utilitarianism, 36, 38, 66
Adequacy, 220
Adjudication, 92
Administrative operability, 220
Advice, 24
Advisers, responsibility of, 43–44
Advising, decision making vs., 16–17
Advocacy, 41
  of alternatives, 334
  by analyst, 28
  definition, 255
  multiple, 334
  of others' position, 15–16
  process, 15–16
A fortiori analysis, 288–89
  definition, 318
Agencies, data from, 79, 80
Agency files, 95–96
Aggregated selection methods, contrasted with disaggregated, 350
Aggregation, pros and cons, 355
AIDS, 149

Alexander, Christopher, 245
Alexander, Ernest R., 51, 228, 251, 254
Allocation formulas, 289–95
  arbitrary nature, 292
  citizen involvement in establishing, 293–94
  example, 290–95
  guidelines, 294–95
  political aspects, 294
  process, 290–93
Alternative(s):
  characteristics of good, 230–31
  compared with the status quo, 230
  creating, 228, 245–51
  contrasted with finding, 228
  contrasted with searching for, 245
  through feasible manipulations, 246–48
  guiding principles for, 231
  by modifying existing solutions, 248–51
  morphological approach to, 245
  pitfalls to avoid in, 251–53
  deriving, 233–45
  by brainstorming, 241–44
  by comparison with an ideal, 244–45
  from experience, 238
  through analogy, 239–41

  through literature reviews, 238
  through passive means, 238–39
  through quick surveys, 237–38
  through research, 234–35
  through synectics, 239–41
  through typologies, 239
  design process, 228
  dominated, 341–49, 359
  do-nothing, 150
  errors in generating, 228
  evaluating, 60–61, 257–332
  identifying, 58–59
  identifying through evaluation, 234
  limitation on number evaluated, 229
  methods of comparing, 337–39
  methods of identifying, 233–34
  no-action, 150–51
  no-action as an alternative, 235–37
  nondominated, 341–43
  Pareto optimal, 341–42
  and policy envelope, 17
  politically viable, 62
  quality contrasted with quantity, 229
  in quick decision analysis, 159
  requirements for creating, 228

  riskless, 159
  risky, 159
  selecting, 61–63
  selection, 340–55
  by equivalent-alternatives method, 343–47
  by lexicographic ordering, 341
  by matrix display systems, 349–52
  by nondominated-alternatives method, 341–43
  by paired comparisons, 341
  by satisficing, 341
  by standard-alternative method, 347–49
  sources, 59, 231–33
  technically superior, 62
  teen-age driver example, 59
  value of considering many, 228–29
  value of segmenting, 237
Alternatives-consequence matrix, 351–52
  definition, 359
Altman, Stanley M., 113, 115–17
American Institute of Aeronautics and Astronautics (AIAA), 89
American Institute of Certified Planners' Code of Ethics and Professional Conduct, 189–90

American Medical
  Association, 154
Analogy, 239–41
  cautions, 241
  definition, 255
  direct, 240
  examples, 240–41
  fantasy, 240–41
  personal, 240
  symbolic, 240
  tragedy of the commons,
    241
  use in synectics, 240
Analysis:
  benefits of investment in,
    176–77
  communicating, 134–41
  ethical, 33–39
  indicators of quality in,
    364–65
Analyst (*see* Policy analysts)
Analytic approach, possible
  work plan, 163
Analytic success, 364
AND command, 83
Annual net benefits, 318
Anticipatory policy analysis,
  66
Antilogs, 266–67
Apgar, William C., Jr., 192
Arrow, Kenneth J., 244, 336,
  359
Art-criticism evaluation
  approach, 394
Association:
  definition, 130
  statistical, 130–33
Athey, Thomas H., 232
Average cost, 201–2
  definition, 220

Back-of-the-envelope
  calculations:
  definition, 178
  heroin example, 157
  highway cost example, 158
  political analysis, 169–70
  in problem definition, 153,
    154
  questions answered by,
    156–57
  types, 154–58
Backward mapping, 307, 313
Backward problem solving,
  54
Bail-out (worst-case) scenario,
  313, 314
Bar charts, 116, 119, 141
Bardach, Eugene, 82, 151,
  152, 310–11
Basic analysis (*see also* Basic
  methods; Data
  analysis):
  contrasted with researched
    analysis, 3–4, 18
  definition, 19
  interrupted time-series
    approach in, 383
  relationship to basic
    methods, 3
  underlying tenet, 356
  use, 4
  versus issue paper, 176–78
Basic methods (*see also* Basic
  analysis):

before-and-after
  comparisons, pros and
  cons, 376
  contrasted with researched
    methods, 3–4, 362
  definition, 19
  goals, 4
  introduction, 2–6
  relationship to basic
    analysis, 3
  by steps in the policy
    analysis process, 65
  used during problem
    definition, 154
Behn, Robert, 158–59
Beliefs, political analysis in
  terms of, 170, 303
Bellavita, Christopher, 27,
  309
Benefit-cost analysis (*see* Cost-
  benefit analysis)
Benefit-cost ratio:
  computation, 280
  contrasted with net present
    value, 280
  definition, 318
  limitations, 213, 284
Benefits, 195
  net, 276
  short run contrasted with
    long run, 298
  types, 195, 210–14
Benjamin Franklin's letter,
  340
Bickner, Robert, 194
Blair, Louis, 310
Bluhm, William T., 32, 41
Bottom-up implementation,
  307
Bowen, Kenneth C., 316
Brainstorming:
  criticism, 242–43
  definition, 255
  guidelines, 242
  types, 241–42
  value, 242
Brainwriting, 243, 255
Braybrooke, David, 188–91,
  229–30
Break-even analysis:
  definition, 318
  example, 287–88, 300
  use, 287–88
Brightman, Harvey J., 229,
  233, 312, 351, 364
Bromiley, Philip, 51
Brown, H. James, 192
Browne, Angela, 366
Bryson, John M., 51
Buchanan, James M., 192–93
Byrne, John, 281

Callahan, Joan C., 37
Campbell, Donald T., 370,
  380, 384
Case law, 92, 94–95
Cases:
  purposes, 394
  time needed to solve, 394
Case study evaluation
  approach, 394
Causality:
  contrasted with association,
    134
  establishing, 385

Census data (*see* U.S. Census)
Change, magnitude of,
  309–10
Citizen analysts, 301
Citizenship, ethical, 40
Cleveland airport example,
  75–76
Clients:
  analyst relationship with,
    258
  communicating with,
    134–41
  and decision criterion, 9
  and decision making,
    16–17
  guidance from, 29
  role, 148
  types, 5
Client's advocate role, 42
Cluster sampling, 109, 141
Coleman, James, 356
Collective-goods dilemma,
  149–50
Collectively exhaustive
  outcomes, 297
Collective rationality:
  conflict with individual
    rationality, 335–36
  definition, 359
Communicability of
  alternatives, 230
Community development
  example, 170–76
Compatibility of alternatives,
  230
Competing objectives:
  analyst's role, 188
  ethical issues, 189–90
Compound interest formula,
  277
Comprehensive planning:
  characteristics, 5
  definition, 5
Computer-based data
  searches, 83–84
Conduct, professional, 42–46
Confidence interval, 109,
  141–42
Confidence level, 109, 142
Conflict of duties, 31
Congress, data from, 89
Congressional Information
  Services, 90
Congressional Quarterly, 90
Consensus, degree of,
  309–10
Consequence, 178
Content analysis of
  documents, 111
Contingency analysis
  example, 288
Control variable (*see* Test
  variable,
  interpretation)
Cook, Thomas J., 380, 384,
  389
Cooper, Terry L., 38, 40, 41
Coplin, William D., 168,
  305–6
Correlation, 130–33 (*see also*
  Association)
Correlation coefficient, 132,
  142
Cost(s), 194–95
  of alternatives, 230

and equity issues, 194
  identifying, 194
  types, 194–95, 201–2,
    210–14
Cost-benefit analysis, 36
  and conflicting objectives,
    337–38
  contrasted with net benefit
    and cost-effectiveness,
    338
  criticisms of, 280–81
  definition, 220
  for measuring efficiency,
    213
  in postprogram evaluation,
    385
  standing in, 196–99
Cost-benefit ratio, 280 (*see
  also* Benefit-cost ratio)
Cost effectiveness, 214
  contrasted with net benefit
    and cost-benefit, 338
  definition, 220
  example, 214
  in postprogram evaluation,
    385
Cost-revenue analysis:
  definition, 220
  use, 213–14
Criteria:
  administrative operability,
    208, 218–19
  analyst's role in
    establishing, 191
  decision, 9
  definition, 187, 220
  discovering, 191
  economic and financial
    possibility, 208,
    210–14
  equity issues, 206
  establishing, 57–58
  ethical issues, 215
  examples, 187–88, 333
  measurement, 187
  operationalizing, 187
  policy termination, 367
  political viability, 208,
    214–18
  problems with ranking, 189
  reluctance of decision
    makers to establish,
    188
  secondary, use, 338
  sources, 57, 191
  stating before evaluation,
    186
  technical feasibility, 208–10
  trading off, 344–48
  types, 57, 332
  use, 186
Criterion:
  acceptability, 215–16
  administrative operability,
    218–19
  appropriateness, 216
  authority, 218
  benefit-cost ratio, 213
  capability, 218–19
  central decision, 9
  change in net worth, 212
  characteristics, 219
  cost effectiveness, 214
  economic efficiency,
    212–13

economic feasibility, 213
equity, 216–17
expected value, 298, 300
institutional commitment, 218
internal rate of return, 281, 282
legality, 216
net present value, 213
organizational support, 219
profitability, 213–14
responsiveness, 216
Crosscutting methods (*see* Data analysis; Data collection)
Cross-impact analysis:
  contrasted with the Delphi method, 275
  definition, 318
  principles, 275
Cross-sectional survey, 107, 142
Cross-tabulation analysis, 130

Daneke, George A., 218, 309–10, 312
Data:
  categorizing, 125–27
  controlling, 132
  evaluating, 109–13
  grouped, 91, 117, 121, 129–30, 142
  level, 131
  library search methods, 82–84
  quality and consistency of, 96
  transforming non-linear, 264–65
Data analysis, 113–34
  association vs. correlation issue in, 130–33
  communicating the (reporting), 134–41
  criteria for, 134–36
  graphics in, 137–38
  in-person, 140–41
  organization, 138–40
  on paper, 136–37
  defined, 114
  descriptive statistics, 114–15, 129–30, 142
  graphic techniques, 115–24
  bar charts, 116, 119, 141
  cautions, 123
  documentation, 123–24
  dot diagrams, 116, 120, 121, 142
  histograms, 116, 119–20, 142
  hypothesis formulation in, 117
  pie charts, 116, 118–19, 142
  scatter diagrams, 116, 121, 122, 143
  selecting measures in, 117–18
  time series, 116, 121–22, 143
  maps, 127–29
  measures of significance, 133–34, 142, 143
  tables, 124–27

Data collection, 77–113
  elite interviews, 97–105
  conducting, 102–4
  definition, 142
  investigative approach, 98–99
  making contact, 101–2
  selecting, 100–101
  structure and closure, 99–100
  time considerations, 104–5
  value of, 98
  from federal government, 87–91
  indexes, abstracts, and guides, 85–86
  journals, 85
  legal searches, 91–95
  library searches, 82–84
  literature reviews, 81–82
  management records, 95–96
  newspapers, 86–87
  observation, 96–97
  quick surveys, 105–9, 237–38
  methods of, 107–8
  questionnaire construction, 108
  sample selection, 109
  types of, 107
  search strategy, 78
  sources for, 78–81
Data plotting, extrapolation and, 261
Data sources:
  agency and program, 79, 80
  checklist, 79
  federal, 79, 80
  local, 79, 80
  private, 79, 81
  public, 79, 80
  state, 79, 80
Davidson, Ian, 307
Deciding among objectives, economic rule, 337–38
Decision, 178
Decision analysis (*see also* Quick decision analysis):
  expected value, 297
  and sensitivity analysis, 298–300
  value, 298
Decision criteria, 9 (*see also* Criteria)
Decision makers:
  and defining criteria, 188
  and ranking goals, 150
  risk neutral, 297
  values of, 169
Decision making:
  advising vs., 16–17
  analyst's role in, 28
  by client, 16–17
Decision-making evaluation approach, 394
Decision node, 160, 178
Decision process, preferences and, 300
Decisions, inconsistent, 357
Decision tree, 160–61, 172–73

definition, 178
value, 159
Deduction, contrasted with induction, 273
Defense Department, 154–55
Delphi method, 273–75, 318
Demand, price elasticity of, 200, 221
Deontological theories, 36, 66
Dependent variable, 117, 142
Descriptive ethics, 34
Descriptive policy analysis, 23–24
  definition, 66
Descriptive statistics, 114–15, 129–30
  definition, 142
Dexter, Lewis Anthony, 113
Dialing, random-digit, 108
Dilemmas, ethical, 30–32
Diminishing returns:
  definition, 221
  law, 203–4
Dimock, Marshall, 356–57
Direct benefits examples, 211
Direct costs:
  definition, 220
  examples, 194–95, 211
Direct impact, 208, 220
Disaggregated selection methods, contrasted with aggregated methods, 350
Disaggregation, pros and cons, 356
Discounted cost model, 271
Discount factor, formula, 279
Discounting, 276–80
  formula, 277
  procedure, 277
  risk and uncertainty in, 276
  theory, 276
Discount rate:
  definition, 318
  derivation, 277
  federal rate, 283
  and inflation, 283–84
  low contrasted with high, 282
  as political decision, 282
  relationship to interest rate, 277
  selecting, 282
  and sensitivity analysis, 283
Discount tables, 330–31
  explanation, 279
Discretion, administrative, 38–39
Diseconomies of scale, 201, 204
  definition, 220
Disproportionate sampling, 107, 142
Document analysis:
  content analysis, 111
  process, 111–13
  structured, 111
  types, 111
  unstructured, 111
Documentation, in graphic analysis, 123–24
Doing nothing, as a policy, 150
Dominant alternative, 341–49, 359

Dominated alternative:
  definition, 359
  example, 341–49
Dominated solutions, in portfolio analysis, 338
Dormitory example, 192–93
Dot diagrams, 116, 120, 121, 142
Downs, Anthony, 158
Driver education issue, 55
Dror, Yehezkel, 315
Drucker, Peter, 366
Dunn, William N., 32, 232, 273, 275
Duties, conflict of, 31

Early retirement example, 247–51, 351
Ecological correlation (*see* Ecological fallacy)
Ecological fallacy, 165–66
  definition, 178
Economic analysis, limitations, 338
Economic and financial possibility, 220
Economic efficiency, 193, 212–13, 220
Economic feasibility, 213
Economic rationality, decisions inconsistent with, 357
Economies of scale, 201, 204
  definition, 220
Edwards, George C., 308, 309, 333–34
Effectiveness:
  contrasted with efficiency, 212
  as a criterion, 208–9
  definition, 220
  example, 212
  political analysis in terms of, 303
Efficiency:
  contrasted with effectiveness, 212
  contrasted with equity, 204
  economic, 193, 212–13, 220
  example, 212
  limitation as a criterion, 334
  measures of, 280–84
Elasticity, types, 200–201
Elite interviewing (*see under* Interviewing)
Enthoven, Alain, 154–55
Entrepreneur, policy analyst as, 26–27
Equity, 204–7, 220
  compensation issues, 217
  contrasted with efficiency, 204
  distributional issues, 217
  examples of issues, 205–6
  related to cost, 194
  and subgroups, 205–6
  tests for fairness, 217
Equivalent-alternatives method, 343–47
  contrasted with standard-alternative method, 347–48
  definition, 359

Estimating unknown
numbers, 155
guessing, 155, 156
using experts, 156
using reference sources,
155
using surveys, 155
Ethical considerations, 30–46
categories of involvement,
37–38
in deciding among
objectives, 189–90
ethical analysis, 33–39
ethical dilemmas, 30–32
and policy advocacy, 16
principles and rules, 39–42
professional conduct,
42–46
values in analysis, 32–33
Ethics, 25, 66
Etzioni, Amitai, 49–50
Evaluating alternatives,
60–61, 257–332 (see
also Alternative(s))
through political analysis,
301–15
through quick decision
analysis, 295–300
uncertainty and, 315–16
Evaluation:
ex-ante, 257
ex-post, 257, 368–69
implementation and,
366–67
of interview data, 113
literature, 373–75
need for flexibility, 390–
91
pitfalls, 389
postprogram, 63–64
preprogram, 63–64
process, 368–69
reasons for opposing, 388
role of program staff,
391–92
sources of data, 387
values and, 372
Evaluation designs, basic and
researched, 64
Evaluation methods, 59,
275–300
actual-versus-planned
performance
comparisons, 377–78
allocation formulas,
289–95
before-and-after
comparisons, 376
cost-oriented approaches,
385–86
development, 370–73
discounting, 276–80
experimental designs,
378–79
experimental models,
378–79
internal rate of return,
280, 281–82
limitations, 375–76
limitations of experimental
approach, 388
naive criteria, 188–89
and political issues, 387
quasi-experimental models,
379–84

quick decision analysis,
295–300
selecting, 386–87
sensitivity analysis, 283,
284–89
types, 261–62, 276
with-and-without
comparisons, 376–77
Evaluative policy analysis, 66
Evaluator neutrality, 371–73
Ex-ante evaluation, 368
definition, 318
example, 362
link to ex-post evaluation,
362–63
Executive order 12291, 196
Expected value, 318
Expected value criterion, 298
Expected value of an
outcome, 297
Experimental design, 378–79
definition, 394
example, 378
process, 378–79
Experimental evaluation
approach, pros and
cons, 388
Experts, interviewing,
97–105
Ex-post evaluation, 318,
368–87
example, 362
link to ex-ante evaluation,
362–63
process, 368–69
purposes of quick, 368–69
types, 369–86
Externalities, 193–94,
199–200
definition, 220
External validity:
definition, 394
example, 377–78
and limits to
generalization, 384
reducing threats to, 384
threats to, 379
Extrapolative techniques,
260–68
applied to populations,
261–68
assumptions of, 267–68
data plotting and, 261
definition, 318
example, 259
linear phenomena and,
261–64
nonlinear phenomena and,
264–67
ratio technique, 267–68
uses of, 260–61
virtues of, 260

Fact checking, 14–15
Failures of policy, types of,
365–67
Feasibility, economic, 213
Feasibility analysis:
modeling, 270–72
political, 302–6
phases of, 302–4
PRINCE (PRobe,
INteract, Calculate,
Execute) method,
305–6, 319

rationale for, 305
rational model and, 51
Feasible manipulations:
to create alternatives,
246–48
definition, 255
examples, 246–48
Federal agencies, data from,
79, 80
Federal court decisions, data
on, 93–94
Federal government, data
from, 87–91
Ferry replacement example,
285–86
Fiduciary model of
professional-client
relationships, 40–41
Fiscal impact analysis, use,
214
Fischer, Frank, 33, 41
Fisk, Donald, 310
Fixed costs, 201
definition, 220
Flexibility of alternative,
230
Focused interviewing (see
Interviewing: elite)
Forecasting, 258–75
extrapolative techniques of,
260–68
applied to populations,
261–68
assumptions of, 267–68
data plotting and, 261
definition, 318
example, 259
linear phenomena and,
261–64
nonlinear phenomena
and, 264–67
ratio technique, 267–68
uses of, 260–61
virtues of, 260
intuitive, 273–75
theoretical forecasting
(modeling), 259–60,
268–73
definition, 319
discounted-cost, 271
game theory, 271–72
grain elevator example,
270–72
in implementation
analysis, 311–12
involvement of decision
makers, 273
probability, 272
types of, 269
Forecasts:
population, 261–68
types, 258
Forester, John, 33
Formaini, Robert, 50
Forward mapping, 313
Fractional measurement:
definition, 178
and operational definitions,
164
Franklin, Benjamin, 339–40,
345
Free market, 192–94
conditions for, 193
failure, 192–94
Function, 142

Gallery method of
brainwriting, 243
Gamblers, compulsive,
157–58
Games approach to
implementation
analysis, 310–11
Game theory, 271–72
Gamma (Yule's Q), 132, 142
Garson, G. David, 38
Generalizing, from
evaluations, 384
Generic solutions
(prepackaged designs),
232
Goal-based evaluation
approach, 394
Goal-free evaluation method,
394
Goals:
ambiguous, 149–50
of decision makers, 334
definition, 187, 220
inconsistent, 150
reluctance to rank, 150
specifying during
evaluation, 390
vague, 150, 390
Goals-achievement matrix,
353–54
definition, 359
Goals and objectives, of
actors, 153
Goeller, Bruce F., 364
Goeller scorecard, 350–51
advantages, 351
definition, 359
Gordon, William J.J., 240
Government, data from,
87–91
Grain elevator example,
270–72
Graphic analysis, 115–24
bar charts, 116, 119, 141
cautions, 123
documentation, 123–24
dot diagrams, 116, 120,
121, 142
histograms, 116, 119–20,
142
hypothesis formulation in,
117
pie charts, 116, 118–19,
142
scatter diagrams, 116, 121,
122, 143
selecting measures in,
117–18
time series, 116, 121–22,
143
Graphics in reports, 137–38
Gravitation, formula, 268–
69
Gravity example, 268–70
Gravity model example, 13
Greenwood Publishing
Group, 90
Grouped data, 91, 117, 121,
129–30, 142
Guba, Egon G., 372
Guides, data from, 85–86

Hatry, Harry, 310, 387, 389
Hawthorne effect, 97, 142

Health care example, 152–54
  heroin abuse example, 157,
    239
Heineman, Robert A., 32, 41
Highway cost example, 158
Hill, Morris, 353
Histograms, 116, 119–20,
    142
Hoaglin, David, 88
Hofferbert, Richard, 50
Horizontal equity, 205
House, Ernest R., 371, 373,
    374
Howe, Elizabeth, 38, 190
Hypothesis, use in
    forecasting, 261
Hypothesis formulation in
    graphic techniques,
    117

Ideal alternative, value,
    244–45
Implementation:
  bottom-up, 307
  policy evaluation and,
    366–67
  top-down, 307
Implementation analysis,
    307–13
  checklists for, 310
  consensus/change
    dimensions of, 309–10
  games approach to, 310–11
  models in, 311–12
  rationale for, 307–9
Impossibility theorem, 336,
    359
Income elasticity, 201, 220
Inconsistent decisions,
    example, 357
Incrementalism, contrasted
    with rational model, 49
Independent probabilities,
    318
Independent reviewers,
    value, 154
Independent variable, 117,
    142
Indexes, data from, 85–86
Indirect benefits, examples,
    211
Indirect costs:
  definition, 220
  examples, 195, 211
Indirect impact, 220
Indirect measurement:
  definition, 179
  as a problem in developing
    operational measures,
    165
Individual rationality:
  conflict with collective
    rationality, 335–36
  definition, 359
Induction, contrasted with
    deduction, 273
Inductive forecasting, 318–19
Inelasticity, types, 200–201
Inferential statistics, 114,
    133–34, 142
Inflation, discount rate
    example, 283–84
Information, evaluating,
    109–13
Ingram, Helen, 311

Innes, Judith, 95, 169
In-person interviews, 108
Intangible benefits,
    definition, 220–21
Intangible costs, definition,
    220–21
Intangibles, importance of,
    13
Intensive interviewing (see
    Interviewing: elite)
Interest rate:
  contrasted with discount
    rate, 277
  definition, 319
Intergenerational equity,
    206–7
Internal rate of return,
    computation, 281–82
  contrasted with net present
    value, 281
  definition, 319
  use in selecting projects,
    281
Internal validity:
  controlling for, 379–81
  definition, 395
  example, 377
  reducing threats to,
    382–83
  threats, 382–83
International City
    Management
    Association, 90
Interrupted time-series
    evaluation design,
    382–84, 395
Interval data, 131
  considered as ordinal,
    291–92
  definition, 142
Interviewing:
  determining truth, 113
  elite, 97–105
    conducting, 102–4
    definition, 142
    investigative approach,
    98–99
    making contact, 101–2
    selecting, 100–101
    structure and closure,
    99–100
    time considerations,
    104–5
    value of, 98
  information sought, 99
  in-person, 108
  process, 97–105
  reluctant respondent, 102
  use of tape recorder, 104
Intuitionism, 37
Intuitive forecasting, 273–75
  Delphi method, 273–75,
    318
  scenario writing, 274–75
Intuitive prediction,
    forecasting method,
    260
Inverse (negative)
    relationship, 124–25,
    132, 142
Investigative approach to
    interviewing, 98–99
Investment:
  in levels of analysis,
    176–77

Invulnerability of alternative,
    230
Issue advocate role, 42
Issue paper, 176–78, 179
Issue table, in political
    analysis, 171, 172

Japanese decision-making
    example, 366
Journals, data from, 85
Jung, Yoon Soo, 51

Kant, Immanuel, 36
Kaufman, Jerome, 37, 190
Kearny, Edward N., 32, 41
Kenneth Arrow's
    Impossibility Theorem,
    359
Kimmel, Wayne, 310
Kiss, Istvan, 316
Krone, Robert M., 338

Lasswell, Harold D., 32–33
Law of diminishing returns,
    221
Lawrence, John E.S., 389
Legal cases, analyzing, 94–95
Legal context, standing and,
    197–98
Legal searches, 91–95
Leung, Hok Lin, 32, 170
Levin, Martin A., 311
Lexicographic ordering, 341,
    359
Libraries, data from, 79–80
Library searches, 82–84
Lincoln, Yvonna S., 372
Lindblom, Charles E., 41, 43,
    49, 188–91, 229–30
Linear phenomena,
    extrapolation and,
    261–64
Lineberry, Robert, 29
Linner, John, 75–76
Litchfield, Nathaniel, 354
Literature reviews, 81–82
Local agencies, data from,
    79, 80
Local government, analysis
    in, 6
Logarithms, example, 265–67
  table, 327–29
Longitudinal surveys, 107,
    142
Lumsdaine, Edward, 243
Lumsdaine, Monika, 243

McKenna, Christopher K.,
    347, 354
MacRae, Duncan, Jr., 47,
    193, 196, 197, 219,
    229, 301
Magazines, surveys conducted
    by, 81
Mail surveys, 107–8
Majone, Giandomenico, 32,
    310
Management records, 95–96
Managers, obligations of,
    29–30
Maps and mapping, 127–29
  backward, 307, 313
  forward, 313
  political, 304
March, James, 190

Marginal analysis, 201–4
  decision rules, 204
  definition, 221
  parking garage example,
    204
  versus average costs, 201–2
  when to use, 202
Marginal cost, 194, 202, 221
Market failure, reasons for,
    192–94
Matrix display systems,
    349–52
  comparative advantages,
    355
  contrasted with a summary
    statistic, 350
  limitations, 350
Matrix methods, researched,
    353–55
May, Ernest, 241
May, Peter J., 246, 304
Mead Data Central, 93
Measurement, scales of, 123,
    132–33, 143
Measures:
  definition, 221
  of efficiency, 280–84
  as related to criteria, 187
  selection of, 117–18
  of significance, 133–34,
    142, 143
Media, data from local, 87
Meltsner, Arnold J., 168,
    215, 239, 302, 304,
    305, 309
Merit of alternative, 230
Metaethics, 34
Metaphor (see Analogy)
Methods, selecting
    appropriate, 11, 74
Middle-range scenarios, 313,
    314
Miser, Hugh J., 364–65
Modeling (see Theoretical
    forecasting (modeling))
Modifying alternatives, to
    create new alternatives,
    248, 250
Monetarizable benefits,
    210–11, 221
Monetarizable costs, 210–11,
    221
Monetary policies, 9–11
Monitoring policy outcomes:
  rationale, 63–64
  value, 363–64
Monte Carlo sampling,
    288–89
Moore, Mark, 239
Moral problems, 30–32
Moral thinking, 34–39
Morphological approach, 255
Mosteller, Frederick, 155
Motivations, political analysis
    in terms of, 170, 303
Multiple advocacy, 334
Multiple criteria:
  conflict among, 337–39
  dealing with, 339
Multiple measures:
  in evaluation, 390–91
  problems with, 189
Multiple objectives, criticism
    of sophisticated
    approaches, 190–91

Murphy, Jerome T., 113
Mutually exclusive outcomes, 297

Nagel, Stuart S., 51–52
Naive criteria, as evaluation method, 188–89
Nakamura, Robert T., 308, 310
National Aeronautics and Space Administration (NASA), 89
National Archives and Records Administration, 89
National Association of Counties, and International City Management Association, 90
National Library of Medicine, 89
National Municipal League, 90
National Technical Information Services (NTIS), 89
Negative findings, value, 364
Negative (inverse) relationship, 124–25, 132, 142
Net-benefit rule, 337–38
contrasted with cost-benefit and cost-effectiveness, 338
Net present value, 213
computation, 277–78
contrasted with benefit-cost ratio, 280
contrasted with internal rate of return, 281
definition, 221
preference of analysts for, 284
Net present worth (see Present value)
Net worth, change in, 212
Neutrality, evaluator, 371–73
Newspapers:
data from, 86–87
surveys conducted by, 81
No-action alternative, 58, 235, 255
No-action (status quo) analysis, 235–37
Nominal data, 131, 142
Nondominated-alternatives method, 341–49
definition, 359
limitations, 343
Nonequivalent control group evaluation design, 380–82
advantages, 380
definition, 395
example, 381
Nonlinear phenomena, extrapolation and, 264–67
Nonmonetary policies, 9–11
Normalizing scores, 291–92
Normative ethics, 34, 66
NOT command, 83

Objective function:
definition, 359
to determine priorities, 349
source, 349
Objectives:
competing, 9
conflict among, 337–39
deciding among competing, 189, 337–38
definition, 187, 221
difficulty in identifying, 54
multiple, 189
sources, 191
utility values, 354
Objective technician role, 42
Obligation, ethics and, 38, 40
Observation:
during interviews, 105
as a source of policy data, 96–97
value, 97
O'Leary, Michael K., 168, 305–6
Operational definitions:
attributes, 166
creating, 187
energy-cost assistance example, 166
process, 187
Operationalize, 221
Opportunity costs, 194
definition, 221
example, 211–12
Optimal decisions, and conflict among criteria, 336, 337
Optimistic scenario, 313, 314
Ordinal data, 131
definition, 142
interval considered as, 291–92
Osborn, Alex F., 229, 241, 248, 253
Outcome, 179
Outcome branches, 160–61
Outcome success, 364

Paired comparisons:
definition, 359
method, 341
Palumbo, Dennis J., 371
Paradox of voting, 336, 340
Parameters, allocating time to identifying, 12
Pareto criterion, 192, 221
Pareto optimum, 192
alternative, 341–42
definition, 221
determination of standing by, 197, 198
example, 192
Paris, David C., 50
Parking garage example, 202–4
Partial correlation coefficient, 132
Pendleton Act of 1883, 33
Perceptual maps, 304
Perfect market (see Free market)
Persuasion, oral and written, 21
Persuasion, political, 301
Persuasive advice, 24
Peterson, Steven A., 32, 41

Pie charts, 116, 118–19, 142
Plan, 66
Planning, contrasted with policy analysis, 4
Planning balance sheet, 354–55
definition, 359
Policies
contrasted with plans, 4
evaluating, 60–61
Policy, 66
Policy actions, types of, 9–11
Policy analysis, 21–73
alternative definitions, 22–23
anticipatory, 23
characteristics, 5
contrasted with planning, 4
definition, 20, 21–22
descriptive, 66
evaluative, 23, 66
ex ante, 23, 66, 368
ex post, 23, 66
identification of topics, 29
methods of, 20
post hoc, 23, 66
predictive, 23–24, 66
pre hoc, 23, 66
prescriptive, 23–24, 66
principles, 8–18
advising vs. decision making, 16–17
advocating position of others, 15–16
boundaries of analysis, 17
central decision criterion, 9
fact checking, 14–15
quality of analysis, 17–18
simplicity and transparency of analysis, 13–14
tool-box approach and, 11–12
types of actions to be taken, 9–11
uncertainty and, 12
use of numbers, 12–13
prospective, 23–24, 66
purpose, 333
as quick analysis, 158
as researched analysis, 158
retrospective, 23, 66
Policy analysts:
and advocacy, 28
challenges faced by, 27–28
citizen, 301
relationship to client, 148
roles of, 26–30, 42, 188
types of, 2, 26–27
Policy entrepreneur, 26–27
Policy envelope:
definition, 20, 179
identifying, 153
and problem definition, 17
Policy failures, types of, 365–67
Policy impacts
adequate contrasted with inadequate, 210–11
direct contrasted with indirect, 209
long-term contrasted with short-term, 209–10

Policy maintenance:
definition, 395
purpose, 368
Policy makers (see Decision makers)
Policy options, subjective nature of, 170–71
Policy planning process, 6
Policy research, 2
Policy studies (see Policy research)
Policy termination:
criteria, 367
types, 367
Political analysis, 301–15
analysts' role, 175
community development budget example, 170–76
definition, 179
feasibility analysis, 302–6
phases of, 302–4
PRINCE (PRobe, INteract, Calculate, Execute) method, 305–6, 319
rationale for, 305
rational model and, 51
guidelines, 175–76
implementation analysis, 307–13
checklists for, 310
consensus/change dimensions of, 309–10
games approach to, 310–11
models in, 311–12
rationale for, 307–9
issue table, 171, 172
meanings of, 301
in the policy analysis process, 169
scenario writing, 274–75, 313–15, 319
terminology, 170
types, 168
Political criteria:
types, 214–18
use, 219
Political data, methods for classifying, 171
Political feasibility (see under Political analysis)
Political mapping, 304
Political persuasion, 301
Political viability:
contrasted with technical feasibility, 333
definition, 221
Politicians:
demands of, 75
policy analyst as, 26–27
serving the needs of, 75–76
Politics, 25
Policy monitoring, 368
definition, 395
Population forecasts:
formulas, 263–64
mathematical, 262–63
regression method, 263–64, 265
visual, 258–59
Portfolio analysis, 338
Position maps, 304